W9-BUK-142

More critical acclaim for *A History of God*

"Highly readable and ought to be read. . . . Karen Armstrong has read widely, has missed nothing, and gives us as solid a purview of the God of the past as it would be possible to find in a book."

—Anthony Burgess
The Observer

"She refreshes the understanding of what one knows, and provides a clear introduction to the unfamiliar . . . 'Yearning,' said Augustine, 'makes the heart deep.' That is the theme which runs through this lucid book, and the note of hope on which it ends."

—Robert Runcie
Former Archbishop of Canterbury

"An enormously intellectually challenging book. A fascinating way of approaching the subject."

—Rabbi Julia Neuberger

"Magisterial and brilliant . . . An extraordinary survey, [a] superb kaleidoscopic history of religion . . . thorough, intelligent, and highly readable."

—*Kirkus Reviews*

"Besides providing a great deal of religious history, [Armstrong] discusses the various philosophers, mystics, and reformers associated with these religions . . . An excellent and informative book."

—*Library Journal*

"This searching, profound comparative history . . . fearlessly illuminates the sociopolitical ground in which religious ideas take root, blossom and mutate."

—*Publishers Weekly*

A HISTORY OF GOD

Also by Karen Armstrong

Islam: A Short History

Holy War: The Crusades and Their Impact

The Battle for God

In the Beginning: A New Interpretation of Genesis

Jerusalem: One City, Three Faiths

Visions of God: Four Medieval Mystics and Their Writings

A HISTORY OF GOD

*The 4000-Year Quest of Judaism,
Christianity and Islam*

by
Karen Armstrong

GRAMERCY BOOKS
NEW YORK

This 2004 edition is published by Gramercy Books, an imprint of Random House Value Publishing, a division of Random House, Inc., New York, by arrangement with Alfred A. Knopf, Inc.

Gramercy is a registered trademark and the colophon is a trademark of Random House, Inc.

Grateful acknowledgment is made to the following for permission to reprint previously published material:

Doubleday and Darton, Longman & Todd Ltd.: Excerpts from *The Jerusalem Bible*, copyright © 1966, 1967, 1968 by Darton, Longman & Todd Ltd. and Doubleday, a division of Bantam Doubleday Dell Publishing Group, Inc. Reprinted by permission.

Oxford University Press: Excerpts from *The Confessions of St. Augustine*, translated by Henry Chadwick, copyright © 1991 by Henry Chadwick. Reprinted by permission of Oxford University Press, Oxford, England.

Peters Fraser & Dunlop: Excerpts from *The Pursuit of the Millennium, Revolutionary Millennarians and Mystical Anarchists of the Middle Ages* by Norman Cohn (Secker & Warburg). Reprinted by permission of Peters Fraser & Dunlop on behalf of the author.

Random House
New York • Toronto • London • Sydney • Auckland
www.randomhouse.com

Printed and bound in the United States

Library of Congress Cataloging-in-Publication Data

Armstrong, Karen, 1944-
    A history of God : the 4000-year quest of Judaism, Christianity, and Islam / Karen Armstrong.
        p. cm.
    Originally published: New York : Ballantine Books, 1993.
    Includes index.
    ISBN 0-517-22312-0
    1. God–Comparative studies. 2. God–Biblical teaching. 3. God–History of doctrines.
    4. God (Islam)–History of doctrines. 5. God (Judaism)–History of doctrines. 6. Judaism–Doctrines–History. 7. Islam–Doctrines–History. I. Title.

BT98.A65 2004
202'.11–dc22

2003062755

10 9 8 7 6 5 4 3

Contents

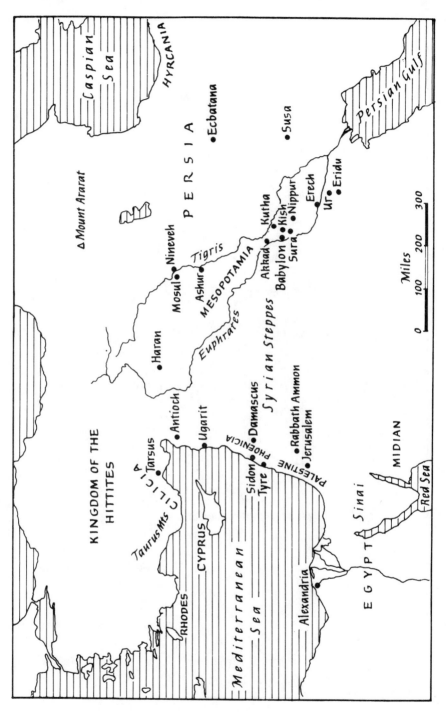

The Ancient Middle East

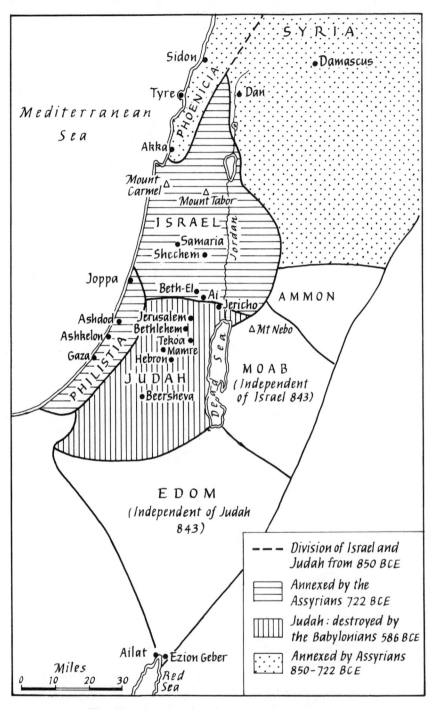

The Kingdoms of Israel and Judah 722–586 BCE

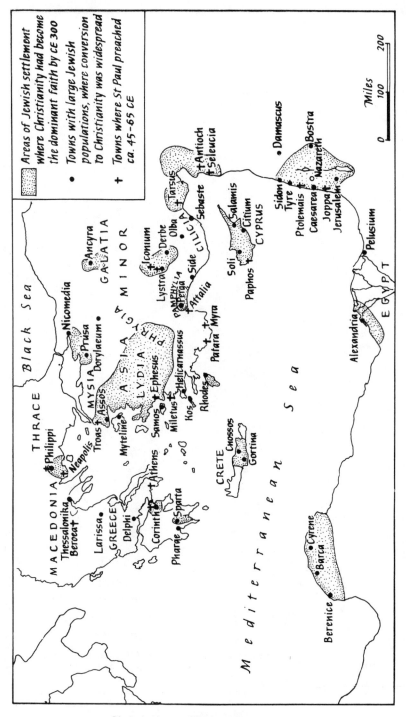

Christianity and Judaism 50–300 CE

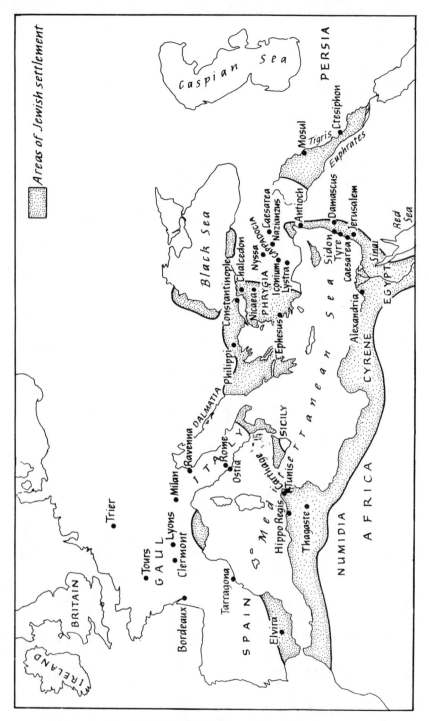

The World of the Fathers of the Church

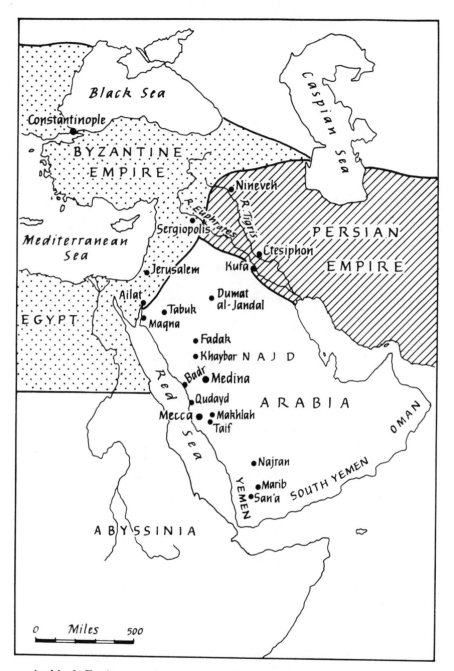

Arabia & Environs at the time of the Prophet Muhammad (570–632 CE)

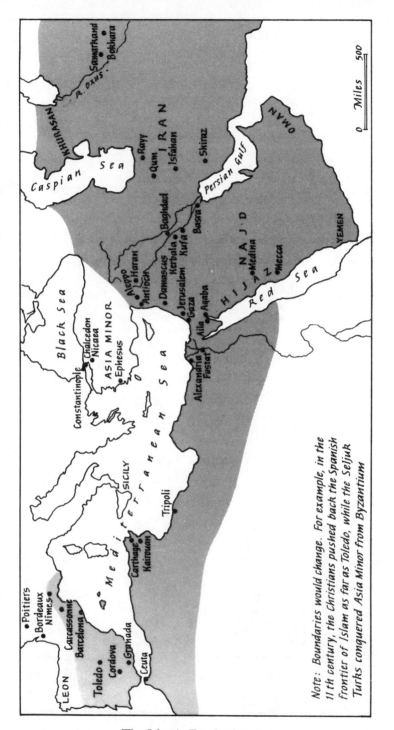

Note: Boundaries would change. For example, in the 11th century, the Christians pushed back the Spanish frontier of Islam as far as Toledo, while the Seljuk Turks conquered Asia Minor from Byzantium

The Islamic Empire by 750

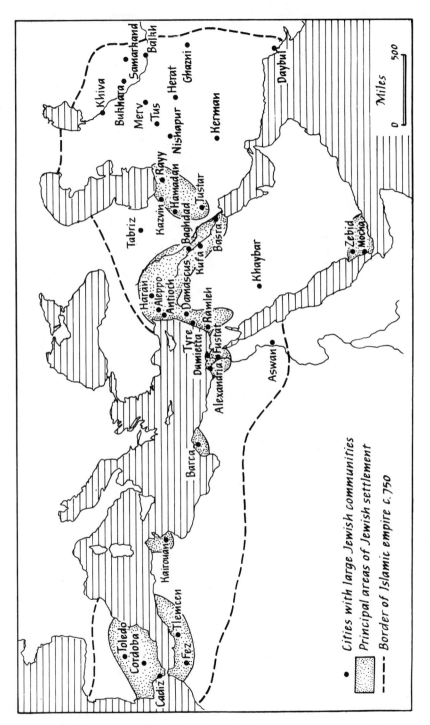

The Jews of Islam c. 750

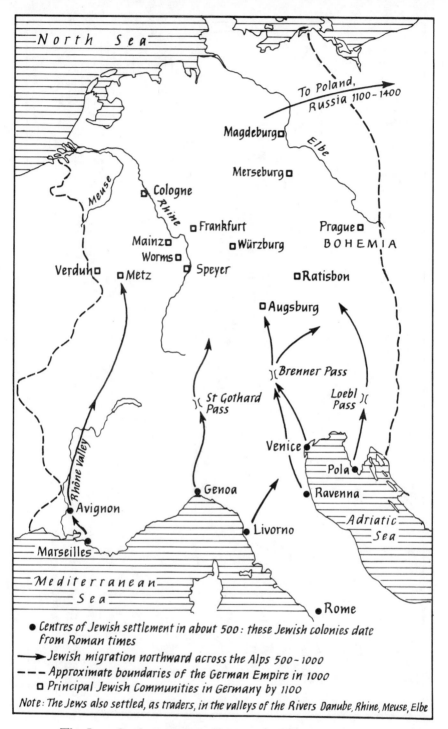

The Jews Settle in Eastern France and Germany 500–1100

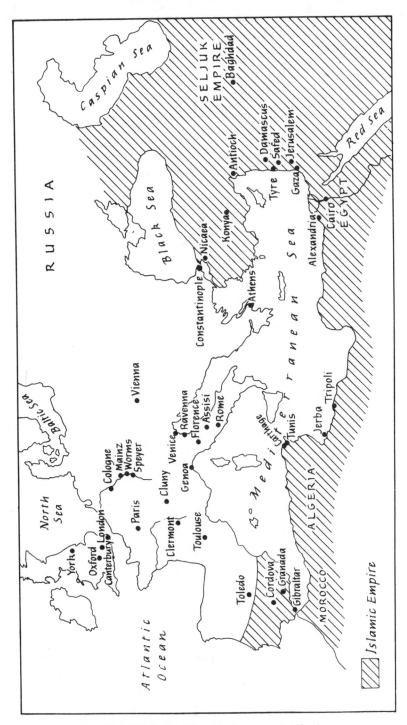

The New Christian West during the Middle Ages

Introduction

AS A CHILD, I had a number of strong religious beliefs but little faith in God. There is a distinction between *belief* in a set of propositions and a *faith* which enables us to put our trust in them. I believed implicitly in the existence of God; I also believed in the Real Presence of Christ in the Eucharist, the efficacy of the sacraments, the prospect of eternal damnation and the objective reality of Purgatory. I cannot say, however, that my belief in these religious opinions about the nature of ultimate reality gave me much confidence that life here on earth was good or beneficent. The Roman Catholicism of my childhood was a rather frightening creed. James Joyce got it right in *Portrait of the Artist as a Young Man*: I listened to my share of hellfire sermons. In fact Hell seemed a more potent reality than God, because it was something that I could grasp imaginatively. God, on the other hand, was a somewhat shadowy figure, defined in intellectual abstractions rather than images. When I was about eight years old, I had to memorize this catechism answer to the question, "What is God?": "God is the Supreme Spirit, Who alone exists of Himself and is infinite in all perfections." Not surprisingly, it meant little to me, and I am bound to say that it still leaves me cold. It has always seemed a singularly arid, pompous and arrogant definition. Since writing this book, however, I have come to believe that it is also incorrect.

As I grew up, I realized that there was more to religion than fear. I read the lives of the saints, the metaphysical poets, T. S. Eliot and some of the simpler writings of the mystics. I began to be moved by the beauty of the liturgy and, though God remained distant, I felt that it was possible to break through to him and that the vision would transfigure the whole of created reality. To do this I entered a religious order and, as a novice and a young nun, I learned a good deal more about the faith. I applied myself to apologetics, scripture, theology and church history. I delved into the history of the monastic life and embarked on a minute discussion of the Rule of my own order, which we had to learn by heart. Strangely enough, God figured very little in any of this. Attention seemed focused on secondary details and the more peripheral aspects of religion. I wrestled with myself in prayer, trying to force my mind to encounter God, but he remained a stern taskmaster who observed my every infringement of the Rule, or tantalizingly absent. The more I read about the raptures of the saints, the more of a failure I felt. I was unhappily aware that what little religious experience I had, had somehow been manufactured by myself as I worked upon my own feelings and imagination. Sometimes a sense of devotion was an aesthetic response to the beauty of the Gregorian chant and the liturgy. But nothing had actually *happened* to me from a source beyond myself. I never glimpsed the God described by the prophets and mystics. Jesus Christ, about whom we talked far more than about "God," seemed a purely historical figure, inextricably embedded in late antiquity. I also began to have grave doubts about some of the doctrines of the Church. How could anybody possibly know for certain that the man Jesus had been God incarnate and what did such a belief mean? Did the New Testament really teach the elaborate—and highly self-contradictory—doctrine of the Trinity or was this, like so many other articles of the faith, a fabrication by theologians centuries after the death of Christ in Jerusalem?

Eventually, with regret, I left the religious life, and, once freed of the burden of failure and inadequacy, I felt my belief in God slip quietly away. He had never really impinged upon my life, though I had done my best to enable him to do so. Now that I no longer felt so guilty and anxious about him, he became too remote to be a reality. My interest in religion continued, however, and I made a number of television programs about the early history of Christianity and the nature of the religious experience. The more I learned about the history of religion, the more my earlier misgivings appeared justified. The doctrines that I had accepted without question as a child were indeed man-made, constructed over a long period. Science seemed to have disposed of the Creator God, and biblical scholars had proved that Jesus had never claimed to be divine. As an epileptic, I had flashes of vision that I knew to be a mere neurological defect: had the visions and raptures of the saints also been a mere mental quirk? Increasingly, God seemed an aberration, something that the human race had outgrown.

Despite my years as a nun, I do not believe that my experience of God is unusual. My ideas about God were formed in childhood and did not keep abreast of my growing knowledge in other disciplines. I had revised simplistic childhood views of Father Christmas; I had come to a more mature understanding of the complexities of the human predicament than had been possible in kindergarten. Yet my early, confused ideas about God had not been modified or developed. People without my peculiarly religious background may also find that their notion of God was formed in infancy. Since those days, we have put away childish things and have discarded the God of our first years.

Yet my study of the history of religion has revealed that human beings are spiritual animals. Indeed, there is a case for arguing that *Homo sapiens* is also *Homo religiosus*. Men and women started to worship gods as soon as they became recognizably human; they created religions at the same time as they created works of art. This was not simply because they wanted to propitiate powerful forces; these early faiths expressed the wonder and mystery that seem always to have been an essential component of the human experience of this beautiful yet terrifying world. Like art, religion has been an attempt to find meaning and value in life, despite the suffering that flesh is heir to. Like any other human activity, religion can be abused, but it seems to have been something that we have always done. It was not tacked on to a primordially secular nature by manipulative kings and priests but was natural to humanity. Indeed, our current secularism is an entirely new experiment, unprecedented in human history. We have yet to see how it will work. It is also true to say that our Western liberal humanism is not something that comes naturally to us; like an appreciation of art or poetry, it has to be cultivated. Humanism is itself a religion without God—not all religions, of course, are theistic. Our ethical secular ideal has its own disciplines of mind and heart and gives people the means of finding faith in the ultimate meaning of human life that were once provided by the more conventional religions.

When I began to research this history of the idea and experience of God in the three related monotheistic faiths of Judaism, Christianity and Islam, I expected to find that God had simply been a projection of human needs and desires. I thought that "he" would mirror the fears and yearnings of society at each stage of its development. My predictions were not entirely unjustified, but I have been extremely surprised by some of my findings, and I wish that I had learned all this thirty years ago, when I was starting out in the religious life. It would have saved me a great deal of anxiety to hear—from eminent monotheists in all three faiths—that instead of waiting for God to descend from on high, I should deliberately create a sense of him for myself. Other rabbis, priests and Sufis would have taken me to task for assuming that God was—in any sense—a reality "out there"; they would have warned me not to expect to experience him as an objective fact that could be discovered by the ordinary process of rational thought. They would have told me that in an important sense God was a product of the creative imagination, like the poetry and music that I found so inspiring. A few highly respected monotheists would have told me quietly and firmly that God did not really exist—and yet that "he" was the most important reality in the world.

This book will not be a history of the ineffable reality of God itself, which is beyond time and change, but a history of the way men and women have perceived him from Abraham to the present day. The human idea of God has a history, since it has always meant something slightly different to each group of people who have used it at various points of time. The idea of God formed in one generation by one set of human beings could be meaningless in another. Indeed, the statement "I believe in God" has no objective meaning, as such, but like any other statement only means something in context, when proclaimed by a particular community. Consequently there is no one unchanging idea contained in the word "God"; instead, the word contains a whole spectrum of meanings, some of which are contradictory or even mutually exclusive. Had the notion of God not had this flexibility, it would not have survived to become one of the great human ideas. When one conception of God has ceased to have meaning or relevance, it has been quietly discarded and replaced by a new theology. A fundamentalist would deny this, since fundamentalism is antihistorical: it believes that Abraham, Moses and the later prophets all experienced their God in exactly the same way as people do today. Yet if we look at our three religions, it becomes clear that there is no objective view of "God": each generation has to create the image of God that works for it. The same is true of atheism. The statement "I do not believe in God" has meant something slightly different at each period of history. The people who have been dubbed "atheists" over the years have always denied a particular conception of the divine. Is the "God" who is rejected by atheists today, the God of the patriarchs, the God of the prophets, the God of the philosophers, the God of the mystics or the God of the eighteenth-century deists? All these deities have been venerated as the God of the Bible and the Koran by Jews, Christians and Muslims at various points of their history. We shall see that they are very different from one another. Atheism has often been a transitional state: thus Jews, Christians and Muslims were all called "atheists" by their pagan contemporaries because they had adopted a revolutionary notion of divinity and transcendence. Is modern atheism a similar denial of a "God" which is no longer adequate to the problems of our time?

Despite its otherworldliness, religion is highly pragmatic. We shall see that it is far more important for a particular idea of God to *work* than for it to be logically or scientifically sound. As soon as it ceases to be effective it will be changed—sometimes for something radically different. This did not disturb most monotheists before our own day because they were quite clear that their ideas about God were not sacrosanct but could only be provisional. They were entirely man-made—they could be nothing else—and quite separate from the indescribable Reality they symbolized. Some developed quite audacious ways of emphasizing this essential distinction. One medieval mystic went so far as to say that this ultimate Reality—mistakenly called "God"—was not even mentioned in the Bible. Throughout history, men and women have experienced a dimension of the spirit that seems to transcend the mundane world. Indeed, it is an arresting characteristic of the human mind to be able to conceive concepts that go beyond it in this way. However we choose to interpret it, this human experience of transcendence has been a fact of life. Not everybody would regard it as divine: Buddhists, as we shall see, would deny that their visions and insights are derived from a supernatural source; they see them as natural to humanity. All the major religions, however, would agree that it is impossible to describe this transcendence in normal conceptual language. Monotheists have called this transcendence "God," but they have hedged this around with important provisos. Jews, for example, are forbidden to pronounce the sacred Name of God, and Muslims must not attempt to depict the divine in visual imagery. The discipline is a reminder that the reality that we call "God" exceeds all human expression.

This will not be a history in the usual sense, since the idea of God has not evolved from one point and progressed in a linear fashion to a final conception. Scientific notions work like that, but the ideas of art and religion do not. Just as there are only a given number of themes in love poetry, so too people have kept saying the same things about God over and over again. Indeed, we shall find a striking similarity in Jewish, Christian and Muslim ideas of the divine. Even though Jews and Muslims both find the Christian doctrines of the Trinity and Incarnation almost blasphemous, they have produced their own versions of these controversial theologies. Each expression of these universal themes is slightly different, however, showing the ingenuity and inventiveness of the human imagination as it struggles to express its sense of "God."

Because this is such a big subject, I have deliberately confined myself to the One God worshipped by Jews, Christians and Muslims, though I have occasionally considered pagan, Hindu and Buddhist conceptions of ultimate reality to make a monotheistic point clearer. It seems that the idea of God is remarkably close to ideas in religions that developed quite independently. Whatever conclusions we reach about the reality of God, the history of this idea must tell us something important about the human mind and the nature of our aspiration. Despite the secular tenor of much Western society, the idea of God still affects the lives of millions of people. Recent surveys have shown that ninety-nine percent of Americans say that they believe in God: the question is which "God" of the many on offer do they subscribe to?

Theology often comes across as dull and abstract, but the history of God has been passionate and intense. Unlike some other conceptions of the ultimate, it was originally attended by agonizing struggle and stress. The prophets of Israel experienced their God as a physical pain that wrenched their every limb and filled them with rage and elation. The reality that they called God was often experienced by monotheists in a state of extremity: we shall read of mountaintops, darkness, desolation, crucifixion and terror. The Western experience of God seemed particularly traumatic. What was the reason for this inherent strain? Other monotheists spoke of light and transfiguration. They used very daring imagery to express the complexity of the reality they experienced, which went far beyond the orthodox theology. There has recently been a revived interest in mythology, which may indicate a widespread desire for a more imaginative expression of religious truth. The work of the late American scholar Joseph Campbell has become extremely popular: he has explored the perennial mythology of mankind, linking ancient myths with those still current in traditional societies. It is often assumed that the three God-religions are devoid of mythology and poetic symbolism. Yet, although monotheists originally rejected the myths of their pagan neighbors, these often crept back into the faith at a later date. Mystics have seen God incarnated in a woman, for example. Others reverently speak of God's sexuality and have introduced a female element into the divine.

This brings me to a difficult point. Because this God began as a specifically male deity, monotheists have usually referred to it as "he." In recent years, feminists have understandably objected to this. Since I shall be recording the thoughts and insights of people who called God "he," I have used the conventional masculine terminology, except when "it" has been more appropriate. Yet it is perhaps worth mentioning that the masculine tenor of God-talk is particularly problematic in English. In Hebrew, Arabic and French, however, grammatical gender gives theological discourse a sort of sexual counterpoint and dialectic, which provides a balance that is often lacking in English. Thus in Arabic *al-Lah* (the supreme name for God) is grammatically masculine, but the word for the divine and inscrutable essence of God—*al-Dhat*—is feminine.

All talk about God staggers under impossible difficulties. Yet monotheists have all been very positive about language at the same time as they have denied its capacity to express the transcendent reality. The God of Jews, Christians and Muslims is a God who—in some sense—speaks. His Word is crucial in all three faiths. The Word of God has shaped the history of our culture. We have to decide whether the word "God" has any meaning for us today.

Note: Since I am looking at the history of God from the Jewish and the Muslim as well as the Christian perspective, the terms "BC" and "AD," which are conventionally used in the West, are not appropriate. I have therefore had recourse to the alternatives "BCE" (Before the Common Era) and "CE" (Common Era).

A HISTORY OF GOD

1

In the Beginning . . .

I N THE BEGINNING, human beings created a God who was the First
Cause of all things and Ruler of heaven and earth. He was not represented by images and had no temple or priests in his service. He was
too exalted for an inadequate human cult. Gradually he faded from the
consciousness of his people. He had become so remote that they decided
that they did not want him anymore. Eventually he was said to have
disappeared.

That, at least, is one theory, popularized by Father Wilhelm Schmidt
in *The Origin of the Idea of God*, first published in 1912. Schmidt suggested
that there had been a primitive monotheism before men and women had
started to worship a number of gods. Originally they had acknowledged
only one Supreme Deity, who had created the world and governed human
affairs from afar. Belief in such a High God (sometimes called the Sky
God, since he is associated with the heavens) is still a feature of the
religious life in many indigenous African tribes. They yearn toward
God in prayer; believe that he is watching over them and will punish
wrongdoing. Yet he is strangely absent from their daily lives: he has no
special cult and is never depicted in effigy. The tribesmen say that he is
inexpressible and cannot be contaminated by the world of men. Some
people say that he has "gone away." Anthropologists suggest that this
God has become so distant and exalted that he has in effect been replaced
by lesser spirits and more accessible gods. So too, Schmidt's theory goes,
in ancient times, the High God was replaced by the more attractive gods
of the pagan pantheons. In the beginning, therefore, there was One God.
If this is so, then monotheism was one of the earliest ideas evolved by

human beings to explain the mystery and tragedy of life. It also indicates some of the problems that such a deity might have to face.

It is impossible to prove this one way or the other. There have been many theories about the origin of religion. Yet it seems that creating gods is something that human beings have always done. When one religious idea ceases to work for them, it is simply replaced. These ideas disappear quietly, like the Sky God, with no great fanfare. In our own day, many people would say that the God worshipped for centuries by Jews, Christians and Muslims has become as remote as the Sky God. Some have actually claimed that he has died. Certainly he seems to be disappearing from the lives of an increasing number of people, especially in Western Europe. They speak of a "God-shaped hole" in their consciousness where he used to be, because, irrelevant though he may seem in certain quarters, he has played a crucial role in our history and has been one of the greatest human ideas of all time. To understand what we are losing—if, that is, he really is disappearing—we need to see what people were doing when they began to worship this God, what he meant and how he was conceived. To do that we need to go back to the ancient world of the Middle East, where the idea of our God gradually emerged about 14,000 years ago.

One of the reasons why religion seems irrelevant today is that many of us no longer have the sense that we are surrounded by the unseen. Our scientific culture educates us to focus our attention on the physical and material world in front of us. This method of looking at the world has achieved great results. One of its consequences, however, is that we have, as it were, edited out the sense of the "spiritual" or the "holy" which pervades the lives of people in more traditional societies at every level and which was once an essential component of our human experience of the world. In the South Sea Islands, they call this mysterious force *mana*; others experience it as a presence or spirit; sometimes it has been felt as an impersonal power, like a form of radioactivity or electricity. It was believed to reside in the tribal chief, in plants, rocks or animals. The Latins experienced *numina* (spirits) in sacred groves; Arabs felt that the landscape was populated by the *jinn*. Naturally people wanted to get in touch with this reality and make it work for them, but they also simply wanted to admire it. When they personalized the unseen forces and made them gods, associated with the wind, sun, sea and stars but possessing human characteristics, they were expressing their sense of affinity with the unseen and with the world around them.

Rudolf Otto, the German historian of religion who published his important book *The Idea of the Holy* in 1917, believed that this sense of the "numinous" was basic to religion. It preceded any desire to explain the origin of the world or find a basis for ethical behavior. The numinous power was sensed by human beings in different ways—sometimes it inspired wild, bacchanalian excitement; sometimes a deep calm; sometimes people felt dread, awe and humility in the presence of the mysterious force inherent in every aspect of life. When people began to devise their myths and worship their gods, they were not seeking a literal explanation for natural phenomena. The symbolic stories, cave paintings and carvings were an attempt to express their wonder and to link this pervasive mystery with their own lives; indeed, poets, artists and musicians are often impelled by a similar desire today. In the Palaeolithic period, for example, when agriculture was developing, the cult of the Mother Goddess expressed a sense that the fertility which was transforming human life was actually sacred. Artists carved those statues depicting her as a naked, pregnant woman which archaeologists have found all over Europe, the Middle East and India. The Great Mother remained imaginatively important for centuries. Like the old Sky God, she was absorbed into later pantheons and took her place alongside the older deities. She was usually one of the most powerful of the gods, certainly more powerful than the Sky God, who remained a rather shadowy figure. She was called Inana in ancient Sumeria, Ishtar in Babylon, Anat in Canaan, Isis in Egypt and Aphrodite in Greece, and remarkably similar stories were devised in all these cultures to express her role in the spiritual lives of the people. These myths were not intended to be taken literally, but were metaphorical attempts to describe a reality that was too complex and elusive to express in any other way. These dramatic and evocative stories of gods and goddesses helped people to articulate their sense of the powerful but unseen forces that surrounded them.

Indeed, it seems that in the ancient world people believed that it was only by participating in this divine life that they would become truly human. Earthly life was obviously fragile and overshadowed by mortality, but if men and women imitated the actions of the gods they would share to some degree their greater power and effectiveness. Thus it was said that the gods had shown men how to build their cities and temples, which were mere copies of their own homes in the divine realm. The sacred world of the gods—as recounted in myth—was not just an ideal toward which men and women should aspire, but was the prototype of human existence; it was the original pattern or the archetype on which our life here below had been modeled. Everything on earth was thus believed to be a replica of something in the divine world, a perception that informed the mythology, ritual and social organization of most of the cultures of antiquity and continues to influence more traditional societies in our own day.[1] In ancient Iran, for example, every single person or object in the mundane world (*getik*) was held to have its counterpart in the archetypal world of sacred reality (*menok*). This is a perspective that is difficult for us to appreciate in the modern world, since we see autonomy and independence as supreme human values. Yet the famous tag *post coitum omne animal tristis est* still expresses a common experience: after an intense and eagerly anticipated moment, we often feel that we have missed something greater that remains just beyond our grasp. The imitation of a god is still an important religious notion: resting on the Sabbath or washing somebody's feet on Maundy Thursday—actions that are meaningless in themselves—are now significant and sacred because people believe that they were once performed by God.

A similar spirituality had characterized the ancient world of Mesopotamia. The Tigris-Euphrates valley, in what is now Iraq, had been inhabited as early as 4000 BCE by the people known as the Sumerians, who had established one of the first great cultures of the Oikumene (the civilized world). In their cities of Ur, Erech and Kish, the Sumerians devised their cuneiform script, built the extraordinary temple-towers called ziggurats and evolved an impressive law, literature and mythology. Not long afterward the region was invaded by the Semitic Akkadians, who had adopted the language and culture of Sumer. Later still, in about 2000 BCE, the Amorites had conquered this Sumerian-Akkadian civilization and made Babylon their capital. Finally, some 500 years later, the Assyrians had settled in nearby Ashur and eventually conquered Babylon itself during the eighth century BCE. This Babylonian tradition also affected the mythology and religion of Canaan, which would become the Promised Land of the ancient Israelites. Like other people in the ancient world, the Babylonians attributed their cultural achievements to the gods, who had revealed their own lifestyle to their mythical ancestors. Thus Babylon itself was supposed to be an image of heaven, with each of its temples a replica of a celestial palace. This link with the divine world was celebrated and perpetuated annually in the great New Year Festival, which had been firmly established by the seventeenth century BCE. Celebrated in the holy city of Babylon during the month of Nisan—our April—the Festival solemnly enthroned the king and established his reign for another year. Yet this political stability could only endure insofar as it participated in the more enduring and effective government of the gods, who had brought order out of primordial chaos when they had created the world. The eleven sacred days of the Festival thus projected the participants outside profane time into the sacred and eternal world of the gods by means of ritual gestures. A scapegoat was killed to cancel the old, dying year; the public humiliation of the king and the enthronement of a carnival king in his place reproduced the original chaos; a mock battle reenacted the struggle of the gods against the forces of destruction.

These symbolic actions thus had a sacramental value; they enabled the people of Babylon to immerse themselves in the sacred power or *mana* on which their own great civilization depended. Culture was felt to be a fragile achievement, which could always fall prey to the forces of disorder and disintegration. On the afternoon of the fourth day of the Festival, priests and choristers filed into the Holy of Holies to recite the *Enuma Elish*, the epic poem which celebrated the victory of the gods over chaos. The story was not a factual account of the physical origins of life upon earth, but was a deliberately symbolic attempt to suggest a great mystery and to release its sacred power. A literal account of creation was impossible, since nobody had been present at these unimaginable events: myth and symbol were thus the only suitable way of describing them. A brief look at the *Enuma Elish* gives us some insight into the spirituality which gave birth to our own Creator God centuries later. Even though the biblical and Koranic account of creation would ultimately take a very different form, these strange myths never entirely disappeared, but would reenter the history of God at a much later date, clothed in a monotheistic idiom.

The story begins with the creation of the gods themselves—a theme which, as we shall see, would be very important in Jewish and Muslim mysticism. In the beginning, said the *Enuma Elish*, the gods emerged two by two from a formless, watery waste—a substance which was itself divine. In Babylonian myth—as later in the Bible—there was no creation out of nothing, an idea that was alien to the ancient world. Before either the gods or human beings existed, this sacred raw material had existed from all eternity. When the Babylonians tried to imagine this primordial divine stuff, they thought that it must have been similar to the swampy wasteland of Mesopotamia, where floods constantly threatened to wipe out the frail works of men. In the *Enuma Elish*, chaos is not a fiery, seething mass, therefore, but a sloppy mess where everything lacks boundary, definition and identity:

> When sweet and bitter
> mingled together, no reed was plaited, no rushes
> muddied the water,
> the gods were nameless, natureless, futureless.[2]

Then three gods did emerge from the primal wasteland: Apsu (identified with the sweet waters of the rivers), his wife, Tiamat (the salty sea), and Mummu, the Womb of chaos. Yet these gods were, so to speak, an early, inferior model which needed improvement. The names "Apsu" and "Tiamat" can be translated "abyss," "void" or "bottomless gulf." They share the shapeless inertia of the original formlessness and had not yet achieved a clear identity.

Consequently, a succession of other gods emerged from them in a process known as emanation, which would become very important in the history of our own God. The new gods emerged, one from the other, in pairs, each of which had acquired a greater definition than the last as the divine evolution progressed. First came Lahmu and Lahamn (their names mean "silt": water and earth are still mixed together). Next came Ansher and Kishar, identified respectively with the horizons of sky and sea. Then Anu (the heavens) and Ea (the earth) arrived and seemed to complete the process. The divine world had sky, rivers and earth, distinct and separate from one another. But creation had only just begun: the forces of chaos and disintegration could only be held at bay by means of a painful and incessant struggle. The younger, dynamic gods rose up against their parents, but even though Ea was able to overpower Apsu and Mummu, he could make no headway against Tiamat, who produced a whole brood of misshapen monsters to fight on her behalf. Fortunately Ea had a wonderful child of his own: Marduk, the Sun God, the most perfect specimen of the divine line. At a meeting of the Great Assembly of gods, Marduk promised to fight Tiamat on condition that he became their ruler. Yet he only managed to slay Tiamat with great difficulty and after a long, dangerous battle. In this myth, creativity is a struggle, achieved laboriously against overwhelming odds.

Eventually, however, Marduk stood over Tiamat's vast corpse and decided to create a new world: he split her body in two to form the arch of the sky and the world of men; next he devised the laws that would keep everything in its appointed place. Order must be achieved. Yet the victory was not complete. It had to be reestablished, by means of a special liturgy, year after year. Consequently the gods met at Babylon, the center of the new earth, and built a temple where the celestial rites could be performed. The result was the great ziggurat in honor of Marduk, "the earthly temple, symbol of infinite heaven." When it was completed, Marduk took his seat at the summit and the gods cried aloud: "This is Babylon, dear city of the god, your beloved home!" Then they performed the liturgy "from which the universe receives its structure, the hidden world is made plain and the gods assigned their places in the universe."[3] These laws and rituals are binding upon everybody; even the gods must observe them to ensure the survival of creation. The myth expresses the inner meaning of civilization, as the Babylonians saw it. They knew perfectly well that their own ancestors had built the ziggurat, but the story of the *Enuma Elish* articulated their belief that their creative enterprise could only endure if it partook of the power of the divine. The liturgy they celebrated at the New Year had been devised before human beings had come into existence: it was written into the very nature of things, to which even the gods had to submit. The myth also expressed their conviction that Babylon was a sacred place, the center of the world and the home of the gods—a notion that was crucial in almost all the religious systems of antiquity. The idea of a holy city, where men and women felt that they were closely in touch with sacred power, the source of all being and efficacy, would be important in all three of the monotheistic religions of our own God.

Finally, almost as an afterthought, Marduk created humanity. He seized Kingu (the oafish consort of Tiamat, created by her after the defeat of Apsu), slew him and shaped the first man by mixing the divine blood with the dust. The gods watched in astonishment and admiration. There is, however, some humor in this mythical account of the origin of humanity, which is by no means the pinnacle of creation but derives from one of the most stupid and ineffectual of the gods. But the story made another important point. The first man had been created from the substance of a god: he therefore shared the divine nature, in however limited a way. There was no gulf between human beings and the gods. The natural world, men and women and the gods themselves all shared the same nature and derived from the same divine substance. The pagan vision was holistic. The gods were not shut off from the human race in a separate, ontological sphere: divinity was not essentially different from humanity. There was thus no need for a special revelation of the gods or for a divine law to descend to earth from on high. The gods and human beings shared the same predicament, the only difference being that the gods were more powerful and were immortal.

This holistic vision was not confined to the Middle East but was com-

mon in the ancient world. In the sixth century BCE, Pindar expressed the
Greek version of this belief in his ode on the Olympic games:

> Single is the race, single
> Of men and gods;
> From a single mother we both draw breath.
> But a difference of power in everything
> Keeps us apart;
> For one is as nothing, but the brazen sky
> Stays a fixed habituation for ever.
> Yet we can in greatness of mind
> Or of body be like the Immortals.[4]

Instead of seeing his athletes as on their own, each striving to achieve his
personal best, Pindar sets them against the exploits of the gods, who were
the pattern for all human achievement. Men were not slavishly imitating
the gods as hopelessly distant beings but living up to the potential of their
own essentially divine nature.

The myth of Marduk and Tiamat seems to have influenced the people
of Canaan, who told a very similar story about Baal-Habad, the god of
storm and fertility, who is often mentioned in extremely unflattering
terms in the Bible. The story of Baal's battle with Yam-Nahar, the god
of the seas and rivers, is told on tablets that date to the fourteenth century
BCE. Baal and Yam both lived with El, the Canaanite High God. At the
Council of El, Yam demands that Baal be delivered up to him. With two
magic weapons, Baal defeats Yam and is about to kill him when Asherah
(El's wife and mother of the gods) pleads that it is dishonorable to slay a
prisoner. Baal is ashamed and spares Yam, who represents the hostile
aspect of the seas and rivers which constantly threaten to flood the earth,
while Baal, the Storm God, makes the earth fertile. In another version of
the myth, Baal slays the seven-headed dragon Lotan, who is called Levia-
than in Hebrew. In almost all cultures, the dragon symbolizes the latent,
the unformed and the undifferentiated. Baal has thus halted the slide back
to primal formlessness in a truly creative act and is rewarded by a beautiful
palace built by the gods in his honor. In very early religion, therefore,
creativity was seen as divine: we still use religious language to speak of
creative "inspiration" which shapes reality anew and brings fresh meaning
to the world.

But Baal undergoes a reverse: he dies and has to descend to the world
of Mot, the god of death and sterility. When he hears of his son's fate,

the High God El comes down from his throne, puts on sackcloth and gashes his cheeks, but he cannot redeem his son. It is Anat, Baal's lover and sister, who leaves the divine realm and goes in search of her twin soul, "desiring him as a cow her calf or a ewe her lamb."[5] When she finds his body, she makes a funeral feast in his honor, seizes Mot, cleaves him with her sword, winnows, burns and grinds him like corn before sowing him in the ground. Similar stories are told about the other great goddesses—Inana, Ishtar and Isis—who search for the dead god and bring new life to the soil. The victory of Anat, however, must be perpetuated year after year in ritual celebration. Later—we are not sure how, since our sources are incomplete—Baal is brought back to life and restored to Anat. This apotheosis of wholeness and harmony, symbolized by the union of the sexes, was celebrated by means of ritual sex in ancient Canaan. By imitating the gods in this way, men and women would share their struggle against sterility and ensure the creativity and fertility of the world. The death of a god, the quest of the goddess and the triumphant return to the divine sphere were constant religious themes in many cultures and would recur in the very different religion of the One God worshipped by Jews, Christians and Muslims.

This religion is attributed in the Bible to Abraham, who left Ur and eventually settled in Canaan some time between the twentieth and nineteenth centuries BCE. We have no contemporary record of Abraham, but scholars think that he may have been one of the wandering chieftains who had led their people from Mesopotamia toward the Mediterranean at the end of the third millennium BCE. These wanderers, some of whom are called Abiru, Apiru or Habiru in Mesopotamian and Egyptian sources, spoke West Semitic languages, of which Hebrew is one. They were not regular desert nomads like the Bedouin, who migrated with their flocks according to the cycle of the seasons, but were more difficult to classify and, as such, were frequently in conflict with the conservative authorities. Their cultural status was usually superior to that of the desert folk. Some served as mercenaries, others became government employees, others worked as merchants, servants or tinkers. Some became rich and might then try to acquire land and settle down. The stories about Abraham in the Book of Genesis show him serving the King of Sodom as a mercenary and describe his frequent conflicts with the authorities of Canaan and its environs. Eventually, when his wife, Sarah, died, Abraham bought land in Hebron, now on the West Bank.

The Genesis account of Abraham and his immediate descendants may indicate that there were three main waves of early Hebrew settlement in

Canaan, the modern Israel. One was associated with Abraham and Hebron and took place in about 1850 BCE. A second wave of immigration
was linked with Abraham's grandson Jacob, who was renamed Israel
("May God show his strength!"); he settled in Shechem, which is now
the Arab town of Nablus on the West Bank. The Bible tells us that Jacob's
sons, who became the ancestors of the twelve tribes of Israel, emigrated
to Egypt during a severe famine in Canaan. The third wave of Hebrew
settlement occurred in about 1200 BCE when tribes who claimed to be
descendants of Abraham arrived in Canaan from Egypt. They said that
they had been enslaved by the Egyptians but had been liberated by a
deity called Yahweh, who was the god of their leader, Moses. After
they had forced their way into Canaan, they allied themselves with the
Hebrews there and became known as the people of Israel. The Bible
makes it clear that the people we know as the ancient Israelites were a
confederation of various ethnic groups, bound together principally by
their loyalty to Yahweh, the God of Moses. The biblical account was
written down centuries later, however, in about the eighth century BCE,
though it certainly drew on earlier narrative sources.

During the nineteenth century, some German biblical scholars developed a critical method which discerned four different sources in the
first five books of the Bible: Genesis, Exodus, Leviticus, Numbers and
Deuteronomy. These were later collated into the final text of what we
know as the Pentateuch during the fifth century BCE. This form of criticism has come in for a good deal of harsh treatment, but nobody has yet
come up with a more satisfactory theory which explains why there are
two quite different accounts of key biblical events, such as the Creation
and the Flood, and why the Bible sometimes contradicts itself. The two
earliest biblical authors, whose work is found in Genesis and Exodus,
were probably writing during the eighth century, though some would
give them an earlier date. One is known as "J" because he calls his God
"Yahweh," the other "E" since he prefers to use the more formal divine
title "Elohim." By the eighth century, the Israelites had divided Canaan
into two separate kingdoms. J was writing in the southern Kingdom of
Judah, while E came from the northern Kingdom of Israel. (See map
p. viii.) We will discuss the two other sources of the Pentateuch—the
Deuteronomist (D) and Priestly (P) accounts of the ancient history of
Israel—in Chapter 2.

We shall see that in many respects both J and E shared the religious
perspectives of their neighbors in the Middle East, but their accounts do
show that by the eighth century BCE, the Israelites were beginning to

develop a distinct vision of their own. J, for example, starts his history of God with an account of the creation of the world which, compared with the *Enuma Elish*, is startlingly perfunctory:

> At the time when Yahweh God made earth and heaven, there was as yet no wild bush on the earth nor had any wild plant yet sprung up, for Yahweh God had not sent rain on the earth nor was there any man to till the soil. However, a flood was rising from the earth and watering all the surface of the soil. Yahweh God fashioned man (*adām*) of dust from the soil (*adāmah*). Then he breathed into his nostrils the breath of life and thus man became a living being.[6]

This was an entirely new departure. Instead of concentrating on the creation of the world and on the prehistoric period like his pagan contemporaries in Mesopotamia and Canaan, J is more interested in ordinary historical time. There would be no real interest in creation in Israel until the sixth century BCE, when the author whom we call "P" wrote his majestic account in what is now the first chapter of Genesis. J is not absolutely clear that Yahweh *is* the sole creator of heaven and earth. Most noticeable, however, is J's perception of a certain distinction between man and the divine. Instead of being composed of the same divine stuff as his god, man (*adām*), as the pun indicates, belongs to the earth (*adāmah*).

Unlike his pagan neighbors, J does not dismiss mundane history as profane, feeble and insubstantial compared with the sacred, primordial time of the gods. He hurries through the events of prehistory until he comes to the end of the mythical period, which includes such stories as the Flood and the Tower of Babel, and arrives at the start of the history of the people of Israel. This begins abruptly in Chapter 12 when the man Abram, who will later be renamed Abraham ("Father of a Multitude"), is commanded by Yahweh to leave his family in Haran, in what is now eastern Turkey, and migrate to Canaan near the Mediterranean Sea. We have been told that his father, Terah, a pagan, had already migrated westward with his family from Ur. Now Yahweh tells Abraham that he has a special destiny: he will become the father of a mighty nation that will one day be more numerous than the stars in the sky, and one day his descendants will possess the land of Canaan as their own. J's account of the call of Abraham sets the tone for the future history of this God. In the ancient Middle East, the divine *mana* was experienced in ritual and myth. Marduk, Baal and Anat were not expected to involve themselves in the ordinary, profane lives of their worshippers: their actions had been performed in sacred time. The God of Israel, however, made his power effective in current events in the real world. He was experienced as an imperative in the here and now. His first revelation of himself consists of a command: Abraham is to leave his people and travel to the land of Canaan.

But who is Yahweh? Did Abraham worship the same God as Moses or did he know him by a different name? This would be a matter of prime importance to us today, but the Bible seems curiously vague on the subject and gives conflicting answers to this question. J says that men had worshipped Yahweh ever since the time of Adam's grandson, but in the sixth century, P seems to suggest that the Israelites had never heard of Yahweh until he appeared to Moses in the Burning Bush. P makes Yahweh explain that he really *was* the same God as the God of Abraham, as though this were a rather controversial notion: he tells Moses that Abraham had called him "El Shaddai" and did not know the divine name Yahweh.[7] The discrepancy does not seem to worry either the biblical writers or their editors unduly. J calls his god "Yahweh" throughout: by the time he was writing, Yahweh *was* the God of Israel and that was all that mattered. Israelite religion was pragmatic and less concerned with the kind of speculative detail that would worry us. Yet we should not assume that either Abraham or Moses believed in their God as we do today. We are so familiar with the Bible story and the subsequent history of Israel that we tend to project our knowledge of later Jewish religion back onto these early historical personages. Accordingly, we assume that the three patriarchs of Israel—Abraham, his son Isaac and his grandson Jacob—were monotheists, that they believed in only one God. This does not seem to have been the case. Indeed, it is probably more accurate to call these early Hebrews pagans who shared many of the religious beliefs of their neighbors in Canaan. They would certainly have believed in the existence of such deities as Marduk, Baal and Anat. They may not all have worshipped the same deity: it is possible that the God of Abraham, the "Fear" or "Kinsman" of Isaac and the "Mighty One" of Jacob were three separate gods.[8]

We can go further. It is highly likely that Abraham's God was El, the High God of Canaan. The deity introduces himself to Abraham as El Shaddai (El of the Mountain), which was one of El's traditional titles.[9] Elsewhere he is called El Elyon (The Most High God) or El of Bethel. The name of the Canaanite High God is preserved in such Hebrew names as Isra-El or Ishma-El. They experienced him in ways that would not have been unfamiliar to the pagans of the Middle East. We shall see that centuries later Israelites found the *mana* or "holiness" of Yahweh a terrifying experience. On Mount Sinai, for example, he would appear to Moses in the midst of an awe-inspiring volcanic eruption, and the Israelites had to keep their distance. In comparison, Abraham's god El is a very mild deity. He appears to Abraham as a friend and sometimes even assumes human form. This type of divine apparition, known as an epiphany, was quite common in the pagan world of antiquity. Even though in general the gods were not expected to intervene directly in the lives of mortal men and women, certain privileged individuals in mythical times had encountered their gods face to face. The *Iliad* is full of such epiphanies. The gods and goddesses appear to both Greeks and Trojans in dreams, when the boundary between the human and divine worlds was believed to be lowered. At the very end of the *Iliad*, Priam is guided to the Greek ships by a charming young man who finally reveals himself as Hermes.[10] When the Greeks looked back to the golden age of their heroes, they felt that they had been closely in touch with the gods, who were, after all, of the same nature as human beings. These stories of epiphanies expressed the holistic pagan vision: when the divine was not essentially distinct from either nature or humanity, it could be experienced without great fanfare. The world was full of gods, who could be perceived unexpectedly at any time, around any corner or in the person of a passing stranger. It seems that ordinary folk may have believed that such divine encounters were possible in their own lives: this may explain the strange story in the Acts of the Apostles when, as late as the first century CE, the apostle Paul and his disciple Barnabas were mistaken for Zeus and Hermes by the people of Lystra in what is now Turkey.[11]

In much the same way, when the Israelites looked back to their own golden age, they saw Abraham, Isaac and Jacob living on familiar terms with their god. El gives them friendly advice, like any sheikh or chieftain: he guides their wanderings, tells them whom to marry and speaks to them in dreams. Occasionally they seem to see him in human form—an idea that would later be anathema to the Israelites. In Chapter 18 of Genesis, J tells us that God appeared to Abraham by the oak tree of Mamre, near Hebron. Abraham had looked up and noticed three strangers approaching his tent during the hottest part of the day. With typical Middle Eastern courtesy, he insisted that they sit down and rest while he hurried to prepare food for them. In the course of conversation, it transpired, quite naturally, that one of these men was none other than his god, whom J always calls "Yahweh." The other two men turn out to be angels. Nobody seems particularly surprised by this revelation. By the time J was writing in the eighth century BCE, no Israelite would have expected to "see" God in this way: most would have found it a shocking notion. J's contemporary, "E," finds the old stories about the patriarchs' intimacy with God unseemly: when E tells stories about Abraham's or Jacob's dealings with God, he prefers to distance the event and make the old legends less anthropomorphic. Thus he will say that God speaks to Abraham through an angel. J, however, does not share this squeamishness and preserves the ancient flavor of these primitive epiphanies in his account.

Jacob also experienced a number of epiphanies. On one occasion, he had decided to return to Haran to find a wife among his relatives there. On the first leg of his journey, he slept at Luz near the Jordan valley, using a stone as a pillow. That night he dreamed of a ladder which stretched between earth and heaven: angels were going up and down between the realms of god and man. We cannot but be reminded of Marduk's ziggurat: on its summit, suspended as it were between heaven and earth, a man could meet his gods. At the top of his own ladder, Jacob dreamed that he saw El, who blessed him and repeated the promises that he had made to Abraham: Jacob's descendants would become a mighty nation and possess the land of Canaan. He also made a promise that made a significant impression on Jacob, as we shall see. Pagan religion was often territorial: a god had jurisdiction only in a particular area, and it was always wise to worship the local deities when you went abroad. But El promised Jacob that he would protect him when he left Canaan and wandered in a strange land: "I am with you; I will keep you safe wherever you go."[12] The story of this early epiphany shows that the High God of Canaan was beginning to acquire a more universal implication.

When he woke up, Jacob realized that he had unwittingly spent the night in a holy place where men could have converse with their gods: "Truly Yahweh is in this place, and I never knew it!" J makes him say. He was filled with the wonder that often inspired pagans when they encountered the sacred power of the divine: "How awe-inspiring this place is! This is nothing less than a house of God (*beth El*); this is the gate of heaven."[13] He had instinctively expressed himself in the religious language of his time and culture: Babylon itself, the abode of the gods, was called "Gate of the gods" (*Bab-ili*). Jacob decided to consecrate this holy ground in the traditional pagan manner of the country. He took the stone he had used as a pillow, upended it and sanctified it with a libation of oil. Henceforth the place would no longer be called Luz but Beth-El, the House of El. Standing stones were a common feature of Canaanite fertility cults, which, we shall see, flourished at Beth-El until the eighth century BCE. Although later Israelites vigorously condemned this type of religion, the pagan sanctuary of Beth-El was associated in early legend with Jacob and his God.

Before he left Beth-El, Jacob had decided to make the god he had encountered there his *elohim*: this was a technical term, signifying everything that the gods could mean for men and women. Jacob had decided that if El (or Yahweh, as J calls him) could really look after him in Haran, he was particularly effective. He struck a bargain: in return for El's special protection, Jacob would make him his *elohim*, the only god who counted. Israelite belief in God was deeply pragmatic. Abraham and Jacob both put their faith in El because he worked for them: they did not sit down and prove that he existed; El was not a philosophical abstraction. In the ancient world, *mana* was a self-evident fact of life, and a god proved his worth if he could transmit this effectively. This pragmatism would always be a factor in the history of God. People would continue to adopt a particular conception of the divine because it worked for them, not because it was scientifically or philosophically sound.

Years later Jacob returned from Haran with his wives and family. As he reentered the land of Canaan, he experienced another strange epiphany. At the ford of Jabbok on the West Bank, he met a stranger who wrestled with him all night. At daybreak, like most spiritual beings, his opponent said that he had to leave, but Jacob held on to him: he would not let him go until he had revealed his name. In the ancient world, knowing somebody's name gave you a certain power over him, and the stranger seemed reluctant to reveal this piece of information. As the strange encounter developed, Jacob became aware that his opponent had been none other than El himself:

> Jacob then made this request, "I beg you, tell me your name." But he replied, "Why do you ask my name?" and he blessed him there. Jacob named the place Peni-El [El's Face] "Because I have seen El face to face," he said, "and I have survived."[14]

The spirit of this epiphany is closer to the spirit of the *Iliad* than to later Jewish monotheism, when such intimate contact with the divine would have seemed a blasphemous notion.

Yet even though these early tales show the patriarchs encountering their god in much the same way as their pagan contemporaries, they do introduce a new category of religious experience. Throughout the Bible, Abraham is called a man of "faith." Today we tend to define faith as an intellectual assent to a creed, but, as we have seen, the biblical writers did not view faith in God as an abstract or metaphysical belief. When they praise the "faith" of Abraham, they are not commending his ortho-doxy (the acceptance of a correct theological opinion about God) but his trust, in rather the same way as when we say that we have faith *in* a person or an ideal. In the Bible, Abraham is a man of faith because he trusts that God would make good his promises, even though they seem absurd. How could Abraham be the father of a great nation when his wife, Sarah, is barren? Indeed, the very idea that she could have a child is so ridiculous—Sarah has passed menopause—that when they hear this promise both Sarah and Abraham burst out laughing. When, against all the odds, their son is finally born, they call him Isaac, a name that may mean "laughter." The joke turns sour, however, when God makes an appalling demand: Abraham must sacrifice his only son to him.

Human sacrifice was common in the pagan world. It was cruel but had a logic and rationale. The first child was often believed to be the offspring of a god, who had impregnated the mother in an act of *droit de seigneur*. In begetting the child, the god's energy had been depleted, so to replenish this and to ensure the circulation of all the available *mana*, the firstborn was returned to its divine parent. The case of Isaac was quite different, however. Isaac had been a gift of God but not his natural son. There was no reason for the sacrifice, no need to replenish the divine energy. Indeed, the sacrifice would make nonsense of Abraham's entire life, which had been based on the promise that he would be the father of a great nation. This god was already beginning to be conceived differently from most other deities in the ancient world. He did not share the human predica-ment; he did not require an input of energy from men and women. He was in a different league and could make whatever demands he chose. Abraham decided to trust his god. He and Isaac set off on a three-day journey to the Mount of Moriah, which would later be the site of the Temple in Jerusalem. Isaac, who knew nothing of the divine command, even had to carry the wood for his own holocaust. It was not until the very last moment, when Abraham actually had the knife in his hand, that God relented and told him that it had only been a test. Abraham had proved himself worthy of becoming the father of a mighty nation, which would be as numerous as the stars in the sky or the grains of sand on the seashore.

Yet to modern ears, this is a horrible story: it depicts God as a despotic and capricious sadist, and it is not surprising that many people today who have heard this tale as children reject such a deity. The myth of the

Exodus from Egypt, when God led Moses and the children of Israel to freedom, is equally offensive to modern sensibilities. The story is well known. Pharaoh was reluctant to let the people of Israel go, so to force his hand, God sent ten fearful plagues upon the people of Egypt. The Nile was turned to blood; the land ravaged with locusts and frogs; the whole country plunged into impenetrable darkness. Finally God unleashed the most terrible plague of all: he sent the Angel of Death to kill the firstborn sons of all the Egyptians, while sparing the sons of the Hebrew slaves. Not surprisingly, Pharaoh decided to let the Israelites leave but later changed his mind and pursued them with his army. He caught up with them at the Sea of Reeds, but God saved the Israelites by opening the sea and letting them cross dry-shod. When the Egyptians followed in their wake, he closed the waters and drowned the Pharaoh and his army.

This is a brutal, partial and murderous god: a god of war who would be known as Yahweh Sabaoth, the God of Armies. He is passionately partisan, has little compassion for anyone but his own favorites and is simply a tribal deity. If Yahweh had remained such a savage god, the sooner he vanished, the better it would have been for everybody. The final myth of the Exodus, as it has come down to us in the Bible, is clearly not meant to be a literal version of events. It would, however, have had a clear message for the people of the ancient Middle East, who were used to gods splitting the seas in half. Yet unlike Marduk and Baal, Yahweh was said to have divided a physical sea in the profane world of historical time. There is little attempt at realism. When the Israelites recounted the story of the Exodus, they were not as interested in historical accuracy as we would be today. Instead, they wanted to bring out the significance of the original event, whatever that may have been. Some modern scholars suggest that the Exodus story is a mythical rendering of a successful peasants' revolt against the suzerainty of Egypt and its allies in Canaan.[15] This would have been an extremely rare occurrence at the time and would have made an indelible impression on everybody involved. It would have been an extraordinary experience of the empowerment of the oppressed against the powerful and the mighty.

We shall see that Yahweh did not remain the cruel and violent god of the Exodus, even though the myth has been important in all three of the monotheistic religions. Surprising as it may seem, the Israelites would transform him beyond recognition into a symbol of transcendence and compassion. Yet the bloody story of the Exodus would continue to inspire dangerous conceptions of the divine and a vengeful theology. We shall see that during the seventh century BCE, the Deuteronomist author (D) would use the old myth to illustrate the fearful theology of election, which has, at different times, played a fateful role in the history of all three faiths. Like any human idea, the notion of God can be exploited and abused. The myth of a Chosen People and a divine election has often inspired a narrow, tribal theology from the time of the Deuteronomist right up to the Jewish, Christian and Muslim fundamentalism that is unhappily rife in our own day. Yet the Deuteronomist has also preserved an interpretation of the Exodus myth that has been equally and more positively effective in the history of monotheism, which speaks of a God who is on the side of the impotent and the oppressed. In Deuteronomy 26, we have what may be an early interpretation of the Exodus story before it was written down in the narratives of J and E. The Israelites are commanded to present the first fruits of the harvest to the priests of Yahweh and make this affirmation:

> My father was a wandering Aramaean. He went down to Egypt to find refuge there, few in numbers; but there he became a nation, great, mighty and strong. The Egyptians ill-treated us, they gave us no peace and inflicted harsh slavery upon us. But we called on Yahweh the God of our fathers. Yahweh heard our voice and saw our misery, our toil and our oppression; and Yahweh brought us out of Egypt with mighty hand and outstretched arm, with great terror, and with signs and wonders. He brought us here [to Canaan] and gave us this land, a land where milk and honey flow. Here then I bring the first-fruits of the produce of the soil that you, Yahweh, have given me.[16]

The God who may have inspired the first successful peasants' uprising in history is a God of revolution. In all three faiths, he has inspired an ideal of social justice, even though it has to be said that Jews, Christians and Muslims have often failed to live up to this ideal and have transformed him into the God of the status quo.

The Israelites called Yahweh "the God of our fathers," yet it seems that he may have been quite a different deity from El, the Canaanite High God worshipped by the patriarchs. He may have been the god of other people before he became the God of Israel. In all his early appearances to Moses, Yahweh insists repeatedly and at some length that he is indeed the God of Abraham, even though he had originally been called El Shaddai. This insistence may preserve the distant echoes of a very early debate about the identity of the God of Moses. It has been suggested that Yahweh was originally a warrior god, a god of volcanoes, a god worshipped in Midian, in what is now Jordan.[17] We shall never know where the Israelites discovered Yahweh, if indeed he really was a completely new deity. Again, this would be a very important question for us today, but it was not so crucial for the biblical writers. In pagan antiquity, gods were often merged and amalgamated, or the gods of one locality accepted as identical with the god of another people. All we can be sure of is that, whatever his provenance, the events of the Exodus made Yahweh the definitive God of Israel and that Moses was able to convince the Israelites that he really was one and the same as El, the God beloved by Abraham, Isaac and Jacob.

The so-called "Midianite Theory"—that Yahweh was originally a god of the people of Midian—is usually discredited today, but it was in Midian that Moses had his first vision of Yahweh. It will be recalled that Moses had been forced to flee Egypt for killing an Egyptian who was ill-treating an Israelite slave. He had taken refuge in Midian, married there, and it was while he was tending his father-in-law's sheep that he had seen a strange sight: a bush that burned without being consumed. When he went closer to investigate, Yahweh had called to him by name and Moses had cried: "Here I am!" (*hineni!*), the response of every prophet of Israel when he encountered the God who demanded total attention and loyalty:

> "Come no nearer" [God] said, "Take off your shoes for the place on which you stand is holy ground. I am the god of your father," he said, "the God of Abraham, the God of Isaac and the God of Jacob." At that Moses covered his face, afraid to look at God.[18]

Despite the first of the assertions that Yahweh is indeed the God of Abraham, this is clearly a very different kind of deity from the one who had sat and shared a meal with Abraham as his friend. He inspires terror and insists upon distance. When Moses asks his name and credentials, Yahweh replies with a pun which, as we shall see, would exercise mono-theists for centuries. Instead of revealing his name directly, he answers: "I Am Who I Am (*Ehyeh asher ehyeh*)."[19] What did he mean? He certainly did not mean, as later philosophers would assert, that he was self-subsist-ent Being. Hebrew did not have such a metaphysical dimension at this stage, and it would be nearly 2000 years before it acquired one. God seems to have meant something rather more direct. *Ehyeh asher ehyeh* is a Hebrew idiom to express a deliberate vagueness. When the Bible uses a phrase like "they went where they went," it means: "I haven't the faintest idea where they went." So when Moses asks who he is, God replies in effect: "Never you mind who I am!" or "Mind your own business!" There was to be no discussion of God's nature and certainly no attempt to manipulate him as pagans sometimes did when they recited the names of their gods. Yahweh is the Unconditioned One: I shall be that which I shall be. He will be exactly as he chooses and will make no guarantees. He simply promised that he would participate in the history of his people. The myth of the Exodus would prove decisive: it was able to engender hope for the future, even in impossible circumstances.

There was a price to be paid for this new sense of empowerment. The old Sky Gods had been experienced as too remote from human concerns; the younger deities like Baal, Marduk and the Mother Goddesses had come close to mankind, but Yahweh had opened the gulf between man and the divine world once again. This is graphically clear in the story of Mount Sinai. When they arrived at the mountain, the people were told to purify their garments and keep their distance. Moses had to warn the Israelites: "Take care not to go up the mountain or touch the foot of it. Whoever touches the mountain will be put to death." The people stood back from the mountain and Yahweh descended in fire and cloud:

> Now at daybreak on the third day there were peals of thunder on the mountain and lightning flashes, a dense cloud, and a loud trumpet blast, and inside the camp all the people trembled. Then Moses led the people out of the camp to meet God and they stood at the bottom of the mountain. The mountain of Sinai was entirely wrapped in smoke, because Yahweh had descended on it in the form of fire. Like smoke from a furnace, the smoke went up and the whole mountain shook violently.[20]

Moses alone went up to the summit and received the tablets of the Law. Instead of experiencing the principles of order, harmony and justice in the very nature of things, as in the pagan vision, the Law is now handed down from on high. The God of history can inspire a greater attention to the mundane world, which is the theater of his operations, but there is also the potential for a profound alienation from it.

In the final text of Exodus, edited in the fifth century BCE, God is said to have made a covenant with Moses on Mount Sinai (an event which is supposed to have happened around 1200). There has been a scholarly debate about this: some critics believe that the covenant did not become important in Israel until the seventh century BCE. But whatever its date, the idea of the covenant tells us that the Israelites were not yet monotheists, since it only made sense in a polytheistic setting. The Israelites did not believe that Yahweh, the God of Sinai, was the *only* God but promised, in their covenant, that they would ignore all the other deities and worship him alone. It is very difficult to find a single monotheistic statement in the whole of the Pentateuch. Even the Ten Commandments delivered on Mount Sinai take the existence of other gods for granted: "There shall be no strange gods for you before my face."[21] The worship of a single deity was an almost unprecedented step: the Egyptian pharaoh Akhenaton had attempted to worship the Sun God and to ignore the other traditional deities of Egypt, but his policies were immediately reversed by his successor. To ignore a potential source of *mana* seemed frankly foolhardy, and the subsequent history of the Israelites shows that they were very reluctant to neglect the cult of the other gods. Yahweh had proved his expertise in war, but he was not a fertility god. When they settled in Canaan, the Israelites turned instinctively to the cult of Baal, the Landlord of Canaan, who had made the crops grow from time immemorial. The prophets would urge the Israelites to remain true to the covenant, but the majority would continue to worship Baal, Asherah and Anat in the traditional way. Indeed, the Bible tells us that while Moses was up on Mount Sinai, the rest of the people turned back to the older pagan religion of Canaan. They made a golden bull, the traditional effigy of El, and performed the ancient rites before it. The placing of this incident in stark juxtaposition to the awesome revelation on Mount Sinai may be an attempt by the final editors of the Pentateuch to indicate the bitterness of the division in Israel. Prophets like Moses preached the lofty religion of Yahweh, but most of the people wanted the older rituals, with their holistic vision of unity among the gods, nature and mankind.

Yet the Israelites *had* promised to make Yahweh their only god after the Exodus, and the prophets would remind them of this agreement in later years. They had promised to worship Yahweh alone as their *elohim*, and, in return, he had promised that they would be his special people and enjoy his uniquely efficacious protection. Yahweh had warned them that if they broke this agreement, he would destroy them mercilessly. Yet the Israelites had entered into the covenant agreement, nonetheless. In the book of Joshua we find what may be an early text of the celebration of this covenant between Israel and its God. The covenant was a formal treaty that was frequently used in Middle Eastern politics to bind two parties together. It followed a set form. The text of the agreement would begin by introducing the king who was the more powerful partner and would then trace the history of the relations between the two parties to the present time. Finally, it stated the terms, conditions and penalties that would accrue if the covenant were neglected. Essential to the whole covenant idea was the demand for absolute loyalty. In the fourteenth-century covenant between the Hittite King Mursilis II and his vassal Duppi Tashed, the king made this demand: "Do not turn to anyone else. Your fathers presented tribute in Egypt; you shall not do that. . . . With my friend you shall be friend and with my enemy you shall be enemy." The Bible tells us that when the Israelites had arrived in Canaan and joined up with their kinsfolk there, all the descendants of Abraham made a covenant with Yahweh. The ceremony was conducted by Moses' successor Joshua, who represented Yahweh. The agreement follows the traditional pattern. Yahweh was introduced; his dealings with Abraham, Isaac and Jacob recalled; then the events of the Exodus were related. Finally Joshua stipulated the terms of the agreement and demanded the formal assent of the assembled people of Israel:

> So now, fear Yahweh and serve him perfectly and sincerely; put away the gods that you once served beyond the River [Jordan] and in Egypt and serve Yahweh. But if you will not serve Yahweh, choose today whom you wish to serve, whether the gods your ancestors served beyond the River or the gods of the Amorites in whose land you are now living.[22]

The people had a choice between Yahweh and the traditional gods of Canaan. They did not hesitate. There was no other god like Yahweh; no other deity had ever been so effective on behalf of his worshippers. His powerful intervention in their affairs had demonstrated beyond reasonable doubt that Yahweh was up to the job of being their *elohim*: they would worship him alone and cast away the other gods. Joshua warned them that Yahweh was exceedingly jealous. If they neglected the terms of the covenant, he would destroy them. The people stood firm: they chose Yahweh alone as their *elohim*. "Then cast away the alien gods from among you!" Josuah cried, "and give your hearts to Yahweh, the God of Israel!"[23]

The Bible shows that the people were not true to the covenant. They remembered it in times of war, when they needed Yahweh's skilled military protection, but when times were easy they worshipped Baal, Anat and Asherah in the old way. Although Yahweh's cult was fundamentally different in its historical bias, it often expressed itself in terms of the old paganism. When King Solomon built a Temple for Yahweh in Jerusalem, the city that his father, David, had captured from the Jebusites, it was similar to the temples of the Canaanite gods. It consisted of three square areas, which culminated in the small, cube-shaped room known as the Holy of Holies which contained the Ark of the Covenant, the portable altar which the Israelites had with them during their years in the wilderness. Inside the Temple was a huge bronze basin, representing Yam, the primeval sea of Canaanite myth, and two forty-foot freestanding pillars, indicating the fertility cult of Asherah. The Israelites continued to worship Yahweh in the ancient shrines which they had inherited from the Canaanites at Beth-El, Shiloh, Hebron, Bethlehem and Dan, where there were frequently pagan ceremonies. The Temple soon became special, however, even though, as we shall see, there were some remarkably unorthodox activities there too. The Israelites began to see the Temple as the replica of Yahweh's heavenly court. They had their own New Year Festival in the autumn, beginning with the scapegoat ceremony on the Day of Atonement, followed five days later by the harvest festival of the Feast of Tabernacles, which celebrated the beginning of the agricultural year. It has been suggested that some of the psalms celebrated the enthronement of Yahweh in his Temple on the Feast of Tabernacles, which, like the enthronement of Marduk, re-enacted his primal subjugation of chaos.[24] King Solomon himself was a great syncretist: he had many pagan wives, who worshipped their own gods, and had friendly dealings with his pagan neighbors.

There was always a danger that the cult of Yahweh would eventually be submerged by the popular paganism. This became particularly acute during the latter half of the ninth century. In 869 King Ahab had succeeded to the throne of the northern Kingdom of Israel. His wife, Jezebel, daughter of the King of Tyre and Sidon in what is now Lebanon, was an ardent pagan, intent upon converting the country to the religion of Baal and Asherah. She imported priests of Baal, who quickly acquired a following among the northerners, who had been conquered by King David and were lukewarm Yahwists. Ahab remained true to Yahweh but did not try to curb Jezebel's proselytism. When a severe drought struck the land toward the end of his reign, however, a prophet named Eli-Jah ("Yahweh is my god!") began to wander through the land, clad in a hairy mantle and a leather loincloth, fulminating against the disloyalty to Yahweh. He summoned King Ahab and the people to a contest on Mount Carmel between Yahweh and Baal. There, in the presence of 450 prophets of Baal, he harangued the people: how long would they dither between the two deities? Then he called for two bulls, one for himself and one for the prophets of Baal, to be placed on two altars. They would call upon their gods and see which one sent down fire from heaven to consume the holocaust. "Agreed!" cried the people. The prophets of Baal shouted his name for the whole morning, performing their hobbling dance around their altar, yelling and gashing themselves with swords and spears. But "there was no voice, no answer." Elijah jeered: "Call louder!" he cried, "for he is a god: he is preoccupied or he is busy, or he has gone on a journey; perhaps he is asleep and he will wake up." Nothing happened: "there was no voice, no answer, no attention given them."

Then it was Elijah's turn. The people crowded around the altar of Yahweh while he dug a trench around it which he filled with water, to make it even more difficult to ignite. Then Elijah called upon Yahweh. Immediately, of course, fire fell from heaven and consumed the altar and the bull, licking up all the water in the trench. The people fell upon their faces: "Yahweh is God," they cried, "Yahweh is God." Elijah was not a generous victor. "Seize the prophets of Baal!" he ordered. Not one was to be spared: he took them to a nearby valley and slaughtered the lot.[25] Paganism did not usually seek to impose itself on other people—Jezebel is an interesting exception—since there was always room for another god in the pantheon alongside the others. These early mythical events show that from the first Yahwism demanded a violent repression and denial of other faiths, a phenomenon we shall examine in more detail in the next chapter. After the massacre, Elijah climbed up to the top of Mount Carmel and sat in prayer with his head between his knees, sending his servant from time to time to scan the horizon. Eventually he brought news of a small cloud—about the size of a man's hand—rising up from the sea, and Elijah told him to go and warn King Ahab to hurry home before the rain stopped him. Almost as he spoke, the sky darkened with storm clouds and the rain fell in torrents. In an ecstasy, Elijah tucked up his cloak and ran alongside Ahab's chariot. By sending rain, Yahweh had usurped the function of Baal, the Storm God, proving that he was just as effective in fertility as in war.

Fearing a reaction against his massacre of the prophets, Elijah fled to the Sinai peninsula and took refuge on the mountain where God had revealed himself to Moses. There he experienced a theophany which manifested the new Yahwist spirituality. He was told to stand in the crevice of a rock to shield himself from the divine impact:

Then Yahweh himself went by. Thence came a mighty wind, so strong it tore the mountains and shattered the rocks before Yahweh. But Yahweh was not in the wind. After the wind came an earthquake. But Yahweh was not in the earthquake. After the earthquake came a fire. But Yahweh was not in the fire. And after the fire came the sound of a gentle breeze. And when Elijah heard this, he covered his face with a cloak.[26]

Unlike the pagan deities, Yahweh was not in any of the forces of nature but in a realm apart. He is experienced in the scarcely perceptible timbre of a tiny breeze in the paradox of a voiced silence.

The story of Elijah contains the last mythical account of the past in the Jewish scriptures. Change was in the air throughout the Oikumene. The period 800–200 BCE has been termed the Axial Age. In all the main regions of the civilized world, people created new ideologies that have continued to be crucial and formative. The new religious systems reflected the changed economic and social conditions. For reasons that we do not entirely understand, all the chief civilizations developed along parallel lines, even when there was no commercial contact (as between China and the European area). There was a new prosperity that led to the rise of a merchant class. Power was shifting from king and priest, temple and palace, to the marketplace. The new wealth led to intellectual and cultural florescence and also to the development of the individual conscience. Inequality and exploitation became more apparent as the pace of change accelerated in the cities and people began to realize that their own behavior could affect the fate of future generations. Each region developed a distinctive ideology to address these problems and concerns: Taoism and Confucianism in China, Hinduism and Buddhism in India and philosophical rationalism in Europe. The Middle East did not produce a uniform solution, but in Iran and Israel, Zoroaster and the Hebrew prophets respectively evolved different versions of monotheism. Strange as it may seem, the idea of "God," like the other great religious insights of the period, developed in a market economy in a spirit of aggressive capitalism.

I propose to look briefly at two of these new developments before proceeding in the next chapter to examine the reformed religion of Yahweh. The religious experience of India developed along similar lines, but its different emphasis will illuminate the peculiar characteristics and problems of the Israelite notion of God. The rationalism of Plato and Aristotle is also important because Jews, Christians and Muslims all drew upon their ideas and tried to adapt them to their own religious experience, even though the Greek God was very different from their own.

In the seventeenth century BCE, Aryans from what is now Iran had invaded the Indus valley and subdued the indigenous population. They had imposed their religious ideas, which we find expressed in the collection of odes known as the *Rig-Veda*. There we find a multitude of gods, expressing many of the same values as the deities of the Middle East and presenting the forces of nature as instinct with power, life and personality. Yet there were signs that people were beginning to see that the various gods might simply be manifestations of one divine Absolute that transcended them all. Like the Babylonians, the Aryans were quite aware that their myths were not factual accounts of reality but expressed a mystery that not even the gods themselves could explain adequately. When they tried to imagine how the gods and the world had evolved from primal chaos, they concluded that nobody—not even the gods—could understand the mystery of existence:

> Who then knows whence it has arisen,
> Whence this emanation hath arisen,
> Whether God disposed it, or whether he did not,—
> Only he who is its overseer in highest heaven knows.
> Or perhaps he does not know![27]

The religion of the Vedas did not attempt to explain the origins of life or to give privileged answers to philosophical questions. Instead, it was designed to help people to come to terms with the wonder and terror of existence. It asked more questions than it answered, designed to hold the people in an attitude of reverent wonder.

By the eighth century BCE, when J and E were writing their chronicles, changes in the social and economic conditions of the Indian subcontinent meant that the old Vedic religion was no longer relevant. The ideas of the indigenous population that had been suppressed in the centuries following the Aryan invasions surfaced and led to a new religious hunger. The revived interest in karma, the notion that one's destiny is determined by one's own actions, made people unwilling to blame the gods for the irresponsible behavior of human beings. Increasingly the gods were seen as symbols of a single transcendent Reality. Vedic religion had become preoccupied with the rituals of sacrifice, but the revived interest in the old Indian practice of Yoga (the "yoking" of the powers of the mind by special disciplines of concentration) meant that people became dissatisfied with a religion that concentrated on externals. Sacrifice and liturgy were not enough: they wanted to discover the inner meaning of these rites. We shall note that the prophets of Israel felt the same dissatisfaction. In India, the gods were no longer seen as other beings who were external to their worshippers; instead men and women sought to achieve an inward realization of truth.

The gods were no longer very important in India. Henceforth they would be superseded by the religious teacher, who would be considered higher than the gods. It was a remarkable assertion of the value of humanity and the desire to take control of destiny: it would be the great religious insight of the subcontinent. The new religions of Hinduism and Buddhism did not deny the existence of the gods, nor did they forbid the people to worship them. In their view, such repression and denial would be damaging. Instead, Hindus and Buddhists sought new ways to transcend the gods, to go beyond them. During the eighth century, sages began to address these issues in the treatises called the *Aranyakas* and the *Upanishads*, known collectively as the *Vedanta*: the end of the Vedas. More and more *Upanishads* appeared, until by the end of the fifth century BCE there were about 200 of them. It is impossible to generalize about the religion we call Hinduism because it eschews systems and denies that one exclusive interpretation can be adequate. But the *Upanishads* did evolve a distinctive conception of godhood that transcends the gods but is found to be intimately present in all things.

In Vedic religion, people had experienced a holy power in the sacrificial ritual. They had called this sacred power Brahman. The priestly caste (known as Brahmanas) were also believed to possess this power. Since the ritual sacrifice was seen as the microcosm of the whole universe, Brahman gradually came to mean a power which sustains everything. The whole world was seen as the divine activity welling up from the mysterious being of Brahman, which was the inner meaning of all existence. The *Upanishads* encouraged people to cultivate a sense of Brahman in all things. It was a process of revelation in the literal meaning of the word: it was an unveiling of the hidden ground of all being. Everything that happens became a manifestation of Brahman: true insight lay in the perception of the unity behind the different phenomena. Some of the *Upanishads* saw Brahman as a personal power, but others saw it as strictly impersonal. Brahman cannot be addressed as "thou"; it is a neutral term, so is neither he nor she; nor is it experienced as the will of a sovereign deity. Brahman does not speak to mankind. It cannot meet men and women; it transcends all such human activities. Nor does it respond to us in a personal way: sin does not "offend" it, and it cannot be said to "love" us or be "angry." Thanking or praising it for creating the world would be entirely inappropriate.

This divine power would be utterly alien were it not for the fact that it also pervades, sustains and inspires *us*. The techniques of Yoga had made people aware of an inner world. These disciplines of posture, breathing, diet and mental concentration have also been developed independently in other cultures, as we shall see, and seem to produce an experience of enlightenment and illumination which have been interpreted differently but which seem natural to humanity. The *Upanishads* claimed that this experience of a new dimension of self was the same holy power that sustained the rest of the world. The eternal principle within each individual was called Atman: it was a new version of the old holistic vision of paganism, a rediscovery in new terms of the One Life within us and abroad which was essentially divine. The *Chandoga Upanishad* explains this in the parable of the salt. A young man called Sretaketu had studied the Vedas for twelve years and was rather full of himself. His father, Uddalaka, asked him a question which he was unable to answer, and then proceeded to teach him a lesson about the fundamental truth of which he was entirely ignorant. He told his son to put a piece of salt into water and report back to him the following morning. When his father asked him to produce the salt, Sretaketu could not find it because it had completely dissolved. Uddalaka began to question him:

> "Would you please sip it at this end? What is it like?" he said.
> "Salt."
> "Sip it in the middle. What is it like?"
> "Salt."
> "Sip it at the far end. What is it like?"
> "Salt."
> "Throw it away and then come to me."
> He did as he was told but [that did not stop the salt from] remaining the same.
> [His father] said to him: "My dear child, it is true that you cannot perceive Being here, but it is equally true that it *is* here. This first essence—the whole universe has as its Self: That is the Real: That is the Self: that *you* are, Sretaketu!"

Thus, even though we cannot see it, Brahman pervades the world and, as Atman, is found eternally within each one of us.[28]

Atman prevented God from becoming an idol, an exterior Reality "out there," a projection of our own fears and desires. God is not seen in Hinduism as a Being added on to the world as we know it, therefore, nor is it identical with the world. There was no way that we could fathom this out by reason. It is only "revealed" to us by an experience (*anubhara*) which cannot be expressed in words or concepts. Brahman is "What cannot be spoken in words, but that whereby words are spoken . . . What cannot be thought with the mind, but that whereby the mind can think."[29] It is impossible to speak *to* a God that is as immanent as this or to think *about* it, making it a mere object of thought. It is a Reality that can only be discerned in ecstasy in the original sense of going beyond the self: God

> comes to the thought of those who know It beyond thought, not to those who imagine It can be attained by thought. It is unknown to the learned and known to the simple.
>
> It is known in the ecstasy of an awakening that opens the door of life eternal.[30]

Like the gods, reason is not denied but transcended. The experience of Brahman or Atman cannot be explained rationally any more than a piece of music or a poem. Intelligence is necessary for the making of such a work of art and its appreciation, but it offers an experience that goes beyond the purely logical or cerebral faculty. This will also be a constant theme in the history of God.

The ideal of personal transcendence was embodied in the Yogi, who would leave his family and abandon all social ties and responsibilities to seek enlightenment, putting himself in another realm of being. In about 538 BCE, a young man named Siddhartha Gautama also left his beautiful wife, his son, his luxurious home in Kapilavashtu, about 100 miles north of Benares, and became a mendicant ascetic. He had been appalled by the spectacle of suffering and wanted to discover the secret to end the pain of existence that he could see in everything around him. For six years, he sat at the feet of various Hindu gurus and undertook fearful penances, but made no headway. The doctrines of the sages did not appeal to him, and his mortifications had simply made him despair. It was not until he abandoned these methods completely and put himself into a trance one night that he gained enlightenment. The whole cosmos rejoiced, the earth rocked, flowers fell from heaven, fragrant breezes blew and the gods in their various heavens rejoiced. Yet again, as in the pagan vision, the gods, nature and mankind were bound together in sympathy.

There was a new hope of liberation from suffering and the attainment of nirvana, the end of pain. Gautama had become the Buddha, the Enlightened One. At first, the demon Mara tempted him to stay where he was and enjoy his newfound bliss: it was no use trying to spread the word because nobody would believe him. But two of the gods of the traditional pantheon—Maha Brahma and Sakra, Lord of the *devas*—came to the Buddha and begged him to explain his method to the world. The Buddha agreed and for the next forty-five years he tramped all over India, preaching his message: in this world of suffering, only one thing was stable and firm. This was Dharma, the truth about right living, which alone could free us from pain.

This was nothing to do with God. The Buddha believed implicitly in the existence of the gods since they were a part of his cultural baggage, but he did not believe them to be much use to mankind. They too were caught up in the realm of pain and flux; they had not helped him to achieve enlightenment; they were involved in the cycle of rebirth like all other beings and eventually they would disappear. Yet at crucial moments of his life—as when he made the decision to preach his message—he imagined the gods influencing him and playing an active role. The Buddha did not deny the gods, therefore, but believed that the ultimate Reality of nirvana was higher than the gods. When Buddhists experience bliss or a sense of transcendence in meditation, they do not believe that this results from contact with a supernatural being. Such states are natural to humanity; they can be attained by anybody who lives in the correct way and learns the techniques of Yoga. Instead of relying on a god, therefore, the Buddha urged his disciples to save themselves.

When he met his first disciples at Benares after his enlightenment, the Buddha outlined his system, which was based on one essential fact: all existence was *dukkha*. It consisted entirely of suffering; life was wholly awry. Things come and go in meaningless flux. Nothing has permanent significance. Religion starts with the perception that something is wrong. In pagan antiquity it had led to the myth of a divine, archetypal world corresponding to our own which could impart its strength to humanity. The Buddha taught that it was possible to gain release from *dukkha* by living a life of compassion for all living beings, speaking and behaving gently, kindly and accurately and refraining from anything like drugs or intoxicants that cloud the mind. The Buddha did not claim to have invented this system. He insisted that he had *discovered* it: "I have seen an ancient path, an ancient Road, trodden by Buddhas of a bygone age."[31]

Like the laws of paganism, it was bound up with the essential structure of existence, inherent in the condition of life itself. It had objective reality not because it could be demonstrated by logical proof but because anybody who seriously tried to live that way would find that it worked. Effectiveness rather than philosophical or historical demonstration has always been the hallmark of a successful religion: for centuries Buddhists in many parts of the world have found that this lifestyle does yield a sense of transcendent meaning.

Karma bound men and women to an endless cycle of rebirth into a series of painful lives. But if they could reform their egotistic attitudes, they could change their destiny. The Buddha compared the process of rebirth to a flame which lights a lamp, from which a second lamp is lit, and so on until the flame is extinguished. If somebody is still aflame at death with a wrong attitude, he or she will simply light another lamp. But if the fire is put out, the cycle of suffering will cease and nirvana will be attained. "Nirvana" literally means "cooling off" or "going out." It is not a merely negative state, however, but plays a role in Buddhist life that is analogous to God. As Edward Conze explains in *Buddhism: its Essence and Development*, Buddhists often use the same imagery as theists to describe nirvana, the ultimate reality:

> We are told that Nirvana is permanent, stable, imperishable, immoveable, ageless, deathless, unborn, and unbecome, that it is power, bliss and happiness, the secure refuge, the shelter and the place of unassailable security; that it is the real Truth and the supreme Reality; that it is the *good*, the supreme goal and the one and only consummation of our life, the eternal, hidden and incomprehensible Peace.[32]

Some Buddhists might object to this comparison because they find the concept of "God" too limiting to express their conception of ultimate reality. This is largely because theists use the word "God" in a limited way to refer to a being who is not very different from us. Like the sages of the *Upanishads*, the Buddha insisted that nirvana could not be defined or discussed as though it were any other human reality.

Attaining nirvana is not like "going to heaven" as Christians often understand it. The Buddha always refused to answer questions about nirvana or other ultimate matters because they were "improper" or "inappropriate." We could not define nirvana because our words and concepts are tied to the world of sense and flux. Experience was the only reliable "proof." His disciples would know that nirvana existed simply because their practice of the good life would enable them to glimpse it.

> There is, monks, an unborn, an unbecome, an unmade, uncompounded. If, monks, there were not there this unborn, unbecome, unmade, uncompounded, there would not here be an escape from the born, the become, the made, the compounded. But because there is an unborn, an unbecome, an unmade, an uncompounded, therefore, there is an escape from the born, the become, the made, the compounded.[33]

His monks should not speculate about the nature of nirvana. All that the Buddha could do was provide them with a raft to take them across to "the farther shore." When asked if a Buddha who had attained nirvana lived after death, he dismissed the question as "improper." It was like asking what direction a flame went when it "went out." It was equally wrong to say that a Buddha existed in nirvana as that he did not exist: the word "exist" bore no relation to any state that we can understand. We shall find that over the centuries, Jews, Christians and Muslims have made the same reply to the question of the "existence" of God. The Buddha was trying to show that language was not equipped to deal with a reality that lay beyond concepts and reason. Again, he did not deny reason but insisted on the importance of clear and accurate thinking and use of language. Ultimately, however, he held that a person's theology or beliefs, like the ritual he took part in, were unimportant. They could be interesting but not a matter of final significance. The only thing that counted was the good life; if it were attempted, Buddhists would find that the Dharma was true, even if they could not express this truth in logical terms.

The Greeks, on the other hand, were passionately interested in logic and reason. Plato (ca. 428–ca. 348 BCE) was continually occupied with problems of epistemology and the nature of wisdom. Much of his early work was devoted to the defense of Socrates, who had forced men to clarify their ideas by his thought-provoking questions but had been sentenced to death in 399 on the charges of impiety and the corruption of youth. In a way that was not dissimilar to that of the people of India, he had become dissatisfied with the old festivals and myths of religion, which he found demeaning and inappropriate. Plato had also been influenced by the sixth-century philosopher Pythagoras, who may have been influenced by ideas from India, transmitted via Persia and Egypt. He had believed that the soul was a fallen, polluted deity incarcerated in the body as in a tomb and doomed to a perpetual cycle of rebirth. He had articulated the common human experience of feeling a stranger in a world that does not seem to be our true element. Pythagoras had taught that the soul could be liberated by means of ritual purifications, which would enable it to achieve harmony with the ordered universe. Plato also believed in the existence of a divine, unchanging reality beyond the world of the senses, that the soul was a fallen divinity, out of its element, imprisoned in the body but capable of regaining its divine status by the purification of the reasoning powers of the mind. In the famous myth of the cave, Plato described the darkness and obscurity of man's life on earth: he perceives only shadows of the eternal realities flickering on the wall of the cave. But gradually he can be drawn out and achieve enlightenment and liberation by accustoming his mind to the divine light.

Later in his life, Plato may have retreated from his doctrine of the eternal forms or ideas, but they became crucial to many monotheists when they tried to express their conception of God. These ideas were stable, constant realities which could be apprehended by the reasoning powers of the mind. They are fuller, more permanent and effective realities than the shifting, flawed material phenomena we encounter with our senses. The things of this world only echo, "participate in" or "imitate" the eternal forms in the divine realm. There is an idea corresponding to every general conception we have, such as Love, Justice and Beauty. The highest of all the forms, however, is the idea of the Good. Plato had cast the ancient myth of the archetypes into a philosophical form. His eternal ideas can be seen as a rational version of the mythical divine world, of which mundane things are the merest shadow. He did not discuss the nature of God but confined himself to the divine world of the forms, though occasionally it seems that ideal Beauty or the Good does represent a supreme reality. Plato was convinced that the divine world was static and changeless. The Greeks saw movement and change as signs of inferior reality: something that had true identity remained always the same, characterized by permanence and immutability. The most perfect motion, therefore, was the circle because it was perpetually turning and returning to its original point: the circling celestial spheres imitate the divine world as best they can. This utterly static image of divinity would have an immense influence on Jews, Christians and Muslims, even though it had little in common with the God of revelation, who is constantly active, innovative and, in the Bible, even changes his mind, as when he repents of having made man and decides to destroy the human race in the Flood.

There was a mystical aspect of Plato which monotheists would find most congenial. Plato's divine forms were not realities "out there" but could be discovered within the self. In his dramatic dialogue the *Symposium*, Plato showed how love of a beautiful body could be purified and transformed into an ecstatic contemplation (*theoria*) of ideal Beauty. He makes Diotima, Socrates' mentor, explain that this Beauty is unique, eternal and absolute, quite unlike anything that we experience in this world:

> This Beauty is first of all eternal; it neither comes into being nor passes away; neither waxes nor wanes; next it is not beautiful in part and ugly in part, nor beautiful at one time and ugly at another, nor beautiful in this relation and ugly in that, nor beautiful here and ugly there, as varying according to its beholders; nor again will this beauty appear to the imagination like the beauty of a face or hands or anything else corporeal, or like the beauty of a thought or science, or like beauty which has its seat in something other than itself, be it in a living thing or the earth or the sky or anything else whatsoever; he will see it as absolute, existing alone within itself, unique, eternal.[34]

In short, an idea like Beauty has much in common with what many theists would call "God." Yet despite its transcendence, the ideas were to be found within the mind of man. We moderns experience thinking as an activity, as something that we *do*. Plato envisaged it as something which happens to the mind: the objects of thought were realities that were active in the intellect of the man who contemplated them. Like Socrates, he saw thought as a process of recollection, an apprehension of something that we had always known but had forgotten. Because human beings were fallen divinities, the forms of the divine world were within them and could be "touched" by reason, which was not simply a rational or cerebral activity but an intuitive grasp of the eternal reality within us. This notion would greatly influence mystics in all three of the religions of historical monotheism.

Plato believed that the universe was essentially rational. This was another myth or imaginary conception of reality. Aristotle (384–322 BCE) took it a step further. He was the first to appreciate the importance of logical reasoning, the basis of all science, and was convinced that it was possible to arrive at an understanding of the universe by applying this method. As well as attempting a theoretical understanding of the truth in the fourteen treatises known as the *Metaphysics* (the term was coined by his editor, who put these treatises "after the *Physics*": *meta ta physika*), he also studied theoretical physics and empirical biology. Yet he possessed profound intellectual humility, insisting that nobody was able to attain an adequate conception of truth but that everybody could make a small contribution to our collective understanding. There has been much controversy about his assessment of Plato's work. He seems to have been temperamentally opposed to Plato's transcendent view of the forms, rejecting the notion that they had a prior, independent existence. Aristotle maintained that the forms only had reality in so far as they existed in concrete, material objects in our own world.

Despite his earthbound approach and his preoccupation with scientific fact, Aristotle had an acute understanding of the nature and importance of religion and mythology. He pointed out that people who had become initiates in the various mystery religions were not required to learn any facts "but to experience certain emotions and to be put in a certain disposition."[35] Hence his famous literary theory that tragedy effected a purification (*katharsis*) of the emotions of terror and pity that amounted to an experience of rebirth. The Greek tragedies, which originally formed part of a religious festival, did not necessarily present a factual account of historical events but were attempting to reveal a more serious truth. Indeed, history was more trivial than poetry and myth: "The one describes what has happened, the other what might. Hence poetry is something more philosophic and serious than history; for poetry speaks of what is universal, history of what is particular."[36] There may or may not have been a historical Achilles or Oedipus, but the facts of their lives were irrelevant to the characters we have experienced in Homer and Sophocles, which express a different but more profound truth about the human condition. Aristotle's account of the *katharsis* of tragedy was a philosophic presentation of a truth that *Homo religiosus* had always understood intuitively: a symbolic, mythical or ritual presentation of events that would be unendurable in daily life can redeem and transform them into something pure and even pleasurable.

Aristotle's idea of God had an immense influence on later monotheists, particularly on Christians in the Western world. In the *Physics*, he had examined the nature of reality and the structure and substance of the universe. He developed what amounted to a philosophical version of the old emanation accounts of creation: there was a hierarchy of existences, each one of which imparts form and change to the one below it, but unlike the old myths, in Aristotle's theory the emanations grew weaker the further they were from their source. At the top of this hierarchy was the Unmoved Mover, which Aristotle identified with God. This God was pure being and, as such, eternal, immobile and spiritual. God was pure thought, at one and the same time thinker and thought, engaged in an eternal moment of contemplation of himself, the highest object of knowledge. Since matter is flawed and mortal, there is no material element in God or the higher grades of being. The Unmoved Mover causes all the motion and activity in the universe, since each movement must have a cause that can be traced back to a single source. He activates the world by a process of attraction, since all beings are drawn toward Being itself.

Man is in a privileged position: his human soul has the divine gift of intellect, which makes him kin to God and a partaker in the divine nature. This godly capacity of reason puts him above plants and animals. As body and soul, however, man is a microcosm of the whole universe, containing within himself its basest materials as well as the divine attribute of reason. It is his duty to become immortal and divine by purifying his intellect. Wisdom (*sophia*) was the highest of all the human virtues; it was expressed in contemplation (*theoria*) of philosophical truth which, as in Plato, makes us divine by imitating the activity of God himself. *Theoria* was not achieved by logic alone, but was a disciplined intuition resulting in an esctatic self-transcendence. Very few people are capable of this wisdom, however, and most can achieve only *phronesis*, the exercise of foresight and intelligence in daily life.

Despite the important position of the Unmoved Mover in his system, Aristotle's God had little religious relevance. He had not created the world, since this would have involved an inappropriate change and temporal activity. Even though everything yearns toward him, this God remains quite indifferent to the existence of the universe, since he cannot contemplate anything inferior to himself. He certainly does not direct or guide the world and can make no difference to our lives, one way or the other. It is an open question whether God even knows of the existence of the cosmos, which has emanated from him as a necessary effect of his existence. The question of the existence of such a God must be entirely peripheral. Aristotle himself may have abandoned his theology later in life. As men of the Axial Age, he and Plato were both concerned with the individual conscience, the good life and the question of justice in society. Yet their thought was elitist. The pure world of Plato's forms or the remote God of Aristotle could make little impact on the lives of ordinary mortals, a fact which their later Jewish and Muslim admirers were forced to acknowledge.

In the new ideologies of the Axial Age, therefore, there was a general agreement that human life contained a transcendent element that was essential. The various sages we have considered interpreted this transcendence differently, but they were united in seeing it as crucial to the development of men and women as full human beings. They had not jettisoned the older mythologies absolutely but reinterpreted them and helped people to rise above them. At the same time as these momentous ideologies were being formed, the prophets of Israel developed their own traditions to meet the changing conditions, with the result that Yahweh eventually became the *only* God. But how would irascible Yahweh measure up to these other lofty visions?

2

One God

IN 742 BCE, a member of the Judaean royal family had a vision of Yahweh in the Temple which King Solomon had built in Jerusalem. It was an anxious time for the people of Israel. King Uzziah of Judah had died that year and was succeeded by his son Ahaz, who would encourage his subjects to worship pagan gods alongside Yahweh. The northern Kingdom of Israel was in a state of near-anarchy: after the death of King Jeroboam II, five kings had sat on the throne between 746 and 736, while King Tigleth Pilesar III, King of Assyria, looked hungrily at their lands, which he was anxious to add to his expanding empire. In 722, his successor, King Sargon II, would conquer the northern Kingdom and deport the population: the ten northern tribes of Israel were forced to assimilate and disappeared from history, while the little Kingdom of Judah feared for its own survival. As Isaiah prayed in the Temple shortly after King Uzziah's death, he was probably full of foreboding; at the same time he may have been uncomfortably aware of the inappropriateness of the lavish Temple ceremonial. Isaiah may have been a member of the ruling class, but he had populist and democratic views and was highly sensitive to the plight of the poor. As the incense filled the sanctuary before the Holy of Holies and the place reeked with the blood of the sacrificial animals, he may have feared that the religion of Israel had lost its integrity and inner meaning.

Suddenly he seemed to see Yahweh himself sitting on his throne in heaven directly above the Temple, which was the replica of his celestial court on earth. Yahweh's train filled the sanctuary and he was attended by two seraphs, who covered their faces with their wings lest they look upon his face. They cried out to one another antiphonally: "Holy! holy! holy is Yahweh Sabaoth. His glory fills the whole earth."[1] At the sound of their voices, the whole Temple seemed to shake on its foundations and was filled with smoke, enveloping Yahweh in an impenetrable cloud, similar to the cloud and smoke that had hidden him from Moses on Mount Sinai. When we use the word "holy" today, we usually refer to a state of moral excellence. The Hebrew *kaddosh*, however, has nothing to do with morality as such but means "otherness," a radical separation. The apparition of Yahweh on Mount Sinai had emphasized the immense gulf that had suddenly yawned between man and the divine world. Now the seraphs were crying: "Yahweh is other! other! other!" Isaiah had experienced that sense of the numinous which has periodically descended upon men and women and filled them with fascination and dread. In his classic book *The Idea of the Holy*, Rudolf Otto described this fearful experience of transcendent reality as *mysterium terribile et fascinans*: it is *terribile* because it comes as a profound shock that severs us from the consolations of normality and *fascinans* because, paradoxically, it exerts an irresistible attraction. There is nothing rational about this overpowering experience, which Otto compares to that of music or the erotic: the emotions it engenders cannot adequately be expressed in words or concepts. Indeed, this sense of the Wholly Other cannot even be said to "exist" because it has no place in our normal scheme of reality.[2] The new Yahweh of the Axial Age was still "the god of the armies" (*sabaoth*) but was no longer a mere god of war. Nor was he simply a tribal deity, who was passionately biased in favor of Israel: his glory was no longer confined to the Promised Land but filled the whole earth.

Isaiah was no Buddha experiencing an enlightenment that brought tranquillity and bliss. He had not become the perfected teacher of men. Instead he was filled with mortal terror, crying aloud:

> What a wretched state I am in! I am lost,
> for I am a man of unclean lips
> and I live among a people of unclean lips,
> and my eyes have looked at the King, Yahweh Sabaoth.[3]

Overcome by the transcendent holiness of Yahweh, he was conscious only of his own inadequacy and ritual impurity. Unlike the Buddha or a Yogi, he had not prepared himself for this experience by a series of spiritual exercises. It had come upon him out of the blue and he was completely shaken by its devastating impact. One of the seraphs flew toward him with a live coal and purified his lips, so that they could utter the word of God. Many of the prophets were either unwilling to speak on God's behalf or unable to do so. When God had called Moses, prototype of all prophets, from the Burning Bush and commanded him to be his messenger to Pharaoh and the children of Israel, Moses had protested that he was "not able to speak well."[4] God had made allowances for this impediment and permitted his brother, Aaron, to speak in Moses' stead. This regular motif in the stories of prophetic vocations symbolizes the difficulty of speaking God's word. The prophets were not eager to proclaim the divine message and were reluctant to undertake a mission of great strain and anguish. The transformation of Israel's God into a symbol of transcendent power would not be a calm, serene process but attended with pain and struggle.

Hindus would never have described Brahman as a great king because their God could not be described in such human terms. We must be careful not to interpret the story of Isaiah's vision too literally: it is an attempt to describe the indescribable, and Isaiah reverts instinctively to the mythological traditions of his people to give his audience some idea of what had happened to him. The psalms often describe Yahweh enthroned in his temple as king, just as Baal, Marduk and Dagon,[5] the gods of their neighbors, presided as monarchs in their rather similar temples. Beneath the mythological imagery, however, a quite distinctive conception of the ultimate reality was beginning to emerge in Israel: the experience with this God is an encounter with a person. Despite his terrifying otherness, Yahweh can speak and Isaiah can answer. Again, this would have been inconceivable to the sages of the *Upanishads*, since the idea of having a dialogue or meeting with Brahman-Atman would be inappropriately anthropomorphic.

Yahweh asked: "Whom shall I send? Who will be our messenger?" and, like Moses before him, Isaiah immediately replied: "Here I am! (*hineni!*) send me!" The point of this vision was not to enlighten the prophet but to give him a practical job to do. Primarily the prophet is one who stands in God's presence, but this experience of transcendence results not in the imparting of knowledge—as in Buddhism—but in action. The prophet will not be characterized by mystical illumination but by obedience. As one might expect, the message is never easy. With typical Semitic paradox, Yahweh told Isaiah that the people would not accept it: he must not be dismayed when they reject God's words: "Go and say to this people: 'Hear and hear again, but do not understand; see and see again, but do not perceive.' "[6] Seven hundred years later, Jesus would quote these words when people refused to hear his equally tough message.[7] Humankind cannot bear very much reality. The Israelites of Isaiah's day were on the brink of war and extinction, and Yahweh had no cheerful message for them: their cities would be devastated, the countryside ravaged and the houses emptied of their inhabitants. Isaiah would live to see the destruction of the northern kingdom in 722 and the deportation of the ten tribes. In 701 Sennacherib would invade Judah with a vast Assyrian army, lay siege to forty-six of its cities and fortresses, impale the defending officers on poles, deport about 2000 people and imprison the Jewish king in Jerusalem "like a bird in a cage."[8] Isaiah had the thankless task of warning his people of these impending catastrophes:

> There will be great emptiness in the country
> and, though a tenth of the people remain,
> it will be stripped like a terebinth
> of which, once felled, only the stock remains.[9]

It would not have been difficult for any astute political observer to foresee these catastrophes. What was chillingly original in Isaiah's message was his analysis of the situation. The old partisan God of Moses would have cast Assyria in the role of the enemy; the God of Isaiah saw Assyria as his instrument. It was not Sargon II and Sennacherib who would drive the Israelites into exile and devastate the country. It is "Yahweh who drives the people out."[10]

This was a constant theme in the message of the prophets of the Axial Age. The God of Israel had originally distinguished himself from the pagan deities by revealing himself in concrete current events, not simply in mythology and liturgy. Now, the new prophets insisted, political catastrophe as well as victory revealed the God who was becoming the lord and master of history. He had all the nations in his pocket. Assyria would come to grief in its turn simply because its kings had not realized that they were only tools in the hand of a being greater than themselves.[11] Since Yahweh had foretold the ultimate destruction of Assyria, there was a distant hope for the future. But no Israelite would have wanted to hear that his own people had brought political destruction upon its own head by its shortsighted policies and exploitative behavior. Nobody would have been happy to hear that Yahweh had masterminded the successful Assyrian campaigns of 722 and 701, just as he had captained the armies of Joshua, Gideon and King David. What did he think he was doing with the nation that was supposed to be his Chosen People? There was no wish fulfillment in Isaiah's depiction of Yahweh. Instead of offering the people a panacea, Yahweh was being used to make people confront unwelcome reality. Instead of taking refuge in the old cultic observances which projected people back into mythical time, prophets like Isaiah were trying to make their countrymen look the actual events of history in the face and accept them as a terrifying dialogue with their God.

While the God of Moses had been triumphalist, the God of Isaiah was full of sorrow. The prophecy, as it has come down to us, begins with a lament that is highly unflattering to the people of the covenant: the ox and the ass know their owners, but "Israel knows nothing, my people understand nothing."[12] Yahweh was utterly revolted by the animal sacrifices in the Temple, sickened by the fat of calves, blood of bulls and goats and the reeking blood that smoked from the holocausts. He could not bear their festivals, New Year ceremonies and pilgrimages.[13] This would have shocked Isaiah's audience: in the Middle East these cultic celebrations were of the essence of religion. The pagan gods depended upon the ceremonies to renew their depleted energies; their prestige depended in part upon the magnificence of their temples. Now Yahweh was actually saying that these things were utterly meaningless. Like other sages and philosophers in the Oikumene, Isaiah felt that exterior observance was not enough. Israelites must discover the inner meaning of their religion. Yahweh wanted compassion rather than sacrifice:

> You may multiply your prayers,
> I shall not listen.
> Your hands are covered with blood,
> wash, make yourselves clean.
> Take your wrong-doing out of my sight.
> Cease to do evil.
> Learn to do good,
> search for justice,
> help the oppressed,
> be just to the orphan,
> plead for the widow.[14]

The prophets had discovered for themselves the overriding duty of compassion, which would become the hallmark of all the major religions formed in the Axial Age. The new ideologies that were developing in the Oikumene during this period all insisted that the test of authenticity was that religious experience be integrated successfully with daily life. It was no longer sufficient to comfine observance to the Temple and to the extratemporal world of myth. After enlightenment, a man or woman must return to the marketplace and practice compassion for all living beings.

The social ideal of the prophets had been implicit in the cult of Yahweh since Sinai: the story of the Exodus had stressed that God was on the side of the weak and oppressed. The difference was that now Israelites themselves were castigated as oppressors. At the time of Isaiah's prophetic vision, two prophets were already preaching a similar message in the chaotic northern kingdom. The first was Amos, who was no aristocrat like Isaiah but a shepherd who had originally lived in Tekoa in the southern kingdom. In about 752, Amos had also been overwhelmed by a sudden imperative that had swept him to the kingdom of Israel in the north. He had burst into the ancient shrine of Beth-El and shattered the ceremonial there with a prophecy of doom. Amaziah, the priest of Beth-El, had tried to send him away. We can hear the superior voice of the establishment in his pompous rebuke to the uncouth herdsman. He naturally imagined that Amos belonged to one of the guilds of soothsayers, who wandered around in groups telling fortunes for a living. "Go away, seer!" he said disdainfully. "Get back to the land of Judah; earn your bread there, do your prophesying there. We want no more prophesying in Beth-El; this is the royal sanctuary, the national temple." Unabashed, Amos drew himself to his full height and replied scornfully that he was no guild prophet but had a direct mandate from Yahweh: "I was no prophet, neither did I belong to any of the brotherhoods of prophets. I was a shepherd and looking after sycamores: but it was Yahweh who took me from herding the flock and Yahweh who said: 'Go, prophesy to my people Israel.' "[15] So the people of Beth-El did not want to hear Yahweh's message? Very well, he had another oracle for them: their wives would be forced onto the streets, their children slaughtered, and they themselves would die in exile, far from the land of Israel.

It was of the essence of the prophet to be solitary. A figure like Amos was on his own; he had broken with the rhythms and duties of his past. This was not something he had chosen but something that had happened to him. It seemed as though he had been jerked out of the normal patterns of consciousness and could no longer operate the usual controls. He was forced to prophesy, whether he wanted to or not. As Amos put it:

> The lion roars; who can help feeling afraid?
> The Lord Yahweh speaks: who can refuse to prophesy?[16]

Amos had not been absorbed like the Buddha into the selfless annihilation of nirvana; instead, Yahweh had taken the place of his ego and snatched him into another world. Amos was the first of the prophets to emphasize the importance of social justice and compassion. Like the Buddha, he was acutely aware of the agony of suffering humanity. In Amos's oracles, Yahweh was speaking on behalf of the oppressed, giving voice to the voiceless, impotent suffering of the poor. In the very first line of his prophecy as it has come down to us, Yahweh is roaring with horror from his Temple in Jerusalem as he contemplates the misery in all the countries of the Near East, including Judah and Israel. The people of Israel were just as bad as the *goyim*, the Gentiles: they might be able to ignore the cruelty and oppression of the poor, but Yahweh could not. He noted every instance of swindling, exploitation and breathtaking lack of compassion: "Yahweh swears it by the pride of Jacob: 'Never will I forget a single thing that you have done.' "[17] Did they really have the temerity to look forward to the Day of the Lord, when Yahweh would exalt Israel and humiliate the *goyim*? They had a shock coming: "What will this Day of Yahweh mean to you? It will mean darkness, not light!"[18] They thought they were God's Chosen People? They had entirely misunderstood the nature of the covenant, which meant responsibility, not privilege: "Listen sons of Israel, to this oracle Yahweh speaks against you!" Amos cried, "against the whole family I brought out of the land of Egypt:

> You alone, of all the families of the earth, have I acknowledged,
> therefore it is for your sins that I mean to punish you."[19]

The covenant meant that *all* the people of Israel were God's elect and had, therefore, to be treated decently. God did not simply intervene in history to glorify Israel but to secure social justice. This was his stake in history and, if need be, he would use the Assyrian army to enforce justice in his own land.

Not surprisingly, most Israelites declined the prophet's invitation to enter into a dialogue with Yahweh. They preferred a less demanding religion of cultic observance either in the Jerusalem Temple or in the old fertility cults of Canaan. This continues to be the case: the religion of compassion is followed only by a minority; most religious people are content with decorous worship in synagogue, church, temple and mosque. The ancient Canaanite religions were still flourishing in Israel. In the tenth century, King Jeroboam I had set up two cultic bulls at the sanctuaries of Dan and Beth-El. Two hundred years later, the Israelites were still taking part in fertility rites and sacred sex there, as we see in the oracles of the prophet Hosea, Amos's contemporary.[20] Some Israelites appear to have thought that Yahweh had a wife, like the other gods: archaeologists have recently unearthed inscriptions dedicated "To Yahweh and his Asherah." Hosea was particularly disturbed by the fact that Israel was breaking the terms of the covenant by worshipping other gods, such as Baal. Like all of the new prophets, he was concerned with the inner meaning of religion. As he makes Yahweh say: "What I want is love (*hesed*), not sacrifice; knowledge of God (*daath Elohim*), not holocausts."[21] He did not mean theological knowledge: the word *daath* comes from the Hebrew verb *yada*: to know, which has sexual connotations. Thus J says that Adam "knew" his wife, Eve.[22] In the Old Canaanite religion, Baal had married the soil and the people had celebrated this with ritual orgies, but Hosea insisted that since the covenant, Yahweh had taken the place of Baal and had wedded the people of Israel. They had to understand that it was Yahweh, not Baal, who would bring fertility to the soil.[23] He was still wooing Israel like a lover, determined to lure her back from the Baals who had seduced her:

> When that day comes—it is Yahweh who speaks—
> she will call me, "My husband,"
> no longer will she call me, "My Baal."
> I will take the names of the Baals off her lips,
> their names shall never be uttered again.[24]

Where Amos attacked social wickedness, Hosea dwelt on the lack of inwardness in Israelite religion: the "knowledge" of God was related to "*hesed*," implying an interior appropriation and attachment to Yahweh that must supersede exterior observance.

Hosea gives us a startling insight into the way the prophets were developing their image of God. At the very beginning of his career, Yahweh seemed to have issued a shocking command. He told Hosea to go off and marry a whore (*esheth zeuunim*) because the whole country had "become nothing but a whore abandoning Yahweh."[25] It appears, however, that God had not ordered Hosea to scour the streets for a prostitute: *esheth zeuunim* (literally, "a wife of prostitution") meant either a woman with a promiscuous temperament or a sacred prostitute in a fertility cult. Given Hosea's preoccupation with fertility rituals, it seems likely that his wife, Gomer, had become one of the sacred personnel in the cult of Baal. His marriage was, therefore, an emblem of Yahweh's relationship with the faithless Israel. Hosea and Gomer had three children, who were given fateful, symbolic names. The elder son was called Jezreel, after a famous battlefield, their daughter was Lo-Ruhamah (Unloved) and their younger son Lo-Ammi (Not-My-People). At his birth, Yahweh had annulled the covenant with Israel: "You are not my people and I am not your God."[26] We shall see that the prophets were often inspired to perform elaborate mimes to demonstrate the predicament of their people, but it appears that Hosea's marriage was not coldly planned from the beginning. The text makes it clear that Gomer did not become an *esheth zeuunim* until after their children had been born. It was only with hindsight that it seemed to Hosea that his marriage had been inspired by God. The loss of his wife had been a shattering experience, which gave Hosea an insight into the way Yahweh must feel when his people deserted him and went whoring after deities like Baal. At first Hosea was tempted to denounce Gomer and have nothing more to do with her: indeed, the law stipulated that a man must divorce an unfaithful wife. But Hosea still loved Gomer, and eventually he went after her and bought her back from her new master. He saw his own desire to win Gomer back as a sign that Yahweh was willing to give Israel another chance.

When they attributed their own human feelings and experiences to Yahweh, the prophets were in an important sense creating a god in their own image. Isaiah, a member of the royal family, had seen Yahweh as a king. Amos had ascribed his own empathy with the suffering poor to Yahweh; Hosea saw Yahweh as a jilted husband, who still continued to feel a yearning tenderness for his wife. All religion must begin with some anthropomorphism. A deity which is utterly remote from humanity, such as Aristotle's Unmoved Mover, cannot inspire a spiritual quest. As long as this projection does not become an end in itself, it can be useful and beneficial. It has to be said that this imaginative portrayal of God in human terms has inspired a social concern that has not been present in Hinduism. All three of the God-religions have shared the egalitarian and socialist ethic of Amos and Isaiah. The Jews would be the first people in the ancient world to establish a welfare system that was the admiration of their pagan neighbors.

Like all the other prophets, Hosea was haunted by the horror of idolatry. He contemplated the divine vengeance that the northern tribes would bring upon themselves by worshipping gods that they had actually made themselves:

And now they add sin to sin,
they smelt images from their silver,
idols of their own manufacture,
smith's work, all of it.
"Sacrifice to them," they say.
Men blow kisses to calves!²⁷

This was, of course, a most unfair and reductive description of Canaanite religion. The people of Canaan and Babylon had never believed that their effigies of the gods were themselves divine; they had never bowed down to worship a statue *tout court*. The effigy had been a symbol of divinity. Like their myths about the unimaginable primordial events, it had been devised to direct the attention of the worshipper beyond itself. The statue of Marduk in the Temple of Esagila and the standing stones of Asherah in Canaan had never been seen as identical with the gods but had been a focus that had helped people to concentrate on the transcendent element of human life. Yet the prophets frequently jeered at the deities of their pagan neighbors with a most unattractive contempt. These homemade gods, in their view, were nothing but gold and silver; they had been knocked together by a craftsman in a couple of hours; they had eyes that did not see, ears that did not hear; they could not walk and had to be carted about by their worshippers; they were brutish and stupid subhuman beings that were no better than scarecrows in a melon patch. Compared with Yahweh, the Elohim of Israel, they were *elilim*, Nothings. The *goyim* who worshipped them were fools and Yahweh hated them.²⁸

Today we have become so familiar with the intolerance that has unfortunately been a characteristic of monotheism that we may not appreciate that this hostility toward other gods was a new religious attitude. Paganism was an essentially tolerant faith: provided that old cults were not threatened by the arrival of a new deity, there was always room for another god alongside the traditional pantheon. Even where the new ideologies of the Axial Age were replacing the old veneration of the gods, there was no such vitriolic rejection of the ancient deities. We have seen that in Hinduism and Buddhism people were encouraged to go beyond the gods rather than to turn upon them with loathing. Yet the prophets of Israel were unable to take this calmer view of the deities they saw as Yahweh's rivals. In the Jewish scriptures, the new sin of "idolatry," the worship of "false" gods, inspires something akin to nausea. It is a reaction that is, perhaps, similar to the revulsion that some of the Fathers of the Church would feel for sexuality. As such, it is not a rational, considered reaction but expressive of deep anxiety and repression. Were the prophets harboring a buried worry about their own religious behavior? Were they, perhaps, uneasily aware that their own conception of Yahweh was similar to the idolatry of the pagans, since they too were creating a god in their own image?

The comparison with the Christian attitude toward sexuality is illuminating in another way. At this point, most Israelites believed implicitly in the existence of the pagan deities. It is true that Yahweh was gradually taking over some of the functions of the *elohim* of the Canaanites in certain circles: Hosea, for example, was trying to argue that he was a better fertility god than Baal. But it was obviously difficult for the irredeemably masculine Yahweh to usurp the function of a goddess like Asherah, Ishtar or Anat, who still had a great following among the Israelites, particularly among the women. Even though monotheists would insist that their God transcended gender, he would remain essentially male, though we shall see that some would try to remedy this imbalance. In part, this was due to his origins as a tribal god of war. Yet his battle with the goddesses reflects a less positive characteristic of the Axial Age, which generally saw a decline in the status of women and the female. It seems that in more primitive societies, women were sometimes held in higher esteem than men. The prestige of the great goddesses in traditional religion reflects the veneration of the female. The rise of the cities, however, meant that the more masculine qualities of martial, physical strength were exalted over female characteristics. Henceforth women were marginalized and became second-class citizens in the new civilizations of the Oikumene. Their position was particularly poor in Greece, for example—a fact that Western people should remember when they decry the patriarchal attitudes of the Orient. The democratic ideal did not extend to the women of Athens, who lived in seclusion and were despised as inferior beings. Israelite society was also becoming more masculine in tone. In the early days, women were forceful and clearly saw themselves as the equals of their husbands. Some, like Deborah, had led armies into battle. Israelites would continue to celebrate such heroic women as Judith and Esther, but after Yahweh had successfully vanquished the other gods and goddesses of Canaan and the Middle East and become the *only* God, his religion would be managed almost entirely by men. The cult of the goddesses would be superseded, and this would be a symptom of a cultural change that was characteristic of the newly civilized world.

We shall see that Yahweh's victory was hard-won. It involved strain, violence and confrontation and suggests that the new religion of the One

God was not coming as easily to the Israelites as Buddhism or Hinduism to the people of the subcontinent. Yahweh did not seem able to transcend the older deities in a peaceful, natural manner. He had to fight it out. Thus in Psalm 82 we see him making a play for the leadership of the Divine Assembly, which had played such an important role in both Babylonian and Canaanite myth:

> Yahweh takes his stand in the Council of El
> to deliver judgments among the gods.[29]
>
> "No more mockery of justice
> no more favoring the wicked!
> Let the weak and the orphan have justice,
> be fair to the wretched and the destitute,
> rescue the weak and needy,
> save them from the clutches of the wicked!"
>
> Ignorant and senseless, they carry on blindly,
> undermining the very basis of human society.
> I once said, "You too are gods,
> sons of El Elyon, all of you";
> but all the same, you shall die like men;
> as one man, gods, you shall fall.

When he stood up to confront the Council over which El has presided from time immemorial, Yahweh accused the other gods of failing to meet the social challenge of the day. He represented the modern compassionate ethos of the prophets, but his divine colleagues had done nothing to promote justice and equity over the years. In the old days, Yahweh had been prepared to accept them as *elohim*, the sons of El Elyon ("God Most High"),[30] but now the gods had proved that they were obsolete. They would wither away like mortal men. Not only did the psalmist depict Yahweh condemning his fellow gods to death, but in doing so he had usurped the traditional prerogative of El, who, it would seem, still had his champions in Israel.

Despite the bad press it has in the Bible, there is nothing wrong with idolatry per se: it becomes objectionable or naive only if the image of God, which has been constructed with such loving care, is confused with the ineffable reality to which it refers. We shall see that later in the history of God, some Jews, Christians and Muslims worked on this early image of the absolute reality and arrived at a conception that was closer to the Hindu or Buddhist visions. Others, however, never quite managed to take this step, but assumed that their conception of God was identical with the ultimate mystery. The dangers of an "idolatrous" religiosity became clear in about 622 BCE during the reign of King Josiah of Judah. He was anxious to reverse the syncretist policies of his predecessors, King Manasseh (687–42) and King Amon (642–40), who had encouraged their people to worship the gods of Canaan alongside Yahweh. Manasseh had actually put up an effigy to Asherah in the Temple, where there was a flourishing fertility cult. Since most Israelites were devoted to Asherah and some thought that she was Yahweh's wife, only the strictest Yahwists would have considered this blasphemous. Determined to promote the cult of Yahweh, however, Josiah had decided to make extensive repairs in the Temple. While the workmen were turning everything upside down, the High Priest Hilkiah is said to have discovered an ancient manuscript which purported to be an account of Moses' last sermon to the children of Israel. He gave it to Josiah's secretary, Shapan, who read it aloud in the king's presence. When he heard it, the young king tore his garments in horror: no wonder Yahweh had been so angry with his ancestors! They had totally failed to obey his strict instructions to Moses.[31]

It is almost certain that the "Book of the Law" discovered by Hilkiah was the core of the text that we now know as Deuteronomy. There have been various theories about its timely "discovery" by the reforming party. Some have even suggested that it had been secretly written by Hilkiah and Shapan themselves with the assistance of the prophetess Huldah, whom Josiah immediately consulted. We shall never know for certain, but the book certainly reflected an entirely new intransigence in Israel, which reflects a seventh-century perspective. In his last sermon, Moses is made to give a new centrality to the covenant and the idea of the special election of Israel. Yahweh had marked his people out from all the other nations, not because of any merit of their own but because of his great love. In return, he demanded complete loyalty and a fierce rejection of all other gods. The core of Deuteronomy includes the declaration which would later become the Jewish profession of faith:

> Listen (*shema*), Israel! Yahweh is our Elohim, Yahweh alone (*ehad*)!
> You shall love Yahweh with all your heart, with all your soul, with
> all your strength. Let these words I urge upon you today be written
> on your hearts.[32]

The election of God had set Israel apart from the *goyim*, so, the author makes Moses say, when they arrived in the Promised Land they were to have no dealings whatever with the native inhabitants. They "must make no covenant with them or show them any pity."³³ There must be no intermarriage and no social mixing. Above all, they were to wipe out the Canaanite religion: "Tear down their altars, smash their standing stones, cut down their sacred poles and set fire to their idols," Moses commands the Israelites, "For you are a people consecrated to Yahweh your Elohim; it is you that Yahweh our Elohim has chosen to be his very own people out of all the peoples in the earth."³⁴

When they recite the *Shema* today, Jews give it a monotheistic interpretation: Yahweh our God is One and unique. The Deuteronomist had not yet reached this perspective. "Yahweh *ehad*" did not mean God is One, but that Yahweh was the only deity whom it was permitted to worship. Other gods were still a threat: their cults were attractive and could lure Israelites from Yahweh, who was a jealous God. If they obeyed Yahweh's laws, he would bless them and bring them prosperity, but if they deserted him the consequences would be devastating:

> You will be torn from the land which you are entering to make your own. Yahweh will scatter you among the peoples, from one end of the earth to the other; there you will serve other gods of wood and of stone that neither you nor your fathers have known . . . Your life from the outset will be a burden to you . . . In the morning you will say, "how I wish it were evening!" and in the evening, "how I wish it were morning!" such terror will grip your heart, such sights your eyes will see.³⁵

When King Josiah and his subjects heard these words at the end of the seventh century, they were about to be confronted by a new political threat. They had managed to keep the Assyrians at bay and had thus avoided the fate of the ten northern tribes, who *had* endured the punishments described by Moses. But in 606 BCE, the Babylonian King Nebupolassar would crush the Assyrians and begin to build his own empire.

In this climate of extreme insecurity, the Deuteronomist's policies made a great impact. Far from obeying Yahweh's commands, the last two kings of Israel had deliberately courted disaster. Josiah instantly began a reform, acting with exemplary zeal. All the images, idols and fertility symbols were taken out of the Temple and burned. Josiah also pulled down the large effigy of Asherah and destroyed the apartments of the Temple prostitutes, who wove garments for her there. All the ancient shrines in the country, which had been enclaves of paganism, were destroyed. Henceforth the priests were only allowed to offer sacrifice to Yahweh in the purified Jerusalem Temple. The chronicler, who recorded Josiah's reforms nearly 300 years later, gives an eloquent description of this piety of denial and suppression:

> [Josiah] looked on as the altars of the Baals were demolished; he tore down the altars of incense standing on them, he smashed the sacred poles and the carved and cast idols; he reduced them to dust, scattering it over the graves of those who had offered them sacrifices. He burned the bones of their priests on their altars, and so purified Judah and Jerusalem; he did the same in the towns of Manasseh, Ephraim, Simeon, and even Naphtali, and in the ravaged districts around them. He demolished the altars and the sacred poles, smashed the idols and ground them to powder, and tore down all the altars of incense throughout the land of Israel.[36]

We are far from the Buddha's serene acceptance of the deities he believed he had outgrown. This wholesale destruction springs from a hatred that is rooted in buried anxiety and fear.

The reformers rewrote Israelite history. The historical books of Joshua, Judges, Samuel and Kings were revised according to the new ideology and, later, the editors of the Pentateuch added passages that gave a Deuteronomist interpretation of the Exodus myth to the older narratives of J and E. Yahweh was now the author of a holy war of extermination in Canaan. The Israelites are told that the native Canaanites must not live in their country,[37] a policy which Joshua is made to implement with unholy thoroughness:

> Then Joshua came and wiped out the Anakim from the highlands, from Hebron, from Debir, from Anoth, from all the highlands of Judah and all the inhabitants of Israel; he delivered them and their towns over to the ban. No more Anakim were left in Israelite territory except at Gaza, Gath and Ashod.[38]

In fact we know nothing about the conquest of Canaan by Joshua and the Judges, though doubtless a good deal of blood was shed. Now, however, the bloodshed had been given a religious rationale. The dangers of such theologies of election, which are not qualified by the transcendent perspective of an Isaiah, are clearly shown in the holy wars that have scarred the history of monotheism. Instead of making God a symbol to challenge our prejudice and force us to contemplate our own shortcomings, it can be used to endorse our egotistic hatred and make it absolute. It makes God behave exactly like us, as though he were simply another human being. Such a God is likely to be more attractive and popular than the God of Amos and Isaiah, who demands ruthless self-criticism.

The Jews have often been criticized for their belief that they are the Chosen People, but their critics have often been guilty of the same kind of denial that fueled the diatribes against idolatry in biblical times. All three of the monotheistic faiths have developed similar theologies of election at different times in their history, sometimes with even more devastating results than those imagined in the Book of Joshua. Western Christians have been particularly prone to the flattering belief that they are God's elect. During the eleventh and twelfth centuries, the Crusaders justified their holy wars against Jews and Muslims by calling themselves the new Chosen People, who had taken up the vocation that the Jews had lost. Calvinist theologies of election have been largely instrumental in encouraging Americans to believe that they are God's own nation. As in Josiah's Kingdom of Judah, such a belief is likely to flourish at a time of political insecurity when people are haunted by the fear of their own destruction. It is for this reason, perhaps, that it has gained a new lease of life in the various forms of fundamentalism that are rife among Jews, Christians and Muslims at this writing. A personal God like Yahweh can be manipulated to shore up the beleaguered self in this way, as an impersonal deity like Brahman can not.

We should note that not all the Israelites subscribed to Deuteronomism in the years that led up to the destruction of Jerusalem by Nebuchadnezzar in 587 BCE and the deportation of the Jews to Babylon. In 604, the year of Nebuchadnezzar's accession, the prophet Jeremiah revived the iconoclastic perspective of Isaiah which turned the triumphalist doctrine of the Chosen People on its head: God was using Babylon as his instrument to punish Israel, and it was now Israel's turn to be "put under a ban."[39] They would go into exile for seventy years. When King Jehoiakim heard this oracle, he snatched the scroll from the hands of the scribe, cut it in pieces and threw it on the fire. Fearing for his life, Jeremiah was forced to go into hiding.

Jeremiah's career shows the immense pain and effort involved in the forging of this more challenging image of God. He hated being a prophet

and was profoundly distressed to have to condemn the people he loved.[40]
He was not a natural firebrand but a tenderhearted man. When the call
had come to him, he cried out in protest: "Ah, Lord Yahweh; look, I do
not know how to speak: I am a child!" and Yahweh had "put out his
hand" and touched his lips, putting his words on his mouth. The message
that he had to articulate was ambiguous and contradictory: "to tear up
and to knock down, to destroy and to overthrow, to build and to plant."[41]
It demanded an agonizing tension between irreconcilable extremes. Jeremiah experienced God as a pain that convulsed his limbs, broke his heart
and made him stagger about like a drunk.[42] The prophetic experience of
the *mysterium terribile et fascinans* was at one and the same time rape and
seduction:

> Yahweh, you have seduced me and I am seduced,
> You have raped me and I am overcome . . .
> I used to say, "I will not think about him,
> I will not speak his name anymore."
> Then there seemed to be a fire burning in my heart,
> imprisoned in my bones.
> The effort to restrain it wearied me,
> I could not bear it.[43]

God was pulling Jeremiah in two different directions: on the one hand,
he felt a profound attraction toward Yahweh that had all the sweet surrender of a seduction, but at other times he felt ravaged by a force that
carried him along against his will.

Ever since Amos, the prophet had been a man on his own. Unlike the
other areas of the Oikumene at this time, the Middle East did not adopt
a broadly united religious ideology.[44] The God of the prophets was forcing
Israelites to sever themselves from the mythical consciousness of the
Middle East and go in quite a different direction from the mainstream.
In the agony of Jeremiah, we can see what an immense wrench and
dislocation this involved. Israel was a tiny enclave of Yahwism surrounded
by a pagan world, and Yahweh was also rejected by many of the Israelites
themselves. Even the Deuteronomist, whose image of God was less threatening, saw a meeting with Yahweh as an abrasive confrontation: he makes
Moses explain to the Israelites, who are appalled by the prospect of
unmediated contact with Yahweh, that God will send them a prophet in
each generation to bear the brunt of the divine impact.

There was as yet nothing to compare with Atman, the immanent divine principle, in the cult of Yahweh. Yahweh was experienced as an external, transcendent reality. He needed to be humanized in some way to make him appear less alien. The political situation was deteriorating: the Babylonians invaded Judah and carried the king and the first batch of Israelites off into exile; finally Jerusalem itself was besieged. As conditions got worse, Jeremiah continued the tradition of ascribing human emotions to Yahweh: he makes God lament his own homelessness, affliction and desolation; Yahweh felt as stunned, offended and abandoned as his people; like them he seemed bemused, alienated and paralyzed. The anger that Jeremiah felt welling up in his own heart was not his own but the wrath of Yahweh.[45] When the prophets thought about "man," they automatically also thought "God," whose presence in the world seems inextricably bound up with his people. Indeed, God is dependent upon man when he wants to act in the world—an idea that would become very important in the Jewish conception of the divine. There are even hints that human beings can discern the activity of God in their own emotions and experiences, that Yahweh is part of the human condition.

As long as the enemy stood at the gate, Jeremiah raged at his people in God's name (though, before God, he pleaded on their behalf). Once Jerusalem had been conquered by the Babylonians in 587, the oracles from Yahweh became more comforting: he promised to save his people, now that they had learned their lesson, and bring them home. Jeremiah had been allowed by the Babylonian authorities to stay behind in Judah, and to express his confidence in the future, he bought some real estate: "For Yahweh Sabaoth says this: 'People will buy fields and vineyards in this land again.' "[46] Not surprisingly, some people blamed Yahweh for the catastrophe. During a visit to Egypt, Jeremiah encountered a group of Jews who had fled to the Delta area and had no time at all for Yahweh. Their women claimed that everything had been fine as long as they had performed the traditional rites in honor of Ishtar, Queen of Heaven, but as soon as they stopped them, at the behest of the likes of Jeremiah, disaster, defeat and penury had followed. Yet the tragedy seemed to deepen Jeremiah's own insight.[47] After the fall of Jerusalem and the destruction of the Temple, he began to realize that such external trappings of religion were simply symbols of an internal, subjective state. In the future, the covenant with Israel would be quite different: "Deep within them I will plant my Law, writing it in their hearts."[48]

Those who had gone into exile were not forced to assimilate, as the ten northern tribes had been in 722. They lived in two communities: one in Babylon itself and the other on the banks of a canal leading from the

Euphrates called the Chebar, not far from Nippur and Ur, in an area which they named Tel Aviv (Springtime Hill). Among the first batch of exiles to be deported in 597 had been a priest called Ezekiel. For about five years he stayed alone in his house and did not speak to a soul. Then he had a shattering vision of Yahweh, which literally knocked him out. It is important to describe his first vision in some detail because—centuries later—it would become very important to Jewish mystics, as we shall see in Chapter 7. Ezekiel had seen a cloud of light, shot through with lightning. A strong wind blew from the north. In the midst of this stormy obscurity, he *seemed* to see—he is careful to emphasize the provisional nature of the imagery—a great chariot pulled by four strong beasts. They were similar to the *karibu* carved on the palace gates in Babylon, yet Ezekiel makes it almost impossible to visualize them: each one had four heads: with the face of a man, a lion, a bull and an eagle. Each one of the wheels rolled in a different direction from the others. The imagery simply served to emphasize the alien impact of the visions that he was struggling to articulate. The beating of the creatures' wings was deafening; it "sounded like rushing water, like the voice of Shaddai, a voice like a storm, like the noise of a camp." On the chariot there was something that was "like" a throne and, sitting in state, was a "being that looked like a man": it shone like brass, fire shooting from its limbs. It was also "something that looked like the glory (*kavod*) of Yahweh."[49] At once Ezekiel fell upon his face and heard a voice addressing him.

The voice called Ezekiel "son of man," as if to emphasize the distance that now existed between humanity and the divine realm. Yet again, the vision of Yahweh was to be followed by a practical plan of action. Ezekiel was to speak the word of God to the rebellious sons of Israel. The nonhuman quality of the divine message was conveyed by a violent image: a hand stretched toward the prophet clasping a scroll, covered with wailings and moanings. Ezekiel was commanded to eat the scroll, to ingest the Word of God and make it part of himself. As usual, the *mysterium* was *fascinans* as well as *terribile:* the scroll turned out to taste as sweet as honey. Finally, Ezekiel said, "the spirit lifted me and took me; my heart, as I went, overflowed with bitterness and anger, and the hand of Yahweh lay heavy on me."[50] He arrived at Tel Aviv and lay "like one stunned" for a whole week.

Ezekiel's strange career emphasizes how alien and foreign the divine world had become to humanity. He himself was forced to become a sign of this strangeness. Yahweh frequently commanded him to perform weird mimes, which set him apart from normal beings. They were also designed to demonstrate the plight of Israel during this crisis and, at a deeper level, showed that Israel was itself becoming an outsider in the pagan world. Thus, when his wife died, Ezekiel was forbidden to mourn; he had to lie on one side for 390 days and on the other for 40; once he had to pack his bags and walk around Tel Aviv like a refugee, with no abiding city. Yahweh afflicted him with such acute anxiety that he could not stop trembling and moving about restlessly. On another occasion, he was forced to eat excrement, as a sign of the starvation that his countrymen would have to endure during the siege of Jerusalem. Ezekiel had become an icon of the radical discontinuity that the cult of Yahweh involved: nothing could be taken for granted, and normal responses were denied.

The pagan vision, on the other hand, had celebrated the continuity that was felt to exist between the gods and the natural world. Ezekiel found nothing consoling about the old religion, which he habitually called "filth." During one of his visions, he was conducted on a guided tour of the Temple in Jerusalem. To his horror he saw that, poised as they were on the brink of destruction, the people of Judah were still worshipping pagan gods in the Temple of Yahweh. The Temple itself had become a nightmarish place: the walls of its rooms were painted with writhing snakes and repulsive animals; the priests performing the "filthy" rites were presented in a sordid light, almost as if they were engaged in back-room sex: "Son of man, have you seen what the elders of the throne of Israel do in the dark, each in his painted room?"[51] In another room, women sat weeping for the suffering god Tammuz. Others worshipped the sun, with their backs toward the sanctuary. Finally, the prophet watched the strange chariot he had seen in his first vision fly away, taking the "glory" of Yahweh with it. Yet Yahweh was not an entirely distant deity. In the final days before the destruction of Jerusalem, Ezekiel depicts him fulminating against the people of Israel in a vain attempt to catch their attention and force them to acknowledge him. Israel had only itself to blame for the impending catastrophe. Alien as Yahweh frequently seemed, he was encouraging Israelites like Ezekiel to see that the blows of history were not random and arbitrary but had a deeper logic and justice. He was trying to find a meaning in the cruel world of international politics.

As they sat beside the rivers of Babylon, some of the exiles inevitably felt that they could not practice their religion outside the Promised Land. Pagan gods had always been territorial, and for some it seemed impossible to sing the songs of Yahweh in a foreign country: they relished the prospect of hurling Babylonian babies against a rock and dashing their brains out.[52] A new prophet, however, preached tranquillity. We know nothing about him, and this may be significant because his oracles and psalms give no sign of a personal struggle, such as those endured by his predecessors. Because his work was later added to the oracles of Isaiah, he is usually called the Second Isaiah. In exile, some of the Jews would have gone over to the worship of the ancient gods of Babylon, but others were pushed into a new religious awareness. The Temple of Yahweh was in ruins; the old cultic shrines in Beth-El and Hebron were destroyed. In Babylon they could not take part in the liturgies that had been central to their religious life at home. Yahweh was all they had. Second Isaiah took this one step further and declared that Yahweh was the *only* God. In his rewriting of Israelite history, the myth of the Exodus is clad in imagery that reminds us of the victory of Marduk over Tiamat, the primal sea:

> And Yahweh will dry up the gulf of the Sea of Egypt
> with the heat of his breath,
> and stretch out his hand over the River [Euphrates]
> and divide it into seven streams,
> for men to cross dry-shod,
> to make a pathway for the remnant of his people . . .
> as there was for Israel
> when it came out of Egypt.[53]

First Isaiah had made history a divine warning; after the catastrophe, in his Book of Consolation, Second Isaiah made history generate new hope for the future. If Yahweh had rescued Israel once in the past, he could do it again. He was masterminding the affairs of history; in his eyes, all the *goyim* were nothing more than a drop of water in a bucket. He was indeed the only God who counted. Second Isaiah imagined the old deities of Babylon being bundled onto carts and trundling off into the sunset.[54] Their day was over: "Am I not Yahweh?" he asked repeatedly, "there is no other god beside me."[55]

> No god was formed before me,
> nor will be after me.
> I, I am Yahweh,
> there is no other savior but me.[56]

Second Isaiah wasted no time denouncing the gods of the *goyim*, who, since the catastrophe, could have been seen as victorious. He calmly assumed that Yahweh—not Marduk or Baal—had performed the great mythical deeds that brought the world into being. For the first time, the Israelites became seriously interested in Yahweh's role in creation, perhaps because of renewed contact with the cosmological myths of Babylon. They were not, of course, attempting a scientific account of the physical origins of the universe but were trying to find comfort in the harsh world of the present. If Yahweh had defeated the monsters of chaos in primordial time, it would be a simple matter for him to redeem the exiled Israelites. Seeing the similarity between the Exodus myth and the pagan tales of victory over watery chaos at the beginning of time, Second Isaiah urged his people to look forward confidently to a new show of divine strength. Here, for example, he refers to the victory of Baal over Lotan, the seamonster of Canaanite creation mythology, who was also called Rahab, the Crocodile (*tannīn*) and the Abyss (*tehōm*):

> Awake, awake! clothe yourself in strength,
> arm of Yahweh,
> Awake, as in the past,
> in times of generations long ago.
> Did you not split Rahab in two,
> and pierce the Dragon (*tannīn*) through?
> Did you not dry up the sea,
> the waters of the great Abyss (*tehōm*),
> to make the seabed a road
> for the redeemed to cross?[57]

Yahweh had finally absorbed his rivals in the religious imagination of Israel; in exile, the lure of paganism had lost its attraction and the religion of Judaism had been born. At a time when the cult of Yahweh might reasonably have been expected to perish, he became the means that enabled people to find hope in impossible circumstances.

Yahweh, therefore, had become the one and only God. There was no attempt to justify his claim philosophically. As always, the new theology succeeded not because it could be demonstrated rationally but because it was effective in preventing despair and inspiring hope. Dislocated and displaced as they were, the Jews no longer found the discontinuity of the cult of Yahweh alien and disturbing. It spoke profoundly to their condition.

Yet there was nothing cozy about Second Isaiah's image of God. He remained beyond the grasp of the human mind:

> For my thoughts are not your thoughts,
> my ways not your ways—it is Yahweh who speaks.
> Yes, the heavens are as high above earth
> as my ways are above your ways,
> my thoughts above your thoughts.[58]

The reality of God lay beyond the reach of words and concepts. Nor would Yahweh always do what his people expected. In a very daring passage, which has particular poignancy today, the prophet looks forward to a time when Egypt and Assyria would also become the people of Yahweh, alongside Israel. Yahweh would say: "Blessed be my people Egypt, Assyria my creature, and Israel my heritage."[59] He had become the symbol of transcendent reality that made narrow interpretations of election seem petty and inadequate.

When Cyrus, King of Persia, conquered the Babylonian empire in 539 BCE, it seemed as though the prophets had been vindicated. Cyrus did not impose the Persian gods on his new subjects but worshipped at the Temple of Marduk when he entered Babylon in triumph. He also restored the effigies of the gods belonging to the peoples conquered by the Babylonians to their original homes. Now that the world had become accustomed to living in giant international empires, Cyrus probably did not need to impose the old methods of deportation. It would ease the burden of rule if his subject peoples worshipped their own gods in their own territories. Throughout his empire, he encouraged the restoration of ancient temples, claiming repeatedly that their gods had charged him with the task. He was an example of the tolerance and breadth of vision of some forms of pagan religion. In 538 Cyrus issued an edict permitting the Jews to return to Judah and rebuild their own temple. Most of them, however, elected to stay behind: henceforth only a minority would live in the Promised Land. The Bible tells us that 42,360 Jews left Babylon and Tel Aviv and began the trek home, where they imposed their new Judaism on their bewildered brethren who had remained behind.

We can see what this entailed in the writings of the Priestly tradition (P), which were written after the exile and inserted into the Pentateuch. This gave its own interpretation of the events described by J and E and added two new books, Numbers and Leviticus. As we might expect, P had an exalted and sophisticated view of Yahweh. He did not believe, for example, that anybody could actually *see* God in the way that J had suggested. Sharing many of the perspectives of Ezekiel, he believed that there was a distinction between the human perception of God and the reality itself. In P's story of Moses on Sinai, Moses begs for a vision of Yahweh, who replies: "You cannot see my face, for no man can see me and live."[60] Instead, Moses must shield himself from the divine impact in a crevice of the rock, where he would catch a glimpse of Yahweh as he departed, in a kind of hindsight. P had introduced an idea that would become extremely important in the history of God. Men and women can see only an afterglow of the divine presence, which he calls "the glory (*kavod*) of Yahweh," a manifestation of his presence, which is not to be confused with God himself.[61] When Moses came down from the mountain, his own face had reflected this "glory" and shone with such unbearable light that the Israelites could not look upon him.[62]

The "glory" of Yahweh was a symbol of his presence on earth and, as such, it emphasized the difference between the limited images of God created by men and women and the holiness of God himself. It was thus a counterbalance to the idolatrous nature of Israelite religion. When P looked back to the old stories of the Exodus, he did not imagine that Yahweh had himself accompanied the Israelites during their wanderings: that would be unseemly anthropomorphism. Instead, he shows the "glory" of Yahweh filling the tent where he met with Moses. Similarly it would only be the "glory of Yahweh" that would dwell in the Temple.[63]

P's most famous contribution to the Pentateuch was, of course, the account of creation in the first chapter of Genesis, which drew upon the *Enuma Elish*. P began with the waters of the primordial abyss (*tĕhom*, a corruption of "Tiamat"), out of which Yahweh fashioned the heavens and earth. There was no battle of the Gods, however, or struggle with Yam, Lotan or Rahab. Yahweh alone was responsible for calling all things into being. There was no gradual emanation of reality; instead Yahweh achieved order by an effortless act of will. Naturally, P did not conceive the world as divine, composed of the same stuff as Yahweh. Indeed, the notion of "separation" is crucial to P's theology: Yahweh made the cosmos an ordered place by separating night from day, water from dry land and light from darkness. At each stage, Yahweh blessed and sanctified the creation and pronounced it "good." Unlike in the Babylonian story, the making of man was the climax of creation, not a comic afterthought. Men and women might not share the divine nature, but they had been created in the image of God: they must carry on his creative tasks. As in the *Enuma Elish*, the six days of creation were followed by a sabbatical rest on the seventh day: in the Babylonian account, this had been the day when the Great Assembly had met to "fix the destinies" and confer the divine titles upon Marduk. In P, the sabbath stood in symbolic contrast to the primordial chaos that had prevailed on Day One. The didactic tone and repetitions suggest that P's creation story was also designed for liturgical recital, like the *Enuma Elish*, to extol the work of Yahweh and enthrone him as Creator and Ruler of Israel.[64]

Naturally the new Temple was central to P's Judaism. In the Near East, the temple had often been seen as a replica of the cosmos. Temple-building had been an act of *imitatio dei*, enabling humanity to participate in the creativity of the gods themselves. During the exile, many of the Jews had found consolation in the old stories of the Ark of the Covenant, the portable shrine in which God had "set up his tent" (*shakan*) with his people and shared their homelessness. When he described the building of the sanctuary, the Tent of Meeting in the wilderness, P drew upon the old mythology. Its architectural design was not original but a copy of the divine model: Moses is given very long and detailed instructions by Yahweh on Sinai: "Build me a sanctuary so that I may dwell among you. In making the tabernacle and the furnishings, you must follow exactly the pattern I shall show you."[65] The long account of the construction of this sanctuary is clearly not intended to be taken literally; nobody imagined that the ancient Israelites had really built such an elaborate shrine of "gold, silver and bronze, purple stuffs, of violet shade and red, crimson stuffs, fine linen, goats hair, rams skin, acacia wood . . ." and so forth.[66] This lengthy interpolation is heavily reminiscent of P's creation story. At each stage of the construction, Moses "saw all the work," and "blessed" the people, like Yahweh on the six days of creation. The sanctuary was built on the first day of the first month of the year; Bezalel, the architect of the shrine, was inspired by the spirit of God (*ruach elohim*) which also brooded over the creation of the world; and both accounts emphasize the importance of the sabbath rest.[67] Temple-building was also a symbol of the original harmony that had prevailed before mankind had ruined the world.

In Deuteronomy the sabbath had been designed to give everybody, slaves included, a day off and to remind the Israelites of the Exodus.[68] P has given the sabbath a new significance: it becomes an act of the imitation of God and a commemoration of his creation of the world. When they observed the sabbath rest, Jews were participating in a ritual that God had originally observed alone: it was a symbolic attempt to live the divine life. In the old paganism, every human act had imitated the actions of the gods, but the cult of Yahweh had revealed a huge gulf between the divine and human worlds. Now Jews were encouraged to come closer to Yahweh by observing the Torah of Moses. Deuteronomy had listed a number of obligatory laws, which had included the Ten Commandments. During and immediately after the exile, this had been elaborated into a complex legislation consisting of the 613 commandments (*mitzvot*) in the Pentateuch. These minute directives seem off-putting to an outsider and have been presented in a very negative light by New Testament polemic. Jews did not find them a crushing burden, as Christians tend to imagine, but found that they were a symbolic way of living in the presence of God. In Deuteronomy, the dietary laws had been a sign of Israel's special status.[69] P also saw them as a ritualized attempt to share the holy separateness of God, healing the painful severance between man and the divine. Human nature could be sanctified when Israelites imitated God's creative actions by separating milk from meat, clean from unclean and sabbath from the rest of the week.

The work of the Priestly tradition was included in the Pentateuch alongside the narratives of J and E and the Deuteronomist. This is a reminder that any major religion consists of a number of independent visions and spiritualities. Some Jews would always feel more drawn to the Deuteronomic God, who had chosen Israel to be aggressively separate from the *goyim*; some extended this into the Messianic myths that looked forward to the Day of Yahweh at the end of time, when he would exalt Israel and humiliate the other nations. These mythological accounts tended to see God as a very distant being. It had been tacitly agreed that after the exile, the era of prophecy had ceased. There was to be no more direct contact with God: this was only achieved in the symbolic visions attributed to the great figures of the remote past, such as Enoch and Daniel.

One of these distant heroes, venerated in Babylon as an example of patience in suffering, was Job. After the exile, one of the survivors used this old legend to ask fundamental questions about the nature of God and his responsibility for the sufferings of humanity. In the old story, Job had been tested by God; because he had borne his unmerited sufferings with patience, God had rewarded him by restoring his former prosperity. In the new version of the Job story, the author split the old legend in half and made Job rage against God's behavior. Together with his three comforters, Job dares to question the divine decrees and engages in a fierce intellectual debate. For the first time in Jewish religious history, the religious imagination had turned to speculation of a more abstract nature. The prophets had claimed that God had allowed Israel to suffer because of its sins; the author of Job shows that some Israelites were no longer satisfied by the traditional answer. Job attacks this view and reveals

its intellectual inadequacy, but God suddenly cuts into his furious speculation. He reveals himself to Job in a vision, pointing to the marvels of
the world he has created: how could a puny little creature like Job dare
to argue with the transcendent God? Job submits, but a modern reader,
who is looking for a more coherent and philosophical answer to the
problem of suffering, will not be satisfied with this solution. The author
of Job is not denying the right to question, however, but suggesting that
the intellect alone is not equipped to deal with these imponderable matters. Intellectual speculation must give way to a direct revelation from
God such as the prophets received.

The Jews had not yet begun to philosophize, but during the fourth
century they came under the influence of Greek rationalism. In 332 BCE
Alexander of Macedonia defeated Darius III of Persia and the Greeks
began to colonize Asia and Africa. They founded city-states in Tyre,
Sidon, Gaza, Philadelphia (Amman) and Tripolis and even at Shechem.
The Jews of Palestine and the diaspora were surrounded by a Hellenic
culture which some found disturbing, but others were excited by Greek
theater, philosophy, sport and poetry. They learned Greek, exercised at
the gymnasium and took Greek names. Some fought as mercenaries in
the Greek armies. They even translated their own scriptures into Greek,
producing the version known as the Septuagint. Thus some Greeks came
to know the God of Israel and decided to worship Yahweh (or Iao, as
they called him) alongside Zeus and Dionysus. Some were attracted to
the synagogues or meeting houses which the diaspora Jews had evolved
in place of the Temple worship. There they read their scriptures, prayed
and listened to sermons. The synagogue was unlike anything else in the
rest of the ancient religious world. Since there was no ritual or sacrifice,
it must have seemed more like a school of philosophy, and many flocked
to the synagogue if a well-known Jewish preacher came to town, as they
would queue up to hear their own philosophers. Some Greeks even
observed selected parts of the Torah and joined Jews in syncretist sects.
During the fourth century BCE, there were isolated instances of Jews and
Greeks merging Yahweh with one of the Greek gods.

Most Jews held aloof, however, and tension developed between Jews
and Greeks in the Hellenistic cities of the Middle East. In the ancient
world, religion was not a private matter. The gods were extremely important to the city, and it was believed that they would withdraw their
patronage if their cult were neglected. Jews, who claimed that these gods
did not exist, were called "atheists" and enemies of society. By the second
century BCE this hostility was entrenched: in Palestine there had even

been a revolt when Antiochus Epiphanes, the Seleucid governor, had attempted to Hellenize Jerusalem and introduce the cult of Zeus into the Temple. Jews had started to produce their own literature, which argued that wisdom was not Greek cleverness but the fear of Yahweh. Wisdom literature was a well-established genre in the Middle East; it tried to delve into the meaning of life, not by philosophical reflection, but by inquiring into the best way to live: it was often highly pragmatic. The author of the Book of Proverbs, who was writing in the third century BCE, went a little further and suggested that Wisdom was the master plan that God had devised when he had created the world and, as such, was the first of his creatures. This idea would be very important to the early Christians, as we shall see in Chapter 4. The author personifies Wisdom so that she seems a separate person:

> Yahweh created me when his purpose first unfolded
>   before the oldest of his works.
> From everlasting I was firmly set,
>   from the beginning, before earth came into being . . .
>   when he laid the foundations of the earth,
> I was at his side, a master craftsman,
>   delighting him day after day, ever at play in his presence,
> at play everywhere in the world,
>   delighting to be with the sons of men.[70]

Wisdom was not a divine being, however, but is specifically said to have been created by God. She is similar to the "glory" of God described by the Priestly authors, representing the plan of God that human beings could glimpse in creation and in human affairs: the author represents Wisdom (*Hokhmah*) wandering through the streets, calling people to fear Yahweh. In the second century BCE, Jesus ben Sira, a devout Jew of Jerusalem, painted a similar portrait of Wisdom. He makes her stand up in the Divine Council and sing her own praises: she had come forth from the mouth of the Most High as the divine Word by which God had created the world; she is present everywhere in creation but has taken up permanent residence among the people of Israel.[71]

Like the "glory" of Yahweh, the figure of Wisdom was a symbol of God's activity in the world. Jews were cultivating such an exalted notion of Yahweh that it was difficult to imagine him intervening directly in human affairs. Like P, they preferred to distinguish the God we could know and experience from the divine reality itself. When we read of the

divine Wisdom leaving God to wander through the world in search of
humanity, it is hard not to be reminded of the pagan goddesses such as
Ishtar, Anat and Isis, who had also descended from the divine world in
a redemptive mission. Wisdom literature acquired a polemic edge in
Alexandria in about 50 BCE. In *The Wisdom of Solomon*, a Jew of Alexandria,
where there was an important Jewish community, warned Jews to resist
the seductive Hellenic culture around them and to remain true to their
own traditions: it is the fear of Yahweh, not Greek philosophy, which
constitutes true wisdom. Writing in Greek, he also personified Wisdom
(*Sophia*) and argued that it could not be separated from the Jewish God:

> [Sophia] is the breath of the power of God,
> pure emanation of the glory of the Almighty;
> hence nothing impure can find a way into her.
> She is a reflection of the eternal light,
> untarnished mirror of God's active power,
> image of his goodness.[72]

This passage would also be extremely important to Christians when they
came to discuss the status of Jesus. The Jewish author, however, simply
saw Sophia as an aspect of the unknowable God who has adapted himself
to human understanding. She is God-as-he-has-revealed-himself-to-man,
the human perception of God, mysteriously distinct from the full reality
of God, which would always elude our understanding.

The author of *The Wisdom of Solomon* was right to sense a tension
between Greek thought and Jewish religion. We have seen that there is
a crucial and, perhaps, an irreconcilable difference between the God of
Aristotle, which is scarcely aware of the world it has created, and the
God of the Bible, who is passionately involved in human affairs. The
Greek God could be discovered by human reason, whereas the God of
the Bible only made himself known by means of revelation. A chasm
separated Yahweh from the world, but Greeks believed that the gift of
reason made human beings kin to God; they could, therefore, reach him
by their own efforts. Yet whenever monotheists fell in love with Greek
philosophy, they inevitably wanted to try to adapt its God to their own.
This will be one of the major themes of our story. One of the first
people to make this attempt was the eminent Jewish philosopher Philo of
Alexandria (ca. 30 BCE–45 CE). Philo was a Platonist and had a distinguished reputation as a rationalist philosopher in his own right. He wrote
in beautiful Greek and does not seem to have spoken Hebrew, yet he

was also a devout Jew and an observer of the *mitzvot*. He could see no incompatibility between his God and the God of the Greeks. It must be said, however, that Philo's God seems very different from Yahweh. For one thing, Philo seemed embarrassed by the historical books of the Bible, which he tried to turn into elaborate allegories: Aristotle, it will be recalled, had considered history unphilosophical. His God has no human qualities: it is quite incorrect, for example, to say that he is "angry." All we can know about God is the bare fact of his existence. Yet, as a practicing Jew, Philo *did* believe that God had revealed himself to the prophets. How had this been possible?

Philo solved the problem by making an important distinction between God's essence (*ousia*), which is entirely incomprehensible, and his activities in the world, which he called his "powers" (*dynameis*) or "energies" (*energeiai*). Basically, it was similar to the solution of P and the Wisdom writers. We can never know God as he is in himself. Philo makes him tell Moses: "The apprehension of me is something more than human nature, yea, even the whole heaven and universe, will be able to contain."[73] To adapt himself to our limited intellect, God communicates through his "powers," which seem equivalent to Plato's divine forms (though Philo is not always consistent about this). They are the highest realities that the human mind can grasp. Philo sees them emanating from God, rather as Plato and Aristotle had seen the cosmos emanating eternally from the First Cause. Two of these powers were especially important. Philo called them the Kingly power, which reveals God in the order of the universe, and the Creative power, whereby God reveals himself in the blessings he bestows upon humanity. Neither of these powers is to be confused with the divine essence (*ousia*), which remains shrouded in impenetrable mystery. They simply enable us to catch a glimpse of a reality which is beyond anything we can conceive. Sometimes Philo speaks of God's essential being (*ousia*) flanked by the Kingly and Creative powers in a kind of trinity. When he interprets the story of Yahweh's visit to Abraham at Mamre with the two angels, for example, he argues that this is an allegorical presentation of God's *ousia*—He Who Is—with the two senior powers.[74]

J would have been astonished by this and, indeed, Jews have always found Philo's conception of God somewhat inauthentic. Christians, however, would find him enormously helpful, and the Greeks, as we shall see, seized upon this distinction between God's unknowable "essence" and the "energies" that make him known to us. They would also be influenced by his theory of the divine Logos. Like the Wisdom writers,

Philo imagined that God had formed a master plan (*logos*) of creation, which corresponded to Plato's realm of the forms. These forms were then incarnated in the physical universe. Again, Philo is not always consistent. Sometimes he suggests that Logos is one of the powers; at other times he seems to think it is higher than the powers, the highest idea of God that human beings can attain. When we contemplate the Logos, however, we form no positive knowledge of God: we are taken beyond the reach of discursive reason to an intuitive apprehension which is "higher than a way of thinking, more precious than anything which is merely thought."[75] It was an activity similar to Plato's contemplation (*theoria*). Philo insisted that we will never reach God as he is in himself: the highest truth we can apprehend is the rapturous recognition that God utterly transcends the human mind.

This is not as bleak as it sounds. Philo described a passionate, joyful voyage into the unknown, which brought him liberation and creative energy. Like Plato, he saw the soul as in exile, trapped in the physical world of matter. It must ascend to God, its true home, leaving passion, the senses and even language behind, because these bind us to the imperfect world. Finally, it will achieve an ecstasy that lifts it above the dreary confines of the ego to a larger, fuller reality. We have seen that the conception of God has often been an imaginative exercise. Prophets had reflected upon their experience and felt that it could be ascribed to the being they called God. Philo shows that religious contemplation had much in common with other forms of creativity. There were times, he says, when he struggled grimly with his books and made no headway, but sometimes he felt possessed by the divine:

> I . . . have suddenly become full, the ideas descending like snow, so that under the impact of divine possession, I have been filled with Corybantic frenzy and become ignorant of everything, place, people, present, myself, what was said and what was written. For I acquired expression, ideas, an enjoyment of life, sharp-sighted vision, exceedingly distinct clarity of objects such as might occur through the eyes as a result of clearest display.[76]

Soon it would be impossible for Jews to achieve such a synthesis with the Greek world. In the year of Philo's death there were pogroms against the Jewish community in Alexandria and widespread fears of Jewish insurrection. When the Romans had established their empire in North Africa and the Middle East in the first century BCE they had themselves succumbed to the Greek culture, merging their ancestral deities with the Greek pantheon and adopting Greek philosophy with enthusiasm. They had not, however, inherited the Greek hostility to the Jews. Indeed, they often favored the Jews over the Greeks, regarding them as useful allies in Greek cities where there was residual hostility to Rome. Jews were given full religious liberty: their religion was known to be of great antiquity, and this was respected. Relations between Jews and Romans were usually good even in Palestine, where foreign rule was accepted less easily. By the first century CE, Judaism was in a very strong position in the Roman empire. One-tenth of the whole empire was Jewish: in Philo's Alexandria, forty percent of the population were Jews. People in the Roman empire were searching for new religious solutions; monotheistic ideas were in the air, and local gods were increasingly seen as mere manifestations of a more encompassing divinity. The Romans were drawn to the high moral character of Judaism. Those who were understandably reluctant to be circumcised and observe the whole Torah often became honorary members of the synagogues, known as the "Godfearers." They were on the increase: it has even been suggested that one of the Flavian emperors might have converted to Judaism, as Constantine would later convert to Christianity. In Palestine, however, a group of political zealots fiercely opposed Roman rule. In 66 CE they orchestrated a rebellion against Rome and, incredibly, managed to hold the Roman armies at bay for four years. The authorities feared that the rebellion would spread to the Jews of the diaspora and were forced to crush it mercilessly. In 70 CE the armies of the new emperor Vespasian finally conquered Jerusalem, burned the Temple to the ground and made the city a Roman city called Aelia Capitolana. Yet again the Jews were forced into exile.

The loss of the Temple, which had been the inspiration of the new Judaism, was a great grief, but with hindsight it seems that the Jews of Palestine, who were often more conservative than the Hellenized Jews of the diaspora, had already prepared themselves for the catastrophe. Various sects had sprung up in the Holy Land which had in different ways dissociated themselves from the Jerusalem Temple. The Essenes and the Qumran sect believed that the Temple had become venal and corrupt; they had withdrawn to live in separate communities, such as the monastic-style community beside the Dead Sea. They believed that they were building a new Temple, not made with hands. Theirs would be a Temple of the Spirit; instead of the old animal sacrifices, they purified themselves and sought forgiveness of sins by baptismal ceremonies and communal meals. God would live in a loving brotherhood, not in a stone temple.

The most progressive of all the Jews of Palestine were the Pharisees, who found the solution of the Essenes too elitist. In the New Testament, the Pharisees are depicted as whited sepulchres and blatant hypocrites. This is due to the distortions of first-century polemic. The Pharisees were passionately spiritual Jews. They believed that the whole of Israel was called to be a holy nation of priests. God could be present in the humblest home as well as in the Temple. Consequently, they lived like the official priestly caste, observing the special laws of purity that applied only to the Temple in their own homes. They insisted on eating their meals in a state of ritual purity because they believed that the table of every single Jew was like God's altar in the Temple. They cultivated a sense of God's presence in the smallest detail of daily life. Jews could now approach him directly without the mediation of a priestly caste and an elaborate ritual. They could atone for their sins by acts of loving-kindness to their neighbor; charity was the most important *mitzvah* in the Torah; when two or three Jews studied the Torah together, God was in their midst. During the early years of the century, two rival schools had emerged: one led by Shammai the Elder, which was more rigorous, and the other led by the great Rabbi Hillel the Elder, which became by far the most popular Pharisaic party. There is a story that one day a pagan had approached Hillel and told him that he would be willing to convert to Judaism if the Master could recite the whole of the Torah to him while he stood on one leg. Hillel replied: "Do not do unto others as you would not have done unto you. That is the whole of the Torah: go and learn it."[77]

By the disastrous year 70, the Pharisees had become the most respected and important sect of Palestinian Judaism; they had already shown their people that they did not need a Temple to worship God, as this famous story shows:

> Once as Rabbi Yohannan ben Zakkai was coming forth from Jerusalem, Rabbi Joshua followed after him and beheld the Temple in ruins.
> "Woe unto us!" Rabbi Joshua said, "that this, the place where the iniquities of Israel were atoned for, is laid waste!"
> "My son," Rabbi Yohannan said, "be not grieved. We have another atonement as effective as this. And what is it? It is acts of loving kindness, as it is said: 'For I desire mercy and not sacrifice.' "[78]

It is said that after the conquest of Jerusalem, Rabbi Yohannan had been smuggled out of the burning city in a coffin. He had been opposed to the

Jewish revolt and thought that the Jews would be better off without a state. The Romans allowed him to found a self-governing Pharisaic community at Jabneh, to the west of Jerusalem. Similar communities were founded in Palestine and Babylonia, which maintained close links. These communities produced the scholars known as the *tannaim*, including rabbinic heroes like Rabbi Yohannan himself, Rabbi Akiva the mystic and Rabbi Ishmael: they compiled the Mishnah, the codification of an oral law which brought the Mosaic law up to date. Next a new set of scholars, known as the *amoraim*, began a commentary on the Mishnah and produced the treatises known collectively as the Talmud. In fact two Talmuds had been compiled; the Jerusalem Talmud, which was completed by the end of the fourth century, and the Babylonian Talmud, which is considered the more authoritative and which was not completed until the end of the fifth century. The process continued as each generation of scholars began to comment in their turn on the Talmud and the exegesis of their predecessors. This legal contemplation is not as desiccated as outsiders tend to imagine. It was an endless meditation on the Word of God, the new Holy of Holies; each layer of exegesis represented the walls and courts of a new Temple, enshrining the presence of God among his people.

Yahweh had always been a transcendent deity, who directed human beings from above and without. The Rabbis made him intimately present within mankind and the smallest details of life. After the loss of the Temple and the harrowing experience of yet another exile, the Jews needed a God in their midst. The Rabbis did not construct any formal doctrines about God. Instead, they experienced him as an almost tangible presence. Their spirituality has been described as a state of "normal mysticism."[79] In the very earliest passages of the Talmud, God was experienced in mysterious physical phenomena. The Rabbis spoke about the Holy Spirit, which had brooded over creation and the building of the sanctuary, making its presence felt in a rushing wind or a blazing fire. Others heard it in the clanging of a bell or a sharp knocking sound. One day, for example, Rabbi Yohannan had been sitting discussing Ezekiel's vision of the chariot, when a fire descended from heaven and angels stood nearby: a voice from heaven confirmed that the Rabbi had a special mission from God.[80]

So strong was their sense of presence that any official, objective doctrines would have been quite out of place. The Rabbis frequently suggested that on Mount Sinai, each one of the Israelites who had been standing at the foot of the mountain had experienced God in a different way. God had, as it were, adapted himself to each person "according to the comprehension of each."[81] As one Rabbi put it, "God does not come to man oppressively but commensurately with a man's power of receiving him."[82] This very important rabbinic insight meant that God could not be described in a formula as though he were the same for everybody: he was an essentially subjective experience. Each individual would experience the reality of "God" in a different way to answer the needs of his or her own particular temperament. Each one of the prophets had experienced God differently, the Rabbis insisted, because his personality had influenced his conception of the divine. We shall see that other monotheists would develop a very similar notion. To this day, theological ideas about God are private matters in Judaism and are not enforced by the establishment.

Any official doctrine would limit the essential mystery of God. The Rabbis pointed out that he was utterly incomprehensible. Not even Moses had been able to penetrate the mystery of God: after lengthy research, King David had admitted that it was futile to try to understand him, because he was too much for the human mind.[83] Jews were even forbidden to pronounce his name, a powerful reminder that any attempt to express him was bound to be inadequate: the divine name was written YHWH and not pronounced in any reading of the scripture. We could admire God's deeds in nature but, as Rabbi Huna said, this only gave us an infinitesimal glimpse of the whole reality: "Man cannot conceive the meaning of thunder, hurricane, storm, the order of the universe, his own nature; how then can he boast of being able to understand the ways of the King of all Kings?"[84] The whole point of the idea of God was to encourage a sense of the mystery and wonder of life, not to find neat solutions. The Rabbis even warned the Israelites against praising God too frequently in their prayers, because their words were bound to be defective.[85]

How did this transcendent and incomprehensible being relate to the world? The Rabbis expressed their sense of this in a paradox: "God is the place of the world, but the world is not his place:"[86] God enveloped and encircled the world, as it were, but he did not live *in* it as mere creatures did. In another of their favorite images, they used to say that God filled the world as the soul fills the body: it informs but transcends it. Again, they said that God was like the rider of a horse: while he is on the horse, the rider depends upon the animal, but he is superior to it and has control of the reins. These were only images and, inevitably, inadequate: they were imaginative depictions of a huge and indefinable "something" in which we live and move and have our being. When they spoke of God's presence on earth, they were as careful as the biblical writers to distinguish those traces of God that he allows us to see from the greater divine mystery which is inaccessible. They liked the images of the "glory" (*kavod*) of YHWH and of the Holy Spirit, which were constant reminders that the God that we experience does not correspond to the essence of the divine reality.

One of their favorite synonyms for God was the Shekinah, which derived from the Hebrew *shakan*, to dwell with or to pitch one's tent. Now that the Temple was gone, the image of God who had accompanied the Israelites on their wanderings in the wilderness suggested the accessibility of God. Some said that the Shekinah, who dwelt with his people on earth, still lived on the Temple Mount, even though the Temple was in ruins. Other Rabbis argued that the destruction of the Temple had freed the Shekinah from Jerusalem and enabled it to inhabit the rest of the world.[87] Like the divine "glory" or the Holy Spirit, the Shekinah was not conceived as a separate divine being but as the presence of God on earth. The Rabbis looked back on the history of their people and saw that it had always accompanied them:

> Come and see how beloved are the Israelites before God, for wherever they went the Shekinah followed them, as it is said, "Did I plainly reveal myself to thy father's house when they were in Egypt?" In Babylon, the Shekinah was with them, as it is said, "For your sake I have [been] sent to Babylon." And when in the future Israel will be redeemed, the Shekinah will then be with them, as it is said, "The Lord thy God will turn thy captivity." That is, God will return with thy captivity.[88]

The connection between Israel and its God was so strong that, when he had redeemed them in the past, the Israelites used to tell God: "Thou hast redeemed *thyself*."[89] In their own distinctly Jewish way, the Rabbis were developing that sense of God as identified with the self, which the Hindus had called Atman.

The image of the Shekinah helped the exiles to cultivate a sense of God's presence wherever they were. The Rabbis spoke of the Shekinah skipping from one synagogue of the diaspora to another; others said that it stood at the door of the synagogue, blessing each step that a Jew took on his way to the House of Studies; the Shekinah also stood at the door of the synagogue when the Jews recited the *Shema* there together.[90] Like the early Christians, the Israelites were encouraged by their Rabbis to see themselves as a united community with "one body and one soul."[91] The community was the new Temple, enshrining the immanent God: thus when they entered the synagogue and recited the *Shema* in perfect unison "with devotion, with one voice, one mind and one tone," God was present among them. But he hated any lack of harmony in the community and returned to heaven, where the angels chanted the divine praises "with one voice and one melody."[92] The higher union of God and Israel could only exist when the lower union of Israelite with Israelite was complete: constantly, the Rabbis told them that when a group of Jews studied the Torah together, the Shekinah sat among them.[93]

In exile, the Jews felt the harshness of the surrounding world; this sense of presence helped them to feel enveloped by a benevolent God. When they bound their phylacteries (*tfillin*) to their hands and fore-heads, wore ritual fringes (*tzitzit*) and nailed the *mezuzah* containing the words of the *Shema* over their doors, as Deuteronomy prescribed, they should not try to explain these obscure and peculiar practices. That would limit their value. Instead they should allow the performance of these *mitzvot* to nudge them into an awareness of God's enveloping love; "Israel is beloved! The Bible surrounds him with *mitzvot*: *tfillin* on the head and arm, a *mezuzah* on the door, *tzitzit* on their clothes."[94] They were like the gifts of jewels that a king gave to his wife to make her more beautiful to him. It was not easy. The Talmud shows that some people were wondering whether God made much difference in such a dark world.[95] The spirituality of the Rabbis became normative in Judaism, not merely among those who had fled Jerusalem but among Jews who had always lived in the diaspora. This was not because it was based on a sound theoretical foundation: many of the practices of the Law made no logical sense. The religion of the Rabbis was accepted because it worked. The vision of the Rabbis had prevented their people from falling into despair.

This type of spirituality was for men only, however, since women were not required—and therefore not permitted—to become Rabbis, to study Torah or to pray in the synagogue. The religion of God was becoming as patriarchal as most of the other ideologies of the period. The woman's role was to maintain the ritual purity of the home. Jews had long sanctified creation by separating its various items, and in this spirit women were relegated to a separate sphere from their menfolk, just as they were to keep milk separate from meat in their kitchens. In practice, this meant that they were regarded as inferior. Even though the Rabbis taught that women were blessed by God, men were commanded to thank God during the morning prayer for not making them Gentiles, slaves or women. Yet marriage was regarded as a sacred duty and family life was holy. The Rabbis stressed its sanctity in legislation that has often been misunderstood. When sexual intercourse was forbidden during menstruation, this was not because a woman was to be regarded as dirty or disgusting. The period of abstinence was designed to prevent a man from taking his wife for granted: "Because a man may become overly familiar with his wife, and thus repelled by her, the Torah says that she should be a *niddah* [sexually unavailable] for seven days [after menses] so that she will be as beloved to him [afterward] as on the day of marriage."[96] Before going to the synagogue on a festival day, a man was commanded to take a ritual bath, not because he was unclean in any simplistic way but to make himself more holy for the sacred divine service. It is in this spirit that a woman was commanded to take a ritual bath after the menstrual period, to prepare herself for the holiness of what came next: sexual relations with her husband. The idea that sex could be holy in this way would be alien to Christianity, which would sometimes see sex and God as mutually incompatible. True, later Jews often gave a negative interpretation to these rabbinic directives, but the Rabbis themselves did not preach a lugubrious, ascetic, life-denying spirituality.

On the contrary, they insisted that Jews had a duty to keep well and happy. They frequently depict the Holy Spirit "leaving" or "abandoning" such biblical characters as Jacob, David or Esther when they were sick or unhappy.[97] Sometimes they made them quote Psalm 22 when they felt the Spirit leave them: "My God, my God, why have you deserted me?" This raises an interesting question about Jesus' mysterious cry from the cross, when he quoted these words. The Rabbis taught that God did not want men and women to suffer. The body should be honored and cared for, since it was in the image of God: it could even be sinful to avoid such pleasures as wine or sex, since God had provided them for man's enjoyment. God was not to be found in suffering and asceticism. When they urged their people to practical ways of "possessing" the Holy Spirit, they were in one sense asking them to create their own image of God for themselves. They taught that it was not easy to say where God's work began and man's ended. The prophets had always made God visible on earth by attributing their *own* insights to him. Now the Rabbis were seen to be engaged in a task that was at once human and divine. When they formulated new legislation, it was seen both as God's and as their own. By increasing the amount of Torah in the world, they were extending his presence in the world and making it more effective. They themselves came to be revered as the incarnations of Torah; they were more "like God" than anybody else because of their expertise in the Law.[98]

This sense of an immanent God helped Jews to see humanity as sacred. Rabbi Akiva taught that the *mitzvah* "Thou shalt love thy neighbor as thyself" was "the great principle of Torah."[99] Offenses against a fellow human being were a denial of God himself, who had made men and women in his image. It was tantamount to atheism, a blasphemous attempt to ignore God. Thus murder was the greatest of all crimes because it was a sacrilege: "Scripture instructs us that whatsoever sheds human blood is regarded as if he had diminished the divine image."[100] Serving another human being was an act of *imitatio dei*: it reproduced God's benevolence and compassion. Because all were created in God's image, all were equal: even the High Priest should be beaten if he injured his fellow man, because it was tantamount to denying the existence of God.[101] God created *adām*, a single man, to teach us that whoever destroyed a single human life would be punished as though he had destroyed the whole world; similarly to save a life was to redeem the whole world.[102] This was not just a lofty sentiment but a basic legal principle: it meant that no one individual could be sacrificed for the sake of a group during a pogrom, for example. To humiliate anybody, even a *goy* or a slave, was one of the most serious offenses, because it was equivalent to murder, a sacrilegious denial of God's image.[103] The right to liberty was crucial: it is difficult to find a single reference to imprisonment in the whole of rabbinic literature, because only God can curtail the freedom of a human being. Spreading scandal about somebody was tantamount to denying the existence of God.[104] Jews were not to think of God as a Big Brother, watching their every move from above; instead they were to cultivate a sense of God within each human being so that our dealings with others became sacred encounters.

Animals have no difficulty in living up to their nature, but men and women seem to find it hard to be fully human. The God of Israel had sometimes seemed to encourage a most unholy and inhumane cruelty. But over the centuries Yahweh had become an idea that could help people to cultivate a compassion and respect for their fellow human beings, which had always been a hallmark of the religions of the Axial Age. The ideals of the Rabbis were close to the second of the God-religions, which had its roots in exactly the same tradition.

3

A Light to the Gentiles

AT THE SAME TIME as Philo was expounding his Platonized Judaism in Alexandria and Hillel and Shammai were arguing in Jerusalem, a charismatic faith healer began his own career in the north of Palestine. We know very little about Jesus. The first full-length account of his life was St. Mark's Gospel, which was not written until about the year 70, some forty years after his death. By that time, historical facts had been overlaid with mythical elements which expressed the meaning Jesus had acquired for his followers. It is this meaning that St. Mark primarily conveys rather than a reliable straightforward portrayal. The first Christians saw him as a new Moses, a new Joshua, the founder of a new Israel. Like the Buddha, Jesus seemed to encapsulate some of the deepest aspirations of many of his contemporaries and to give substance to dreams that had haunted the Jewish people for centuries. During his lifetime, many Jews in Palestine had believed that he was the Messiah: he had ridden into Jerusalem and been hailed as the Son of David, but, only a few days later, he was put to death by the agonizing Roman punishment of crucifixion. Yet despite the scandal of a Messiah who had died like a common criminal, his disciples could not believe that their faith in him had been misplaced. There were rumors that he had risen from the dead. Some said that his tomb had been found empty three days after his crucifixion; others saw him in visions, and on one occasion 500 people saw him simultaneously. His disciples believed that he would soon return to inaugurate the Messianic Kingdom of God, and, since there was nothing heretical about such a belief, their sect was accepted as authentically Jewish by no less a person than Rabbi Gamaliel, the grandson of Hillel and one of the greatest of the *tannaim*. His followers worshipped in the Temple every day as fully observant Jews. Ultimately, however, the New Israel, inspired by the life, death and resurrection of Jesus, would become a Gentile faith, which would evolve its own distinctive conception of God.

By the time of Jesus' death in about 30 CE, the Jews were passionate monotheists, so nobody expected the Messiah to be a divine figure: he would simply be an ordinary, if privileged, human being. Some of the Rabbis suggested that his name and identity were known to God from all eternity. In that sense, therefore, the Messiah could be said to have been "with God" from before the beginning of time in the same symbolic way as the figure of divine Wisdom in Proverbs and Ecclesiasticus. Jews expected the Messiah, the anointed one, to be a descendant of King David, who, as king and spiritual leader, had founded the first independent Jewish kingdom in Jerusalem. The Psalms sometimes called David or the Messiah "the Son of God," but that was simply a way of expressing his intimacy with Yahweh. Nobody since the return from Babylon had imagined that Yahweh actually had a son, like the abominable deities of the *goyim*.

Mark's Gospel, which as the earliest is usually regarded as the most reliable, presents Jesus as a perfectly normal man, with a family that included brothers and sisters. No angels announced his birth or sang over his crib. He had not been marked out during his infancy or adolescence as remarkable in any way. When he began to teach, his townsmen in Nazareth were astonished that the son of the local carpenter should have turned out to be such a prodigy. Mark begins his narrative with Jesus' career. It seems that he may originally have been the disciple of one John the Baptist, a wandering ascetic who had probably been an Essene: John had regarded the Jerusalem establishment as hopelessly corrupt and preached excoriating sermons against it. He urged the populace to repent and to accept the Essene rite of purification by baptism in the River Jordan. Luke suggests that Jesus and John were actually related. Jesus had made the long journey from Nazareth to Judaea to be baptized by John. As Mark tells us: "No sooner had he come out of the water than he saw the heavens torn apart and the Spirit, like a dove, descending on him. And a voice came from heaven, 'You are my Son, the Beloved; my favor rests upon you.' "[1] John the Baptist had immediately recognized Jesus as the Messiah. The next thing we hear about Jesus is that he began to preach in all the towns and villages of Galilee, announcing: "The Kingdom of God has arrived!"[2]

There has been much speculation about the exact nature of Jesus' mission. Very few of his actual words seem to have been recorded in the Gospels, and much of their material has been affected by later developments in the churches that were founded by St. Paul after his death. Nevertheless, there are clues that point to the essentially Jewish nature of his career. It has been pointed out that faith healers were familiar religious figures in Galilee: like Jesus, they were mendicants, who preached, healed the sick and exorcised demons. Like Jesus again, these Galilean holy men often had a large number of women disciples. Others argue that Jesus was probably a Pharisee of the same school as Hillel, just as Paul, who claimed to have been a Pharisee before his conversion to Christianity, was said to have sat at the feet of Rabbi Gamaliel.[3] Certainly Jesus' teaching was in accord with major tenets of the Pharisees, since he also believed that charity and loving-kindness were the most important of the *mitzvot*. Like the Pharisees, he was devoted to the Torah and was said to have preached a more stringent observance than many of his contemporaries.[4] He also taught a version of Hillel's Golden Rule, when he argued that the whole of the Law could be summed up in the maxim: do unto others as you would have them do unto you.[5] In St. Matthew's Gospel, Jesus is made to utter violent and rather unedifying diatribes against "the Scribes and Pharisees," presenting them as worthless hypocrites.[6] Apart from this being a libelous distortion of the facts and a flagrant breach of the charity that was supposed to characterize his mission, the bitter denunciation of the Pharisees is almost certainly inauthentic. Luke, for example, gives the Pharisees a fairly good press in both his Gospel and the Acts of the Apostles, and Paul would scarcely have flaunted his Pharisaic background if the Pharisees really had been the sworn enemies of Jesus who had hounded him to death. The anti-Semitic tenor of Matthew's Gospel reflects the tension between Jews and Christians during the 80s. The Gospels often show Jesus arguing with the Pharisees, but the discussion is either amicable or may reflect a disagreement with the more rigorous school of Shammai.

After his death, his followers decided that Jesus had been divine. This did not happen immediately; as we shall see, the doctrine that Jesus had been God in human form was not finalized until the fourth century. The development of Christian belief in the Incarnation was a gradual, complex process. Jesus himself certainly never claimed to be God. At his baptism he had been called the Son of God by a voice from heaven, but this was probably simply a confirmation that he was the beloved Messiah. There was nothing particularly unusual about such a proclamation from above:

the Rabbis often experienced what they called a *bat qol* (literally, "Daughter of the Voice"), a form of inspiration that had replaced the more direct prophetic revelations.[7] Rabbi Yohannan ben Zakkai had heard such a *bat qol* confirming his own mission on the occasion when the Holy Spirit had descended upon him and his disciples in the form of fire. Jesus himself used to call himself "the Son of Man." There has been much controversy about this title, but it seems that the original Aramaic phrase (*bar nasha*) simply stressed the weakness and mortality of the human condition. If this is so, Jesus seems to have gone out of his way to emphasize that he was a frail human being who would one day suffer and die.

The Gospels tell us that God had given Jesus certain divine "powers" (*dunamis*), however, which enabled him, mere mortal though he was, to perform the God-like tasks of healing the sick and forgiving sins. When people saw Jesus in action, therefore, they had a living, breathing image of what God was like. On one occasion, three of his disciples claimed to have seen this more clearly than usual. The story has been preserved in all three of the Synoptic Gospels and would be very important to later generations of Christians. It tells us that Jesus had taken Peter, James and John up a very high mountain, which is traditionally identified with Mount Tabor in Galilee. There he was "transfigured" before them: "his face shone like the sun and his clothes became white as the light."[8] Moses and Elijah, representing respectively the Law and the prophets, suddenly appeared beside him and the three conversed together. Peter was quite overcome and cried aloud, not knowing what he said, that they should build three tabernacles to commemorate the vision. A bright cloud, like that which had descended on Mount Sinai, covered the mountaintop and a *bat qol* declared: "This is my Son, the Beloved; he enjoys my favor. Listen to him."[9] Centuries later, when Greek Christians pondered the meaning of this vision, they decided that the "powers" of God had shone through Jesus' transfigured humanity.

They also noted that Jesus had never claimed that these divine "powers," or *dynameis*, were confined to him alone. Again and again, Jesus had promised his disciples that if they had "faith" they would enjoy these "powers" too. By faith, of course, he did not mean adopting the correct theology but cultivating an inner attitude of surrender and openness to God. If his disciples laid themselves open to God without reserve, they would be able to do everything that he could do. Like the Rabbis, Jesus did not believe that the Spirit was just for a privileged elite but for all men of goodwill: some passages even suggest that, again like some of the Rabbis, Jesus believed that even the *goyim* could receive the

Spirit. If his disciples had "faith," they would be able to do even greater things. Not only would they be able to forgive sins and exorcise demons, but they would be able to hurl a mountain into the sea.[10] They would discover that their frail, mortal lives had been transfigured by the "powers" of God that were present and active in the world of the Messianic Kingdom.

After his death, the disciples could not abandon their faith that Jesus had somehow presented an image of God. From a very early date, they had begun to pray to him. St. Paul believed that the powers of God should be made accessible to the *goyim* and preached the Gospel in what is now Turkey, Macedonia and Greece. He was convinced that non-Jews could become members of the New Israel even though they did not observe the full Law of Moses. This offended the original group of disciples, who wanted to remain a more exclusively Jewish sect, and they broke with Paul after a passionate dispute. Most of Paul's converts were either diaspora Jews or Godfearers, however, so the New Israel remained deeply Jewish. Paul never called Jesus "God." He called him "the Son of God" in its Jewish sense: he certainly did not believe that Jesus had been the incarnation of God himself: he had simply possessed God's "powers" and "Spirit," which manifested God's activity on earth and were not to be identified with the inaccessible divine essence. Not surprisingly, in the Gentile world the new Christians did not always retain the sense of these subtle distinctions, so that eventually a man who had stressed his weak, mortal humanity was believed to have been divine. The doctrine of the Incarnation of God in Jesus has always scandalized Jews, and, later, Muslims would also find it blasphemous. It is a difficult doctrine with certain dangers; Christians have often interpreted it crudely. Yet this type of Incarnational devotion has been a fairly constant theme in the history of religion: we shall see that even Jews and Muslims developed some strikingly similar theologies of their own.

We can see the religious impulse behind this startling divinization of Jesus by looking briefly at some developments in India at about the same time. In both Buddhism and Hinduism there had been a surge of devotion to exalted beings, such as the Buddha himself or Hindu gods which had appeared in human form. This kind of personal devotion, known as *bhakti*, expressed what seems to be a perennial human yearning for humanized religion. It was a completely new departure and yet, in both faiths, it was integrated into the religion without compromising essential priorities.

After the Buddha had died at the end of the sixth century BCE, people naturally wanted a memento of him, yet they felt that a statue was inappropriate, since in nirvana he no longer "existed" in any normal sense. Yet personal love of the Buddha developed and the need to contemplate his enlightened humanity became so strong that in the first century BCE the first statues appeared at Gandhara in northwest India and Mathura on the Jumna River. The power and inspiration of such images gave them a central importance in Buddhist spirituality, even though this devotion to a being outside the self was very different from the interior discipline preached by Gautama. All religions change and develop. If they do not, they will become obsolete. The majority of Buddhists found *bhakti* extremely valuable and felt that it reminded them of some essential truths which were in danger of being lost. When the Buddha had first achieved enlightenment, it will be recalled that he had been tempted to keep it to himself, but his compassion for suffering humanity had compelled him to spend the next forty years preaching the Way. Yet by the first century BCE, Buddhist monks who were locked away in their monasteries trying to reach nirvana on their own seemed to have lost sight of this. The monastic was also a daunting ideal, which many felt to be quite beyond them. During the first century CE, a new kind of Buddhist hero emerged: the *bodhisattva*, who followed the Buddha's example and put off his own nirvana, sacrificing himself for the sake of the people. He was ready to endure rebirth in order to rescue people in pain. As the *Prajna-paramita Sutras* (Sermons on the Perfection of Wisdom), which were compiled at the end of the first century BCE, explain, the *bodhisattvas*

> do not wish to attain their own private *nirvana*. On the contrary, they have surveyed the highly painful world of being, and yet desirous of winning supreme enlightenment, they do not tremble at birth-and-death. They have set out for the benefit of the world, for the ease of the world, out of pity for the world. They have resolved: "We will become a shelter for the world, the world's place of rest, the final relief of the world, islands of the world, lights of the world, the guides of the world's means of salvation."[11]

Further, the *bodhisattva* had acquired an infinite source of merit, which could help the less spiritually gifted. A person who prayed to a *bodhisattva* could be reborn into one of the paradises in the Buddhist cosmology, where conditions made the attainment of enlightenment easier.

The texts emphasize that these ideas were not to be interpreted literally. They had nothing to do with ordinary logic or events in this world, but were merely symbols of a more elusive truth. In the early second century

CE, Nagarjuna, the philosopher who founded the Void School, used paradox and a dialectical method to demonstrate the inadequacy of normal conceptual language. The ultimate truths, he insisted, could only be grasped intuitively through the mental disciplines of meditation. Even the Buddha's teachings were conventional, man-made ideas that did no justice to the reality he had tried to convey. Buddhists who adopted this philosophy developed a belief that everything we experience is an illusion: in the West, we would call them idealists. The Absolute, which is the inner essence of all things, is a void, a nothing, which has no existence in the normal sense. It was natural to identify the void with nirvana. Since a Buddha such as Gautama had attained nirvana, it followed that in some ineffable way he had *become* nirvana and was identical with the Absolute. Thus everybody who sought nirvana was also seeking identity with the Buddhas.

It is not difficult to see that this *bhakti* (devotion) to the Buddhas and the *bodhisattvas* was similar to the Christian devotion to Jesus. It also made the faith accessible to more people, rather as Paul had wished to make Judaism available to the *goyim*. There had been a similar welling up of *bhakti* in Hinduism at the same time, which centred on the figures of Shiva and Vishnu, two of the most important Vedic deities. Yet again, popular devotion proved stronger than the philosophical austerity of the *Upanishads*. In effect, Hindus developed a Trinity: Brahman, Shiva and Vishnu were three symbols or aspects of a single, ineffable reality.

Sometimes it would be more helpful to contemplate the mystery of God under the aspect of Shiva, the paradoxical deity of good and evil, fertility and asceticism, who was both creator and destroyer. In popular legend, Shiva was also a great Yogi, so he also inspired his devotees to transcend personal concepts of divinity by means of meditation. Vishnu was usually kinder and more playful. He liked to show himself to mankind in various incarnations or *avatars*. One of his more famous *personae* was the character of Krishna, who had been born into a noble family but was brought up as a cowherd. Popular legend loved the stories of his dalliance with the cowgirls, which depicted God as the Lover of the Soul. Yet when Vishnu appears to Prince Arjuna as Krishna in the *Bhagavad-Gita*, it is a terrifying experience:

> I see the gods
> in your body, O God,
> and hordes of varied creatures:
> Brahman, the cosmic creator,

on his lotos throne,
all the seers and celestial serpents.[12]

Everything is somehow present in the body of Krishna: he has no beginning or end, he fills space, and includes all possible deity: "Howling storm
gods, sun gods, bright gods and gods of ritual."[13] He is also "man's tireless
spirit," the essence of humanity.[14] All things rush toward Krishna, as
rivers roil toward the sea or as moths fly into a blazing flame. All Arjuna
can do as he gazes at this awe-ful sight is quake and tremble, having
entirely lost his bearings.

The development of *bhakti* answered a deep-rooted popular need for
some kind of personal relationship with the ultimate. Having established
Brahman as utterly transcendent, there is a danger that it could become
too rarefied and, like the ancient Sky God, fade from human consciousness. The evolution of the *bodhisattva* ideal in Buddhism and the *avatars*
of Vishnu seem to represent another stage in religious development when
people insist that the Absolute cannot be less than human. These symbolic
doctrines and myths deny that the Absolute can be expressed in only *one*
epiphany, however: there were numerous Buddhas and *bodhisattvas*, and
Vishnu had a variety of *avatars*. These myths also express an ideal for
humanity: they show mankind enlightened or deified, as he was meant
to be.

By the first century CE, there had been a similar thirst for divine
immanence in Judaism. The person of Jesus had seemed to answer that
need. St. Paul, the earliest Christian writer, who created the religion that
we now know as Christianity, believed that Jesus had replaced the Torah
as God's principal revelation of himself to the world.[15] It is not easy to
know exactly what he meant by this. Paul's letters were occasional responses to specific questions rather than a coherent account of a fully
articulated theology. He certainly believed that Jesus had been the Messiah: the word "Christ" was a translation of the Hebrew *Massiach*: the
Anointed One. Paul also talked about the man Jesus as though he had
been more than an ordinary human being, even though, as a Jew, Paul
did not believe that he had been God incarnate. He constantly used the
phrase "in Christ" to describe his experience of Jesus: Christians live "in
Christ"; they have been baptized into his death; the Church somehow
constitutes his body.[16] This was not a truth which Paul argued logically.
Like many Jews, he took a dim view of Greek rationalism, which he
described as mere "foolishness."[17] It was a subjective and mystical experience that made him describe Jesus as a sort of atmosphere in which "we

live and move and have our being."[18] Jesus had become the source of Paul's religious experience: he was, therefore, talking about him in ways that some of his contemporaries might have talked about a god.

When Paul explained the faith that had been handed on to him, he said that Jesus had suffered and died "for our sins,"[19] showing that at a very early stage, Jesus' disciples, shocked by the scandal of his death, had explained it by saying that it had somehow been for our benefit. In Chapter 9, we shall see that during the seventeenth century other Jews would find a similar explanation for the scandalous end of yet another Messiah. The early Christians felt that Jesus was in some mysterious way still alive and that the "powers" that he had possessed were now embodied in them, as he had promised. We know from Paul's epistles that the first Christians had all kinds of unusual experiences that could have indicated the advent of a new type of humanity: some had become faith healers, some spoke in heavenly languages, others delivered what they believed were inspired oracles from God. Church services were noisy, charismatic affairs, quite different from a tasteful evensong today at the parish church. It seemed that Jesus' death had indeed been beneficial in some way: it had released a "new kind of life" and a "new creation"—a constant theme in Paul's letters.[20]

There were, however, no detailed theories about the crucifixion as an atonement for some "original sin" of Adam: we shall see that this theology did not emerge until the fourth century and was only important in the West. Paul and the other New Testament writers never attempted a precise, definitive explanation of the salvation they had experienced. Yet the notion of Christ's sacrificial death was similar to the ideal of the *bodhisattva*, which was developing at this time in India. Like the *bodhisattva*, Christ had, in effect, become a mediator between humanity and the Absolute, the difference being that Christ was the *only* mediator and the salvation he effected was not an unrealized aspiration for the future, like that of the *bodhisattva*, but a *fait accompli*. Paul insisted that Jesus' sacrifice had been unique. Although he believed that his own sufferings on behalf of others were beneficial, Paul was quite clear that Jesus' suffering and death were in quite a different league.[21] There is a potential danger here. The innumerable Buddhas and the elusive, paradoxical *avatars* all reminded the faithful that ultimate reality could not be adequately expressed in any one form. The single Incarnation of Christianity, suggesting that the whole of the inexhaustible reality of God *had* been manifest in just one human being, could lead to an immature type of idolatry.

Jesus had insisted that the "powers" of God were not for him alone. Paul developed this insight by arguing that Jesus had been the first example of a new type of humanity. Not only had he done everything that the old Israel had failed to achieve, but he had become the new *adām*, the new humanity in which all human beings, *goyim* included, must somehow participate.[22] Again, this is not dissimilar to the Buddhist belief that, since all Buddhas had become one with the Absolute, the human ideal was to participate in Buddhahood.

In his letter to the Church at Philippi, Paul quotes what is generally considered to be a very early Christian hymn which raises some important issues. He tells his converts that they must have the same self-sacrificing attitude as Jesus,

> Who subsisting in the form of God
> did not cling
> to his equality with God
> but emptied himself,
> to assume the condition of a slave,
> and became as men are;
> and being as men are,
> he was humbler yet,
> even to accepting death,
> death on a cross.
> But God raised him high
> and gave him the name
> which is above all names
> so that all beings
> in the heavens, on earth and in the underworld,
> should bend the knee at the name of Jesus
> and that every tongue should acclaim
> Jesus Christ as Lord (*kyrios*)
> to the glory of God the Father.[23]

The hymn seems to reflect a belief among the first Christians that Jesus had enjoyed some kind of prior existence "with God" before becoming a man in the act of "self-emptying" (*kenosis*) by which, like a *bodhisattva*, he had decided to share the suffering of the human condition. Paul was too Jewish to accept the idea of Christ existing as a second divine being beside YHWH from all eternity. The hymn shows that after his exaltation he is still distinct from and inferior to God, who raises him and confers the title *kyrios* upon him. He cannot assume it himself but is given this title only "to the glory of God the Father."

Some forty years later, the author of St. John's Gospel (written ca. 100) made a similar suggestion. In his prologue, he described the Word (*logos*) which had been "with God from the beginning" and had been the agent of creation: "Through him all things came to be, not one thing had its being but through him."[24] The author was not using the Greek word *logos* in the same way as Philo: he appears to have been more in tune with Palestinian than Hellenized Judaism. In the Aramaic translations of the Hebrew scriptures known as the *targums*, which were being composed at this time, the term *Memra* (word) is used to describe God's activity in the world. It performs the same function as other technical terms like "glory," "Holy Spirit" and "Shekinah" which emphasized the distinction between God's presence in the world and the incomprehensible reality of God itself. Like the divine Wisdom, the "Word" symbolized God's original plan for creation. When Paul and John spoke about Jesus as though he had some kind of preexistent life, they were not suggesting that he was a second divine "person" in the later Trinitarian sense. They were indicating that Jesus had transcended temporal and individual modes of existence. Because the "power" and "wisdom" that he represented were activities that derived from God, he had in some way expressed "what was there from the beginning."[25]

These ideas were comprehensible in a strictly Jewish context, though later Christians with a Greek background would interpret them differently. In the Acts of the Apostles, written as late as 100 CE, we can see that the first Christians still had an entirely Jewish conception of God. On the feast of Pentecost, when hundreds of Jews had congregated in Jerusalem from all over the diaspora to celebrate the gift of the Torah on Sinai, the Holy Spirit had descended upon Jesus' companions. They heard "what sounded like a powerful wind from heaven . . . and something appeared to them that seemed like tongues of fire."[26] The Holy Spirit had manifested itself to these first Jewish Christians as it had to their contemporaries, the *tannaim*. Immediately the disciples rushed outside and began preaching to the crowds of Jews and Godfearers from "Mesopotamia, Judaea and Cappadocia, Pontus and Asia, Phrygia and Pamphylia, Egypt and the parts of Libya around Cyrene."[27] To their amazement, everybody heard the disciples preaching in his own language. When Peter rose to address the crowd, he presented this phenomenon as the apogee of Judaism. The prophets had foretold the day when God would pour out his Spirit upon mankind so that even women and slaves would have visions and dream dreams.[28] This day would inaugurate the Messianic Kingdom, when God would live on earth with his people. Peter did not claim that Jesus of Nazareth was God. He "was a man, commended to you by God by the miracles and portents and signs that God worked through him when he was among you." After his cruel death, God had raised him to life and had exalted him to a specially high status "by God's right hand." The prophets and Psalmists had all foretold these events; thus the "whole House of Israel" could be certain that Jesus was the long-awaited Messiah.[29] This speech appears to have been the message (*kerygma*) of the earliest Christians.

By the end of the fourth century, Christianity had become strong in precisely the places listed above by the author of Acts: it took root among Jewish synagogues in the diaspora which had attracted a large number of Godfearers or proselytes. Paul's reformed Judaism appeared to address many of their dilemmas. They also "spoke in many tongues," lacking a united voice and a coherent position. Many diaspora Jews had come to regard the Temple in Jerusalem, drenched as it was in the blood of animals, as a primitive and barbarous institution. The Acts of the Apostles preserves this viewpoint in the story of Stephen, a Hellenistic Jew who had converted to the Jesus sect and was stoned to death by the Sanhedrin, the Jewish governing council, for blasphemy. In his last impassioned speech, Stephen had claimed that the Temple was an insult to the nature of God: "The Most High does not live in a home that human hands have built."[30] Some diaspora Jews adopted the Talmudic Judaism developed by the Rabbis after the destruction of the Temple; others found that Christianity answered some of their other queries about the status of the Torah and the universality of Judaism. It was, of course, especially attractive to the Godfearers, who could become full members of the New Israel without the burden of all 613 *mitzvot*.

During the first century, Christians continued to think about God and pray to him like Jews; they argued like Rabbis, and their churches were similar to the synagogues. There were some acrimonious disputes in the 80s with the Jews when Christians were formally ejected from the synagogues because they refused to observe the Torah. We have seen that Judaism had attracted many converts in the early decades of the first century, but after 70, when Jews were in trouble with the Roman empire, their position declined. The defection of the Godfearers to Christianity made Jews suspicious of converts, and they were no longer anxious to proselytize. Pagans who would formerly have been attracted to Judaism now turned to Christianity, but these tended to be slaves and members of the lower classes. It was not until the end of the second century that highly educated pagans became Christians and were able to explain the new religion to a suspicious pagan world.

In the Roman empire, Christianity was first seen as a branch of Judaism, but when Christians made it clear that they were no longer members of the synagogue, they were regarded with contempt as a *religio* of fanatics who had committed the cardinal sin of impiety by breaking with the parent faith. The Roman ethos was strictly conservative: it valued the authority of the paterfamilias and ancestral custom. "Progress" was seen as a return to a golden age, not as a fearless march forward into the future. A deliberate break with the past was not seen as potentially creative, as in our own society, which has institutionalized change. Innovation was regarded as dangerous and subversive. Romans were highly suspicious of mass movements that threw off the restraints of tradition and were on their guard to protect their citizens from religious "quackery." There was a spirit of restlessness and anxiety in the empire, however. The experience of living in a huge international empire had made the old gods seem petty and inadequate; people had become aware of cultures that were alien and disturbing. They were looking for new spiritual solutions. Oriental cults were imported into Europe: deities like Isis and Semele were worshipped alongside the traditional gods of Rome, the guardians of the state. During the first century CE, the new mystery religions offered their initiates salvation and what purported to be inside knowledge of the next world. But none of these new religious enthusiasms threatened the old order. The Eastern deities did not demand a radical conversion and a rejection of the familiar rites but were like new saints, providing a fresh and novel outlook and a sense of a wider world. You could join as many different mystery cults as you liked: provided that they did not attempt to jeopardize the old gods and kept a reasonably low profile, the mystery religions were tolerated and absorbed into the established order.

Nobody expected religion to be a challenge or to provide an answer to the meaning of life. People turned to philosophy for that kind of enlightenment. In the Roman empire of late antiquity, people worshipped the gods to ask for help during a crisis, to secure a divine blessing for the state and to experience a healing sense of continuity with the past. Religion was a matter of cult and ritual rather than ideas; it was based on emotion, not on ideology or consciously adopted theory. This is not an unfamiliar attitude today: many of the people who attend religious services in our own society are not interested in theology, want nothing too exotic and dislike the idea of change. They find that the established rituals provide them with a link with tradition and give them a sense of security. They do not expect brilliant ideas from the sermon and are disturbed by changes in the liturgy. In rather the same way, many of the pagans of late antiquity loved to worship the ancestral gods, as generations had done before them. The old rituals gave them a sense of identity, celebrated local traditions and seemed an assurance that things would continue as they were. Civilization seemed a fragile achievement and should not be threatened by wantonly disregarding the patronal gods, who would ensure its survival. They would feel obscurely threatened if a new cult set out to abolish the faith of their fathers. Christianity, therefore, had the worst of both worlds. It lacked the venerable antiquity of Judaism and had none of the attractive rituals of paganism, which everybody could see and appreciate. It was also a potential threat, since Christians insisted that theirs was the *only* God and that all the other deities were delusions. Christianity seemed an irrational and eccentric movement to the Roman biographer Gaius Suetonius (70–160), a *superstitio nova et prava*, which was "depraved" precisely because it was "new."[31]

Educated pagans looked to philosophy, not religion, for enlightenment. Their saints and luminaries were such philosophers of antiquity as Plato, Pythagoras and Epictetus. They even saw them as "sons of God": Plato, for example, was held to have been the son of Apollo. The philosophers had maintained a cool respect for religion but saw it as essentially different from what they were doing. They were not dried-up academics in ivory towers but men with a mission, anxious to save the souls of their contemporaries by attracting them to the disciplines of their particular school. Both Socrates and Plato had been "religious" about their philosophy, finding that their scientific and metaphysical studies had inspired them with a vision of the glory of the universe. By the first century CE, therefore, intelligent and thoughtful people turned to them for an explanation of the meaning of life, for an inspiring ideology and for ethical motivation. Christianity seemed a barbaric creed. The Christian God seemed a ferocious, primitive deity, who kept intervening irrationally in human affairs: he had nothing in common with the remote, changeless God of a philosopher like Aristotle. It was one thing to suggest that men of the caliber of Plato or Alexander the Great had been sons of a god, but a Jew who had died a disgraceful death in an obscure corner of the Roman empire was quite another matter.

Platonism was one of the most popular philosophies of late antiquity. The new Platonists of the first and second century were not attracted to Plato the ethical and political thinker but to Plato the mystic. His teachings would help the philosopher to realize his true self, by liberating his soul from the prison of the body and enabling him to ascend to the divine world. It was a noble system, which used cosmology as an image of continuity and harmony. The One existed in serene contemplation of itself beyond the ravages of time and change at the pinnacle of the great chain of being. All existence derived from the One as a necessary consequence of its pure being: the eternal forms had emanated from the One and had in their turn animated the sun, stars and moon, each in their respective sphere. Finally the gods, who were now seen as the angelic ministers of the One, transmitted the divine influence to the sublunary world of men. The Platonist needed no barbaric tales of a deity who suddenly decided to create the world or who ignored the established hierarchy to communicate directly with a small group of human beings. He needed no grotesque salvation by means of a crucified Messiah. Since he was akin to the God who had given life to all things, a philosopher could ascend to the divine world by means of his own efforts in a rational, ordered way.

How could the Christians explain their faith to the pagan world? It seemed to fall between two stools, appearing to be neither a religion, in the Roman sense, nor a philosophy. Moreover, Christians would have found it hard to list their "beliefs" and may not have been conscious of evolving a distinctive system of thought. In this they resembled their pagan neighbors. Their religion had no coherent "theology" but could more accurately be described as a carefully cultivated attitude of commitment. When they recited their "creeds," they were not assenting to a set of propositions. The word *credere*, for example, seems to have derived from *cor dare*: to give one's heart. When they said "*credo!*" (or *pisteno* in Greek), this implied an emotional rather than an intellectual position. Thus Theodore, Bishop of Mopsuestia in Cilicia from 392 to 428, explained to his converts:

> When you say "I engage myself" (*pisteuo*) before God, you show that you will remain steadfastly with him, that you will never separate yourself from him and that you will think it higher than anything else to be and to live with him and to conduct yourself in a way that is in harmony with his commandments.[32]

Later Christians would need to give a more theoretical account of their faith and would develop a passion for theological debate that is unique in the history of world religion. We have seen, for example, that there was no official orthodoxy in Judaism but that ideas about God were essentially private matters. The early Christians would have shared this attitude.

During the second century, however, some pagan converts to Christianity tried to reach out to their unbelieving neighbors in order to show that their religion was not a destructive breach with tradition. One of the first of these apologists was Justin of Caesarea (100–165), who died a martyr for the faith. In his restless search for meaning, we can sense the spiritual anxiety of the period. Justin was neither a profound nor a brilliant thinker. Before turning to Christianity, he had sat at the feet of a Stoic, a peripatetic philosopher and a Pythagorean but had clearly failed to understand what was involved in their systems. He lacked the temperament and intelligence for philosophy but seemed to need more than the worship of cult and ritual. He found his solution in Christianity. In his two *apologiae* (ca. 150 and 155), he argued that Christians were simply following Plato, who had also maintained that there was only one God. Both the Greek philosophers and the Jewish prophets had foretold the coming of Christ—an argument which would have impressed the pagans of his day, since there was a fresh enthusiasm for oracles. He also argued that Jesus was the incarnation of the *logos* or divine reason, which the Stoics had seen in the order of the cosmos; the *logos* had been active in the world throughout history, inspiring Greeks and Hebrews alike. He did not, however, explain the implications of this somewhat novel idea: how could a human being incarnate the *logos*? was the *logos* the same as such biblical images as Word or Wisdom? What was its relation to the One God?

Other Christians were developing far more radical theologies, not out of love of speculation for its own sake but to assuage a profound anxiety. In particular, the *gnostikoi*, the Knowing Ones, turned from philosophy to mythology to explain their acute sense of separation from the divine world. Their myths confronted their ignorance about God and the divine, which they clearly experienced as a source of grief and shame. Basilides, who taught in Alexandria between 130 and 160, and his contemporary Valentinus, who left Egypt to teach in Rome, both acquired a huge following and showed that many of the people who converted to Christianity felt lost, adrift and radically displaced.

The Gnostics all began with an utterly incomprehensible reality which they called the Godhead, since it was the source of the lesser being that we call "God." There was nothing at all that we could say about it, since it entirely eludes the grasp of our limited minds. As Valentinus explained, the Godhead was perfect and pre-existent . . . dwelling in invisible and unnameable heights: this is the prebeginning and forefather and depth. It is uncontainable and invisible, eternal and ungenerated, is Quiet and deep Solitude for infinite aeons. With It was thought, which is also called Grace and Silence.[33]

Men have always speculated about this Absolute, but none of their explanations have been adequate. It is impossible to describe the Godhead, which is neither "good" nor "evil" and cannot even be said to "exist." Basilides taught that in the beginning, there had been not God but only the Godhead, which, strictly speaking, was Nothing because it did not exist in any sense that we can understand.[34]

But this Nothingness had wished to make itself known and was not content to remain alone in Depth and Silence. There was an inner revolution in the depths of its unfathomable being which resulted in a series of emanations similar to those described in the ancient pagan mythologies. The first of these emanations was the "God," which we know and pray to. Yet even "God" was inaccessible to us and needed further elucidation. Consequently new emanations proceeded from God in pairs, each of which expressed one of his divine attributes. "God" lay beyond gender but, as in the *Enuma Elish*, each pair of emanations consisted of a male and female—a scheme which attempted to neutralize the masculine tenor of more conventional monotheism. Each pair of emanations grew weaker and more attenuated, since they were getting ever further from their divine Source. Finally, when thirty such emanations (or aeons) had emerged, the process stopped and the divine world, the Pleroma, was complete. The Gnostics were not proposing an entirely outrageous cosmology, since everybody believed that the cosmos was teeming with such aeons, demons and spiritual powers. St. Paul had referred to Thrones, Dominations, Sovereignties and Powers, while the philosophers had believed that these invisible powers were the ancient gods and had made them intermediaries between man and the One.

There had been a catastrophe, a primal fall, which the Gnostics described in various ways. Some said that Sophia (Wisdom), the last of the emanations, fell from grace because she aspired to a forbidden knowledge of the inaccessible Godhead. Because of her overweening presumption, she had fallen from the Pleroma and her grief and distress had formed the world of matter. Exiled and lost, Sophia had wandered through the cosmos, yearning to return to her divine Source. This amalgam of oriental and pagan ideas expressed the Gnostics' profound sense that our world was in some sense a perversion of the celestial, born of ignorance and dislocation. Other Gnostics taught that "God" had not created the material world, since he could have had nothing to do with base matter. This had been the work of one of the aeons, which they called the *demiourgos* or Creator. He had become envious of "God" and aspired to be the center of the Pleroma. Consequently he fell and had created the world in a fit of defiance. As Valentinus explained, he had "made heaven without knowledge; he formed man in ignorance of man; he brought earth to light without understanding earth."[35] But the Logos, another of the aeons, had come to the rescue and descended to earth, assuming the physical appearance of Jesus in order to teach men and women the way back to God. Eventually this type of Christianity would be suppressed, but we shall see that centuries later Jews, Christians and Muslims would return to this type of mythology, finding that it expressed their religious experience of "God" more accurately than orthodox theology.

These myths were never intended as literal accounts of creation and salvation; they were symbolic expressions of an inner truth. "God" and the Pleroma were not external realities "out there" but were to be found within:

> Abandon the search for God and the creation and other matters of a similar sort. Look for him by taking yourself as the starting point. Learn who it is within you makes everything his own and says, My God, my mind, my thought, my soul, my body. Learn the sources of sorrow, joy, love, hate. Learn how it happens that one watches without willing, loves without willing. If you carefully investigate these matters, you will find him in yourself.[36]

The Pleroma represented a map of the soul. The divine light could be discerned even in this dark world, if the Gnostic knew where to look: during the Primal Fall—of either Sophia or the Demiurge—some divine sparks had also fallen from the Pleroma and been trapped in matter. The Gnostic could find a divine spark in his own soul, could become aware of a divine element within himself which would help him to find his way home.

The Gnostics showed that many of the new converts to Christianity were not satisfied with the traditional idea of God which they had inherited from Judaism. They did not experience the world as "good," the work of a benevolent deity. A similar dualism and dislocation marked the doctrine of Marcion (100–165), who founded his own rival church in

Rome and attracted a huge following. Jesus had said that a sound tree produced good fruit:[37] how could the world have been created by a good God when it was manifestly full of evil and pain? Marcion was also appalled by the Jewish scriptures, which seemed to describe a harsh, cruel God who exterminated whole populations in his passion for justice. He decided that it was this Jewish God, who was "lustful for war, inconstant in his attitudes and self-contradictory,"[38] who had created the world. But Jesus had revealed that another God existed, who had never been mentioned by the Jewish scriptures. This second God was "placid, mild and simply good and excellent."[39] He was entirely different from the cruel "juridical" Creator of the world. We should, therefore, turn away from the world, which, since it was not his doing, could tell us nothing about this benevolent deity and should also reject the "Old" Testament, concentrating simply upon those New Testament books which had preserved the spirit of Jesus. The popularity of Marcion's teachings showed that he had voiced a common anxiety. At one time it seemed as though he were about to found a separate Church. He had put his finger on something important in the Christian experience; generations of Christians have found it difficult to relate positively to the material world, and there are still a significant number who do not know what to make of the Hebrew God.

The North African theologian Tertullian (160–220), however, pointed out that Marcion's "good" God had more in common with the God of Greek philosophy than the God of the Bible. This serene deity, who had nothing to do with this flawed world, was far closer to the Unmoved Mover described by Aristotle than the Jewish God of Jesus Christ. Indeed, many people in the Greco-Roman world found the biblical God a blundering, ferocious deity who was unworthy of worship. In about 178 the pagan philosopher Celsus accused the Christians of adopting a narrow, provincial view of God. He found it appalling that the Christians should claim a special revelation of their own: God was available to all human beings, yet the Christians huddled together in a sordid little group, asserting: "God has even deserted the whole world and the motions of the heavens and disregarded the vast earth to give attention to us alone."[40] When Christians were persecuted by the Roman authorities, they were accused of "atheism" because their conception of divinity gravely offended the Roman ethos. By failing to give the traditional gods their due, people feared that the Christians would endanger the state and overturn the fragile order. Christianity seemed a barbarous creed that ignored the achievements of civilization.

By the end of the second century, however, some truly cultivated pagans began to be converted to Christianity and were able to adapt the Semitic God of the Bible to the Greco-Roman ideal. The first of these was Clement of Alexandria (ca. 150–215), who may have studied philosophy in Athens before his conversion. Clement had no doubt that Yahweh and the God of the Greek philosophers were one and the same: he called Plato the Attic Moses. Yet both Jesus and St. Paul would have been surprised by his theology. Like the God of Plato and Aristotle, Clement's God was characterized by his *apatheia*: he was utterly impassible, unable to suffer or change. Christians could participate in this divine life by imitating the calmness and imperturbability of God himself. Clement devised a rule of life that was remarkably similar to the detailed rules of conduct prescribed by the Rabbis except that it had more in common with the Stoic ideal. A Christian should imitate the serenity of God in every detail of his life: he must sit correctly, speak quietly, refrain from violent, convulsive laughter and even burp gently. By this diligent exercise of studied calm, Christians would become aware of a vast Quietness within, which was the image of God inscribed in their own being. There was no gulf between God and humanity. Once Christians had conformed to the divine ideal, they would find that they had a Divine Companion "sharing our house with us, sitting at table, sharing in the whole moral effort of our life."[41]

Yet Clement also believed that Jesus was God, "the living God that suffered and is worshipped."[42] He who had "washed their feet, girded with a towel," had been "the prideless God and Lord of the Universe."[43] If Christians imitated Christ, they too would become deified: divine, incorruptible and impassible. Indeed, Christ had been the divine *logos* who had become man "so that you might learn from a man how to become God."[44] In the West, Irenaeus, Bishop of Lyons (130–200), had taught a similar doctrine. Jesus had been the incarnate Logos, the divine reason. When he had become man, he had sanctified each stage of human development and become a model for Christians. They should imitate him in rather the same way as an actor was believed to become one with the character he was portraying and would thus fulfill their human potential.[45] Clement and Irenaeus were both adapting the Jewish God to notions that were characteristic of their own time and culture. Even though it had little in common with the God of the prophets, who was chiefly characterized by his pathos and vulnerability, Clement's doctrine of *apatheia* would become fundamental to the Christian conception of God. In the Greek world, people longed to rise above the mess of emotion and mutability and achieve a superhuman calm. This ideal prevailed, despite its inherent paradox.

Clement's theology left crucial questions unanswered. How could a mere man have been the Logos or divine reason? What exactly did it mean to say that Jesus had been divine? Was the Logos the same as the "Son of God," and what did this Jewish title mean in the Hellenic world? How could an impassible God have suffered in Jesus? How could Christians believe that he had been a divine being and yet, at the same time, insist that there was only *one* God? Christians were becoming increasingly aware of these problems during the third century. In the early years of the century in Rome, one Sabellius, a rather shadowy figure, had suggested that the biblical terms "Father," "Son" and "Spirit" could be compared to the masks (*personae*) worn by actors to assume a dramatic role and to make their voices audible to the audience. The One God had thus donned different *personae* when dealing with the world. Sabellius attracted some disciples, but most Christians were distressed by his theory: it suggested that the impassible God had in some sense suffered when playing the role of the Son, an idea that they found quite unacceptable. Yet when Paul of Samosata, Bishop of Antioch from 260 to 272, had suggested that Jesus had simply been a man, in whom the Word and Wisdom of God had dwelt as in a temple, this was considered equally unorthodox. Paul's theology was condemned at a synod at Antioch in 264, though he managed to hold on to his see with the support of Queen Zenobia of Palmyra. It was clearly going to be very difficult to find a way of accommodating the Christian conviction that Jesus had been divine with the equally strong belief that God was One.

When Clement had left Alexandria in 202 to become a priest in the service of the Bishop of Jerusalem, his place at the catechetical school was taken by his brilliant young pupil Origen, who was about twenty years old at the time. As a youth Origen had been passionately convinced that martyrdom was the way to heaven. His father, Leonides, had died in the arena four years earlier, and Origen had tried to join him. His mother, however, saved him by hiding his clothes. Origen had started by believing that the Christian life meant turning against the world, but he later abjured this position and developed a form of Christian Platonism. Instead of seeing an impassible gulf between God and the world, which could only be bridged by the radical dislocation of martyrdom, Origen developed a theology that stressed the continuity of God with the world. His was a spirituality of light, optimism and joy. Step by step, a Christian could ascend the chain of being until he reached God, his natural element and home.

As a Platonist, Origen was convinced of the kinship between God and the soul: the knowledge of the divine was natural to humanity. It could be "recollected" and awakened by special disciplines. To adapt his Platonic philosophy to the Semitic scriptures, Origen developed a symbolic method of reading the Bible. Thus the virgin birth of Christ in the womb of Mary was not primarily to be understood as a literal event but as the birth of the divine Wisdom in the soul. He also adopted some of the ideas of the Gnostics. Originally, all the beings in the spiritual world had contemplated the ineffable God who had revealed himself to them in the Logos, the divine Word and Wisdom. But they had grown tired of this perfect contemplation and fallen from the divine world into bodies, which had arrested their fall. All was not lost, however. The soul could ascend to God in a long, steady journey that would continue after death. Gradually it would cast aside the fetter of the body and rise above gender to become pure spirit. By means of contemplation (*theoria*), the soul would advance in the knowledge (*gnosis*) of God, which would transform it until, as Plato himself had taught, it would itself become divine. God was deeply mysterious and none of our human words or concepts could adequately express him, but the soul had the capacity to know God, since it shared his divine nature. Contemplation of the Logos was natural to us, since all spiritual beings (*logikoi*) had originally been equal to one another. When they had fallen, only the future mind of the man Jesus Christ had been content to remain in the divine world contemplating God's Word, and our own souls were equal to his. Belief in the divinity of Jesus the man was only a phase; it would help us on our way, but would eventually be transcended when we would see God face to face.

In the ninth century, the Church would condemn some of Origen's ideas as heretical. Neither Origen nor Clement believed that God had created the world out of nothing (*ex nihilo*), which would later become orthodox Christian doctrine. Origen's view of the divinity of Jesus and the salvation of humanity certainly did not conform to later official Christian teaching: he did not believe that we had been "saved" by the death of Christ, but that we ascended to God under our own steam. The point is that when Origen and Clement were writing and teaching their Christian Platonism there *was* no official doctrine. Nobody knew for certain if God had created the world or how a human being had been divine. The turbulent events of the fourth and fifth centuries would lead to a definition of orthodox belief only after an agonizing struggle.

Origen is, perhaps, best known for his self-castration. In the Gospels, Jesus said that some people had made themselves eunuchs for the sake of the Kingdom of Heaven, and Origen took him at his word. Castration was quite a common operation in late antiquity; Origen did not rush at himself with a knife, nor was his decision inspired by the kind of neurotic loathing of sexuality that would characterize some Western theologians, such as St. Jerome (342–420). The British scholar Peter Brown suggests that it may have been an attempt to demonstrate his doctrine of the indeterminacy of the human condition, which the soul must soon transcend. Apparently immutable factors such as gender would be left behind in the long process of divinization, since in God there was neither male nor female. In an age where the philosopher was characterized by his long beard (a sign of wisdom), Origen's smooth cheeks and high voice would have been a startling sight.

Plotinus (205–270) had studied in Alexandria under Origen's old teacher Ammonius Saccus and had later joined the Roman army, hoping that it would take him to India, where he was anxious to study. Unfortunately the expedition came to grief and Plotinus fled to Antioch. Later he founded a prestigious school of philosophy in Rome. We know little else about him, since he was an extremely reticent man who never spoke about himself and did not even celebrate his own birthday. Like Celsus, Plotinus found Christianity a thoroughly objectionable creed, yet he influenced generations of future monotheists in all three of the God-religions. It is important, therefore, to give some detailed consideration to his vision of God. Plotinus has been described as a watershed: he had absorbed the main currents of some 800 years of Greek speculation and transmitted it in a form which has continued to influence such crucial figures in our own century as T. S. Eliot and Henri Bergson. Drawing on Plato's ideas, Plotinus evolved a system designed to achieve an understanding of the self. Again, he was not at all interested in finding a scientific explanation of the universe or attempting to explain the physical origins of life; instead of looking outside the world for an objective explanation, Plotinus urged his disciples to withdraw into themselves and begin their exploration in the depths of the psyche.

Human beings are aware that something is wrong with their condition; they feel at odds with themselves and others, out of touch with their inner nature and disoriented. Conflict and a lack of simplicity seem to characterize our existence. Yet we are constantly seeking to unite the multiplicity of phenomena and reduce them to some ordered whole. When we glance at a person, we do not see a leg, an arm, another arm and a head, but automatically organize these elements into an integrated human being. This drive for unity is fundamental to the way our minds work and must, Plotinus believed, also reflect the essence of things in general. To find the underlying truth of reality, the soul must refashion itself, undergo a period of purification (*katharsis*) and engage in contemplation (*theoria*), as Plato had advised. It will have to look beyond the cosmos, beyond the sensible world and even beyond the limitations of the intellect to see into the heart of reality. This will not be an ascent to a reality outside ourselves, however, but a descent into the deepest recesses of the mind. It is, so to speak, a climb inward.

The ultimate reality was a primal unity, which Plotinus called the One. All things owe their existence to this potent reality. Because the One is simplicity itself, there was nothing to say about it: it had no qualities distinct from its essence that would make ordinary description possible. It just *was*. Consequently, the One is nameless: "If we are to think positively of the One," Plotinus explained, "there would be more truth in Silence."[46] We cannot even say that it exists, since as Being itself, it is "not *a* thing but is distinct from all things."[47] Indeed, Plotinus explained, it "is Everything and Nothing; it can be none of the existing things, and yet it is all."[48] We shall see that this perception will be a constant theme in the history of God.

But this Silence cannot be the whole truth, Plotinus argued, since we are able to arrive at some knowledge of the divine. This would be impossible if the One had remained shrouded in its impenetrable obscurity. The One must have transcended itself, gone beyond its Simplicity in order to make itself apprehensible to imperfect beings like ourselves. This divine transcendence could be described as "ecstasy" properly so called, since it is a "going out of the self" in pure generosity: "Seeking nothing, possessing nothing, lacking nothing, the One is perfect and, in metaphor, has overflowed, and its exuberance has produced the new."[49] There was nothing personal in all this; Plotinus saw the One as beyond all human categories, including that of personality. He returned to the ancient myth of emanation to explain the radiation of all that exists from this utterly simple Source, using a number of analogies to describe this process: it was like a light shining from the sun or the heat that radiates from a fire and becomes warmer as you draw nearer to its blazing core. One of Plotinus's favorite similes was the comparison of the One to the point at the center of a circle, which contained the possibility of all the future circles that could derive from it. It was similar to the ripple effect achieved by dropping a stone into a pool. Unlike the emanations in a myth such as the *Enuma Elish*, where each pair of gods that evolved from one another became more perfect and effective, the opposite was the case in Plotinus's scheme. As in the Gnostic myths, the further a being got from its source in the One, the weaker it became.

Plotinus regarded the first two emanations to radiate from the One as divine, since they enabled us to know and to participate in the life of God. Together with the One, they formed a Triad of divinity which was in some ways close to the final Christian solution of the Trinity. Mind (*nous*), the first emanation, corresponded in Plotinus's scheme to Plato's realm of ideas: it made the simplicity of the One intelligible, but knowledge here was intuitive and immediate. It was not laboriously acquired through research and reasoning processes but was absorbed in rather the same way as our senses drink in the objects they perceive. Soul (*psyche*), which emanates from Mind in the same way as Mind emanates from the One, is a little further from perfection, and in this realm knowledge can only be acquired discursively, so that it lacks absolute simplicity and coherence. Soul corresponds to reality as we know it: all the rest of physical and spiritual existence emanates from Soul, which gives to our world whatever unity and coherence it possesses. Again, it must be emphasized that Plotinus did not envisage this trinity of One, Mind and Soul as a god "out there." The divine comprised the whole of existence. God was all in all, and lesser beings only existed insofar as they participated in the absolute being of the One.[50]

The outward flow of emanation was arrested by a corresponding movement of return to the One. As we know from the workings of our own minds and our dissatisfaction with conflict and multiplicity, all beings yearn for unity; they long to return to the One. Again, this is not an ascent to an external reality but an interior descent into the depths of the mind. The soul must recollect the simplicity it has forgotten and return to its true self. Since all souls were animated by the same Reality, humanity could be compared to a chorus standing around a conductor. If any one individual were distracted, there would be dissonance and disharmony, but if all turned toward the conductor and concentrated on him, the whole community would benefit, since "they would sing as they ought, and really be with him."[51]

The One is strictly impersonal; it has no gender and is entirely oblivious of us. Similarly Mind (*nous*) is grammatically masculine and Soul (*psyche*) feminine, which could show a desire on Plotinus's part to preserve the old pagan vision of sexual balance and harmony. Unlike the biblical God, it does not come out to meet us and guide us home. It does not yearn toward us, or love us, or reveal itself to us. It has no knowledge of anything beyond itself.[52] Nevertheless, the human soul was occasionally rapt in ecstatic apprehension of the One. Plotinus's philosophy was not a logical process but a spiritual quest:

> We here, for our part, must put aside all else and be set on This alone, become This alone, stripping off all our encumbrances; we must make haste to escape from here, impatient of our earthly bonds, to embrace God with all our being, that there may be no part of us that does not cling to God. There we may see God and ourself as by law revealed: ourself in splendor, filled with the light of Intellect, or rather, light itself, pure, buoyant, aerial, become—in truth, being—a god.[53]

This god was not an alien object but our best self. It comes "neither by knowing, nor by Intellection that discovers the Intellectual beings [in the Mind or *nous*] but by a presence (*parousia*) overpassing all knowledge."[54]

Christianity was coming into its own in a world where Platonic ideas predominated. Thereafter, when Christian thinkers tried to explain their own religious experience, they turned naturally to the Neoplatonic vision of Plotinus and his later pagan disciples. The notion of an enlightenment that was impersonal, beyond human categories and natural to humanity was also close to the Hindu and Buddhist ideal in India, where Plotinus had been so keen to study. Thus despite the more superficial differences, there were profound similarities between the monotheistic and other visions of reality. It seems that when human beings contemplate the absolute, they have very similar ideas and experiences. The sense of presence, ecstasy and dread in the presence of a reality—called nirvana, the One, Brahman or God—seems to be a state of mind and a perception that are natural and endlessly sought by human beings.

Some Christians were determined to make friends with the Greek world. Others wanted nothing whatever to do with it. During an outbreak of persecution in the 170s, a new prophet called Montanus arose in Phrygia in modern Turkey, who claimed to be a divine *avatar*: "I am the Lord God Almighty, who descended to a man," he used to cry; "I am Father, son and Paraclete." His companions Priscilla and Maximilla made similar claims.[55] Montanism was a fierce apocalyptic creed which painted a fearsome portrait of God. Not only were its adherents obliged to turn their backs upon the world and lead celibate lives, but they were told that martyrdom was the only sure path to God. Their agonizing death for the faith would hasten the coming of Christ: the martyrs were soldiers of God engaged in a battle with the forces of evil. This terrible creed appealed to a latent extremism in the Christian spirit: Montanism spread like wildfire in Phrygia, Thrace, Syria and Gaul. It was particularly strong in North Africa, where the people were used to gods who demanded human sacrifice. Their cult of Baal, which had entailed the sacrifice of the firstborn, had been suppressed by the emperor only during the second century. Soon the heresy had attracted no less a person than Tertullian, the leading theologian of the Latin Church. In the East, Clement and Origen preached a peaceful, joyous return to God, but in the Western Church a more frightening God demanded hideous death as a condition of salvation. At this stage, Christianity was a struggling religion in Western Europe and North Africa, and from the start there was a tendency toward extremism and rigor.

Yet in the East Christianity was making great strides, and by 235 it had become one of the most important religions of the Roman empire. Christians now spoke of a Great Church with a single rule of faith that shunned extremity and eccentricity. These orthodox theologians had outlawed the pessimistic visions of the Gnostics, Marcionites and Montanists and had settled for the middle road. Christianity was becoming an urbane creed that eschewed the complexities of the mystery cults and an inflexible asceticism. It was beginning to appeal to highly intelligent men who were able to develop the faith along lines that the Greco-Roman world could understand. The new religion also appealed to women: its scriptures taught that in Christ there was neither male nor female and insisted that men cherished their wives as Christ cherished his church. Christianity had all the advantages that had once made Judaism such an attractive faith without the disadvantages of circumcision and an alien Law. Pagans were particularly impressed by the welfare system that the churches had established and by the compassionate behavior of Christians toward one another. During its long struggle to survive persecution from without and dissension from within, the Church had also evolved an efficient organization that made it almost a microcosm of the empire itself: it was multiracial, catholic, international, ecumenical and administered by efficient bureaucrats.

As such it had become a force for stability and appealed to the emperor Constantine, who became a Christian himself after the battle of Milvian

Bridge in 312, and legalized Christianity the following year. Christians were now able to own property, worship freely and make a distinctive contribution to public life. Even though paganism flourished for another two centuries, Christianity became the state religion of the empire and began to attract new converts who made their way into the Church for the sake of material advancement. Soon the Church, which had begun life as a persecuted sect pleading for toleration, would demand conformity to its own laws and creeds. The reasons for the triumph of Christianity are obscure; it certainly would not have succeeded without the support of the Roman empire, though this inevitably brought its own problems. Supremely a religion of adversity, it has never been at its best in prosperity. One of the first problems that had to be solved was the doctrine of God: no sooner had Constantine brought peace to the Church than a new danger arose from within which split Christians into bitterly warring camps.

4

Trinity: The Christian God

IN ABOUT 320 a fierce theological passion had seized the churches of Egypt, Syria and Asia Minor. Sailors and travelers were singing versions of popular ditties that proclaimed that the Father alone was true God, inaccessible and unique, but that the Son was neither coeternal nor uncreated, since he received life and being from the Father. We hear of a bath attendant who harangued the bathers, insisting that the Son came from nothingness, of a money changer who, when asked for the exchange rate, prefaced his reply with a long disquisition on the distinction between the created order and the uncreated God, and of a baker who informed his customer that the Father was greater than the Son. People were discussing these abstruse questions with the same enthusiasm as they discuss football today.[1] The controversy had been kindled by Arius, a charismatic and handsome presbyter of Alexandria, who had a soft, impressive voice and a strikingly melancholy face. He had issued a challenge which his bishop, Alexander, found impossible to ignore but even more difficult to rebut: how could Jesus Christ have been God in the same way as God the Father? Arius was not denying the divinity of Christ; indeed, he called Jesus "strong God" and "full God,"[2] but he argued that it was blasphemous to think that he was divine by nature: Jesus had specifically said that the Father was greater than he. Alexander and his brilliant young assistant Athanasius immediately realized that this was no mere theological nicety. Arius was asking vital questions about the nature of God. In the meantime, Arius, a skillful propagandist, had set his ideas to music, and soon the laity were debating the issue as passionately as their bishops.

The controversy became so heated that the emperor Constantine himself intervened and summoned a synod to Nicaea in modern Turkey to settle the issue. Today Arius's name is a byword for heresy, but when the conflict broke out there was no officially orthodox position and it was by no means certain why or even whether Arius was wrong. There was nothing new about his claim: Origen, whom both sides held in high esteem, had taught a similar doctrine. Yet the intellectual climate in Alexandria had changed since Origen's day, and people were no longer convinced that the God of Plato could be successfully wedded with the God of the Bible. Arius, Alexander and Athanasius, for example, had come to believe a doctrine that would have startled any Platonist: they considered that God had created the world out of nothing (*ex nihilo*), basing their opinion on scripture. In fact, Genesis had not made this claim. The Priestly author had implied that God had created the world out of the primordial chaos, and the notion that God had summoned the whole universe from an absolute vacuum was entirely new. It was alien to Greek thought and had not been taught by such theologians as Clement and Origen, who had held to the Platonic scheme of emanation. But by the fourth century, Christians shared the Gnostic view of the world as inherently fragile and imperfect, separated from God by a vast chasm. The new doctrine of creation *ex nihilo* emphasized this view of the cosmos as quintessentially frail and utterly dependent upon God for being and life. God and humanity were no longer akin, as in Greek thought. God had summoned every single being from an abysmal nothingness, and at any moment he could withdraw his sustaining hand. There was no longer a great chain of being emanating eternally from God; there was no longer an intermediate world of spiritual beings who transmitted the divine *mana* to the world. Men and women could no longer ascend the chain of being to God by their own efforts. Only the God who had drawn them from nothingness in the first place and kept them perpetually in being could ensure their eternal salvation.

Christians knew that Jesus Christ had saved them by his death and resurrection; they had been redeemed from extinction and would one day share the existence of God, who was Being and Life itself. Somehow Christ had enabled them to cross the gulf that separated God from humanity. The question was how had he done it? On which side of the Great Divide was he? There was now no longer a Pleroma, a Place of Fullness of intermediaries and aeons. Either Christ, the Word, belonged to the divine realm (which was now the domain of God alone) or he belonged to the fragile created order. Arius and Athanasius put him on opposite sides of the gulf: Athanasius in the divine world and Arius in the created order.

Arius wanted to emphasize the essential difference between the unique God and all his creatures. As he wrote to Bishop Alexander, God was "the only unbegotten, the only eternal, the only one without beginning, the only true, the only one who has immortality, the only wise, the only good, the only potentate."[3] Arius knew the scriptures well, and he produced an armory of texts to support his claim that Christ the Word could only be a creature like ourselves. A key passage was the description of the divine Wisdom in Proverbs, which stated explicitly that God had *created* Wisdom at the very beginning.[4] This text also stated that Wisdom had been the agent of creation, an idea repeated in the Prologue of St. John's Gospel. The Word had been *with* God in the beginning:

> Through him all things came to be,
> not one thing had its being but through him.[5]

The Logos had been the instrument used by God to call other creatures into existence. It was, therefore, entirely different from all other beings and of exceptionally high status, but because it had been created by God, the Logos was essentially different and distinct from God himself.

St. John made it clear that Jesus was the Logos; he also said that the Logos was God.[6] Yet he was not God by nature, Arius insisted, but had been promoted by God to divine status. He was different from the rest of us, because God had created him directly but all other things through him. God had foreseen that when the Logos became man he would obey him perfectly and had, so to speak, conferred divinity upon Jesus in advance. But Jesus' divinity was not natural to him: it was only a reward or gift. Again, Arius could produce many texts that seemed to support his view. The very fact that Jesus had called God his "Father" implied a distinction; paternity by its very nature involves prior existence and a certain superiority over the son. Arius also emphasized the biblical passages that stressed the humility and vulnerability of Christ. Arius had no intention of denigrating Jesus, as his enemies claimed. He had a lofty notion of Christ's virtue and obedience unto death, which had ensured our salvation. Arius's God was close to the God of the Greek philosophers, remote and utterly transcending the world; so too he adhered to a Greek concept of salvation. The Stoics, for example, had always taught that it was possible for a virtuous human being to become divine; this had also been essential to the Platonic view. Arius passionately believed that

Christians had been saved and made divine, sharers in the nature of God. This was only possible because Jesus had blazed a trail for us. He had lived a perfect human life; he had obeyed God even unto the death of the Cross; as St. Paul said, it was *because* of this obedience unto death that God had raised him up to a specially exalted status and given him the divine title of Lord (*kyrios*).[7] If Jesus had not been a human being, there would be no hope for us. There would have been nothing meritorious in his life if he had been God by nature, nothing for us to imitate. It was by contemplating Christ's life of perfectly obedient sonship that Christians would become divine themselves. By imitating Christ, the perfect creature, they too would become "unalterable and unchangeable, perfect creature[s] of God."[8]

But Athanasius had a less optimistic view of man's capacity for God. He saw humanity as inherently fragile: we had come from nothing and had fallen back into nothingness when we had sinned. When he contemplated his creation, therefore, God

> saw that all created nature, if left to its own principles, was in flux and subject to dissolution. To prevent this and to keep the universe from disintegrating back into nonbeing, he made all things by his very own eternal Logos and endowed the creation with being.[9]

It was only by participating in God, through his Logos, that man could avoid annihilation because God alone was perfect Being. If the Logos himself were a vulnerable creature, he would not be able to save mankind from extinction. The Logos had been made flesh to give us life. He had descended into the mortal world of death and corruption in order to give us a share of God's impassibility and immortality. But this salvation would have been impossible if the Logos himself had been a frail creature, who could himself lapse back into nothingness. Only he who had created the world could save it, and that meant that Christ, the Logos made flesh, must be of the same nature as the Father. As Athanasius said, the Word became man in order that we could become divine.[10]

When the bishops gathered at Nicaea on May 20, 325, to resolve the crisis, very few would have shared Athanasius's view of Christ. Most held a position midway between Athanasius and Arius. Nevertheless, Athanasius managed to impose his theology on the delegates and, with the emperor breathing down their necks, only Arius and two of his brave companions refused to sign his Creed. This made creation *ex nihilo* an official Christian doctrine for the first time, insisting that Christ was no mere creature or aeon. The Creator and Redeemer were one.

> We believe in one God,
> the Father Almighty,
> maker of all things, visible and invisible,
> and in one Lord, Jesus Christ,
> the Son of God,
> the only-begotten of the Father,
> that is, of the substance (*ousia*) of the Father,
> God from God,
> light from light,
> true God from true God,
> begotten not made,
> of one substance (*homoousion*) with the Father,
> through whom all things were made,
> those things that are in heaven and
>   those things that are on earth,
> who for us men and for our salvation
>   came down and was made man,
> suffered,
> rose again on the third day,
> ascended into the heavens
> and will come
> to judge the living and the dead.
> And we believe in the Holy Spirit.[11]

The show of agreement pleased Constantine, who had no understanding of the theological issues, but in fact there was no unanimity at Nicaea. After the council, the bishops went on teaching as they had before, and the Arian crisis continued for another sixty years. Arius and his followers fought back and managed to regain imperial favor. Athanasius was exiled no fewer than five times. It was very difficult to make his creed stick. In particular the term *homoousion* (literally, "made of the same stuff") was highly controversial because it was unscriptural and had materialistic association. Thus two copper coins could be said to be *homoousion*, because both derived from the same substance.

Further, Athanasius's creed begged many important questions. It stated that Jesus was divine but did not explain how the Logos could be "of the same stuff" as the Father without being a second God. In 339 Marcellus, Bishop of Ancyra—a loyal friend and colleague of Athanasius, who had even gone into exile with him on one occasion—argued that the Logos could not possibly be an eternal divine being. He was only a quality or potential inherent *within* God: as it stood, the Nicene formula could be accused of tritheism, the belief that there were three gods: Father, Son and Spirit. Instead of the controversial *homoousion*, Marcellus proposed the compromise term *homoiousion*, of like or similar nature. The tortuous nature of this debate has often excited ridicule, notably by Gibbon, who found it absurd that Christian unity should have been threatened by a mere diphthong. What is remarkable, however, is the tenacity with which Christians held on to their sense that the divinity of Christ was essential, even though it was so difficult to formulate in conceptual terms. Like Marcellus, many Christians were troubled by the threat to the divine unity. Marcellus seems to have believed that the Logos was only a passing phase: it had emerged from God at the creation, had become incarnate in Jesus and, when the redemption was complete, would melt back into the divine nature, so that the One God would be all in all.

Eventually Athanasius was able to convince Marcellus and his disciples that they should join forces, because they had more in common with one another than with the Arians. Those who said that the Logos was of the *same* nature as the Father and those who believed that he was *similar* in nature to the Father were "brethren, who mean what we mean and are disputing only about terminology."[12] The priority must be to oppose Arius, who declared that the Son was entirely distinct from God and of a fundamentally different nature. To an outsider, these theological arguments inevitably seem a waste of time: nobody could possibly prove anything definitively, one way or the other, and the dispute proved to be simply divisive. However, for the participants, this was no arid debate but concerned the nature of the Christian experience. Arius, Athanasius and Marcellus were all convinced that something new had come into the world with Jesus, and they were struggling to articulate this experience in conceptual symbols to explain it to themselves and to others. The words could only be symbolic, because the realities to which they pointed were ineffable. Unfortunately, however, a dogmatic intolerance was creeping into Christianity, which would ultimately make the adoption of the "correct" or orthodox symbols crucial and obligatory. This doctrinal obsession, unique to Christianity, could easily lead to a confusion between the human symbol and the divine reality. Christianity had always been a paradoxical faith: the powerful religious experience of the early Christians had overcome their ideological objections to the scandal of a crucified Messiah. Now at Nicaea the Church had opted for the paradox of the Incarnation, despite its apparent incompatibility with monotheism.

In his *Life of Antony*, the famous desert ascetic, Athanasius tried to show how his new doctrine affected Christian spirituality. Antony, known as the father of monasticism, had lived a life of formidable austerity in the Egyptian desert. Yet in *The Sayings of the Fathers*, an anonymous anthology of maxims of the early desert monks, he comes across as a human and vulnerable man, troubled by boredom, agonizing over human problems and giving simple, direct advice. In his biography, however, Athanasius presents him in an entirely different light. He is, for example, transformed into an ardent opponent of Arianism; he had already begun to enjoy a foretaste of his future apotheosis, since he shares the divine *apatheia* to a remarkable degree. When, for example, he emerged from the tombs where he had spent twenty years wrestling with demons, Athanasius says that Antony's body showed no signs of ageing. He was a perfect Christian, whose serenity and impassibility set him apart from other men: "his soul was unperturbed, and so his outward appearance was calm."[13] He had perfectly imitated Christ: just as the Logos had taken flesh, descended into the corrupt world and fought the powers of evil, so Antony had descended into the abode of demons. Athanasius never mentions contemplation, which according to such Christian platonists as Clement or Origen had been the means of deification and salvation. It was no longer considered possible for mere mortals to ascend to God in this way by their own natural powers. Instead, Christians must imitate the descent of the Word made flesh into the corruptible, material world.

But Christians were still confused: if there was only one God, how could the Logos also be divine? Eventually three outstanding theologians of Cappadocia in eastern Turkey came up with a solution that satisfied the Eastern Orthodox Church. They were Basil, Bishop of Caesarea (ca. 329–79), his younger brother Gregory, Bishop of Nyssa (335–95) and his friend Gregory of Nazianzus (329–91). The Cappadocians, as they are called, were all deeply spiritual men. They thoroughly enjoyed speculation and philosophy but were convinced that religious experience alone could provide the key to the problem of God. Trained in Greek philosophy, they were all aware of a crucial distinction between the factual content of truth and its more elusive aspects. The early Greek rationalists had drawn attention to this: Plato had contrasted philosophy (which was expressed in terms of reason and was thus capable of proof) with the equally important teaching handed down by means of mythology, which eluded scientific demonstration. We have seen that Aristotle had made a similar distinction when he had noted that people attended the mystery religions not to learn (*mathein*) anything but to experience (*pathein*) something. Basil expressed the same insight in a Christian sense when he distinguished between *dogma* and *kerygma*. Both kinds of Christian teaching were essential to religion. *Kerygma* was the public teaching of the Church, based on the scriptures. *Dogma*, however, represented the deeper meaning of biblical truth, which could only be apprehended through religious experience and expressed in symbolic form. Besides the clear message of the Gospels, a secret or esoteric tradition had been handed down "in a mystery" from the apostles; this had been a "private and secret teaching,"

> which our holy fathers have preserved in a silence that prevents anxiety and curiosity . . . so as to safeguard by this silence the sacred character of the mystery. The uninitiated are not permitted to behold these things: their meaning is not to be divulged by writing it down.[14]

Behind the liturgical symbols and the lucid teachings of Jesus, there was a secret dogma which represented a more developed understanding of the faith.

A distinction between esoteric and exoteric truth will be extremely important in the history of God. It was not to be confined to Greek Christians, but Jews and Muslims would also develop an esoteric tradition. The idea of a "secret" doctrine was not to shut people out. Basil was not talking about an early form of Freemasonry. He was simply calling attention to the fact that not all religious truth was capable of being expressed and defined clearly and logically. Some religious insights had an inner resonance that could only be apprehended by each individual in his own time during what Plato had called *theoria*, contemplation. Since all religion was directed toward an ineffable reality that lay beyond normal concepts and categories, speech was limiting and confusing. If they did not "see" these truths with the eye of the spirit, people who were not yet very experienced could get quite the wrong idea. Besides their literal meaning, therefore, the scriptures also had a spiritual significance which it was not always possible to articulate. The Buddha had also noted that certain questions were "improper" or inappropriate, since they referred to realities that lay beyond the reach of words. You would only discover them by undergoing the introspective techniques of contemplation: in some sense you had to create them for yourself. The attempt to describe them in words was likely to be as grotesque as a verbal account of one of Beethoven's late quartets. As Basil said, these elusive religious realities could only be suggested in the symbolic gestures of the liturgy or, better still, by silence.[15]

Western Christianity would become a much more talkative religion and would concentrate on the *kerygma*: this would be one of its chief problems with God. In the Greek Orthodox Church, however, all good theology would be silent or apophatic. As Gregory of Nyssa said, every concept of God is a mere simulacrum, a false likeness, an idol: it could not reveal God himself.[16] Christians must be like Abraham, who, in Gregory's version of his life, laid aside all ideas about God and took hold of a faith which was "unmixed and pure of any concept."[17] In his *Life of Moses*, Gregory insisted that "the true vision and the knowledge of what we seek consists precisely in *not* seeing, in an awareness that our goal transcends all knowledge and is everywhere cut off from us by the darkness of incomprehensibility."[18] We cannot "see" God intellectually, but if we let ourselves be enveloped in the cloud that descended upon Mount Sinai, we will *feel* his presence. Basil reverted to the distinction that Philo had made between God's essence (*ousia*) and his activities (*energeiai*) in the world: "We know our God only by his operations (*energeiai*) but we do not undertake to approach his essence."[19] This would be the keynote of all future theology in the Eastern Church.

The Cappadocians were also anxious to develop the notion of the Holy Spirit, which they felt had been dealt with very perfunctorily at Nicaea: "And we believe in the Holy Spirit" seemed to have been added to Athanasius's creed almost as an afterthought. People were confused about the Holy Spirit. Was it simply a synonym for God or was it something more? "Some have conceived [the Spirit] as an activity," noted Gregory of Nazianzus, "some as a creature, some as God and some have been uncertain what to call him."[20] St. Paul had spoken of the Holy Spirit as renewing, creating and sanctifying, but these activities could only be performed by God. It followed, therefore, that the Holy Spirit, whose presence within us was said to *be* our salvation, must be divine, not a mere creature. The Cappadocians employed a formula that Athanasius had used in his dispute with Arius: God had a single essence (*ousia*) which remained incomprehensible to us—but three expressions (*hypostases*) which made him known.

Instead of beginning their consideration of God with his unknowable *ousia*, the Cappadocians began with mankind's experience of his *hypostases*. Because God's *ousia* is unfathomable, we can only know him through those manifestations which have been revealed to us as Father, Son and Spirit. This did not mean that the Cappadocians believed in three divine beings, however, as some Western theologians imagined. The word *hypostasis* was confusing to people who were not familiar with Greek, because it had a variety of senses: some Latin scholars like St. Jerome believed that the word *hypostasis* meant the same as *ousia* and thought that the Greeks believed in three divine essences. But the Cappadocians insisted that there was an important difference between *ousia* and *hypostasis*, which it was essential to bear in mind. Thus the *ousia* of an object was that which made something what it was; it was usually applied to an object as it was *within* itself. *Hypostasis*, on the other hand, was used to denote an object viewed from *without*. Sometimes the Cappadocians liked to use the word *prosopon* instead of *hypostasis*. *Prosopon* had originally meant "force" but had acquired a number of secondary meanings: thus it could refer to the expression on a person's face which was an outward depiction of his state of mind; it was also used to denote a role that he had consciously adopted or a character that he intended to act. Consequently, like *hypostasis*, *prosopon* meant the exterior expression of somebody's inner nature, or the individual self as it was presented to an onlooker. So when the Cappadocians said that God was one *ousia* in three *hypostases*, they meant that God as he is in himself was One: there was only a single, divine self-consciousness. But when he allows something of himself to be glimpsed by his creatures, he is three *prosopoi*.

Thus the *hypostases* Father, Son and Spirit should not be identified with God himself, because, as Gregory of Nyssa explained, "the divine nature (*ousia*) is unnameable and unspeakable"; "Father," "Son" and "Spirit" are only "terms that we use" to speak of the *energeiai* by which he has made himself known.[21] Yet these terms have symbolic value because they translate the ineffable reality into images that we can understand. Men have experienced God as transcendent (the Father, hidden in inaccessible light), as creative (the Logos) and as immanent (the Holy Spirit). But these three *hypostases* are only partial and incomplete glimpses of the Divine Nature itself, which lies far beyond such imagery and conceptualization.[22] The Trinity, therefore, should not be seen as a literal fact but as a paradigm that corresponds to real facts in the hidden life of God.

In his letter *To Alabius: That There Are Not Three Gods*, Gregory of Nyssa outlined his important doctrine of the inseparability or coinherence of the three divine persons or *hypostases*. One should not think of God splitting himself up into three parts; that was a grotesque and indeed blasphemous idea. God expressed himself wholly and totally in each one of these three manifestations when he wished to reveal himself to the world. Thus the Trinity gives us an indication of the pattern of "every operation which extends from God to creation": as Scripture shows, it has its origin in the Father, proceeds through the agency of the Son and is made effective in the world by means of the immanent Spirit. But the Divine Nature is equally present in each phase of the operation. In our own experience we can see the interdependence of the three *hypostases*: we should never have known about the Father were it not for the revelation of the Son, nor could we recognize the Son without the indwelling Spirit who makes him known to us. The Spirit accompanies the divine Word of the Father, just as the breath (Greek, *pneuma*; Latin, *spiritus*) accompanies the word spoken by a man. The three persons do not exist side by side in the divine world. We can compare them to the presence of different fields of knowledge in the mind of an individual: philosophy may be different from medicine, but it does not inhabit a separate sphere of consciousness. The different sciences pervade one another, fill the whole mind and yet remain distinct.[23]

Ultimately, however, the Trinity only made sense as a mystical or spiritual experience: it had to be lived, not thought, because God went far beyond human concepts. It was not a logical or intellectual formulation but an imaginative paradigm that confounded reason. Gregory of Nazianzus made this clear when he explained that contemplation of the Three in One induced a profound and overwhelming emotion that confounded thought and intellectual clarity.

> No sooner do I conceive of the One than I am illumined by the splendor of the Three; no sooner do I distinguish Three than I am carried back into the One. When I think of any of the Three, I think of him as the whole, and my eyes are filled, and the greater part of what I am thinking escapes me.[24]

Greek and Russian Orthodox Christians continue to find that the contemplation of the Trinity is an inspiring religious experience. For many Western Christians, however, the Trinity is simply baffling. This could be because they consider only what the Cappadocians would have called its *kerygmatic* qualities, whereas for the Greeks it was a *dogmatic* truth that was only grasped intuitively and as a result of religious experience. Logically, of course, it made no sense at all. In an earlier sermon, Gregory of Nazianzus had explained that the very incomprehensibility of the *dogma* of the Trinity brings us up against the absolute mystery of God; it reminds

us that we must not hope to understand him.[25] It should prevent us from
making facile statements about a God who, when he reveals himself, can
only express his nature in an ineffable manner. Basil also warned us
against imagining that we could work out the way in which the Trinity
operated, so to speak: it was no good, for example, attempting to puzzle
out how the three *hypostases* of the Godhead were at one and the same
time identical and distinct. This lay beyond words, concepts and human
powers of analysis.[26]

Thus the Trinity must not be interpreted in a literal manner; it was
not an abstruse "theory" but the result of *theoria*, contemplation. When
Christians in the West became embarrassed by this *dogma* during the
eighteenth century and tried to jettison it, they were trying to make God
rational and comprehensible to the Age of Reason. This was one of the
factors that would lead to the so-called Death of God in the nineteenth
and twentieth centuries, as we shall see. One of the reasons why the
Cappadocians evolved this imaginative paradigm was to prevent God
from becoming as rational as he was in Greek philosophy, as understood
by such heretics as Arius. The theology of Arius was a little too clear and
logical. The Trinity reminded Christians that the reality that we called
"God" could not be grasped by the human intellect. The doctrine of the
Incarnation, as expressed at Nicaea, was important but could lead to a
simplistic idolatry. People might start thinking about God himself in too
human a way: it might even be possible to imagine "him" thinking,
acting and planning like us. From there, it was only a very short step to
attributing all kinds of prejudiced opinions to God and thus making them
absolute. The Trinity was an attempt to correct this tendency. Instead
of seeing it as a statement of fact about God, it should, perhaps, be seen
as a poem or a theological dance between what is believed and accepted
by mere mortals about "God" and the tacit realization that any such
statement or *kerygma* could only be provisional.

The difference between the Greek and the Western use of the word
"theory" is instructive. In Eastern Christianity, *theoria* would always
mean contemplation. In the West, "theory" has come to mean a rational
hypothesis which must be logically demonstrated. Developing a "theory"
about God implied that "he" could be contained in a human system of
thought. There had only been three Latin theologians at Nicaea. Most
Western Christians were not up to this level of discussion and, since they
would not understand some of the Greek terminology, many felt unhappy
with the doctrine of the Trinity. Perhaps it was not wholly translatable
into another idiom. Every culture has to create its own idea of God. If

Westerners found the Greek interpretation of the Trinity alien, they would have to come up with a version of their own.

The Latin theologian who defined the Trinity for the Latin Church was Augustine. He was also an ardent Platonist and devoted to Plotinus and was, therefore, more sympathetically disposed to this Greek doctrine than some of his Western colleagues. As he explained, misunderstanding was often simply due to terminology:

> For the sake of describing things ineffable that we may be able in some way to express what we are in no way able to express fully, our Greek friends have spoken of one essence and three substances, but the Latins of one essence or substance and three persons (*personae*).[27]

Where the Greeks approached God by considering the three *hypostases*, refusing to analyze his single, unrevealed essence, Augustine himself and Western Christians after him have begun with the divine unity and then proceeded to discuss its three manifestations. Greek Christians venerated Augustine, seeing him as one of the great Fathers of the Church, but they were mistrustful of his Trinitarian theology, which they felt made God seem too rational and anthropomorphic. Augustine's approach was not metaphysical, like the Greeks', but psychological and highly personal.

Augustine can be called the founder of the Western spirit. No other theologian, apart from St. Paul, has been more influential in the West. We know him more intimately than any other thinker of late antiquity, largely because of his *Confessions*, the eloquent and passionate account of his discovery of God. From his earliest years, Augustine had sought a theistic religion. He saw God as essential to humanity: "Thou hast made us for thyself," he tells God at the beginning of the *Confessions*, "and our hearts are restless till they rest in thee!"[28] While teaching rhetoric in Carthage, he was converted to Manicheism, a Mesopotamian form of Gnosticism, but eventually he abandoned it because he found its cosmology unsatisfactory. He found the notion of the Incarnation offensive, a defilement of the idea of God, but while he was in Italy, Ambrose, Bishop of Milan, was able to convince him that Christianity was not incompatible with Plato and Plotinus. Yet Augustine was reluctant to take the final step and accept baptism. He felt that for him Christianity entailed celibacy and he was loath to take that step: "Lord, give me chastity," he used to pray, "but not yet."[29]

His final conversion was an affair of *Sturm und Drang*, a violent wrench from his past life and a painful rebirth, which has been characteristic of Western religious experience. One day, while he was sitting with his friend Alypius in their garden at Milan, the struggle came to a head:

> From a hidden depth a profound self-examination had dredged up a heap of all my misery and set it "in the sight of my heart" (Psalm 18:15). That precipitated a vast storm bearing a massive downpour of tears. To pour it all out with the accompanying groans, I got up from beside Alypius (solitude seemed to me more appropriate for the business of weeping). . . . I threw myself down somehow under a certain fig tree and let my tears flow freely. Rivers streamed from my eyes, a sacrifice acceptable to you (Psalm 50:19), and—though not in these words, yet in this sense—I repeatedly said to you, "How long, O Lord, how long will you be angry to the uttermost?" (Psalm 6:4)[30]

God has not always come easily to us in the West. Augustine's conversion seems like a psychological abreaction, after which the convert falls exhausted into the arms of God, all passion spent. As Augustine lay weeping on the ground, he suddenly heard a child's voice in a nearby house chanting the phrase "*Tolle, lege*: pick up and read, pick up and read!" Taking this as an oracle, Augustine leapt to his feet, rushed back to the astonished and long-suffering Alypius and snatched up his New Testament. He opened it at St. Paul's words to the Romans: "Not in riots and drunken parties, not in eroticism and indecencies, not in strife and rivalry, but put on the Lord Jesus Christ and make no provision for the flesh and its lusts." The long struggle was over: "I neither wished nor needed to read further," Augustine recalled. "At once, with the last words of this sentence, it was as if a light of relief from all anxiety flooded my heart. All the shadows of doubt were dispelled."[31]

God could also be a source of joy, however: not long after his conversion, Augustine experienced an ecstasy one night with his mother, Monica, at Ostia on the River Tiber. We shall discuss this in more detail in Chapter 7. As a Platonist, Augustine knew that God was to be found in the mind, and in Book X of the *Confessions*, he discussed the faculty of what he called *Memoria*, memory. This was something far more complex than the faculty of recollection and is closer to what psychologists would call the unconscious. For Augustine, memory represented the whole mind, conscious and unconscious alike. Its complexity and diversity filled him with astonishment. It was an "awe-inspiring mystery," an unfathomable world of images, presences of our past and countless plains, caverns and caves.[32] It was through this teeming inner world that Augustine descended to find his God, who was paradoxically both within and above him. It was no good simply searching for proof of God in the external world. He could only be discovered in the *real* world of the mind:

> Late have I loved you, beauty so old and so new; late have I loved you. And see, you were within and I was in the external world and sought you there, and in my unlovely state I plunged into those lovely created things which you made. You were with me, and I was not with you. The lovely things kept me far from you, though if they did not have their existence in you, they had no existence at all.[33]

God, therefore, was not an objective reality but a spiritual presence in the complex depths of the self. Augustine shared this insight not only with Plato and Plotinus but also with Buddhists, Hindus and Shamans in the nontheistic religions. Yet his was not an impersonal deity but the highly personal God of the Judeo-Christian tradition. God had condescended to man's weakness and gone in search of him:

> You called and cried out loud and shattered my deafness. You were radiant and resplendent, you put to flight my blindness. You were fragrant, and I drew in my breath and now pant after you. I tasted you and I feel but hunger and thirst for you. You touched me, and I am set on fire to attain that peace which was yours.[34]

The Greek theologians did not generally bring their own personal experience into their theological writing, but Augustine's theology sprang from his own highly individual story.

Augustine's fascination with the mind led him to develop his own psychological Trinitarianism in the treatise *De Trinitate*, written in the early years of the fifth century. Since God had made us in his own image, we should be able to discern a trinity in the depths of our minds. Instead of starting with the metaphysical abstractions and verbal distinctions that the Greeks enjoyed, Augustine began this exploration with a moment of truth that most of us have experienced. When we hear such phrases as "God is Light" or "God is truth," we instinctively feel a quickening of spiritual interest and feel that "God" can give meaning and value to our lives. But after this momentary illumination, we fall back into our normal frame of mind, when we are obsessed with "things accustomed and earthly."[35] Try as we might, we cannot recapture that moment of inarticulate longing. Normal thought processes cannot help us; instead we must listen to "what the heart means" by such phrases as "He is Truth."[36] But is it possible to love a reality that we do not know? Augustine goes on to show that since there is a trinity in our own minds which mirrors God, like any Platonic image, we yearn toward our Archetype—the original pattern on which we were formed.

If we start by considering the mind loving itself, we find not a trinity but a duality: love and the mind. But unless the mind is aware of itself, with what we should call self-consciousness, it cannot love itself. Anticipating Descartes, Augustine argues that knowledge of ourselves is the bedrock of all other certainty. Even our experience of doubt makes us conscious of ourselves.[37]

Within the soul there are three properties, therefore: memory, understanding and will, corresponding to knowledge, self-knowledge and love. Like the three divine persons, these mental activities are essentially one because they do not constitute three separate minds, but each fills the whole mind and pervades the other two: "I remember that I possess memory and understanding and will; I understand that I understand, will and remember. I will my own willing and remembering and understanding."[38] Like the Divine Trinity described by the Cappadocians, all three properties, therefore, "constitute one life, one mind, one essence."[39]

This understanding of our mind's workings, however, is only the first step: the trinity we encounter within us is not God himself but is a trace of the God who made us. Both Athanasius and Gregory of Nyssa had used the imagery of a reflection in a mirror to describe God's transforming presence within the soul of man, and to understand this correctly we must recall that the Greeks believed that the mirror image was real, formed when the light from the eye of the beholder mingled with the light beaming from the object and reflected on the surface of the glass.[40] Augustine believed that the trinity in the mind was also a reflection that included the presence of God and was directed toward him.[41] But how do we get beyond this image, reflected as in a glass darkly, to God himself? The immense distance between God and man cannot be traversed by human effort alone. It is only because God has come to meet us in the person of the incarnate Word that we can restore the image of God within us, which has been damaged and defaced by sin. We open ourselves to the divine activity which will transform us by a threefold discipline, which Augustine calls the trinity of faith: *retineo* (holding the truths of the

Incarnation in our minds), *contemplatio* (contemplating them) and *dilectio* (delighting in them). Gradually, by cultivating a continual sense of God's presence within our minds in this way, the Trinity will be disclosed.[42] This knowledge was not just the cerebral acquisition of information but a creative discipline that would transform us from within by revealing a divine dimension in the depths of the self.

These were dark and terrible times in the Western world. The barbarian tribes were pouring into Europe and bringing down the Roman empire: the collapse of civilization in the West inevitably affected Christian spirituality there. Ambrose, Augustine's great mentor, preached a faith that was essentially defensive: *integritas* (wholeness) was its most important virtue. The Church had to preserve its doctrines intact, and, like the pure body of the Virgin Mary, it must remain unpenetrated by the false doctrines of the barbarians (many of whom had converted to Arianism). A deep sadness also informed Augustine's later work: the fall of Rome influenced his doctrine of Original Sin, which would become central to the way Western people would view the world. Augustine believed that God had condemned humanity to an eternal damnation, simply because of Adam's one sin. The inherited guilt was passed on to all his descendants through the sexual act, which was polluted by what Augustine called "concupiscence." Concupiscence was the irrational desire to take pleasure in mere creatures instead of God; it was felt most acutely during the sexual act, when our rationality is entirely swamped by passion and emotion, when God is utterly forgotten and creatures revel shamelessly in one another. This image of reason dragged down by the chaos of sensations and lawless passions was disturbingly similar to Rome, source of rationality, law and order in the West, brought low by the barbarian tribes. By implication, Augustine's harsh doctrine paints a terrible picture of an implacable God:

> Banished [from Paradise] after his sin, Adam bound his offspring also with the penalty of death and damnation, that offspring which by sinning he had corrupted in himself, as in a root; so that whatever progeny was born (through carnal concupiscence, by which a fitting retribution for his disobedience was bestowed upon him) from himself and his spouse—who was the cause of his sin and the companion of his damnation—would drag through the ages the burden of Original Sin, by which it would itself be dragged through manifold errors and sorrows, down to that final and never-ending torment with the rebel angels. . . . So the matter stood; the damned lump of humanity

was lying prostrate, no, was wallowing in evil, it was falling headlong from one wickedness to another; and joined to the faction of the angels who had sinned, it was paying the most righteous penalty of its impious treason.[43]

Neither Jews nor Greek Orthodox Christians regarded the fall of Adam in such a catastrophic light; nor, later, would Muslims adopt this dark theology of Original Sin. Unique to the West, the doctrine compounds the harsh portrait of God suggested earlier by Tertullian.

Augustine left us with a difficult heritage. A religion which teaches men and women to regard their humanity as chronically flawed can alienate them from themselves. Nowhere is this alienation more evident than in the denigration of sexuality in general and women in particular. Even though Christianity had originally been quite positive for women, it had already developed a misogynistic tendency in the West by the time of Augustine. The letters of Jerome teem with loathing of the female which occasionally sounds deranged. Tertullian had castigated women as evil temptresses, an eternal danger to mankind:

> Do you not know that you are each an Eve? The sentence of God on this sex of yours lives in this age: the guilt must of necessity live too. *You* are the devil's gateway; *you* are the unsealer of that forbidden tree; *you* are the first deserter of the divine law; *you* are she who persuaded him whom the devil was not valiant enough to attack. *You* so carelessly destroyed man, God's image. On account of *your* desert, even the Son of God had to die.[44]

Augustine agreed; "What is the difference," he wrote to a friend, "whether it is in a wife or a mother, it is still Eve the temptress that we must beware of in any woman."[45] In fact Augustine is clearly puzzled that God should have made the female sex: after all, "if it was good company and conversation that Adam needed, it would have been much better arranged to have two men together as friends, not a man and a woman."[46] Woman's only function was the childbearing which passed the contagion of Original Sin to the next generation, like a venereal disease. A religion which looks askance upon half the human race and which regards every involuntary motion of mind, heart and body as a symptom of fatal concupiscence can only alienate men and women from their condition. Western Christianity never fully recovered from this neurotic misogyny, which can still be seen in the unbalanced reaction to the very notion of the ordination of women. While Eastern women shared the burden of inferiority carried by all women of the Oikumene at this time, their sisters in the West carried the additional stigma of a loathsome and sinful sexuality which caused them to be ostracized in hatred and fear.

This is doubly ironic, since the idea that God had become flesh and shared our humanity should have encouraged Christians to value the body. There had been further debates about this difficult belief. During the fourth and fifth centuries, "heretics" such as Apollinarius, Nestorius and Eutyches asked very difficult questions. How had the divinity of Christ been able to cohere with his humanity? Surely Mary was not the mother of God but the mother of the man Jesus? How could God have been a helpless, puling baby? Was it not more accurate to say that he had dwelt with Christ in particular intimacy, as in a temple? Despite the obvious inconsistencies, the orthodox stuck to their guns. Cyril, Bishop of Alexandria, reiterated the faith of Athanasius: God had indeed descended so deeply into our flawed and corrupt world that he had even tasted death and abandonment. It seemed impossible to reconcile this belief with the equally firm conviction that God was utterly impassible, unable to suffer or change. The remote God of the Greeks, characterized chiefly by the divine *apatheia*, seemed an entirely different deity from the God who was supposed to have become incarnate in Jesus Christ. The orthodox felt that the "heretics," who found the idea of a suffering, helpless God deeply offensive, wanted to drain the divine of its mystery and wonder. The paradox of the Incarnation seemed an antidote to the Hellenic God who did nothing to shake our complacency and who was so entirely reasonable.

In 529 the emperor Justinian closed the ancient school of philosophy in Athens, the last bastion of intellectual paganism: its last great master had been Proclus (412–485), an ardent disciple of Plotinus. Pagan philosophy went underground and seemed defeated by the new religion of Christianity. Four years later, however, four mystical treatises appeared which were purportedly written by Denys the Areopagite, St. Paul's first Athenian convert. They were, in fact, written by a sixth-century Greek Christian, who has preserved his anonymity. The pseudonym had a symbolic power, however, which was more important than the identity of the author: Pseudo-Denys managed to baptize the insights of Neoplatonism and wed the God of the Greeks to the Semitic God of the Bible.

Denys was also the heir of the Cappadocian Fathers. Like Basil, he took the distinction between *kerygma* and *dogma* very seriously. In one of his letters, he affirmed that there were two theological traditions, both of which derived from the apostles. The kerygmatic gospel was clear and knowable; the dogmatic gospel was silent and mystical. Both were mutually interdependent, however, and essential to the Christian faith. One was "symbolic and presupposing initiation," the other "philosophical and capable of proof—and the ineffable is woven with what can be uttered."[47] The *kerygma* persuades and exhorts by its clear, manifest truth, but the silent or hidden tradition of *dogma* was a mystery that required initiation: "It effects and establishes the soul with God by initiations that do not teach anything,"[48] Denys insisted, in words that recalled Aristotle. There was a religious truth which could not adequately be conveyed by words, logic or rational discourse. It was expressed symbolically, through the language and gestures of the liturgy or by doctrines which were "sacred veils" that hid the ineffable meaning from view but which also adapted the utterly mysterious God to the limitations of human nature and expressed the Reality in terms that could be grasped imaginatively if not conceptually.[49]

The hidden or esoteric meaning was not for a privileged elite but for all Christians. Denys was not advocating an abstruse discipline that was suitable for monks and ascetics only. The liturgy, attended by all the faithful, was the chief path to God and dominated his theology. The reason that these truths were hidden behind a protective veil was not to exclude men and women of goodwill but to lift all Christians above sense perceptions and concepts to the inexpressible reality of God himself. The humility which had inspired the Cappadocians to claim that all theology should be apophatic became for Denys a bold method of ascending to the inexpressible God.

In fact, Denys did not like to use the word "God" at all—probably because it had acquired such inadequate and anthropomorphic connotations. He preferred to use Proclus's term *theurgy*, which was primarily liturgical: *theurgy* in the pagan world had been a tapping of the divine *mana* by means of sacrifice and divination. Denys applied this to God-talk, which, properly understood, could also release the divine *energeiai* inherent in the revealed symbols. He agreed with the Cappadocians that all our words and concepts for God were inadequate and must not be taken as an accurate description of a reality which lies beyond our ken. Even the word "God" itself was faulty, since God was "above God," a "mystery beyond being."[50] Christians must realize that God is not the Supreme Being, the highest being of all heading a hierarchy of lesser beings. Things and people do not stand over against God as a separate reality or an alternative being, which can be the object of knowledge.

God is not one of the things that exist and is quite unlike anything else in our experience. In fact, it is more accurate to call God "Nothing": we should not even call him a Trinity since he is "neither a unity nor a trinity in the sense in which we know them."[51] He is above all names just as he is above all being.[52] Yet we can use our incapacity to speak about God as a method of achieving a union with him, which is nothing less than a "deification" (*theosis*) of our own nature. God had revealed some of his Names to us in scripture, such as "Father," "Son" and "Spirit," yet the purpose of this had not been to impart information *about* him but to draw men and women toward himself and enable them to share his divine nature.

In each chapter of his treatise *The Divine Names*, Denys begins with a *kerygmatic* truth, revealed by God: his goodness, wisdom, paternity and so forth. He then proceeds to show that although God has revealed something of himself in these titles, what he reveals is not himself. If we really want to understand God, we must go on to deny those attributes and names. Thus we must say that he is both "God" and "not-God," "good" and then go on to say that he is "not-good." The shock of this paradox, a process that includes both knowing and unknowing, will lift us above the world of mundane ideas to the inexpressible reality itself. Thus, we begin by saying that:

> of him there is understanding, reason, knowledge, touch, perception, imagination, name and many other things. But he is not understood, nothing can be said of him, he cannot be named. He is not one of the things that are.[53]

Reading the Scriptures is not a process of discovering facts about God, therefore, but should be a paradoxical discipline that turns the *kerygma* into *dogma*. This method is a *theurgy*, a tapping of the divine power that enables us to ascend to God himself and, as Platonists had always taught, become ourselves divine. It is a method to stop us thinking! "We have to leave behind us all our conceptions of the divine. We call a halt to the activities of our minds."[54] We even have to leave our denials of God's attributes behind. Then and only then shall we achieve an ecstatic union with God.

When Denys talks about ecstasy, he is not referring to a peculiar state of mind or an alternative form of consciousness achieved by an obscure yogic discipline. This is something that every Christian can manage in this paradoxical method of prayer and *theoria*. It will stop us talking and bring us to the place of silence: "As we plunge into that darkness which is beyond intellect, we shall find ourselves not simply running short of words but actually speechless and unknowing."[55] Like Gregory of Nyssa, he found the story of Moses' ascent of Mount Sinai instructive. When Moses had climbed the mountain, he did not see God himself on the summit but had only been brought to the place where God was. He had been enveloped by a thick cloud of obscurity and could see nothing: thus everything that we *can* see or understand is only a symbol (the word Denys uses is "paradigm") which reveals the presence of a reality beyond all thought. Moses had passed into the darkness of ignorance and thus achieved union with that which surpasses all understanding: we will achieve a similar ecstasy that will "take us out of ourselves" and unite us to God.

This is only possible because, as it were, God comes to meet us on the mountain. Here Denys departs from Neoplatonism, which perceived God as static and remote, entirely unresponsive to human endeavor. The God of the Greek philosophers was unaware of the mystic who occasionally managed to achieve an ecstatic union with him, whereas the God of the Bible turns toward humanity. God also achieves an "ecstasy" which takes him beyond himself to the fragile realm of created being:

> And we must dare to affirm (for it is the truth) that the Creator of the universe himself, in his beautiful and good yearning towards the universe . . . is transported outside himself in his providential activities towards all things that have being . . . and so is drawn from his transcendent throne above all things to dwell within the heart of all things, through an ecstatic power that is above being and whereby he yet stays within himself.[56]

Emanation had become a passionate and voluntary outpouring of love, rather than an automatic process. Denys's way of negation and paradox was not just something that we do but something that happens to us.

For Plotinus, ecstasy had been a very occasional rapture: it had been achieved by him only two or three times in his life. Denys saw ecstasy as the constant state of every Christian. This was the hidden or esoteric message of Scripture and liturgy, revealed in the smallest gestures. Thus when the celebrant leaves the altar at the beginning of the Mass to walk through the congregation, sprinkling it with holy water before returning to the sanctuary, this is not just a rite of purification—though it is that too. It imitates the divine ecstasy, whereby God leaves his solitude and merges himself with his creatures. Perhaps the best way of viewing Denys's theology is as that spiritual dance between what we can affirm about God and the appreciation that everything we can say about him can only be symbolic. As in Judaism, Denys's God has two aspects: one is turned toward us and manifests himself in the world; the other is the far side of God as he is in himself, which remains entirely incomprehensible. He "stays within himself" in his eternal mystery, at the same time as he is totally immersed in creation. He is not another being, additional to the world. Denys's method became normative in Greek theology. In the West, however, theologians would continue to talk and explain. Some imagined that when they said "God," the divine reality actually coincided with the idea in their minds. Some would attribute their own thoughts and ideas to God—saying that God wanted this, forbade that and had planned the other—in a way that was dangerously idolatrous. The God of Greek Othodoxy, however, would remain mysterious, and the Trinity would continue to remind Eastern Christians of the provisional nature of their doctrines. Eventually, the Greeks decided that an authentic theology must meet Denys's two criteria: it must be silent and paradoxical.

Greeks and Latins also developed significantly different views of the divinity of Christ. The Greek concept of the incarnation was defined by Maximus the Confessor (ca. 580–662), who is known as the father of Byzantine theology. This approximates more closely to the Buddhist ideal than does the Western view. Maximus believed that human beings would only fulfill themselves when they had been united to God, just as Buddhists believed that enlightenment was humanity's proper destiny. "God" was thus not an optional extra, an alien, external reality tacked on to the human condition. Men and women had a potential for the divine and would become fully human only if this was realized. The Logos had not become man to make reparation for the sin of Adam; indeed, the Incarnation would have occurred even if Adam had not sinned. Men and women had been created in the likeness of the Logos, and they would achieve their full potential only if this likeness was perfected. On Mount Tabor, Jesus' glorified humanity showed us the deified human condition to which we could all aspire. The Word was made flesh in order that "the whole human being would become God, deified by the grace of God become man—whole man, soul and body, by nature and becoming whole God, soul and body, by grace."[57] Just as enlightenment and Buddhahood did not involve invasion by a supernatural reality but were an enhancement of powers that were natural to humanity, so too the deified Christ showed us the state that we could acquire by means of God's grace. Christians could venerate Jesus the God-Man in rather the same way as Buddhists had come to revere the image of the enlightened Gautama: he had been the first example of a truly glorified and fulfilled humanity.

Where the Greek view of Incarnation brought Christianity closer to the oriental tradition, the Western view of Jesus took a more eccentric course. The classic theology was expressed by Anselm, Bishop of Canterbury (1033–1109), in his treatise *Why God Became Man*. Sin, he argued, had been an affront of such magnitude that atonement was essential if God's plans for the human race were not to be completely thwarted. The Word had been made flesh to make reparation on our behalf. God's justice demanded that the debt be repaid by one who was both God and man: the magnitude of the offense meant that only the Son of God could effect our salvation, but, as a man had been responsible, the redeemer also had to be a member of the human race. It was a tidy, legalistic scheme that depicted God thinking, judging and weighing things up as though he were a human being. It also reinforced the Western image of a harsh God who could only be satisfied by the hideous death of his own Son, who had been offered up as a kind of human sacrifice.

The doctrine of the Trinity has often been misunderstood in the Western world. People tend to imagine three divine figures or else ignore the doctrine altogether and identify "God" with the Father and make Jesus a divine friend—not quite on the same level. Muslims and Jews have also found the doctrine puzzling and even blasphemous. Yet we shall see that in both Judaism and Islam mystics developed remarkably similar conceptions of the divine. The idea of a *kenosis*, the self-emptying ecstasy of God, would, for example, be crucial in both Kabbalah and Sufism. In the Trinity, the Father transmits all that he *is* to the Son, giving up everything—even the possibility of expressing himself in another Word. Once that Word has been spoken, as it were, the Father remains silent: there is nothing that we can say about him, since the only God we know is the Logos or Son. The Father, therefore, has no identity, no "I" in the normal sense, and confounds our notion of personality. At the very source of Being is the Nothing glimpsed not only by Denys but also by Plotinus, Philo and even the Buddha. Since the Father is commonly presented as the End of the Christian quest, the Christian journey becomes a progress toward no place, no where and No One. The idea of a personal God or a personalized Absolute has been important to humanity: Hindus and Buddhists had to permit the personalistic devotionalism of *bhakti*. But the paradigm or symbol of the Trinity suggests that personalism must be transcended and that it is not enough to imagine God as man writ large, behaving and reacting in much the same way as we ourselves.

The doctrine of the Incarnation can be seen as another attempt to neutralize the danger of idolatry. Once "God" is seen as a wholly other reality "out there," he can easily become a mere idol and a projection, which enables human beings to externalize and worship their own prejudice and desires. Other religious traditions have attempted to prevent this by insisting that the Absolute is somehow bound up with the human condition, as in the Brahman-Atman paradigm. Arius—and later Nestorius and Eutyches—all wanted to make Jesus either human or divine, and they were resisted partly because of this tendency to keep humanity and divinity in separate spheres. True, their solutions were more rational, but *dogma*—as opposed to *kerygma*—should not be confined by the wholly explicable, any more than poetry or music. The doctrine of the Incarnation—as fumblingly expressed by Athanasius and Maximus—was an attempt to articulate the universal insight that "God" and man must be inseparable. In the West, where the Incarnation was not formulated in this way, there has been a tendency for God to remain external to man and an alternative reality to the world that we know. Consequently, it has been all too easy to make this "God" a projection, which has recently become discredited.

Yet by making Jesus the only *avatar*, we have seen that Christians would adopt an exclusive notion of religious truth: Jesus was the first and last Word of God to the human race, rendering future revelation unnecessary. Consequently, like Jews, they were scandalized when a prophet arose in Arabia during the seventh century who claimed to have received a direct revelation from their God and to have brought a new scripture to his people. Yet the new version of monotheism, which eventually became known as "Islam," spread with astonishing rapidity throughout the Middle East and North Africa. Many of its enthusiastic converts in these lands (where Hellenism was not on home ground) turned with relief from Greek Trinitarianism, which expressed the mystery of God in an idiom that was alien to them, and adopted a more Semitic notion of the divine reality.

5

Unity: The God of Islam

IN ABOUT THE YEAR 610 an Arab merchant of the thriving city of Mecca in the Hijaz, who had never read the Bible and probably never heard of Isaiah, Jeremiah and Ezekiel, had an experience that was uncannily similar to theirs. Every year Muhammad ibn Abdallah, a member of the Meccan tribe of Quraysh, used to take his family to Mount Hira just outside the city to make a spiritual retreat during the month of Ramadan. This was quite a common practice among the Arabs of the peninsula. Muhammad would have spent the time praying to the High God of the Arabs and distributing food and alms to the poor who came to visit him during this sacred period. He probably also spent much time in anxious thought. We know from his later career that Muhammad was acutely aware of a worrying malaise in Mecca, despite its recent spectacular success. Only two generations earlier, the Quraysh had lived a harsh nomadic life in the Arabian steppes, like the other Bedouin tribes: each day had required a grim struggle for survival. During the last years of the sixth century, however, they had become extremely successful in trade and made Mecca the most important settlement in Arabia. They were now rich beyond their wildest dreams. Yet their drastically altered lifestyle meant that the old tribal values had been superseded by a rampant and ruthless capitalism. People felt obscurely disoriented and lost. Muhammad knew that the Quraysh were on a dangerous course and needed to find an ideology that would help them to adjust to their new conditions.

At this time, any political solution tended to be of a religious nature. Muhammad was aware that the Quraysh were making a new religion out of money. This was hardly surprising, because they must have felt that their new wealth had "saved" them from the perils of the nomadic life, cushioning them from the malnutrition and tribal violence that were endemic to the steppes of Arabia, where each Bedouin tribe daily faced the possibility of extinction. They now had almost enough to eat and were making Mecca an international center of trade and high finance. They felt that they had become the masters of their own fate, and some even seem to have believed that their wealth would give them a certain immortality. But Muhammad believed that this new cult of self-sufficiency (*istaqa*) would mean the disintegration of the tribe. In the old nomadic days the tribe had had to come first and the individual second: each one of its members knew that they all depended upon one another for survival. Consequently they had a duty to take care of the poor and vulnerable people of their ethnic group. Now individualism had replaced the communal ideal and competition had become the norm. Individuals were starting to build personal fortunes and took no heed of the weaker Qurayshis. Each of the clans, or smaller family groups of the tribe, fought one another for a share of the wealth of Mecca, and some of the least successful clans (like Muhammad's own clan of Hashim) felt that their very survival was in jeopardy. Muhammad was convinced that unless the Quraysh learned to put another transcendent value at the center of their lives and overcome their egotism and greed, his tribe would tear itself apart morally and politically in internecine strife.

In the rest of Arabia the situation was also bleak. For centuries the Bedouin tribes of the regions of the Hijaz and Najd had lived in fierce competition with one another for the basic necessities of life. To help the people cultivate the communal spirit that was essential for survival, the Arabs had evolved an ideology called *muruwah*, which fulfilled many of the functions of religion. In the conventional sense, the Arabs had little time for religion. There was a pagan pantheon of deities and the Arabs worshipped at their shrines, but they had not developed a mythology that explained the relevance of these gods and holy places to the life of the spirit. They had no notion of an afterlife but believed instead that *darh*, which can be translated as "time" or "fate," was supreme—an attitude that was probably essential in a society where the mortality rate was so high. Western scholars often translate *muruwah* as "manliness" but it had a far wider range of significance: it meant courage in battle, patience and endurance in suffering and absolute dedication to the tribe. The virtues of *muruwah* required an Arab to obey his *sayyid* or chief at a second's notice, regardless of his personal safety; he had to dedicate himself to the chivalrous duties of avenging any wrong committed against the tribe and protecting its more vulnerable members. To ensure the survival of the tribe, the *sayyid* shared its wealth and possessions equally and avenged the death of a single one of his people by killing a member of the murderer's tribe. It is here that we see the communal ethic most clearly: there was no duty to punish the killer himself because an individual could vanish without trace in a society like pre-Islamic Arabia. Instead one member of the enemy tribe was equivalent to another for such purposes. The vendetta or blood feud was the only way of ensuring a modicum of social security in a region where there was no central authority, where every tribal group was a law unto itself and where there was nothing comparable to a modern police force. If a chief failed to retaliate, his tribe would lose respect and others would feel free to kill its members with impunity. The vendetta was thus a rough-and-ready form of justice which meant that no one tribe could easily gain ascendancy over any of the others. It also meant that the various tribes could easily become involved in an unstoppable cycle of violence, in which one vendetta would lead to another if people felt that the revenge taken was disproportionate to the original offense.

Brutal as it undoubtedly was, however, *muruwah* had many strengths. It encouraged a deep and strong egalitarianism and an indifference to material goods which, again, was probably essential in a region where there were not enough of the essentials to go round: the cults of largesse and generosity were important virtues and taught the Arabs to take no heed for the morrow. These qualities would become very important in Islam, as we shall see. *Muruwah* had served the Arabs well for centuries, but by the sixth century it was no longer able to answer the conditions of modernity. During the last phase of the pre-Islamic period, which Muslims call the *jahiliyyah* (the time of ignorance), there seems to have been widespread dissatisfaction and spiritual restlessness. The Arabs were surrounded on all sides by the two mighty empires of Sassanid Persia and Byzantium. Modern ideas were beginning to penetrate Arabia from the settled lands; merchants who traveled into Syria or Iraq brought back stories of the wonders of civilization.

Yet it seemed that the Arabs were doomed to perpetual barbarism. The tribes were involved in constant warfare, which made it impossible for them to pool their meager resources and become the united Arab people that they were dimly aware of being. They could not take their destiny into their own hands and found a civilization of their own. Instead they were constantly open to exploitation by the great powers: indeed, the more fertile and sophisticated region of Southern Arabia in what is now Yemen (which had the benefit of the monsoon rains) had become a mere province of Persia. At the same time, the new ideas that were infiltrating the region brought intimations of individualism that undermined the old communal ethos. The Christian doctrine of the afterlife, for example, made the eternal fate of each individual a sacred value: how could that be squared with the tribal ideal which subordinated the individual to the group and insisted that a man or woman's sole immortality lay in the survival of the tribe?

Muhammad was a man of exceptional genius. When he died in 632, he had managed to bring nearly all the tribes of Arabia into a new united community, or *ummah*. He had brought the Arabs a spirituality that was uniquely suited to their own traditions and which unlocked such reserves of power that within a hundred years they had established their own great empire, which stretched from the Himalayas to the Pyrenees, and founded a unique civilization. Yet as Muhammad sat in prayer in the tiny cave at the summit of Mount Hira during his Ramadan retreat of 610, he could not have envisaged such phenomenal success. Like many of the Arabs, Muhammad had come to believe that al-Lah, the High God of the ancient Arabian pantheon, whose name simply meant "the God," was identical to the God worshipped by the Jews and the Christians. He also believed that only a prophet of this God could solve the problems of his people, but he never believed for one moment that *he* was going to be that prophet. Indeed, the Arabs were unhappily aware that al-Lah had never sent them a prophet or a scripture of their own, even though they had had his shrine in their midst from time immemorial. By the seventh century, most Arabs had come to believe that the Kabah, the massive cube-shaped shrine in the heart of Mecca, which was clearly of great antiquity, had originally been dedicated to al-Lah, even though at present the Nabatean deity Hubal presided there. All Meccans were fiercely proud of the Kabah, which was the most important holy place in Arabia. Each year Arabs from all over the peninsula made the *hajj* pilgrimage to Mecca, performing the traditional rites over a period of several days. All violence was forbidden in the sanctuary, the sacred area around the Kabah, so that in Mecca the Arabs could trade with one another peacefully, knowing that old tribal hostilities were temporarily in abeyance. The Quraysh knew that without the sanctuary they could never have achieved their mercantile success and that a great deal of their prestige among the other tribes depended upon their guardianship of the Kabah and upon their preservation of its ancient sanctities. Yet though al-Lah had clearly singled the Quraysh out for his special favor, he had never sent them a messenger like Abraham, Moses or Jesus, and the Arabs had no scripture in their own language.

There was, therefore, a widespread feeling of spiritual inferiority. Those Jews and Christians with whom the Arabs came in contact used to taunt them for being a barbarous people who had received no revelation from God. The Arabs felt a mingled resentment and respect for these people who had knowledge that they did not. Judaism and Christianity had made little headway in the region, even though the Arabs acknowledged that this progressive form of religion was superior to their own traditional paganism. There were some Jewish tribes of doubtful provenance in the settlements of Yathrib (later Medina) and Fadak, to the north of Mecca, and some of the northern tribes on the borderland between the Persian and Byzantine empires had converted to Monophysite or Nestorian Christianity. Yet the Bedouin were fiercely independent, were determined not to come under the rule of the great powers like their brethren in Yemen and were acutely aware that both the Persians and the Byzantines had used the religions of Judaism and Christianity to promote their imperial designs in the region. They were probably also instinctively aware that they had suffered enough cultural dislocation, as their own traditions eroded. The last thing they needed was a foreign ideology, couched in alien languages and traditions.

Some Arabs seem to have attempted to discover a more neutral form of monotheism not tainted by imperialistic associations. As early as the fifth century, the Palestinian Christian historian Sozomenos tells us that some of the Arabs in Syria had rediscovered what they called the authentic religion of Abraham, who had lived before God had sent either the Torah or the Gospel and who was, therefore, neither a Jew nor a Christian. Shortly before Muhammad received his own prophetic call, his first biographer, Muhammad ibn Ishaq (d. 767), tells us that four of the Quraysh of Mecca had decided to seek the *hanifiyyah*, the true religion of Abraham. Some Western scholars have argued that this little *hanifiyyah* sect is a pious fiction, symbolizing the spiritual restlessness of the *jahiliyyah*, but it must have some factual basis. Three of the four *hanifs* were well known to the first Muslims: Ubaydallah ibn Jahsh was Muhammad's cousin, Waraqa ibn Nawfal, who eventually became a Christian, was one of his earliest spiritual advisers, and Zayd ibn Amr was the uncle of Umar ibn al-Khattab, one of Muhammad's closest companions and the second caliph of the Islamic empire. There is a story that one day, before he had left Mecca to search in Syria and Iraq for the religion of Abraham, Zayd had been standing by the Kabah, leaning against the shrine and telling the

Quraysh who were making the ritual circumambulations around it in the time-honored way: "O Quraysh, by him in whose hand is the soul of Zayd, not one of you follows the religion of Abraham but I." Then he added sadly, "O God, if I knew how you wish to be worshipped I would so worship you; but I do not know."[1]

Zayd's longing for a divine revelation was fulfilled on Mount Hira in 610 on the seventeenth night of Ramadan, when Muhammad was torn from sleep and felt himself enveloped by a devastating divine presence. Later he explained this ineffable experience in distinctively Arabian terms. He said that an angel had appeared to him and given him a curt command: "Recite!" (*iqra!*) Like the Hebrew prophets who were often reluctant to utter the Word of God, Muhammad refused, protesting, "I am not a reciter!" He was no *kahin*, one of the ecstatic soothsayers of Arabia who claimed to recite inspired oracles. But, Muhammad said, the angel simply enveloped him in an overpowering embrace, so that he felt as if all the breath was being squeezed from his body. Just as he felt he could bear it no longer, the angel released him and again commanded him to "Recite!" (*iqra!*). Again Muhammad refused and again the angel embraced him until he felt he had reached the limits of his endurance. Finally, at the end of a third terrifying embrace, Muhammad found the first words of a new scripture pouring from his mouth:

> Recite in the name of thy Sustainer, who has created—created man out of a germ-cell! Recite—for thy Sustainer is the Most Bountiful, One who has taught [man] the use of the pen—taught him what he did not know![2]

The word of God had been spoken for the first time in the Arabic language, and this scripture would ultimately be called the *qur'an*: the Recitation.

Muhammad came to himself in terror and revulsion, horrified to think that he might have become a mere disreputable *kahin* whom people consulted if one of their camels went missing. A *kahin* was supposedly possessed by a *jinni*, one of the sprites who were thought to haunt the landscape and who could be capricious and lead people into error. Poets also believed that they were possessed by their personal *jinni*. Thus Hassan ibn Thabit, a poet of Yathrib who later became a Muslim, says that when he received his poetic vocation his *jinni* had appeared to him, thrown him to the ground and forced the inspired words from his mouth. This was the only form of inspiration that was familiar to Muhammad, and the thought that he might have become *majnun*, *jinni*-possessed, filled him with such despair that he no longer wished to live. He thoroughly despised the *kahins*, whose oracles were usually unintelligible mumbo jumbo, and was always very careful to distinguish the Koran from conventional Arabic poetry. Now, rushing from the cave, he resolved to fling himself from the summit to his death. But on the mountainside he had another vision of a being which, later, he identified with the angel Gabriel:

> When I was midway on the mountain, I heard a voice from heaven saying, "O Muhammad! thou art the apostle of God and I am Gabriel." I raised my head towards heaven to see who was speaking, and lo, Gabriel in the form of a man with feet astride the horizon. . . . I stood gazing at him, moving neither backward or forward; then I began to turn my face away from him, but towards whatever region of the sky I looked, I saw him as before.[3]

In Islam Gabriel is often identified with the Holy Spirit of revelation, the means by which God communicates with men. This was no pretty naturalistic angel, but an overwhelming ubiquitous presence from which escape was impossible. Muhammad had had that overpowering apprehension of numinous reality, which the Hebrew prophets had called *kaddosh*, holiness, the terrifying otherness of God. They too had felt near to death and at a physical and psychological extremity when they experienced it. But unlike Isaiah or Jeremiah, Muhammad had none of the consolations of an established tradition to support him. The terrifying experience seemed to have fallen upon him out of the blue and left him in a state of profound shock. In his anguish, he turned instinctively to his wife, Khadija.

Crawling on his hands and knees, trembling violently, Muhammad flung himself into her lap. "Cover me! cover me!" he cried, begging her to shield him from the divine presence. When the fear had abated somewhat, Muhammad asked her whether he really had become *majnun*, and Khadija hastened to reassure him: "You are kind and considerate towards your kin. You help the poor and forlorn and bear their burdens. You are striving to restore the high moral qualities that your people have lost. You honor the guest and go to the assistance of those in distress. This cannot be, my dear!"[4] God did not act in such an arbitrary way. Khadija suggested that they consult her cousin Waraqa ibn Nawfal, now a Christian and learned in the scriptures. Waraqa had no doubts at all: Muhammad had received a revelation from the God of Moses and the prophets and had become the divine envoy to the Arabs. Eventually, after a period of several years, Muhammad was convinced that this was indeed the case and began to preach to the Quraysh, bringing them a scripture in their own language.

Unlike the Torah, however, which according to the biblical account was revealed to Moses in one session on Mount Sinai, the Koran was revealed to Muhammad bit by bit, line by line and verse by verse over a period of twenty-three years. The revelations continued to be a painful experience. "Never once did I receive a revelation without feeling that my soul was being torn away from me," Muhammad said in later years.[5] He had to listen to the divine words intently, struggling to make sense of a vision and significance that did not always come to him in a clear, verbal form. Sometimes, he said, the content of the divine message was clear: he seemed to see Gabriel and heard what he was saying. But at other times the revelation was distressingly inarticulate: "Sometimes it comes unto me like the reverberations of a bell, and that is the hardest upon me; the reverberations abate when I am aware of their message."[6] The early biographers of the classical period often show him listening intently to what we should perhaps call the unconscious, rather as a poet describes the process of "listening" to a poem that is gradually surfacing from the hidden recesses of his mind, declaring itself with an authority and integrity that seem mysteriously separate from him. In the Koran, God tells Muhammad to listen to the incoherent meaning carefully and with what Wordsworth would call "a wise passiveness."[7] He must not rush to force words or a particular conceptual significance upon it until the true meaning revealed itself in its own good time:

> Move not thy tongue in haste [repeating the words of the revelation];
>   for, behold, it is for Us to gather it [in thy heart], and cause it to
>   be recited [as it ought to be recited].
> Thus when We recite it, follow thou its wordings [with all thy mind]:
>   and then, behold, it will be for Us to make its meaning clear.[8]

Like all creativity, it was a difficult process. Muhammad used to enter a tranced state and sometimes seemed to lose consciousness; he used to sweat profusely, even on a cold day, and often felt an interior heaviness like grief that impelled him to lower his head between his knees, a position adopted by some contemporary Jewish mystics when they entered an alternative state of consciousness—though Muhammad could not have known this.

It is not surprising that Muhammad found the revelations such an immense strain: not only was he working through to an entirely new political solution for his people, but he was composing one of the great spiritual and literary classics of all time. He believed that he was putting the ineffable Word of God into Arabic, for the Koran is as central to the spirituality of Islam as Jesus, the Logos, is to Christianity. We know more about Muhammad than about the founder of any other major religion, and in the Koran, whose various suras or chapters can be dated with reasonable accuracy, we can see how his vision gradually evolved and developed, becoming ever more universal in scope. He did not see at the outset all that he had to accomplish, but this was revealed to him little by little, as he responded to the inner logic of events. In the Koran we have, as it were, a contemporaneous commentary on the beginnings of Islam that is unique in the history of religion. In this sacred book, God seems to comment on the developing situation: he answers some of Muhammad's critics, explains the significance of a battle or a conflict within the early Muslim community and points to the divine dimension of human life. It did not come to Muhammad in the order we read today but in a more random manner, as events dictated and as he listened to their deeper meaning. As each new segment was revealed, Muhammad, who could neither read nor write, recited it aloud, the Muslims learned it by heart and those few who were literate wrote it down. Some twenty years after Muhammad's death, the first official compilation of the revelations was made. The editors put the longest suras at the beginning and the shortest at the end. This arrangement is not as arbitrary as it might appear, because the Koran is neither a narrative nor an argument that needs a sequential order. Instead, it reflects on various themes: God's presence in the natural world, the lives of the prophets or the Last Judgment. To a Westerner, who cannot appreciate the extraordinary beauty of the Arabic, the Koran seems boring and repetitive. It seems to go over the same ground again and again. But the Koran was not meant for private perusal but for liturgical recitation. When Muslims hear a sura chanted in the mosque, they are reminded of all the central tenets of their faith.

When Muhammad began to preach in Mecca, he had only a modest conception of his role. He did not believe that he was founding a new universal religion but saw himself bringing the old religion of the one God to the Quraysh. At first he did not even think that he should preach to the other Arab tribes but only to the people of Mecca and its environs.[9] He had no dreams of founding a theocracy and would probably not have known what a theocracy was: he himself should have no political function

in the city but was simply its *nadhir*, the Warner.[10] Al-Lah had sent him
to warn the Quraysh of the perils of their situation. His early message
was not doom-laden, however. It was a joyful message of hope. Muhammad did not have to prove the existence of God to the Quraysh. They all
believed implicitly in al-Lah, who was the creator of heaven and earth,
and most believed him to be the God worshipped by the Jews and Christians. His existence was taken for granted. As God says to Muhammad
in an early sura of the Koran:

> And thus it is [with most people]: if thou ask them, "Who is it that
> has created the heavens and the earth and made the sun and moon
> subservient [to his laws]?"—they will surely answer al-Lah.
> And thus it is, if thou ask them, "Who is it that sends down water
> from the skies, giving life thereby to the earth after it had been
> lifeless?" they will surely answer "al-Lah."[11]

The trouble was that the Quraysh were not thinking through the implications of this belief. God had created each one of them from a drop of
semen, as the very first revelation had made clear; they depended upon
God for their food and sustenance, and yet they still regarded themselves
as the center of the universe in an unrealistic presumption (*yatqa*) and
self-sufficiency (*istaqa*)[12] that took no account of their responsibilities as
members of a decent Arab society.

Consequently the early verses of the Koran all encourage the Quraysh
to become aware of God's benevolence, which they can see wherever they
look. They will then realize how many things they still owe to him,
despite their new success, and appreciate their utter dependency upon
the Creator of the natural order:

> [Only too often] man destroys himself: how stubbornly does he deny
> the truth!
> [Does man ever consider] out of what substance [God] creates him?
> Out of a drop of sperm he creates him, and then determines his
> nature and then makes it easy for him to go through life; and in
> the end he causes him to die and brings him to the grave; and
> then, if it be his will, he shall raise him again to life.
> Nay but [man] has never yet fulfilled what he has enjoined upon
> him.
> Let man, then, consider [the sources of] his food: [how it is] that we
> pour down waters, pouring it down abundantly; and then we

cleave the earth [with new growth] cleaving it asunder, and there-
upon we cause grain to grow out of it, and vines and edible plants,
and olive trees and date palms, and gardens dense with foliage,
and fruits and herbage, for you and for your animals to enjoy.[13]

The existence of God is not in question, therefore. In the Koran an
"unbeliever" (*kafir bi na'mat al-Lah*) is not an atheist in our sense of the
word, somebody who does not believe in God, but one who is ungrateful
to him, who can see quite clearly what is owing to God but refuses to
honor him in a spirit of perverse ingratitude.

The Koran was not teaching the Quraysh anything new. Indeed, it
constantly claims to be "a reminder" of things known already, which it
throws into more lucid relief. Frequently the Koran introduces a topic
with a phrase like: "Have you not seen . . . ?" or "Have you not considered . . . ?" The Word of God was not issuing arbitrary commands from
on high but was entering into a dialogue with the Quraysh. It reminds
them, for example, that the Kabah, the House of al-Lah, accounted in
large measure for their success, which was really in some sense owing to
God. The Quraysh loved to make the ritual circumambulations around
the shrine, but when they put themselves and their own material success
into the center of their lives they had forgotten the meaning of these
ancient rites of orientation. They should look at the "signs" (*ayat*) of God's
goodness and power in the natural world. If they failed to reproduce
God's benevolence in their own society, they would be out of touch with
the true nature of things. Consequently, Muhammad made his converts
bow down in ritual prayer (*salat*) twice a day. This external gesture would
help Muslims to cultivate the internal posture and reorient their lives.
Eventually Muhammad's religion would be known as *islām*, the act of
existential surrender that each convert was expected to make to al-Lah: a
muslīm was a man or woman who has surrendered his or her whole being
to the Creator. The Quraysh were horrified when they saw these first
Muslims making the *salat*: they found it unacceptable that a member of the
haughty clan of Quraysh with centuries of proud Bedouin independence
behind him should be prepared to grovel on the ground like a slave, and
the Muslims had to retire to the glens around the city to make their prayer
in secret. The reaction of the Quraysh showed that Muhammad had
diagnosed their spirit with unerring accuracy.

In practical terms, *islām* meant that Muslims had a duty to create a
just, equitable society where the poor and vulnerable are treated decently.
The early moral message of the Koran is simple: it is wrong to stockpile

wealth and to build a private fortune, and good to share the wealth of society fairly by giving a regular proportion of one's wealth to the poor.[14] Alms-giving (*zakat*) accompanied by prayer (*salat*) represented two of the five essential "pillars" (*rukn*) or practices of Islam. Like the Hebrew prophets, Muhammad preached an ethic that we might call socialist as a consequence of his worship of the one God. There were no obligatory doctrines about God: indeed, the Koran is highly suspicious of theological speculation, dismissing it as *zanna*, self-indulgent guesswork about things that nobody can possibly know or prove. The Christian doctrines of the Incarnation and the Trinity seemed prime examples of *zanna* and, not surprisingly, the Muslims found these notions blasphemous. Instead, as in Judaism, God was experienced as a moral imperative. Having practically no contact with either Jews or Christians and their scriptures, Muhammad had cut straight into the essence of historical monotheism.

In the Koran, however, al-Lah is more impersonal than YHWH. He lacks the pathos and passion of the biblical God. We can only glimpse something of God in the "signs" of nature, and so transcendent is he that we can only talk about him in "parables."[15] Constantly, therefore, the Koran urges Muslims to see the world as an epiphany; they must make the imaginative effort to see *through* the fragmentary world to the full power of original being, to the transcendent reality that infuses all things. Muslims were to cultivate a sacramental or symbolic attitude:

> Verily, in the creation of the heavens and of the earth and the succession of night and day and in the ships that speed through the sea with what is useful to man: and in the waters which God sends down from the sky, giving life thereby to the earth after it had been lifeless, and causing all manner of living creatures to multiply thereon: and in the change of the winds, and the clouds that run their appointed courses between sky and earth: [in all this] there are messages (*ayat*) indeed for a people who use their reason.[16]

The Koran constantly stresses the need for intelligence in deciphering the "signs" or "messages" of God. Muslims are not to abdicate their reason but to look at the world attentively and with curiosity. It was this attitude that later enabled Muslims to build a fine tradition of natural science, which has never been seen as such a danger to religion as in Christianity. A study of the workings of the natural world showed that it had a transcendent dimension and source, whom we can talk about only in signs

and symbols: even the stories of the prophets, the accounts of the Last
Judgment and the joys of paradise should not be interpreted literally but
as parables of a higher, ineffable reality.

But the greatest sign of all was the Koran itself: indeed its individual
verses are called *ayat*. Western people find the Koran a difficult book, and
this is largely a problem of translation. Arabic is particularly difficult to
translate: even ordinary literature and the mundane utterances of politi-
cians frequently sound stilted and alien when translated into English, for
example, and this is doubly true of the Koran, which is written in dense
and highly allusive, elliptical speech. The early suras in particular give
the impression of human language crushed and splintered under the divine
impact. Muslims often say that when they read the Koran in a translation,
they feel that they are reading a different book because nothing of the
beauty of the Arabic has been conveyed. As its name suggests, it is meant
to be recited aloud, and the sound of the language is an essential part of
its effect. Muslims say that when they hear the Koran chanted in the
mosque they feel enveloped in a divine dimension of sound, rather as
Muhammad was enveloped in the embrace of Gabriel on Mount Hira or
when he saw the angel on the horizon no matter where he looked. It is
not a book to be read simply to acquire information. It is meant to yield
a sense of the divine, and must not be read in haste:

> And thus have We bestowed from on high this [divine writ] as a
> discourse in the Arabic tongue, and have given therein many facets
> to all manner of warnings, so that men might remain conscious of
> Us, or that it give rise to a new awareness in them.
> [Know] then, [that] God is sublimely exalted, the Ultimate Sovereign
> (*al-Malik*), the Ultimate Truth (*al-Haqq*): and [knowing this], do
> not approach the Koran in haste, ere it has been revealed unto
> thee in full, but [always] say: "O my Sustainer, cause me to grow
> in knowledge!"[17]

By approaching the Koran in the right way, Muslims claim that they do
experience a sense of transcendence, of an ultimate reality and power that
lie behind the transient and fleeting phenomena of the mundane world.
Reading the Koran is therefore a spiritual discipline, which Christians
may find difficult to understand because they do not have a sacred language, in the way that Hebrew, Sanskrit and Arabic are sacred to Jews,
Hindus and Muslims. It is Jesus who is the Word of God, and there is
nothing holy about the New Testament Greek. Jews, however, have a

similar attitude toward the Torah. When they study the first five books of the Bible, they do not simply run their eyes over the page. Frequently they recite the words aloud, savoring the words that God himself is supposed to have used when he revealed himself to Moses on Sinai. Sometimes they sway backward and forward, like a flame before the breath of the Spirit. Obviously Jews who read their Bible in this way are experiencing a very different book than Christians who find most of the Pentateuch extremely dull and obscure.

The early biographers of Muhammad constantly describe the wonder and shock felt by the Arabs when they heard the Koran for the first time. Many were converted on the spot, believing that God alone could account for the extraordinary beauty of the language. Frequently a convert would describe the experience as a divine invasion that tapped buried yearnings and released a flood of feelings. Thus the young Qurayshi Umar ibn al-Khattab had been a virulent opponent of Muhammad; he had been devoted to the old paganism and ready to assassinate the Prophet. But this Muslim Saul of Tarsus was converted not by a vision of Jesus the Word but by the Koran. There are two versions of his conversion story, both worthy of note. The first has Umar discovering his sister, who had secretly become a Muslim, listening to a recitation of a new sura. "What was that balderdash?" he had roared angrily as he strode into the house, knocking poor Fatimah to the ground. But when he saw that she was bleeding, he probably felt ashamed because his face changed. He picked up the manuscript, which the visiting Koran reciter had dropped in the commotion, and, being one of the few Qurayshis who were literate, he started to read. Umar was an acknowledged authority on Arabic oral poetry and was consulted by poets as to the precise significance of the language, but he had never come across anything like the Koran. "How fine and noble is this speech!" he said wonderingly, and was instantly converted to the new religion of al-Lah.[18] The beauty of the words had reached through his reserves of hatred and prejudice to a core of receptivity that he had not been conscious of. We have all had a similar experience, when a poem touches a chord of recognition that lies at a level deeper than the rational. In the other version of Umar's conversation, he encountered Muhammad one night at the Kabah, reciting the Koran quietly to himself before the shrine. Thinking that he would like to listen to the words, Umar crept under the damask cloth that covered the huge granite cube and edged his way around until he was standing directly in front of the Prophet. As he said, "There was nothing between us but the cover of the Kabah"—all his defenses but one were down. Then the magic of the

Arabic did its work: "When I heard the Koran, my heart was softened and I wept and Islam entered into me."[19] It was the Koran which prevented God from being a mighty reality "out there" and brought him into the mind, heart and being of each believer.

The experience of Umar and the other Muslims who were converted by the Koran can perhaps be compared to the experience of art described by George Steiner in his book *Real Presences: Is there anything* in *what we say?* He speaks of what he calls "the indiscretion of serious art, literature and music" which "queries the last privacies of our existence." It is an invasion or an annunciation, which breaks into "the small house of our cautionary being" and commands us "change your life!" After such a summons, the house "is no longer habitable in quite the same way as it was before."[20] Muslims like Umar seem to have experienced a similar unsettling of sensibility, an awakening and a disturbing sense of significance which enabled them to make the painful break with the traditional past. Even those Qurayshis who refused to accept Islam were disturbed by the Koran and found that it lay outside all their familiar categories: it was nothing like the inspiration of the *kahin* or the poet; nor was it like the incantations of a magician. Some stories show powerful Qurayshis who remained steadfastly with the opposition being visibly shaken when they listened to a sura. It is as though Muhammad had created an entirely new literary form that some people were not ready for but which thrilled others. Without this experience of the Koran, it is extremely unlikely that Islam would have taken root. We have seen that it took the ancient Israelites some 700 years to break with their old religious allegiances and accept monotheism, but Muhammad managed to help the Arabs achieve this difficult transition in a mere 23 years. Muhammad as poet and prophet and the Koran as text and theophany are surely an unusually striking instance of the deep congruence that exists between art and religion.

During the first years of his mission, Muhammad attracted many converts from the younger generation, who were becoming disillusioned with the capitalistic ethos of Mecca, as well as from underprivileged and marginalized groups, which included women, slaves and members of the weaker clans. At one point, the early sources tell us, it seemed as though the whole of Mecca would accept Muhammad's reformed religion of al-Lah. The richer establishment, who were more than happy with the status quo, understandably held aloof, but there was no formal rupture with the leading Qurayshis until Muhammad forbade the Muslims to worship the pagan gods. For the first three years of his mission it seems that Muhammad did not emphasize the monotheistic content of his mes-

sage, and people probably imagined that they could go on worshipping
the traditional deities of Arabia alongside al-Lah, the High God, as they
always had. But when he condemned these ancient cults as idolatrous,
he lost most of his followers overnight and Islam became a despised and
persecuted minority. We have seen that the belief in only one God demands a painful change of consciousness. Like the early Christians, the
first Muslims were accused of an "atheism" which was deeply threatening
to society. In Mecca, where urban civilization was so novel and must
have seemed a fragile achievement for all the proud self-sufficiency of the
Quraysh, many seem to have felt the same sinking dread and dismay as
those citizens of Rome who had clamored for Christian blood. The
Quraysh seem to have found a rupture with the ancestral gods profoundly
threatening, and it would not be long before Muhammad's own life was
imperiled. Western scholars have usually dated this rupture with the
Quraysh to the possibly apocryphal incident of the Satanic Verses, which
has become notorious since the tragic Salman Rushdie affair. Three of
the Arabian deities were particularly dear to the Arabs of the Hijaz: al-
Lat (whose name simply meant "the Goddess") and al-Uzza (the Mighty
One), who had shrines at Taif and Nakhlah respectively, to the southeast
of Mecca, and Manat, the Fateful One, who had her shrine at Qudayd
on the Red Sea coast. These deities were not fully personalized like Juno
or Pallas Athene. They were often called the *banat al-Lah*, the Daughters
of God, but this does not necessarily imply a fully developed pantheon.
The Arabs used such kinship terms to denote an abstract relationship:
thus *banat al-dahr* (literally, "daughters of fate") simply meant misfortunes
or vicissitudes. The term *banat al-Lah* may simply have signified "divine
beings." These deities were not represented by realistic statues in their
shrines but by large standing stones, similar to those in use among the
ancient Canaanites, which the Arabs worshipped not in any crudely
simplistic way but as a focus of divinity. Like Mecca with its Kabah, the
shrines at Taif, Nakhlah and Qudayd had become essential spiritual
landmarks in the emotional landscape of the Arabs. Their forefathers had
worshipped there from time immemorial, and this gave a healing sense
of continuity.

The story of the Satanic Verses is not mentioned either in the Koran
or in any of the early oral or written sources. It is not included in Ibn
Ishaq's *Sira*, the most authoritative biography of the Prophet, but only in
the work of the tenth-century historian Abu Jafar at-Tabari (d. 923). He
tells us that Muhammad was distressed by the rift that had developed
between him and most of his tribe after he had forbidden the cult of the

goddesses and so, inspired by "Satan," he uttered some rogue verses which allowed the *banat al-Lah* to be venerated as intercessors, like the angels. In these so-called "Satanic" verses, the three goddesses were not on a par with al-Lah but were lesser spiritual beings who could intercede with him on behalf of mankind. Later, however, Tabari says that Gabriel told the Prophet that these verses were of "Satanic" origin and should be excised from the Koran to be replaced by these lines which declared that the *banat al-Lah* were mere projections and figments of the imagination:

> Have you, then, ever considered [what you are worshipping in] al-Lat, al-Uzza, as well as [in] Manat, the third and last [of this triad]? . . .
> These [allegedly divine beings] are nothing but empty names which you have invented—you and your forefathers—[and] for which God has bestowed no warrant from on high. They [who worship them] follow nothing but surmise and their own wishful thinking—although right guidance has now indeed come unto them from their Sustainer.[21]

This was the most radical of all the Koranic condemnations of the ancestral pagan gods, and after these verses had been included in the Koran there was no chance of a reconciliation with the Quraysh. From this point, Muhammad became a jealous monotheist, and *shirk* (idolatry; literally, associating other beings with al-Lah) became the greatest sin of Islam.

Muhammad had not made any concession to polytheism in the incident of the Satanic Verses—if, that is, it ever happened. It is also incorrect to imagine that the role of "Satan" meant that the Koran was momentarily tainted by evil: in Islam Satan is a much more manageable character than he became in Christianity. The Koran tells us that he will be forgiven on the Last Day, and Arabs frequently used the word "Shaitan" to allude to a purely human tempter or a natural temptation.[22] The incident may indicate the difficulty Muhammad certainly experienced when he tried to incarnate the ineffable divine message in human speech: it is associated with canonical Koranic verses which suggest that most of the other prophets had made similar "Satanic" slips when they conveyed the divine message but that God always rectified their mistakes and sent down a new and superior revelation in their stead. An alternative and more secular way of looking at this is to see Muhammad revising his work in the light of new insights like any other creative artist. The sources show that Muhammad absolutely refused to compromise with the Quraysh on the matter of idolatry. He was a pragmatic man and would readily make a concession on what he deemed to be inessential, but whenever the Quraysh asked him to adopt a monolatrous solution, allowing them to worship their ancestral gods while he and his Muslims worshipped al-Lah alone, Muhammad vehemently rejected the proposal. As the Koran has it: "I do not worship that which you worship, and neither do you worship that which I worship . . . Unto you your moral law, and, unto me, mine!"[23] The Muslims would surrender to God alone and would not succumb to the false objects of worship—be they deities or values—espoused by the Quraysh.

The perception of God's uniqueness was the basis of the morality of the Koran. To give allegiance to material goods or to put trust in lesser beings was *shirk* (idolatry), the greatest sin of Islam. The Koran pours scorn on the pagan deities in almost exactly the same way as the Jewish scriptures: they are totally ineffective. These gods cannot give food or sustenance; it is no good putting them at the center of one's life because they are powerless. Instead the Muslim must realize that al-Lah is the ultimate and unique reality:

Say: "He is the One God;
God, the Eternal, the Uncaused Cause of all being.
He begets not, and neither is he begotten
and there is nothing that could be compared to him.[24]

Christians like Athanasius had also insisted that only the Creator, the Source of Being, had the power to redeem. They had expressed this insight in the doctrines of the Trinity and the Incarnation. The Koran returns to a Semitic idea of the divine unity and refuses to imagine that God can "beget" a son. There is no deity but al-Lah the Creator of heaven and earth, who alone can save man and send him the spiritual and physical sustenance that he needs. Only by acknowledging him as *as-Samad*, "the Uncaused Cause of all being," would Muslims address a dimension of reality beyond time and history and which would take them beyond the tribal divisions that were tearing their society apart. Muhammad knew that monotheism was inimical to tribalism: a single deity who was the focus of all worship would integrate society as well as the individual.

There is no simplistic notion of God, however. This single deity is not a being like ourselves whom we can know and understand. The phrase *"Allahu Akhbah!"* (God is greater!) that summons Muslims to *salat* distinguishes between God and the rest of reality, as well as between God as he is in himself (*al-Dhat*) and anything that we can say about him. Yet this incomprehensible and inaccessible God had wanted to make himself known. An early tradition (*hadith*) has God say to Muhammad: "I was a hidden treasure; I wanted to be known. Hence, I created the world so that I might be known."[25] By contemplating the signs (*ayat*) of nature and the verses of the Koran, Muslims could glimpse that aspect of divinity which has turned toward the world, which the Koran calls the Face of God (*wajh al-Lah*). Like the two older religions, Islam makes it clear that we only see God in his activities, which adapt his ineffable being to our limited understanding. The Koran urges Muslims to cultivate a perpetual consciousness (*taqwa*) of the Face or the Self of God that surrounds them on all sides: "Wheresoever you turn, there is the Face of al-Lah."[26] Like the Christian Fathers, the Koran sees God as the Absolute, who alone has true existence: "All that lives on earth or in the heavens is bound to pass away: but forever will abide thy Sustainer's Self, full of majesty and glory."[27] In the Koran, God is given ninety-nine names or attributes. These emphasize that he is "greater," the source of all positive qualities that we find in the universe. Thus the world only exists because he is *al-Ghani* (rich and infinite); he is the giver of life (*al-Muhyi*), the knower of all things (*al-Alim*), the producer of speech (*al-Kalimah*): without him, therefore, there would not be life, knowledge or speech. It is an assertion that only God has true existence and positive value. Yet frequently the divine names seem to cancel one another out. Thus God is *al-Qahtar*, he who dominates and who breaks the back of his enemies, and *al-Halim*, the utterly forbearing one; he is *al-Qabid*, he who takes away, and *al-Basit*, he who gives abundantly; *al-Khafid*, he who brings low, and *ar-Rafic*, he who exalts. The Names of God play a central role in Muslim piety: they are recited, counted on rosary beads and chanted as a mantra. All this has reminded Muslims that the God they worship cannot be contained by human categories and refuses simplistic definition.

The first of the "pillars" of Islam would be the Shahadah, the Muslim profession of faith: "I bear witness that there is no god but al-Lah and that Muhammad is his Messenger." This was not simply an affirmation of God's existence but an acknowledgment that al-Lah was the only true reality, the only true form of existence. He was the only true reality, beauty or perfection: all the beings that seem to exist and possess these qualities have them only insofar as they participate in this essential being. To make this assertion demands that Muslims integrate their lives by making God their focus and sole priority. The assertion of the unity of God was not simply a denial that deities like the *banat al-Lah* were worthy of worship. To say that God was One was not a mere numerical definition: it was a call to make that unity the driving factor of one's life and society. The unity of God could be glimpsed in the truly integrated self. But the divine unity also required Muslims to recognize the religious aspirations of others. Because there was only one God, all rightly guided religions must derive from him alone. Belief in the supreme and sole Reality would be culturally conditioned and would be expressed by different societies in different ways, but the focus of all true worship must have been inspired by and directed toward the being whom the Arabs had always called al-Lah. One of the divine names of the Koran is *an-Nur*, the Light. In these famous verses of the Koran, God is the source of all knowledge as well as the means whereby men catch a glimpse of transcendence:

> God is the light of the heavens and the earth. The parable of his light is, as it were (*ka*), that of a niche containing a lamp; the lamp is [enclosed] in glass, the glass [shining] like a radiant star: [a lamp] lit from a blessed tree—an olive tree that is neither of the east nor of the west—the oil whereof [is so bright that it] would well-nigh give light [of itself] even though fire had not touched it: light upon light.[28]

The participle *ka* is a reminder of the essentially symbolic nature of the Koranic discourse about God. *An-Nur*, the Light, is not God himself, therefore, but refers to the enlightenment which he bestows on a particular revelation (the lamp) which shines in the heart of an individual (the niche). The light itself cannot be identified wholly with any one of its bearers but is common to them all. As Muslim commentators pointed out from the very earliest days, light is a particularly good symbol for the divine Reality, which transcends time and space. The image of the olive tree in these verses has been interpreted as an allusion to the continuity of revelation, which springs from one "root" and branches into a multifarious variety of religious experience that cannot be identified with or confined by any one particular tradition or locality: it is neither of the East nor the West.

When the Christian Waraqa ibn Nawfal had acknowledged Muhammad as a true prophet, neither he nor Muhammad expected him to convert to Islam. Muhammad never asked Jews or Christians to convert to his religion of al-Lah unless they particularly wished to do so, because they had received authentic revelations of their own. The Koran did not see revelation as canceling out the messages and insights of previous prophets, but instead it stressed the continuity of the religious experience of mankind. It is important to stress this point because tolerance is not a virtue that many Western people today would feel inclined to attribute to Islam. Yet from the start, Muslims saw revelation in less exclusive terms than either Jews or Christians. The intolerance that many people condemn in Islam today does not always spring from a rival vision of God but from quite another source:[29] Muslims are intolerant of injustice, whether this is committed by rulers of their own—like Shah Muhammad Reza Pahlavi of Iran—or by the powerful Western countries. The Koran does not condemn other religious traditions as false or incomplete but shows each new prophet as confirming and continuing the insights of his predecessors. The Koran teaches that God had sent messengers to every people on the face of the earth: Islamic tradition says there had been 124,000 such prophets, a symbolic number suggesting infinitude. Thus the Koran repeatedly points out that it is not bringing a message that is essentially new and that Muslims must emphasize their kinship with the older religions:

> Do not argue with the followers of earlier revelation otherwise than in the most kindly manner—unless it be such of them as are set on evil doing—and say: "We believe in that which has been bestowed upon us, as well as that which has been bestowed upon you: for our God and your God is one and the same, and it is unto him that we [all] surrender ourselves."[30]

The Koran naturally singles out apostles who were familiar to the Arabs— like Abraham, Noah, Moses and Jesus, who were the prophets of the Jews and Christians. It also mentions Hud and Salih, who had been sent to the ancient Arab peoples of Midian and Thamood. Today Muslims insist that if Muhammad had known about Hindus and Buddhists, he would have included their religious sages: after his death they were allowed full religious liberty in the Islamic empire, like the Jews and Christians. On the same principle, Muslims argue, the Koran would also have honored the shamans and holy men of the American Indians or the Australian aborigines.

Muhammad's belief in the continuity of the religious experience was soon put to the test. After the rift with the Quraysh, life became impossible for the Muslims in Mecca. The slaves and freedmen who had no tribal protection were persecuted so severely that some died under the treatment, and Muhammad's own clan of Hashim were boycotted in an attempt to starve them into submission: the privation probably caused the death of his beloved wife, Khadija. Eventually Muhammad's own life would be in danger. The pagan Arabs of the northern settlement of Yathrib had invited the Muslims to abandon their clan and to emigrate there. This was an absolutely unprecedented step for an Arab: the tribe had been the sacred value of Arabia and such a defection violated essential principles. Yathrib had been torn by apparently incurable warfare between its various tribal groups, and many of the pagans were ready to accept Islam as a spiritual and political solution to the problems of the oasis. There were three large Jewish tribes in the settlement, and they had prepared the minds of the pagans for monotheism. This meant that they were not as offended as the Quraysh by the denigration of the Arabian deities. Accordingly during the summer of 622, about seventy Muslims and their families set off for Yathrib.

In the year before the *hijra* or migration to Yathrib (or Medina, the City, as the Muslims would call it), Muhammad had adapted his religion to bring it closer to Judaism as he understood it. After so many years of working in isolation he must have been looking forward to living with members of an older, more established tradition. Thus he prescribed a fast for Muslims on the Jewish Day of Atonement and commanded Muslims to pray three times a day like the Jews, instead of only twice as hitherto. Muslims could marry Jewish women and should observe some of the dietary laws. Above all, Muslims must now pray facing Jerusalem like the Jews and Christians. The Jews of Medina were at first prepared to give Muhammad a chance: life had become intolerable in the oasis, and like many of the committed pagans of Medina they were ready to give him the benefit of the doubt, especially since he seemed so positively inclined toward their faith. Eventually, however, they turned against Muhammad and joined those pagans who were hostile to the newcomers from Mecca. The Jews had sound religious reasons for their rejection: they believed that the era of prophecy was over. They were expecting a Messiah, but no Jew or Christian at this stage would have believed that they were prophets. Yet they were also motivated by political considerations: in the old days, they had gained power in the oasis by throwing in their lot with one or the other warring Arab tribe. Muhammad, however, had joined both these tribes with the Quraysh in the new Muslim *ummah*, a kind of super-tribe of which the Jews were also members. As they saw their position in Medina decline, the Jews became antagonistic. They used to assemble in the mosque "to listen to the stories of the Muslims and laugh and scoff at their religion."[31] It was very easy for them, with their superior knowledge of scripture, to pick holes in the stories of the

Koran—some of which differed markedly from the biblical version. They also jeered at Muhammad's pretensions, saying that it was very odd that a man who claimed to be a prophet could not even find his camel when it went missing.

Muhammad's rejection by the Jews was probably the greatest disappointment in his life, and it called his whole religious position into question. But some of the Jews were friendly and seem to have joined the Muslims in an honorary capacity. They discussed the Bible with him and showed him how to rebuff the criticisms of other Jews, and this new knowledge of scripture also helped Muhammad to develop his own insights. For the first time Muhammad learned the exact chronology of the prophets, about which he had previously been somewhat hazy. He could now see that it was very important that Abraham had lived before either Moses or Jesus. Hitherto Muhammad probably thought that Jews and Christians both belonged to one religion, but now he learned that they had serious disagreements with one another. To outsiders like the Arabs there seemed little to choose between the two positions, and it seemed logical to imagine that the followers of the Torah and the Gospel had introduced inauthentic elements into the *hanifiyyah*, the pure religion of Abraham, such as the Oral Law elaborated by the Rabbis and the blasphemous doctrine of the Trinity. Muhammad also learned that in their own scriptures the Jews were called a faithless people, who had turned to idolatry to worship the Golden Calf. The polemic against the Jews in the Koran is well developed and shows how threatened the Muslims must have felt by the Jewish rejection, even though the Koran still insists that not all "the people of earlier revelation"[32] have fallen into error and that essentially all religions are one.

From the friendly Jews of Medina, Muhammad also learned the story of Ishmael, Abraham's elder son. In the Bible, Abraham had had a son by his concubine Hagar, but when Sarah had borne Isaac she had become jealous and demanded that he get rid of Hagar and Ishmael. To comfort Abraham, God promised that Ishmael would also be the father of a great nation. The Arabian Jews had added some local legends of their own, saying that Abraham had left Hagar and Ishmael in the valley of Mecca, where God had taken care of them, revealing the sacred spring of Zamzam when the child was dying of thirst. Later Abraham had visited Ishmael and together father and son had built the Kabah, the first temple of the one God. Ishmael had become the father of the Arabs, so, like the Jews, they too were sons of Abraham. This must have been music to Muhammad's ears: he was bringing the Arabs their own scripture and now he could root their faith in the piety of their ancestors. In January 624, when it was clear that the hostility of the Medinan Jews was permanent, the new religion of al-Lah declared its independence. Muhammad commanded the Muslims to pray facing Mecca instead of Jerusalem. This changing of the direction of prayer (*qibla*) has been called Muhammad's most creative religious gesture. By prostrating themselves in the direction of the Kabah, which was independent of the two older revelations, Muslims were tacitly declaring that they belonged to no established religion but were surrendering themselves to God alone. They were not joining a sect that impiously divided the religion of the one God into warring groups. Instead they were returning to the primordial religion of Abraham, who had been the first *muslim* to surrender to God and who had built his holy house:

> And they say, "Be Jews"—or "Christians"—"and you shall be on the right path." Say: "nay, but [ours is] the creed of Abraham, who turned away from all that is false and was not of those who ascribe divinity to aught beside God."
>
> Say: "We believe in God and in that which had been bestowed from on high upon us, and in that which has been bestowed upon Abraham and Ishmael and Isaac and Jacob and their descendants, and that which has been vouchsafed to Moses and Jesus, and that which has been vouchsafed to all the [other] prophets by their Sustainer: we make no distinction between any of them. And it is unto him that we surrender ourselves."[33]

It was, surely, idolatry to prefer a merely human interpretation of the truth to God himself.

Muslims date their era not from the birth of Muhammad nor from the year of the first revelations—there was, after all, nothing new about these—but from the year of the *hijra* (the migration to Medina) when Muslims began to implement the divine plan in history by making Islam a political reality. We have seen that the Koran teaches that all religious people have a duty to work for a just and equal society, and Muslims have taken their political vocation very seriously indeed. Muhammad had not intended to become a political leader at the outset, but events that he could not have foreseen had pushed him toward an entirely new political solution for the Arabs. During the ten years between the *hijra* and his death in 632 Muhammad and his first Muslims were engaged in a desperate struggle for survival against his opponents in Medina and the Quraysh of Mecca, all of whom were ready to exterminate the *ummah*. In the West,

Muhammad has often been presented as a warlord, who imposed Islam on a reluctant world by force of arms. The reality was quite different. Muhammad was fighting for his life, was evolving a theology of the just war in the Koran with which most Christians would agree, and never forced anybody to convert to his religion. Indeed the Koran is clear that there is to be "no compulsion in religion." In the Koran war is held to be abhorrent; the only just war is a war of self-defense. Sometimes it is necessary to fight in order to preserve decent values, as Christians believed it necessary to fight against Hitler. Muhammad had political gifts of a very high order. By the end of his life most of the Arabian tribes had joined the *ummah*, even though, as Muhammad well knew, their *islām* was either nominal or superficial for the most part. In 630 the city of Mecca opened its gates to Muhammad, who was able to take it without bloodshed. In 632, shortly before his death, he made what has been called the Farewell Pilgrimage, in which he Islamized the old Arabian pagan rites of the *hajj* and made this pilgrimage, which was so dear to the Arabs, the fifth "pillar" of his religion.

All Muslims have a duty to make the *hajj* at least once in a lifetime if their circumstances permit. Naturally the pilgrims remember Muhammad, but the rites have been interpreted to remind them of Abraham, Hagar and Ishmael rather than their prophet. These rites look bizarre to an outsider—as do any alien social or religious rituals—but they are able to unleash an intense religious experience and perfectly express the communal and personal aspects of Islamic spirituality. Today many of the thousands of pilgrims who assemble at the appointed time in Mecca are not Arabs, but they have been able to make the ancient Arabic ceremonies their own. As they converge on the Kabah, clad in the traditional pilgrim dress that obliterates all distinctions of race or class, they feel that they have been liberated from the egotistic preoccupations of their daily lives and been caught up into a community that has one focus and orientation. They cry in unison, "Here I am at your service, O al-Lah," before they begin the circumambulations around the shrine. The essential meaning of this rite is brought out well by the late Iranian philosopher Ali Shariati:

> As you circumambulate and move closer to the Kabah, you feel like a small stream merging with a big river. Carried by a wave you lose touch with the ground. Suddenly, you are floating, carried on by the flood. As you approach the centre, the pressure of the crowd squeezes you so hard that you are given a new life. You are now

part of the People; you are now a Man, alive and eternal. . . . The Kabah is the world's sun whose face attracts you into its orbit. You have become part of this universal system. Circumambulating around Al-lah, you will soon forget yourself. . . . You have been transformed into a particle that is gradually melting and disappearing. This is absolute love at its peak.[34]

Jews and Christians have also emphasized the spirituality of community. The *hajj* offers each individual Muslim the experience of a personal integration in the context of the *ummah*, with God at its center. As in most religions, peace and harmony are important pilgrimage themes, and once the pilgrims have entered the sanctuary violence of any kind is forbidden. Pilgrims may not even kill an insect or speak a harsh word. Hence the outrage throughout the Muslim world during the *hajj* of 1987, when Iranian pilgrims instigated a riot in which 402 people were killed and 649 injured.

Muhammad died unexpectedly after a short illness in June 632. After his death, some of the Bedouin tried to break away from the *ummah*, but the political unity of Arabia held firm. Eventually the recalcitrant tribes also accepted the religion of the one God: Muhammad's astonishing success had shown the Arabs that the paganism which had served them well for centuries no longer worked in the modern world. The religion of al-Lah introduced the compassionate ethos which was the hallmark of the more advanced religions: brotherhood and social justice were its crucial virtues. A strong egalitarianism would continue to characterize the Islamic ideal.

During Muhammad's lifetime, this had included the equality of the sexes. Today it is common in the West to depict Islam as an inherently misogynistic religion, but, like Christianity, the religion of al-Lah was originally positive for women. During the *jahiliyyah*, the pre-Islamic period, Arabia had preserved the attitudes toward women which had prevailed before the Axial Age. Polygamy, for example, was common, and wives remained in their father's households. Elite women enjoyed considerable power and prestige—Muhammad's first wife, Khadija, for example, was a successful merchant—but the majority were on a par with slaves; they had no political or human rights, and female infanticide was common. Women had been among Muhammad's earliest converts, and their emancipation was a project that was dear to his heart. The Koran strictly forbade the killing of female children and rebuked the Arabs for their dismay when a girl was born. It also gave women legal rights of inheritance and divorce: most Western women had nothing comparable until the nineteenth century. Muhammad encouraged women to play an active role in the affairs of the *ummah*, and they expressed their views forthrightly, confident that they would be heard. On one occasion, for example, the women of Medina had complained to the Prophet that the men were outstripping them in the study of the Koran and asked him to help them catch up. This Muhammad did. One of their most important questions was why the Koran addressed men only when women had also made their surrender to God. The result was a revelation that addressed women as well as men and emphasized the absolute moral and spiritual equality of the sexes.[35] Thereafter the Koran quite frequently addressed women explicitly, something that rarely happens in either the Jewish or Christian scriptures.

Unfortunately, as in Christianity, the religion was later hijacked by the men, who interpreted texts in a way that was negative for Muslim women. The Koran does not prescribe the veil for all women but only for Muhammad's wives, as a mark of their status. Once Islam had taken its place in the civilized world, however, Muslims adopted those customs of the Oikumene which relegated women to second-class status. They adopted the customs of veiling women and secluding them in harems from Persia and Christian Byzantium, where women had long been marginalized in this way. By the time of the Abbasid caliphate (750–1258), the position of Muslim women was as bad as that of their sisters in Jewish and Christian society. Today Muslim feminists urge their menfolk to return to the original spirit of the Koran.

This reminds us that, like any other faith, Islam could be interpreted in a number of different ways; consequently it evolved its own sects and divisions. The first of these—that between the Sunnah and Shiah—was prefigured in the struggle for the leadership after Muhammad's sudden death. Abu Bakr, Muhammad's close friend, was elected by the majority, but some believed that he would have wanted Ali ibn Abi Talib, his cousin and son-in-law, to be his successor (*kalipha*). Ali himself accepted Abu Bakr's leadership, but during the next few years he seems to have been the focus of the loyalty of dissidents who disapproved of the policies of the first three caliphs: Abu Bakr, Umar ibn al-Khattab and Uthman ibn Affan. Finally Ali became the fourth caliph in 656: the Shiah would eventually call him the first Imam or Leader of the *ummah*. Concerned with the leadership, the split between Sunnis and Shiis was political rather than doctrinal, and this heralded the importance of politics in Muslim religion, including its conception of God. The *Shiah-i-Ali* (the

Partisans of Ali) remained a minority and would develop a piety of protest, typified by the tragic figure of Muhammad's grandson Husayn ibn Ali, who refused to accept the Ummayads (who had seized the caliphate after the death of his father Ali) and was killed with his small band of supporters by the Ummayad Caliph Yazid in 680 on the plain of Karbala, near Kufa in modern Iraq. All Muslims regard the immoral slaughter of Husayn with horror, but he has become a particular hero of the Shiah, a reminder that it is sometimes necessary to fight tyranny to the death. By this time, the Muslims had begun to establish their empire. The first four caliphs had been concerned only to spread Islam among the Arabs of the Byzantine and Persian empires, which were both in a state of decline. Under the Ummayads, however, the expansion continued into Asia and North Africa, inspired not by religion so much as by Arab imperialism.

Nobody in the new empire was forced to accept the Islamic faith; indeed, for a century after Muhammad's death, conversion was not encouraged and, in about 700, was actually forbidden by law: Muslims believed that Islam was for the Arabs as Judaism was for the sons of Jacob. As the "people of the book" (*ahl al-kitab*), Jews and Christians were granted religious liberty as *dhimmis*, protected minority groups. When the Abbasid caliphs began to encourage conversion, many of the Semitic and Aryan peoples in their empire were eager to accept the new religion. The success of Islam was as formative as the failure and humiliation of Jesus have been in Christianity. Politics is not extrinsic to a Muslim's personal religious life, as in Christianity, which mistrusts mundane success. Muslims regard themselves as committed to implementing a just society in accord with God's will. The *ummah* has sacramental importance, as a "sign" that God has blessed this endeavor to redeem humanity from oppression and injustice; its political health holds much the same place in a Muslim's spirituality as a particular theological option (Catholic, Protestant, Methodist, Baptist) in the life of a Christian. If Christians find the Muslims' regard for politics strange, they should reflect that their passion for abstruse theological debate seems equally bizarre to Jews and Muslims.

In the early years of Islamic history, therefore, speculation about the nature of God often sprang from a political concern about the state of the caliphate and the establishment. Learned debates about who and what manner of man should lead the *ummah* proved to be as formative in Islam as debates about the person and nature of Jesus in Christianity. After the period of the *rashidun* (the first four "rightly guided" caliphs), Muslims found that they were living in a world very different from the small, embattled society of Medina. They were now masters of an expanding empire, and their leaders seemed motivated by worldliness and greed. There were a luxury and corruption among the aristocracy and in the court that were very different from the austere lives led by the Prophet and his companions. The most pious Muslims challenged the establishment with the socialist message of the Koran and tried to make Islam relevant to the new conditions. A number of different solutions and sects emerged.

The most popular solution was found by legists and traditionists who attempted to return to the ideals of Muhammad and the *rashidun*. This resulted in the formation of the Shariah law, a code similar to the Torah which was based on the Koran and the life and maxims of the Prophet. A bewildering number of oral traditions were in circulation about the words (*hadith*) and practice (*sunnah*) of Muhammad and his early companions, and these were collected during the eighth and ninth centuries by a number of editors, the most famous of whom were Muhammad ibn Ismail al-Bukhari and Muslim ibn al-Hijjaj al-Qushayri. Because Muhammad was believed to have surrendered perfectly to God, Muslims were to imitate him in their daily lives. Thus by imitating the way Muhammad spoke, loved, ate, washed and worshipped, the Islamic Holy Law helped Muslims to live a life that was open to the divine. By modeling themselves on the Prophet, they hoped to acquire his interior receptivity to God. Thus when Muslims follow a *sunnah* by greeting one another with the words "*Salaam alaykum*" (Peace be with you) as Muhammad used to do, when they are kind to animals, to orphans and the poor as he was and are generous and reliable in their dealings with others, they are reminded of God. The external gestures are not to be regarded as ends in themselves but as a means of acquiring *taqwa*, the "God-consciousness" prescribed by the Koran and practiced by the Prophet, which consists of a constant remembrance of God (*dhikr*). There has been much debate about the validity of the *sunnah* and *hadith*: some are regarded as more authentic than others. But ultimately the question of the historical validity of these traditions is less important than the fact that they have worked: they have proved able to bring a sacramental sense of the divine into the lives of millions of Muslims over the centuries.

The *hadith* or collected maxims of the Prophet are mostly concerned with everyday matters but also with metaphysics, cosmology and theology. A number of these sayings are believed to have been spoken by God himself to Muhammad. These *hadith qudsi* (sacred traditions) emphasize God's immanence and presence in the believer: one famous *hadith*, for example, lists the stages whereby a Muslim apprehends a divine presence which seems almost incarnate in the believer: you begin by observing the commandments of the Koran and Shariah and then progress to voluntary acts of piety:

> My servant draws near to me by means of nothing dearer to me than that which I have established as a duty to him. And my servant continues drawing nearer to me through supererogatory acts until I love him: and when I love him, I become his ear through which he hears, his eye with which he sees, his hand with which he grasps and his foot whereon he walks.[36]

As in Judaism and Christianity, the transcendent God is also an immanent presence encountered here below. The Muslims could cultivate a sense of this divine presence by methods very similar to those discovered by the two older religions.

The Muslims who promoted this type of piety based on the imitation of Muhammad are generally known as the *ahl al-hadith*, the Traditionists. They appealed to the ordinary people, because theirs was a fiercely egalitarian ethic. They opposed the luxury of the Ummayad and Abbasid courts but were not in favor of the revolutionary tactics of the Shiah. They did not believe that the caliph need have exceptional spiritual qualities: he was simply an administrator. Yet by stressing the divine nature of the Koran and the *sunnah*, they provided each Muslim with the means of direct contact with God that was potentially subversive and highly critical of absolute power. There was no need for a caste of priests to act as mediators. Each Muslim was responsible before God for his or her own fate.

Above all, the Traditionists taught that the Koran was an eternal reality which, like the Torah or the Logos, was somehow of God himself; it had dwelt in his mind from before the beginning of time. Their doctrine of the uncreated Koran meant that when it was recited, Muslims could hear the invisible God directly. The Koran represented the presence of God in their very midst. His speech was on their lips when they recited its sacred words, and when they held the holy book it was as though they had touched the divine itself. The early Christians had thought of Jesus the man in a similar way:

> Something which has existed since the beginning,
> that we have heard,

and we have seen with our own eyes;
that we have watched
and touched with our hands;
the Word, who is life—
this is our subject.[37]

The exact status of Jesus, the Word, had greatly exercised Christians. Now Muslims would begin to debate the nature of the Koran: in what sense was the Arabic text really the Word of God? Some Muslims found this elevation of the Koran as blasphemous as those Christians who had been scandalized by the idea that Jesus had been the incarnate Logos.

The Shiah, however, gradually evolved ideas that seemed even closer to Christian Incarnation. After the tragic death of Husayn, Shiis became convinced that only the descendants of his father, Ali ibn Abi Talib, should lead the *ummah*, and they became a distinctive sect within Islam. As his cousin and son-in-law, Ali had a double blood tie with Muhammad. Since none of the Prophet's sons had survived infancy, Ali was his chief male relative. In the Koran, prophets often ask God to bless their descendants. The Shiis extended this notion of divine blessing and came to believe that only members of Muhammad's family through the house of Ali had true knowledge (*ilm*) of God. They alone could provide the *ummah* with divine guidance. If a descendant of Ali came to power, Muslims could look forward to a golden age of justice, and the *ummah* would be led according to God's will.

The enthusiasm for the person of Ali would develop in some surprising ways. Some of the more radical Shii groups would elevate Ali and his descendants to a position above that of Muhammad himself and give them near-divine status. They were drawing on ancient Persian tradition of a chosen god-begotten family which transmitted the divine glory from one generation to another. By the end of the Ummayad period, some Shiis had come to believe that the authoritative *ilm* was retained in one particular line of Ali's descendants. Muslims would only find the person designated by God as the true Imam (leader) of the *ummah* in this family. Whether he was in power or not, his guidance was absolutely necessary, so every Muslim had a duty to look for him and accept his leadership. Since these Imams were seen as a focus of disaffection, the caliphs regarded them as enemies of state: according to Shii tradition, several of the Imams were poisoned and some had to go into hiding. When each Imam died, he would choose one of his relatives to inherit the *ilm*. Gradually the Imams were revered as *avatars* of the divine: each one had been a "proof" (*hujjah*) of God's presence on earth and, in some mysterious sense, made the divine incarnate in a human being. His words, decisions and commands were God's. As Christians had seen Jesus as the Way, the Truth and the Light that would lead men to God, Shiis revered their Imams as the gateway (*bab*) to God, the road (*sabil*) and the guide of each generation.

The various branches of the Shiah traced the divine succession differently. "Twelver Shiis," for example, venerated twelve descendants of Ali through Husayn, until in 939 the last Imam went into hiding and disappeared from human society; since he had no descendants, the line died out. The Ismailis, known as the Seveners, believed that the seventh of these Imams had been the last. A messianic strain appeared among the Twelvers, who believed that the Twelfth or Hidden Imam would return to inaugurate a golden age. These were obviously dangerous ideas. Not only were they politically subversive, but they could easily be interpreted in a crude, simplistic way. The more extreme Shiis developed an esoteric tradition, therefore, based on a symbolic interpretation of the Koran, as we shall see in the next chapter. Their piety was too abstruse for most Muslims, who regarded this incarnational idea as blasphemous, so Shiis were usually found among the more aristocratic classes and the intellectuals. Since the Iranian revolution, we have tended in the West to depict Shiism as an inherently fundamentalist sect of Islam, but that is an inaccurate assessment. Shiism became a sophisticated tradition. In fact, Shiis had much in common with those Muslims who attempted to apply rational arguments systematically to the Koran. These rationalists, known as Mutazilis, formed their own distinctive group; they also had a firm political commitment: like the Shiis, Mutazilis were highly critical of the luxury of the court and were frequently politically active against the establishment.

The political question inspired a theological debate about God's government of human affairs. Supporters of the Ummayads had rather disingenuously claimed that their un-Islamic behavior was not their fault because they had been predestined by God to be the kind of people they were. The Koran has a very strong conception of God's absolute omnipotence and omniscience, and many texts could be used to support this view of predestination. But the Koran is equally emphatic about human responsibility: "Verily, God does not change men's condition unless they change their inner selves." Consequently the critics of the establishment stressed free will and moral responsibility. The Mutazilis took a middle road and withdrew (*i'tazahu*, to stand aloof) from an extreme position. They defended free will in order to safeguard the ethical nature of humanity. Muslims who believed that God was above mere human notions of right and wrong were decrying his justice. A God who violated all decent principles and got away with it simply because he was God would be a monster, no better than a tyrannical caliph. Like the Shiis, the Mutazilis declared that justice was of the essence of God: he *could* not wrong anybody; he *could* not enjoin anything contrary to reason.

Here they came into conflict with the Traditionists, who argued that by making man the author and creator of his own fate, the Mutazilis were insulting the omnipotence of God. They complained that the Mutazilis were making God *too* rational and too like a man. They adopted the doctrine of predestination in order to emphasize God's essential incomprehensibility: if we claimed to understand him, he could not be God but was a mere human projection. God transcended mere human notions of good and evil and could not be tied down to our standards and expectations: an act was evil or unjust because God had decreed it to be so, not because these human values had a transcendent dimension binding upon God himself. The Mutazilis were wrong to say that justice, a purely human ideal, was of the essence of God. The problem of predestination and free will, which has also exercised Christians, indicates a central difficulty in the idea of a personal God. An impersonal God, such as Brahman, can more easily be said to exist beyond "good" and "evil," which are regarded as masks of the inscrutable divinity. But a God who is in some mysterious way a person and who takes an active part in human history lays himself open to criticism. It is all too easy to make this "God" a larger-than-life tyrant or judge and make "him" fulfill our expectations. We can turn "God" into a Republican or a socialist, a racist or a revolutionary according to our personal views. The danger of this has led some to see a personal God as an unreligious idea, because it simply embeds us in our own prejudice and makes our human ideas absolute.

To avoid this danger, the Traditionists came up with the time-honored distinction, used by both Jews and Christians, between God's essence and his activities. They claimed that some of those attributes which enabled the transcendent God to relate to the world—such as power, knowledge, will, hearing, sight and speech, which are all attributed to al-Lah in the Koran—had existed with him from all eternity in much the same way as the uncreated Koran. They were distinct from God's unknowable essence, which would always elude our understanding. Just as Jews had imagined that God's Wisdom or the Torah had existed with

God from before the beginning of time, Muslims were now developing a similar idea to account for the personality of God and to remind Muslims that he could not be wholly contained by the human mind. Had not the Caliph al-Mamum (813–832) sided with the Mutazilis and attempted to make their ideas official Muslim doctrine, this abstruse argument would probably have affected a mere handful of people. But when the caliph began to torture the Traditionists in order to impose the Mutazili belief, the ordinary folk were horrified by this un-Islamic behavior. Ahmad ibn Hanbal (780–855), a leading Traditionist who narrowly escaped death in al-Mamun's inquisition, became a popular hero. His sanctity and charisma—he had prayed for his torturers—challenged the caliphate, and his belief in the uncreated Koran became the watchword of a populist revolt against the rationalism of the Mutazilah.

Ibn Hanbal refused to countenance any kind of rational discussion about God. Thus when the moderate Mutazili al-Huayan al-Karabisi (d. 859) put forward a compromise solution—that the Koran considered as God's speech was indeed uncreated but that when it was put into human words it became a created thing—Ibn Hanbal condemned the doctrine. Al-Karabisi was quite ready to modify his view again, and declared that the written and spoken Arabic of the Koran was *un*created in so far as it partook of God's eternal speech. Ibn Hanbal, however, declared that this was unlawful too because it was useless and dangerous to speculate about the origin of the Koran in this rationalistic way. Reason was not an appropriate tool for exploring the unutterable God. He accused the Mutazilis of draining God of all mystery and making him an abstract formula that had no religious value. When the Koran used anthropomorphic terms to describe God's activity in the world or when it said that God "speaks" and "sees" and "sits upon his throne," Ibn Hanbal insisted that it be interpreted literally but "without asking how" (*bila kayf*). He can perhaps be compared to radical Christians like Athanasius, who insisted on an extreme interpretation of the doctrine of Incarnation against the more rational heretics. Ibn Hanbal was stressing the essential ineffability of the divine, which lay beyond the reach of all logic and conceptual analysis.

Yet the Koran constantly emphasizes the importance of intelligence and understanding, and Ibn Hanbal's position was somewhat simpleminded. Many Muslims found it perverse and obscurantist. A compromise was found by Abu al-Hasan ibn Ismail al-Ashari (878–941). He had been a Mutazili but was converted to Traditionism by a dream in which the

Prophet had appeared to him and urged him to study *hadith*. Al-Ashari then went to the other extreme, became an ardent Traditionist and preached against the Mutazilah as the scourge of Islam. Then he had another dream, in which Muhammad looked rather irritated and said: "I did not tell you to give up rational arguments but to support the true *hadiths*!"[38] Henceforth al-Ashari used the rationalist techniques of the Mutazilah to promote the agnostic spirit of Ibn Hanbal. Where the Mutazilis claimed that God's revelation could not be unreasonable, al-Ashari used reason and logic to show that God was beyond our understanding. The Mutazilis had been in danger of reducing God to a coherent but arid concept; al-Ashari wanted to return to the full-blooded God of the Koran, despite its inconsistency. Indeed, like Denys the Areopagite, he believed that paradox would enhance our appreciation of God. He refused to reduce God to a concept that could be discussed and analyzed like any other human idea. The divine attributes of knowledge, power, life and so on were real; they *had* belonged to God from all eternity. But they were distinct from God's essence, because God was essentially one, simple and unique. He could not be regarded as a complex being because he was simplicity itself; we could not analyze him by defining his various characteristics or splitting him up into smaller parts. Al-Ashari refused any attempt to resolve the paradox: thus he insisted that when the Koran says that God "sits on his throne," we must accept that this is a fact even though it is beyond our understanding to conceive of a pure spirit "sitting."

Al-Ashari was trying to find a middle course between deliberate obscurantism and extreme rationalism. Some literalists claimed that if the blessed were going to "see" God in heaven, as the Koran said, he must have a physical appearance. Hisham ibn Hakim went so far as to say that:

> Allah has a body, defined, broad, high and long, of equal dimensions, radiating with light, of a broad measure in its three dimensions, in a place beyond place, like a bar of pure metal, shining as a round pearl on all sides, provided with color, taste, smell and touch.[39]

Some Shiis accepted such views, because of their belief that the Imams were incarnations of the divine. The Mutazilis insisted that when the Koran speaks of God's "hands," for example, this must be interpreted allegorically to refer to his generosity and munificence. Al-Ashari opposed the literalists by pointing out that the Koran insisted that we could talk about God only in symbolic language. But he also opposed the Traditionist wholesale rejection of reason. He argued that Muhammad had not encountered these problems or he would have given the Muslims guidance; as it was, all Muslims had a duty to use such interpretive tools as analogy (*qiyas*) to retain a truly religious concept of God.

Constantly al-Ashari opted for a compromise position. Thus he argued that the Koran was the eternal and uncreated Word of God but that the ink, paper and Arabic words of the sacred text were created. He condemned the Mutazili doctrine of free will, because God alone could be the "creator" of man's deeds, but he also opposed the Traditionist view that men did not contribute at all to their salvation. His solution was somewhat tortuous: God creates the deeds but allows men to acquire merit or discredit for them. Unlike Ibn Hanbal, however, Al-Ashari *was* prepared to ask questions and to explore these metaphysical problems, even though ultimately he concluded that it was wrong to try to contain the mysterious and ineffable reality that we call God in a tidy, rationalistic system. Al-Ashari had founded the Muslim tradition of *Kalam* (literally, "word" or "discourse"), which is usually translated "theology." His successors in the tenth and eleventh centuries refined the methodology of Kalam and developed his ideas. The early Asharites wanted to set up a metaphysical framework for a valid discussion of God's sovereignty. The first major theologian of the Asharite school was Abu Bakr al-Baqillani (d. 1013). In his treatise *al-Tawhid* (Unity), he agreed with the Mutazilah that men could prove the existence of God logically with rational arguments: indeed the Koran itself shows Abraham discovering the eternal Creator by meditating systematically on the natural world. But al-Baqillani denied that we could distinguish between good and evil without a revelation, since these are not natural categories but have been decreed by God: al-Lah is not bound by human notions of what is right or wrong.

Al-Baqillani developed a theory known as "atomism" or "occasionalism" which attempted to find a metaphysical rationale for the Muslim profession of faith: that there was no god, no reality or certainty but al-Lah. He claimed that everything in the world is absolutely dependent upon God's direct attention. The whole universe was reduced to innumerable individual atoms: time and space were discontinuous and nothing had a specific identity of its own. The phenomenal universe was reduced to nothingness by al-Baqillani as radically as it had been by Athanasius. God alone had reality, and only he could redeem us from nothingness. He sustained the universe and summoned his creation into existence at every second. There were no natural laws that explained the survival of the cosmos. Although other Muslims were applying themselves to science with great success, Asharism was fundamentally antagonistic to the natural sciences, yet it had a religious relevance. It was a metaphysical attempt to explain the presence of God in every detail of daily life and a reminder that faith did not depend upon ordinary logic. If used as a discipline rather than a factual account of reality it could help Muslims to develop that God-consciousness prescribed by the Koran. Its weakness lay in the exclusion of the scientific evidence to the contrary and its overliteral interpretation of an essentially elusive religious attitude. It could effect a dislocation between the way a Muslim viewed God and the way he regarded other matters. Both the Mutazilis and the Asharites had attempted, in different ways, to connect the religious experience of God with ordinary rational thought. This was important. Muslims were trying to find out whether it was possible to talk about God as we discuss other matters. We have seen that the Greeks had decided on balance that it was not and that silence was the only appropriate form of theology. Ultimately most Muslims would come to the same conclusion.

Muhammad and his companions had belonged to a far more primitive society than that of al-Baqillani. The Islamic empire had spread to the civilized world, and the Muslims had to confront more intellectually sophisticated ways of regarding God and the world. Muhammad had instinctively relived much in the old Hebrew encounter with the divine, and later generations also had to live through some of the problems encountered by the Christian churches. Some had even resorted to an incarnational theology, despite the Koran's condemnation of the Christian deification of Christ. The Islamic venture shows that the notion of a transcendent yet personal God tends to bring up the same kind of problems and lead to the same type of solutions.

The experiment of Kalam showed that though it was possible to use rational methods to show that "God" was rationally incomprehensible, this would make some Muslims uneasy. Kalam never became as important as theology in Western Christianity. The Abbasid caliphs who had supported the Mutazilah found that they could not impose its doctrines on the faithful because they did not "take." Rationalism continued to influence future thinkers throughout the medieval period, but it remained a minority pursuit, and most Muslims came to distrust the whole enterprise. Like Christianity and Judaism, Islam had emerged from a Semitic experience but had collided with the Greek rationalism in the Hellenic centers of the Middle East. Other Muslims were attempting an even more radical Hellenization of the Islamic God and introduced a new philosophical element into the three monotheistic religions. The three faiths of Judaism, Christianity and Islam would come to different but highly significant conclusions about the validity of philosophy and its relevance to the mystery of God.

6

The God of the Philosophers

URING THE NINTH CENTURY, the Arabs came into contact with Greek science and philosophy, and the result was a cultural florescence which, in European terms, can be seen as a cross between the Renaissance and the Enlightenment. A team of translators, most of whom were Nestorian Christians, made Greek texts available in Arabic and did a brilliant job. Arab Muslims now studied astronomy, alchemy, medicine and mathematics with such success that, during the ninth and tenth centuries, more scientific discoveries had been achieved in the Abbasid empire than in any previous period of history. A new type of Muslim emerged, dedicated to the ideal that he called *Falsafah*. This is usually translated "philosophy" but has a broader, richer meaning: like the French *philosophes* of the eighteenth century, the Faylasufs wanted to live rationally in accordance with the laws that they believed governed the cosmos, which could be discerned at every level of reality. At first, they concentrated on natural science, but then, inevitably, they turned to Greek metaphysics and determined to apply its principles to Islam. They believed that the God of the Greek philosophers was identical with al-Lah. Greek Christians had also felt an affinity with Hellenism but had decided that the God of the Greeks must be modified by the more paradoxical God of the Bible: eventually, as we shall see, they turned their backs on their own philosophical tradition in the belief that reason and logic had little to contribute to the study of God. The Faylasufs, however, came to the opposite conclusion: they believed that rationalism represented the most advanced form of religion and had evolved a higher notion of God than the revealed God of scripture.

Today, we generally see science and philosophy as antagonistic to religion, but the Faylasufs were usually devout men and saw themselves as loyal sons of the Prophet. As good Muslims, they were politically aware, despised the luxury of the court and wanted to reform their society according to the dictates of reason. Their venture was important: since their scientific and philosophic studies were dominated by Greek thought, it was imperative to find a link between their faith and this more rationalistic, objective outlook. It can be most unhealthy to relegate God to a separate intellectual category and to see faith in isolation from other human concerns. The Faylasufs had no intention of abolishing religion, but wanted to purify it of what they regarded as primitive and parochial elements. They had no doubt that God existed—indeed they regarded his existence as self-evident—but felt that it was important to prove this logically in order to show that al-Lah was compatible with their rationalist ideal.

There were problems, however. We have seen that the God of the Greek philosophers was very different from the God of revelation: the Supreme Deity of Aristotle or Plotinus was timeless and impassible; he took no notice of mundane events, did not reveal himself in history, had not created the world and would not judge it at the end of time. Indeed history, the major theophany of the monotheistic faiths, had been dismissed by Aristotle as inferior to philosophy. It had no beginning, middle or end, since the cosmos emanated eternally from God. The Faylasufs wanted to get beyond history, which was a mere illusion, to glimpse the changeless, ideal world of the divine. Despite the emphasis on rationality, Falsafah demanded a faith of its own. It took great courage to believe that the cosmos, where chaos and pain seemed more in evidence than a purposeful order, was really ruled by the principle of reason. They too had to cultivate a sense of an ultimate meaning amid the frequently disastrous and botched events of the world around them. There was a nobility in Falsafah, a search for objectivity and a timeless vision. They wanted a universal religion, which was not limited to a particular manifestation of God or rooted in a definite time and place; they believed that it was their duty to translate the revelation of the Koran into the more advanced idiom developed through the ages by the best and noblest minds in all cultures. Instead of seeing God as a mystery, the Faylasufs believed that he was reason itself.

Such faith in a wholly rational universe seems naive to us today, since our own scientific discoveries have long since revealed the inadequacy of Aristotle's proofs for the existence of God. This perspective was impossible for anybody in the ninth and tenth centuries, but the experience of Falsafah is relevant to our current religious predicament. The scientific revolution of the Abbasid period involved its participants in more than an acquisition of new information. As in our own day, scientific discoveries demanded the cultivation of a different mentality that transformed the way the Faylasufs viewed the world. Science demands the fundamental belief that there is a rational explanation for everything; it also requires an imagination and courage which are not dissimilar to religious creativity. Like the prophet or the mystic, the scientist also forces himself to confront the dark and unpredictable realm of uncreated reality. Inevitably this affected the Faylasufs' perception of God and made them revise and even abandon the older beliefs of their contemporaries. In the same way, the scientific vision of our own day has made much classic theism impossible for many people. To cling to the old theology is not only a failure of nerve but could involve a damaging loss of integrity. The Faylasufs attempted to wed their new insights with mainstream Islamic faith and came up with some revolutionary Greek-inspired ideas about God. Yet the ultimate failure of their rational deity has something important to tell us about the nature of religious truth.

The Faylasufs were attempting a more thoroughgoing merging of Greek philosophy and religion than any previous monotheists. The Mutazilis and the Asharites had both tried to build a bridge between revelation and natural reason but, with them, the God of revelation had come first. Kalam was based on the traditionally monotheistic view of history as a theophany; it argued that concrete, particular events were crucial because they provided the only certainty we had. Indeed, the Asharis doubted that there *were* general laws and timeless principles. Though this atomism had a religious and imaginative value, it was clearly alien to the scientific spirit and could not satisfy the Faylasufs. Their Falsafah discounted history, the concrete and the particular but cultivated a reverence for the general laws that the Asharis rejected. Their God was to be discovered in logical arguments, not in particular revelations at various moments in time to individual men and women. This search for objective, generalized truth characterized their scientific studies and conditioned the way they experienced the ultimate reality. A God who was not the same for everybody, give or take inevitable cultural coloration, could not provide a satisfactory solution to the fundamental religious question: "What is the ultimate meaning of life?" You could not seek scientific solutions that had a universal application in the laboratory and pray to a God who was increasingly regarded by the faithful as the sole possession of the Muslims. Yet the study of the Koran revealed that Muhammad himself had had a universal vision and had insisted that all rightly guided religions came from God. The Faylasufs did not feel that there was any need to jettison the Koran. Instead they tried to show the relationship between the two: both were valid paths to God, suited to the needs of individuals. They saw no fundamental contradiction between revelation and science, rationalism and faith. Instead, they evolved what has been called a prophetic philosophy. They wanted to find the kernel of truth that lay at the heart of all the various historical religions, which, since the dawn of history, had been trying to define the reality of the same God.

Falsafah had been inspired by the encounter with Greek science and metaphysics but was not slavishly dependent upon Hellenism. In their Middle Eastern colonies, the Greeks had tended to follow a standard curriculum, so that though there were different emphases in Hellenistic philosophy, each student was expected to read a set of texts in a particular order. This had led to a degree of unity and coherence. However, the Faylasufs did not observe this curriculum, but read the texts as they became available. This inevitably opened up new perspectives. Besides their own distinctively Islamic and Arab insights, their thinking was also affected by Persian, Indian and Gnostic influence.

Thus Yaqub ibn Ishaq al-Kindi (d. ca. 870), the first Muslim to apply the rational method to the Koran, was closely associated with the Muta-zilis and disagreed with Aristotle on several major issues. He had been educated at Basra but settled in Baghdad, where he enjoyed the patronage of the Caliph al-Mamun. His output and influence were immense, including mathematics, science and philosophy. But his chief concern was religion. With his Mutazili background, he could only see philosophy as the handmaid of revelation: the inspired knowledge of the prophets had always transcended the merely human insights of the philosophers. Most later Faylasufs would not share this perspective. Al-Kindi was also anxious to seek out the truth in other religious traditions, however. Truth was one, and it was the task of the philosopher to search for it in whatever cultural or linguistic garments it had assumed over the centuries.

> We should not be ashamed to acknowledge truth and to assimilate it from whatever source it comes to us, even if it is brought to us by former generations and foreign peoples. For him who seeks the truth there is nothing of higher value than truth itself; it never cheapens or debases him who reaches for it but ennobles and honors him.[1]

Here al-Kindi was in line with the Koran. But he went further, since he did not confine himself to the prophets but also turned to the Greek philosophers. He used Aristotle's arguments for the existence of a Prime Mover. In a rational world, he argued, everything had a cause. There must, therefore, be an Unmoved Mover to start the ball rolling. This First Principle was Being itself, unchangeable, perfect and indestructible. But having reached this conclusion, al-Kindi departed from Aristotle by adhering to the Koranic doctrine of creation *ex nihilo*. Action can be defined as the bringing of something out of nothing. This, al-Kindi maintained, was God's prerogative. He is the only Being who can truly act in this sense, and it is he who is the real cause of all the activity that we see in the world around us.

Falsafah came to reject creation *ex nihilo*, so al-Kindi cannot really be described as a true Faylasuf. But he was a pioneer in the Islamic attempt to harmonize religious truth with systematic metaphysics. His successors were more radical. Thus Abu Bakr Muhammad ibn Zakaria ar-Razi (d. ca. 930), who has been described as the greatest nonconformist in Muslim history, rejected Aristotle's metaphysics and, like the Gnostics, saw the creation as the work of a demiurge: matter could not have proceeded from a wholly spiritual God. He also rejected the Aristotelian solution of a Prime Mover, as well as the Koranic doctrines of revelation and prophecy. Only reason and philosophy could save us. Ar-Razi was not really a monotheist, therefore: he was perhaps the first freethinker to find the concept of God incompatible with a scientific outlook. He was a brilliant physician and a kindly, generous man, who worked for years as the head of the hospital of his native Rayy in Iran. Most Faylasufs did not take their rationalism to such an extreme. In a debate with a more conventional Muslim, he argued that no true Faylasuf could rely on an established tradition, but had to think things through for himself, since reason alone could lead us to truth. Reliance on revealed doctrines was useless because the religions could not agree. How could anybody tell which one was correct? But his opponent—who, rather confusingly, was also called ar-Razi[2]—made an important point. What about the common people? he asked. Most of them were quite incapable of philosophic thought: were they therefore lost, doomed to error and confusion? One of the reasons that Falsafah remained a minority sect in Islam was its elitism. It necessarily only appealed to those with a certain IQ and was thus against the egalitarian spirit that was beginning to characterize Muslim society.

The Turkish Faylasuf Abu Nasr al-Farabi (d. 980) dealt with the problem of the uneducated masses, who were not capable of philosophic rationalism. He can be regarded as the founder of authentic Falsafah and showed the attractive universality of this Muslim ideal. Al-Farabi was what we would call a Renaissance Man; he was not only a physician but also a musician and a mystic. In his *Opinions of the Inhabitants of a Virtuous City*, he also demonstrated the social and political concern that were central to Muslim spirituality. In the *Republic*, Plato had argued that a good society must be led by a philosopher who ruled according to rational principles, which he was able to put across to the ordinary people. Al-Farabi maintained that the Prophet Muhammad had been exactly the kind of ruler that Plato had envisaged. He had expressed the timeless truths in an imaginative form that the people could understand, so Islam was ideally suited to create Plato's ideal society. The Shiah was perhaps the form of Islam best suited to carry out this project, because of its cult of the wise Imam. Even though he was a practicing Sufi, al-Farabi saw revelation as a wholly natural process. The God of the Greek philosophers, who was remote from human concerns, could not possibly "talk to" human beings and interfere in mundane events, as the traditional doctrine of revelation implied. That did not mean that God was remote from al-Farabi's main concerns, however. God was central to his philosophy, and his treatise began with a discussion of God. This was the God of Aristotle and Plotinus, however: he was the First of all beings. A Greek Christian brought up on the mystical philosophy of Denys the Areopagite would have objected to a theory that simply made God another being, albeit of a superior nature. But al-Farabi stayed close to Aristotle. He did not believe that God had "suddenly" decided to create the world. That would have involved the eternal and static God in unseemly change.

Like the Greeks, al-Farabi saw the chain of being proceeding eternally from the One in ten successive emanations or "intellects," each of which generates one of the Ptolemaic spheres: the outer heavens, the sphere of the fixed stars, the spheres of Saturn, Jupiter, Mars, Sun, Venus, Mercury and the Moon. Once we arrive in our own sublunary world, we become aware of a hierarchy of being that evolves in the opposite direction, beginning with inanimate matter, progressing through plants and animals to culminate in humanity, whose soul and intellect partake of the divine Reason, while his body comes from the earth. By the process of purification, described by Plato and Plotinus, human beings can cast off their earthly fetters and return to God, their natural home.

There were obvious differences from the Koranic vision of reality, but al-Farabi saw philosophy as a superior way of understanding truths which the prophets had expressed in a poetic, metaphorical way, in order to appeal to the people. Falsafah was not for everybody. By the middle of the tenth century, an esoteric element was beginning to enter Islam. Falsafah was one such esoteric discipline. Sufism and Shiism also interpreted Islam differently from the *ulema*, the clerics who adhered solely to the Holy Law and the Koran. Again, they kept their doctrines secret not because they wanted to exclude the populace but because Faylasufs, Sufis and Shiis all understood that their more adventurous and inventive versions of Islam could easily be misunderstood. A literal or simplistic interpretation of the doctrines of Falsafah, the myths of Sufism or the Imamology of the Shiah could confuse people who had not the capacity, training or temperament for a more symbolic, rationalistic or imaginative approach to ultimate truth. In these esoteric sects, initiates were carefully prepared for the reception of these difficult notions, by means of special disciplines of mind and heart. We have seen that Greek Christians had developed a similar notion, in the distinction between *dogma* and *kerygma*. The West did not develop an esoteric tradition but adhered to the *kerygmatic* interpretation of religion, which was supposed to be the same for everybody. Instead of allowing their so-called deviants to go private, Western Christians simply persecuted them and attempted to wipe out nonconformists. In Islamdom, esoteric thinkers usually died in their beds.

Al-Farabi's doctrine of emanation became generally accepted by the Faylasufs. Mystics, as we shall see, also found the notion of emanation more sympathetic than the doctrine of the creation *ex nihilo*. Far from seeing philosophy and reason as inimical to religion, Muslim Sufis and Jewish Kabbalists often found that the insights of the Faylasufs were an inspiration to their more imaginative mode of religion. This was particularly evident in the Shiah. Although they remained a minority form of Islam, the tenth century is known as the Shii century since Shiis managed to establish themselves in leading political posts throughout the empire. The most successful of these Shii ventures was the establishment of a caliphate in Tunis in 909 in opposition to the Sunni caliphate in Baghdad. This was the achievement of the Ismaili sect, known as "Fatimids" or "Seveners" to distinguish them from the more numerous "Twelver" Shiis, who accepted the authority of twelve Imams. The Ismailis broke away from the Twelvers after the death of Jafar ibn Sadiq, the saintly Sixth Imam, in 765. Jafar had designated his son Ismail as his successor, but when Ismail died young the Twelvers accepted the authority of his brother Musa. The Ismailis, however, remained true to Ismail and believed that the line had ended with him. Their North African caliphate became extremely powerful: in 973 they moved their capital to al-Qahirah, the site of modern Cairo, where they built the great mosque of al-Azhar.

The veneration of the Imams was no mere political enthusiasm, however. As we have seen, Shiis had come to believe that their Imams embodied God's presence on earth in some mysterious way. They had evolved an esoteric piety of their own which depended upon a symbolic reading of the Koran. It was held that Muhammad had imparted a secret knowledge to his cousin and son-in-law Ali ibn Abi Talib and that this *ilm* had been passed down the line of designated Imams, who were his direct descendants. Each of the Imams embodied the "Light of Muhammad" (*al-nur al-Muhammad*), the prophetic spirit which had enabled Muhammad to surrender perfectly to God. Neither the Prophet nor the Imams were divine, but they had been so totally open to God that he could be said to dwell within them in a more complete way than he dwelt in more ordinary mortals. The Nestorians had held a similar view of Jesus. Like the Nestorians, Shiis saw their Imams as "temples" or "treasuries" of the divine, brimful of that enlightening divine knowledge. This *ilm* was not simply secret information but a means of transformation and inner conversion. Under the guidance of his *da'i* (spiritual director), the disciple was roused from sloth and insensitivity by a vision of dreamlike clarity. This so transformed him that he was able to understand the esoteric interpretation of the Koran. This primal experience was an act of awakening, as we see in this poem by Nasiri al-Khusraw, a tenth-century Ismaili philosopher, which describes the vision of the Imam which changed his life:

> Have you ever heard of a sea which flows from fire?
> Have you ever seen a fox become a lion?
> The sun can transmute a pebble, which even the hand
> of nature can never change, into a gem.
> I am that precious stone, my Sun is he
> by whose rays this tenebrous world is filled with light.
> In jealousy I cannot speak [the Imam's] name
> in this poem, but can only say that for him
> Plato himself would become a slave. He
> is the teacher, healer of souls, favored by God,
> image of wisdom, fountain of knowledge and truth.
> O Countenance of Knowledge, Virtue's Form,
> Heart of Wisdom, Goal of Humankind,
> O Pride of Pride, I stood before thee, pale
> and skeletal, clad in a woolen cloak,

and kissed thine hand as if it were the grave
of the Prophet or Black Stone of the Kabah.[3]

As Christ on Mount Tabor represented deified humanity to Greek Orthodox Christians and as the Buddha embodied that enlightenment that is
possible for all mankind, so too had the human nature of the Imam been
transfigured by his total receptivity to God.

The Ismailis feared that the Faylasufs were concentrating too much on
the external and rationalistic elements of religion and were neglecting its
spiritual kernel. They had, for example, opposed the free thinker ar-Razi.
But they had also developed their own philosophy and science, which
were not regarded as ends in themselves but as spiritual disciplines to
enable them to perceive the inner meaning (*batin*) of the Koran. Contemplating the abstractions of science and mathematics purified their minds
of sensual imagery and freed them from the limitations of their workaday
consciousness. Instead of using science to gain an accurate and literal
understanding of external reality, as we do, the Ismailis used it to develop
their imaginations. They turned to the old Zoroastrian myths of Iran,
fused them with some Neoplatonic ideas and evolved a new perception
of salvation history. It will be recalled that in more traditional societies,
people believed that their experience here below repeated events that had
taken place in the celestial world: Plato's doctrine of the forms or eternal
archetypes had expressed this perennial belief in a philosophical idiom.
In pre-Islamic Iran, for example, reality had a double aspect: there was
thus a visible (*getik*) sky and a heavenly (*menok*) sky that we could not see
with our normal perception. The same was true of more abstract, spiritual
realities: every prayer or virtuous deed that we perform here and now in
the *getik* was duplicated in the celestial world which gave it true reality
and eternal significance.

These heavenly archetypes were felt to be true in the same way as the
events and forms that inhabit our imaginations often seem more real and
significant to us than our mundane existence. It can be seen as an attempt
to explain our conviction that, despite the mass of dispiriting evidence to
the contrary, our lives and the world we experience have meaning and
importance. In the tenth century, the Ismailis revived this mythology,
which had been abandoned by Persian Muslims when they converted to
Islam but which was still part of their cultural inheritance, and fused it
imaginatively with the Platonic doctrine of emanation. Al-Farabi had
envisaged ten emanations between God and the material world which
presided over the Ptolemaic spheres. Now the Ismailis made the Prophet

and the Imams the "souls" of this celestial scheme. In the highest "prophetic" sphere of the First Heaven was Muhammad; in the Second Heaven was Ali, and each of the seven Imams presided over the succeeding spheres in due order. Finally in the sphere nearest to the material world was Muhammad's daughter Fatimah, Ali's wife, who had made this sacred line possible. She was, therefore, the Mother of Islam and corresponded with Sophia, the divine Wisdom. This image of the apotheosized Imams reflected the Ismaili interpretation of the true meaning of Shii history. This had not just been a succession of external, mundane events—many of them tragic. The lives of these illustrious human beings here on earth had corresponded to events in the *menok*, the archetypal order.[4]

We should not be too quick to deride this as a delusion. Today in the West we pride ourselves on our concern for objective accuracy, but the Ismaili *batinis*, who sought the "hidden" (*batin*) dimension of religion, were engaged in a quite different quest. Like poets or painters, they used symbolism which bore little relation to logic but which they felt revealed a deeper reality than could be perceived by the senses or expressed in rational concepts. Accordingly they developed a method of reading the Koran which they called *tawil* (literally, "carrying back"). They felt that this would take them back to the original archetypal Koran, which had been uttered in the *menok* at the same time as Muhammad had recited it in the *getik*. Henri Corbin, the late historian of Iranian Shiism, has compared the discipline of *tawil* to that of harmony in music. It was as though the Ismaili could hear a "sound"—a verse of the Koran or a *hadith*—on several levels at the same time; he was trying to train himself to hear its heavenly counterpart as well as the Arabic words. The effort stilled his clamorous critical faculty and made him conscious of the silence that surrounds each word in much the same way as a Hindu listens to the ineffable silence surrounding the sacred syllable *OUM*. As he listened to the silence, he became aware of the gulf that exists between our words and ideas of God and the full reality.[5] It was a discipline that helped Muslims to understand God as he deserved to be understood, Abu Yaqub al-Sijistani, a leading Ismaili thinker (d. 971), explained. Muslims often spoke about God anthropomorphically, making him a larger-than-life man, while others drained him of all religious meaning and reduced God to a concept. Instead, al-Sijistani advocated the use of the double negative. We should begin by talking about God in negatives, saying, for example, that he was "nonbeing" rather than "being," "not ignorant" rather than "wise" and so forth. But we should immediately negate that rather lifeless and abstract negation, saying that God is "not not-ignorant" or that he is "not No-thing" in the way that we normally use the word. He does not correspond to any human way of speaking. By a repeated use of this linguistic discipline, the *batini* would become aware of the inadequacy of language when it tried to convey the mystery of God.

Hamid al-Din Kirmani (d. 1021), a later Ismaili thinker, described the immense peace and satisfaction that this exercise produced in his *Rahaf al-aql* (Balm for the Intellect). It was by no means an arid, cerebral discipline, a pedantic trick, but invested every detail of the Ismaili's life with a sense of significance. Ismaili writers frequently spoke of their *batin* in terms of illumination and transformation. *Tawil* was not designed to provide information about God but to create a sense of wonder that enlightened the *batini* at a level deeper than the rational. Nor was it escapism. The Ismailis were political activists. Indeed, Jafar ibn Sadiq, the Sixth Imam, had defined faith as action. Like the Prophet and the Imams, the believer had to make his vision of God effective in the mundane world.

These ideals were also shared by the *Ikwan al-Safa*, the Brethren of Purity, an esoteric society that arose in Basra during the Shii century. The Brethren were probably an offshoot of Ismailism. Like the Ismailis, they dedicated themselves to the pursuit of science, particularly mathematics and astrology, as well as to political action. Like the Ismailis, the Brethren were searching for the *batin*, the hidden meaning of life. Their Epistles (*Rasail*), which became an encyclopedia of the philosophical sciences, were extremely popular and spread as far west as Spain. Again, the Brethren combined science and mysticism. Mathematics was seen as a prelude to philosophy and psychology. The various numbers revealed the different qualities inherent in the soul and were a method of concentration that enabled the adept to become aware of the workings of his mind. Just as St. Augustine had seen self-knowledge as indispensable to the knowledge of God, a deep understanding of the self became the kingpin of Islamic mysticism. The Sufis, the Sunni mystics with whom the Ismailis felt great affinity, had an axiom: "He who knows himself, knows his Lord." This was quoted in the First Epistle of the Brethren.[6] As they contemplated the numbers of the soul, they were led back to the primal One, the principle of the human self in the heart of the psyche. The Brethren were also very close to the Faylasufs. Like the Muslim rationalists, they emphasized the unity of truth, which must be sought everywhere. A seeker after truth must "shun no science, scorn no book, nor cling fanatically to a single creed."[7] They developed a Neoplatonic conception of God, whom they saw as the ineffable, incomprehensible One of Plotinus. Like the Faylasufs, they adhered to the Platonic doctrine of emanation rather than the traditional Koranic doctrine of creation *ex nihilo*: the world expressed the divine Reason, and man could participate in the divine and return to the One by purifying his rational powers.

Falsafah reached its apogee in the work of Abu Ali ibn Sina (980–1037), who was known in the West as Avicenna. Born of a family of Shii officials near Bukhara in Central Asia, Ibn Sina was also influenced by the Ismailis who used to come and argue with his father. He became a child prodigy: by the time he was sixteen he was the adviser of important physicians, and at eighteen he had mastered mathematics, logic and physics. He had difficulty with Aristotle, however, but saw the light when he came across al-Farabi's *Intentions of Aristotle's Metaphysics*. He lived as a peripatetic physician, wandering through the Islamic empire, dependent upon the whim of his patrons. At one point he became the vizier of the Shii Buyid dynasty, which ruled in what is now western Iran and southern Iraq. A brilliant, lucid intellectual, he was no dried-up pedant. He was also a sensualist and was said to have died at the quite early age of fifty-eight because of excessive indulgence in wine and sex.

Ibn Sina had realized that Falsafah needed to adapt to the changing conditions within the Islamic empire. The Abbasid caliphate was in decline, and it was no longer so easy to see the caliphal state as the ideal philosophic society described by Plato in the *Republic*. Naturally Ibn Sina sympathized with the spiritual and political aspirations of the Shiah, but he was more attracted to the Neoplatonism of Falsafah, which he Is-lamized with more success than any previous Faylasuf. He believed that if Falsafah was to live up to its claims of presenting a complete picture of reality, it must make more sense of the religious belief of ordinary people, which—however one chose to interpret it—was a major fact of political, social and personal life. Instead of seeing revealed religion as an inferior version of Falsafah, Ibn Sina held that a prophet like Muhammad was superior to any philosopher because he was not dependent upon human reason but enjoyed a direct and intuitive knowledge of God. This was similar to the mystical experience of the Sufis and had been described by Plotinus himself as the highest form of wisdom. This did not mean, however, that the intellect could make no sense of God. Ibn Sina worked out a rational demonstration of the existence of God based on Aristotle's proofs which became standard among later medieval philosophers in both Judaism and Islam. Neither he nor the Faylasufs had the slightest doubt that God existed. They never doubted that unaided human reason could arrive at a knowledge of the existence of a Supreme Being. Reason was man's most exalted activity: it partook of the divine reason and clearly had an important role in the religious quest. Ibn Sina saw it as a religious duty for those who had the intellectual ability to discover God for themselves in this way to do so, because reason could refine the conception of God and free it of superstition and anthropomorphism. Ibn Sina and those of his successors who put their minds to a rational demonstration of God's existence were not arguing with atheists in our sense of the word. They wanted to use reason to discover as much as they could about the nature of God.

Ibn Sina's "proof" begins with a consideration of the way our minds work. Wherever we look in the world, we see composite beings that consist of a number of different elements. A tree, for example, consists of wood, bark, pith, sap and leaves. When we try to understand something, we "analyze" it, breaking it up into its component parts until no further division is possible. The simple elements seem primary to us and the composite beings that they form seem secondary. We are continually looking for simplicity, therefore, for beings that are irreducibly themselves. It was an axiom of Falsafah that reality forms a logically coherent whole; that meant that our endless quest for simplicity must reflect things on a large scale. Like all Platonists, Ibn Sina felt that the multiplicity we see all around us must be dependent upon a primal unity. Since our minds *do* regard composite things as secondary and derivative, this tendency must have been caused by something outside them that is a simple, higher reality. Multiple things are contingent, and contingent beings are inferior to the realities upon which they depend, rather as in a family children are inferior in status to the father who gave them being. Something that is Simplicity itself will be what the philosophers call a "Necessary Being," that is, it will not depend on anything else for its existence. Is there such a being? A Faylasuf like Ibn Sina took it for granted that the cosmos was rational and in a rational universe there must be an Uncaused Being, an Unmoved Mover at the apex of the hierarchy of existence. Something must have started the chain of cause and effect. The absence of such a supreme being would mean that our minds were not in sympathy with reality as a whole. That, in turn, would mean that the universe was not coherent and rational. This utterly simple being upon which the whole of multiple, contingent reality depended was what the religions called "God." Because it is the highest thing of all, it must be absolutely perfect and worthy of honor and worship. But because its existence was so different from that of anything else, it was not just another item in the chain of being.

The philosophers and the Koran were in agreement that God was simplicity itself: he was One. It follows, therefore, that he cannot be analyzed or broken down into component parts or attributes. Because this being is absolutely simple, it has no cause, no qualities, no temporal dimension, and there is absolutely nothing that we can say about it. God cannot be the object of discursive thought, because our brains cannot deal with him in the way that they deal with everything else. Because God is essentially unique, he cannot be compared to any of the things that exist in the normal, contingent sense. Consequently when we talk about God it is better to use negatives to distinguish him absolutely from everything else that we talk about. But since God is the source of all things, we can postulate certain things about him. Because we know that goodness exists, God must be essential or "necessary" Goodness; because we know that life, power and knowledge exist, God must be alive, powerful and intelligent in the most essential and complete manner. Aristotle had taught that since God is pure Reason—at one and the same time, the act of reasoning as well as the object and subject of thought—he could only contemplate himself and take no cognizance of lesser, contingent reality. This did not agree with the portrait of God in revelation, who is said to know all things and to be present and active in the created order. Ibn Sina attempted a compromise: God is far too exalted to descend to the knowledge of such ignoble, particular beings as men and their doings. As Aristotle had said, "There are some things which it is better not to see than to see."[8] God could not sully himself with some of the really base and trivial minutiae of life on earth. But in his eternal act of self-knowledge, God apprehends everything that has emanated from him and that he has brought into being. He knows that he is the cause of contingent creatures. His thought is so perfect that thinking and doing are one and the same act, so his eternal contemplation of himself generates the process of emanation described by the Faylasufs. But God knows us and our world only in general and universal terms; he does not deal in particulars.

Yet Ibn Sina was not content with this abstract account of God's nature: he wanted to relate it to the religious experience of believers, Sufis and *batinis*. Interested in religious psychology, he used the Plotinan scheme of emanation to explain the experience of prophecy. At each of the ten phases of the descent of being from the One, Ibn Sina speculated that the ten pure Intelligences, together with the souls or angels which set each

of the ten Ptolemaic spheres in motion, form an intermediate realm between man and God, which corresponds to the world of archetypal reality
imagined by the *batinis*. These Intelligences also possess imagination;
indeed, they *are* Imagination in its pure state and it is through this intermediate realm of imagination—not through discursive reason—that men
and women reach their most complete apprehension of God. The last of
the Intelligences in our own sphere—the tenth—is the Holy Spirit of
Revelation, known as Gabriel, the source of light and knowledge. The
human soul is composed of practical intellect, which relates to this world,
and the contemplative intellect, which is able to live in close intimacy
with Gabriel. Thus it is possible for the prophets to gain an intuitive,
imaginative knowledge of God, akin to that enjoyed by the Intelligences,
that transcends practical, discursive reason. The experience of the Sufis
showed that it was possible for people to attain a vision of God that
was philosophically sound without using logic and rationality. Instead of
syllogisms, they used the imaginative tools of symbolism and imagery.
The Prophet Muhammad had perfected this direct union with the divine
world. This psychological interpretation of vision and revelation would
enable the more philosophically inclined Sufis to discuss their own religious experience, as we shall see in the next chapter.

Indeed at the end of his life Ibn Sina seems to have become a mystic
himself. In his treatise *Kitab al-Asherat* (The Book of Admonitions), he
was clearly becoming critical of the rational approach to God, which
he found frustrating. He was turning toward what he called "Oriental
Philosophy" (*al-hikmat al-mashriqiyyeh*). This did not refer to the geographical location of the East but to the source of light. He intended to write
an esoteric treatise in which the methods would be based on a discipline
of illumination (*ishraq*) as well as ratiocination. We are not sure whether
he ever wrote this treatise: if he did, it has not survived. But, as we
shall also see in the next chapter, the great Iranian philosopher Yahya
Suhrawardi would found the Ishraqi school, which did fuse philosophy
with spirituality in the way envisaged by Ibn Sina.

The disciplines of Kalam and Falsafah had inspired a similar intellectual
movement among the Jews of the Islamic empire. They began to write
their own philosophy in Arabic, introducing a metaphysical and speculative element into Judaism for the first time. Unlike the Muslim Faylasufs,
the Jewish philosophers did not concern themselves with the full range
of philosophical science but concentrated almost entirely on religious
matters. They felt that they had to answer the challenge of Islam on its
own terms, and that involved squaring the personalistic God of the Bible

with the God of the Faylasufs. Like the Muslims, they worried about the anthropomorphic portrait of God in the scriptures and the Talmud and asked themselves how he could be the same as the God of the philosophers. They worried about the problem of the creation of the world and about the relation between revelation and reason. They naturally came to different conclusions, but they were deeply dependent upon the Muslim thinkers. Thus Saadia ibn Joseph (882–942), the first to undertake a philosophical interpretation of Judaism, was a Talmudist but also a Mutazili. He believed that reason could attain a knowledge of God by means of its own powers. Like a Faylasuf, he saw the attainment of a rational conception of God as a *mitzvah*, a religious duty. Yet like the Muslim rationalists, Saadia had no doubts whatever about the existence of God. The reality of the Creator God seemed so obvious to Saadia that it was the possibility of religious doubt rather than faith that he felt needed to be proven in his *Book of Beliefs and Opinions*.

A Jew was not required to strain his reason to accept the truths of revelation, Saadia argued. But that did not mean that God was entirely accessible to human reason. Saadia acknowledged that the idea of the creation *ex nihilo* was fraught with philosophical difficulties and impossible to explain in rational terms, because the God of Falsafah is not capable of making a sudden decision and initiating change. How could a material world have its origin in a wholly spiritual God? Here we had reached the limits of reason and must simply accept that the world was not eternal, as Platonists believed, but had a beginning in time. This was the only possible explanation that agreed with scripture and common sense. Once we have accepted this, we can deduce other facts about God. The created order is intelligently planned; it has life and energy: therefore God, who created it, must also have Wisdom, Life and Power. These attributes are not separate *hypostases*, as the Christian doctrine of the Trinity suggested, but mere aspects of God. It is only because our human language cannot adequately express the reality of God that we have to analyze him in this way and seem to destroy his absolute simplicity. If we want to be as exact about God as possible, we can only properly say that he exists. Saadia does not forbid all positive description of God, however, nor does he put the remote and impersonal God of the philosophers above the personal, anthropomorphic God of the Bible. When, for example, he tries to explain the suffering that we see in the world, Saadia resorts to the solutions of the Wisdom writers and the Talmud. Suffering, he says, is a punishment for sin; it purifies and disciplines us in order to make us humble. This would not have satisfied a true Faylasuf because it makes God far too human and attributes plans and intentions to him. But Saadia does not see the revealed God of scripture as inferior to the God of Falsafah. The prophets were superior to any philosopher. Ultimately reason could only attempt to demonstrate systematically what the Bible had taught.

Other Jews went further. In his *Fountain of Life*, the Neoplatonist Solomon ibn Gabirol (ca. 1022–ca. 1070) could not accept the doctrine of creation *ex nihilo* but tried to adapt the theory of emanation to allow God some degree of spontaneity and free will. He claimed that God had willed or desired the process of emanation, thereby attempting to make it less mechanical and indicate that God was in control of the laws of existence instead of subject to the same dynamic. But Gabirol failed to explain adequately how matter could derive from God. Others were less innovative. Bahya ibn Pakudah (d. ca. 1080) was not a strict Platonist but retreated to the methods of Kalam whenever it suited him. Thus, like Saadia, he argued that God had created the world at a particular moment. The world had certainly not come into being by accident: that would be as ridiculous an idea as imagining that a perfectly written paragraph came into being when ink was spilled on a page. The order and purposiveness of the world shows that there must be a Creator, as scripture had revealed. Having thus put forward this highly unphilosophical doctrine, Bahya switched from Kalam to Falsafah, listing Ibn Sina's proof that a Necessary, Simple Being had to exist.

Bahya believed that the only people who worshipped God properly were prophets and philosophers. The prophet had a direct, intuitive knowledge of God, the philosopher a rational knowledge of him. Everybody else was simply worshipping a projection of himself, a God made in his own image. They were all like blind men, led by other human beings, if they did not try to prove the existence and unity of God for themselves. Bahya was as elitist as any Faylasuf, but he also had strong Sufi leanings: reason could tell us *that* God existed but could not tell us anything about him. As its title suggests, Bahya's treatise *Duties of the Heart* used reason to help us to cultivate a proper attitude toward God. If Neoplatonism conflicted with his Judaism, he simply jettisoned it. His religious experience of God took precedence over any rationalistic method.

But if reason could not tell us anything about God, what was the point of rational discussion of theological matters? This question agonized the Muslim thinker Abu Hamid al-Ghazzali (1058–1111), a crucial and emblematic figure in the history of religious philosophy. Born in Khurasan, he had studied Kalam under Juwayni, the outstanding Asharite theologian, to such effect that at the age of thirty-three he was appointed director of the prestigious Nizamiyyah mosque in Baghdad. His brief was to defend Sunni doctrines against the Shii challenge of the Ismailis. Al-Ghazzali, however, had a restless temperament that made him struggle with truth like a terrier, worrying problems to the bitter death and refusing to be content with an easy, conventional answer. As he tells us,

> I have poked into every dark recess, I have made an assault on every problem, I have plunged into every abyss. I have scrutinized the creed of every sect, I have tried to lay bare the inmost doctrines of every community. All this I have done that I might distinguish between true and false, between sound tradition and heretical innovation.[9]

He was searching for the kind of indubitable certainty that a philosopher like Saadia felt, but he became increasingly disillusioned. No matter how exhaustive his research, absolute certainty eluded him. His contemporaries sought God in several ways, according to their personal and temperamental needs: in Kalam, through an Imam, in Falsafah and in Sufi mysticism. Al-Ghazzali seems to have studied each of these disciplines in his attempt to understand "what all things really are in themselves."[10] The disciples of all four of the main versions of Islam that he researched claimed total conviction but, al-Ghazzali asked, how could this claim be verified objectively?

Al-Ghazzali was as aware as any modern skeptic that certainty was a psychological condition that was not necessarily objectively true. Faylasufs said that they acquired certain knowledge by rational argument; mystics insisted that they had found it through the Sufi disciplines; Ismailis felt that it was only found in the teachings of their Imam. But the reality that we call "God" cannot be tested empirically, so how could we be sure that our beliefs were not mere delusions? The more conventionally rational proofs failed to satisfy al-Ghazzali's strict standards. The theologians of Kalam began with propositions found in scripture, but these had not been verified beyond reasonable doubt. The Ismailis depended upon the teachings of a hidden and inaccessible Imam, but how could we be certain that the Imam was divinely inspired, and if we cannot find him what is the point of this inspiration? Falsafah was particularly unsatisfactory. Al-Ghazzali directed a considerable part of his polemic against al-Farabi and Ibn Sina. Believing that they could only be refuted by an expert in their own discipline, al-Ghazzali studied Falsafah for three years until he had completely mastered it.[11] In his treatise *The Incoherence of the*

Philosophers, he argued that the Faylasufs were begging the question. If Falsafah confined itself to mundane, observable phenomena as in medicine, astronomy or mathematics, it was extremely useful but it could tell us nothing about God. How could anybody prove the doctrine of emanation, one way or the other? By what authority did the Faylasufs assert that God knew only general, universal things rather than particulars? Could they prove this? Their argument that God was too exalted to know the baser realities was inadequate: since when was ignorance about anything excellent? There was no way that any of these propositions could be satisfactorily verified, so the Faylasufs had been irrational and unphilosophical by seeking knowledge that lay beyond the capacity of the mind and could not be verified by the senses.

But where did that leave the honest seeker after truth? Was a sound, unshakable faith in God impossible? The strain of his quest caused al-Ghazzali such personal distress that he had a breakdown. He found himself unable to swallow or to eat and felt overwhelmed by a weight of doom and despair. Finally in about 1094 he found that he could not speak or give his lectures:

> God shriveled my tongue until I was prevented from giving instruction. So I used to force myself to teach on a particular day for the benefit of my various pupils but my tongue would not utter a single word.[12]

He fell into a clinical depression. The doctors rightly diagnosed a deep-rooted conflict and told him that until he was delivered from his hidden anxiety, he would never recover. Fearing that he was in danger of hellfire if he did not recover his faith, al-Ghazzali resigned his prestigious academic post and went off to join the Sufis.

There he found what he was looking for. Without abandoning his reason—he always distrusted the more extravagant forms of Sufism—al-Ghazzali discovered that the mystical disciplines yielded a direct but intuitive sense of something that could be called "God." The British scholar John Bowker shows that the Arabic word for existence (*wujud*) derives from the root *wajada*: "he found."[13] Literally, therefore, *wujud* means "that which is findable": it was more concrete than the Greek metaphysical terms and yet gave Muslims more leeway. An Arabic-speaking philosopher who attempted to prove that God existed did not have to produce God as another object among many. He simply had to prove that he could be found. The only absolute proof of God's *wujud* would appear—or not—when the believer came face to face with the divine reality after death, but the reports of such people as the prophets and mystics who claimed to have experienced it in this life should be considered carefully. The Sufis certainly claimed that they had experienced the *wujud* of God: the word *wajd* was a technical term for their ecstatic apprehension of God which gave them complete certainty (*yaqin*) that it was a reality, not just a fantasy. Admittedly those reports could be mistaken in their claims, but after living for ten years as a Sufi, al-Ghazzali found that the religious experience was the only way of verifying a reality that lay beyond the reach of the human intellect and cerebral process. The Sufis' knowledge of God was not a rational or metaphysical knowledge, but it was clearly akin to the intuitive experience of the prophets of old: Sufis thus *found* the essential truths of Islam for themselves by reliving its central experience.

Al-Ghazzali therefore formulated a mystical creed that would be acceptable to the Muslim establishment, who had often looked askance at the mystics of Islam, as we shall see in the following chapter. Like Ibn Sina, he looked back to the ancient belief in an archetypal realm beyond this mundane world of sensory experience. The visible world (*alam al-shahadah*) is an inferior replica of what he called the world of the Platonic intelligence (*alam al-malakut*), as any Faylasuf acknowledged. The Koran and the Bible of the Jews and Christians had spoken of this spiritual world. Man straddled both realms of reality: he belonged to the physical as well as the higher world of the spirit because God had inscribed the divine image within him. In his mystical treatise *Mishkat al-Anwar*, al-Ghazzali interprets the Koranic Sura of Light, which I quoted in the last chapter.[14] The light in these verses refers both to God and to the other illuminating objects: the lamp, the star. Our reason is also enlightening. Not only does it enable us to perceive other objects but, like God himself, it can transcend time and space. It partakes of the same reality as the spiritual world, therefore. But in order to make it clear that by "reason" he did not merely refer to our cerebral, analytic powers, al-Ghazzali reminds his readers that his explanation cannot be understood in a literal sense: we can only discuss these matters in the figurative language that is the preserve of the creative imagination.

Some people possess a power that is higher than reason, however, which al-Ghazzali calls "the prophetic spirit." People who lack this faculty should not deny that it exists simply because they have no experience of it. That would be as absurd as if somebody who was tone-deaf claimed that music was an illusion, simply because he himself could not appreciate it. We can learn something about God by means of our reasoning and imaginative powers, but the highest type of knowledge can be attained only by people like the prophets or the mystics who have this special God-enabling faculty. This sounds elitist, but mystics in other traditions have also claimed that the intuitive, receptive qualities demanded by a discipline like Zen or Buddhist meditation are a special gift, comparable to the gift of writing poetry. Not everybody has this mystical talent. Al-Ghazzali describes this mystical knowledge as an awareness that the Creator alone exists or has being. This results in the fading away of self and an absorption in God. Mystics are able to rise above the world of metaphor, which has to satisfy less gifted mortals; they

> are able to see that there is no being in the world other than God and that the face of everything is perishing save his Face (Koran 28:88). . . . Indeed, everything other than he is pure non being and, considered from the standpoint of the being which it receives from the First Intelligence [in the Platonic scheme], has being not in itself but in regard to the face of its Maker, so that the only thing which truly is is God's Face.[15]

Instead of being an external, objectified Being whose existence can be proved rationally, God is an all-enveloping reality and the ultimate existence which cannot be perceived as we perceive the beings that depend upon it and partake of its necessary existence: we have to cultivate a special mode of seeing.

Al-Ghazzali eventually returned to his teaching duties in Baghdad but never lost his conviction that it was impossible to demonstrate the existence of God by logic and rational proof. In his biographical treatise *Al-Mundiqh min al-dalal* (The Deliverance from Error), he argued passionately that neither Falsafah nor Kalam could satisfy somebody who was in danger of losing his faith. He himself had been brought to the brink of skepticism (*safsafah*) when he realized that it was absolutely impossible to prove God's existence beyond reasonable doubt. The reality that we call "God" lay outside the realm of sense perception and logical thought, so science and metaphysics could neither prove nor disprove the *wujud* of al-Lah. For those who were not blessed with the special mystical or prophetic talent, al-Ghazzali devised a discipline to enable Muslims to cultivate a consciousness of God's reality in the minutiae of daily life. He made an indelible impression on Islam. Never again would Muslims make the facile assumption that God was a being like any other, whose existence could be demonstrated scientifically or philosophically. Henceforth Muslim philosophy would become inseparable from spirituality and a more mystical discussion of God.

He also had an effect on Judaism. The Spanish philosopher Joseph ibn Saddiq (d. 1143) used Ibn Sina's proof of the existence of God but was careful to make the point that God was not simply another being—one of the things that "exist" in our usual sense of the word. If we claimed to understand God, that would mean that he was finite and imperfect. The most exact statement that we could make about God was that he was incomprehensible, utterly transcending our natural intellectual powers. We could speak about God's activity in the world in positive terms but not about God's essence (*al-Dhat*), which would always elude us. The Toledan physician Judah Halevi (1085–1141) followed al-Ghazzali closely. God could not be proved rationally; that did not mean that faith in God was irrational but simply that a logical demonstration of his existence had no religious value. It could tell us very little: there was no way of establishing beyond reasonable doubt how such a remote and impersonal God could have created this imperfect material world or whether he related to the world in any meaningful way. When the philosophers claimed that they became united to the divine Intelligence that informs the cosmos through the exercise of reason, they were deluding themselves. The only people who had any direct knowledge of God were the prophets, who had had nothing to do with Falsafah.

Halevi did not understand philosophy as well as al-Ghazzali, but he agreed that the only reliable knowledge of God was by religious experience. Like al-Ghazzali, he also postulated a special religious faculty but claimed that it was the prerogative of the Jews alone. He tried to soften this by suggesting that the *goyim* could come to a knowledge of God through the natural law, but the purpose of *The Kuzari*, his great philosophical work, was to justify the unique position of Israel among the nations. Like the Rabbis of the Talmud, Halevi believed that any Jew could acquire the prophetic spirit by careful observance of the *mitzvot*. The God he would encounter was not an objective fact whose existence could be demonstrated scientifically but an essentially subjective experience. He could even be seen as an extension of the Jew's "natural" self:

> This Divine principle waits, as it were, for him to whom it is meet that it should attach itself, so that it should become his God, as was the case with the prophets and saints. . . . It is just as the soul which waits for its entry into the fetus until the latter's vital powers are

sufficiently completed to enable it to receive this higher state of things. It is just the same way as Nature itself waits for a temperate climate, in order that she might exert her effort upon the soil and produce vegetation.[16]

God is not an alien, intrusive reality, therefore, nor is the Jew an autonomous being sealed off from the divine. God can be seen—yet again—as the completion of humanity, the fulfillment of a man or woman's potential; furthermore, the "God" he encounters is uniquely his own, an idea that we shall explore in more depth in the following chapter. Halevi is careful to distinguish the God that Jews are able to experience from the essence of God himself. When prophets and saints claim to have experienced "God," they have not known him as he is in himself but only in the divine activities within him that are a sort of afterglow of the transcendent, inaccessible reality.

Falsafah was not entirely dead as a result of al-Ghazzali's polemic, however. In Cordova a distinguished Muslim philosopher attempted to revive it and to argue that it was the highest form of religion. Abu al-Walid ibn Ahmad ibn Rushd (1126–1198), known in Europe as Averroës, became an authority in the West among both Jews and Christians. During the thirteenth century he was translated into Hebrew and Latin, and his commentaries on Aristotle had an immense influence on such distinguished theologians as Maimonides, Thomas Aquinas and Albert the Great. In the nineteenth century, Ernest Renan would hail him as a free spirit, the champion of rationalism against blind faith. In the Islamic world, however, Ibn Rushd was a more marginal figure. In his career and his posthumous effect, we can see a parting of the ways between East and West in their approach to and conception of God. Ibn Rushd passionately disapproved of al-Ghazzali's condemnation of Falsafah and the way he had discussed these esoteric matters openly. Unlike his predecessors al-Farabi and Ibn Sina, he was a Qadi, a jurist of the Shariah law, as well as a philosopher. The *ulema* had always been suspicious of Falsafah and its fundamentally different God, but Ibn Rushd had managed to unite Aristotle with a more traditional Islamic piety. He was convinced that there was no contradiction whatsoever between religion and rationalism. Both expressed the same truth in different ways; both looked toward the same God. Not everybody was capable of philosophical thought, however, so Falsafah was only for an intellectual elite. It would confuse the masses and lead them into an error that imperiled their eternal salvation. Hence the importance of the esoteric tradition, which kept these dangerous doctrines from those unfitted to receive them. It was just the same with Sufism and the *batini* studies of the Ismailis; if unsuitable people attempted these mental disciplines they could become seriously ill and develop all kinds of psychological disorders. Kalam was equally dangerous. It fell short of true Falsafah and gave people the misleading idea that they were engaged in a proper rational discussion when they were not. Consequently it merely stirred up fruitless doctrinal disputes, which could only weaken the faith of uneducated people and make them anxious.

Ibn Rushd believed that the acceptance of certain truths was essential to salvation—a novel view in the Islamic world. The Faylasufs were the chief authorities on doctrine: they alone were capable of interpreting the scriptures and were the people described in the Koran as "deeply rooted in knowledge."[17] Everybody else should take the Koran at face value and read it literally, but the Faylasuf could attempt a symbolic exegesis. But even the Faylasufs had to subscribe to the "creed" of obligatory doctrines, which Ibn Rushd listed as follows:

1. The existence of God as Creator and Sustainer of the world.
2. The Unity of God.
3. The attributes of knowledge, power, will, hearing, seeing and speech, which are given to God throughout the Koran.
4. The uniqueness and incomparability of God, clearly asserted in Koran 42:9: "There is nothing like unto him."
5. The creation of the world by God.
6. The validity of prophecy.
7. The justice of God.
8. The resurrection of the body on the Last Day.[18]

These doctrines about God must be accepted *in toto*, as the Koran is quite unambiguous about them. Falsafah had not always subscribed to belief in the creation of the world, for example, so it is not clear how such Koranic doctrines should be understood. Although the Koran says unequivocally that God has created the world, it does not say *how* he did this or whether the world was created at a particular moment in time. This left the Faylasuf free to adopt the belief of the rationalists. Again, the Koran says that God has such attributes as knowledge, but we do not know exactly what this means because our concept of knowledge is necessarily human and inadequate. The Koran does not necessarily contradict the philosophers, therefore, when it says that God knows everything that we do.

In the Islamic world, mysticism was so important that Ibn Rushd's conception of God, based as it was on a strictly rationalist theology, had little influence. Ibn Rushd was a revered but secondary figure in Islam, but he became very important indeed in the West, which discovered Aristotle through him and developed a more rationalistic conception of God. Most Western Christians had a very limited knowledge of Islamic culture and were ignorant of philosophical developments after Ibn Rushd. Hence it is often assumed that the career of Ibn Rushd marked the end of Islamic philosophy. In fact during Ibn Rushd's lifetime, two distinguished philosophers who would both be extremely influential in the Islamic world were writing in Iraq and Iran. Yahya Suhrawardi and Muid ad-Din ibn al-Arabi followed in the footsteps of Ibn Sina rather than Ibn Rushd and attempted to fuse philosophy with mystical spirituality. We shall consider their work in the next chapter.

Ibn Rushd's great disciple in the Jewish world was the great Talmudist and philosopher Rabbi Moses ibn Maimon (1135–1204), who is usually known as Maimonides. Like Ibn Rushd, Maimonides was a native of Cordova, the capital of Muslim Spain, where there was a growing consensus that some kind of philosophy was essential for a deeper understanding of God. Maimonides was forced to flee Spain, however, when it fell prey to the fanatical Berber sect of the Almoravids, who persecuted the Jewish community. This painful collision with medieval fundamentalism did not make Maimonides hostile to Islam as a whole. He and his parents settled in Egypt, where he held high office in the government and even became the physician of the sultan. There, too, he wrote his famous treatise *The Guide for the Perplexed*, which argued that the Jewish faith was not an arbitrary set of doctrines but was based on sound rational principles. Like Ibn Rushd, Maimonides believed that Falsafah was the most advanced form of religious knowledge and the royal road to God, which must not be revealed to the masses but should remain the preserve of a philosophical elite. Unlike Ibn Rushd, however, he did believe that the ordinary people could be taught to interpret the scriptures symbolically, so as not to acquire an anthropomorphic view of God. He also believed that certain doctrines were necessary for salvation and published a creed of thirteen articles that was markedly similar to Ibn Rushd's:

1. The existence of God.
2. The unity of God.
3. The incorporeality of God.

4. The eternity of God.
5. The prohibition of idolatry.
6. The validity of prophecy.
7. Moses was the greatest of the prophets.
8. The divine origin of truth.
9. The eternal validity of the Torah.
10. God knows the deeds of men.
11. He judges them accordingly.
12. He will send a Messiah.
13. The resurrection of the dead.[19]

This was an innovation in Judaism and never became entirely accepted. As in Islam, the notion of orthodoxy (as opposed to orthopraxy) was alien to the Jewish religious experience. The creeds of Ibn Rushd and Maimonides suggest that a rationalistic and intellectualist approach to religion leads to dogmatism and to an identification of "faith" with "correct belief."

Yet Maimonides was careful to maintain that God was essentially incomprehensible and inaccessible to human reason. He proved God's existence by means of the arguments of Aristotle and Ibn Sina but insisted that God remains ineffable and indescribable because of his absolute simplicity. The prophets themselves had used parables and taught us that it was only possible to talk about God in any meaningful or extensive way in symbolic, allusive language. We know that God cannot be compared to any of the things that exist. It is better, therefore, to use negative terminology when we attempt to describe him. Instead of saying that "he exists," we should deny his nonexistence and so on. As with the Ismailis, the use of the negative language was a discipline that would enhance our appreciation of God's transcendence, reminding us that the reality was quite distinct from any idea that we poor humans can conceive of him. We cannot even say that God is "good" because he is far more than anything that we can mean by "goodness." This is a way of excluding our imperfections from God, preventing us from projecting our hopes and desires onto him. That would create a God in our own image and likeness. We can, however, use the *Via Negativa* to form some positive notions of God. Thus, when we say that God is "not impotent" (instead of saying that he is powerful), it follows logically that God must be able to act. Since God is "not imperfect" his actions must also be perfect. When we say that God is "not ignorant" (meaning that he is wise), we can deduce that he is perfectly wise and fully informed. This kind of deduction can only be made about God's activities, *not* about his essence, which remains beyond the reach of our intellect.

When it came to a choice between the God of the Bible and the God of the philosophers, Maimonides always chose the former. Even though the doctrine of the creation *ex nihilo* was philosophically unorthodox, Maimonides adhered to the traditional biblical doctrine and jettisoned the philosophic idea of emanation. As he pointed out, neither creation *ex nihilo* nor emanation could be proven definitively by reason alone. Again, he considered prophecy superior to philosophy. Both the prophet and the philosopher spoke about the same God, but the prophet had to be imaginatively as well as intellectually gifted. He had a direct, intuitive knowledge of God which was higher than the knowledge achieved by discursive reasoning. Maimonides seems to have been something of a mystic himself. He speaks of the trembling excitement that accompanied this kind of intuitive experience of God, an emotion "consequent upon the perfection of the imaginative faculties."[20] Despite Maimonides' emphasis on rationality, he maintained that the highest knowledge of God derived more from the imagination than from the intellect alone.

His ideas spread among the Jews of Southern France and Spain, so that by the beginning of the fourteenth century, there was what amounted to a Jewish philosophical enlightenment in the area. Some of these Jewish Faylasufs were more vigorously rationalistic than Maimonides. Thus Levi ben Gershom (1288–1344) of Bagnols in Southern France denied that God had knowledge of mundane affairs. His was the God of the philosophers, not the God of the Bible. Inevitably a reaction set in. Some Jews turned to mysticism and developed the esoteric discipline of Kabbalah, as we shall see. Others recoiled from philosophy when tragedy struck, finding that the remote God of Falsafah was unable to console them. During the thirteenth and fourteenth centuries, the Christian Wars of Reconquest began to push back the frontiers of Islam in Spain and brought the anti-Semitism of Western Europe to the peninsula. Eventually this would culminate in the destruction of Spanish Jewry, and during the sixteenth century the Jews turned away from Falsafah and developed an entirely new conception of God that was inspired by mythology rather than scientific logic.

The crusading religion of Western Christendom had separated it from the other monotheistic traditions. The First Crusade of 1096–99 had been the first cooperative act of the new West, a sign that Europe was beginning to recover from the long period of barbarism known as the Dark Ages.

The new Rome, backed by the Christian nations of Northern Europe, was fighting its way back onto the international scene. But the Christianity of the Angles, the Saxons and the Franks was rudimentary. They were aggressive and martial people and they wanted an aggressive religion. During the eleventh century, the Benedictine monks of the Abbey of Cluny and its affiliated houses had tried to tether their martial spirit to the church and teach them true Christian values by means of such devotional practices as the pilgrimage. The first Crusaders had seen their expedition to the Near East as a pilgrimage to the Holy Land, but they still had a very primitive conception of God and of religion. Soldier saints like St. George, St. Mercury and St. Demetrius figured more than God in their piety and, in practice, differed little from pagan deities. Jesus was seen as the feudal lord of the Crusaders rather than as the incarnate Logos: he had summoned his knights to recover his patrimony—the Holy Land—from the infidel. As they began their journey, some of the Crusaders resolved to avenge his death by slaughtering the Jewish communities along the Rhine Valley. This had not been part of Pope Urban II's original idea when he had summoned the Crusade, but it seemed simply perverse to many of the Crusaders to march 3,000 miles to fight the Muslims, about whom they knew next to nothing, when the people who had—or so they thought—actually killed Christ were alive and well on their very doorsteps. During the long terrible march to Jerusalem, when the Crusaders narrowly escaped extinction, they could only account for their survival by assuming that they must be God's Chosen People, who enjoyed his special protection. He was leading them to the Holy Land as he had once led the ancient Israelites. In practical terms, their God was still the primitive tribal deity of the early books of the Bible. When they finally conquered Jerusalem in the summer of 1099, they fell on the Jewish and Muslim inhabitants of the city with the zeal of Joshua and massacred them with a brutality that shocked even their contemporaries.

Thenceforth Christians in Europe regarded Jews and Muslims as the enemies of God; for a long time they had also felt a deep antagonism toward the Greek Orthodox Christians of Byzantium, who made them feel barbarous and inferior.[21] This had not always been the case. During the ninth century, some of the more educated Christians of the West had been inspired by Greek theology. Thus the Celtic philosopher Duns Scotus Erigena (810–877), who left his native Ireland to work in the court of Charles the Bold, King of the West Franks, had translated many of the Greek Fathers of the Church into Latin for the benefit of Western Christians, in particular the works of Denys the Areopagite. Erigena passionately believed that faith and reason were not mutually exclusive. Like the Jewish and Muslim Faylasufs, he saw philosophy as the royal road to God. Plato and Aristotle were the masters of those who demanded a rational account of the Christian religion. Scripture and the writings of the Fathers could be illuminated by the disciplines of logic and rational inquiry, but that did not mean a literal interpretation: some passages of scripture had to be interpreted symbolically because, as Erigena explained in his *Exposition of Denys's Celestial Hierarchy*, theology was "a kind of poetry."[22]

Erigena used the dialectical method of Denys in his own discussion of God, who could only be explained by a paradox that reminded us of the limitations of our human understanding. Both the positive and the negative approaches to God were valid. God is incomprehensible: even the angels do not know or understand his essential nature, but it is acceptable to make a positive statement, such as "God is wise," because when we refer it to God we know that we are not using the word "wise" in the usual way. We remind ourselves of this by going on to make a negative statement, saying "God is *not* wise." The paradox forces us to move on to Denys's third way of talking about God, when we conclude: "God is *more than* wise." This was what the Greeks called an apophatic statement because we do not understand what "more than wise" can possibly mean. Again, this was not simply a verbal trick but a discipline that by juxtaposing two mutually exclusive statements helps us to cultivate a sense of the mystery that our word "God" represents, since it can never be confined to a merely human concept.

When he applied this method to the statement "God exists," Erigena arrived, as usual, at the synthesis: "God is more than existence." God does not exist like the things he has created and is not just another being existing alongside them, as Denys had pointed out. Again, this was an incomprehensible statement, because, Erigena comments, "what that is which is more than 'being' it does not reveal. For it says that God is not one of the things that are, but that he is more than the things that are, but what that 'is' is, it in no way defines."[23] In fact, God is "Nothing." Erigena knew that this sounded shocking and he warned his reader not to be afraid. His method was devised to remind us that God is not an object; he does not possess "being" in any sense that we can comprehend. God is "He who is more than being" (*aliquo modo superesse*).[24] His mode of existence is as different from ours as our being is from an animal's and an animal's from a rock. But if God is "Nothing" he is also "Everything": because this "super-existence" means that God alone has true being; he is the essence of everything that partakes of this. Every one of his creatures, therefore, is a theophany, a sign of God's presence. Erigena's Celtic piety—encapsulated in St. Patrick's famous prayer: "God be in my head and in my understanding"—led him to emphasize the immanence of God. Man, who in the Neoplatonic scheme sums up the whole of creation in himself, is the most complete of these theophanies, and, like Augustine, Erigena taught that we can discover a trinity within ourselves, albeit in a glass darkly.

In Erigena's paradoxical theology, God is both Everything and Nothing; the two terms balance one another and are held in a creative tension to suggest the mystery which our word "God" can only symbolize. Thus when a student asks him what Denys meant when he called God Nothing, Erigena replies that the divine Goodness is incomprehensible because it is "superessential"—that is, more than Goodness itself—and "supernatural." So

> while it is contemplated in itself [it] neither is, nor was, nor shall be, for it is understood to be none of the things that exist because it surpasses all things but when by a certain ineffable descent into the things that are, it is beheld by the mind's eye, it alone is found to be in all things, and it is and was and shall be.[25]

When, therefore, we consider the divine reality in itself, "it is not unreasonably called 'Nothing,' " but when this divine Void decides to proceed "out of Nothing into Something," every single creature it informs "can be called a theophany, that is, a divine apparition."[26] We cannot see God as he is in himself since this God to all intents and purposes does not exist. We only see the God which animates the created world and reveals himself in flowers, birds, trees and other human beings. There are problems in this approach. What about evil? Is this, as Hindus maintain, also a manifestation of God in the world? Erigena does not attempt to deal with the problem of evil in sufficient depth, but Jewish Kabbalists would later attempt to locate evil within God: they also developed a theology that described God proceeding from Nothingness to become Something in a way that is remarkably similar to Erigena's account, though it is highly unlikely that any of the Kabbalists had read him.

Erigena showed that the Latins had much to learn from the Greeks, but in 1054 Eastern and Western Churches broke off relations in a schism which has turned out to be permanent—though at the time nobody intended this. The conflict had a political dimension, which I shall not discuss, but it also centered on a dispute about the Trinity. In 796 a synod of Western bishops had met at Fréjus in Southern France and had inserted an extra clause into the Nicene Creed. This stated that the Holy Spirit proceeded not only from the Father but also from the Son (*filioque*). The Latin bishops wanted to emphasize the equality of the Father and the Son, since some of their flock harbored Arian views. Making the Spirit proceed from both the Father and the Son, they thought, would stress their equal status. Even though Charlemagne, soon to become Emperor of the West, had absolutely no understanding of the theological issues, he approved the new clause. The Greeks, however, condemned it. Yet the Latins held firm and insisted that their *own* Fathers had taught this doctrine. Thus St. Augustine had seen the Holy Spirit as the principle of unity in the Trinity, maintaining that he was the love between Father and Son. It was, therefore, correct to say that the Spirit had proceeded from them both, and the new clause stressed the essential unity of the three persons.

But the Greeks had always distrusted Augustine's Trinitarian theology, because it was too anthropomorphic. Where the West began with the notion of God's unity and then considered the three persons within that unity, the Greeks had always started with the three *hypostases* and declared that God's unity—his essence—was beyond our ken. They thought that the Latins made the Trinity too comprehensible, and they also suspected that the Latin language was not able to express these Trinitarian ideas with sufficient precision. The *filioque* clause overemphasized the unity of the three persons and, the Greeks argued, instead of hinting at the essential incomprehensibility of God, the addition made the Trinity too rational. It made God one with three aspects or modes of being. In fact there was nothing heretical about the Latin assertion, even though it did not suit the Greeks' apophatic spirituality. The conflict could have been patched up if there had been a will for peace, but tension between East and West escalated during the Crusades, especially when the fourth Crusaders sacked the Byzantine capital of Constantinople in 1204 and fatally wounded the Greek empire. What the *filioque* rift had revealed was that the Greeks and Latins were evolving quite different conceptions of God. The Trinity had never been as central to Western spirituality as it has remained for the Greeks. The Greeks felt that by emphasizing the unity of God in this way, the West was identifying God himself with a "simple essence" that *could* be defined and discussed, like the God of the Philosophers.[27] In later chapters we shall see that Western Christians were frequently uneasy about the doctrine of the Trinity and that, during the eighteenth-century Enlightenment, many would drop it altogether. To all intents and purposes, many Western Christians are not really Trinitarians. They complain that the doctrine of Three Persons in One God is incomprehensible, not realizing that for the Greeks that was the whole point.

After the schism, Greeks and Latins took divergent paths. In Greek Orthodoxy, *theologia*, the study of God, remained precisely that. It was confined to the contemplation of God in the essentially mystical doctrines of the Trinity and the Incarnation. They would find the idea of a "theology of grace" or a "theology of the family" contradictions in terms: they were not particularly interested in theoretical discussions and definitions of secondary issues. The West, however, was increasingly concerned to define these questions and to form a correct opinion that was binding on everybody. The Reformation, for example, divided Christendom into yet more warring camps because Catholics and Protestants could not agree on the mechanics of *how* salvation happened and exactly *what* the Eucharist was. Western Christians continually challenged the Greeks to give their opinion on these contentious issues, but the Greeks lagged behind and, if they did reply, their answer frequently sounded rather cobbled together. They had become distrustful of rationalism, finding it an inappropriate tool for the discussion of a God who must elude concepts and logic. Metaphysics was acceptable in secular studies, but increasingly Greeks felt that it could endanger the faith. It appealed to the more talkative, busy part of the mind, whereas their *theoria* was not an intellectual opinion but a disciplined silence before the God who could only be known by means of religious and mystical experience. In 1082, the philosopher and humanist John Italos was tried for heresy because of his excessive use of philosophy and his Neoplatonic conception of creation. This deliberate withdrawal from philosophy happened shortly before al-Ghazzali had his breakdown in Baghdad and quit Kalam in order to become a Sufi.

It is, therefore, poignant and ironic that Western Christians should have begun to get down to Falsafah at the precise moment when Greeks and Muslims were starting to lose faith in it. Plato and Aristotle had not been available in Latin during the Dark Ages, so inevitably the West had been left behind. The discovery of philosophy was stimulating and exciting. The eleventh-century theologian Anselm of Canterbury, whose views on the Incarnation we discussed in Chapter 4, seemed to think that it was possible to prove anything. His God was not Nothing but the highest being of all. Even the unbeliever could form an idea of a supreme being, which was "one nature, highest of all the things that are, alone sufficient unto itself in eternal beatitude."[28] Yet he also insisted that God could only be known in faith. This is not as paradoxical as it might appear. In his famous prayer, Anselm reflected on the words of Isaiah: "Unless you have faith, you will not understand":

> I yearn to understand some measure of thy truth which my heart believes and loves. For I do not seek to understand in order to have faith but I have faith in order to understand (*credo ut intellegam*). For I believe even this: I shall not understand unless I have faith.[29]

The oft-quoted *credo ut intellegam* is not an intellectual abdication. Anselm was not claiming to embrace the creed blindly in the hope of its making sense some day. His assertion should really be translated: "I commit myself in order that I may understand." At this time, the word *credo* still did not have the intellectual bias of the word "belief" today but meant an attitude of trust and loyalty. It is important to note that even in the first flush of Western rationalism, the religious experience of God remained primary, coming before discussion or logical understanding.

Nevertheless, like the Muslim and Jewish Faylasufs, Anselm believed that the existence of God could be argued rationally, and he devised his own proof, which is usually called the "ontological" argument. Anselm defined God as "something than which nothing greater can be thought" (*aliquid quo nihil maius cogitari possit*).[30] Since this implied that God could be an object of thought, the implication was that he could be conceived and comprehended by the human mind. Anselm argued that this Something must exist. Since existence is more "perfect" or complete than nonexistence, the perfect being that we imagine must have existence or it would be imperfect. Anselm's proof was ingenious and effective in a world dominated by Platonic thought, where ideas were believed to point to eternal archetypes. It is unlikely to convince a skeptic today. As the British theologian John Macquarrie has remarked, you may imagine that you have $100, but unfortunately that will not make the money a reality in your pocket.[31]

Anselm's God was Being, therefore, not the Nothing described by Denys and Erigena. Anselm was willing to speak about God in far more positive terms than most of the previous Faylasufs. He did not propose the discipline of a *Via Negativa* but seemed to think it possible to arrive at a fairly adequate idea of God by means of natural reason, which was precisely what had always troubled the Greeks about the Western theology. Once he had proved God's existence to his satisfaction, Anselm set out to demonstrate the doctrines of the Incarnation and the Trinity, which the Greeks had always insisted defied reason and conceptualization. In his treatise *Why God Became Man*, which we considered in Chapter 4, he relies on logic and rational thought more than revelation—his quotations from the Bible and the Fathers seem purely incidental to the thrust of his argument, which, as we saw, ascribed essentially human motivation to God. He was not the only Western Christian to try to explain the mystery of God in rational terms. His contemporary Peter Abelard (1079–1147), the charismatic philosopher of Paris, had also evolved an explanation of the Trinity which emphasized the divine unity somewhat at the expense of the distinction of the Three Persons. He also developed a sophisticated and moving rationale for the mystery of the atonement: Christ had been crucified to awaken compassion in us and by doing so he became our Savior.

Abelard was primarily a philosopher, however, and his theology was usually rather conventional. He had become a leading figure in the intellectual revival in Europe during the twelfth century and had acquired a huge following. This had brought him into conflict with Bernard, the charismatic abbot of the Cistercian Abbey of Clairvaux in Burgundy, who was arguably the most powerful man in Europe. Pope Eugene II and King Louis VII of France were both in Bernard's pocket, and his eloquence had inspired a monastic revolution in Europe: scores of young men had left their homes to follow him into the Cistercian order, which sought to reform the old Cluniac form of Benedictine religious life. When Bernard preached the Second Crusade in 1146, the people of France and Germany—who had previously been somewhat apathetic about the expedition—almost tore him to pieces in their enthusiasm, flocking to join the army in such numbers that, Bernard complacently wrote to the Pope, the countryside seemed deserted. Bernard was an intelligent man, who had given the rather external piety of Western Europe a new interior dimension. Cistercian piety seems to have influenced the legend of the Holy Grail, which describes a spiritual journey to a symbolic city that is not of this world but which represents the vision of God. Bernard heartily distrusted the intellectualism of scholars like Abelard, however, and vowed to silence him. He accused Abelard of "attempting to bring the merit of the Christian faith to naught because he supposes that by human reason he can comprehend all that is God."[32] Referring to St. Paul's hymn to charity, Bernard claimed that the philosopher was lacking in Christian love: "He sees nothing as an enigma, nothing as in a mirror, but looks on everything face to face."[33] Love and the exercise of reason, therefore, were incompatible. In 1141 Bernard summoned Abelard to appear before the Council of Sens, which he packed with his own supporters, some of whom stood outside to intimidate Abelard when he arrived. That was not difficult to do since, by this time, Abelard had probably developed Parkinson's disease. Bernard attacked him with such eloquence that he simply collapsed and died the following year.

It was a symbolic moment, which marked a split between mind and heart. In the Trinitarianism of Augustine, heart and mind had been inseparable. Muslim Faylasufs such as Ibn Sina and al-Ghazzali may have decided that the intellect alone could not find God, but they had both eventually envisaged a philosophy which was informed by the ideal of love and by the disciplines of mysticism. We shall see that during the twelfth and thirteenth centuries, the major thinkers of the Islamic world attempted to fuse mind and heart and saw philosophy as inseparable from the spirituality of love and imagination promoted by the Sufis. Bernard, however, seemed afraid of the intellect and wanted to keep it separate from the more emotional, intuitive parts of the mind. This was dangerous: it could lead to an unhealthy dissociation of sensibility that was in its own way just as worrying as an arid rationalism. The Crusade preached by Bernard was a disaster partly because it relied on an idealism that was untempered by common sense and was in flagrant denial of the Christian ethos of compassion.[34] Thus Bernard's treatment of Abelard was conspicuously lacking in charity, and he had urged the Crusaders to show their love for Christ by killing the infidels, and driving them out of the Holy Land. Bernard was right to fear a rationalism that attempted to explain the mystery of God and threatened to dilute the religious sense of awe and wonder, but unbridled subjectivity that fails to examine its prejudices critically can lead to the worst excesses of religion. What was required was an informed and intelligent subjectivity, not an emotionalism of "love," which represses the intellect violently and abandons the compassion which was supposed to be the hallmark of the religion of God.

Few thinkers have made such a lasting contribution to Western Christianity as Thomas Aquinas (1225–74), who attempted a synthesis of Augustine and the Greek philosophy which had recently been made available in the West. During the twelfth century, European scholars had flocked to Spain, where they encountered Muslim scholarship. With the help of Muslim and Jewish intellectuals they undertook a vast translation project to bring this intellectual wealth to the West. Arabic translations of Plato, Aristotle and the other philosophers of the ancient world were now translated into Latin and became available to the people of Northern Europe for the first time. The translators also worked on more recent Muslim scholarship, including the work of Ibn Rushd as well as the discoveries of Arab scientists and physicians. At the same time as some European Christians were bent on the destruction of Islam in the Near East, Muslims in Spain were helping the West to build up its own civilization. The *Summa Theologiae* of Thomas Aquinas was an attempt to integrate the new philosophy with the Western Christian tradition. Aquinas had been particularly impressed by Ibn Rushd's explication of Aristotle. Yet, unlike Anselm and Abelard, he did not believe that such mysteries as the Trinity could be proved by reason and distinguished carefully between the ineffable reality of God and human doctrines about him. He agreed with Denys that God's real nature was inaccessible to the human mind: "Hence in the last resort all that man knows of God is to know that he does not know him, since he knows that what God is surpasses all that we can understand of him."[35] There is a story that when he had dictated the last sentence of the *Summa*, Aquinas laid his head sadly on his arms. When the scribe asked him what was the matter, he replied that everything that he had written was straw compared with what he had seen.

Aquinas's attempt to set his religious experience in the context of the new philosophy was necessary in order to articulate faith with other reality and not relegate it to an isolated sphere of its own. Excessive intellectualism is damaging to the faith, but if God is not to become an indulgent endorsement of our own egotism, religious experience must be informed by an accurate assessment of its content. Aquinas defined God by returning to God's own definition of himself to Moses: "I am What I Am." Aristotle had said that God was Necessary Being; Aquinas accordingly linked the God of the Philosophers with the God of the Bible by calling God "He Who Is" (*Qui est*). He made it absolutely clear that God was not simply another being like ourselves, however. The definition of God as Being Itself was appropriate "because it does not signify any particular form [of being] but rather being itself (*esse seipsum*)."[36] It would be incorrect to blame Aquinas for the rationalistic view of God that later prevailed in the West.

Unfortunately, however, Aquinas gives the impression that God can be discussed in the same way as other philosophical ideas or natural phenomena by prefacing his discussion of God with a demonstration of God's existence from natural philosophy. This suggests that we can get to know God in much the same way as other mundane realities. Aquinas lists five "proofs" for God's existence that would become immensely important in the Catholic world and would also be used by Protestants:

1. Aristotle's argument for a Prime Mover.
2. A similar "proof" which maintains that there cannot be an infinite series of causes: there must have been a beginning.
3. The argument from contingency, propounded by Ibn Sina, which demands the existence of a "Necessary Being."
4. Aristotle's argument from the *Philosophy* that the hierarchy of excellence in this world implies a Perfection that is the best of all.
5. The argument from design, which maintains that the order and purpose that we see in the universe cannot simply be the result of chance.

These proofs do not hold water today. Even from a religious point of view, they are rather dubious, since, with the possible exception of the argument from design, each proof tacitly implies that "God" is simply an-other being, one more link in the chain of existence. He is the Supreme Being, the Necessary Being, the Most Perfect Being. Now, it is true that the use of such terms as "First Cause" or "Necessary Being" implies that God cannot be anything like the beings we know but rather their ground or the condition for their existence. This was certainly Aquinas's intention. Nevertheless, readers of the *Summa* have not always made this important distinction and have talked about God as if he were simply the Highest Being of all. This is reductive and can make this Super Being an idol, created in our own image and easily turned into a celestial Super Ego. It is probably not inaccurate to suggest that many people in the West regard God as a Being in this way.

It was important to try to link God with the new vogue for Aristotelianism in Europe. The Faylasufs had also been anxious that the idea of God should keep abreast of the times and not be relegated to an archaic ghetto. In each generation, the idea and experience of God would have to be created anew. Most Muslims, however, had—so to speak—voted with their feet and decided that Aristotle did not have much to contribute to the study of God, though he was immensely useful in other spheres, such as natural science. We have seen that Aristotle's discussion of the nature of God had been dubbed *meta ta physica* ("After the *Physics*") by the editor of his work: his God had simply been a continuation of physical reality rather than a reality of a totally different order. In the Muslim world, therefore, most future discussion of God blended philosophy with mysticism. Reason alone could not reach a religious understanding of the reality we call "God," but religious experience needed to be informed by the critical intelligence and discipline of philosophy if it were not to become messy, indulgent—or even dangerous—emotion.

Aquinas's Franciscan contemporary Bonaventure (1217–74) had much the same vision. He also tried to articulate philosophy with religious experience to the mutual enrichment of both spheres. In *The Threefold Way*, he had followed Augustine in seeing "trinities" everywhere in creation and took this "natural trinitarianism" as his starting point in *The Journey of the Mind to God*. He genuinely believed that the Trinity could be proved by unaided natural reason but avoided the dangers of rationalist chauvinism by stressing the importance of spiritual experience as an essential component of the idea of God. He took Francis of Assisi, the founder of his order, as the great exemplar of the Christian life. By looking at the events of his life, a theologian such as himself could find evidence for the doctrines of the Church. The Tuscan poet Dante Alighieri (1265–1321) would also find that a fellow human being—in Dante's case the Florentine woman Beatrice Portinari—could be an epiphany of the divine. This personalistic approach to God looked back to St. Augustine.

Bonaventure also applied Anselm's Ontological Proof for the existence of God to his discussion of Francis as an epiphany. He argued that Francis had achieved an excellence in this life that seemed more than human, so it was possible for us, while still living here below, to "see and understand that the 'best' is . . . that than which nothing better can be imagined."[37] The very fact that we could form such a concept as "the best" proved that it must exist in the Supreme Perfection of God. If we entered into ourselves, as Plato and Augustine had both advised, we would find God's image reflected "in our own inner world."[38] This introspection was essential. It was, of course, important to take part in the liturgy of the Church, but the Christian must first descend into the depths of his own self, where he would be "transported in ecstasy above the intellect" and find a vision of God that transcended our limited human notions.[39]

Both Bonaventure and Aquinas had seen the religious experience as primary. They had been faithful to the tradition of Falsafah, since in both Judaism and Islam, philosophers had often been mystics who were acutely conscious of the limitations of the intellect in theological matters. They had evolved rational proofs of God's existence to articulate their religious faith with their scientific studies and to link it with other more ordinary experiences. They did not personally doubt God's existence, and many were well aware of the limitations of their achievement. These proofs were not designed to convince unbelievers, since there were as yet no atheists in our modern sense. This natural theology was, therefore, not a prelude to religious experience but an accompaniment: the Faylasufs did not believe that you had to convince yourself of God's existence rationally before you could have a mystical experience. If anything, it was the other way around. In the Jewish, Muslim and Greek Orthodox worlds, the God of the philosophers was being rapidly overtaken by the God of the mystics.

7

The God of the Mystics

J UDAISM, CHRISTIANITY and—to a lesser extent—Islam have all developed the idea of a personal God, so we tend to think that this ideal represents religion at its best. The personal God has helped monotheists to value the sacred and inalienable rights of the individual and to cultivate an appreciation of human personality. The Judeo-Christian tradition has thus helped the West to acquire the liberal humanism it values so highly. These values were originally enshrined in a personal God who does everything that a human being does: he loves, judges, punishes, sees, hears, creates and destroys as we do. Yahweh began as a highly personalized deity with passionate human likes and dislikes. Later he became a symbol of transcendence, whose thoughts were not our thoughts and whose ways soared above our own as the heavens tower above the earth. The personal God reflects an important religious insight: that no supreme value can be less than human. Thus personalism has been an important and—for many—an indispensable stage of religious and moral development. The prophets of Israel attributed their own emotions and passions to God; Buddhists and Hindus had to include a personal devotion to *avatars* of the supreme reality. Christianity made a human person the center of the religious life in a way that was unique in the history of religion: it took the personalism inherent in Judaism to an extreme. It may be that without some degree of this kind of identification and empathy, religion cannot take root.

Yet a personal God can become a grave liability. He can be a mere idol carved in our own image, a projection of our limited needs, fears and desires. We can assume that he loves what we love and hates what we hate, endorsing our prejudices instead of compelling us to transcend them. When he seems to fail to prevent a catastrophe or seems even to desire a tragedy, he can seem callous and cruel. A facile belief that a disaster is the will of God can make us accept things that are fundamentally unacceptable. The very fact that, as a person, God has a gender is also limiting: it means that the sexuality of half the human race is sacralized at the expense of the female and can lead to a neurotic and inadequate imbalance in human sexual mores. A personal God can be dangerous, therefore. Instead of pulling us beyond our limitations, "he" can encourage us to remain complacently within them; "he" can make us as cruel, callous, self-satisfied and partial as "he" seems to be. Instead of inspiring the compassion that should characterize all advanced religion, "he" can encourage us to judge, condemn and marginalize. It seems, therefore, that the idea of a personal God can only be a stage in our religious development. The world religions all seem to have recognized this danger and have sought to transcend the personal conception of supreme reality.

It is possible to read the Jewish scriptures as the story of the refinement and, later, of the abandonment of the tribal and personalized Yahweh who became YHWH. Christianity, arguably the most personalized religion of the three monotheistic faiths, tried to qualify the cult of God incarnate by introducing the doctrine of the transpersonal Trinity. Muslims very soon had problems with those passages in the Koran which implied that God "sees," "hears" and "judges" like human beings. All three of the monotheistic religions developed a mystical tradition, which made their God transcend the personal category and become more similar to the impersonal realities of nirvana and Brahman-Atman. Only a few people are capable of true mysticism, but in all three faiths (with the exception of Western Christianity) it was the God experienced by the mystics which eventually became normative among the faithful, until relatively recently.

Historical monotheism was not originally mystical. We have noted the difference between the experience of a contemplative such as the Buddha and the prophets. Judaism, Christianity and Islam are all essentially active faiths, devoted to ensuring that God's will is done on earth as it is in heaven. The central motif of these prophetic religions is confrontation or a personal meeting between God and humanity. This God is experienced as an imperative to action; he calls us to himself; gives us the choice of rejecting or accepting his love and concern. This God relates to human beings by means of a dialogue rather than silent contemplation. He utters a Word, which becomes the chief focus of devotion and which has to be painfully incarnated in the flawed and tragic conditions of earthly life. In Christianity, the most personalized of the three, the relationship with God is characterized by love. But the point of love is that the ego has, in some sense, to be annihilated. In either dialogue or love, egotism is a perpetual possibility. Language itself can be a limiting faculty since it embeds us in the concepts of our mundane experience.

The prophets had declared war on mythology: their God was active in history and in current political events rather than in the primordial, sacred time of myth. When monotheists turned to mysticism, however, mythology reasserted itself as the chief vehicle of religious experience. There is a linguistic connection between the three words "myth," "mysticism" and "mystery." All are derived from the Greek verb *musteion*: to close the eyes or the mouth. All three words, therefore, are rooted in an experience of darkness and silence.[1] They are not popular words in the West today. The word "myth," for example, is often used as a synonym for a lie: in popular parlance, a myth is something that is not true. A politician or a film star will dismiss scurrilous reports of their activities by saying that they are "myths" and scholars will refer to mistaken views of the past as "mythical." Since the Enlightenment, a "mystery" has been seen as something that needs to be cleared up. It is frequently associated with muddled thinking. In the United States, a detective story is called a "mystery" and it is of the essence of this genre that the problem be solved satisfactorily. We shall see that even religious people came to regard "mystery" as a bad word during the Enlightenment. Similarly "mysticism" is frequently associated with cranks, charlatans or indulgent hippies. Since the West has never been very enthusiastic about mysticism, even during its heyday in other parts of the world, there is little understanding of the intelligence and discipline that are essential to this type of spirituality.

Yet there are signs that the tide may be turning. Since the 1960s Western people have been discovering the benefits of certain types of Yoga, and religions such as Buddhism, which have the advantage of being uncontaminated by an inadequate theism, have enjoyed a great flowering in Europe and the United States. The work of the late American scholar Joseph Campbell on mythology has enjoyed a recent vogue. The current enthusiasm for psychoanalysis in the West can be seen as a desire for some kind of mysticism, for we shall find arresting similarities between the two disciplines. Mythology has often been an attempt to explain the inner world of the psyche, and both Freud and Jung turned instinctively to ancient myths, such as the Greek story of Oedipus, to explain their new science. It may be that people in the West are feeling the need for an alternative to a purely scientific view of the world.

Mystical religion is more immediate and tends to be more help in time of trouble than a predominantly cerebral faith. The disciplines of mysticism help the adept to return to the One, the primordial beginning, and to cultivate a constant sense of presence. Yet the early Jewish mysticism that developed during the second and third centuries, which was very difficult for Jews, seemed to emphasize the gulf between God and man. Jews wanted to turn away from a world in which they were persecuted and marginalized to a more powerful divine realm. They imagined God as a mighty king who could only be approached in a perilous journey through the seven heavens. Instead of expressing themselves in the simple direct style of the Rabbis, the mystics used sonorous, grandiloquent language. The Rabbis hated this spirituality, and the mystics were anxious not to antagonize them. Yet this "Throne Mysticism," as it was called, must have fulfilled an important need since it continued to flourish alongside the great rabbinic academies until it was finally incorporated into Kabbalah, the new Jewish mysticism, during the twelfth and thirteenth centuries. The classic texts of Throne Mysticism, which were edited in Babylon in the fifth and sixth centuries, suggest that the mystics, who were reticent about their experiences, felt a strong affinity with rabbinic tradition, since they make such great *tannaim* as Rabbi Akiva, Rabbi Ishmael and Rabbi Yohannan the heroes of this spirituality. They revealed a new extremity in the Jewish spirit, as they blazed a new trail to God on behalf of their people.

The Rabbis had had some remarkable religious experiences, as we have seen. On the occasion when the Holy Spirit descended upon Rabbi Yohannan and his disciples in the form of fire from heaven, they had apparently been discussing the meaning of Ezekiel's strange vision of God's chariot. The chariot and the mysterious figure that Ezekiel had glimpsed sitting upon its throne seem to have been the subject of early esoteric speculation. The Study of the Chariot (*Ma'aseh Merkavah*) was often linked to speculation about the meaning of the creation story (*Ma'aseh Bereshit*). The earliest account we have of the mystical ascent to God's throne in the highest heavens emphasized the immense perils of this spiritual journey:

> Our Rabbis taught: Four entered an orchard and these are they: Ben Azzai, Ben Zoma, Aher and Rabbi Akiva. Rabbi Akiva said to them:

"When you reach the stones of pure marble, do not say 'Water! water!' For it is said: 'He that speaketh falsehood shall not be established before mine eyes.' " Ben Azzai gazed and died. Of him, Scripture says: "Precious in the sight of the Lord is the death of his saints." Ben Zoma gazed and was stricken. Of him Scripture says: "Hast thou found honey? Eat as much as is sufficient for thee, lest thou be filled therewith, and vomit it." Aher cut the shoots [that is, became a heretic]. Rabbi Akiva departed in peace.[2]

Only Rabbi Akiva was mature enough to survive the mystical way unscathed. A journey to the depths of the mind involves great personal risks because we may not be able to endure what we find there. That is why all religions have insisted that the mystical journey can only be undertaken under the guidance of an expert, who can monitor the experience, guide the novice past the perilous places and make sure that he is not exceeding his strength, like poor Ben Azzai, who died, and Ben Zoma, who went mad. All mystics stress the need for intelligence and mental stability. Zen masters say that it is useless for a neurotic person to seek a cure in meditation, for that will only make him sicker. The strange and outlandish behavior of some European Catholic saints who were revered as mystics must be regarded as aberrations. This cryptic story of the Talmudic sages shows that Jews had been aware of the dangers from the very beginning: later, they would not let young people become initiated into the disciplines of Kabbalah until they were fully mature. A mystic also had to be married, to ensure that he was in good sexual health.

The mystic had to journey to the Throne of God through the mythological realm of the seven heavens. Yet this was only an imaginary flight. It was never taken literally but was always seen as a symbolic ascent through the mysterious regions of the mind. Rabbi Akiva's strange warning about the "stones of pure marble" may refer to the password that the mystic had to utter at various crucial points in his imaginary journey. These images were visualized as part of an elaborate discipline. Today we know that the unconscious is a teeming mass of imagery that surfaces in dreams, in hallucinations and in aberrant psychic or neurological conditions such as epilepsy or schizophrenia. Jewish mystics did not imagine that they were "really" flying through the sky or entering God's palace but were marshaling the religious images that filled their minds in a controlled and ordered way. This demanded great skill and a certain disposition and training. It required the same kind of concentration as the disciplines of Zen or Yoga, which also help the adept to find his way through the labyrinthine paths of the psyche. The Babylonian sage Hai Gaon (939–1038) explained the story of the four sages by means of contemporary mystical practice. The "orchard" refers to the mystical ascent of the soul to the "Heavenly Halls" (*hekhalot*) of God's palace. A man who wishes to make this imaginary, interior journey must be "worthy" and "blessed with certain qualities" if he wishes "to gaze at the heavenly chariot and the halls of the angels on high." It will not happen spontaneously. He has to perform certain exercises that are similar to those practiced by Yogis and contemplatives all the world over:

> He must fast for a specified number of days, he must place his head between his knees whispering softly to himself the while certain praises of God with his face towards the ground. As a result he will gaze in the innermost recesses of his heart and it will seem as if he saw the seven halls with his own eyes, moving from hall to hall to observe that which is therein to be found.[3]

Although the earliest texts of this Throne Mysticism date only to the second or third centuries, this kind of contemplation was probably older. Thus St. Paul refers to a friend "who belonged to the Messiah" who had been caught up to the third heaven some fourteen years earlier. Paul was not sure how to interpret this vision but believed that the man "was caught up into paradise and heard things which must not and cannot be put into human language."[4]

The visions are not ends in themselves but means to an ineffable religious experience that exceeds normal concepts. They will be conditioned by the particular religious tradition of the mystic. A Jewish visionary will see visions of the seven heavens because his religious imagination is stocked with these particular symbols. Buddhists see various images of Buddhas and *bodhisattvas*; Christians visualize the Virgin Mary. It is a mistake for the visionary to see these mental apparitions as objective or as anything more than symbols of transcendence. Since hallucination is often a pathological state, considerable skill and mental balance is required to handle and interpret the symbols that emerge during the course of concentrated meditation and inner reflection.

One of the strangest and most controversial of these early Jewish visions is found in the *Shiur Qomah* (The Measurement of the Height), a fifth-century text which describes the figure that Ezekiel had seen on God's throne. The *Shiur Qomah* calls this being Yotzrenu, "Our Creator." Its peculiar description of this vision of God is probably based on a passage from the *Song of Songs*, which was Rabbi Akiva's favorite biblical text. The Bride describes her Lover:

> My beloved is fresh and ruddy,
> to be known among ten thousand.
> His head is golden, purest gold,
> his locks are palm fronds
> and black as the raven.
> His eyes are doves
> at a pool of water,
> bathed in milk,
> at rest on a pool;
> his cheeks are beds of spices,
> banks sweetly scented.
> His lips are lilies,
> distilling pure myrrh,
> His hands are golden, rounded,
> set with jewels of Tarshish.
> His belly a block of ivory
> covered with sapphires.
> His legs are alabaster columns.[5]

Some saw this as a description of God: to the consternation of generations of Jews, the *Shiur Qomah* proceeded to measure each one of God's limbs listed here. In this strange text, the measurements of God are baffling. The mind cannot cope. The "parasang"—the basic unit—is equivalent to 180 trillion "fingers" and each "finger" stretches from one end of the earth to the other. These massive dimensions boggle the mind, which gives up trying to follow them or even to conceive a figure of such size. That is the point. The *Shiur* is trying to tell us that it is impossible to measure God or contain him in human terms. The mere attempt to do so demonstrates the impossibility of the project and gives us a new experience of God's transcendence. Not surprisingly, many Jews have found this odd attempt to measure the wholly spiritual God blasphemous. That is why an esoteric text such as the *Shiur* was kept hidden from the unwary. Seen in context, the *Shiur Qomah* would give to those adepts who were prepared to approach it in the right way, under the guidance of their spiritual director, a new insight into the transcendence of a God

which exceeds all human categories. It is certainly not meant to be taken
literally; it certainly conveys no secret information. It is a deliberate
evocation of a mood that created a sense of wonder and awe.

The *Shiur* introduces us to two essential ingredients in the mystical
portrait of God, which are common in all three faiths. First, it is essentially imaginative; secondly, it is ineffable. The figure described in the
Shiur is the image of God whom the mystics see sitting enthroned at the
end of their ascent. There is absolutely nothing tender, loving or personal
about this God; indeed his holiness seems alienating. When they see him,
however, the mystical heroes burst into songs which give very little
information about God but which leave an immense impression:

> A quality of holiness, a quality of power, a fearful quality, a dreaded-
>   quality, a quality of awe, a quality of dismay, a quality of terror—
> Such is the quality of the garment of the Creator, Adonai, God of
>   Israel, who, crowned, comes to the thone of his glory;
> His garment is engraved inside and outside and entirely covered
>   with YHWH, YHWH.
> No eyes are able to behold it, neither the eyes of flesh and blood,
>   nor the eyes of his servants.[6]

If we cannot imagine what Yahweh's cloak is like, how can we think to
behold God himself?

Perhaps the most famous of the early Jewish mystical texts is the fifth-
century *Sefer Yezirah* (The Book of Creation). There is no attempt to
describe the creative process realistically; the account is unashamedly
symbolic and shows God creating the world by means of language as
though he were writing a book. But language has been entirely transformed, and the message of creation is no longer clear. Each letter of the
Hebrew alphabet is given a numerical value; by combining the letters
with the sacred numbers, rearranging them in endless configurations, the
mystic weaned his mind away from the normal connotations of words.
The purpose was to bypass the intellect and remind Jews that no words
or concepts could represent the reality to which the Name pointed. Again,
the experience of pushing language to its limits and making it yield a non-
linguistic significance created a sense of the otherness of God. Mystics
did not want a straightforward dialogue with a God whom they experienced as an overwhelming holiness rather than a sympathetic friend and
father.

Throne Mysticism was not unique. The Prophet Muhammad is said to have had a very similar experience when he made his Night Journey from Arabia to the Temple Mount in Jerusalem. He had been transported in sleep by Gabriel on a celestial horse. On arrival, he was greeted by Abraham, Moses, Jesus and a crowd of other prophets, who confirmed Muhammad in his own prophetic mission. Then Gabriel and Muhammad began their perilous ascent up a ladder (*miraj*) through the seven heavens, each of which was presided over by a prophet. Finally Muhammad reached the divine sphere. The early sources reverently keep silent about the final vision, to which these verses in the Koran are believed to refer.

> And indeed he saw him a second time by the lote-tree of the furthest
>   limit, near unto the garden of promise, with the lote-tree veiled
>   in a veil of nameless splendor . . .
> [And withal] the eye did not waver, nor yet did it stray: truly did
>   he see some of the most profound of his Sustainer's symbols.[7]

Muhammad did not see God himself but only symbols that pointed to the divine reality: in Hinduism the lote-tree marks the limit of rational thought. There is no way in which the vision of God can appeal to the normal experiences of thought or language. The ascent to heaven is a symbol of the furthest reach of the human spirit, which marks the threshold of ultimate meaning.

The imagery of ascent is common. St. Augustine had experienced an ascent to God with his mother at Ostia, which he described in the language of Plotinus:

> Our minds were lifted up by an ardent affection towards eternal
> being itself. Step by step we climbed beyond all corporate objects
> and the heaven itself, where sun, moon and stars shed light on the
> earth. We ascended even further by internal reflection and dialogue
> and wonder at your works and entered into our own minds.[8]

Augustine's mind was filled with the Greek imagery of the great chain of being instead of the Semitic images of the seven heavens. This was not a literal journey through outer space to a God "out there" but a mental ascent to a reality within. This rapturous flight seems something given, from without, when he says "our minds were lifted up" as though he and Monica were passive recipients of grace, but there is a deliberation in this steady climb toward "eternal being." Similar imagery of ascent has also been noted in the trance experiences of Shamans "from Siberia to Tierra del Fuego," as Joseph Campbell puts it.[9]

The symbol of an ascent indicates that worldly perceptions have been left far behind. The experience of God that is finally attained is utterly indescribable, since normal language no longer applies. The Jewish mystics describe anything *but* God! They tell us about his cloak, his palace, his heavenly court and the veil that shields him from human gaze, which represents the eternal archetypes. Muslims who speculated about Muhammad's flight to heaven stress the paradoxical nature of his final vision of God: he both saw and did not see the divine presence.[10] Once the mystic has worked through the realm of imagery in his mind, he reaches the point where neither concepts nor imagination can take him any further. Augustine and Monica were equally reticent about the climax of their flight, stressing its transcendence of space, time and ordinary knowledge. They "talked and panted" for God, and "touched it in some small degree by a moment of total concentration of heart."[11] Then they had to return to normal speech, where a sentence has a beginning, a middle and an end:

> Therefore we said: If to anyone the tumult of the flesh has fallen silent, if the images of earth, water, and air are quiescent, if the heavens themselves are shut out and the very soul itself is making no sound and is surpassing itself by no longer thinking about itself, if all dreams and visions in the imagination are excluded, if all language and everything transitory is silent—for if anyone could hear then this is what all of them would be saying, "We did not make ourselves, we were made by him who abides for eternity" (Psalm 79:3,5). . . . That is how it was when at that moment we extended our reach and in a flash of mental energy attained the eternal wisdom which abides beyond all things.[12]

This was no naturalistic vision of a personal God: they had not, so to speak, "heard his voice" through any of the normal methods of naturalistic communication: through ordinary speech, the voice of an angel, through nature or the symbolism of a dream. It seemed that they had "touched" the Reality which lay beyond all these things.[13]

Although it is clearly culturally conditioned, this kind of "ascent" seems an incontrovertible fact of life. However we choose to interpret it, people all over the world and in all phases of history have had this type of contemplative experience. Monotheists have called the climactic insight a "vision of God"; Plotinus had assumed that it was the experience of the One; Buddhists would call it an intimation of nirvana. The point is that this is something that human beings who have a certain spiritual talent have always wanted to do. The mystical experience of God has certain characteristics that are common to all faiths. It is a subjective experience that involves an interior journey, not a perception of an objective fact outside the self; it is undertaken through the image-making part of the mind—often called the imagination—rather than through the more cerebral, logical faculty. Finally, it is something that the mystic creates in himself or herself deliberately: certain physical or mental exercises yield the final vision; it does not always come upon them unawares.

Augustine seems to have imagined that privileged human beings were sometimes able to see God in this life: he cited Moses and St. Paul as examples. Pope Gregory the Great (540–604), who was an acknowledged master of the spiritual life as well as being a powerful pontiff, disagreed. He was not an intellectual and, as a typical Roman, had a more pragmatic view of spirituality. He used the metaphors of cloud, fog or darkness to suggest the obscurity of all human knowledge of the divine. His God remained hidden from human beings in an impenetrable darkness that was far more painful than the cloud of unknowing experienced by such Greek Christians as Gregory of Nyssa and Denys. God was a distressing experience for Gregory. He insisted that God was difficult of access. There was certainly no way we could talk about him familiarly, as though we had something in common. We knew nothing at all about God. We could make no predictions about his behavior on the basis of our knowledge of people: "Then only is there truth in what we know concerning God, when we are made sensible that we cannot fully know anything about him."[14] Frequently Gregory dwells upon the pain and effort of the approach to God. The joy and peace of contemplation could only be attained for a few moments after a mighty struggle. Before tasting God's sweetness, the soul has to fight its way out of the darkness that is its natural element: It

> cannot fix its mind's eyes on that which it has with hasty glance seen within itself, because it is compelled by its own habits to sink downwards. It meanwhile pants and struggles and endeavors to go above itself but sinks back, overpowered with weariness, into its own familiar darkness.[15]

God could only be reached after "a great effort of the mind," which had to wrestle with him as Jacob had wrestled with the angel. The path to God was beset with guilt, tears and exhaustion; as it approached him, "the soul could do nothing but weep." "Tortured" by its desire for God, it only "found rest in tears, being wearied out."[16] Gregory remained an important spiritual guide until the twelfth century; clearly the West continued to find God a strain.

In the East, the Christian experience of God was characterized by light rather than darkness. The Greeks evolved a different form of mysticism, which is also found worldwide. This did not depend on imagery and vision but rested on the apophatic or silent experience described by Denys the Areopagite. They naturally eschewed all rationalistic conceptions of God. As Gregory of Nyssa had explained in his *Commentary on the Song of Songs*, "every concept grasped by the mind becomes an obstacle in the quest to those who search." The aim of the contemplative was to go beyond ideas and also beyond all images whatsoever, since these could only be a distraction. Then he would acquire "a certain sense of presence" that was indefinable and certainly transcended all human experiences of a relationship with another person.[17] This attitude was called *hesychia*, "tranquillity" or "interior silence." Since words, ideas and images can only tie us down in the mundane world, in the here and now, the mind must be deliberately stilled by the techniques of concentration, so that it could cultivate a waiting silence. Only then could it hope to apprehend a Reality that transcended anything that it could conceive.

How was it possible to know an incomprehensible God? The Greeks loved that kind of paradox, and the *hesychasts* turned to the old distinction between God's essence (*ousia*) and his "energies" (*energeiai*) or activities in the world, which enabled us to experience something of the divine. Since we could never know God as he is in himself, it was the "energies" not the "essence," that we experienced in prayer. They could be described as the "rays" of divinity, which illuminated the world and were an out-pouring of the divine, but as distinct from God himself as sunbeams were distinct from the sun. They manifested a God who was utterly silent and unknowable. As St. Basil had said: "It is by his energies that we know our God; we do not assert that we come near to the essence itself, for his energies descend to us but his essence remains unapproachable."[18] In the Old Testament, this divine "energy" had been called God's "glory" (*ka-vod*). In the New Testament, it had shone forth in the person of Christ on Mount Tabor, when his humanity had been transfigured by the divine rays. Now they penetrated the whole created universe and deified those who had been saved. As the word *energeiai* implied, this was an active and dynamic conception of God. Where the West would see God making himself known by means of his eternal attributes—his goodness, justice, love and omnipotence—the Greeks saw God making himself accessible in a ceaseless activity in which he was somehow present.

When we experienced the "energies" in prayer, therefore, we were in some sense communing with God directly, even though the unknowable reality itself remained in obscurity. The leading *hesychast* Evagrius Pontus (d. 399) insisted that the "knowledge" that we had of God in prayer had nothing whatever to do with concepts or images but was an immediate experience of the divine which transcended these. It was important, therefore, for *hesychasts* to strip their souls naked: "When you are praying," he told his monks, "do not shape within yourself any image of the deity and do not let your mind be shaped by the impress of any form." Instead, they should "approach the Immaterial in an immaterial manner."[19] Evagrius was proposing a sort of Christian Yoga. This was not a process of reflection; indeed, "prayer means the shedding of thought."[20] It was rather an intuitive apprehension of God. It will result in a sense of the unity of all things, a freedom from distraction and multiplicity, and the loss of ego—an experience that is clearly akin to that produced by contemplatives in nontheistic religions like Buddhism. By systematically weaning their minds away from their "passions"—such as pride, greed, sadness or anger which tied them to the ego—*hesychasts* would transcend themselves and become deified like Jesus on Mount Tabor, transfigured by the divine "energies."

Diodochus, the fifth-century bishop of Photice, insisted that this deification was not delayed until the next world but could be experienced consciously here below. He taught a method of concentration that involved breathing: as they inhaled, *hesychasts* should pray: "Jesus Christ, Son of God"; they should exhale to the words: "have mercy upon us." Later *hesychasts* refined this exercise: contemplatives should sit with head and shoulders bowed, looking toward their heart or navel. They should breathe ever more slowly in order to direct their attention inward, to certain psychological foci like the heart. It was a rigorous discipline that must be used carefully; it could only be safely practiced under an expert director. Gradually, like a Buddhist monk, the *hesychast* would find that he or she could set rational thoughts gently to one side, the imagery that thronged the mind would fade away and the *hesychast* would feel totally one with the prayer. Greek Christians had discovered for themselves techniques that had been practiced for centuries in the oriental religions.

They saw prayer as a psychosomatic activity, whereas Westerners like Augustine and Gregory thought that prayer should liberate the soul from the body. Maximus the Confessor had insisted: "The whole man should become God, deified by the grace of the God-become-man, becoming whole man, soul and body, by nature and becoming whole god, soul and body, by grace."[21] The *hesychast* would experience this as an influx of energy and clarity that was so powerful and compelling that it could only be divine. As we have seen, the Greeks saw this "deification" as an enlightenment that was natural to man. They found inspiration in the transfigured Christ on Mount Tabor, just as Buddhists were inspired by the image of the Buddha, who had attained the fullest realization of humanity. The Feast of the Transfiguration is very important in the Eastern Orthodox Churches; it is called an "epiphany," a manifestation of God. Unlike their Western brethren, the Greeks did not think that strain, dryness and desolation were an inescapable prelude to the experience of God: these were simply disorders that must be cured. Greeks had no cult of a dark night of the soul. The dominant motif was Tabor rather than Gethsemane and Calvary.

Not everybody could achieve these higher states, however, but other Christians could glimpse something of this mystical experience in the icons. In the West, religious art was becoming predominantly representational: it depicted historical events in the lives of Jesus or the saints. In Byzantium, however, the icon was not meant to represent anything in *this* world but was an attempt to portray the ineffable mystical experience of the *hesychasts* in a visual form to inspire the nonmystics. As the British historian Peter Brown explains, "Throughout the Eastern Christian world, icon and vision validated one another. Some deep gathering into one focal point of the collective imagination . . . ensured that by the sixth century, the supernatural had taken on the precise lineaments, in dreams and in each person's imagination, in which it was commonly portrayed in art. The icon had the validity of a realized dream."[22] Icons were not meant to instruct the faithful or to convey information, ideas or doctrines. They were a focus of contemplation (*theoria*) which provided the faithful with a sort of window on the divine world.

They became so central to the Byzantine experience of God, however, that by the eighth century they had become the center of a passionate doctrinal dispute in the Greek Church. People were beginning to ask *what* exactly the artist was painting when he painted Christ. It was impossible to depict his divinity, but if the artist claimed that he was only painting the humanity of Jesus, was he guilty of Nestorianism, the heretical belief that Jesus' human and divine natures were quite distinct? The iconoclasts wanted to ban icons altogether, but icons were defended by two leading monks: John of Damascus (656–747) of the monastery of Mar Sabbas near Bethlehem, and Theodore (759–826), of the monastery of Studius near Constantinople. They argued that the iconoclasts were wrong to forbid the depiction of Christ. Since the Incarnation, the material world and the human body had both been given a divine dimension, and an artist *could* paint this new type of deified humanity. He was also painting an image of God, since Christ the Logos was the icon of God *par excellence*. God could not be contained in words or summed up in human concepts, but he could be "described" by the pen of the artist or in the symbolic gestures of the liturgy.

The piety of the Greeks was so dependent upon icons that by 820 the iconoclasts had been defeated by popular acclaim. This assertion that God was in some sense describable did not amount to an abandonment of Denys's apophatic theology, however. In his *Greater Apology for the Holy Images*, the monk Nicephoras claimed that icons were "expressive of the silence of God, exhibiting in themselves the ineffability of a mystery that transcends being. Without ceasing and without speech, they praise the goodness of God in that venerable and thrice-illumined melody of theology."[23] Instead of instructing the faithful in the dogmas of the Church and helping them to form lucid ideas about their faith, the icons held them in a sense of mystery. When describing the effect of these religious paintings, Nicephoras could only compare it to the effect of music, the most ineffable of the arts and possibly the most direct. Emotion and experience are conveyed by music in a way that bypasses words and concepts. In the nineteenth century, Walter Pater would assert that all art aspired to the condition of music; in ninth-century Byzantium, Greek Christians saw theology as aspiring to the condition of iconography. They found that God was better expressed in a work of art than in rationalistic discourse. After the intensely wordy Christological debates of the fourth and fifth centuries, they were evolving a portrait of God that depended upon the imaginative experience of Christians.

This was definitively expressed by Symeon (949–1022), Abbot of the small monastery of St. Macras in Constantinople, who became known as the "New Theologian." This new type of theology made no attempt to define God. This, Symeon insisted, would be presumptuous; indeed, to speak about God in any way at all implied that "that which is incomprehensible is comprehensible."[24] Instead of arguing rationally about God's nature, the "new" theology relied on direct, personal religious experience.

It was impossible to know God in conceptual terms, as though he were just another being about which we could form ideas. God was a mystery. A true Christian was one who had a conscious experience of the God who had revealed himself in the transfigured humanity of Christ. Symeon had himself been converted from a worldly life to contemplation by an experience that seemed to come to him out of the blue. At first he had had no idea what was happening, but gradually he became aware that he was being transformed and, as it were, absorbed into a light that was of God himself. This was not light as we know it, of course; it was beyond "form, image or representation and could only be experienced intuitively, through prayer."[25] But this was not an experience for the elite or for monks only; the kingdom announced by Christ in the Gospels was a union with God that everybody could experience here and now, without having to wait until the next life.

For Symeon, therefore, God was known and unknown, near and far. Instead of attempting the impossible task of describing "ineffable matters by words alone,"[26] he urged his monks to concentrate on what could be experienced as a transfiguring reality in their own souls. As God had said to Symeon during one of his visions: "Yes, I am God, the one who became man for your sake. And behold, I have created you, as you see, and I shall make you God."[27] God was not an external, objective fact but an essentially subjective and personal enlightenment. Yet Symeon's refusal to speak *about* God did not lead him to break with the theological insights of the past. The "new" theology was based firmly on the teachings of the Fathers of the Church. In his *Hymns of Divine Love*, Symeon expressed the old Greek doctrine of the deification of humanity, as described by Athanasius and Maximus:

> O Light that none can name, for it is altogether nameless.
> O Light with many names, for it is at work in all things . . .
> How do you mingle yourself with grass?
> How, while continuing unchanged, altogether inaccessible,
> do you preserve the nature of the grass unconsumed?[28]

It was useless to define the God who affected this transformation, since he was beyond speech and description. Yet as an experience that fulfilled and transfigured humanity without violating its integrity, "God" was an incontrovertible reality. The Greeks had developed ideas about God— such as the Trinity and the Incarnation—that separated them from other monotheists, yet the actual experience of their mystics had much in common with those of Muslims and Jews.

Even though the Prophet Muhammad had been primarily concerned with the establishment of a just society, he and some of his closest companions had been mystically inclined, and the Muslims had quickly developed their own distinctive mystical tradition. During the eighth and ninth centuries, an ascetical form of Islam had developed alongside the other sects; the ascetics were as concerned as the Mutazilis and the Shiis about the wealth of the court and the apparent abandonment of the austerity of the early *ummah*. They attempted to return to the simpler life of the first Muslims in Medina, dressing in the coarse garments made of wool (Arabic *SWF*) that were supposed to have been favored by the Prophet. Consequently, they were known as Sufis. Social justice remained crucial to their piety, as Louis Massignon, the late French scholar, has explained:

> The mystic call is as a rule the result of an inner rebellion of the conscience against social injustices, not only those of others but primarily and particularly against one's own faults with a desire intensified by inner purification to find God at any price.[29]

At first Sufis had much in common with the other sects. Thus the great Mutazili rationalist Wasil ibn Ata (d. 748) had been a disciple of Hasan al-Basri (d. 728), the ascetic of Medina who was later revered as one of the fathers of Sufism.

The *ulema* were beginning to distinguish Islam sharply from other religions, seeing it as the one, true faith, but Sufis by and large remained true to the Koranic vision of the unity of all rightly guided religion. Jesus, for example, was revered by many Sufis as the prophet of the interior life. Some even amended the Shahadah, the profession of faith, to say: "There is no god but al-Lah and Jesus is his Messenger," which was technically correct but intentionally provocative. Where the Koran speaks of a God of justice who inspires fear and awe, the early woman ascetic Rabiah (d. 801) spoke of love, in a way that Christians would have found familiar:

> Two ways I love Thee: selfishly,
> And next, as worthy is of Thee.
> 'Tis selfish love that I do naught
> Save think on Thee with every thought.

> 'Tis purest love when Thou dost raise
> The veil to my adoring gaze.
> Not mine the praise in that or this:
> Thine is the praise in both, I wis.[30]

This is close to her famous prayer: "O God! If I worship thee in fear of Hell, burn me in Hell; and if I worship Thee in hope of Paradise, exclude me from Paradise; but if I worship Thee for Thine own sake, withhold not Thine Everlasting Beauty!"[31] The love of God became the hallmark of Sufism. Sufis may well have been influenced by the Christian ascetics of the Near East, but Muhammad remained a crucial influence. They hoped to have an experience of God that was similar to that of Muhammad when he had received his revelations. Naturally, they were also inspired by his mystical ascent to heaven, which became the paradigm of their own experience of God.

They also evolved the techniques and disciplines that have helped mystics all over the world to achieve an alternative state of consciousness. Sufis added the practices of fasting, night vigils and chanting the Divine Names as a mantra to the basic requirements of Muslim law. The effect of these practices sometimes resulted in behavior which seemed bizarre and unrestrained, and such mystics were known as "drunken" Sufis. The first of these was Abu Yazid Bistami (d. 874), who, like Rabiah, approached God as a lover. He believed that he should strive to please al-Lah as he would a woman in a human love affair, sacrificing his own needs and desires so as to become one with the Beloved. Yet the introspective disciplines he adopted to achieve this led him beyond this personalized conception of God. As he approached the core of his identity, he felt that nothing stood between God and himself; indeed, everything that he understood as "self" seemed to have melted away:

> I gazed upon [al-Lah] with the eye of truth and said to Him: "Who is this?" He said, "This is neither I nor other than I. There is no God but I." Then he changed me out of my identity into His Selfhood. . . . Then I communed with Him with the tongue of His Face, saying: "How fares it with me with Thee?" He said, "I am through Thee; there is no god but Thou."[32]

Yet again, this was no external deity "out there," alien to mankind: God was discovered to be mysteriously identified with the inmost self. The systematic destruction of the ego led to a sense of absorption in a larger, ineffable reality. This state of annihilation (*'fana*) became central to the Sufi ideal. Bistami had completely reinterpreted the Shahadah in a way that could have been construed as blasphemous, had it not been recognized by so many other Muslims as an authentic experience of that *islām* commanded by the Koran.

Other mystics, known as the "sober" Sufis, preferred a less extravagant spirituality. Al-Junayd of Baghdad (d. 910), who mapped out the ground plan of all future Islamic mysticism, believed that al-Bistami's extremism could be dangerous. He taught that *'fana* (annihilation) must be succeeded by *baqa* (revival), a return to an enhanced self. Union with God should not destroy our natural capabilities but fulfill them: a Sufi who had ripped away obscuring egotism to discover the divine presence at the heart of his own being would experience greater self-realization and self-control. He would become more fully human. When they experienced *'fana* and *baqa*, therefore, Sufis had achieved a state that a Greek Christian would call "deification." Al-Junayd saw the whole Sufi quest as a return to man's primordial state on the day of creation: he was returning to the ideal humanity that God had intended. He was also returning to the Source of his being. The experience of separation and alienation was as central to the Sufi as to the Platonic or Gnostic experience; it is, perhaps not dissimilar to the "separation" of which Freudians and Kleinians speak today, although the psychoanalysts attribute this to a nontheistic source. By means of disciplined, careful work under the expert guidance of a Sufi master (*pir*) like himself, al-Junayd taught that a Muslim could be reunited with his Creator and achieve that original sense of God's immediate presence that he had experienced when, as the Koran says, he had been drawn from Adam's loins. It would be the end of separation and sadness, a reunion with a deeper self that was also the self he or she was meant to be. God was not a separate, external reality and judge but somehow one with the ground of each person's being:

> Now I have known, O Lord,
> What lies within my heart;
> In secret, from the world apart,
> My tongue hath talked with my Adored.

> So in a manner we
> United are, and One;
> Yet otherwise disunion
> is our estate eternally.

> Though from my gaze profound
> Deep awe hath hid Thy Face,
> In wondrous and ecstatic Grace
> I feel Thee touch my inmost ground.[33]

The emphasis on unity harks back to the Koranic ideal of *tawhid*: by drawing together his dissipated self, the mystic would experience the divine presence in personal integration.

Al-Junayd was acutely aware of the dangers of mysticism. It would be easy for untrained people, who did not have the benefit of the advice of a *pir* and the rigorous Sufi training, to misunderstand the ecstasy of a mystic and get a very simplistic idea of what he meant when he said that he was one with God. Extravagant claims like those of al-Bistami would certainly arouse the ire of the establishment. At this early stage, Sufism was very much a minority movement, and the *ulema* often regarded it as an inauthentic innovation. Junayd's famous pupil Husain ibn Mansur (usually known as al-Hallaj, the Wool-Carder) threw all caution to the winds, however, and became a martyr for his mystical faith. Roaming the Iraq, preaching the overthrow of the caliphate and the establishment of a new social order, he was imprisoned by the authorities and crucified like his hero, Jesus. In his ecstasy, al-Hallaj had cried aloud: "I am the Truth!" According to the Gospels, Jesus had made the same claim, when he had said that he was the Way, the Truth and the Life. The Koran repeatedly condemned the Christian belief in God's Incarnation in Christ as blasphemous, so it was not surprising that Muslims were horrified by al-Hallaj's ecstatic cry. *Al-Haqq* (the Truth) was one of the names of God, and it was idolatry for any mere mortal to claim this title for himself. Al-Hallaj had been expressing his sense of a union with God that was so close that it felt like identity. As he said in one of his poems:

> I am He whom I love, and He whom I love is I:
> We are two spirits dwelling in one body.
> If thou seest me, thou seest Him,
> And if thou seest Him, thou seest us both.[34]

It was a daring expression of that annihilation of self and union with God that his master al-Junayd had called *'fana*. Al-Hallaj refused to recant when accused of blasphemy and died a saintly death.

When he was brought to be crucified and saw the cross and the nails, he turned to the people and uttered a prayer, ending with the words: "And these Thy servants who are gathered to slay me, in zeal for Thy religion and in desire to win Thy favors, forgive them, O Lord, and have mercy upon them; for verily if Thou hadst revealed to them that which Thou hast revealed to me, they would not have done what they have done; and if Thou hadst hidden from me that which Thou hast hidden from them, I should not have suffered this tribulation. Glory unto Thee in whatsoever Thou doest, and glory unto Thee in whatsoever Thou willest."[35]

Al-Hallaj's cry *ana al-Haqq*: "I am the Truth!" shows that the God of the mystics is not an objective reality but profoundly subjective. Later al-Ghazzali argued that he had not been blasphemous but only unwise in proclaiming an esoteric truth that could be misleading to the uninitiated. Because there is no reality but al-Lah—as the Shahadah maintains—all men are essentially divine. The Koran taught that God had created Adam in his own image so that he could contemplate himself as in a mirror.[36] That is why he ordered the angels to bow down and worship the first man. The mistake of the Christians had been to assume that one man had contained the whole incarnation of the divine, Sufis would argue. A mystic who had regained his original vision of God had rediscovered the divine image within himself, as it had appeared on the day of creation. The Sacred Tradition (*hadith qudsi*) beloved by the Sufis shows God drawing a Muslim toward him so closely that he seems to have become incarnate in each one of his servants: "When I love him, I become his Ear through which he hears, his Eye with which he sees, his Hand with which he grasps, and his Foot with which he walks." The story of al-Hallaj shows the deep antagonism that can exist between the mystic and the religious establishment who have different notions of God and revelation. For the mystic the revelation is an event that happens within his own soul, while for more conventional people like some of the *ulema* it is an event that is firmly fixed in the past. We have seen, however, that during the eleventh century, Muslim philosophers such as Ibn Sina and al-Ghazzali himself had found that objective accounts of God were unsatisfactory and had turned toward mysticism. Al-Ghazzali had made Sufism acceptable to the establishment and had shown that it was the most authentic form of Muslim spirituality. During the twelfth century the Iranian philosopher Yahya Suhrawardi and the Spanish-born Muid ad-

Din ibn al-Arabi linked Islamic Falsafah indissolubly with mysticism and made the God experienced by the Sufis normative in many parts of the Islamic empire. Like al-Hallaj, however, Suhrawardi was also put to death by the *ulema* in Aleppo in 1191, for reasons that remain obscure. He had made it his life's work to link what he called the original "Oriental" religion with Islam, thus completing the project that Ibn Sina had proposed. He claimed that all the sages of the ancient world had preached a single doctrine. Originally it had been revealed to Hermes (whom Suhrawardi identified with the prophet known as Idris in the Koran or Enoch in the Bible); in the Greek world it had been transmitted through Plato and Pythagoras and in the Middle East through the Zoroastrian Magi. Since Aristotle, however, it had been obscured by a more narrowly intellectual and cerebral philosophy, but it had been secretly passed from one sage to another until it had finally reached Suhrawardi himself via al-Bistami and al-Hallaj. This perennial philosophy was mystical and imaginative but did not involve the abandonment of reason. Suhrawardi was as intellectually rigorous as al-Farabi, but he also insisted on the importance of intuition in the approach to truth. As the Koran had taught, all truth came from God and should be sought wherever it could be found. It could be found in paganism and Zoroastrianism as well as in the monotheistic tradition. Unlike dogmatic religion, which lends itself to sectarian disputes, mysticism often claims that there are as many roads to God as people. Sufism in particular would evolve an outstanding appreciation of the faith of others.

Suhrawardi is often called the Sheikh al-Ishraq or the Master of Illumination. Like the Greeks, he experienced God in terms of light. In Arabic, *ishraq* refers to the first light of dawn that issues from the East as well as to enlightenment: the Orient, therefore, is not the geographical location but the source of light and energy. In Suhrawardi's Oriental faith, therefore, human beings dimly remember their Origin, feeling uneasy in this world of shadow, and long to return to their first abode. Suhrawardi claimed that his philosophy would help Muslims to find their true orientation, to purify the eternal wisdom within them by means of the imagination.

Suhrawardi's immensely complex system was an attempt to link all the religious insights of the world into a spiritual religion. Truth must be sought wherever it could be found. Consequently his philosophy linked the pre-Islamic Iranian cosmology with the Ptolemaic planetary system and the Neoplatonic scheme of emanation. Yet no other Faylasuf had ever quoted so extensively from the Koran. When he discussed cosmology, Suhrawardi was not primarily interested in accounting for the physical origins of the universe. In his masterwork *The Wisdom of Illumination* (*Hiqmat al-Ishraq*), Suhrawardi began by considering problems of physics and natural science, but this was only a prelude to the mystical part of his work. Like Ibn Sina, he had grown dissatisfied with the wholly rational and objective orientation of Falsafah, though he did believe that rational and metaphysical speculation had their place in the perception of total reality. The true sage, in his opinion, excelled in both philosophy and mysticism. There was always such a sage in the world. In a theory that was very close to Shii Imamology, Suhrawardi believed that this spiritual leader was the true pole (*qutb*) without whose presence the world could not continue to exist, even if he remained in obscurity. Suhrawardi's Ishraqi mysticism is still practiced in Iran. It is an esoteric system not because it is exclusive but because it requires spiritual and imaginative training of the sort undergone by Ismailis and Sufis.

The Greeks, perhaps, would have said that Suhrawardi's system was *dogmatic* rather than *kerygmatic*. He was attempting to discover the imaginative core that lay at the heart of all religion and philosophy and, though he insisted that reason was not enough, he never denied its right to probe the deepest mysteries. Truth had to be sought in scientific rationalism as well as esoteric mysticism; sensibility must be educated and informed by the critical intelligence.

As its name suggests, the core of Ishraqi philosophy was the symbol of light, which was seen as the perfect synonym for God. It was (at least in the twelfth century!) immaterial and indefinable, yet was also the most obvious fact of life in the world: totally self-evident, it required no definition but was perceived by everybody as the element that made life possible. It was all-pervasive: whatever luminosity belonged to material bodies came directly from light, a source outside themselves. In Suhrawardi's emanationist cosmology, the Light of Lights corresponded to the Necessary Being of the Faylasufs, which was utterly simple. It generated a succession of lesser lights in a descending hierarchy; each light, recognizing its dependency upon the Light of Lights, developed a shadow-self that was the source of a material realm, which corresponded to one of the Ptolemaic spheres. This was a metaphor of the human predicament. There was a similar combination of light and darkness within each one of us: the light or soul was conferred upon the embryo by the Holy Spirit (also known, as in Ibn Sina's scheme, as the Angel Gabriel, the light of our world). The soul longs to be united with the higher world of Lights and, if it is properly instructed by the *qutb* saint of the time or by one of his disciples, can even catch a glimpse of this here below.

Suhrawardi described his own enlightenment in the *Hiqmat*. He had been obsessed with the epistemological problem of knowledge but could make no headway: his book-learning had nothing to say to him. Then he had a vision of the Imam, the *qutb*, the healer of souls:

> Suddenly I was wrapped in gentleness; there was a blinding flash, then a diaphanous light in the likeness of a human being. I watched attentively and there he was. . . . He came towards me, greeting me so kindly that my bewilderment faded and my alarm gave way to a feeling of familiarity. And then I began to complain to him of the trouble I had with this problem of knowledge.
>
> "Awaken to yourself," he said to me, "and your problem will be solved."[37]

The process of awakening or illumination was clearly very different from the wrenching, violent inspiration of prophecy. It had more in common with the tranquil enlightenment of the Buddha: mysticism was introducing a calmer spirituality into the religions of God. Instead of a collision with a Reality without, illumination would come from within the mystic himself. There was no imparting of facts. Instead, the exercise of the human imagination would enable people to return to God by introducing them to the *alam al-mithal*, the world of pure images.

Suhrawardi drew upon the ancient Iranian belief in an archetypal world by which every person and object in the *getik* (the mundane, physical world) had its exact counterpart in the *menok* (the heavenly realm). Mysticism would revive the old mythology that the God-religions had ostensibly abandoned. The *menok*, which in Suhrawardi's scheme became the *alam al-mithal*, was now an intermediate realm that existed between our world and God's. This could not be perceived by means of reason or by the senses. It was the faculty of the creative imagination which enabled us to dis-cover the realm of hidden archetypes, just as the symbolic interpretation of the Koran revealed its true spiritual meaning. The *alam al-mithal* was close to the Ismaili perception of the spiritual history of Islam which was the real meaning of the earthly events or Ibn Sina's angelology, which we discussed in the last chapter. It would be crucial to all future mystics of Islam as a way of interpreting their experiences and visions. Suhrawardi was examining the visions that are so strikingly similar, whether they are seen by shamans, mystics or ecstatics, in many different cultures. There has recently been much interest in this phenomenon. Jung's conception of the collective unconscious is a more scientific attempt to examine this common imaginative experience of humanity. Other scholars, such as the Rumanian-American philosopher of religion Mircea Eliade, have attempted to show how the epics of ancient poets and certain kinds of fairy tales derive from ecstatic journeys and mystical flights.[38]

Suhrawardi insisted that the visions of mystics and the symbols of scripture—such as Heaven, Hell and the Last Judgment—were as real as the phenomena we experience in this world, but not in the same way. They could not be empirically proven but could only be discerned by the trained imaginative faculty, which enabled visionaries to see the spiritual dimension of earthly phenomena. This experience was nonsensical to anybody who had not had the requisite training, just as the Buddhist enlightenment could only be experienced when the necessary moral and mental exercises had been undertaken. All our thoughts, ideas, desires, dreams and visions corresponded to realities in the *alam al-mithal*. The Prophet Muhammad, for example, had awakened to this intermediate world during the Night Vision, which had taken him to the threshold of the divine world. Suhrawardi would also have claimed that the visions of the Jewish Throne Mystics took place when they had learned to enter the *alam al-mithal* during their spiritual exercises of concentration. The path to God, therefore, did not lie solely through reason, as the Faylasufs had thought, but through the creative imagination, the realm of the mystic.

Today many people in the West would be dismayed if a leading theologian suggested that God was in some profound sense a product of the imagination. Yet it should be obvious that the imagination is the chief religious faculty. It has been defined by Jean-Paul Sartre as *the ability to think of what is not*.[39] Human beings are the only animals who have the capacity to envisage something that is not present or something that does not yet exist but which is merely possible. The imagination has thus been the cause of our major achievements in science and technology as well as in art and religion. The idea of God, however it is defined, is perhaps the prime example of an absent reality which, despite its inbuilt problems, has continued to inspire men and women for thousands of years. The only way we can conceive of God, who remains imperceptible to the senses and to logical proof, is by means of symbols, which it is the chief function of the imaginative mind to interpret. Suhrawardi was attempting an imaginative explanation of those symbols that have had a crucial influence on human life, even though the realities to which they refer remain elusive. A symbol can be defined as an object or a notion that we can perceive with our senses or grasp with our minds but in which we see something other than itself. Reason alone will not enable us to perceive the special, the universal or the eternal in a particular, temporal object. That is the task of the creative imagination, to which mystics, like artists, attribute their insights. As in art, the most effective religious symbols are those informed by an intelligent knowledge and understanding of the human condition. Suhrawardi, who wrote in extraordinarily beautiful Arabic and was a highly skilled metaphysician, was a creative artist as well as a mystic. Yoking apparently unrelated things together—science with mysticism, pagan philosophy with monotheistic religion—he was able to help Muslims create their own symbols and find new meaning and significance in life.

Even more influential than Suhrawardi was Muid ad-Din ibn al-Arabi (1165–1240), whose life we can, perhaps, see as a symbol of the parting of the ways between East and West. His father was a friend of Ibn Rushd, who was very impressed by the piety of the young boy on the one occasion when they met. During a severe illness, Ibn al-Arabi was converted to Sufism, however, and at the age of thirty he left Europe for the Middle East. He made the *hajj* and spent two years praying and meditating at the Kabah but eventually settled at Malatya on the Euphrates. Frequently called Sheikh al-Akbah, the Great Master, he profoundly affected the Muslim conception of God, but his thought did not influence the West, which imagined that Islamic philosophy had ended with Ibn Rushd. Western Christendom would embrace Ibn Rushd's Aristotelian God, while most of Islamdom opted, until relatively recently, for the imaginative God of the mystics.

In 1201, while making the circumambulations around the Kabah, Ibn al-Arabi had a vision which had a profound and lasting effect upon him: he had seen a young girl, named Nizam, surrounded by a heavenly aura and he realized that she was an incarnation of Sophia, the divine Wisdom. This epiphany made him realize that it would be impossible for us to love God if we relied only on the rational arguments of philosophy. Falsafah emphasized the utter transcendence of al-Lah and reminded us that nothing could resemble him. How could we love such an alien Being? Yet we can love the God we see in his creatures: "If you love a being for his beauty, you love none other than God, for he is *the* Beautiful Being," he explained in the *Futuhat al-Makkiyah* (The Meccan Revelations). "Thus in all its aspects, the object of love is God alone."[40] The Shahadah reminded us that there was no god, no absolute reality but al-Lah. Consequently, there was no beauty apart from him. We cannot see God himself, but we can see him as he has chosen to reveal himself in such creatures as Nizam, who inspire love in our hearts. Indeed, the mystic had a duty to create his own epiphanies for himself in order to see a girl like Nizam as she really was. Love is essentially a yearning for something that remains absent; that is why so much of our human love remains disappointing. Nizam had become "the object of my Quest and my hope, the Virgin Most Pure." As he explained in the prelude to *The Diwan*, a collection of love poems:

> In the verses I have composed for the present book, I never cease to allude to the divine inspirations, the spiritual visitations, the correspondences [of our world] with the world of Angelic Intelligences. In this I conformed to my usual manner of thinking in symbols; this because the things of the invisible world attract me more than those of actual life and because this young girl knew exactly what I was referring to.[41]

The creative imagination had transformed Nizam into an *avatar* of God.

Some eighty years later, the young Dante Alighieri had a similar experience in Florence when he saw Beatrice Portinari. As soon as he caught sight of her, he felt his spirit tremble violently and seemed to hear it cry: "Behold a god more powerful than I who comes to rule over me." From that moment, Dante was ruled by his love of Beatrice, which acquired a mastery "owing to the power which my imagination gave him."[42] Beatrice remained the image of divine love for Dante, and in *The Divine Comedy*, he shows how this brought him, through an imaginary journey through Hell, Purgatory and Heaven, to a vision of God. Dante's poem had been inspired by Muslim accounts of Muhammad's ascent to heaven; certainly his view of the creative imagination was similar to that of Ibn al-Arabi. Dante argued that it was not true that *imaginativa* simply combined images derived from perception of the mundane world, as Aristotle had maintained; it was in part an inspiration from God:

> O fantasy (*imaginativa*), that reav'st us oft away
> So from ourselves that we remain distraught,
> Deaf though a thousand trumpets round us bray.

What moves thee when the senses show thee naught?
Light moves thee, formed in Heaven, by will maybe
Of Him who sends it down, or else self-wrought.[43]

Throughout the poem, Dante gradually purges the narrative of sensuous and visual imagery. The vividly physical descriptions of Hell give way to the difficult, emotional climb up Mount Purgatory to the earthly paradise, where Beatrice upbraids him for seeing her physical being as an end in itself: instead, he should have seen her as a symbol or an *avatar* that pointed him away from the world to God. There are scarcely any physical descriptions in Paradise; even the blessed souls are elusive, reminding us that no human personality can become the final object of human yearning. Finally, the cool intellectual imagery expresses the utter transcendence of God, who is beyond all imagination. Dante has been accused of painting a cold portrait of God in the *Paradiso*, but the abstraction reminds us that ultimately we know nothing at all about him.

Ibn al-Arabi was also convinced that the imagination was a God-given faculty. When a mystic created an epiphany for himself, he was bringing to birth here below a reality that existed more perfectly in the realm of archetypes. When we saw the divine in other people, we were making an imaginative effort to uncover the true reality: "God made the creatures like veils," he explained, "He who knows them as such is led back to Him, but he who takes them as real is barred from His presence."[44] Thus—as seemed to be the way of Sufism—what started as a highly personalized spirituality, centering on a human being, led Ibn al-Arabi to a transpersonal conception of God. The image of the female remained important to him: he believed that women were the most potent incarnations of Sophia, the divine Wisdom, because they inspired a love in men that was ultimately directed toward God. Admittedly, this is a very male view, but it was an attempt to bring a female dimension to the religion of a God who was often conceived as wholly masculine.

Ibn al-Arabi did not believe that the God he knew had an objective existence. Even though he was a skilled metaphysician, he did not believe that God's existence could be proved by logic. He liked to call himself a disciple of Khidr, a name given to the mysterious figure who appears in the Koran as the spiritual director of Moses, who brought the external Law to the Israelites. God has given Khidr a special knowledge of himself, so Moses begs him for instruction, but Khidr tells him that he will not be able to put up with this, since it lies outside his own religious experience.[45] It is no good trying to understand religious "information" that we have not experienced ourselves. The name Khidr seems to have meant "the Green One," indicating that his wisdom was ever fresh and eternally renewable. Even a prophet of Moses' stature cannot necessarily comprehend esoteric forms of religion, for, in the Koran, he finds that indeed he cannot put up with Khidr's method of instruction. The meaning of this strange episode seems to suggest that the external trappings of a religion do not always correspond to its spiritual or mystical element. People, such as the *ulema*, might be unable to understand the Islam of a Sufi like Ibn al-Arabi. Muslim tradition makes Khidr the master of all who seek a mystic truth, which is inherently superior to and quite different from the literal, external forms. He does not lead his disciple to a perception of a God which is the same as everybody else's but to a God who is in the deepest sense of the word subjective.

Khidr was also important to the Ismailis. Despite the fact that Ibn al-Arabi was a Sunni, his teachings were very close to Ismailism and were subsequently incorporated into their theology—yet another instance of mystical religion being able to transcend sectarian divisions. Like the Ismailis, Ibn al-Arabi stressed the pathos of God, which was in sharp contrast to the *apatheia* of the God of the philosophers. The God of the mystics yearned to be known by his creatures. The Ismailis believed that the noun *ilah* (god) sprang from the Arabic root *WLH*: to be sad, to sigh for.[46] As the Sacred Hadith had made God say: "I was a hidden treasure and I yearned to be known. Then I created creatures in order to be known by them." There is no rational proof of God's sadness; we know it only by our own longing for something to fulfill our deepest desires and to explain the tragedy and pain of life. Since we are created in God's image, we must reflect God, the supreme archetype. Our yearning for the reality that we call "God" must, therefore, mirror a sympathy with the pathos of God. Ibn al-Arabi imagined the solitary God sighing with longing, but this sigh (*nafas rahmani*) was not an expression of maudlin self-pity. It had an active, creative force which brought the whole of our cosmos into existence; it also exhaled human beings, who became *logoi*, words that express God to himself. It follows that each human being is a unique epiphany of the Hidden God, manifesting him in a particular and unrepeatable manner.

Each one of these divine *logoi* are the names that God has called himself, making himself totally present in each one of his epiphanies. God cannot be summed up in one human expression since the divine reality is inexhaustible. It also follows that the revelation that God has made in each one of us is unique, different from the God known by the other innumerable men and women who are also his *logoi*. We will only know our own "God" since we cannot experience him objectively; it is impossible to know him in the same way as other people. As Ibn al-Arabi said: "Each being has as his god only his particular Lord; he cannot possibly have the whole." He liked to quote the *hadith*: "Meditate upon God's blessings, but not upon his essence (*al-Dhat*)."[47] The whole reality of God is unknowable; we must concentrate on the particular Word spoken in our own being. Ibn al-Arabi also liked to call God *al-Ama*, "the Cloud" or "The Blindness"[48] to emphasize his inaccessibility. But these human *logoi* also reveal the Hidden God to *himself*. It is a two-way process: God sighs to become known and is delivered from his solitude by the people in whom he reveals himself. The sorrow of the Unknown God is assuaged by the Revealed God in each human being who makes him known to himself; it is also true that the Revealed God in every individual yearns to return to its source with a divine nostalgia that inspires our own longing.

Divinity and humanity were thus two aspects of the divine life that animates the entire cosmos. This insight was not dissimilar to the Greek understanding of the Incarnation of God in Jesus, but Ibn al-Arabi could not accept the idea that one single human being, however holy, could express the infinite reality of God. Instead he believed that each human person was a unique *avatar* of the divine. Yet he did develop the symbol of the Perfect Man (*insan i-kamil*) who embodied the mystery of the Revealed God in each generation for the benefit of his contemporaries, though he did not, of course, incarnate the whole reality of God or his hidden essence. The Prophet Muhammad had been the Perfect Man of his generation and a particularly effective symbol of the divine.

This introspective, imaginative mysticism was a search for the ground of being in the depths of the self. It deprived the mystic of the certainties that characterize the more dogmatic forms of religion. Since each man and woman had had a unique experience of God, it followed that no one religion could express the whole of the divine mystery. There was no objective truth about God to which all must subscribe; since this God transcended the category of personality, predictions about his behavior and inclinations were impossible. Any consequent chauvinism about one's own faith at the expense of other people's was obviously unacceptable, since no one religion had the whole truth about God. Ibn al-Arabi developed the positive attitude toward other religions which could be found in the Koran and took it to a new extreme of tolerance:

My heart is capable of every form.
A cloister for the monk, a fane for idols,
A pasture for gazelles, the votary's Kabah
The tables of the Torah, the Koran.
Love is the faith I hold: wherever turn
His camels, still the one true faith is mine.[49]

The man of God was equally at home in synagogue, temple, church and mosque, since all provided a valid apprehension of God. Ibn al-Arabi often used the phrase "the God created by the faiths" (*Khalq al-haqq fi'l-itiqad*); it could be pejorative if it referred to the "god" that men and women created in a particular religion and considered identical with God himself. This only bred intolerance and fanaticism. Instead of such idolatry, Ibn al-Arabi gave this advice:

Do not attach yourself to any particular creed exclusively, so that you may disbelieve all the rest; otherwise you will lose much good, nay, you will fail to recognize the real truth of the matter. God, the omnipresent and omnipotent, is not limited by any one creed, for, he says, "Wheresoever ye turn, there is the face of al-Lah" (Koran 2:109). Everyone praises what he believes; his god is his own creature, and in praising it he praises himself. Consequently he blames the beliefs of others, which he would not do if he were just, but his dislike is based on ignorance.[50]

We *never* see any god but the personal Name that has been revealed and given concrete existence in each one of us; inevitably our understanding of our personal Lord is colored by the religious tradition into which we were born. But the mystic (*arif*) knows that this "God" of ours is simply an "angel" or a particular symbol of the divine, which must never be confused with the Hidden Reality itself. Consequently he sees all the different religions as valid theophanies. Where the God of the more dogmatic religions divides humanity into warring camps, the God of the mystics is a unifying force.

It is true that Ibn al-Arabi's teachings were too abstruse for the vast majority of Muslims, but they did percolate down to the more ordinary people. During the twelfth and thirteenth centuries, Sufism ceased to be a minority movement and became the dominant Islamic mood in many parts of the Muslim empire. This was the period when the various Sufi orders or *tariqas* were founded, each with its particular interpretation of the mystical faith. The Sufi sheikh had a great influence on the populace and was often revered as a saint in rather the same way as the Shii Imams. It was a period of political upheaval: the Baghdad caliphate was disintegrating, and the Mongol hordes were devastating one Muslim city after another. People wanted a God who was more immediate and sympathetic than the remote God of the Faylasufs and the legalistic God of the *ulema*. The Sufi practices of *dhikr*, the recitation of the Divine Names as a mantra to induce ecstasy, spread beyond the *tariqas*. The Sufi disciplines of concentration, with their carefully prescribed techniques of breathing and posture, helped people to experience a sense of transcendent presence within. Not everybody was capable of the higher mystical states, but these spiritual exercises did help people to abandon simplistic and anthropomorphic notions of God and to experience him as a presence within the self. Some orders used music and dancing to enhance concentration, and their *pirs* became heroes to the people.

The most famous of the Sufi orders was the Mawlawiyyah, whose members are known in the West as the "whirling dervishes." Their stately and dignified dance was a method of concentration. As he spun around and around, the Sufi felt the boundaries of selfhood dissolve as he melted into his dance, giving him a foretaste of the annihilation of *'fana*. The founder of the order was Jalal ad-Din Rumi (ca. 1207–73), known to his disciples as Mawlana, our Master. He had been born in Khurusan in Central Asia but had fled to Konya in modern Turkey before the advancing Mongol armies. His mysticism can be seen as a Muslim response to this scourge, which might have caused many to lose faith in al-Lah. Rumi's ideas are similar to those of his contemporary Ibn al-Arabi, but his poem the *Masnawi*, known as the Sufi Bible, had a more popular appeal and helped to disseminate the God of the mystics among ordinary Muslims who were not Sufis. In 1244 Rumi had come under the spell of the wandering dervish Shams ad-Din, whom he saw as the Perfect Man of his generation. Indeed, Shams ad-Din believed that he was a reincarnation of the Prophet and insisted upon being addressed as "Muhammad." He had a dubious reputation and was known not to observe the Shariah, the Holy Law of Islam, thinking himself above such trivialities. Rumi's disciples were understandably worried by their Master's evident infatuation. When Shams was killed in a riot, Rumi was inconsolable and devoted still more time to mystical music and dancing. He was able to transform his grief imaginatively into a symbol of the love of God—of God's yearning for humanity and humanity's longing for al-Lah. Whether knowingly or not, everybody was searching for the absent God, obscurely aware that he or she was separated from the Source of being.

> Listen to the reed, how it tells a tale, complaining of separateness. Ever since I was parted from the reed-bed, my lament has caused men and women to moan. I want a bosom torn by severance, that I may unfold [to such a person] the power of love-desire: everyone who is left far from his source wishes back the time when he was united to it.[51]

The Perfect Man was believed to inspire more ordinary mortals to seek God: Shams ad-Din had unlocked in Rumi the poetry of the *Masnawi*, which recounted the agonies of this separation.

Like other Sufis, Rumi saw the universe as a theophany of God's myriad Names. Some of these revealed God's wrath or severity, while others expressed those qualities of mercy which were intrinsic to the divine nature. The mystic was engaged in a ceaseless struggle (*jihad*) to distinguish the compassion, love and beauty of God in all things and to strip away everything else. The *Masnawi* challenged the Muslim to find the transcendent dimension in human life and to see through appearances to the hidden reality within. It is the ego which blinds us to the inner mystery of all things, but once we have got beyond that we are not isolated, separate beings but one with the Ground of all existence. Again, Rumi emphasized that God could only be a subjective experience. He tells the humorous tale of Moses and the Shepherd to illustrate the respect we must show to other people's conceptions of the divine. One day Moses overheard a shepherd talking familiarly to God: he wanted to help God, wherever he was—to wash his clothes, pick the lice off, kiss his hands and feet at bedtime. "All I can say, remembering You," the prayer concluded, "is *ayyyy* and *ahhhhhhhh*." Moses was horrified. Who on earth did the shepherd imagine he was talking to? The Creator of heaven and earth? It sounded as though he were talking to his uncle! The shepherd repented and wandered disconsolately off into the desert, but God rebuked Moses. He did not want orthodox words but burning love and humility. There *were* no correct ways of talking about God:

> What seems wrong to you is right for him
> What is poison to one is honey to someone else.

Purity and impurity, sloth and diligence in worship,
These mean nothing to Me.
        I am apart from all that.
Ways of worshipping are not to be ranked as better
or worse than one another.

        Hindus do Hindu things.
The Dravidian Muslims in India do what they do.
It's all praise, and it's all *right*.

It's not I that's glorified in acts of worship.
It's the worshippers! I don't hear the words
they say. I look inside at the humility.
That broken-open lowliness is the Reality,   '
not the language! Forget phraseology.
I want burning, *burning*.
        Be Friends
with your burning. Burn up your thinking
and your forms of expression![52]

Any speech about God was as absurd as the shepherd's, but when a
believer looked through the veils to how things really were, he would
find that it belied all his human preconceptions.

By this time tragedy had also helped the Jews of Europe to form a new
conception of God. The crusading anti-Semitism of the West was making
life intolerable for the Jewish communities, and many wanted a more
immediate, personal God than the remote deity experienced by the
Throne Mystics. During the ninth century, the Kalonymos family had
emigrated from southern Italy to Germany and had brought some mystical literature with them. But by the twelfth century, persecution had
introduced a new pessimism into Ashkenazic piety, and this was expressed in the writings of three members of the Kalonymos clan: Rabbi
Samuel the Elder, who wrote the short treatise *Sefer ha-Yirah* (The Book
of the Fear of God) in about 1150; Rabbi Judah the Pietist, author of *Sefer
Hasidim* (The Book of the Pietists), and his cousin Rabbi Eliezar ben Judah
of Worms (d. 1230), who edited a number of treatises and mystical texts.
They were not philosophers or systematic thinkers, and their work shows
that they had borrowed their ideas from a number of sources that might
seem incompatible. They had been greatly impressed by the dry Faylasuf

Saadia ibn Joseph, whose books had been translated into Hebrew, and by such Christian mystics as Francis of Assisi. From this strange amalgam of sources, they managed to create a spirituality which remained important to the Jews of France and Germany until the seventeenth century.

The Rabbis, it will be recalled, had declared it sinful to deny oneself pleasure created by God. But the German Pietists preached a renunciation that resembled Christian asceticism. A Jew would only see the Shekinah in the next world if he turned his back on pleasure and gave up such pastimes as keeping pets or playing with children. Jews should cultivate an *apatheia* like God's, remaining impervious to scorn and insults. But God could be addressed as Friend. No Throne Mystic would have dreamt of calling God "Thou," as Eliezar did. This familiarity crept into the liturgy, depicting a God who was immanent and intimately present at the same time as he was transcendent:

> Everything is in Thee and Thou art in everything; Thou fillest everything and dost encompass it; when everything was created, Thou was in everything; before everything was created, Thou wast everything.[53]

They qualified this immanence by showing that nobody could approach God himself but only God as he manifested himself to mankind in his "glory" (*kavod*) or in "the great radiance called Shekinah." The Pietists were not worried by the apparent inconsistency. They concentrated on practical matters rather than theological niceties, teaching their fellow Jews methods of concentration (*kawwanah*) and gestures that would enhance their sense of God's presence. Silence was essential; a Pietist should close his eyes tightly, cover his head with a prayer shawl to avoid distraction, pull in his stomach and grind his teeth. They devised special ways of "drawing out prayer," which was found to encourage this sense of Presence. Instead of simply repeating the words of the liturgy, the Pietist should count the letters of each word, calculating their numerical value and getting beyond the literal meaning of the language. He must direct his attention upward, to encourage his sense of a higher reality.

The situation of the Jews in the Islamic empire, where there was no anti-Semitic persecution, was far happier, and they had no need of this Ashkenazic pietism. They were evolving a new type of Judaism, however, as a response to Muslim developments. Just as the Jewish Faylasufs had attempted to explain the God of the Bible philosophically, other Jews tried to give their God a mystical, symbolic interpretation. At first these mystics constituted only a tiny minority. Theirs was an esoteric discipline, handed on from master to disciple: they called it Kabbalah, or "inherited tradition." Eventually, however, the God of Kabbalah would appeal to the majority and take hold of the Jewish imagination in a way that the God of the Philosophers never did. Philosophy threatened to turn God into a remote abstraction, but the God of the Mystics was able to touch those fears and anxieties that lie deeper than the rational. Where the Throne Mystics had been content to gaze upon the glory of God from without, the Kabbalists attempted to penetrate the inner life of God and the human consciousness. Instead of speculating rationally about the nature of God and the metaphysical problems of his relationship with the world, the Kabbalists turned to the imagination.

Like the Sufis, the Kabbalists made use of the Gnostic and Neoplatonic distinction between the essence of God and the God whom we glimpse in revelation and creation. God himself is essentially unknowable, inconceivable and impersonal. They called the hidden God En Sof, (literally, "without end"). We know nothing whatever about En Sof: he is not even mentioned in either the Bible or the Talmud. An anonymous thirteenth-century author wrote that En Sof is incapable of becoming the subject of a revelation to humanity.[54] Unlike YHWH, En Sof had no documented name; "he" is not a person. Indeed it is more accurate to refer to the Godhead as "It." This was a radical departure from the highly personal God of the Bible and the Talmud. The Kabbalists evolved their own mythology to help them to explore a new realm of the religious consciousness. To explain the relationship between En Sof and YHWH, without yielding to the Gnostic heresy that they were two different beings, the Kabbalists developed a symbolic method of reading scripture. Like the Sufis, they imagined a process whereby the hidden God made himself known to humanity. En Sof had manifested himself to the Jewish mystics under ten different aspects or *sefiroth* ("numerations") of the divine reality which had emanated from the inscrutable depths of the unknowable Godhead. Each *sefirah* represented a stage in En Sof's unfolding revelation and had its own symbolic name, but each of these divine spheres contained the whole mystery of God considered under a particular heading. The Kabbalistic exegesis made every single word of the Bible refer to one or other of the ten *sefiroth*: each verse described an event or phenomenon that had its counterpart in the inner life of God himself.

Ibn al-Arabi had seen God's sigh of compassion, which had revealed him to mankind, as the Word which had created the world. In rather the same way, the *sefiroth* were both the names that God had given to himself and the means whereby he had created the world. Together these ten names formed his one great Name, which was not known to men. They represented the stages whereby En Sof had descended from his lonely inaccessibility to the mundane world. They are usually listed as follows:

1. Kether Elyon: the "Supreme Crown."
2. Hokhmah: "Wisdom."
3. Binah: "Intelligence."
4. Hesed: "Love" or "Mercy."
5. Din: "Power" (usually manifested in stern judgment).
6. Rakhamim: "Compassion"; sometimes called "Tifereth": "Beauty."
7. Netsakh: "Lasting Endurance."
8. Hod: "Majesty."
9. Yesod: "Foundation."
10. Malkuth: "Kingdom"; also called "Shekinah."

Sometimes the *sefiroth* are depicted as a tree, growing upside down with its roots in the incomprehensible depths of En Sof [see diagram] and its summit in the Shekinah, in the world. The organic image expresses the unity of this Kabbalistic symbol. En Sof is the sap that runs through the branches of the tree and gives them life, unifying them in a mysterious and complex reality. Although there is a distinction between En Sof and the world of his names, the two are one in rather the same way as a coal and a flame. The *sefiroth* represent the worlds of light that manifest the darkness of En Sof, which remains in impenetrable obscurity. It is yet another way of showing that our notions of "God" cannot fully express the reality to which they point.

The world of the *sefiroth* is not an alternative reality "out there" between the Godhead and the world, however. They are not the rungs of a ladder between heaven and earth but underlie the world experienced by the senses. Because God is all in all, the *sefiroth* are present and active in everything that exists. They also represent the stages of human consciousness by which the mystic ascends to God by descending into his own mind. Yet again, God and man are depicted as inseparable. Some Kabbalists saw the *sefiroth* as the limbs of primordial man as originally intended by God. This was what the Bible had meant when it said that man had been created in God's image: the mundane reality here below corres-

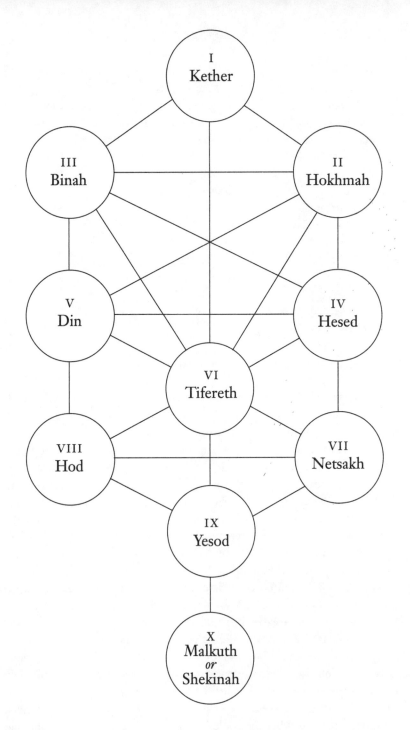

The Tree of the Sefiroth

ponded to an archetypal reality in the heavenly world. The images of God as a tree or as a man were imaginative depictions of a reality that defied rational formulation. The Kabbalists were not antagonistic toward Falsafah—many of them revered figures like Saadia Gaon and Maimonides—but they found symbolism and mythology more satisfying than metaphysics for penetrating the mystery of God.

The most influential Kabbalistic text was *The Zohar*, which was probably written in about 1275 by the Spanish mystic Moses of Leon. As a young man, he had studied Maimonides but had gradually felt the attraction of mysticism and the esoteric tradition of Kabbalah. *The Zohar* (The Book of Splendour) is a sort of mystical novel, which depicts the third-century Talmudist Simeon ben Yohai wandering around Palestine with his son Eliezar, talking to his disciples about God, nature and human life. There is no clear structure and no systematic development of theme or ideas. Such an approach would be alien to the spirit of *The Zohar*, whose God resists any neat system of thought. Like Ibn al-Arabi, Moses of Leon believed that God gives each mystic a unique and personal revelation, so there is no limit to the way the Torah can be interpreted: as the Kabbalist progresses, layer upon layer of significance is revealed. *The Zohar* shows the mysterious emanation of the ten *sefiroth* as a process whereby the impersonal En Sof becomes a personality. In the three highest *sefiroth*—Kether, Hokhmah and Binah—when, as it were, En Sof has only just "decided" to express himself, the divine reality is called "he." As "he" descends through the middle *sefiroth*—Hesed, Din, Tifereth, Netsakh, Hod and Yesod—"he" becomes "you." Finally, when God becomes present in the world in the Shekinah, "he" calls himself "I." It is at this point, where God has, as it were, become an individual and his self-expression is complete, that man can begin his mystical journey. Once the mystic has acquired an understanding of his own deepest self, he becomes aware of the Presence of God within him and can then ascend to the more impersonal higher spheres, transcending the limits of personality and egotism. It is a return to the unimaginable Source of our being and the hidden world of uncreated reality. In this mystical perspective, our world of sense impression is simply the last and outermost shell of the divine reality.

In Kabbalah, as in Sufism, the doctrine of the creation is not really concerned with the physical origins of the universe. *The Zohar* sees the Genesis account as a symbolic version of a crisis within En Sof, which causes the Godhead to break out of its unfathomable introspection and reveal itself. As *The Zohar* says:

In the beginning, when the will of the King began to take effect, he engraved signs into the divine aura. A dark flame sprang forth from the innermost recesses of En Sof, like a fog which forms out of the formless, enclosed in the ring of this aura, neither white nor black, red nor green and of no color whatever.[55]

In Genesis, God's first creative word had been: "Let there be light!" In *The Zohar*'s commentary on Genesis (called *Bereshit* in Hebrew after its opening word: "in the beginning") this "dark flame" is the first *sefirah*: Kether Elyon, the Supreme Crown of Divinity. It has no color or form: other Kabbalists prefer to call it Nothing (*ayin*). The highest form of divinity that the human mind can conceive is equated with nothingness because it bears no comparison with any of the other things in existence. All the other *sefiroth*, therefore, emerge from the womb of Nothingness. This is a mystical interpretation of the traditional doctrine of the creation *ex nihilo*. The process of the Godhead's self-expression continues as the welling of light, which spreads in ever wider spheres. *The Zohar* continues:

But when this flame began to assume size and extension, it produced radiant colors. For in the inmost center a well sprang forth from which flames poured upon everything below, hidden in the mysterious secrets of En Sof. The well broke through, and yet did not entirely break through, the eternal aura which surrounded it. It was entirely recognizable until under the impact of its breakthrough, a hidden supernal point shone forth. Beyond this point nothing may be known or understood, and it is called *Bereshit*, the Beginning; the first word of creation.[56]

This "point" is Hokhmah (Wisdom), the second *sefirah* which contains the ideal form of all created things. The point develops into a palace or a building, which becomes Binah (Intelligence), the third *sefirah*. These three highest *sefiroth* represent the limit of human comprehension. Kabbalists say that God exists in Binah as the great "Who?" (*Mi*) which stands at the beginning of every question. But it is not possible to get an answer. Even though En Sof is gradually adapting Itself to human limitations, we have no way of knowing "Who" he is: the higher we ascend, the more "he" remains shrouded in darkness and mystery.

The next seven *sefiroth* are said to correspond to the seven days of creation in Genesis. During the biblical period, YHWH had eventually triumphed over the ancient goddesses of Canaan and their erotic cults.

But as Kabbalists struggled to express the mystery of God, the old mythologies reasserted themselves, albeit in a disguised form. *The Zohar* describes Binah as the Supernal Mother, whose womb is penetrated by the "dark flame" to give birth to the seven lower *sefiroth*. Again Yesod, the ninth *sefirah*, inspires some phallic speculation: it is depicted as the channel through which the divine life pours into the universe in an act of mystical procreation. It is in the Shekinah, the tenth *sefirah*, however, that the ancient sexual symbolism of creation and theogony appears most clearly. In the Talmud, the Shekinah was a neutral figure: it had neither sex nor gender. In Kabbalah, however, the Shekinah becomes the female aspect of God. The *Bahir* (ca. 1200), one of the earliest Kabbalistic texts, had identified the Shekinah with the Gnostic figure of Sophia, the last of the divine emanations which had fallen from the Pleroma and now wandered, lost and alienated from the Godhead, through the world. *The Zohar* links this "exile of the Shekinah" with the fall of Adam as recounted in Genesis. It says that Adam was shown the "middle *sefiroth*" in the Tree of Life and the Shekinah in the Tree of Knowledge. Instead of worshipping the seven *sefiroth* together, he chose to venerate the Shekinah alone, sundering life from knowledge and rupturing the unity of the *sefiroth*. The divine life could no longer flow uninterruptedly into the world, which was isolated from its divine Source. But by observing the Torah, the community of Israel could heal the exile of the Shekinah and reunite the world to the Godhead. Not surprisingly, many strict Talmudists found this an abhorrent idea, but the exile of the Shekinah, which echoed the ancient myths of the goddess who wandered far from the divine world, became one of the most popular elements of Kabbalah. The female Shekinah brought some sexual balance into the notion of God, which tended to be too heavily weighted toward the masculine, and it clearly fulfilled an important religious need.

The notion of the divine exile also addressed that sense of separation which is the cause of so much human anxiety. *The Zohar* constantly defines evil as something which has become separated or which has entered into a relationship for which it is unsuited. One of the problems of ethical monotheism is that it isolates evil. Because we cannot accept the idea that there is evil in our God, there is a danger that we will not be able to endure it within ourselves. It can then be pushed away and made monstrous and inhuman. The terrifying image of Satan in Western Christendom was such a distorted projection. *The Zohar* finds the root of evil in God himself: in Din or Stern Judgment, the fifth *sefirah*. Din is depicted as God's left hand, Hesed (Mercy) as his right. As long as Din operates harmoniously with the divine Mercy, it is positive and beneficial. But if it breaks away and becomes separate from the other *sefiroth*, it becomes evil and destructive. *The Zohar* does not tell us how this separation came about. In the next chapter, we shall see that later Kabbalists reflected on the problem of evil, which they saw as the result of a kind of primordial "accident" that occurred in the very early stages of God's self-revelation. Kabbalah makes little sense if interpreted literally, but its mythology proved psychologically satisfying. When disaster and tragedy engulfed Spanish Jewry during the fifteenth century, it was the Kabbalistic God which helped them to make sense of their suffering.

We can see the psychological acuity of Kabbalah in the work of the Spanish mystic Abraham Abulafia (1240–after 1291). The bulk of his work was composed at about the same time as *The Zohar*, but Abulafia concentrated on the practical method of achieving a sense of God rather than with the nature of God itself. These methods are similar to those employed today by psychoanalysts in their secular quest for enlightenment. As the Sufis had wanted to experience God like Muhammad, Abulafia claimed to have found a way of achieving prophetic inspiration. He evolved a Jewish form of Yoga, using the usual disciplines of concentration such as breathing, the recitation of a mantra and the adoption of a special posture to achieve an alternative state of consciousness. Abulafia was an unusual Kabbalist. He was a highly erudite man, who had studied Torah, Talmud and Falsafah before being converted to mysticism by an overwhelming religious experience at the age of thirty-one. He seems to have believed that he was the Messiah, not only to Jews but also to Christians. Accordingly, he traveled extensively throughout Spain making disciples and even ventured as far as the Near East. In 1280 he visited the Pope as a Jewish ambassador. Although Abulafia was often very outspoken in his criticism of Christianity, he seems to have appreciated the similarity between the Kabbalistic God and the theology of the Trinity. The three highest *sefiroth* are reminiscent of the Logos and Spirit, the Intellect and Wisdom of God, which proceed from the Father, the Nothingness lost in inaccessible light. Abulafia himself liked to speak about God in a Trinitarian manner.

To find this God, Abulafia taught that it was necessary "to unseal the soul, to untie the knots which bind it." The phrase "untying the knots" is also found in Tibetan Buddhism, another indication of the fundamental agreement of mystics worldwide. The process described can perhaps be compared to the psychoanalytic attempt to unlock those complexes that impede the mental health of the patient. As a Kabbalist, Abulafia was more concerned with the divine energy that animates the whole of creation but which the soul cannot perceive. As long as we clog our minds with ideas based on sense perception, it is difficult to discern the transcendent element of life. By means of his yogic disciplines, Abulafia taught his disciples to go beyond normal consciousness to discover a whole new world. One of his methods was the *Hokhmah ha-Tseruf* (The Science of the Combination of the Letters), which took the form of a meditation on the Name of God. The Kabbalist was to combine the letters of the divine Name in different combinations with a view to divorcing his mind from the concrete to a more abstract mode of perception. The effects of this discipline—which sound remarkably unpromising to an outsider—appear to have been remarkable. Abulafia himself compared it to the sensation of listening to musical harmonies, the letters of the alphabet taking the place of notes in a scale. He also used a method of associating ideas, which he called *dillug* (jumping) and *kefitsah* (skipping), which is clearly similar to the modern analytic practice of free association. Again, this is said to have achieved astonishing results. As Abulafia explained, it brings to light hidden mental processes and liberated the Kabbalist from "the prison of the natural spheres and leads [him] to the boundaries of the divine sphere."[57] In this way, the "seals" of the soul were unlocked and the initiate discovered resources of psychic power that enlightened his mind and assuaged the pain of his heart.

In rather the same way as a psychoanalytic patient needs the guidance of his therapist, Abulafia insisted that the mystical journey into the mind could only be undertaken under the supervision of a master of Kabbalah. He was well aware of the dangers because he himself had suffered from a devastating religious experience in his youth which had almost caused him to despair. Today patients will often internalize the person of the analyst in order to appropriate the strength and health that he or she represents. Similarly Abulafia wrote that the Kabbalist would often "see" and "hear" the person of his spiritual director, who became "the mover from inside, who opens the closed doors within him." He felt a new surge of power and an inner transformation that was so overwhelming that it seemed to issue from a divine source. A disciple of Abulafia gave another interpretation of the ecstasy: the mystic, he said, became his own Messiah. In ecstasy he was confronted with a vision of his own liberated and enlightened self:

> Know that the complete spirit of prophecy consists for the prophet
> in that he suddenly sees the shape of his self standing before him

and he forgets his self and it is disengaged from him . . . and of this
secret our teachers said [in the Talmud]: "Great is the strength of
the prophets, who compare the form of Him who formed it" [that
is, "who compare men to God"].[58]

Jewish mystics were always reluctant to claim union with God. Abulafia
and his disciples would only say that by experiencing union with a spiritual director or by realizing a personal liberation the Kabbalist had been
touched by God indirectly. There are obvious differences between medieval mysticism and modern psychotherapy, but both disciplines have
evolved similar techniques to achieve healing and personal integration.

In the West Christians were slower to develop a mystical tradition.
They had fallen behind the monotheists in the Byzantine and Islamic
empires and were perhaps not ready for this new development. During
the fourteenth century, however, there was a veritable explosion of mystical religion, especially in Northern Europe. Germany in particular produced a flock of mystics: Meister Eckhart (1260–?1327), Johannes Tauler
(1300–61), Gertrude the Great (1256–1302) and Henry Suso (ca.
1295–1306). England also made a significant contribution to this Western
development and produced four great mystics who quickly attracted a
following on the Continent as well as in their own country: Richard Rolle
of Hampole (1290–1349), the unknown author of *The Cloud of Unknowing*,
Walter Hilton (d. 1346) and Dame Julian of Norwich (ca. 1342–1416).
Some of these mystics were more advanced than others. Richard Rolle,
for example, seems to have gotten trapped in the cultivation of exotic
sensations, and his spirituality was sometimes characterized by a certain
egotism. But the greatest of them discovered for themselves many of the
insights already achieved by the Greeks, Sufis and Kabbalists.

Meister Eckhart, for example, who greatly influenced Tauler and Suso,
was himself influenced by Denys the Areopagite and Maimonides. A
Dominican friar, he was a brilliant intellectual and lectured on Aristotelian philosophy at the University of Paris. In 1325, however, his mystical
teaching brought him into conflict with his bishop, the Archbishop of
Cologne, who arraigned him for heresy: he was charged with denying
the goodness of God, with claiming that God himself was born in the
soul and with preaching the eternity of the world. Yet even some of
Eckhart's severest critics believed that he was orthodox: the mistake lay
in interpreting some of his remarks literally instead of symbolically, as
intended. Eckhart was a poet, who thoroughly enjoyed paradox and
metaphor. While he believed that it was rational to believe in God, he

denied that reason alone could form any adequate conception of the divine nature: "The proof of a knowable thing is made to either the senses or the intellect," he argued, "but as regards the knowledge of God there can be neither a demonstration from sensory perception, since He is incorporeal, nor from the intellect, since He lacks any form known to us."[59] God was not another being whose existence could be proved like any normal object of thought.

God, Eckhart declared, was Nothing.[60] This did not mean that he was an illusion but that God enjoyed a richer, fuller type of existence than that known to us. He also called God "darkness," not to denote the absence of light but to indicate the presence of something brighter. Eckhart also distinguished between the "Godhead," which was best described in negative terms, such as "desert," "wilderness," "darkness" and "nothing," and the God who is known to us as Father, Son and Spirit.[61] As a Westerner, Eckhart liked to use Augustine's analogy of the Trinity in the human mind and implied that even though the doctrine of the Trinity could not be known by reason, it was only the intellect which perceived God as Three persons: once the mystic had achieved union with God, he or she saw him as One. The Greeks would not have liked this idea, but Eckhart would have agreed with them that the Trinity was essentially a mystical doctrine. He liked to talk about the Father engendering the Son in the soul, rather as Mary had conceived Christ in the womb. Rumi had also seen the Virgin Birth of the Prophet Jesus as a symbol for the birth of the soul in the heart of the mystic. It was, Eckhart insisted, an allegory of the cooperation of the soul with God.

God could only be known by mystical experience. It was better to speak of him in negative terminology, as Maimonides had suggested. Indeed, we had to purify our conception of God, getting rid of our ridiculous preconceptions and anthropomorphic imagery. We should even avoid using the term "God" itself. This is what Eckhart meant when he said: "Man's last and highest parting is when, for God's sake, he takes leave of God."[62] It would be a painful process. Since God was Nothing, we had to be prepared to be nothing too in order to become one with him. In a process similar to that *fana* described by the Sufis, Eckhart spoke of "detachment" or, rather, "separateness" (*Abgeschiedenheit*).[63] In much the same way as a Muslim considers the veneration of anything other than God himself as idolatry (*shirk*), Eckhart taught that the mystic must refuse to be enslaved by any finite ideas about the divine. Only thus would he achieve identity with God, whereby "God's existence must be my existence and God's Is-ness (*Istigkeit*) is my is-ness."[64] Since God was the ground of being, there was no need to seek him "out there" or envisage an ascent to something beyond the world we knew.

Al-Hallaj had antagonized the *ulema* by crying: "I am the Truth" and Eckhart's mystical doctrine shocked the bishops of Germany: what did it mean to say that a mere man or woman could become one with God? During the fourteenth century, Greek theologians debated this question furiously. Since God was essentially inaccessible, how could he communicate himself to mankind? If there was a distinction between God's essence and his "activities" or "energies," as the Fathers had taught, surely it was blasphemous to compare the "God" that a Christian encountered in prayer with God himself? Gregory Palamas, Archbishop of Saloniki, taught that, paradoxical as it might seem, any Christian could enjoy such a direct knowledge of God himself. True, God's essence was always beyond our comprehension, but his "energies" were not distinct from God and should not be considered a mere divine afterglow. A Jewish mystic would have agreed: God En Sof would always remain shrouded in impenetrable darkness, but his *sefiroth* (which corresponded to the Greeks' "energies") were themselves divine, flowing eternally from the heart of the Godhead. Sometimes men and women could see or experience these "energies" directly, as when the Bible said that God's "glory" had appeared. Nobody had ever seen God's essence, but that did not mean that a direct experience of God himself was impossible. The fact that this assertion was paradoxical did not distress Palamas in the least. It had long been agreed by the Greeks that any statement about God *had* to be a paradox. Only thus could people retain a sense of his mystery and ineffability. Palamas put it this way:

> We attain to participation in the divine nature, and yet at the same time it remains totally inaccessible. We need to affirm both at the same time and *to preserve the antimony as a criterion for right doctrine.*[65]

There was nothing new in Palamas's doctrine: it had been outlined during the eleventh century by Symeon the New Theologian. But Palamas was challenged by Barlaam the Calabrian, who had studied in Italy and been strongly influenced by the rationalistic Aristotelianism of Thomas Aquinas. He opposed the traditional Greek distinction between God's "essence" and his "energies," accusing Palamas of splitting God into two separate parts. Barlaam proposed a definition of God that went back to the ancient Greek rationalists and emphasized his absolute simplicity. Greek philosophers like Aristotle, who, Barlaam claimed, had been specially enlightened by God, taught that God was unknowable and remote from the world. It was not possible, therefore, for men and women to "see" God: human beings could only sense his influence indirectly in scripture or the wonders of creation. Barlaam was condemned by a Council of the Orthodox Church in 1341 but was supported by other monks who had also been influenced by Aquinas. Basically this had become a conflict between the God of the mystics and the God of the philosophers. Barlaam and his supporters Gregory Akindynos (who liked to quote the Greek version of the *Summa Theologiae*), Nicephoras Gregoras and the Thomist Prochoros Cydones had all become alienated from the apophatic theology of Byzantium with its stress on silence, paradox and mystery. They preferred the more positive theology of Western Europe, which defined God as Being rather than as Nothing. Against the mysterious deity of Denys, Symeon and Palamas, they set up a God about which it was possible to make statements. The Greeks had always distrusted this tendency in Western thought and, in the face of this infiltration of rationalistic Latin ideas, Palamas reasserted the paradoxical theology of Eastern Orthodoxy. God must not be reduced to a concept that could be expressed by a human word. He agreed with Barlaam that God was unknowable but insisted that he had nonetheless been experienced by men and women. The light that had transfigured the humanity of Jesus on Mount Tabor was not God's essence, which no man had seen, but was in some mysterious way God himself. The liturgy which, according to Greek theology, enshrined orthodox opinion, proclaimed that on Tabor: "We have seen the Father as light and the Spirit as light." It had been a revelation of "what we once were and what we are to be" when, like Christ, we become deified.[66] Again, what we "saw" when we contemplated God in this life was not a substitute for God but was somehow God himself. Of course this was a contradiction, but the Christian God *was* a paradox: antimony and silence represented the only correct posture before the mystery that we called "God"—not a philosophical *hubris* which tried to iron out the difficulties.

Barlaam had tried to make the concept of God too consistent: in his view, either God was to be identified with his essence or he was not. He had tried, as it were, to confine God to his essence and say that it was impossible for him to be present outside it in his "energies." But that was to think about God as though he were any other phenomenon and was based on purely human notions of what was or was not possible. Palamas insisted that the vision of God was a mutual ecstasy: men and women transcend themselves *but* God also underwent the ecstasy of transcendence by going beyond "himself" in order to make himself known to his creatures: "God also comes out of himself and becomes united with our minds by condescension."[67] The victory of Palamas, whose theology remained normative in Orthodox Christianity, over the Greek rationalists of the fourteenth century represents a wider triumph for mysticism in all three monotheistic religions. Since the eleventh century, Muslim philosophers had come to the conclusion that reason—which was indispensable for such studies as medicine or science—was quite inadequate when it came to the study of God. To rely on reason alone was like attempting to eat soup with a fork.

The God of the Sufis had gained ascendency over the God of the philosophers in most parts of the Islamic empire. In the next chapter we shall see that the God of the Kabbalists became dominant in Jewish spirituality during the sixteenth century. Mysticism was able to penetrate the mind more deeply than the more cerebral or legalistic types of religion. Its God could address more primitive hopes, fears and anxieties before which the remote God of the philosophers was impotent. By the fourteenth century the West had launched its own mystical religion and made a very promising start. But mysticism in the West would never become as widespread as in the other traditions. In England, Germany and the Lowlands, which had produced such distinguished mystics, the Protestant Reformers of the sixteenth century decried this unbiblical spirituality. In the Roman Catholic Church, leading mystics like St. Teresa of Avila were often threatened by the Inquisition of the Counter-Reformation. As a result of the Reformation, Europe began to see God in still more rationalistic terms.

8

A God for Reformers

THE FIFTEENTH AND SIXTEENTH centuries were decisive for all the people of God. It was a particularly crucial period for the Christian West, which had not only succeeded in catching up with the other cultures of the Oikumene but was about to overtake them. These centuries saw the Italian Renaissance, which quickly spread to Northern Europe, the discovery of the New World and the beginning of the scientific revolution, which would have fateful consequences for the rest of the world. By the end of the sixteenth century, the West was about to create an entirely different kind of culture. It was, therefore, a time of transition and, as such, characterized by anxiety as well as achievement. This was evident in the Western conception of God at this time. Despite their secular success, people in Europe were more concerned about their faith than ever before. The laity were especially dissatisfied with the medieval forms of religion that no longer answered their needs in the brave new world. Great reformers gave voice to this disquiet and discovered new ways of considering God and salvation. This split Europe into two warring camps—Catholic and Protestant—which have never entirely lost their hatred and suspicion of one another. During the Reformation, Catholic and Protestant reformers urged the faithful to rid themselves of peripheral devotion to saints and angels and to concentrate on God alone. Indeed, Europe seemed obsessed by God. Yet by the beginning of the seventeenth century, some were fantasizing about "atheism." Did this mean that they were ready to get rid of God?

It was also a period of crisis for Greeks, Jews and Muslims. In 1453 the Ottoman Turks conquered the Christian capital of Constantinople and destroyed the empire of Byzantium. Henceforth the Christians of Russia would continue the traditions and spirituality developed by the Greeks. In January 1492, the year of Christopher Columbus's discovery of the New World, Ferdinand and Isabella conquered Granada in Spain, the last Muslim stronghold in Europe: later Muslims would be expelled from the Iberian peninsula, which had been their home for 800 years. The destruction of Muslim Spain was fatal for the Jews. In March 1492, a few weeks after the conquest of Granada, the Christian monarchs gave Spanish Jews the choice of baptism or expulsion. Many of the Spanish Jews were so attached to their home that they became Christians, though some continued to practice their faith in secret: like the *Moriscos*, the converts from Islam, these Jewish converts were then hounded by the Inquisition because they were suspected of heresy. Some 150,000 Jews refused baptism, however, and were forcibly deported from Spain: they took refuge in Turkey, the Balkans and North Africa. The Muslims of Spain had given Jews the best home they had ever had in the diaspora, so the annihilation of Spanish Jewry was mourned by Jews throughout the world as the greatest disaster to have befallen their people since the destruction of the Temple in CE 70. The experience of exile entered more deeply into Jewish religious consciousness than ever before: it led to a new form of Kabbalah and the evolution of a new conception of God.

These were also complex years for Muslims in other parts of the world. The centuries which had succeeded the Mongol invasions led—perhaps inevitably—to a new conservatism, as people tried to recover what had been lost. In the fifteenth century, the Sunni *ulema* of the *madrasas*, the schools of Islamic studies, decreed that "the gates of *ijtihad* (independent reasoning) had been closed." Henceforth Muslims should practice "emulation" (*taqlid*) of the great luminaries of the past, especially in the study of Shariah, the Holy Law. It was unlikely that there would be innovative ideas about God in this conservative climate or, indeed, about anything else. Yet it would be mistaken to date this period as the beginning of a decadence in Islam, as Western Europeans have often suggested. As Marshall G. S. Hodgson points out in *The Venture of Islam, Conscience and History in a World Civilisation*, we simply do not know enough about this period to make such sweeping generalizations. It would be wrong, for example, to assume that there was a slackening in Muslim science at this time, as we have insufficient evidence, one way or the other.

The conservative tendency had surfaced during the fourteenth century in champions of the Shariah like Ahmad ibn Taymiyah of Damascus (d. 1328) and his pupil Ibn al-Qayin al-Jawziyah. Ibn Taymiyah, who was dearly loved by the people, wanted to extend the Shariah to enable it to apply to all the circumstances in which Muslims were likely to find themselves. This was not meant to be a repressive discipline: he wanted to shed obsolete rules to make the Shariah more relevant and to assuage the anxiety of Muslims during these difficult times. The Shariah should provide them with a clear, logical answer to their practical religious problems. But in his zeal for Shariah, Ibn Taymiyah attacked Kalam, Falsafah and even Asherism. Like any reformer, he wanted to go back to the sources—to the Koran and the *hadith* (on which the Shariah had been based)—and to shed all later accretions: "I have examined all the theological and philosophical methods and found them incapable of curing any ills or of quenching any thirst. For me the best method is that of the Koran."[1] His pupil al-Jawziyah added Sufism to this list of innovations, advocating a literalist interpretation of scripture and condemning the cult of Sufi saints in a spirit that was not entirely dissimilar to that of the later Protestant Reformers in Europe. Like Luther and Calvin, Ibn Taymiyah and al-Jawziyah were not regarded by their contemporaries as backward-looking: they were seen as progressives, who wanted to lighten the burden of their people. Hodgson warns us not to dismiss the so-called conservatism of this period as "stagnation." He points out that no society before our own could either afford or envisage progress on the scale that we now enjoy.[2] Western scholars have often chided the Muslims of the fifteenth and sixteenth centuries for failing to take account of the Italian Renaissance. True, this was one of the great cultural florescences of history, but it did not exceed or differ much from that of the Sung dynasty in China, for example, which had been an inspiration to Muslims during the twelfth century. The Renaissance was crucial to the West, but nobody could have foreseen the birth of the modern technical age, which, with hindsight, we can see that it foreshadowed. If Muslims were underwhelmed by this Western Renaissance, this did not necessarily reveal an irredeemable cultural inadequacy. Muslims were, not surprisingly, more concerned with their own not inconsiderable achievements during the fifteenth century.

In fact Islam was still the greatest world power during this period, and the West was fearfully aware that it was now on the very threshold of Europe. During the fifteenth and sixteenth centuries, three new Muslim empires were founded: by the Ottoman Turks in Asia Minor and Eastern Europe, by the Safavids in Iran and by the Moghuls in India. These new ventures show that the Islamic spirit was by no means moribund but could still provide Muslims with the inspiration to rise again to new success after catastrophe and disintegration. Each of the empires achieved its own remarkable cultural florescence: the Safavid renaissance in Iran and Central Asia was interestingly similar to the Italian Renaissance: both expressed themselves preeminently in painting and felt that they were returning creatively to the pagan roots of their culture. Despite the power and magnificence of these three empires, however, what has been called the conservative spirit still prevailed. Where earlier mystics and philosophers like al-Farabi and Ibn al-Arabi had been conscious of breaking new ground, this period saw a subtle and delicate restatement of old themes. This makes it more difficult for Westerners to appreciate, because our own scholars have ignored these more modern Islamic ventures for too long, and also because the philosophers and poets expect the minds of their readers to be stocked with the images and ideas of the past.

There were parallels with contemporary Western developments, however. A new type of Twelver Shiism had become the state religion in Iran under the Safavids, and this marks the beginning of a hostility between the Shiah and the Sunnah which was unprecedented. Hitherto Shiis had had much in common with the more intellectual or mystical Sunnis. But during the sixteenth century, the two formed rival camps that were unhappily similar to the sectarian wars in Europe at this time. Shah Ismail, the founder of the Safavid dynasty, had come to power in Azerbaijan in 1503 and had extended his power into western Iran and Iraq. He was determined to wipe out Sunnism and forced the Shiah on his subjects with a ruthlessness rarely attempted before. He saw himself as the Imam of his generation. This movement had similarities with the Protestant Reformation in Europe: both had their roots in traditions of protest, both were against the aristocracy and associated with the establishment of royal governments. The reformed Shiis abolished the Sufi *tariqas* in their territories in a way that recalls the Protestant dissolution of the monasteries. Not surprisingly, they inspired a similar intransigence among the Sunnis of the Ottoman empire, who suppressed the Shiah in their territories. Seeing themselves on the front line of the latest holy war against the crusading West, the Ottomans also cultivated a new intransigence toward their Christian subjects. It would, however, be a mistake to see the whole of the Iranian establishment as fanatical. The Shii *ulema* of Iran looked askance at this reformed Shiah: unlike their Sunni counterparts, they refused to "close the gates of *ijtihad*" and insisted on their right to interpret Islam independently of the shahs. They refused to accept the Safavi—and later the Qajar—dynasty as the successor of the Imams. Instead they allied themselves with the people against the rulers and became the champions of the *ummah* against royal oppression in Isfahan and, later, Teheran. They developed a tradition of upholding the rights of the merchants and of the poor against the encroachments of the shahs, and it was this that enabled them to mobilize the people against Shah Muhammad Reza Pahlavi's corrupt regime in 1979.

The Shiis of Iran also developed their own Falsafah, which continued the mystical traditions of Suhrawardi. Mir Damad (d. 1631), the founder of this Shii Falsafah, was a scientist as well as a theologian. He identified the divine Light with the enlightenment of such symbolic figures as Muhammad and the Imams. Like Suhrawardi, he emphasized the unconscious, psychological element of religious experience. The supreme exponent of this Iranian school, however, was Mir Damad's disciple Sadr al-Din Shirazi, who is usually known as Mulla Sadra (ca. 1571–1640). Many Muslims today regard him as the most profound of all the Islamic thinkers, claiming that his work epitomizes the fusion of metaphysics and spirituality that had come to characterize Muslim philosophy. He is only just becoming known in the West, however, and at this writing only one of his many treatises has been translated into English.

Like Suhrawardi, Mulla Sadra believed that knowledge was not simply a matter of acquiring information but a process of transformation. The *alam al-mithal* described by Suhrawardi was crucial to his thought: he himself saw dreams and visions as the highest form of truth. Iranian Shiism was, therefore, still continuing to see mysticism as the most appropriate tool for the discovery of God rather than pure science and metaphysics. Mulla Sadra taught that the *imitatio dei*, the approximation of God, was the goal of philosophy and could not be confined to any one creed or faith. As Ibn Sina had demonstrated, God, the supreme reality, alone had true existence (*wujud*), and this single reality informs the whole chain of being from the divine realm to the dust. Mulla Sadra was not a pantheist. He simply saw God as the source of all things that exist: the beings that we see and experience are only vessels that contain the divine Light in a limited form. Yet God also transcends mundane reality. The unity of all being does not mean that God alone exists, but is similar to the unity of the sun with the beams of light that radiate from it. Like Ibn al-Arabi, Mulla Sadra distinguished between God's essence or "the Blindness" and its various manifestations. His vision is not dissimilar to that of the Greek *hesychasts* and the Kabbalists. He saw the whole cosmos radiating from the Blindness to form a "single jewel" with many layers, which can also be said to correspond to the gradations of God's unfolding self-revelation in his attributes or "signs" (*ayat*). They also represent the stages of humanity's return to the Source of being.

Union with God was not reserved for the next world. Like some of the *hesychasts*, Mulla Sadra believed that it could be realized in this life by means of knowledge. Needless to say, he did not mean cerebral, rational knowledge alone: in his ascent to God the mystic had to travel through the *alam al-mithal*, the realm of vision and imagination. God is not a reality that can be known objectively, but will be found within the image-making faculty of each individual Muslim. When the Koran or the *hadith* speak of Paradise, Hell or the throne of God, they are not referring to a reality that was in a separate location but to an inner world, hidden beneath the veils of sensible phenomena:

> Everything to which man aspires, everything he desires, is instanta-neously present to him, or rather one should say: to picture his desire *is* itself to experience the real presence of its object. But the sweetness and delight are the expression of Paradise and Hell, good and evil, all that can reach man of what constitutes his retribution in the world beyond, have no other source than the essential "I" of man himself, formed as it is by his intentions and projects, his innermost beliefs, his conduct.[3]

Like Ibn al-Arabi, whom he greatly revered, Mulla Sadra did not envisage God sitting in another world, an external, objective heaven to which all the faithful would repair after death. Heaven and the divine sphere were to be discovered within the self, in the personal *alam al-mithal* which was the inalienable possession of every single human being. No two people would have exactly the same heaven or the same God.

Mulla Sadra, who venerated Sunni, Sufi and Greek philosophers as well as the Shiite Imams, reminds us that Iranian Shiism was not always exclusive and fanatical. In India, many of the Muslims had cultivated a similar tolerance toward other traditions. Although Islam predominated culturally in Moghul India, Hinduism remained vital and creative, and some Muslims and Hindus cooperated in the arts and in intellectual projects. The subcontinent had long been free of religious intolerance, and during the fourteenth and fifteenth centuries the most creative forms of Hinduism stressed the unity of religious aspiration: all paths were valid, provided that they emphasized an interior love for the One God. This clearly resonated with both Sufism and Falsafah, which were the most dominant Islamic moods in India. Some Muslims and Hindus formed interfaith societies, the most important of which became Sikhism, founded by Guru Namak during the fifteenth century. This new form of monotheism believed that al-Lah was identical with the God of Hinduism. On the Muslim side, the Iranian scholar Mir Abu al-Qasim Findiriski (d. 1641), the contemporary of Mir Damad and Mulla Sadra, taught the works of Ibn Sina in Isfahan but also spent a good deal of time in India studying Hinduism and Yoga. It would be difficult to imagine a Roman Catholic expert on Thomas Aquinas at this time showing a similar enthusiasm for a religion that was not even in the Abrahamic tradition.

This spirit of tolerance and cooperation was strikingly demonstrated in the policies of Akbar, the third Moghul emperor, who reigned from 1560 to 1605 and who respected all faiths. Out of sensitivity to the Hindus, he became a vegetarian, gave up hunting—a sport he greatly enjoyed—and forbade the sacrifice of animals on his birthday or in the Hindu holy places. In 1575 he founded a House of Worship, where scholars from all religions could meet to discuss God. Here, apparently, the Jesuit missionaries from Europe were the most aggressive. He founded his own Sufi order, dedicated to "divine monotheism" (*tawhid-e-ilahi*), which proclaimed a radical belief in the one God who could reveal himself in any rightly guided religion. Akbar's own life was eulogized by Abulfazl Allami (1551–1602) in his *Akbar-Namah* (The Book of Akbar), which attempted to apply the principles of Sufism to the history of civilization. Allami saw Akbar as the ideal ruler of Falsafah and the Perfect Man of his time. Civilization could lead to universal peace when a generous, liberal society was created by a ruler like Akbar who made bigotry impossible. Islam in its original sense of "surrender" to God could be achieved by any faith: what he certainly called "Muhammad's religion" did not have the monopoly of God. Not all Muslims shared the vision of Akbar, however, and many saw him as a danger to the faith. His tolerant policy could only be sustained while the Moghuls were in a position of strength. When their power began to decline and various groups began to revolt against the Moghul rulers, religious conflicts escalated among Muslims, Hindus and Sikhs. The emperor Aurengzebe (1618–1707) may have believed that unity could be restored by greater discipline within the Muslim camp: he enacted legislation to put a stop to various laxities like wine-drinking, made cooperation with Hindus impossible, reduced the number of Hindu festivals and doubled the taxes of Hindu merchants. The most spectacular expression of his communalist policies was the widespread destruction of Hindu temples. These policies, which had completely reversed the tolerant approach of Akbar, were abandoned after Aureng-zebe's death, but the Moghul empire never recovered from the destructive bigotry he had unleashed and sanctified in the name of God.

One of Akbar's most vigorous opponents during his lifetime had been the outstanding scholar Sheikh Ahmad Sirhindi (1564–1624), who was also a Sufi and, like Akbar, was venerated as the Perfect Man by his own disciples. Sirhindi stood out against the mystical tradition of Ibn al-Arabi, whose disciples had come to see God as the *only* reality. As we have seen, Mulla Sadra had asserted this perception of the Oneness of Existence (*wahdat al-wujud*). It was a mystical restatement of the Shahadah: there was no reality but al-Lah. Like mystics in other religions, the Sufis had experienced a unity and felt one with the whole of existence. Sirhindi, however, dismissed this perception as purely subjective. While the mystic was concentrating on God alone, everything else tended to fade from his consciousness, but this did not correspond to an objective reality. Indeed, to speak of any unity or identity between God and the world was an awful misconception. In fact, there was no possibility of a direct experience of God, who was entirely beyond the reach of mankind: "He is the Holy One, beyond the Beyond, again beyond the Beyond, again beyond the Beyond."[4] There could be no relation between God and the world, except indirectly through the contemplation of the "signs" of nature. Sirhindi claimed that he himself had passed beyond the ecstatic condition of mystics like Ibn al-Arabi to a higher and more sober state of consciousness. He used mysticism and religious experience to reaffirm belief in the distant God of the philosophers, who was an objective but inaccessible reality. His views were ardently embraced by his disciples but not by the majority of Muslims, who remained true to the immanent, subjective God of the mystics.

While Muslims like Findiriski and Akbar were seeking understanding with people of other faiths, the Christian West had demonstrated in 1492 that it could not even tolerate proximity with the two other religions of Abraham. During the fifteenth century, anti-Semitism had increased throughout Europe and Jews were expelled from one city after another: from Linz and Vienna in 1421, Cologne in 1424, Augsburg in 1439, Bavaria in 1442 (and again in 1450) and Moravia in 1454. They were driven out of Perugia in 1485, Vicenza in 1486, Parma in 1488, Lucca and Milan in 1489 and Tuscany in 1494. The expulsion of the Sephardic Jews of Spain must be seen in the context of this larger European trend. The Spanish Jews who had settled in the Ottoman empire continued to suffer from a sense of dislocation coupled with the irrational but indelible guilt of the survivor. It is, perhaps, not dissimilar to the guilt experienced by those who managed to survive the Nazi Holocaust and it is significant, therefore, that today some Jews feel drawn to the spirituality that the Sephardic Jews evolved during the sixteenth century to help them to come to terms with their exile.

This new form of Kabbalism probably originated in the Balkan provinces of the Ottoman empire, where many of the Sephardim had established communities. The tragedy of 1492 seems to have caused a widespread yearning for the redemption of Israel foretold by the prophets. Some Jews led by Joseph Karo and Solomon Alkabaz migrated from Greece to Palestine, the homeland of Israel. Their spirituality sought to heal the humiliation that the expulsion had inflicted upon the Jews and their God. They wanted, they said, "to raise the Shekinah from the dust." But they were not seeking a political solution, nor did they envisage a more widespread return of the Jews to the Promised Land. They settled in Safed in Galilee and initiated a remarkable mystical revival which discovered a profound significance in their experience of homelessness. Hitherto Kabbalah had appealed only to an elite, but after the disaster Jews all over the world turned eagerly to a more mystical spirituality. The consolations of philosophy now seemed hollow: Aristotle sounded arid and his God distant and inaccessible. Indeed, many blamed Falsafah for the catastrophe, claiming that it had weakened Judaism and diluted the sense of Israel's special vocation. Its universality and accommodation of Gentile philosophy had persuaded too many Jews to accept baptism. Never again would Falsafah be an important spirituality within Judaism.

People longed for a more direct experience of God. In Safed this yearning acquired an almost erotic intensity. Kabbalists used to wander through the hills of Palestine and lie on the graves of the great Talmudists, seeking, as it were, to absorb their vision into their own troubled lives. They used to stay awake all night, sleepless as frustrated lovers, singing love songs to God and calling him fond names. They found that the mythology and disciplines of Kabbalah broke down their reserves and touched the pain in their souls in a way that metaphysics or the study of Talmud no longer could. But because their condition was so different from that of Moses of Leon, the author of *The Zohar*, the Spanish exiles needed to adapt his vision so that it could speak to their particular circumstances. They came up with an extraordinarily imaginative solution which equated absolute homelessness with absolute Godliness. The exile of the Jews symbolized the radical dislocation at the heart of all existence. Not only was the whole of creation no longer in its proper place, but God was in exile from himself. The new Kabbalah of Safed achieved almost overnight popularity and became a mass movement that not only inspired the Sephardim but also gave new hope to the Ashkenazim of Europe, who had discovered that they had no abiding city in Christendom. This extraordinary success shows that the strange and—to an outsider—bewildering myths of Safed had the power to speak to the condition of the Jews. It was the last Jewish movement to be accepted by almost everybody and wrought a profound change in the religious consciousness of world Jewry. The special disciplines of Kabbalah were only for an initiated elite, but its ideas—and its conception of God—became a standard expression of Jewish piety.

In order to do justice to this new vision of God, we must understand that these myths were not intended to be taken literally. The Safed Kabbalists were aware that the imagery they used was very daring and constantly hedged around it with such expressions as "as it were" or "one might suppose." But any talk about God was problematic, not least the biblical doctrine of the creation of the universe. The Kabbalists found this as difficult in their own way as had the Faylasufs. Both accepted the Platonic metaphor of emanation, which involves God with the world that eternally flows from him. The prophets had stressed God's holiness and separation from the world, but *The Zohar* had suggested that the world of God's *sefiroth* comprised the whole of reality. How could he be separate from the world if he was all in all? Moses ben Jacob Cordovero of Safed (1522–1570) saw the paradox clearly and attempted to deal with it. In his theology, God En Sof was no longer the incomprehensible Godhead but the thought of the world: he was one with all created things in their ideal Platonic state but separate from their flawed embodiment below: "Insofar as everything that exists is contained in his existence, [God] encompasses all existence," he explained, "his substance is present in his *sefiroth* and He Himself is everything and nothing exists outside him."[5] He was very close to the monism of Ibn al-Arabi and Mulla Sadra.

But Isaac Luria (1534–1572), the hero and saint of the Kabbalism of Safed, tried to explain the paradox of the divine transcendence and immanence more fully with one of the most astonishing ideas ever formulated about God. Most Jewish mystics were very reticent about their experience of the divine. It is one of the contradictions of this type of spirituality that mystics claim that their experiences are ineffable but are yet quite ready to write it all down. Kabbalists were wary of this, however. Luria was one of the first Zaddikim, or holy men, who attracted disciples to his brand of mysticism by his personal charisma. He was not a writer, and our knowledge of his Kabbalistic system is based on the conversations recorded by his disciples Hayim Vital (1542–1620) in his treatise *Etz Hayim* (The Tree of Life) and Joseph ibn Tabul, whose manuscript was not published until 1921.

Luria confronted the question that had troubled monotheists for centuries: how could a perfect and infinite God have created a finite world riddled with evil? Where had evil come from? Luria found his answer by imagining what had happened *before* the emanation of the *sefiroth*, when En Sof had been turned in upon itself in sublime introspection. In order to make room for the world, Luria taught, En Sof had, as it were, vacated a region within himself. In this act of "shrinking" or "withdrawal" (*tsimtsum*), God had thus created a place where he was not, an empty space that he could fill by the simultaneous process of self-revelation and creation. It was a daring attempt to illustrate the difficult doctrine of creation out of nothing: the very first act of En Sof was a self-imposed exile from a part of himself. He had, as it were, descended more deeply into his own being and put a limit upon himself. It is an idea that is not dissimilar to the primordial *kenosis* that Christians have imagined in the Trinity, whereby God emptied himself into his Son in an act of self-expression. For sixteenth-century Kabbalists, *tsimtsum* was primarily a symbol of exile, which underlay the structure of all created existence and had been experienced by En Sof himself.

The "empty space" created by God's withdrawal was conceived as a circle, which was surrounded on all sides by En Sof. This was *tohu u-bohu*, the formless waste mentioned in Genesis. Before the recoil of *tsimtsum*, all God's various "powers" (later to become the *sefiroth*) mingled harmoniously together. They were not differentiated from one another. In particular, God's Hesed (Mercy) and Din (Stern Judgment) existed within God in perfect harmony. But during the process of *tsimtsum*, En Sof separated Din from the rest of his attributes and thrust it into the empty space that he had abandoned. Thus *tsimtsum* was not simply an act of self-emptying love but could be seen as a sort of divine purge: God had eliminated his Wrath or Judgment (which *The Zohar* had seen as the root of evil) from his inmost being. His primal act, therefore, showed a harshness and ruthlessness toward himself. Now that Din was separate from Hesed and the rest of God's attributes, it was potentially destructive. Yet En Sof did not abandon the empty space entirely. A "thin line" of the divine light penetrated this circle, which took the form of what *The Zohar* had called Adam Kadmon, Primordial Man.

Then came the emanation of the *sefiroth*, though not as this is said to

have occurred in *The Zohar*. Luria taught that the *sefiroth* had formed in
Adam Kadmon: the three highest *sefiroth*—Kether (The Crown), Hokhmah (Wisdom) and Binah (Intelligence)—radiated from his "nose," "ears"
and "mouth," respectively. But then a catastrophe occurred, which Luria
called "the Breaking of the Vessels" (*Shevirath Ha-Kelim*). The *sefiroth*
needed to be contained in special coverings or "vessels" to distinguish and
separate them from one another and to prevent them from merging again
into their former unity. These "vessels" or "pipes" were not material, of
course, but were composed of a sort of thicker light that served as "shells"
(*kelipot*) for the purer light of the *sefiroth*. When the three highest *sefiroth*
had radiated from Adam Kadmon, their vessels had functioned perfectly.
But when the next six *sefiroth* issued from his "eyes," their vessels were
not strong enough to contain the divine light and they smashed. Consequently the light was scattered. Some of it rose upward and returned to
the Godhead, but some divine "sparks" fell into the empty waste and
remained trapped in chaos. Thenceforth nothing was in its proper place.
Even the three highest *sefiroth* had fallen to a lower sphere as a result of
the catastrophe. The original harmony had been ruined and the divine
sparks were lost in the formless waste of *tohu u-bohu*, in exile from the
Godhead.

This strange myth is reminiscent of the earlier Gnostic myths of a
primordial dislocation. It expresses the tension involved in the whole
creative process, which is far closer to the Big Bang envisaged by scientists
today than the more peaceful, orderly sequence described by Genesis. It
was not easy for En Sof to emerge from his hidden state: he could only
do so—as it were—in a sort of trial and error. In the Talmud, the Rabbis
had had a similar idea. They had said that God had made other worlds
and had destroyed them before he created this one. But all was not lost.
Some Kabbalists compared this "Breaking" (*Shevirath*) to the breakthrough
of birth or the bursting of a seed pod. The destruction had simply been
a prelude to a new creation. Although everything was in disarray, En Sof
would bring new life out of this apparent chaos by means of the process
of *Tikkun* or reintegration.

After the catastrophe, a new stream of light issued from En Sof and
broke through the "forehead" of Adam Kadmon. This time the *sefiroth*
were reorganized into new configurations: they were no longer to be
generalized aspects of God. Each one became a "Countenance" (*parzuf*)
in which the entire personality of God was revealed, with—as it were—
distinctive features, in rather the same way as in the three *personae* of the
Trinity. Luria was trying to find a new way of expressing the old Kabba-

listic idea of the inscrutable God giving birth to himself as a person. In the process of *Tikkun*, Luria used the symbolism of the conception, birth and development of a human personality to suggest a similar evolution in God. It is complicated and perhaps best explained in diagrammatic form. In the reintegration of *Tikkun*, God restored order by regrouping the ten *sefiroth* into five "Countenances" (*parzufim*) in the following stages:

1. Kether (The Crown), the highest *sefirah*, which *The Zohar* had called "Nothing," becomes the first *parzuf*, called "Arik" Anpin: the Forebearing One.
2. Hokhmah (Wisdom) becomes the second *parzuf*, called Abba: Father.
3. Binah (Intelligence) becomes the third *parzuf*, called Ima: Mother.
4. Din (Judgment); Hesed (Mercy); Rakhamim (Compassion); Netsakh (Patience); Hod (Majesty); Yesod (Foundation) all become the fourth *parzuf*, called Zeir Anpin: the Impatient One. His consort is:
5. The last *sefirah*, called Malkuth (Kingdom) or the Shekinah: it becomes the fifth *parzuf*, which is called Nuqrah de Zeir: Zeir's Woman.

The sexual symbolism is a bold attempt to depict the reunification of the *sefiroth*, which will heal the rupture that occurred when the vessels were broken and restore the original harmony. The two "couples"—Abba and Ima, Zeir and Nuqrah—engage in *ziwwug* (copulation), and this mating of the male and female elements within God symbolizes the restored order. The Kabbalists constantly warn their readers not to take this literally. It is a fiction designed to hint at a process of integration that cannot be described in clear, rational terms and to neutralize the overwhelmingly masculine imagery of God. The salvation envisaged by the mystics did not depend upon historical events like the coming of the Messiah but was a process that God himself must undergo. God's first plan had been to make humanity his helpmate in the process of redeeming those divine sparks that had been scattered and trapped in chaos at the Breaking of the Vessels. But Adam had sinned in the Garden of Eden. Had he not done so, the original harmony would have been restored and the divine exile ended on the first Sabbath. But Adam's fall repeated the primal catastrophe of the Breaking of the Vessels. The created order fell and the divine light in his soul was scattered abroad and imprisoned in broken matter. Consequently, God evolved yet another plan. He had chosen Israel to be his helpmate in the struggle for sovereignty and control. Even though Israel, like the divine sparks themselves, is scattered throughout the cruel and Godless realm of the diaspora, Jews have a special mission. As long as the divine sparks are separated and lost in matter, God is incomplete. By careful observance of Torah and the discipline of prayer, each Jew could help to restore the sparks to their divine source and so redeem the world. In this vision of salvation, God is not gazing down on humanity condescendingly but, as Jews had always insisted, is actually dependent upon mankind. Jews have the unique privilege of helping to re-form God and create him anew.

Luria gave a new meaning to the original image of the exile of the Shekinah. It will be recalled that in the Talmud, the Rabbis had seen the Shekinah voluntarily going into exile with the Jews after the destruction of the Temple. *The Zohar* had identified the Shekinah with the last *sefirah* and made it the female aspect of divinity. In Luria's myth, the Shekinah fell with the other *sefiroth* when the Vessels were shattered. In the first stage of *Tikkun*, she had become Nuqrah and by mating with Zeir (the six "Middle" *sefiroth*) had almost been reintegrated into the divine world. But when Adam sinned, the Shekinah fell once more and went into exile from the rest of the Godhead. Luria was most unlikely to have encountered the writings of those Christian Gnostics who had developed a very similar mythology. He had spontaneously reproduced the old myths of exile and fall to meet the tragic conditions of the sixteenth century. Tales of divine copulation and the exiled goddess had been rejected by the Jews during the biblical period, when they were evolving their doctrine of the One God. Their connection with paganism and idolatry should logically have revolted the Sephardim. Instead, Luria's mythology was embraced eagerly by Jews from Persia to England, Germany to Poland, Italy to North Africa, Holland to Yemen; recast in Jewish terms, it was able to touch a buried chord and give new hope in the midst of despair. It enabled the Jews to believe that despite the appalling circumstances in which so many of them lived, there was an ultimate meaning and significance.

The Jews could end the exile of the Shekinah. By the observance of the *mitzvot*, they could rebuild their God again. It is interesting to compare this myth with the Protestant theology that Luther and Calvin were creating in Europe at about the same time. The Protestant reformers both preached the absolute sovereignty of God: in their theology, as we shall see, there is absolutely nothing that men and women could contribute to their own salvation. Luria, however, preached a doctrine of works: God needed human beings and would remain somehow incomplete without their prayer and good deeds. Despite the tragedy that had befallen the Jewish people in Europe, they were able to be more optimistic about humanity than the Protestants. Luria saw the mission of *Tikkun* in contemplative terms. Where the Christians of Europe—Catholic and Protestant alike—were formulating more and more dogmas, Luria revived the mystical techniques of Abraham Abulafia to help Jews transcend this kind of intellectual activity and to cultivate a more intuitive awareness. Rearranging the letters of the Divine Name, in Abulafia's spirituality, had reminded the Kabbalist that the meaning of "God" could not adequately be conveyed by human language. In Luria's mythology, it also symbolized the restructuring and re-formation of the divine. Hayyim Vital described the immensely emotional effect of Luria's disciplines: by separating himself from his normal, everyday experience—by keeping vigil when everybody else was asleep, fasting when others were eating, withdrawing into seclusion for a while—a Kabbalist could concentrate on the strange "words" that bore no relation to ordinary speech. He felt that he was in another world, would find himself shaking and trembling as though possessed by a force outside himself.

But there was no anxiety. Luria insisted that before he began his spiritual exercises, the Kabbalist must achieve peace of mind. Happiness and joy were essential: there was to be no breast-beating or remorse, no guilt or anxiety about one's performance. Vital insisted that the Shekinah cannot live in a place of sorrow and pain—an idea that we have seen to be rooted in the Talmud. Sadness springs from the forces of evil in the world, whereas happiness enables the Kabbalist to love God and cleave to him. There should be no anger or aggression in the Kabbalist's heart for anybody whatsoever—even the *goyim*. Luria identified anger with idolatry, since an angry person is possessed by a "strange god." It is easy to criticize Lurianic mysticism. As Gershom Scholem points out, the mystery of God En Sof, which was so strong in *The Zohar*, tends to get lost in the drama of *tsimtsum*, the Breaking of the Vessels and *Tikkun*.[6] In the next chapter, we shall see that it contributed to a disastrous and embarrassing episode in Jewish history. Yet Luria's conception of God was able to help Jews to cultivate a spirit of joy and kindness, together with a positive view of humanity at a time when the guilt and anger of the Jews could have caused many to despair and to lose faith in life altogether.

The Christians of Europe were not able to produce such a positive spirituality. They too had endured historical disasters that could not be assuaged by the philosophical religion of the scholastics. The Black Death of 1348, the fall of Constantinople in 1453, and the ecclesiastical scandals of the Avignon Captivity (1334–42) and the Great Schism (1378–1417) had thrown the impotence of the human condition into vivid relief and brought the Church into disrepute. Humanity seemed unable to extricate itself from its fearful predicament without God's help. During the fourteenth and fifteenth centuries, therefore, theologians like Duns Scotus of Oxford (1265–1308)—not to be confused with Duns Scotus Erigena— and the French theologian Jean de Gerson (1363–1429) both emphasized the sovereignty of God, who controlled human affairs as stringently as an absolute ruler. Men and women could contribute nothing to their salvation; good deeds were not meritorious in themselves but only because God had graciously decreed that they were good. But during these centuries, there was also a shift in emphasis. Gerson himself was a mystic, who believed that it was better to "hold primarily to the love of God without lofty enquiry" rather than to "seek through reasons based on the true faith, to understand the nature of God."[7] There had been an upsurge of mysticism in Europe during the fourteenth century, as we have seen, and the people were beginning to appreciate that reason was inadequate to explain the mystery they called "God." As Thomas à Kempis said in *The Imitation of Christ*:

> Of what use is it to discourse learnedly on the Trinity, if you lack humility and therefore displease the Trinity. . . . I would far rather feel contrition than be able to define it. If you knew the whole Bible by heart, and all the teachings of the philosophers, how would this help you without the grace and love of God?[8]

The Imitation of Christ, with its rather dour, gloomy religiosity, became one of the most popular of all Western spiritual classics. During these centuries, piety centered increasingly on Jesus the man. The practice of making the stations of the cross dwelt in particular detail on Jesus' physical pain and sorrow. Some fourteenth-century meditations written by an anonymous author tell the reader that when he wakes up in the morning after spending most of the night meditating on the Last Supper and the Agony in the Garden, his eyes should still be red with weeping. Immediately he should begin to contemplate Jesus' trial and follow his progress to Calvary, hour by hour. The reader is urged to imagine himself pleading with the authorities to save Christ's life, to sit beside him in prison and to kiss his chained hands and feet.[9] In this dismal program, there is little emphasis on the Resurrection. Instead the stress is on the vulnerable humanity of Jesus. A violence of emotion and what strikes the modern reader as morbid curiosity characterizes many of these descriptions. Even the great mystics Bridget of Sweden or Julian of Norwich speculate in lurid detail about Jesus' physical state:

> I saw his dear face, dry, bloodless, and pallid with death. It became more pale, deathly and lifeless. Then, dead, it turned a blue color, gradually changing to a browny blue, as the flesh continued to die. For me his passion was shown primarily through his blessed face, and particularly by his lips. There too I saw these same four colors, though previously they had been, as I had seen, fresh, red, and lovely. It was a sorry business to see him change as he progressively died. His nostrils too shriveled and dried before my eyes, and his dear body became black and brown as it dried up in death.[10]

This reminds us of the German crucifixes of the fourteenth century with their grotesquely twisted figures and gushing blood, which, of course, reached a climax in the work of Matthias Grünewald (1480–1528). Julian was capable of great insight into the nature of God: she depicts the Trinity living within the soul and not as an external reality "out there," like a true mystic. But the strength of Western concentration on the human Christ seemed too powerful to resist. Increasingly, during the fourteenth and fifteenth centuries, men and women in Europe were making other human beings the center of their spiritual life rather than God. The medieval cult of Mary and of the saints increased alongside the growing devotion to Jesus the man. Enthusiasm for relics and holy places also distracted Western Christians from the one thing necessary. People seemed to be concentrating on anything *but* God.

The dark side of the Western spirit was even manifest during the Renaissance. The philosophers and humanists of the Renaissance were highly critical of much medieval piety. They disliked the scholastics intensely, feeling that their abstruse speculations made God sound alien and boring. Instead, they wanted to return to the sources of the faith, particularly to St. Augustine. The medievals had revered Augustine as a theologian, but the humanists rediscovered the *Confessions* and saw him as a fellow man on a personal quest. Christianity, they argued, was not a body of doctrines but an experience. Lorenzo Valla (1407–57) stressed the futility of mixing sacred dogma with "tricks of dialectics" and "metaphysical quibbles":[11] these "futilities" had been condemned by St. Paul himself. Francesco Petrarch (1304–74) had suggested that "theology is actually poetry, poetry concerning God," effective not because it "proved" anything but because it penetrated the heart.[12] The humanists had rediscovered the dignity of humanity, but this did not cause them to reject God: instead, as true men of their age, they stressed the humanity of God who had become man. But the old insecurities remained. The Renaissance men were deeply aware of the fragility of our knowledge and could also sympathize with Augustine's acute sense of sin. As Petrarch said:

> How many times I have pondered over my own misery and over death; with what floods of tears I have sought to wash away my stains so that I can scarce speak of it without weeping, yet hitherto all is vain. God indeed is the best: and I am the worst.[13]

Hence there was a vast distance between man and God: Coluccio Salutati (1331–1406) and Leonardo Bruni (1369–1444) both saw God as utterly transcendent and inaccessible to the human mind.

Yet the German philosopher and churchman Nicholas of Cusa (1401–64) was more confident about our ability to understand God. He was extremely interested in the new science, which he thought could help us to comprehend the mystery of the Trinity. Mathematics, for example, which dealt only with pure abstractions, could supply a certainty that was impossible in other disciplines. Thus the mathematical idea of "the maximum" and "the minimum" were apparently opposites but in fact could logically be seen as identical. This "coincidence of opposites" contained the idea of God: the idea of "the maximum" includes everything; it implies notions of unity and necessity which point directly to God. Further, the *maximum* line was not a triangle, a circle or a sphere, but all three combined: the unity of opposites was also a Trinity. Yet Nicholas's clever demonstration has little religious meaning. It seems to reduce the idea of God to a logical conundrum. But his conviction that "God embraces everything, even contradictions"[14] was close to the Greek Orthodox perception that all true theology must be paradoxical. When he was writing as a spiritual teacher, rather than as a philosopher and mathematician, Nicholas was aware that the Christian must "leave everything behind" when he sought to approach God, and "even transcend one's intellect" going beyond all sense and reason. The face of God will remain shrouded in "a secret and mystic silence."[15]

The new insights of the Renaissance could not address deeper fears that, like God, lay beyond the reach of reason. Not long after Nicholas's death, a particularly noxious phobia erupted in his native Germany and spread throughout northern Europe. In 1484 Pope Innocent VIII published the Bull *Summa Desiderantes*, which marked the beginning of the great witch craze that raged sporadically throughout Europe during the sixteenth and seventeenth centuries, afflicting Protestant and Catholic communities equally. It revealed the dark underside of the Western spirit. During this hideous persecution, thousands of men and women were cruelly tortured until they confessed to astonishing crimes. They said that they had had sexual intercourse with demons, had flown hundreds of miles through the air to take part in orgies where Satan was worshipped instead of God in an obscene Mass. We now know that there were no witches but that the craze represented a vast collective fantasy, shared by the learned Inquisitors and many of their victims, who had dreamed these things and were easily persuaded that they actually happened. The fantasy was linked with anti-Semitism and a deep sexual fear. Satan had emerged as the shadow of an impossibly good and powerful God. This had not happened in the other God-religions. The Koran, for example, makes it clear that Satan will be forgiven on the Last Day. Some of the Sufis claimed that he had fallen from grace because he had loved God more than any of the other angels. God had commanded him to bow down before Adam on the day of creation, but Satan had refused because he believed that such obeisance should be offered to God alone. In the West, however, Satan became a figure of ungovernable evil. He was increasingly represented as a vast animal with a priapic sexual appetite and huge genitals. As Norman Cohn has suggested in his book *Europe's Inner Demons*, this portrait of Satan was not only a projection of buried fear and anxiety. The witch craze also represented an unconscious but compulsive revolt against a repressive religion and an apparently inexorable God. In their torture chambers, Inquisitors and "witches" together created a fantasy which was an inversion of Christianity. The Black Mass became a horrifying but perversely satisfying ceremony that worshipped the Devil instead of a God who seemed harsh and too frightening to deal with.[16]

Martin Luther (1483–1546) was a firm believer in witchcraft and saw the Christian life as a battle against Satan. The Reformation can be seen as an attempt to address this anxiety even though most of the Reformers did not promote any new conception of God. It is, of course, simplistic to call the immense cycle of religious change that took place in Europe during the sixteenth century "the Reformation." The term suggests a more deliberate and unified movement than actually occurred. The various Reformers—Catholic as well as Protestant—were all trying to articulate a new religious awareness that was strongly felt but had not been conceptualized or consciously thought out. We do not know exactly why "the Reformation" happened: today scholars warn us against the old textbook accounts. The changes were not wholly due to the corruption of the Church, as is often supposed, nor to a decline in religious fervor. Indeed, there seems to have been a religious enthusiasm in Europe which led people to criticize abuses which they had previously taken for granted. The actual ideas of the Reformers all sprang from medieval, Catholic theologies. The rise of nationalism and of the cities in Germany and Switzerland also played a part, as did the new piety and theological awareness of the laity during the sixteenth century. There was also a heightened sense of individualism in Europe, and this always entailed a radical revision of current religious attitudes. Instead of expressing their faith in external, collective ways, the people of Europe were beginning to explore the more interior consequences of religion. All these factors contributed to the painful and frequently violent changes that propelled the West toward modernity.

Before his conversion, Luther had almost despaired of the possibility of pleasing a God he had come to hate:

> Although I lived a blameless life as a monk, I felt that I was a sinner with an uneasy conscience before God. I also could not believe that I had pleased him with my works. Far from loving that righteous God who punished sinners, I actually loathed him. I was a good monk, and kept my order so strictly that if ever a monk could get to heaven by monastic discipline, I was that monk. All my companions in the monastery would confirm this. . . . And yet my conscience would not give me certainty, but I always doubted and said, "You didn't do that right. You weren't contrite enough. You left that out of your confession."[17]

Many Christians today—Protestant as well as Catholic—will recognize this syndrome, which the Reformation could not entirely abolish. Luther's God was characterized by his wrath. None of the saints, prophets or psalmists had been able to endure this divine anger. It was no good simply trying "to do one's best." Because God was eternal and omnipotent, "his fury or wrath toward self-satisfied sinners is also immeasurable and infinite."[18] His will was past finding out. Observance of the Law of

God or the rules of a religious order could not save us. Indeed, the Law could only bring accusation and terror, because it showed us the measure of our inadequacy. Instead of bringing a message of hope, the Law revealed "the wrath of God, sin, death and damnation in the sight of God."[19]

Luther's personal breakthrough came about when he formulated his doctrine of justification. Man could not save himself. God provides everything necessary for "justification," the restoration of a relationship between the sinner and God. God is active and humans only passive. Our "good works" and observance of the Law are not the *cause* of our justification but only the result. We are able to observe the precepts of religion simply because God has saved us. This was what St. Paul had meant by the phrase "justification by faith." There was nothing new about Luther's theory: it had been current in Europe since the early fourteenth century. But once Luther had grasped it and made it his own, he felt his anxieties fall away. The revelation that ensued "made me feel as though I had been born again, and as though I had entered through open gates into paradise itself."[20]

Yet he remained extremely pessimistic about human nature. By the year 1520 he had developed what he called his Theology of the Cross. He had taken the phrase from St. Paul, who had told his Corinthian converts that the cross of Christ had shown that "God's foolishness is wiser than human wisdom, and God's weakness is stronger than human strength."[21] God justified "sinners" who, by purely human standards, could only be regarded as worthy of punishment. God's strength was revealed in what was weakness in the eyes of men. Where Luria had taught his Kabbalists that God could only be found in joy and tranquillity, Luther claimed that "God can be found only in suffering and the Cross."[22] From this position, he developed a polemic against scholasticism, distinguishing the false theologian, who makes a display of human cleverness and "looks upon the invisible things of God as though they were clearly perceptible," from the true theologian "who comprehends the visible and manifest things of God through suffering and the Cross."[23] The doctrines of the Trinity and the Incarnation seemed suspect in the way they had been formulated by the Fathers of the Church; their complexity suggested the false "theology of glory."[24] Yet Luther remained true to the orthodoxy of Nicaea, Ephesus and Chalcedon. Indeed, his theory of justification depended upon the divinity of Christ and his Trinitarian status. These traditional doctrines of God were too deeply embedded in the Christian experience for either Luther or Calvin to question, but Luther rejected the abstruse formulations of the false theologians. "What does it matter to me?" he asked, when confronted with the complex Christological doctrines: all he needed to know was that Christ was his redeemer.[25]

Luther even doubted the possibility of proving the existence of God. The only "God" who could be deduced by logical arguments, such as those used by Thomas Aquinas, was the God of the pagan philosophers. When Luther claimed that we were justified by "faith," he did not mean the adoption of the right ideas about God. "Faith does not require information, knowledge and certainty," he preached in one of his sermons, "but a free surrender and a joyful bet on his unfelt, untried and unknown goodness."[26] He had anticipated the solutions of Pascal and Kierkegaard to the problem of faith. Faith did not mean assent to the propositions of a creed and it was not "belief" in orthodox opinion. Instead, faith was a leap in the dark toward a reality that had to be taken on trust. It was "a sort of knowledge and darkness that can see nothing."[27] God, he insisted, strictly forbade speculative discussion of his nature. To attempt to reach him by means of reason alone could be dangerous and lead to despair, since all that we would discover were the power, wisdom and justice of God, which could only intimidate convicted sinners. Instead of engaging in rationalistic discussion of God, the Christian should appropriate the revealed truths of scripture and make them his own. Luther showed how this should be done in the creed he composed in his *Small Catechism*:

> I believe that Jesus Christ, begotten of the Father from eternity, and also the man, born of the Virgin Mary, is my Lord; who has redeemed *me*, a lost and condemned creature, and delivered *me* from all sins, from death, and from the power of the devil, not with silver and gold but with his holy and precious blood and with his innocent sufferings and death, in order that I may be his, live under him and in his Kingdom and serve him in everlasting righteousness and blessedness, even as he is risen from the dead and reigns to all eternity.[28]

Luther had been trained in scholastic theology but had reverted to simpler forms of faith and had reacted against the arid theology of the fourteenth century, which could do nothing to calm his fears. Yet he himself could be abstruse when, for example, he tried to explain exactly *how* we became justified. Augustine, Luther's hero, had taught that the righteousness bestowed upon the sinner was not his own but God's. Luther gave this a subtle twist. Augustine had said that this divine righteousness became a part of us; Luther insisted that it remained outside the sinner but that

God regarded it *as though* it were our own. Ironically, the Reformation would lead to greater doctrinal confusion and to the proliferation of new doctrines as the banners of the various sects which were just as rarefied and tenuous as some of those they sought to replace.

Luther claimed that he had been reborn when he had formulated his doctrine of justification, but in fact it does not seem as though all his anxieties had been allayed. He remained a disturbed, angry and violent man. All the major religious traditions claim that the acid test of any spirituality is the degree to which it has been integrated into daily life. As the Buddha said, after enlightenment one should "return to the market-place" and practice compassion for all living beings. A sense of peace, serenity and loving-kindness are the hallmarks of all true religious insight. Luther, however, was a rabid anti-Semite, a misogynist, was convulsed with a loathing and horror of sexuality and believed that all rebellious peasants should be killed. His vision of a wrathful God had filled him with personal rage, and it has been suggested that his belligerent character did great harm to the Reformation. At the beginning of his career as a Reformer many of his ideas were held by orthodox Catholics, and they could have given the Church a new vitality, but Luther's aggressive tactics caused them to be regarded with unnecessary suspicion.[29]

In the long term, Luther was less important than John Calvin (1509–64) whose Swiss Reformation, based more than Luther's on the ideals of the Renaissance, had a profound effect on the emerging Western ethos. By the end of the sixteenth century, "Calvinism" had been established as an international religion that, for good or ill, was able to transform society and give people the inspiration to believe that they could achieve whatever they wanted. Calvinistic ideas inspired the Puritan revolution in England under Oliver Cromwell in 1645 and the colonization of New England in the 1620s. Luther's ideas were in the main confined to Germany after his death, but Calvin's seemed the more progressive. His disciples developed his teaching and effected the second wave of the Reformation. As the historian Hugh Trevor Roper has remarked, Calvinism is more easily discarded by its adherents than Roman Catholicism—hence the adage "once a Catholic always a Catholic." Yet Calvinism makes its own impression: once discarded, it can be expressed in secular ways.[30] This has been especially true in the United States. Many Americans who no longer believe in God subscribe to the Puritan work ethic and to the Calvinist notion of election, seeing themselves as a "chosen nation," whose flag and ideals have a semidivine purpose. We have seen that the major religions were all in one sense products of civilization and, more specifically, of the city. They had developed at a time when the wealthy merchant classes were gaining an ascendancy over the old pagan establishment and wanted to take their destiny into their own hands. Calvin's version of Christianity was especially attractive to the bourgeoisie in the newly developing cities of Europe, whose inhabitants wanted to shake off the shackles of a repressive hierarchy.

Like the earlier Swiss theologian Huldrych Zwingli (1484–1531), Calvin was not particularly interested in dogma: his concern was centered on the social, political and economic aspects of religion. He wanted to return to a simpler, scriptural piety but adhered to the doctrine of the Trinity, despite the unbiblical provenance of its terminology. As he wrote in *The Institutes of the Christian Religion*, God had declared that he was One but "clearly sets this before us as existing in three persons."[31] In 1553 Calvin had the Spanish theologian Michael Servetus executed for his denial of the Trinity. Servetus had fled Catholic Spain and had taken refuge in Calvin's Geneva, claiming that he was returning to the faith of the apostles and the earliest Fathers of the Church, who had never heard of this extraordinary doctrine. With some justice, Servetus argued that there was nothing in the New Testament to contradict the strict monotheism of the Jewish scriptures. The doctrine of the Trinity was a human fabrication which had "alienated the minds of men from the knowledge of the true Christ and presented us with a tripartite God."[32] His beliefs were shared by two Italian reformers—Giorgio Blandrata (ca. 1515–1588) and Faustus Socinus (1539–1604)—who had both fled to Geneva but discovered that their theology was too radical for the Swiss Reformation; they did not even adhere to the traditional Western view of the atonement. They did not believe that men and women were justified by Christ's death but simply by their "faith" or trust in God. In his book *Christ the Savior*, Socinus repudiated the so-called orthodoxy of Nicaea: the term "Son of God" was not a statement about Jesus' divine nature but simply meant that he was specially loved by God. He had not died to atone for our sins but was simply a teacher who "showed and taught the way of salvation." As for the doctrine of the Trinity, that was simply a "monstrosity," an imaginary fiction that was "repugnant to reason" and actually encouraged the faithful to believe in three separate gods.[33] After the execution of Servetus, Blandrata and Socinus both fled to Poland and Transylvania, taking their "Unitarian" religion with them.

Zwingli and Calvin relied on more conventional ideas of God and, like Luther, they emphasized his absolute sovereignty. This was not simply an intellectual conviction but the result of an intensely personal experience. In August 1519, shortly after he had begun his ministry in Zurich, Zwingli contracted the plague that eventually wiped out twenty-five percent of the population of the city. He felt completely helpless, realizing that there was absolutely nothing he could do to save himself. It did not occur to him to pray to the saints for help or ask the Church to intercede for him. Instead he threw himself on God's mercy. He composed this short prayer:

> Do as you will
> for I lack nothing.
> I am your vessel
> to be restored or destroyed.[34]

His surrender was similar to the ideal of *islām*: like Jews and Muslims at a comparable stage of their development, Western Christians were no longer willing to accept mediators but were evolving a sense of their inalienable responsibility before God. Calvin also based his reformed religion on God's absolute rule. He has not left us with a full account of his conversion experience. In his *Commentary on the Psalms*, he simply tells us that it was entirely the work of God. He had been completely enthralled by the institutional Church and "the superstitions of the papacy." He was both unable and unwilling to break free, and it had taken an act of God to shift him: "At last God turned my course in a different direction by the hidden bridle of his providence. . . . By a sudden conversion to docility, he tamed a mind too stubborn for its years."[35] God alone was in control and Calvin absolutely powerless, yet he felt singled out for a special mission precisely by his acute sense of his own failure and impotence.

The radical conversion had been characteristic of Western Christianity since the time of Augustine. Protestantism would continue the tradition of breaking abruptly and violently with the past in what the American philosopher William James called a "twice-born" religion for "sick souls."[36] Christians were being "born again" to a new faith in God and a rejection of the host of intermediaries that had stood between them and the divine in the medieval Church. Calvin said that people had venerated the saints out of anxiety; they had wanted to propitiate an angry God by gaining the ear of those closest to him. Yet in their rejection of the cult of the saints, Protestants often betrayed an equal anxiety. When they heard the news that the saints were ineffective, a good deal of the fear and hostility they had felt for this intransigent God seemed to explode in an intense reaction. The English humanist Thomas More detected a personal hatred in many of the diatribes against the "idolatry" of saint-worship.[37] This came out in the violence of their image-smashing. Many Protestants and Puritans took the condemnation of graven images in the Old Testament very seriously when they shattered the statues of the saints and the Virgin Mary and hurled whitewash over the frescoes in the churches and cathedrals. Their frantic zeal showed that they were just as fearful of offending this irritable and jealous God as they had been when they had prayed to the saints to intercede for them. It also showed that this zeal to worship God alone did not spring from a calm conviction but from the anxious denial that had caused the ancient Israelites to tear down the poles of Asherah and pour torrents of abuse upon their neigh-bors' gods.

Calvin is usually remembered for his belief in predestination, but in fact this was not central to his thought: it did not become crucial to "Calvinism" until after his death. The problem of reconciling God's om-nipotence and omniscience with human free will springs from an anthro-pomorphic conception of God. We have seen that Muslims had come up against this difficulty during the ninth century and had found no logical or rational way out of it; instead, they had stressed the mystery and inscrutability of God. The problem had never troubled the Greek Ortho-dox Christians, who enjoyed paradox and found it a source of light and inspiration, but it had been a bone of contention in the West, where a more personalistic view of God prevailed. People tried to talk about "God's will" as though he were a human being, subject to the same constraints as us and literally governing the world, like an earthly ruler. Yet the Catholic Church had condemned the idea that God had predes-tined the damned to hell for all eternity. Augustine, for example, had applied the term "predestination" to God's decision to save the elect but had denied that some lost souls were doomed to perdition, even though this was the logical corollary of his thought. Calvin gave very little space to the topic of predestination in the *Institutes*. When we looked about us, he admitted, it seemed that God did indeed favor some people more than others. Why did some respond to the Gospel while others remained indifferent? Was God acting in a way that was arbitrary or unfair? Calvin denied this: the apparent choice of some and the rejection of others was a sign of the mystery of God.[38] There was no rational solution to the problem, which seemed to imply that God's love and his justice were irreconcilable. This did not trouble Calvin overmuch, since he was not very interested in dogma.

After his death, however, when "Calvinists" needed to distinguish themselves from Lutherans on the one hand and Roman Catholics on the other, Theodorus Beza (1519–1605), who had been Calvin's right-hand man in Geneva and took on the leadership after his death, made predestination the distinguishing mark of Calvinism. He ironed out the paradox with relentless logic. Since God was all-powerful, it followed that man could contribute nothing toward his own salvation. God was changeless and his decrees were just and eternal: thus he had decided from all eternity to save some but had predestined the rest to eternal damnation. Some Calvinists recoiled in horror from this obnoxious doctrine. In the Low Countries, Jakob Arminius argued that this was an example of bad theology, since it spoke of God as though he were a mere human being. But Calvinists believed that God could be discussed as objectively as any other phenomenon. Like other Protestants and Catholics, they were developing a new Aristotelianism, which stressed the importance of logic and metaphysics. This was different from the Aristotelianism of St. Thomas Aquinas, since the new theologians were not as interested in the content of Aristotle's thought as in his rational method. They wanted to present Christianity as a coherent and rational system that could be derived from syllogistic deductions based on known axioms. This was deeply ironic, of course, since the Reformers had all rejected this type of rationalistic discussion of God. The latter-day Calvinist theology of predestination showed what could happen when the paradox and mystery of God were no longer regarded as poetry but were interpreted with a coherent but terrifying logic. Once the Bible begins to be interpreted literally instead of symbolically, the idea of its God becomes impossible. To imagine a deity who is literally responsible for everything that happens on earth involves impossible contradictions. The "God" of the Bible ceases to be a symbol of a transcendent reality and becomes a cruel and despotic tyrant. The doctrine of predestination shows the limitations of such a personalized God.

Puritans based their religious experience on Calvin and clearly found God a struggle: he did not seem to imbue them with either happiness or compassion. Their journals and autobiographies show that they were obsessed with predestination and a terror that they would not be saved. Conversion became a central preoccupation, a violent, tortured drama in which the "sinner" and his spiritual director "wrestled" for his soul. Frequently the penitent had to undergo severe humiliation or experience real despair of God's grace until he appreciated his utter dependence upon God. Often the conversion represented a psychological abreaction, an unhealthy swing from extreme desolation to elation. The heavy emphasis on hell and damnation combined with an excessive self-scrutiny led many into clinical depression: suicide seems to have been prevalent. Puritans attributed this to Satan, who seemed as powerful a presence in their lives as God.[39] Puritanism did have a positive dimension: it gave people pride in their work, which had hitherto been experienced as a slavery but which was now seen as a "calling." Its urgent apocalyptic spirituality inspired some to colonize the New World. But at its worst, the Puritan God inspired anxiety and a harsh intolerance of those who were not among the elect.

Catholics and Protestants now regarded one another as enemies, but in fact their conception and experience of God were remarkably similar. After the Council of Trent (1545–63), Catholic theologians also committed themselves to the neo-Aristotelian theology, which reduced the study of God to a natural science. Reformers like Ignatius of Loyola (1491–1556), founder of the Society of Jesus, shared the Protestant emphasis on direct experience of God and the need to appropriate revelation and make it uniquely one's own. The *Spiritual Exercises* which he evolved for his first Jesuits were intended to induce a conversion, which could be a wracking, painful experience as well as an extremely joyful one. With its emphasis on self-examination and personal decision, this thirty-day retreat undertaken on a one-to-one basis with a director was not dissimilar to Puritan spirituality. The *Exercises* represent a systematic, highly efficient crash course in mysticism. Mystics had often evolved disciplines that were similar to those used today by psychoanalysts and it is, therefore, interesting that the *Exercises* are also being used today by Catholics and Anglicans to provide an alternative type of therapy.

Ignatius was aware of the dangers of false mysticism, however. Like Luria, he stressed the importance of serenity and joy, warning his disciples against the extremes of emotion that pushed some Puritans over the edge in his *Rules for the Discernment of Spirits*. He divides the various emotions that the exercitant is likely to experience during his retreat into those which were likely to come from God and those which came from the devil. God was to be experienced as peace, hope, joy and an "elevation of mind," while disquiet, sadness, aridity and distraction came from "the evil spirit." Ignatius's own sense of God was acute: it used to make him weep with joy, and he once said that without it he would be unable to live. But he distrusted violent swings of emotion and stressed the need for discipline in his journey to a new self. Like Calvin, he saw Christianity as an encounter with Christ, which he plotted in the *Exercises*: the culmination was the "Contemplation for Obtaining Love," which sees "all things as creatures of the goodness of God and reflections of it."[40] For Ignatius the world was full of God. During the canonization process, his disciples recalled:

> We often saw how even the smallest things could make his spirit soar upwards to God, who even in the smallest things is the Greatest. At the sight of a little plant, a leaf, a flower or a fruit, an insignificant worm or a tiny animal Ignatius could soar free above the heavens and reach through into things which lie beyond the senses.[41]

Like the Puritans, Jesuits experienced God as a dynamic force which, at its best, could fill them with confidence and energy. As Puritans braved the Atlantic to settle in New England, Jesuit missionaries traveled the globe: Francis Xavier (1506–1552) evangelized India and Japan, Matteo Ricci (1552–1610) took the Gospel to China and Robert de Nobili (1577–1656) to India. Like the Puritans again, Jesuits were often enthusiastic scientists, and it has been suggested that the first scientific society was not the Royal Society of London or the Accademia del Cimento but the Society of Jesus.

Yet Catholics seemed as troubled as the Puritans. Ignatius, for example, regarded himself as such a great sinner that he prayed that after his death his body might be exposed on a dung heap to be devoured by birds and dogs. His doctors warned him that if he continued to weep so bitterly during Mass, he might lose his sight. Teresa of Avila, who reformed the monastic life of women in the order of discalced Carmelites, had a terrifying vision of the place reserved for her in Hell. The great saints of the period seemed to regard the world and God as irreconcilable opposites: to be saved one had to renounce the world and all natural affections. Vincent de Paul, who lived a life of charity and good works, prayed that God would take away his love for his parents; Jane Francis de Chantal, who founded the Order of the Visitation, stepped over the prone body of her son when she went to join her convent: he had flung himself over the threshold to prevent her departure. Where the Renaissance had tried to reconcile heaven and earth, the Catholic Reformation tried to split them asunder. God may have made the reformed Christians of the West efficient and powerful, but he did not make them happy. The Reformation period was a time of great fear on both sides: there were violent repudiations of the past, bitter condemnations and anathemas, a terror of heresy and doctrinal deviation, a hyperactive awareness of sin and an obsession with Hell. In 1640 the controversial book of the Dutch Catholic Cornelis Jansen was published, which, like the new Calvinism, preached a frightening God who had predestined all men except the elect to eternal damnation. Naturally Calvinists praised the book, finding that it "taught the doctrine of the irresistible power of the grace of God that is correct and in accordance with Reformed doctrine."[42]

How can we account for this widespread fear and dismay in Europe? It was a period of extreme anxiety: a new kind of society, based on science and technology, was beginning to emerge that would shortly conquer the world. Yet God seemed unable to alleviate these fears and provide the consolation that the Sephardic Jews, for example, had found in the myths of Isaac Luria. The Christians of the West had always seemed to find that God was something of a strain and the Reformers, who had sought to allay these religious anxieties, seem ultimately to have made matters worse. The God of the West, who was believed to predestine millions of human beings to everlasting damnation, had become even more frightening than the harsh deity envisaged by Tertullian or Augustine in his darker moments. Could it be that a deliberately imaginative conception of God, based on mythology and mysticism, is more effective as a means of giving his people courage to survive tragedy and distress than a God whose myths are interpreted literally?

Indeed, by the end of the sixteenth century, many people in Europe felt that religion had been gravely discredited. They were disgusted by the killing of Catholics by Protestants and Protestants by Catholics. Hundreds of people had died as martyrs for holding views that it was impossible to prove one way or the other. Sects preaching a bewildering variety of doctrines that were deemed essential for salvation had proliferated alarmingly. There was now too much theological choice: many felt paralyzed and distressed by the variety of religious interpretations on offer. Some may have felt that faith was becoming harder to achieve than ever. It was, therefore, significant that at this point in the history of the Western God, people started spotting "atheists," who seemed to be as numerous as the "witches," the old enemies of God and allies of the devil. It was said that these "atheists" had denied the existence of God, were acquiring converts to their sect and undermining the fabric of society. Yet in fact a full-blown atheism in the sense that we use the word today was impossible. As Lucien Febvre has shown in his classic book *The Problem of Unbelief in the Sixteenth Century*, the conceptual difficulties in the way of a complete denial of God's existence at this time were so great as to be insurmountable. From birth and baptism to death and burial in the churchyard, religion dominated the life of every single man and woman. Every activity of the day, which was punctuated with church bells summoning the faithful to prayer, was saturated with religious beliefs and institutions: they dominated professional and public life—even the guilds and the universities were religious organizations. As Febvre points out, God and religion were so ubiquitous that nobody at this stage thought to say: "So our life, the whole of our life, is dominated by Christianity! How tiny is the area of our lives that is already secularized, compared to everything that is still governed, regulated and shaped by religion!"[43] Even if an exceptional man could have achieved the objectivity necessary to question the nature of religion and the existence of God, he would have found no support in either the philosophy or the science of his time. Until there had formed a body of coherent reasons, each of which was based on another cluster of scientific verifications, nobody could deny the existence of a God whose religion shaped and dominated the moral, emotional, aesthetic and political life of Europe. Without this support, such a denial could only be a personal whim or a passing impulse that was unworthy of serious consideration. As Febvre has shown, a vernacular language such as French lacked either the vocabulary or the syntax for skepticism. Such words as "absolute," "relative," "causality," "concept" and "intuition" were not yet in use.[44] We should also remember that as yet no society in the world had eliminated religion, which was taken for granted as a fact of life. Not until the very end of the eighteenth century would a few Europeans find it possible to deny the existence of God.

What, then, did people mean when they accused one another of "atheism"? The French scientist Marin Mersenne (1588–1648), who was also a member of a strict Franciscan order, declared that there were about 50,000 atheists in Paris alone, but most of the "atheists" he named believed in God. Thus Pierre Carrin, the friend of Michel Montaigne, had defended Catholicism in his treatise *Les Trois Vérités* (1589), but in his chief work, *De La Sagesse*, he had stressed the frailty of reason and claimed that man could only reach God through faith. Mersenne disapproved of this and saw it as tantamount to "atheism." Another of the "unbelievers" he denounced was the Italian rationalist Giordano Bruno (1548–1600), even though Bruno believed in a sort of Stoic God who was the soul, origin and end of the universe. Mersenne called both these men "atheists" because he disagreed with them about God, not because they denied the existence of a Supreme Being. In rather the same way, pagans of the Roman empire had called Jews and Christians "atheists" because their opinion of the divine had differed from their own. During the sixteenth and seventeenth centuries, the word "atheist" was still reserved exclusively for polemic. Indeed, it was possible to call any of your enemies an "atheist" in much the same way as people were dubbed "anarchists" or "communists" in the late nineteenth and early twentieth centuries.

After the Reformation, people had become anxious about Christianity in a new way. Like "the witch" (or, indeed, "the anarchist" or "the communist"), "the atheist" was the projection of a buried anxiety. It reflected a hidden worry about the faith and could be used as a shock tactic to frighten the godly and encourage them in virtue. In the *Laws of Ecclesiastical Polity*, the Anglican theologian Richard Hooker (1554–1600) claimed that there were two kinds of atheists: a tiny group who did not believe in God and a much larger number who lived as though God did not exist. People tended to lose sight of this distinction and concentrated on the latter, practical type of atheism. Thus in *The Theatre of God's Judgements* (1597), Thomas Beard's imaginary "atheist" denied the providence of God, the immortality of the soul and the afterlife but not, apparently, the existence of God. In his tract *Atheism Closed and Open Anatomized* (1634), John Wingfield claimed: "the hypocrite is an Atheist; the loose wicked man is an open Atheist; the secure, bold and proud transgressor is an Atheist: he that will not be taught or reformed is an Atheist."[45] For the Welsh poet William Vaughan (1577–1641), who helped in the colonization of Newfoundland, those who raised rents or enclosed commons were obvious atheists. The English dramatist Thomas Nashe (1567–1601) proclaimed that the ambitious, the greedy, the gluttons, the vainglorious and prostitutes were all atheists.

The term "atheist" was an insult. Nobody would have dreamed of calling *himself* an atheist. It was not yet a badge to be worn with pride. Yet during the seventeenth and eighteenth centuries, people in the West would cultivate an attitude that would make the denial of God's existence not only possible but desirable. They would find support for their views in science. Yet the God of the Reformers could be seen to favor the new science. Because they believed in the absolute sovereignty of God, Luther and Calvin had both rejected Aristotle's view of nature as having intrinsic powers of its own. They believed that nature was as passive as the Christian, who could only accept the gift of salvation from God and could do nothing for himself. Calvin had explicitly commended the scientific study of the natural world in which the invisible God had made himself known. There could be no conflict between science and scripture: God had adapted himself to our human limitations in the Bible, just as a skillful speaker adjusts his thought and speech to the capacity of his audience.

The account of Creation, Calvin believed, was an example of *balbutive* (baby talk), which accommodated complex and mysterious processes to the mentality of simple people so that everybody could have faith in God.[46] It was not to be taken literally.

The Roman Catholic Church had not always been as open-minded, however. In 1530 the Polish astronomer Nicolaus Copernicus had completed his treatise *De revolutionibus*, which claimed that the sun was the center of the universe. It was published shortly before his death in 1543 and placed by the Church on the Index of Proscribed Books. In 1613 the Pisan mathematician Galileo Galilei claimed that the telescope he had invented proved that Copernicus's system was correct. His case became a *cause célèbre*: summoned before the Inquisition, Galileo was commanded to retract his scientific creed and sentenced to indefinite imprisonment. Not all Catholics agreed with this decision, but the Roman Catholic Church was as instinctively opposed to change as any other institution at this period when the conservative spirit prevailed. What made the Church different was that it had the power to enforce its opposition and was a smoothly running machine that had become horribly efficient in imposing intellectual conformity. Inevitably the condemnation of Galileo inhibited scientific study in Catholic countries, even though many distinguished scientists of the early period such as Marin Mersenne, René Descartes and Blaise Pascal remained loyal to their Catholic faith. The case of Galileo is complex and I do not intend to go into all its political ramifications. One fact emerges, however, that is important in our story: the Roman Catholic Church did not condemn the heliocentric theory because it endangered belief in God the Creator but because it contradicted the word of God in scripture.

This also disturbed many Protestants at the time of Galileo's trial. Neither Luther nor Calvin had condemned Copernicus, but Luther's associate Philipp Melanchthon (1497–1560) rejected the idea of the earth's motion around the sun because it was in conflict with certain passages of the Bible. This was not just a Protestant concern. After the Council of Trent, Catholics had developed a new enthusiasm for their own Scripture: the Vulgate, St. Jerome's Latin translation of the Bible. In the words of the Spanish Inquisitor Leon of Castro in 1576: "Nothing may be changed that disagrees with the Latin edition of the Vulgate, be it a single period, a single little conclusion or a single clause, a single word of expression, a single syllable or one iota."[47] In the past, as we have seen, some rationalists and mystics had gone out of their way to depart from a literal reading of the Bible and the Koran in favor of a deliberately symbolic interpretation.

Now Protestants and Catholics had both begun to put their faith in an entirely literal understanding of scripture. The scientific discoveries of Galileo and Copernicus might not have disturbed Ismailis, Sufis, Kabbalists or *hesychasts*, but they did pose problems for those Catholics and Protestants who had embraced the new literalism. How could the theory that the earth moved round the sun be reconciled with the biblical verses: "The world also is established, that it cannot be moved"; "The sun also ariseth, and the sun goeth down and hasteth to his place where he arose"; "He appointed the moon for seasons; the sun knoweth his going down"?[48] Churchmen were highly disturbed by some of Galileo's suggestions. If, as he said, there could be life on the moon, how could these men have descended from Adam and how had they got out of Noah's Ark? How could the theory of the motion of the earth be squared with Christ's ascension into heaven? Scripture said that the heavens and the earth had been created for man's benefit. How could this be so if, as Galileo claimed, the earth was just another planet revolving around the sun? Heaven and Hell were regarded as real places, which it was difficult to locate in the Copernican system. Hell, for example, was widely believed to be situated at the center of the earth, where Dante had put it. Cardinal Robert Bellarmine, the Jesuit scholar who was consulted on the Galileo question by the newly established Congregation for the Propagation of the Faith, came down on the side of tradition: "Hell is a subterranean place distinct from the tombs." He concluded that it must be at the center of the earth, basing his final argument on "natural reason":

> The last is natural reason. There is no doubt that it is indeed reasonable that the place of devils and wicked damned men should be as far as possible from the place where angels and blessed men will be forever. The abode of the blessed (as our adversaries agree) is heaven, and no place is further removed from heaven than the center of the earth.[49]

Bellarmine's arguments sound farcical today. Even the most literal Christians no longer imagine that hell is at the center of the earth. But many have been shaken by other scientific theories that find "no room for God" in a sophisticated cosmology.

At a time when Mulla Sadra was teaching Muslims that heaven and hell were located in the imaginary world within each individual, sophisticated churchmen such as Bellarmine were strenuously arguing that they had a literal geographic location. When Kabbalists were reinterpreting the biblical account of creation in a deliberately symbolic manner and warning their disciples not to take this mythology literally, Catholics and Protestants were insisting that the Bible was factually true in every detail. This would make the traditional religious mythology vulnerable to the new science and would eventually make it impossible for many people to believe in God at all. The theologians were not preparing their people well for this approaching challenge. Since the Reformation and the new enthusiasm for Aristotelianism among Protestants and Catholics, they were beginning to discuss God as though he were any other objective fact. This would ultimately enable the new "atheists" of the late eighteenth and early nineteenth centuries to get rid of God altogether.

Thus Leonard Lessius (1554–1623), the highly influential Jesuit theologian of Louvain, seems to give his allegiance to the God of the philosophers in his treatise *The Divine Providence*. The existence of this God can be demonstrated scientifically like any of the other facts of life. The design of the universe, which could not have happened by chance, points to the existence of a Prime Mover and Sustainer. There is nothing specifically Christian about Lessius's God, however: he is a scientific fact who can be discovered by any rational human being. Lessius scarcely mentions Jesus. He gives the impression that the existence of God could be deduced from ordinary observation, philosophy, the study of comparative religion and common sense. God had become just another being, like the host of other objects that scientists and philosophers were beginning to explore in the West. The Faylasufs had not doubted the validity of their proofs for the existence of God, but their coreligionists had finally decided that this God of the philosophers had little religious value. Thomas Aquinas may have given the impression that God was just another item—albeit the highest—in the chain of being, but he had personally been convinced that these philosophical arguments bore no relation to the mystical God he had experienced in prayer. But by the beginning of the seventeenth century, leading theologians and churchmen continued to argue the existence of God on entirely rational grounds. Many have continued to do so to the present day. When the arguments were disproved by the new science, the existence of God himself came under attack. Instead of seeing the idea of God as a symbol of a reality which had no existence in the usual sense of the word and which could only be discovered by the imaginative disciplines of prayer and contemplation, it was increasingly assumed that God was simply a fact of life like any other. In a theologian such as Lessius we can see that as Europe approached modernity, the theologians themselves were handing the future atheists the ammunition for their rejection of a God who had little religious value and who filled many people with fear rather than with hope and faith. Like the philosophers and scientists, post-Reformation Christians had effectively abandoned the imaginative God of the mystics and sought enlightenment from the God of reason.

9

Enlightenment

B Y THE END of the sixteenth century, the West had embarked on a process of technicalization that would produce an entirely different kind of society and a new ideal of humanity. Inevitably this would affect the Western perception of the role and nature of God. The achievements of the newly industrialized and efficient West also changed the course of world history. The other countries of the Oikumene found it increasingly difficult to ignore the Western world, as in the past when it had lagged behind the other major civilizations, or to come to terms with it. Because no other society had ever achieved anything similar, the West created problems that were entirely new and therefore very difficult to deal with. Until the eighteenth century, for example, Islam had been the dominant world power in Africa, the Middle East and the Mediterranean area. Even though its fifteenth-century Renaissance had put Western Christendom ahead of Islamdom in some respects, the various Muslim powers were easily able to contain the challenge. The Ottomans had continued to advance into Europe, and Muslims had been able to hold their own against the Portuguese explorers and the merchants who followed in their wake. By the end of the eighteenth century, however, Europe had begun to dominate the world, and the very nature of its achievement meant that it was impossible for the rest of the world to catch up. The British had also gained control of India, and Europe was poised to colonize as much of the world as it could. The process of Westernization had begun and with it the cult of secularism that claimed independence of God.

What did the modern technical society involve? All previous civilizations had depended upon agriculture. As its name implied, civilization had been the achievement of the cities, where an elite had lived upon the agricultural surplus produced by the peasantry and had the leisure and resources to create the various cultures. Belief in the One God had developed in the cities of the Middle East and in Europe at the same time as other major religious ideologies. All such agrarianate civilizations were vulnerable, however. They depended upon variables, such as crops, harvests, climate and soil erosion. As each empire spread and increased its commitments and responsibilities, it ultimately outran its limited resources. After it had reached the zenith of its power, it began its inevitable decline and fall. The new West, however, was not dependent upon agriculture. Its technical mastery meant that it had become independent of local conditions and external, temporal reversals. The accumulation of capital had been built into the economic resources that—until recently—seemed to be indefinitely renewable. The process of modernization involved the West in a series of profound changes: it led to industrialization and a consequent transformation of agriculture, an intellectual "enlightenment" and political and social revolutions. Naturally these immense changes affected the way men and women perceived themselves and made them revise their relationship with the ultimate reality that they traditionally called "God."

Specialization was crucial to this Western technical society: all the innovations in the economic, intellectual and social fields demanded a particular expertise in many different fields. Scientists, for example, depended upon the increased efficiency of instrument-makers; industry demanded new machines and sources of energy, as well as theoretical input from science. The various specializations intermeshed and became gradually interdependent: one inspired another in a different and perhaps hitherto unrelated field. It was an accumulative process. The achievements of one specialization were increased by their usage in another, and this in turn affected its own efficiency. Capital was systematically reinvested and multiplied on the basis of continued development. The interlocking changes acquired a progressive and apparently unstoppable momentum. More and more people of all ranks were drawn into the process of modernization in an increasing number of spheres. Civilization and cultural achievement were no longer the preserve of a tiny elite but depended upon factory workers, coal miners, printers and clerks, not only as laborers but also as buyers in the ever-expanding market. Ultimately it would become necessary for these lower orders to become literate and to share—to some degree—in the wealth of society if the overriding need for efficiency was to be preserved. The great increase in productivity, the accumulation of capital and the expansion of mass markets, as well as the new intellectual advances in science, led to social revolution: the power of the landed gentry declined and was replaced by the financial muscle of the bourgeoisie. The new efficiency was also felt in matters of social organization, which gradually brought the West up to the standards already achieved in other parts of the world, such as China and the Ottoman empire, and then enabled it to surpass them. By 1789, the year of the French Revolution, public service was judged by its effectiveness and utility. The various governments in Europe found it necessary to reconstitute themselves and engage in a continuous revision of their laws in order to meet the ever-changing conditions of modernity.

This would have been unthinkable under the old agrarianate dispensation, when law was regarded as immutable and divine. It was a sign of the new autonomy that technicalization was bringing to Western society: men and women felt that they were in charge of their own affairs as never before. We have seen the profound fear that innovation and change had unleashed in traditional societies, where civilization was felt to be a fragile achievement and any break in continuity with the past was resisted. The modern technical society introduced by the West, however, was based upon the expectation of constant development and progress. Change was institutionalized and taken for granted. Indeed, such institutions as the Royal Society in London were dedicated to the collection of new knowledge to replace the old. Specialists in the various sciences were encouraged to pool their findings to aid this process. Instead of keeping their discoveries secret, the new scientific institutions wanted to disseminate knowledge in order to advance future growth in their own and other fields. The old conservative spirit of the Oikumene, therefore, had been replaced in the West by a desire for change and a belief that continual development was practicable. Instead of fearing that the younger generation was going to the dogs, as in former times, the older generation expected their children to live better than they. The study of history was dominated by a new myth: that of Progress. It achieved great things, but now that damage to the environment has made us realize that this way of life is as vulnerable as the old, we are, perhaps, beginning to grasp that it is as fictitious as most of the other mythologies that have inspired humanity over the centuries.

While the pooling of resources and discoveries drew people together, the new specialization inevitably pulled them apart in other ways. Hitherto it had been possible for an intellectual to keep abreast of knowledge on all fronts. The Muslim Faylasufs, for example, had been proficient in medicine, philosophy and aesthetics. Indeed, Falsafah had offered its disciples a coherent and inclusive account of what was believed to be the whole of reality. By the seventeenth century, the process of specialization that would become so marked a feature of Western society was beginning to make itself felt. The various disciplines of astronomy, chemistry and geometry were beginning to become independent and autonomous. Ultimately in our own day it would be impossible for an expert in one field to feel any competence whatever in another. It followed that every major intellectual saw himself less as a conserver of tradition than as a pioneer. He was an explorer, like the navigators who had penetrated to new parts of the globe. He was venturing into hitherto uncharted realms for the sake of his society. The innovator who made such an effort of imagination to break new ground and, in the process, overthrow old sanctities, became a cultural hero. There was new optimism about humanity as control over the natural world, which had once held mankind in thrall, appeared to advance in leaps and bounds. People began to believe that better education and improved laws could bring light to the human spirit. This new confidence in the natural powers of human beings meant that people came to believe that they could achieve enlightenment by means of their own exertions. They no longer felt that they needed to rely on inherited tradition, an institution or an elite—or, even, a revelation from God—to discover the truth.

Yet the experience of specialization meant that people involved in the process of specialization were increasingly unable to see the whole picture. Consequently innovative scientists and intellectuals felt obliged to work out their own theories of life and religion, starting from scratch. They felt that their own enhanced knowledge and effectiveness gave them the duty to look again at the traditional Christian explanations of reality and bring them up to date. The new scientific spirit was empirical, based solely on observation and experiment. We have seen that the old rationalism of Falsafah had depended upon an initial act of faith in a rational universe. The Western sciences could take nothing for granted in this way, and the pioneers were increasingly ready to risk a mistake or knock down established authorities and institutions such as the Bible, the Church and the Christian tradition. The old "proofs" for God's existence were no longer entirely satisfactory, and natural scientists and philosophers, full of enthusiasm for the empirical method, felt compelled to verify the objective reality of God in the same way as they proved other demonstrable phenomena.

Atheism was still felt to be abhorrent. As we shall see, most of the *philosophes* of the Enlightenment believed implicitly in the existence of a God. Yet a few people *were* beginning to see that not even God could be taken for granted. Perhaps one of the first people to appreciate this and to take atheism seriously was the French physicist, mathematician and theologian Blaise Pascal (1623–62). A sickly, precocious child, he had been closeted from other children and educated by his scientist father, who discovered that the eleven-year-old Blaise had secretly worked out for himself the first twenty-three propositions of Euclid. At sixteen, he had published a paper on geometry which scientists like René Descartes refused to believe could have been written by one so young. Later he devised a calculating machine, a barometer and a hydraulic press. The Pascals were not a particularly devout family, but in 1646 they had been converted to Jansenism. Blaise's sister, Jacqueline, entered the Jansenist convent of Port-Royal in southwest Paris and became one of the Catholic sect's most passionate advocates. On the night of November 23, 1654, Blaise himself had a religious experience which lasted "from about half-past ten in the evening till about half an hour after midnight" and which showed him that his faith had been too remote and academic. After his death, his "Memorial" of this revelation was found stitched into his doublet:

Fire

"God of Abraham, God of Isaac, God of Jacob," not of philosophers and scholars.
    Certainty, certainty, heartfelt, joy, peace.
    God of Jesus Christ.
    God of Jesus Christ.
    My God and your God.
"Thy God shall be my God."
    The World forgotten and everything except God.
    He can only be found by the ways taught in the Gospels.[1]

This essentially mystical experience meant that the God of Pascal was different from the God of the other scientists and philosophers we shall consider in this chapter. This was not the God of the philosophers but the God of revelation, and the overwhelming power of his conversion led Pascal to throw in his lot with the Jansenists against the Jesuits, their chief enemies.

Where Ignatius had seen the world as full of God and had encouraged

Jesuits to cultivate a sense of the divine omnipresence and omnipotence, Pascal and the Jansenists found the world to be bleak and empty, bereft of divinity. Despite his revelation, Pascal's God remains "a hidden God" who cannot be discovered by means of rational proof. The *Pensées*, Pascal's jottings on religious matters, which were published posthumously in 1669, are rooted in a profound pessimism about the human condition. Human "vileness" is a constant theme; it cannot even be alleviated by Christ, "who will be in agony until the end of the world."[2] The sense of desolation and of God's terrifying absence characterizes much of the spirituality of the new Europe. The continuing popularity of the *Pensées* shows that Pascal's darker spirituality and his hidden God appealed to something vital in the Western religious consciousness.

Pascal's scientific achievements, therefore, did not give him much confidence in the human condition. When he contemplated the immensity of the universe, he was scared stiff:

> When I see the blind and wretched state of man, when I survey the whole universe in its dumbness and man left to himself with no light, as though lost in this corner of the universe, without knowing who put him there, what he has come to do, what will become of him when he dies, incapable of knowing anything, I am moved to terror, like a man transported in his sleep to some terrifying desert island, who wakes up quite lost with no means of escape. Then I marvel that so wretched a state does not drive people to despair.[3]

This is a salutary reminder that we should not generalize about the buoyant optimism of the scientific age. Pascal could envisage the full horror of a world that seemed empty of ultimate meaning or significance. The terror of waking up in an alien world, which had always haunted humanity, has rarely been more eloquently expressed. Pascal was brutally honest with himself; unlike most of his contemporaries, he was convinced that there was no way of proving the existence of God. When he imagined himself arguing with somebody who was constitutionally unable to believe, Pascal could find no arguments to convince him. This was a new development in the history of monotheism. Hitherto nobody had seriously questioned the existence of God. Pascal was the first person to concede that, in this brave new world, belief in God could only be a matter of personal choice. In this, he was the first modern.

Pascal's approach to the problem of God's existence is revolutionary in its implications, but it has never been accepted officially by any church.

In general, Christian apologists have preferred the rationalistic approach of Leonard Lessius, discussed at the end of the last chapter. Such an approach, however, could only lead to the God of the philosophers, not to the God of revelation experienced by Pascal. Faith, he insisted, was not a rational assent based on common sense. It was a gamble. It was impossible to prove that God exists but equally impossible for reason to disprove his existence: "We are incapable of knowing either what [God] is or whether he is. . . . Reason cannot decide this question. Infinite chaos separates us. At the far end of this infinite distance a coin is being spun which will come down heads or tails. How will you wager?"[4] This gamble is not entirely irrational, however. To opt for God is a win-win solution. In choosing to believe in God, Pascal continued, the risk is finite but the gain infinite. As the Christian progresses in the Faith, he or she will become aware of a continuous enlightenment, an awareness of God's presence that is a sure sign of salvation. It is no good relying on external authority; each Christian is on his own.

Pascal's pessimism is countered by a growing realization in the *Pensées* that once the wager has been made, the hidden God reveals himself to anyone who seeks him. Pascal makes God say: "You would not seek me, if you had not already found me."[5] True, humanity cannot batter its way to the distant God by arguments and logic or by accepting the teaching of an institutional church. But by making the personal decision to surrender to God, the faithful feel themselves transformed, becoming "faithful, honest, humble, grateful, full of good works, a true friend."[6] Somehow the Christian will find that life has acquired meaning and significance, having created faith and constructed a sense of God in the face of meaninglessness and despair. God is a reality because he works. Faith is not intellectual certainty but a leap into the dark and an experience that brings a moral enlightenment.

René Descartes (1596–1650), another of the new men, had far more confidence in the ability of the mind to discover God. Indeed, he insisted that the intellect alone could provide us with the certainty we seek. He would not have approved of Pascal's wager, since it was based on a purely subjective experience, though his own demonstration of the existence of God depended upon another type of subjectivity. He was anxious to refute the skepticism of the French essayist Michel Montaigne (1533–92), who had denied that anything was certain or even probable. Descartes, a mathematician and a convinced Catholic, felt that he had a mission to bring the new empirical rationalism to the fight against such skepticism. Like Lessius, Descartes thought that reason alone could persuade human-

ity to accept the truths of religion and morality, which he saw as the
foundation of civilization. Faith told us nothing that could not be demonstrated rationally: St. Paul himself had asserted as much in the first
chapter of his epistle to the Romans: "For what can be known about God
is perfectly plain to [mankind] since God himself has made it plain. Ever
since God created the world his everlasting power and deity—however
invisible—have been there for the mind to see in the things that he has
made."[7] Descartes went on to argue that God could be known more easily
and certainly (*facilius et certius*) than any of the other things in existence.
This was as revolutionary in its own way as Pascal's wager, especially
since Descartes's proof rejected the witness of the external world that
Paul had put forward in favor of the reflexive introspection of the mind
turning in upon itself.

Using the empirical method of his universal Mathematics, which had
progressed logically toward the simples or first principles, Descartes attempted to establish an equally analytic demonstration of God's existence.
But unlike Aristotle, St. Paul and all previous monotheistic philosophers,
he found the cosmos completely Godless. There was no design in nature.
In fact the universe was chaotic and revealed no sign of intelligent planning. It was impossible for us to deduce any certainty about first principles
from nature, therefore. Descartes had no time for the probable or the
possible: he sought to establish the kind of certainty that mathematics
could provide. It could also be found in simple and self-evident propositions, such as: "What's done cannot be undone," which was irrefutably
true. Accordingly, while he was sitting meditating beside a wood stove,
he hit upon the famous maxim: *Cogito, ergo sum*; I think, therefore I am.
Like Augustine, some twelve centuries earlier, Descartes found evidence
of God in human consciousness: even doubt proved the existence of the
doubter! We cannot be certain of anything in the external world, but we
can be certain of our own inner experience. Descartes's argument turns
out to be a reworking of Anselm's Ontological Proof. When we doubt,
the limitations and finite nature of the ego are revealed. Yet we could not
arrive at the idea of "imperfection" if we did not have a prior conception
of "perfection." Like Anselm, Descartes concluded that a perfection that
did not exist would be a contradiction in terms. Our experience of doubt,
therefore, tells us that a supreme and perfect being—God—must exist.

Descartes went on to deduce facts about the nature of God from this
"proof" of his existence, in much the same way as he had conducted
mathematical demonstrations. As he said in his *Discourse on Method*, "it is
at least as certain that God, who is this perfect being, is or exists, as any

demonstration of geometry can possibly be."[8] Just as a Euclidian triangle must have angles that add up to two right angles, Descartes's perfect being had to have certain attributes. Our experience tells us that the world has objective reality and a perfect God, who must be truthful, could not deceive us. Instead of using the world to prove the existence of God, therefore, Descartes had used the idea of God to give him faith in the reality of the world. In his own way, Descartes felt as alienated from the world as Pascal. Instead of reaching out toward the world, his mind recoils upon itself. Even though the idea of God gives man certainty about his own existence and is, therefore, essential to Descartes's epistemology, the Cartesian method reveals an isolation and an image of autonomy that would become central to the Western image of man in our own century. Alienation from the world and a proud self-reliance would lead many people to reject the whole idea of a God who reduces a man or woman to the condition of a dependent.

From the very beginning, religion had helped people to relate to the world and to root themselves in it. The cult of the holy place had preceded all other reflection upon the world and helped men and women to find a focus in a terrifying universe. The deification of the natural forces had expressed the wonder and awe which had always been part of the human response to the world. Even Augustine had found the world a place of wondrous beauty, despite his anguished spirituality. Descartes, whose philosophy was based on the Augustinian tradition of introspection, had no time at all for wonder. A sense of mystery was to be avoided at all costs because it represented a primitive state of mind that civilized man had outgrown. In the introduction to his treatise *Les météores*, he explained that it was natural for us to "have more admiration for the things above us than for those on our level or below."[9] Poets and painters had, therefore, depicted the clouds as God's throne, had imagined God sprinkling dew upon the clouds or hurling lightning against the rocks with his own hand:

> This leads me to hope that if I here explain the nature of the clouds,
> in such a way that we will no longer have occasion to wonder at
> anything that can be seen of them, or anything that descends from
> them, we will easily believe that it is similarly possible to find the
> causes of everything that is most admirable above the earth.

Descartes would explain clouds, winds, dew and lightning as mere physical events in order, as he explained, to remove "any cause to marvel."[10] The God of Descartes, however, was the God of the philosophers who took no cognizance of earthly events. He was revealed not in the miracles described in scripture but in the eternal laws that he had ordained: *Les météores* also explained that the manna that had fed the ancient Israelites in the desert was a kind of dew. Thus had been born the absurd type of apologetics that attempt to "prove" the veracity of the Bible by finding a rational explanation for the various miracles and myths. Jesus' feeding of the five thousand, for example, has been interpreted as his shaming people in the crowd to produce the picnics that they had surreptitiously brought with them and hand them around. Well-intentioned as it is, this kind of argument misses the point of the symbolism that is of the essence of biblical narrative.

Descartes was always careful to submit to the rulings of the Roman Catholic Church and saw himself as an orthodox Christian. He saw no contradiction between faith and reason. In his treatise *Discourse on Method*, he argued that there was a system that would enable humanity to reach *all* truth. Nothing lay beyond its grasp. All that was necessary—in any discipline—was to apply the method and it would then be possible to piece together a reliable body of knowledge that would disperse all confusion and ignorance. Mystery had become muddle, and the God whom previous rationalists had been careful to separate from all other phenomena had now been contained within a human system of thought. Mysticism had not really had time to take root in Europe before the dogmatic convulsions of the Reformation. Thus the type of spirituality that thrives upon mystery and mythology and is, as its name implies, deeply connected with them was strange to many Christians in the West. Even in Descartes's church, mystics were rare and often suspect. The God of the mystics, whose existence depended upon religious experience, was quite alien to a man like Descartes, for whom contemplation meant purely cerebral activity.

The English physicist Isaac Newton (1642–1727), who also reduced God to his own mechanical system, was equally anxious to rid Christianity of mystery. His starting point was mechanics, not mathematics, because a scientist had to learn to draw a circle accurately before he could master geometry. Unlike Descartes, who had proved the existence of the self, God and the natural world in that order, Newton began with an attempt to explain the physical universe, with God as an essential part of the system. In Newton's physics, nature was entirely passive: God was the sole source of activity. Thus, as in Aristotle, God was simply a continuation of the natural, physical order. In his great work *Philosophiae*

Naturalis Principia (The Principles of Natural Philosophy, 1687), Newton wanted to describe the relations between the various celestial and terrestrial bodies in mathematical terms in such a way as to create a coherent and comprehensive system. The notion of gravitational force, which Newton introduced, drew the component parts of his system together. The notion of gravity offended some scientists, who accused Newton of reverting to Aristotle's idea of the attractive powers of matter. Such a view was incompatible with the Protestant idea of the absolute sovereignty of God. Newton denied this: a sovereign God was central to his whole system, for without such a divine Mechanick it would not exist.

Unlike Pascal and Descartes, when Newton contemplated the universe he was convinced that he had proof of God's existence. Why had the internal gravity of the celestial bodies not pulled them all together into one huge spherical mass? Because they had been carefully disposed throughout infinite space with sufficient distance between them to prevent this. As he explained to his friend Richard Bentley, Dean of St. Paul's, this would have been impossible without an intelligent divine Overseer: "I do not think it explicable by mere natural causes but am forced to ascribe it to ye counsel and contrivance of a voluntary agent."[11] A month later he wrote to Bentley again: "Gravity may put ye planets into motion but without ye divine power it could never put them into such a Circulating motion as they have about ye Sun, and therefore, for this as well as other reasons, I am compelled to ascribe ye frame of this Systeme to an intelligent Agent."[12] If, for example, the earth revolved on its axis at only one hundred miles per hour instead of one thousand miles per hour, night would be ten times longer and the world would be too cold to sustain life; during the long day, the heat would shrivel all the vegetation. The Being which had contrived all this so perfectly had to be a supremely intelligent Mechanick.

Besides being intelligent, this Agent had to be powerful enough to manage these great masses. Newton concluded that the primal force which had set the infinite and intricate system in motion was *dominatio* (dominion), which alone accounted for the universe and made God divine. Edward Pococke, the first professor of Arabic at Oxford, had told Newton that the Latin *deus* derived from the Arabic *du* (Lord). Dominion, therefore, was God's essential attribute rather than the perfection which had been the starting point for Descartes's discussion of God. In the "General Scholium" which concludes the *Principia*, Newton deduced all God's traditional attributes from his intelligence and power:

This most beautiful system of the sun, planets and comets could only proceed from the counsel and dominion of an intelligent and powerful Being. . . . He is eternal and infinite, omnipotent and omniscient; that is, his duration reaches from eternity to eternity; his presence from infinity to infinity; he governs all things, and knows all things that are or can be done. . . . We know him only by his most wise and excellent contrivances of things, and final causes; we admire him for his perfection; but we reverence and adore him on account of his dominion: for we adore him as his servants; and a god without dominion, providence, and final causes, is nothing else but Fate and Nature. Blind metaphysical necessity, which is certainly the same always and everywhere, could produce no variety of things. All that diversity of natural things which we find suited to different times and places could arise from nothing but the ideas and will of a Being necessarily existing.[13]

Newton does not mention the Bible: we know God *only* by contemplating the world. Hitherto the doctrine of the creation had expressed a spiritual truth: it had entered both Judaism and Christianity late and had always been somewhat problematic. Now the new science had moved the creation to center stage and made a literal and mechanical understanding of the doctrine crucial to the conception of God. When people deny the existence of God today they are often rejecting the God of Newton, the origin and sustainer of the universe whom scientists can no longer accommodate.

Newton himself had to resort to some startling solutions to find room for God in his system, which had of its very nature to be comprehensive. If space was unchangeable and infinite—two cardinal features of the system—where did God fit in? Was not space itself somehow divine, possessing as it did the attributes of eternity and infinity? Was it a second divine entity, which had existed beside God from before the beginning of time? Newton had always been concerned about this problem. In the early essay *De Gravitatione et Aequipondio Fluidorum*, he had returned to the old Platonic doctrine of emanation. Since God is infinite, he must exist everywhere. Space is an effect of God's existence, emanating eternally from the divine omnipresence. It was not created by him in an act of will but existed as a necessary consequence or extension of his ubiquitous being. In the same way, because God himself is eternal, he emanates time. We can, therefore, say that God constitutes that space and time in which we live and move and have our being. Matter, on the other hand, *was* created by God on the day of creation by a voluntary act. One could perhaps say that he had decided to endow some parts of space with shape, density, perceptibility and mobility. It was possible to stand by the Christian doctrine of creation out of nothing because God had brought forth material substance from empty space: he had produced matter out of the void.

Like Descartes, Newton had no time for mystery, which he equated with ignorance and superstition. He was anxious to purge Christianity of the miraculous, even if that brought him into conflict with such crucial doctrines as the divinity of Christ. During the 1670s he began a serious theological study of the doctrine of the Trinity and came to the conclusion that it had been foisted on the Church by Athanasius in a specious bid for pagan converts. Arius had been right: Jesus Christ had certainly not been God, and those passages of the New Testament that were used to "prove" the doctrines of the Trinity and the Incarnation were spurious. Athanasius and his colleagues had forged them and added them to the canon of scripture, thus appealing to the base, primitive fantasies of the masses: "Tis the temper of the hot and superstitious part of mankind in matters of religion ever to be fond of mysteries, & for that reason to like best what they understand least."[14] To expunge this mumbo jumbo from the Christian faith became something of an obsession for Newton. In the early 1680s, shortly before publishing the *Principia*, Newton began work on a treatise which he called *The Philosophical Origins of Gentile Theology*. This argued that Noah had founded the primordial religion—a Gentile theology—which had been free of superstition and had advocated a rational worship of one God. The only commandments were love of God and love of neighbor. Men were commanded to contemplate Nature, the only temple of the great God. Later generations had corrupted this pure religion, with tales of miracles and marvels. Some had fallen back into idolatry and superstition. Yet God had sent a succession of prophets to put them back on course. Pythagoras had learned about this religion and brought it to the West. Jesus had been one of these prophets sent to call mankind back to the truth, but his pure religion had been corrupted by Athanasius and his cohorts. The Book of Revelation had prophesied the rise of Trinitarianism—"this strange religion of ye West," "the cult of three equal Gods"—as the abomination of desolation.[15]

Western Christians had always found the Trinity a difficult doctrine, and their new rationalism would make the philosophers and scientists of the Enlightenment anxious to discard it. Newton had clearly no understanding of the role of mystery in the religious life. The Greeks had used

the Trinity as a means of holding the mind in a state of wonder and as a
reminder that human intellect could never understand the nature of God.
For a scientist like Newton, however, it was very difficult to cultivate
such an attitude. In science people were learning that they had to be
ready to scrap the past and start again from first principles in order to
find the truth. Religion, however, like art often consists of a dialogue
with the past in order to find a perspective from which to view the present.
Tradition provides a jumping-off point which enables men and women
to engage with the perennial questions about the ultimate meaning of life.
Religion and art, therefore, do not work like science. During the eighteenth century, however, Christians began to apply the new scientific
methods to the Christian faith and came up with the same solutions as
Newton. In England, radical theologians like Matthew Tindal and John
Toland were anxious to go back to basics, purge Christianity of its mysteries and establish a true rational religion. In *Christianity Not Mysterious*
(1696), Toland argued that mystery simply led to "tyranny and superstition."[16] It was offensive to imagine that God was incapable of expressing
himself clearly. Religion had to be reasonable. In *Christianity as Old as
Creation* (1730), Tindal tried, like Newton, to recreate the primordial
religion and purge it of later accretions. Rationality was the touchstone
of all true religion: "There's a religion of nature and reason written in the
hearts of every one of us from the first creation, by which all mankind
must judge of the truth of any institutional religion whatever."[17] Consequently revelation was unnecessary because the truth could be found by
our own rational inquiries; mysteries like the Trinity and the Incarnation
had a perfectly reasonable explanation and should not be used to keep the
simple faithful in thrall to superstition and an institutional church.

As these radical ideas spread to the Continent, a new breed of historians
began to examine church history objectively. Thus in 1699 Gottfried
Arnold published his nonpartisan *History of the Churches from the Beginning
of the New Testament to 1688*, arguing that what was currently regarded as
orthodox could not be traced back to the primitive church. Johann Lorenz
von Mosheim (1694–1755) deliberately separated history from theology
in his magisterial *Institutions of Ecclesiastical History* (1726) and recorded
the development of doctrine without arguing for its veracity. Other historians like Georg Walch, Giovanni But and Henry Noris examined the
history of difficult doctrinal controversies, such as Arianism, the *filioque*
dispute, and the various Christological debates of the fourth and fifth
centuries. It was disturbing for many of the faithful to see that fundamen-

tal dogmas about the nature of God and Christ had developed over the centuries and were not present in the New Testament: did that mean that they were false? Others went even further and applied this new objectivity to the New Testament itself. Hermann Samuel Reimarus (1694–1768) actually attempted a critical biography of Jesus himself: the question of the humanity of Christ was no longer a mystical or doctrinal matter but was being subjected to the scientific scrutiny of the Age of Reason. Once this had happened, the modern period of skepticism was well and truly launched. Reimarus argued that Jesus had simply wanted to found a godly state and when his messianic mission had failed he had died in despair. He pointed out that in the Gospels Jesus never claimed that he had come to atone for the sins of mankind. That idea, which had become central to Western Christendom, could only be traced to St. Paul, the true founder of Christianity. We should not revere Jesus as God, therefore, but as the teacher of a "remarkable, simple, exalted and practical religion."[18]

These objective studies depended upon a literal understanding of scripture and ignored the symbolic or metaphorical nature of the faith. One might object that this kind of criticism was as irrelevant as it might be to art or poetry. But once the scientific spirit had become normative for many people, it was difficult for them to read the Gospels in any other way. Western Christians were now committed to a literal understanding of their faith and had taken an irrevocable step back from myth: a story was either factually true or it was a delusion. Questions about the origin of religion were more important to Christians than, say, to Buddhists because their monotheistic tradition had always claimed that God was revealed in historical events. If Christians were to preserve their integrity in the scientific age, therefore, these questions had to be addressed. Some Christians who held more conventional beliefs than Tindal or Reimarus were beginning to question the traditional Western understanding of God. In his tract *Wittenburg's Innocence of a Double Murder* (1681), the Lutheran John Friedmann Mayer wrote that the traditional doctrine of the atonement, as outlined by Anselm, which depicted God demanding the death of his own Son, presented an inadequate conception of the divine. He was "the righteous God, the angered God" and "the embittered God," whose demands for strict retribution filled so many Christians with fear and taught them to recoil from their own "sinfulness."[19] More and more Christians were embarrassed by the cruelty of so much Christian history, which had conducted fearful crusades, inquisitions and persecutions in the name of this just God. Coercing people to believe in orthodox doctrines seemed particularly appalling to an age increasingly enamored of liberty and freedom of conscience. The bloodbath unleashed by the Reformation and its aftermath seemed the final straw.

Reason seemed the answer. Yet could a God drained of the mystery that had for centuries made him an effective religious value in other traditions appeal to the more imaginative and intuitive Christians? The Puritan poet John Milton (1608–74) was particularly disturbed by the Church's record of intolerance. A true man of his age, he had attempted, in his unpublished treatise *On Christian Doctrine*, to reform the Reformation and to work out a religious creed for himself that did not rely upon the beliefs and judgments of others. He was also doubtful about such traditional doctrines as the Trinity. Yet it is significant that the true hero of his masterpiece *Paradise Lost* is Satan rather than the God whose actions he intended to justify to man. Satan has many of the qualities of the new men of Europe: he defies authority, pits himself against the unknown, and in his intrepid journeys from Hell, through Chaos to the newly created earth, he becomes the first explorer. Milton's God, however, seems to bring out the inherent absurdity of Western literalism. Without the mystical understanding of the Trinity, the position of the Son is highly ambiguous in the poem. It is by no means clear whether he is a second divine being or a creature similar to, though of higher status than, the angels. At all events, he and the Father are two entirely separate beings who must engage in lengthy conversations of deep tedium to learn each other's intentions, even though the Son is the acknowledged Word and Wisdom of the Father.

It is, however, Milton's treatment of God's foreknowledge of events on earth that makes his deity incredible. Since of necessity God already knows that Adam and Eve will fall—even before Satan has reached the earth—he must engage in some pretty specious justification of his actions before the event. He would have no pleasure in enforced obedience, he explains to the Son, and he had given Adam and Eve the ability to withstand Satan. Therefore they could not, God argues defensively, justly accuse

> Thir maker, or thir making, or thir Fate;
> As if Predestination over-rul'd
> Thir will, dispos'd by absolute Decree
> Or high foreknowledge; they themselves decreed
> Thir own revolt; not I: if I foreknew,
> Foreknowledge had no influence on thir fault,

> Which had no less prov'd certain unforeknown . . .
>
> I formed them free, and free they must remain,
> Till they enthrall themselves: I else must change
> Thir nature, and revoke the high Decree
> Unchangeable, Eternal, which ordaind
> Thir freedom; they themselves ordaind thir fall.[20]

Not only is it difficult to respect this shoddy thinking, but God comes across as callous, self-righteous and entirely lacking in the compassion that his religion was supposed to inspire. Forcing God to speak and think like one of us in this way shows the inadequacies of such an anthropomorphic and personalistic conception of the divine. There are too many contradictions for such a God to be either coherent or worthy of veneration.

The literal understanding of such doctrines as the omniscience of God will not work. Not only is Milton's God cold and legalistic, he is also grossly incompetent. In the last two books of *Paradise Lost*, God sends the Archangel Michael to console Adam for his sin by showing him how his descendants will be redeemed. The whole course of salvation history is revealed to Adam in a series of tableaux, with a commentary by Michael: he sees the murder of Abel by Cain, the Flood and Noah's Ark, the Tower of Babel, the call of Abraham, the Exodus from Egypt and the giving of the Law on Sinai. The inadequacy of the Torah, which oppressed God's unfortunate chosen people for centuries, is, Michael explains, a ploy to make them yearn for a more spiritual law. As this account of the future salvation of the world progresses—through the exploits of King David, the exile to Babylon, the birth of Christ and so forth—it occurs to the reader that there must have been an easier and more direct way to redeem mankind. The fact that this tortuous plan with its constant failures and false starts is decreed *in advance* can only cast grave doubts on the intelligence of its Author. Milton's God can inspire little confidence. It must be significant that after *Paradise Lost* no other major English creative writer would attempt to describe the supernatural world. There would be no more Spensers or Miltons. Henceforth the supernatural and the spiritual would become the domain of more marginal writers, such as George MacDonald and C. S. Lewis. Yet a God who cannot appeal to the imagination is in trouble.

At the very end of *Paradise Lost*, Adam and Eve take their solitary way out of the Garden of Eden and into the world. In the West too, Christians were on the threshold of a more secular age, though they still adhered to belief in God. The new religion of reason would be known as Deism. It had no time for the imaginative disciplines of mysticism and mythology. It turned its back on the myth of revelation and on such traditional "mysteries" as the Trinity, which had for so long held people in the thrall of superstition. Instead it declared allegiance to the impersonal "Deus" which man could discover by his own efforts. François-Marie de Voltaire, the embodiment of the movement that would subsequently become known as the Enlightenment, defined this ideal religion in his *Philosophical Dictionary* (1764). It would, above all, be as simple as possible.

> Would it not be that which taught much morality and very little dogma? that which tended to make men just without making them absurd? that which did not order one to believe in things that are impossible, contradictory, injurious to divinity, and pernicious to mankind, and which dared not menace with eternal punishment anyone possessing common sense? Would it not be that which did not uphold its belief with executioners, and did not inundate the earth with blood on account of unintelligible sophism? . . . which taught only the worship of one god, justice, tolerance and humanity?[21]

The churches had only themselves to blame for this defiance, since for centuries they had burdened the faithful with a crippling number of doctrines. The reaction was inevitable and could even be positive.

The philosophers of the Enlightenment did not reject the idea of God, however. They rejected the cruel God of the orthodox who threatened mankind with eternal fire. They rejected mysterious doctrines about him that were abhorrent to reason. But their belief in a Supreme Being remained intact. Voltaire built a chapel at Ferney with the inscription "Deo Erexit Voltaire" inscribed on the lintel and went so far as to suggest that if God had not existed it would have been necessary to invent him. In the *Philosophical Dictionary*, he had argued that faith in one god was more rational and natural to humanity than belief in numerous deities. Originally people living in isolated hamlets and communities had acknowledged that a single god had control of their destinies: polytheism was a later development. Science and rational philosophy both pointed to the existence of a Supreme Being: "What conclusion can we draw from all this?" Voltaire asks at the end of his essay on "Atheism" in the *Dictionary*. He replies:

That atheism is a monstrous evil in those who govern; and also in learned men even if their lives are innocent, because from their studies they can affect those who hold office; and that, even if it is not as baleful as fanaticism, it is nearly always fatal to virtue. Above all, let me add that there are fewer atheists today than there have ever been, since philosophers have perceived that there is no vegetative being without germ, no germ without design etc.[22]

Voltaire equated atheism with the superstition and fanaticism that the philosophers were so anxious to eradicate. His problem was not God but the doctrines about him which offended against the sacred standard of reason.

The Jews of Europe had also been affected by the new ideas. Baruch Spinoza (1632–77), a Dutch Jew of Spanish descent, had become discontented with the study of Torah and had joined a philosophical circle of Gentile freethinkers. He evolved ideas which were profoundly different from conventional Judaism and which had been influenced by scientific thinkers such as Descartes and the Christian scholastics. In 1656, at the age of twenty-four, he was formally cast out of the synagogue of Amsterdam. While the edict of excommunication was read out, the lights of the synagogue were gradually extinguished until the congregation was left in total darkness, experiencing for themselves the darkness of Spinoza's soul in a God-less world:

Let him be accursed by day and accursed by night; accursed in his lying down and his rising up, in going out and in coming in. May the Lord never more pardon or acknowledge him! May the wrath and displeasure of the Lord burn against this man henceforth, load him with all the curses written in the book of the law, and raze out his name from under the sky.[23]

Henceforth Spinoza belonged to none of the religious communities of Europe. As such, he was the prototype of the autonomous, secular outlook that would become current in the West. In the early twentieth century, many people revered Spinoza as the hero of modernity, feeling an affinity with his symbolic exile, alienation and quest for secular salvation.

Spinoza has been regarded as an atheist, but he did have a belief in a God, even though this was not the God of the Bible. Like the Faylasufs, he saw revealed religion as inferior to the scientific knowledge of God acquired by the philosopher. The nature of religious faith had been misunderstood, he argued in *A Theologico-Political Treatise*. It had become "a mere compound of credulity and prejudices," a "tissue of meaningless mysteries."[24] He looked critically at biblical history. The Israelites had called any phenomenon that they could not understand "God." The prophets, for example, were said to have been inspired by God's Spirit simply because they were men of exceptional intellect and holiness. But this kind of "inspiration" was not confined to an elite but was available to everybody through natural reason: the rites and symbols of the faith could only help the masses who were incapable of scientific, rational thought.

Like Descartes, Spinoza returned to the Ontological Proof for God's existence. The very idea of "God" contains a validation of God's existence because a perfect being which did not exist would be a contradiction in terms. The existence of God was necessary because it alone provided the certainty and confidence necessary to make other deductions about reality. Our scientific understanding of the world shows us that it is governed by immutable laws. For Spinoza God is simply the principle of law, the sum of all the eternal laws in existence. God is a material being, identical with and equivalent to the order which governs the universe. Like Newton, Spinoza returned to the old philosophical idea of emanation. Because God is inherent and immanent in all things—material and spiritual—it can be defined as the law that orders their existence. To speak of God's activity in the world was simply a way of describing the mathematical and causal principles of existence. It was an absolute denial of transcendence.

It seems a bleak doctrine, but Spinoza's God inspired him with a truly mystical awe. As the aggregate of all the laws in existence, God was the highest perfection, which welded everything into unity and harmony. When human beings contemplated the workings of their minds in the way that Descartes had enjoined, they opened themselves to the eternal and infinite being of God at work within them. Like Plato, Spinoza believed that intuitive and spontaneous knowledge reveals the presence of God more than a laborious acquisition of facts. Our joy and happiness in knowledge is equivalent to the love of God, a deity which is not an eternal object of thought but the cause and principle of that thought, deeply one with every single human being. There is no need for revelation or divine law: this God is accessible to the whole of humanity, and the only Torah is the eternal law of nature. Spinoza brought the old metaphysics into line with the new science: his God was not the unknowable One of the Neoplatonists but closer to the absolute Being described by philosophers like Aquinas. But it was also close to the mystical God experienced by orthodox monotheists within themselves. Jews, Christians and philosophers tended to see Spinoza as an atheist: there was nothing personal about this God, which was inseparable from the rest of reality. Indeed, Spinoza had only used the word "God" for historical reasons: he agreed with atheists, who claim that reality cannot be divided into a part which is "God" and a part which is not-God. If God cannot be separated from anything else, it is impossible to say that "he" exists in any ordinary sense. What Spinoza was saying in effect was that there was no God that corresponded to the meaning we usually attach to that word. But mystics and philosophers had been making the same point for centuries. Some had said that there was "Nothing" apart from the world we know. Were it not for the absence of the transcendent En Sof, Spinoza's pantheism would resemble Kabbalah and we could sense an affinity between radical mysticism and the newly emergent atheism.

It was the German philosopher Moses Mendelssohn (1729–86) who opened the way for Jews to enter modern Europe, however, though at first he had no intention of constructing a specifically Jewish philosophy. He was interested in psychology and aesthetics as well as religion, and his early works *Phaedon* and *Morning Hours* were written simply within the context of the broader German Enlightenment: they sought to establish the existence of God on rational grounds and did not consider the question from a Jewish perspective. In countries like France and Germany, the liberal ideas of the Enlightenment brought emancipation and enabled Jews to enter society. It was not difficult for these *maskilim*, as the enlightened Jews were called, to accept the religious philosophy of the German Enlightenment. Judaism had never had the same doctrinal obsession as Western Christianity. Its basic tenets were practically identical with the rational religion of the Enlightenment, which in Germany still accepted the notion of miracles and God's intervention in human affairs. In *Morning Hours*, Mendelssohn's philosophical God was very similar to the God of the Bible. It was a personal God, not a metaphysical abstraction. Human characteristics such as wisdom, goodness, justice, loving-kindness and intellect could in their loftiest sense all be applied to this Supreme Being.

But this makes Mendelssohn's God very much like us. His was a typical Enlightenment faith: cool, dispassionate and tending to ignore the paradoxes and ambiguities of religious experience. Mendelssohn saw life without God as meaningless, but this was not a passionate faith: he was quite content with the knowledge of God attainable by reason. God's goodness is the hinge on which his theology hangs. If human beings had to rely on revelation alone, Mendelssohn argued, this would be inconsistent with God's goodness because so many people had apparently been excluded from the divine plan. Hence his philosophy dispensed with the abstruse intellectual skills demanded by Falsafah—which were only possible for a few people—and relied more on common sense, which was within everybody's grasp. There is a danger in such an approach, however, because it is all too easy to make such a God conform to our own prejudices and make them absolute.

When *Phaedon* had been published in 1767, its philosophic defense of the immortality of the soul was positively, if sometimes patronizingly, received in Gentile or Christian circles. A young Swiss pastor, Johann Caspar Lavater, wrote that the author was ripe for conversion to Christianity and challenged Mendelssohn to defend his Judaism in public. Mendelssohn was, then, drawn almost against his will into a rational defense of Judaism, even though he did not espouse such traditional beliefs as that of a chosen people or a promised land. He had to tread a fine line: he did not want to go the way of Spinoza or bring down the wrath of the Christians upon his own people if his defense of Judaism proved too successful. Like other deists, he argued that revelation could only be accepted if its truths could be demonstrated by reason. The doctrine of the Trinity did not meet his criterion. Judaism was not a revealed religion but a revealed law. The Jewish conception of God was essentially identical to the natural religion that belonged to the whole of humanity and could be demonstrated by unaided reason. Mendelssohn relied on the old cosmological and ontological proofs, arguing that the function of the Law had been to help the Jews to cultivate a correct notion of God and to avoid idolatry. He ended with a plea for toleration. The universal religion of reason should lead to a respect for other ways of approaching God, including Judaism, which the churches of Europe had persecuted for centuries.

Jews were less influenced by Mendelssohn than by the philosophy of Immanuel Kant, whose *Critique of Pure Reason* (1781) was published in the last decade of Mendelssohn's life. Kant had defined the Enlightenment as "man's exodus from his self-imposed tutelage" or reliance upon external authority.[25] The only way to God lay through the autonomous realm of moral conscience, which he called "practical reason." He dismissed many of the trappings of religion, such as the dogmatic authority of the churches, prayer and ritual, which all prevented human beings from relying upon their own powers and encouraged them to depend upon Another. But Kant was not opposed to the idea of God per se. Like al-

Ghazzali centuries earlier, he argued that the traditional arguments for the existence of God were useless because our minds could only understand things that exist in space or time and are not competent to consider realities that lie beyond this category. But he allowed that humanity had a natural tendency to transgress these limits and seek a principle of unity that would give us a vision of reality as a coherent whole. This was the idea of God. It was not possible to prove God's existence logically, but neither was it possible to disprove it. The idea of God was essential to us: it represented the ideal limit that enabled us to achieve a comprehensive idea of the world.

For Kant, therefore, God was simply a convenience, which could be misused. The idea of a wise and omnipotent Creator could undermine scientific research and lead to a lazy reliance on a *deus ex machina*, a god who fills the gaps of our knowledge. It could also be a source of unnecessary mystification, which leads to acrimonious disputes such as those that have scarred the history of the churches. Kant would have denied that he was an atheist. His contemporaries described him as a devout man, who was profoundly aware of mankind's capacity for evil. This made the idea of God essential to him. In his *Critique of Practical Reason*, Kant argued that in order to live a moral life, men and women needed a governor, who would reward virtue with happiness. In this perspective, God was simply tacked on to the ethical system as an afterthought. The center of religion was no longer the mystery of God but man himself. God has become a strategy which enables us to function more efficiently and morally and is no longer the ground of all being. It would not be long before some would take his ideal of autonomy one step further and dispense with this somewhat tenuous God altogether. Kant had been one of the first people in the West to doubt the validity of the traditional proofs, showing that in fact they proved nothing. They would never appear quite so convincing again.

This seemed liberating to some Christians, however, who firmly believed that God had closed one path to faith only to open another. In *A Plain Account of Genuine Christianity*, John Wesley (1703–91) wrote:

> I have sometimes been almost inclined to believe that the wisdom of God has, in most later ages, permitted the external evidence for Christianity to be more or less clogged and encumbered for this very end, that men (of reflection especially) might not altogether rest there but be constrained to look into themselves also and attend to the light shining in their hearts.[26]

A new type of piety developed alongside the rationalism of the Enlightenment, which is often called "the religion of the heart." Although it was
centered in the heart rather than the head, it shared many of the same
preoccupations as Deism. It urged men and women to abandon external
proofs and authorities and discover the God who was within the heart
and capacity of everybody. Like many of the deists, the disciples of the
Wesley brothers or of the German Pietist Count Nikolaus Ludwig von
Zinzendorf (1700–60) felt that they were shaking off the accretions of
centuries and returning to the "plain" and "genuine" Christianity of Christ
and the first Christians.

John Wesley had always been a fervent Christian. When he was a
young Fellow of Lincoln College, Oxford, he and his brother Charles had
founded a society for undergraduates, known as the Holy Club. It was
strong on method and discipline, so its members became known as Methodists. In 1735, John and Charles sailed to the colony of Georgia in
America as missionaries, but John returned disconsolate two years later,
noting in his journal: "I went to America to convert the Indians; but oh,
who will convert me?"[27] During the voyage, the Wesleys had been much
impressed by some missionaries of the Moravian sect, which eschewed
all doctrine and insisted that religion was simply an affair of the heart. In
1738 John underwent a conversion experience during a Moravian meeting
in a chapel in Aldersgate Street, London, which convinced him that
he had received a direct mission from God to preach this new kind of
Christianity throughout England. Thenceforth he and his disciples toured
the country, preaching to the working classes and the peasantry in the
markets and fields.

The experience of being "born again" was crucial. It was "absolutely
necessary" to experience "God *continually* breathing, as it were, upon the
human soul," filling the Christian with "a continual, thankful love to
God" that was consciously felt and which made it "natural and, in a
manner, necessary, to love every child of God with kindness, gentleness
and long suffering."[28] Doctrines about God were useless and could be
damaging. The psychological effect of Christ's words on the believer was
the best proof of the truth of religion. As in Puritanism, an emotional
experience of religion was the only proof of genuine faith and hence of
salvation. But this mysticism-for-everybody could be dangerous. Mystics
had always stressed the perils of the spiritual paths and warned against
hysteria: peace and tranquillity were the signs of a true mysticism. This
Born-Again Christianity could produce frenzied behavior, as in the vio-

lent ecstasies of the Quakers and Shakers. It could also lead to despair: the poet William Cowper (1731–1800) went mad when he no longer felt saved, imagining that this lack of sensation was a sign that he was damned.

In the religion of the heart, doctrines about God were transposed into interior emotional states. Thus Count von Zinzendorf, the patron of several religious communities who lived on his estates in Saxony, argued like Wesley that "faith was not in thoughts nor in the head, but in the heart, a light illuminated in the heart."[29] Academics could go on "chattering about the mystery of the Trinity" but the meaning of the doctrine was not the relations of the three Persons to one another but "what they are to us."[30] The Incarnation expressed the mystery of the new birth of an individual Christian, when Christ became "the King of the heart." This emotive type of spirituality had also surfaced in the Roman Catholic Church in the devotion to the Sacred Heart of Jesus, which established itself in the face of much opposition from the Jesuits and the establishment, who were suspicious of its frequently mawkish sentimentality. It has survived to the present day: many Roman Catholic churches contain a statue of Christ baring his breast to display a bulbous heart surrounded by a nimbus of flames. It was the mode in which he had appeared to Marguerite-Marie Alacoque (1647–90) in her convent in Paray-le-Monial, France. There is no resemblance between this Christ and the abrasive figure of the Gospels. In his whining self-pity, he shows the dangers of concentrating on the heart to the exclusion of the head. In 1682 Marguerite-Marie recalled that Jesus appeared to her at the beginning of Lent:

> covered all over with wounds and bruises. His adorable Blood was streaming over Him on every side: "Will no one," He said in a sad and mournful tone, "have pity on Me and compassionate Me, and take part in My sorrow, in the piteous state to which sinners reduce Me especially at this time."[31]

A highly neurotic woman, who confessed to a loathing of the very idea of sex, suffered from an eating disorder and indulged in unhealthy masochistic acts to prove her "love" for the Sacred Heart, Marguerite-Marie shows how a religion of the heart alone can go awry. Her Christ is often nothing more than a wish fulfillment, whose Sacred Heart compensates her for the love she had never experienced: "You shall be for ever Its beloved disciple, the sport of Its good pleasure and the victim of Its wishes," Jesus tells her. "It shall be the sole delight of all your desires; It will repair and supply for your defects, and discharge your obligations for you."[32] Concentrating solely on Jesus the man, such a piety is simply a projection which imprisons the Christian in a neurotic egotism.

We are clearly far from the cool rationalism of the Enlightenment, yet there was a connection between the religion of the heart, at its best, and Deism. Kant, for example, had been brought up in Königsburg as a Pietist, the Lutheran sect in which Zinzendorf also had his roots. Kant's proposals for a religion within the bounds of unaided reason is akin to the Pietist insistence on a religion "laid down in the very constitution of the soul"[33] rather than in a revelation enshrined in the doctrines of an authoritarian church. When he became known for his radical view of religion, Kant is said to have reassured his Pietist servant by telling him that he had only "destroyed dogma to make room for faith."[34] John Wesley was fascinated by the Enlightenment and was especially sympathetic to the ideal of liberty. He was interested in science and technology, dabbled in electrical experiments and shared the optimism of the Enlightenment about human nature and the possibility of progress. The American scholar Albert C. Outler points out that the new religion of the heart and the rationalism of the Enlightenment were both antiestablishment and both mistrusted external authority; both ranged themselves with the moderns against the ancients, and both shared a hatred of inhumanity and an enthusiasm for philanthropy. Indeed, it seems that a radical piety actually paved the way for the ideals of the Enlightenment to take root among Jews as well as Christians. There is a remarkable similarity in some of these extreme movements. Many of these sects seemed to respond to the immense changes of the period by violating religious taboos. Some appeared blasphemous; some were dubbed atheistic, while others had leaders who actually claimed to be incarnations of God. Many of these sects were Messianic in tone and proclaimed the imminent arrival of a wholly new world.

There had been an outbreak of apocalyptic excitement in England under the Puritan government of Oliver Cromwell, especially after the execution of King Charles I in 1649. The Puritan authorities had found it difficult to control the religious fervor that erupted in the army and among the ordinary people, many of whom believed that the Day of the Lord was at hand. God would pour his Spirit on all his people, as promised in the Bible, and establish his Kingdom definitively in England. Cromwell himself seems to have entertained similar hopes, as had those Puritans who had settled in New England during the 1620s. In 1649 Gerard Winstanley had founded his community of "Diggers" near Cobham in Surrey, determined to restore mankind to its original state when Adam had tilled the Garden of Eden: in this new society, private property, class distinction and human authority would wither away. The first Quakers—George Fox and James Naylor and their disciples—preached that all men and women could approach God directly. There was an Inner Light within each individual, and once it had been discovered and nurtured, everybody, irrespective of class or status, could achieve salvation here on earth. Fox himself preached pacifism, nonviolence and a radical egalitarianism for his Society of Friends. Hope for liberty, equality and fraternity had surfaced in England some 140 years before the people of Paris stormed the Bastille.

The most extreme examples of this new religious spirit had much in common with the late medieval heretics known as the Brethren of the Free Spirit. As the British historian Norman Cohn explains in *The Pursuit of the Millennium, Revolutionary Millenarians and Mystical Anarchists of the Middle Ages*, the Brethren were accused by their enemies of pantheism. They "did not hesitate to say: 'God is all that is,' 'God is in every stone and in each limb of the human body as surely as in the Eucharistic bread.' 'Every created thing is divine.' "[35] It was a reinterpretation of Plotinus's vision. The eternal essence of all things, which had emanated from the One, was divine. Everything that existed yearned to return to its Divine Source and would eventually be reabsorbed into God: even the three Persons of the Trinity would finally be submerged into the primal Unity. Salvation was achieved by the recognition of one's own divine nature here on earth. A treatise by one of the Brethren, found in a hermit's cell near the Rhine, explained: "The divine essence is my essence and my essence is the divine essence." The Brethren repeatedly asserted: "Every rational creature is in its nature blessed."[36] It was not a philosophical creed so much as a passionate longing to transcend the limits of humanity. As the Bishop of Strasbourg said, the Brethren "say they are God by nature, without any distinction. They believe that all divine perfections are in them, that they are eternal and in eternity."[37]

Cohn argues that extremist Christian sects in Cromwell's England, such as the Quakers, the Levelers and the Ranters, were a revival of the fourteenth-century heresy of the Free Spirit. It was not a conscious revival, of course, but these seventeenth-century enthusiasts had independently arrived at a pantheistic vision which it is hard not to see as a popular version of the philosophical pantheism that would shortly be expounded by Spinoza. Winstanley probably did not believe in a transcendent God at all, though he—like the other radicals—was reluctant to formulate his faith in conceptual terms. None of these revolutionary sects really believed that they owed their salvation to the atonement wrought by the historical Jesus. The Christ who mattered to them was a presence diffused through the members of the community which was virtually indistinguishable from the Holy Spirit. All agreed that prophecy was still the prime means of approaching God and that direct inspiration by the Spirit was superior to the teaching of the established religions. Fox taught his Quakers to wait upon God in a silence that was reminiscent of Greek *hesychasm* or the *via negativa* of the medieval philosophers. The old idea of a Trinitarian God was disintegrating: this immanent divine presence could not be divided into three persons. Its hallmark was Oneness, reflected in the unity and egalitarianism of the various communities. Like the Brethren, some of the Ranters thought of themselves as divine: some claimed to be Christ or a new incarnation of God. As Messiahs, they preached a revolutionary doctrine and a new world order. Thus in his polemical tract *Gangraena or a Catalogue and Discovery of Many of the Errours, Heresies, Blasphemies and pernicious Practices of the Sectarians of this time* (1640), their Presbyterian critic Thomas Edwards summarized the beliefs of the Ranters:

> Every creature in the first estate of creation was God, and every creature is God, every creature that hath life and breath being an efflux from God, and shall return unto God again, be swallowed up in him as a drop is in the ocean. . . . A man baptized with the Holy Ghost knows all things even as God knows all things, which point is a deep mystery. . . . That if a man by the spirit knows himself to be in a state of grace, though he did commit murther or drunkennesses, God did see no sin in him. . . . All the earth is the Saints, and there ought to be a community of goods, and the Saints should share in the lands and Estates of Gentlemen and such men.[38]

Like Spinoza, the Ranters were accused of atheism. They deliberately broke Christian taboos in their libertarian creed and blasphemously claimed that there was no distinction between God and man. Not everybody was capable of the scientific abstraction of Kant or Spinoza, but in the self-exaltation of the Ranters or the Inner Light of the Quakers it is possible to see an aspiration that was similar to that expressed a century later by the French revolutionaries who enthroned the Goddess of Reason in the Panthéon.

Several of the Ranters claimed to be the Messiah, a reincarnation of

God, who was to establish the new Kingdom. The accounts that we have of their lives suggest mental disorder in some cases, but they still seem to have attracted a following, obviously addressing a spiritual and social need in the England of their time. Thus William Franklin, a respectable householder, became mentally ill in 1646 after his family had been smitten by plague. He horrified his fellow Christians by declaring himself to be God and Christ, but later recanted and begged pardon. He seemed in full possession of his faculties, but he still left his wife and began to sleep with other women, leading an apparently disreputable, mendicant life. One of these women, Mary Gadbury, began to see visions and hear voices, prophesying a new social order which would abolish all class distinctions. She embraced Franklin as her Lord and Christ. They seem to have attracted a number of disciples but in 1650 were arrested, whipped and imprisoned in Bridewell. At about the same time, one John Robbins was also revered as God: he claimed to be God the Father and believed that his wife would shortly give birth to the Savior of the world.

Some historians deny that men like Robbins and Franklin were Ranters, noting that we only hear about their activities from their enemies, who may have distorted their beliefs for polemical reasons. But some texts by notable Ranters like Jacob Bauthumely, Richard Coppin and Laurence Clarkson have survived which show the same complex of ideas: they also preached a revolutionary social creed. In his treatise *The Light and Dark Sides of God* (1650), Bauthumely speaks of God in terms that recall the Sufi belief that God was the Eye, Ear and Hand of the man who turns to him: "O God, what shall I say thou art?" he asks. "For if I say I see thee, it is nothing but thy seeing of thy selfe; for there is nothing in me capable of seeing thee but thy selfe: If I say I know thee, that is no other but the knowledge of thy selfe."[39] Like the rationalists, Bauthumely rejects the doctrine of the Trinity and, again like a Sufi, qualifies his belief in the divinity of Christ by saying that while he *was* divine, God could not become manifest in only one man: "He as really and substantially dwells in the flesh of other men and Creatures, as well as in the man Christ."[40] The worship of a distinct, localized God is a form of idolatry; Heaven is not a place but the spiritual presence of Christ. The biblical idea of God, Bauthumely believed, was inadequate: sin is not an action but a condition, a falling short of our divine nature. Yet mysteriously, God was present in sin, which was simply "the dark side of God, a mere privation of light."[41] Bauthumely was denounced as an atheist by his enemies, but his outlook is not far in spirit from Fox, Wesley and Zinzenburg, though it is expressed far more crudely. Like the later Pietists and

Methodists, he was trying to internalize a God who had become distant and inhumanly objective and to transpose traditional doctrine into religious experience. He also shared the rejection of authority and essentially optimistic view of humanity shared later by the philosophers of the Enlightenment and those who subscribed to a religion of the heart.

Bauthumely was flirting with the deeply exciting and subversive doctrine of the holiness of sin. If God was everything, sin was nothing—an assertion that Ranters like Laurence Clarkson and Alastair Coppe also tried to demonstrate by flagrantly violating the current sexual code or by swearing and blaspheming in public. Coppe was particularly famous for drunkenness and smoking. Once he had become a Ranter, he had indulged what was obviously a long-suppressed craving to curse and swear. We hear of him cursing for a whole hour in the pulpit of a London church and swearing at the hostess of a tavern so fearfully that she trembled for hours afterward. This could have been a reaction to the repressive Puritan ethic, with its unhealthy concentration on the sinfulness of mankind. Fox and his Quakers insisted that sin was by no means inevitable. He certainly did not encourage his Friends to sin and hated the licentiousness of the Ranters, but he was trying to preach a more optimistic anthropology and restore the balance. In his tract *A Single Eye*, Laurence Clarkson argued that since God had made all things good, "sin" only existed in men's imagination. God himself had claimed in the Bible that he would make the darkness light. Monotheists had always found it difficult to accommodate the reality of sin, though mystics had tried to discover a more holistic vision. Julian of Norwich had believed that sin was "behovely" and somehow necessary. Kabbalists had suggested that sin was mysteriously rooted in God. The extreme libertarianism of Ranters like Coppe and Clarkson can be seen as a rough and ready attempt to shake off an oppressive Christianity which had terrorized the faithful with its doctrine of an angry, vengeful God. Rationalists and "enlightened" Christians were also trying to shake off the fetters of a religion which had presented God as a cruel authority figure, and to discover a milder deity.

Social historians have noted that Western Christianity is unique among world religions for its violent alternations of periods of repression and permissiveness. They have also noted that the repressive phases usually coincide with a religious revival. The more relaxed moral climate of the Enlightenment would be succeeded in many parts of the West by the repressions of the Victorian period, which was accompanied by an upsurge of a more fundamentalist religiosity. In our own day, we have witnessed the permissive society of the 1960s giving way to the more puritan ethic of the 1980s, which has also coincided with the rise of Christian fundamentalism in the West. This is a complex phenomenon, which doubtless has no single cause. It is, however, tempting to connect this with the idea of God, which Westerners have found problematic. The theologians and mystics of the Middle Ages may have preached a God of love, but the fearful Dooms over the cathedral doors depicting the tortures of the damned told another story. The sense of God has often been characterized by darkness and struggle in the West, as we have seen. Ranters like Clarkson and Coppe were flouting Christian taboos and proclaiming the holiness of sin at the same time as the witchcraft craze was raging in various countries of Europe. The radical Christians of Cromwell's England were also rebelling against a God and a religion which was too demanding and frightening.

The new born-again Christianity that was beginning to appear in the West during the seventeenth and eighteenth centuries was frequently unhealthy and characterized by violent and sometimes dangerous emotions and reversals. We can see this in the wave of religious fervor known as the Great Awakening that swept New England during the 1730s. It had been inspired by the evangelical preaching of George Whitfield, a disciple and colleague of the Wesleys, and the hellfire sermons of the Yale graduate Jonathan Edwards (1703–58). Edwards describes this Awakening in his essay "A Faithful Narrative of the Surprising Work of God in Northampton, Connecticut." He describes his parishioners there as nothing out of the ordinary: they were sober, orderly and good but lacking in religious fervor. They were no better or worse than men and women in any of the other colonies. But in 1734 two young people died shockingly sudden deaths, and this (backed up, it would appear, by some fearful words by Edwards himself) plunged the town into a frenzy of religious fervor. People could talk of nothing but religion; they stopped work and spent the whole day reading the Bible. In about six months, there had been about three hundred born-again conversions from all classes of society: sometimes there would be as many as five a week. Edwards saw this craze as the direct work of God himself: he meant this quite literally, it was not a mere pious *façon de parler*. As he repeatedly said, "God seemed to have gone out of his usual way" of behaving in New England and was moving the people in a marvelous and miraculous manner. It must be said, however, that the Holy Spirit sometimes manifested himself in some rather hysterical symptoms. Sometimes, Edwards tells us, they were quite "broken" by the fear of God and "sunk into an abyss, under a sense of guilt that they were ready to think was beyond the mercy of God."

This would be succeeded by an equally extreme elation, when they felt suddenly saved. They used "to break forth into laughter, tears often at the same time issuing like a flood, and intermingling a loud weeping. Sometimes they have not been able to forbear crying out with a loud voice, expressing their great admiration."[42] We are clearly far from the calm control that mystics in all the major religious traditions have believed to be the hallmark of true enlightenment.

These intensely emotional reversals have continued to be characteristic of religious revival in America. It was a new birth, attended by violent convulsions of pain and effort, a new version of the Western struggle with God. The Awakening spread like a contagion to surrounding towns and villages, just as it would a century later when New York state would be called the Burned-Over District, because it was so habitually scorched by the flames of religious fervor. While in this exalted state, Edwards noted that his converts felt that the whole world was delightful. They could not tear themselves away from their Bibles and even forgot to eat. Not surprisingly, perhaps, their emotion died down, and about two years later Edwards noted that "it began to be very sensible that the Spirit of God was gradually withdrawing from us." Again, he was not speaking metaphorically: Edwards was a true Western literalist in religious matters. He was convinced that the Awakening had been a direct revelation of God in their midst, the tangible activity of the Holy Spirit as on the first Pentecost. When God had withdrawn, as abruptly as he had come, his place was—again, quite literally—taken by Satan. Exaltation was succeeded by suicidal despair. First one poor soul killed himself by cutting his throat and: "After this multitudes in this and other towns seemed to have it strongly suggested to them, and pressed upon them, to do as this person had done. Many had it urged upon them as if somebody had spoken to them, 'Cut your own throat, now is a good opportunity. Now!' " Two people went mad with "strange, enthusiastic delusions."[43] There were no more conversions, but the people who survived the experience were calmer and more joyful than they had been before the Awakening, or so Edwards would have us believe. The God of Jonathan Edwards and his converts, who revealed himself in such abnormality and distress, was clearly just as frightening and arbitrary in his dealings with his people as ever. The violent swings of emotion, the manic elation and profound despair, show that many of the less privileged people of America found it difficult to keep their balance when they had dealings with "God." It also shows a conviction that we find also in the scientific religion of

Newton that God is directly responsible for everything that happens in the world, however bizarre.

It is difficult to associate this fervid and irrational religiosity with the measured calm of the Founding Fathers. Edwards had many opponents who were extremely critical of the Awakening. God would only express himself rationally, the liberals claimed, not in violent eruptions into human affairs. But in *Religion and the American Mind; From the Great Awakening to the Revolution*, Alan Heimart argues that the new birth of the Awakening was an evangelical version of the Enlightenment ideal of the pursuit of happiness: it represented an "existential liberation from a world in which 'everything awakens powerful apprehension.' "[44] The Awakening occurred in the poorer colonies, where people had little expectation of happiness in this world, despite the hopes of the sophisticated Enlightenment. The experience of being born again, Edwards had argued, resulted in a feeling of joy and a perception of beauty that were quite different from any natural sensation. In the Awakening, therefore, a God-experience had made the Enlightenment of the New World available to more than a few successful people in the colonies. We should also recall that the philosophical Enlightenment was also experienced as a quasireligious liberation. The terms *éclaircissement* and *Aufklärung* have definite religious connotations. The God of Jonathan Edwards also contributed to the revolutionary enthusiasm of 1775. In the eyes of the revivalists, Britain had lost the new light that had shone so brightly during the Puritan revolution and now seemed decadent and regressive. It was Edwards and his colleagues who led Americans of the lower classes to take the first steps toward revolution. Messianism was essential to Edwards's religion: human effort would hasten the coming of God's Kingdom, which was attainable and imminent in the New World. The Awakening itself (despite its tragic finale) made people believe that the process of redemption described in the Bible had already begun. God was firmly committed to the project. Edwards gave the doctrine of the Trinity a political interpretation: the Son was "the deity generated by God's understanding" and thus the blueprint of the New Commonwealth; the Spirit, "the deity subsisting in act," was the force which would accomplish this master plan in time.[45] In the New World of America, God would thus be able to contemplate his own perfections on earth. The society would express the "excellencies" of God himself. The New England would be a "city on the hill," a light unto the Gentiles "shining with a reflection of the glory of Jehovah risen upon it, which shall be attractive and ravishing to all."[46] The God of

Jonathan Edwards, therefore, would be incarnated in the Commonwealth: Christ was seen as embodied in a good society.

Other Calvinists were in the van of progress: they introduced chemistry into the curriculum in America, and Timothy Dwight, Edwards's grandson, saw scientific knowledge as a prelude to the final perfection of humanity. Their God did not necessarily mean obscurantism, as the American liberals sometimes imagined. The Calvinists disliked Newton's cosmology, which left God with little to do once he had got things started. As we have seen, they preferred a God who was literally active in the world: their doctrine of predestination showed that in their view God was actually responsible for everything that happened here below, for good or ill. This meant that science could only reveal the God who could be discerned in all the activities of his creatures—natural, civil, physical and spiritual— even in those activities which seemed fortuitous. In some respects, the Calvinists were more adventurous in their thinking than the Liberals, who opposed their revivalism and preferred simple faith to the "speculative, perplexing notions" that disturbed them in the preaching of revivalists like Whitfield and Edwards. Alan Heimart argues that the origins of antiintellectualism in American society might not lie with the Calvinists and evangelicals but with the more rational Bostonians like Charles Chauncey or Samuel Quincey, who preferred ideas about God that were "more plain and obvious."[47]

There had been some remarkably similar developments within Judaism which would also prepare the way for the spread of rationalist ideals among Jews and would enable many to assimilate with the Gentile population in Europe. In the apocalyptic year of 1666, a Jewish Messiah declared that redemption was at hand and was accepted ecstatically by Jews all over the world. Shabbetai Zevi had been born on the anniversary of the destruction of the Temple in 1626 to a family of wealthy Sephardic Jews in Smyrna in Asia Minor. As he grew up he developed strange tendencies which we would perhaps diagnose today as manic-depressive. He had periods of deep despair, when he used to withdraw from his family and live in seclusion. These were succeeded by an elation that bordered on ecstasy. During these "manic" periods, he would sometimes deliberately and spectacularly break the Law of Moses: he would publicly eat forbidden foods, utter the sacred Name of God and claim that he had been inspired to do so by a special revelation. He believed that he was the long-awaited Messiah. Eventually the Rabbis could bear it no longer and in 1656 they expelled Shabbetai from the city. He became a wanderer among the Jewish communities of the Ottoman empire. During a manic spell in Istanbul, he announced that the Torah had been abrogated, crying aloud: "Blessed art Thou, O Lord our God, Who permits the forbidden!" In Cairo he caused scandal by marrying a woman who had fled the murderous pogroms in Poland in 1648 and now lived as a prostitute. In 1662 Shabbetai set off for Jerusalem: at this point he was in a depressive phase and believed that he must be possessed by demons. In Palestine he heard about a young, learned Rabbi called Nathan who was a skilled exorcist, so he set out to find him in his home in Gaza.

Like Shabbetai, Nathan had studied the Kabbalah of Isaac Luria. When he met the troubled Jew from Smyrna, he told him that he was not possessed: his dark despair proved that he was indeed the Messiah. When he descended to these depths, he was fighting against the evil powers of the Other Side, releasing the divine sparks in the realm of the *kelipoth* which could only be redeemed by the Messiah himself. Shabbetai had a mission to descend into hell before he could achieve the final redemption of Israel. At first Shabbetai would have none of this, but eventually Nathan's eloquence persuaded him. On May 31, 1665, he was suddenly seized with a manic joy and, with Nathan's encouragement, he announced his Messianic mission. Leading Rabbis dismissed all this as dangerous nonsense, but many of the Jews of Palestine flocked to Shabbetai, who chose twelve disciples to be the judges of the tribes of Israel, which would soon reassemble. Nathan announced the good news to the Jewish communities in letters to Italy, Holland, Germany and Poland, as well as to the cities of the Ottoman empire, and Messianic excitement spread like wildfire through the Jewish world. Centuries of persecution and ostracism had isolated the Jews of Europe from the mainstream, and this unhealthy state of affairs had conditioned many to believe that the future of the world depended upon the Jews alone. The Sephardim, descendants of the exiled Jews of Spain, had taken Lurianic Kabbalah to their hearts, and many had come to believe in the imminent End of Days. All this helped the cult of Shabbetai Zevi. Throughout Jewish history, there had been many Messianic claimants, but none had ever attracted such massive support. It became dangerous for Jews who had their reservations about Shabbetai to speak out. His supporters came from all classes of Jewish society: rich and poor, learned and uneducated. Pamphlets and broadsheets spread the glad tidings in English, Dutch, German and Italian. In Poland and Lithuania there were public processions in his honor. In the Ottoman empire, prophets wandered through the streets describing visions in which they had seen Shabbetai seated upon a throne. All business ceased; ominously, the Jews of Turkey dropped the name of the sultan from the Sabbath prayers and put in Shabbetai's name instead. Eventually, when Shabbetai arrived in Istanbul in January 1666, he was arrested as a rebel and imprisoned in Gallipoli.

After centuries of persecution, exile and humiliation, there was hope. All over the world, Jews had experienced an inner freedom and liberation that seemed similar to the ecstasy that the Kabbalists had experienced for a few moments when they contemplated the mysterious world of the *sefiroth*. Now this experience of salvation was no longer simply the preserve of a privileged few but seemed common property. For the first time, Jews felt that their lives had value; redemption was no longer a vague hope for the future but was real and full of meaning in the present. Salvation had come! This sudden reversal made an indelible impression. The eyes of the whole Jewish world were fixed on Gallipoli, where Shabbetai had even made an impression on his captors. The Turkish vizier housed him in considerable comfort. Shabbetai began to sign his letters: "I am the Lord your God, Shabbetai Zevi." But when he was brought back to Istanbul for his trial, he had fallen once again into a depression. The sultan gave him the choice of conversion to Islam or death: Shabbetai chose Islam and was immediately released. He was given an imperial pension and died as an apparently loyal Muslim on September 17, 1676.

Naturally the appalling news devastated his supporters, many of whom instantly lost their faith. The Rabbis attempted to erase his memory from the earth: they destroyed all the letters, pamphlets and tracts about Shabbetai they could find. To this day, many Jews are embarrassed by this Messianic debacle and find it hard to deal with. Rabbis and rationalists alike have downplayed its significance. Recently, however, scholars have followed the late Gershom Scholem in trying to understand the meaning of this strange episode and its more significant aftermath.[48] Astonishing as it may seem, many Jews remained loyal to their Messiah, despite the scandal of his apostasy. The experience of redemption had been so profound that they could not believe that God had allowed them to be deluded. It is one of the most striking instances of the religious experience of salvation taking precedence over mere facts and reason. Faced with the choice of abandoning their newfound hope or accepting an apostate Messiah, a surprising number of Jews of all classes refused to submit to the hard facts of history. Nathan of Gaza devoted the rest of his life to preaching the mystery of Shabbetai: by converting to Islam, he had continued his lifelong battle with the forces of evil. Yet again, he had been impelled to violate the deepest sanctities of his people in order to descend into the realm of darkness to liberate the *kelipoth*. He had accepted the tragic burden of his mission and descended to the lowest depths to conquer the world of Godlessness from within. In Turkey and Greece, about two hundred families remained loyal to Shabbetai: after his death they decided to follow his example in order to continue his battle with evil and converted to Islam en masse in 1683. They remained secretly loyal to Judaism, keeping in close touch with the Rabbis and congregating in the clandestine synagogues in one another's houses. In 1689 their leader Jacob Querido made the *hajj* pilgrimage to Mecca, and the Messiah's widow declared that he was the reincarnation of Shabbetai Zevi. There is still a small group of *Donmeh* (apostates) in Turkey, who live outwardly impeccable Islamic lives but cling passionately to their Judaism in secret.

Other Sabbatarians did not go to these lengths but remained loyal to their Messiah and to the synagogue. There seem to have been more of these crypto-Sabbatarians than was once believed. During the nineteenth century, many Jews who had assimilated or adopted a more liberal form of Judaism considered it shameful to have had Sabbatarian ancestors, but it appears that many outstanding Rabbis of the eighteenth century believed that Shabbetai had been the Messiah. Scholem argues that even though this Messianism never became a mass movement in Judaism, its numbers should not be underestimated. It had a special appeal to the Marranos, who had been forced by the Spanish to convert to Christianity but eventually reverted to Judaism. The notion of apostasy as a mystery assuaged their guilt and sorrow. Sabbatarianism flourished in Sephardic communities in Morocco, the Balkans, Italy and Lithuania. Some, like Benjamin Kohn of Reggio and Abraham Rorigo of Modena, were eminent Kabbalists who kept their link with the movement secret. From the Balkans, the Messianic sect spread to the Ashkenazic Jews in Poland, who were demoralized and exhausted by the escalating anti-Semitism of Eastern Europe. In 1759 the disciples of the strange and sinister prophet Jacob Frank followed the example of their Messiah and converted en masse to Christianity, adhering to Judaism in secret.

Scholem suggests an illuminating comparison to Christianity. Some sixteen hundred years earlier, another group of Jews had been unable to abandon their hope in a scandalous Messiah, who had died the death of a common criminal in Jerusalem. What St. Paul had called the scandal of the cross was every bit as shocking as the scandal of an apostate Messiah. In both cases, the disciples proclaimed the birth of a new form of Judaism which had replaced the old; they embraced a paradoxical creed. Christian belief that there was new life in the defeat of the Cross was similar to the

Sabbatarians' conviction that apostasy was a sacred mystery. Both groups believed that the grain of wheat had to rot in the earth in order to bear fruit; they believed that the old Torah was dead and had been replaced by the new law of the Spirit. Both developed Trinitarian and Incarnational conceptions of God.

Like many Christians during the seventeenth and eighteenth centuries, Sabbatarians believed that they were standing on the threshold of a new world. Kabbalists had repeatedly argued that in the Last Days the true mysteries of God, which had been obscured during the exile, would be revealed. Sabbatarians who believed that they were living in the Messianic era felt free to break away from traditional ideas about God, even if that meant accepting an apparently blasphemous theology. Thus Abraham Cardazo (d. 1706), who had been born a Marrano and had started by studying Christian theology, believed that because of their sins all Jews had been destined to become apostates. This was to have been their punishment. But God had saved his people from this terrible fate by allowing the Messiah to make the supreme sacrifice on their behalf. He came to the frightening conclusion that during their time in exile, the Jews had lost all true knowledge of God.

Like the Christians and Deists of the Enlightenment, Cardazo was attempting to peel away what he saw as inauthentic accretions from his religion and to return to the pure faith of the Bible. It will be recalled that during the second century, some Christian Gnostics had evolved a kind of metaphysical anti-Semitism by distinguishing the Hidden God of Jesus Christ from the cruel God of the Jews, who was responsible for the creation of the world. Now Cardazo unconsciously revived this old idea but completely reversed it. He also taught that there were two Gods: one who was the God who had revealed himself to Israel and another who was common knowledge. In every civilization people had proved the existence of a First Cause: this was the God of Aristotle, who had been worshipped by the whole pagan world. This deity had no religious significance: he had not created the world and had no interest whatever in humanity; he had, therefore, not revealed himself in the Bible, which never mentions him. The second God, who had revealed himself to Abraham, Moses and the prophets, was quite different: he had created the world out of nothing, had redeemed Israel and was its God. In exile, however, philosophers such as Saadia and Maimonides were surrounded by the *goyim* and had absorbed some of their ideas. Consequently they had confused the two Gods and taught the Jews that they were one and the same. The result was that the Jews had come to worship the God of the philosophers as though he were the God of their Fathers.

How did the two Gods relate to one another? Cardazo evolved a Trinitarian theology to account for this additional deity without abandoning Jewish monotheism. There was a Godhead which consisted of three *hypostases* or *parzufim* (countenances): the first of these was called *Atika Kadisha*, the Holy Ancient One. This was the First Cause. The second *parzuf*, which emanated from the first, was called *Malka Kadisha*; he was the God of Israel. The third *parzuf* was the Shekinah, who had been exiled from the Godhead as Isaac Luria had described. Cardazo argued that these "three knots of the faith" were not three entirely separate gods but were mysteriously one, as they all manifested the same Godhead. Cardazo was a moderate Sabbatarian. He did not believe it his duty to apostasize because Shabbetai Zevi had performed this painful task on his behalf. But in proposing a Trinity, he was breaking a taboo. Over the centuries, Jews had come to hate Trinitarianism, which they considered blasphemous and idolatrous. But a surprising number of Jews were drawn to this forbidden vision. As the years passed without any change in the world, Sabbatarians had to modify their Messianic hopes. Sabbatarians like Nehemiah Hayim, Samuel Primo and Jonathan Eibeschütz came to the conclusion that the "mystery of the Godhead" (*sod ha-elohut*) had not been fully revealed in 1666. The Shekinah had begun to "rise from the dust," as Luria had foretold, but had not yet returned to the Godhead. Redemption would be a gradual process, and during this time of transition it was permissible to continue to practice the Old Law and worship in the synagogue, while adhering secretly to the Messianic doctrine. This revised Sabbatarianism explained how many Rabbis who believed that Shabbetai Zevi had been the Messiah were able to stay in the pulpits during the eighteenth century.

The extremists who did apostasize adopted a theology of Incarnation, thus breaking another Jewish taboo. They came to believe that Shabbetai Zevi had not only been the Messiah but an incarnation of God. As in Christianity, this belief evolved gradually. Abraham Cardazo taught a doctrine that was similar to St. Paul's belief in the glorification of Jesus after his resurrection: when the redemption had begun at the time of his apostasy, Shabbetai had been raised to the Trinity of *parzufim*: "the Holy One [*Malka Kadisha*] blessed be He, removed himself upward and Shabbetai Zevi ascended to be God in his place."[49] He had, therefore, somehow been promoted to divine status and had taken the place of the

God of Israel, the second *parzuf.* Soon the *Donmeh*, who had converted to Islam, took the idea a step further and decided that the God of Israel had descended and been made flesh in Shabbetai. Since they also came to believe that each of their leaders was a reincarnation of the Messiah, it followed that they became *avatars* too, in rather the same way, perhaps, as the Shii Imams. Each generation of apostates, therefore, had a leader who was an incarnation of the divine.

Jacob Frank (1726–1791), who led his Ashkenazic disciples to baptism in 1759, had implied that he was God incarnate at the very beginning of his career. He has been described as the most frightening figure in the entire history of Judaism. He was uneducated and proud of it but had the ability to evolve a dark mythology that attracted many Jews who had found their faith empty and unsatisfying. Frank preached that the Old Law had been abrogated. Indeed, all religions must be destroyed so that God could shine forth clearly. In his *Slowa Panskie* (The Sayings of the Lord), he took Sabbatarianism over the edge into nihilism. Everything had to be broken down: "Wherever Adam trod, a city was built, but wherever I set foot all will be destroyed, for I have come into this world only to destroy and annihilate."[50] There is a disturbing similarity to some of the sayings of Christ, who had also claimed that he had come to bring not peace but the sword. Unlike Jesus and St. Paul, however, Frank proposed to put nothing in the place of the old sanctities. His nihilistic creed was not too dissimilar, perhaps, to that of his younger contemporary the Marquis de Sade. It was only by descending to the depths of degradation that men could ascend to find the Good God. This meant not only the rejection of all religion but the commission of "strange acts" that resulted in voluntary abasement and utter shamelessness.

Frank was not a Kabbalist but preached a cruder version of Cardozo's theology. He believed that each of the three *parzufim* of the Sabbatarian Trinity would be represented on earth by a different Messiah. Shabbetai Zevi, whom Frank used to call "The First One," had been the incarnation of "the Good God," who was Cardozo's *Atika Kadisha* (the Holy Ancient One); he himself was the incarnation of the second *parzuf*, the God of Israel. The third Messiah, who would incarnate the Shekinah, would be a woman whom Frank called "the Virgin." At present, the world was in thrall to evil powers, however. It would not be redeemed until men had adopted Frank's nihilistic gospel. Jacob's ladder was in the shape of a V: to ascend to God, one had first to descend to the depths like Jesus and Shabbetai: "This much I tell you," Frank declared, "Christ, as you know, said that he had come to redeem the world from the power of the devil, but I have come to redeem it from all the laws and customs that have ever existed. It is my task to annihilate all this so that the Good God can reveal himself."[51] Those who wished to find God and liberate themselves from the evil powers had to follow their leader step by step into the abyss, violating all the laws that they held most sacred: "I say to you that all who would be warriors must be without religion, which means that they must reach freedom under their own powers."[52]

In this last saying, we can sense the connection between Frank's dark vision and the rationalist Enlightenment. The Polish Jews who had adopted his gospel had clearly found their religion unable to help them to adjust to their appalling circumstances in a world that was not safe for Jews. After Frank's death, Frankism lost much of its anarchism, retaining only a belief in Frank as God incarnate and what Scholem calls an "intense, luminous feeling of salvation."[53] They had seen the French Revolution as a sign of God on their behalf: they abandoned their antinomianism for political action, dreaming of a revolution which would rebuild the world. Similarly, the *Donmeh* who had converted to Islam would often be active Young Turks in the early years of the twentieth century, and many assimilated completely in the secular Turkey of Kemal Atatürk. The hostility that all Sabbatarians had felt toward external observance was in one sense a rebellion against the conditions of the ghetto. Sabbatarianism, which had seemed such a backward, obscurantist religion, had helped them to liberate themselves from the old ways and made them susceptible to new ideas. The moderate Sabbatarians, who had remained outwardly loyal to Judaism, were often pioneers in the Jewish Enlightenment (*Haskalah*); they were also active in the creation of Reform Judaism during the nineteenth century. Often these reforming *maskilim* had ideas that were a strange amalgam of old and new. Thus Joseph Wehte of Prague, who was writing in about 1800, said that his heroes were Moses Mendelssohn, Immanuel Kant, Shabbetai Zevi and Isaac Luria. Not everybody could make his way into modernity via the difficult paths of science and philosophy: the mystical creeds of radical Christians and Jews enabled them to work toward a secularism that they would once have found abhorrent by addressing the deeper, more primitive regions of the psyche. Some adopted new and blasphemous ideas of God that would enable their children to abandon him altogether.

At the same time as Jacob Frank was evolving his nihilistic gospel, other Polish Jews had found a very different Messiah. Since the pogroms of 1648, Polish Jewry had undergone a trauma of dislocation and demoralization that was as intense as the exile of the Sephardim from Spain.

Many of the most learned and spiritual Jewish families of Poland had either been killed or had migrated to the comparative safety of Western Europe. Tens of thousands of Jews had been displaced and many had become wanderers, roaming from town to town, barred from permanent settlement. The Rabbis who remained were often of low caliber and had allowed the house of study to shield them from the grim reality of the world outside. Wandering Kabbalists spoke of the demonic darkness of the world of the *achra sitra*, the Other Side, which was separated from God. The Shabbetai Zevi disaster had also contributed to the general disillusion and anomie. Some Jews of the Ukraine had been affected by the Christian Pietist movements, which had also sprung up in the Russian Orthodox Church. The Jews had started to produce a similar kind of charismatic religion. There were reports of Jews falling into ecstasy, breaking into song and clapping their hands during prayer. During the 1730s one of these ecstatics emerged as the undisputed leader of this Jewish religion of the heart and founded the school known as Hasidism.

Israel ben Eliezer was not a scholar. He preferred to walk in the woods, singing songs and telling stories to children, to studying the Talmud. He and his wife lived in abject poverty in southern Poland in a hut in the Carpathian Mountains. For a time he dug lime and sold it to the people of the nearby town. Then he and his wife became innkeepers. Finally, when he was about thirty-six years old, he announced that he had become a faith healer and an exorcist. He journeyed through the villages of Poland, healing the illnesses of the peasants and townsfolk with herbal remedies, amulets and prayers. There were many healers at this time, who claimed to cure the afflicted in the Name of the Lord. Israel had thus now become a Baal Shem Tov, a Master of the Good Name. Even though he had never been ordained, his followers began to call him Rabbi Israel Baal Shem Tov, or, simply, the Besht. Most of the healers were content with magic, but the Besht was also a mystic. The Shabbetai Zevi episode had convinced him of the dangers of combining mysticism with Messianism, and he returned to an earlier form of Kabbalism, which was not to be for an elite, however, but for everybody. Instead of seeing the fall of the divine sparks to the world as a disaster, the Besht taught his Hasidim to look on the bright side. These sparks were lodged in every item of creation, and this meant that the whole world was filled with the presence of God. A devout Jew could experience God in the tiniest action of his daily life—while he was eating, drinking or making love to his wife—because the divine sparks were everywhere. Men and women were not surrounded by hosts of demons, therefore, but by a God who was present in every gust of wind or blade of grass: he wanted Jews to approach him with confidence and joy.

The Besht abandoned Luria's grand schemes for the salvation of the world. The Hasid was simply responsible for reuniting the sparks trapped in the items of his personal world—in his wife, his servants, furniture and food. As Hillel Zeitlin, one of the Besht's disciples, explained, the Hasid has a unique responsibility to his particular environment, which he alone can perform: "Every man is a redeemer of a world that is all his own. He beholds only what he, and only he, ought to behold and feels only what he is personally singled out to feel."[54] Kabbalists had devised a discipline of concentration (*devekuth*) which helped mystics to become aware of the presence of God wherever they turned. As a seventeenth-century Kabbalist of Safed had explained, mystics should sit in solitude, take time off from the study of Torah and "imagine the light of the Shekinah above their heads, as though it were flowing all around them and they were sitting in the midst of light."[55] This sense of God's presence had brought them to a tremulous, ecstatic joy. The Besht taught his followers that this ecstasy was not reserved for the privileged mystical elite but that every Jew had a duty to practice *devekuth* and become aware of the all-pervasive presence of God: in fact failure in *devekuth* was tantamount to idolatry, a denial that nothing truly exists apart from God. This brought the Besht into conflict with the establishment, who feared that Jews would abandon the study of Torah in favor of these potentially dangerous and eccentric devotions.

Hasidism spread quickly, however, because it brought the disaffected Jews a message of hope: many of the converts seem to have been former Sabbatarians. The Besht did not want his disciples to abandon the Torah. Instead he gave it a new mystical interpretation: the word *mitzvah* (commandment) meant a bond. When a Hasid performed one of the commandments of the Law while practicing *devekuth*, he was binding himself to God, the Ground of all being, at the same time as he was reuniting the divine sparks in the person or thing he was dealing with at the moment to the Godhead. The Torah had long encouraged Jews to sanctify the world by the performance of the *mitzvot*, and the Besht was simply giving this a mystical interpretation. Sometimes the Hasidim went to somewhat dubious lengths in their zeal to save the world: many of them took to smoking a great deal to rescue the sparks in their tobacco! Baruch of Medzibozh (1757–1810), another of the Besht's grandsons, had a splendid court with wonderful furniture and tapestries, which he justified by claiming that he was only concerned for the sparks in these magnificent trappings. Abraham Joshua Heschel of Apt (d. 1825) used to eat huge meals to reclaim the divine sparks in his food.[56] One can, however, see the Hasidic enterprise as an attempt to find meaning in a cruel and dangerous world. The disciplines of *devekuth* were an imaginative attempt to strip the veil of familiarity from the world to discover the glory within. It was not dissimilar to the imaginative vision of the contemporary English Romantics William Wordsworth (1770–1850) and Samuel Taylor Coleridge (1772–1834), who sensed the One Life that unites the whole of reality in everything they saw. The Hasidim also became aware of what they saw as a divine energy coursing through the whole created world which transformed it into a glorious place, despite the sorrows of exile and persecution. Gradually the material world would fade into insignificance and everything would become an epiphany: Moses Teitelbaum of Ujhaly (1759–1841) said that when Moses had seen the Burning Bush, he had simply seen the divine presence which burns in every single bush and keeps it in existence.[57] The whole world seemed appareled in celestial light, and the Hasidim would shout with joy in their ecstasy, clapping their hands, and break into song. Some even used to turn somersaults, demonstrating that the glory of their vision had turned the whole world upside down.

Unlike Spinoza and some of the Christian radicals, the Besht did not mean that everything was God but that all beings existed in God, who gave them life and being. He was the vital force that kept everything in existence. He did not believe that the Hasidim would become divine through the practice of *devekuth* or even achieve unity with God—such temerity seemed extravagant to all Jewish mystics. Instead, the Hasidim would draw close to God and become aware of his presence. Most were simple, unsophisticated men, and they often expressed themselves extravagantly, but they were aware that their mythology was not to be taken literally. They preferred stories to philosophic or Talmudic discussion, seeing fiction as the best vehicle for conveying an experience which had little to do with facts and reason. Their vision was an imaginative attempt to depict the interdependence of God and mankind. God was no external, objective reality: indeed, the Hasidim believed that in some sense they were creating him by building him up anew after his disintegration. By becoming aware of the Godly spark within them, they would become more fully human. Again, they expressed this insight in the mythological terms of Kabbalah. Dov Baer, the successor of the Besht, said that God and man were a unity: a man would only become *adām* as God had intended on the day of creation when he lost his sense of separation from the rest of existence and was transformed into the "cosmic figure of primordial man, whose likeness Ezekiel beheld on the throne."[58] It was a distinctively Jewish expression of the Greek or Buddhist belief in the enlightenment which made human beings aware of their own transcendent dimension.

The Greeks had expressed this insight in their doctrine of the Incarnation and deification of Christ. The Hasidim developed their own form of Incarnationalism. The Zaddik, the Hasidic Rabbi, became the *avatar* of his generation, a link between heaven and earth and a representative of the divine presence. As Rabbi Menahem Nahum of Chernobyl (1730–1797) wrote, the Zaddik "is truly a part of God, and has a place, as it were, with Him."[59] Just as Christians imitated Christ in an attempt to draw near to God, the Hasid imitated his Zaddik, who had made the ascent to God and practiced perfect *devekuth*. He was a living proof that this enlightenment was possible. Because the Zaddik was close to God, the Hasidim could approach the Master of the Universe through him. They would crowd around their Zaddik, hanging on his every word, as he told them a story about the Besht or expounded a verse of Torah. As in the enthusiastic Christian sects, Hasidism was not a solitary religion but intensely communal. The Hasidim would attempt to follow their Zaddik in his ascent to the ultimate together with their master, in a group. Not surprisingly, the more orthodox Rabbis of Poland were horrified by this personality cult, which completely bypassed the learned Rabbi who had long been seen as the incarnation of Torah. The opposition was led by Rabbi Elijah ben Solomon Zalman (1720–1797), the Gaon or head of the academy of Vilna. The Shabbetai Zevi debacle had made some Jews extremely hostile to mysticism, and the Gaon of Vilna has often been seen as the champion of a more rational religion. Yet he was an ardent Kabbalist as well as a master of Talmud. His close disciple Rabbi Hayyim of Volozhin praised his "complete and mighty mastery of the whole of *The Zohar* . . . which he studied with the flame of the love and fear of the divine majesty, with holiness and purity and a wonderful *devekuth*."[60] Whenever he spoke of Isaac Luria, his whole body would tremble. He had marvelous dreams and revelations, yet always insisted that the study of Torah was his chief way of communing with God. He showed a remarkable understanding of the purpose of dreams in releasing buried intuition, however. As Rabbi Hayyim continues: "He used to say that God created sleep to this end only, that man should attain the insights that he cannot attain, even after much labor and effort, when the soul is joined to the body because the body is like a curtain dividing."[61]

There is not such a great gap between mysticism and rationalism as we tend to imagine. The Gaon of Vilna's remarks about sleep show a clear perception of the role of the unconscious: we have all urged friends to "sleep on" a problem in the hope of finding a solution that has eluded them in their waking hours. When our minds are receptive and relaxed, ideas come from the deeper region of the mind. This has also been the experience of such scientists as Archimedes, who discovered his famous Principle in the bath. A truly creative philosopher or scientist has, like the mystic, to confront the dark world of uncreated reality and the cloud of unknowing in the hope of piercing it. As long as they wrestle with logic and concepts, they are, necessarily, imprisoned in ideas or forms of thought that have already been established. Often their discoveries seem "given" from outside. They speak in terms of vision and inspiration. Thus Edward Gibbon (1737–94), who loathed religious enthusiasm, had what amounts to a moment of vision while musing among the ruins of the Capitol in Rome, which impelled him to write *The Decline and Fall of the Roman Empire*. Commenting on this experience, the twentieth-century historian Arnold Toynbee described it as a "communion": "he was directly aware of the passage of History gently flowing through him in a mighty current, and of his own life welling like a wave in the flow of a vast tide." Such a moment of inspiration, Toynbee concludes, is akin to the "experience that has been described as the Beatific Vision by souls to whom it has been vouchsafed."[62] Albert Einstein also claimed that mysticism was "the sower of all true art and science":

> To know that what is impenetrable to us really exists, manifesting itself to us as the highest wisdom and the most radiant beauty, which our dull faculties can comprehend only in their most primitive forms—this knowledge, this feeling, is at the center of all true religiousness. In this sense, and in this sense only, I belong to the ranks of devoutly religious men.[63]

In this sense, the religious enlightenment discovered by such mystics as the Besht can be seen as akin to some other achievements of the Age of Reason: it was enabling simpler men and women to make the imaginative transition to the New World of modernity.

During the 1780s, Rabbi Shneur Zalman of Lyaday (1745–1813) had not found the emotional exuberance of Hasidism alien to the intellectual quest. He founded a new form of Hasidism which attempted to blend mysticism with rational contemplation. It became known as the Habad, an acrostic of the three attributes of God: Hokhmah (Wisdom), Binah (Intelligence) and Da'at (Knowledge). Like earlier mystics who had amalgamated philosophy with spirituality, Zalman believed that metaphysical speculation was an essential preliminary to prayer because it revealed the limitations of the intellect. His technique started from the fundamental Hasidic vision of God present in all things and led the mystic, by a dialectical process, to realize that God was the *only* reality. Zalman explained: "From the standpoint of the Infinite, blessed be He, all the worlds are as if literally nothing and nihility."[64] The created world has no existence apart from God, its vital force. It is only because of our limited perceptions that it appears to exist separately, but this is an illusion. God, therefore, is not really a transcendent being who occupies an alternative sphere of reality: he is not external to the world. Indeed, the doctrine of God's transcendence is another illusion of our minds, which find it almost impossible to get beyond sense impressions. The mystical disciplines of Habad would help Jews to get beyond sensory perception to see things from God's point of view. To an unenlightened eye the world seems empty of God: the contemplation of Kabbalah will break down the rational boundaries to help us discover the God who is in the world around us.

Habad shared the Enlightenment confidence in the ability of the human mind to reach God but did so through the time-honored method of paradox and mystical concentration. Like the Besht, Zalman was convinced that *anybody* could attain the vision of God: Habad was not for an elite of mystics. Even if people seemed to lack spiritual talent, they could achieve enlightenment. It was hard work, however. As Rabbi Dov Baer of Lubavitch (1773–1827), Zalman's son, explained in his *Tract on Ecstasy*, one had to begin with a heartbreaking perception of inadequacy. Mere cerebral contemplation is not enough: it had to be accompanied by self-analysis, study of Torah and prayer. It was painful to give up our intellectual and imaginative prejudices about the world, and most people were deeply reluctant to give up their point of view. Once they had gone beyond this egotism, the Hasid would realize that there was no reality but God. Like the Sufi who had experienced *'fana*, the Hasid would achieve ecstasy. Baer explained that he would get beyond himself: "his whole being is so absorbed that nothing remains and he has no self-consciousness whatsoever."[65] The disciplines of Habad made Kabbalah a tool of psychological analysis and self-knowledge, teaching the Hasid to descend, sphere by sphere, ever more deeply into his inner world until he reached the center of himself. There he discovered the God that was the only true reality. The mind could discover God by the exercise of reason and imagination, but this would not be the objective God of the *philosophes* and such scientists as Newton, but a profoundly subjective reality inseparable from the self.

The seventeenth and eighteenth centuries had been a period of painful extremity and excitement of spirit which had mirrored the revolutionary turbulence of the political and social world. There had been nothing comparable in the Muslim world at this time, although this is difficult for a Western person to ascertain because eighteenth-century Islamic thought has not been much studied. It has generally been too easily dismissed by Western scholars as an uninteresting period, and it has been held that while Europe had an Enlightenment, Islam went into decline. Recently, however, this perspective has been challenged as being too simplistic. Even though the British had achieved control of India in 1767, the Muslim world was not yet fully aware of the unprecedented nature of the Western challenge. The Indian Sufi Shah Walli-Ullah of Delhi (1703–62) was perhaps the first to sense the new spirit. He was an impressive thinker who was suspicious of cultural universalism but believed that Muslims should unite to preserve their heritage. Even though he did not like the Shiah, he believed that Sunnis and Shiis should find common ground. He tried to reform the Shariah to make it more relevant to the new conditions of India. Walli-Ullah seemed to have had a presentiment of the consequences of colonialism: his son would lead a *jihad* against the British. His religious thought was more conservative, heavily dependent upon Ibn al-Arabi: man could not develop his full potential without God. Muslims were still happy to draw on the riches of the past in religious matters, and Walli-Ullah is an example of the power that Sufism could still inspire. In many parts of the world, however, Sufism had become somewhat decadent, and a new reforming movement in Arabia presaged the swing away from mysticism that would characterize the Muslim perception of God during the nineteenth century and the Islamic response to the challenge of the West.

Like the Christian reformers of the sixteenth century, Muhammad ibn al-Wahhab (d. 1784), a jurist of Najd in the Arabian peninsula, wanted to restore Islam to the purity of its beginnings and get rid of all later accretions. He was particularly hostile to mysticism. All suggestion of an incarnational theology was condemned, including devotion to Sufi saints and the Shii Imams. He even opposed the cult of the Prophet's tomb at Medina: no mere man, however illustrious, should distract attention from God. Al-Wahhab managed to convert Muhammad ibn Saud, ruler of a small principality in Central Arabia, and together they initiated a reform which was an attempt to reproduce the first *ummah* of the Prophet and his companions. They attacked the oppression of the poor, indifference to the plight of widows and orphans, immorality and idolatry. They also waged a *jihad* against their imperial masters the Ottomans, believing that Arabs, not Turks, should lead the Muslim peoples. They managed to wrest a sizable portion of the Hijaz from Ottoman control, which the Turks were not able to regain until 1818, but the new sect had seized the imagination of many people in the Islamic world. Pilgrims to Mecca had been impressed by this new piety, which seemed fresher and more vigorous than much current Sufism. During the nineteenth century, Wahhabism would become the dominant Islamic mood and Sufism increasingly marginalized and, consequently, even more bizarre and superstitious. Like Jews and Christians, Muslims were beginning to step back from the mystical ideal and adopt a more rationalistic type of piety.

In Europe a few people were beginning the trend away from God himself. In 1729 Jean Meslier, a country priest who had led an exemplary life, died an atheist. He left behind a memoir which was circulated by Voltaire. This expressed his disgust with humanity and his inability to believe in God. Newton's infinite space, Meslier believed, was the only eternal reality: nothing but matter existed. Religion was a device used by the rich to oppress the poor and render them powerless. Christianity was distinguished by its particularly ludicrous doctrines, such as the Trinity and the Incarnation. His denial of God was meat too strong even for the *philosophes*. Voltaire removed the specifically atheistic passages and transformed the abbé into a Deist. By the end of the century, however, there were a few philosophers who were proud to call themselves atheists, though they remained a tiny minority. This was an entirely new development. Hitherto "atheist" had been a term of abuse, a particularly nasty slur to hurl at your enemies. Now it was just beginning to be worn as a badge of pride. The Scottish philosopher David Hume (1711–1776) had taken the new empiricism to its logical conclusion. There was no need to go beyond a scientific explanation of reality and no philosophical reason for believing anything that lay beyond our sense experience. In the *Dialogues Concerning Natural Religion*, Hume disposed of the argument that purported to prove God's existence from the design of the universe, arguing that it rested on analogical arguments that were inconclusive. One might be able to argue that the order we discern in the natural world pointed to an intelligent Overseer, but how, then, to account for evil and the manifest disorder? There was no logical answer to this, and Hume, who had written the *Dialogues* in 1750, wisely left them unpublished. Some twelve months earlier, the French philosopher Denis Diderot (1713–84) had been imprisoned for asking the same question in *A Letter to the Blind for the Use of Those Who See*, which introduced a full-blown atheism to the general public.

Diderot himself denied that he was an atheist. He simply said that he did not care whether God existed or not. When Voltaire objected to his book, he replied: "I believe in God, although I live very well with the atheists. . . . It is . . . very important not to mistake hemlock for parsley; but to believe or not to believe in God is not important at all." With unerring accuracy, Diderot had put his finger on the essential point. Once "God" has ceased to be a passionately subjective experience, "he" does not exist. As Diderot pointed out in the same letter, it was pointless to believe in the God of the philosophers who never interferes with the affairs of the world. The Hidden God had become *Deus Otiosus*: "Whether God exists or does not exist, He has come to rank among the most sublime and useless truths."[66] He had come to the opposite conclusion to Pascal, who had seen the wager as of supreme importance and utterly impossible to ignore. In his *Pensées Philosophiques*, published in 1746, Diderot had dismissed Pascal's religious experience as too subjective: he and the Jesuits had both been passionately concerned with God but had very different ideas about him. How to choose between them? Such a "God" was nothing but *tempérament*. At this point, three years before the publication of *A Letter to the Blind*, Diderot did believe that science—and science alone—could refute atheism. He evolved an impressive new interpretation of the argument from design. Instead of examining the vast motion of the universe, he urged people to examine the underlying structure of nature. The organization of a seed, a butterfly or an insect was too intricate to have happened by accident. In the *Pensées* Diderot still believed that reason could prove the existence of God. Newton had got rid of all the superstition and foolishness of religion: a God who worked miracles was on a par with the goblins with which we frighten our children.

Three years later, however, Diderot had come to question Newton and was no longer convinced that the external world provided any evidence for God. He saw clearly that God had nothing whatever to do with the new science. But he could only express this revolutionary and inflammatory thought in fictional terms. In *A Letter to the Blind*, Diderot imagined an argument between a Newtonian, whom he called "Mr. Holmes," and Nicholas Saunderson (1682–1739), the late Cambridge mathematician who had lost his sight as a baby. Diderot makes Saunderson ask Holmes how the argument from design could be reconciled with such "monsters" and accidents as himself, who demonstrated anything but intelligent and benevolent planning:

> What is this world, Mr. Holmes, but a complex, subject to cycles of change, all of which show a continual tendency to destruction: a rapid succession of beings that appear one by one, flourish and disappear; a merely transitory symmetry and a momentary appearance of order.[67]

The God of Newton, and indeed of many conventional Christians, who was supposed to be literally responsible for everything that happens, was not only an absurdity but a horrible idea. To introduce "God" to explain things that we cannot explain at present was a failure of humility. "My good friend, Mr. Holmes," Diderot's Saunderson concludes, "admit your ignorance."

In Diderot's view there was no need of a Creator. Matter was not the passive, ignoble stuff that Newton and the Protestants imagined, but had its own dynamic which obeys its own laws. It is this law of matter—not a Divine Mechanick—which is responsible for the apparent design we think we see. Nothing but matter existed. Diderot had taken Spinoza one step further. Instead of saying that there was no God but nature, Diderot had claimed that there was only nature and no God at all. He was not alone in his belief: scientists such as Abraham Trembley and John Turbeville Needham had discovered the principle of generative matter, which was now surfacing as an hypothesis in biology, microscopy, zoology, natural history and geology. Few were prepared to make a final break with God, however. Even the philosophers who frequented the salon of Paul Heinrich, Baron of Holbach (1723–89), did not publicly espouse atheism, though they enjoyed open and frank discussion. From these debates came Holbach's book *The System of Nature: or Laws of the Moral and Physical World* (1770), which became known as the bible of atheistic materialism. There was no supernatural alternative to nature, which, Holbach argued, was "but an immense chain of causes and effects which unceasingly flow from one another."[68] To believe in a God was dishonest and a denial of our true experience. It was also an act of despair. Religion created gods because people could not find any other explanation to console them for the tragedy of life in this world. They turned to the imaginary comforts of religion and philosophy in an attempt to establish some illusory sense of control, trying to propitiate an "agency" they imagine lurking behind the scenes to ward off terror and disaster. Aristotle had been wrong: philosophy was not the result of a noble desire for knowledge but of the craven longing to avoid pain. The cradle of religion, therefore, was ignorance and fear, and a mature, enlightened man must climb out of it.

Holbach attempted his own history of God. First men had worshipped the forces of nature. This primitive animism had been acceptable because it had not tried to get beyond this world. The rot had set in when people had started to personify the sun, wind and sea to create gods in their own image and likeness. Finally they had merged all these godlings into one big Deity, which was nothing but a projection and a mass of contradictions. Poets and theologians had done nothing over the centuries but

> make a gigantic, exaggerated man, whom they will render illusory by dint of heaping together incompatible qualities. Human beings will never see in God, but a being of the human species, in whom they will strive to aggrandize the proportions, until they have formed a being totally inconceivable.

History shows that it is impossible to reconcile the so-called goodness of God with his omnipotence. Because it lacks coherence, the idea of God is bound to disintegrate. The philosophers and scientists have done their best to save it but they have fared no better than the poets and theologians. The *"hautes perfections"* that Descartes claimed to have proved were simply the product of his imagination. Even the great Newton was "a slave to the prejudices of his infancy." He had discovered absolute space and created a God out of the void who was simply *"un homme puissant,"* a divine despot terrorizing his human creators and reducing them to the condition of slaves.[69]

Fortunately the Enlightenment would enable humanity to rid itself of this infantilism. Science would replace religion. "If the ignorance of nature gave birth to the Gods, the knowledge of nature is calculated to destroy them."[70] There are no higher truths or underlying patterns, no grand design. There is only nature itself;

> Nature is not a work; she has always been self-existent; it is in her bosom that everything is operated; she is an immense laboratory, provided with the materials, and who makes the instruments of which she avails herself to act. All her works are the effects of her

own energy, and of those agents or causes which she makes, which she contains, which she puts in action.[71]

God was not merely unnecessary but positively harmful. By the end of the century, Pierre-Simon de Laplace (1749–1827) had ejected God from physics. The planetary system had become a luminosity extending from the sun, which was gradually cooling. When Napoleon asked him: "Who was the author of this?" Laplace simply replied: "*Je n'avais pas besoin de cette hypothèse-là.*"

For centuries monotheists in each of the God-religions had insisted that God was not merely another being. He did not exist like the other phenomena we experience. In the West, however, Christian theologians had got into the habit of talking about God as though he really *were* one of the things that existed. They had seized upon the new science to prove the objective reality of God as though he could be tested and analyzed like anything else. Diderot, Holbach and Laplace had turned this attempt on its head and come to the same conclusion as the more extreme mystics: there was nothing out there. It was not long before other scientists and philosophers triumphantly declared that God was dead.

10

The Death of God?

B Y THE BEGINNING of the nineteenth century, atheism was definitely on the agenda. The advances in science and technology were creating a new spirit of autonomy and independence which led some to declare their independence of God. This was the century in which Ludwig Feuerbach, Karl Marx, Charles Darwin, Friedrich Nietzsche and Sigmund Freud forged philosophies and scientific interpretations of reality which had no place for God. Indeed, by the end of the century, a significant number of people were beginning to feel that if God was not yet dead, it was the duty of rational, emancipated human beings to kill him. The idea of God which had been fostered for centuries in the Christian West now appeared disastrously inadequate, and the Age of Reason seemed to have triumphed over centuries of superstition and bigotry. Or had it? The West had now seized the initiative, and its activities would have fateful consequences for Jews and Muslims, who would be forced to review their own position. Many of the ideologies which rejected the idea of God made good sense. The anthropomorphic, personal God of Western Christendom was vulnerable. Appalling crimes had been committed in his name. Yet his demise was not experienced as a joyous liberation but attended by doubt, dread and, in some cases, agonizing conflict. Some people tried to save God by evolving new theologies to free him from the inhibiting systems of empirical thought, but atheism had come to stay.

There was also a reaction against the cult of reason. The poets, novelists and philosophers of the Romantic movement pointed out that a thoroughgoing rationalism was reductive, because it left out the imaginative and intuitive activities of the human spirit. Some reinterpreted dogmas and mysteries of Christianity in a secular way. This reconstituted theology translated the old themes of hell and heaven, rebirth and redemption into an idiom that made them intellectually acceptable to the post-Enlightenment, depriving them of their association with a supernatural Reality "out there." One of the themes of this "natural supernaturalism," as the American literary critic M. R. Abrams has called it,[1] was that of the creative imagination. This was seen as a faculty that could engage with external reality in such a way as to create a new truth. The English poet John Keats (1795–1821) put it succinctly: "The imagination is like Adam's dream—he awoke and found it truth." He was referring to the story of the creation of Eve in Milton's *Paradise Lost*, when, after dreaming of an as yet uncreated reality, Adam had woken to find it in the woman confronting him. In the same letter, Keats had written of the imagination as a sacred faculty: "I am certain of nothing but of the holiness of the heart's affections and the truth of the imagination—what the imagination seizes as beauty must be truth—whether it existed before or not."[2] Reason had only a limited role in this creative process. Keats also described a state of mind which he called "Negative Capability," "when a man is capable of being in uncertainties, mysteries, doubts, without any irritable reaching after fact and reason."[3] Like a mystic, the poet had to transcend reason and hold himself in an attitude of silent waiting.

Medieval mystics had described the experience of God in rather the same way. Ibn al-Arabi had even spoken of the imagination creating its own experience of the uncreated reality of God in the depths of the self. Although Keats was critical of William Wordsworth (1770–1850), who had pioneered the Romantic movement in England with Samuel Taylor Coleridge (1772–1834), they shared a similar vision of the imagination. Wordsworth's best poetry celebrated the alliance of the human mind and the natural world, which acted and reacted upon one another to create vision and meaning.[4] Wordsworth was himself a mystic whose experiences of nature were similar to the experience of God. In the *Lines Composed a Few Miles above Tintern Abbey*, he described the receptive state of mind that resulted in an ecstatic vision of reality:

> that blessed mood
> In which the burthen of the mystery,
> In which the heavy and the weary weight
> Of all this unintelligible world,
> Is lightened: that serene and blessed mood

In which the affections gently lead us on,—
Until, the breath of this corporeal frame
And even the motion of our human blood
Almost suspended, we are laid asleep
In body, and become a living soul:
While, with an eye made quiet by the power
Of harmony, and the deep power of joy,
We see into the life of things.[5]

This vision came from the heart and the affections rather than what Wordsworth called "the meddling intellect" whose purely analytic powers could destroy this kind of intuition. People did not need learned books and theories. All that was required was a "wise passiveness" and "a heart that watches and receives."[6] Insight began with a subjective experience, although this had to be "wise," not uninformed and self-indulgent. As Keats would say, a truth did not become true until it was felt upon the pulse and carried alive into the heart by passion.

Wordsworth had discerned a 'spirit' which was at one and the same time immanent in and distinct from natural phenomena:

A presence that disturbs me with the joy
Of elevated thoughts; a sense sublime
Of something far more deeply interfused
Whose dwelling is the light of setting suns,
And the round ocean and the living air,
And the blue sky, and in the mind of man:
A motion and a spirit, that impels
All thinking things, all objects of all thought
And rolls through all things.[7]

Philosophers such as Hegel would find such a spirit in the events of history. Wordsworth was careful not to give this experience a conventionally religious interpretation, though he was quite happy to talk about "God" on other occasions, especially in an ethical context.[8] English Protestants were not familiar with the God of the mystics, which had been discounted by the Reformers. God spoke through the conscience in the summons of duty; he corrected the desires of the heart but seemed to have little in common with the "presence" that Wordsworth had felt in Nature. Always concerned with accuracy of expression, Wordsworth would only call it "something," a word which is often used as a substitute for exact definition. Wordsworth used it to describe the spirit which, with true mystical agnosticism, he refused to name because it did not fit into any of the categories he knew.

Another mystical poet of the period sounded a more apocalyptic note and announced that God was dead. In his early poetry, William Blake (1757–1827) had used a dialectical method: terms such as "innocence" and "experience," which seemed diametrically opposed to one another, were discovered to be half-truths of a more complex reality. Blake had transformed the balanced antithesis, which had characterized the rhymed couplets of poetry during the Age of Reason in England, into a method of forging a personal and subjective vision. In *Songs of Innocence and Experience*, two contrary states of the human soul are both revealed to be inadequate until they are synthesized: innocence must become experience and experience itself fall to the lowest depths before the recovery of true innocence. The poet has become a prophet, "Who Present, Past, & Future, sees" and who listens to the Holy Word that spoke to humanity in primordial time:

> Calling the lapsèd Soul,
> And weeping in the evening dew
> That might controll
> The starry pole,
> And fallen, fallen, light renew.[9]

Like the Gnostics and Kabbalists, Blake envisaged a state of absolute fallenness. There could be no true vision until human beings recognized their lapsed condition. Like these earlier mystics, Blake was using the idea of an original fall to symbolize a process that is continuously present in the mundane reality about us.

Blake had rebelled against the vision of the Enlightenment, which had attempted to systematize truth. He had also rebelled against the God of Christianity, who had been used to alienate men and women from their humanity. This God had been made to promulgate unnatural laws to repress sexuality, liberty and spontaneous joy. Blake railed against the "fearful symmetry" of this inhumane God in "The Tyger," seeing him as remote from the world in unutterably "distant deeps and skies." Yet the wholly other God, Creator of the World, undergoes mutation in the poems. God himself has to fall into the world and die in the person of Jesus.[10] He even becomes Satan, the enemy of mankind. Like the Gnostics, Kabbalists and early Trinitarians, Blake envisaged a *kenosis*, a self-emptying in the Godhead, who falls from his solitary heaven and becomes incarnate in the world. There is no longer an autonomous deity in a world of his own, who demands that men and women submit to an external, heteronymous law. There is no human activity which is alien to God; even the sexuality repressed by the Church is manifest in the passion of Jesus himself. God has died voluntarily in Jesus and the transcendent, alienating God is no more. When the death of God is complete, the Human Face Divine will appear:

> Jesus said; "Wouldst thou love one who never died
> For thee, or ever die for one who had not died for thee?
> And if God dieth not for Man & giveth not himself
> Eternally for Man, Man could not exist; for Man is Love
> As God is Love: every kindness to another is a little Death
> In the Divine Image, nor can Man exist but by brotherhood.[11]

Blake rebelled against the institutional churches, but some theologians were attempting to incorporate the Romantic vision into official Christianity. They also found the idea of a remote transcendent God both abhorrent and irrelevant, stressing instead the importance of subjective religious experience. In 1799, the year after Wordsworth and Coleridge had published the *Lyrical Ballads* in England, Friedrich Schleiermacher (1768–1834) published *On Religion, Speeches to its Cultured Despisers*, his own Romantic manifesto, in Germany. Dogmas were not divine facts but simply "accounts of the Christian religious affections set forth in speech."[12] Religious faith could not be confined to the propositions of the creeds: it involved an emotional apprehension and an interior surrender. Thought and reason had their place, but they could only take us so far. When we had come to the limit of reason, feeling would complete the journey to the Absolute. When he spoke of "feeling," Schleiermacher did not mean a sloppy emotionalism but an intuition which drove men and women toward the infinite. Feeling was not opposed to human reason but an imaginative leap that takes us beyond the particular to an apprehension of the whole. The sense of God thus acquired arose from the depths of each individual rather than a collision with an objective Fact.

Western theology had tended to overemphasize the importance of rationality ever since Thomas Aquinas, a tendency which had increased since the Reformation. Schleiermacher's romantic theology was an attempt to redress the balance. He made it clear that feeling was not an end in itself and could not provide a complete explanation of religion. Reason and feeling both pointed beyond themselves to an indescribable Reality. Schleiermacher defined the essence of religion as "the feeling of absolute dependence."[13] This, as we shall see, was an attitude that would become anathema to progressive thinkers during the nineteenth century, but Schleiermacher did not mean an abject servility before God. In context, the phrase refers to the sense of reverence that arises in us when we contemplate the mystery of life. This attitude of awe sprang from that universal human experience of the numinous. The prophets of Israel had experienced this as a profound shock when they had their visions of holiness. Romantics such as Wordsworth had felt a similar reverence and sense of dependence upon the spirit they encountered in nature. Schleiermacher's distinguished pupil Rudolf Otto would explore this experience in his important book *The Idea of the Holy*, showing that when human beings are confronted with this transcendence, they no longer feel that they are the alpha and omega of existence.

At the end of his life, Schleiermacher felt that he might have overemphasized the importance of feeling and subjectivity. He was aware that Christianity was beginning to seem an outmoded creed: some Christian doctrines were misleading and made the faith vulnerable to the new skepticism. The doctrine of the Trinity, for example, seemed to suggest that there were three gods. Schleiermacher's disciple Albrecht Ritschl (1822–89) saw the doctrine as a flagrant instance of Hellenization. It had corrupted the Christian message by introducing an alien "layer of metaphysical concepts, derived from the natural philosophy of the Greeks," having nothing at all to do with the pristine Christian experience.[14] Yet Schleiermacher and Ritschl had failed to see that each generation had to create its own imaginative conception of God, just as each Romantic poet had to experience truth upon his own pulse. The Greek Fathers were simply trying to make the Semitic concept of God work for them by expressing it in terms of their own culture. As the West entered the modern technical age, the older ideas of God would prove inadequate. Yet right up to the end, Schleiermacher insisted that religious emotion was not opposed to reason. On his deathbed he said: "I must think the deepest, speculative thoughts, and they are to me completely at one with the most intimate religious sensations."[15] Concepts about God were useless unless they were imaginatively transformed by feeling and personal religious experience.

During the nineteenth century, one major philosopher after another rose to challenge the traditional view of God, at least the "God" who prevailed in the West. They were particularly offended by the notion of a supernatural deity "out there" which had an objective existence. We have seen that though the idea of God as the Supreme Being had gained ascendancy in the West, other monotheistic traditions had gone out of their way to separate themselves from this type of theology. Jews, Muslims and Orthodox Christians had all insisted in their different ways that our human idea of God did not correspond to the ineffable reality of which it was a mere symbol. All had suggested, at one time or another, that it was more accurate to describe God as "Nothing" rather than the Supreme Being, since "he" did not exist in any way that we could conceive. Over the centuries, the West had gradually lost sight of this more imaginative conception of God. Catholics and Protestants had come to regard "him" as a Being who was another reality added on to the world we know, overseeing our activities like a celestial Big Brother. Not surprisingly, this notion of God was quite unacceptable to many people in the postrevolutionary world, since it seemed to condemn human beings to an ignoble servitude and an unworthy dependence that was incompatible with human dignity. The atheistic philosophers of the nineteenth century rebelled against this God with good reason. Their criticisms inspired many of their contemporaries to do the same; they seemed to be saying something entirely new, yet when they addressed themselves to the question of "God," they often unconsciously reiterated old insights by other monotheists in the past.

Thus Georg Wilhelm Hegel (1770–1831) evolved a philosophy which was in some respects strikingly similar to Kabbalah. This was ironic, since he regarded Judaism as an ignoble religion which was responsible for the primitive conception of God that had perpetrated great wrong. The Jewish God in Hegel's view was a tyrant who required unquestioning submission to an intolerable Law. Jesus had tried to liberate men and women from this base servitude, but Christians had fallen into the same trap as the Jews and promoted the idea of a divine Despot. It was now time to cast this barbaric deity aside and evolve a more enlightened view of the human condition. Hegel's highly inaccurate view of Judaism, based on the New Testament polemic, was a new type of metaphysical anti-Semitism. Like Kant, Hegel regarded Judaism as an example of everything that was wrong with religion. In *The Phenomenology of Mind* (1807), he substituted the idea of a Spirit which was the life force of the world for the conventional deity. Yet as in Kabbalah, the Spirit was willing to suffer limitation and exile in order to achieve true spirituality and self-consciousness. As in Kabbalah again, the Spirit was dependent upon the world and upon human beings for its fulfillment. Hegel had thus asserted the old monotheistic insight—characteristic also of Christianity and Islam—that "God" was not separate from mundane reality, an optional extra in a world of his own, but was inextricably bound up with humanity. Like Blake, he expressed this insight dialectically, seeing humanity and Spirit, finite and infinite, as two halves of a single truth which are mutually interdependent and involved in the same process of self-realization. Instead of pacifying a distant deity by observing an alien, unwanted Law, Hegel had in effect declared that the divine was a dimension of our humanity. Indeed, Hegel's view of the *kenosis* of the Spirit, which empties itself to become immanent and incarnate in the world, has much in common with the Incarnational theologies that have developed in all three faiths.

Hegel was a man of the Enlightenment as well as a Romantic, however, and he therefore valued reason more than the imagination. Again, he unwittingly echoed the insights of the past. Like the Faylasufs, he saw reason and philosophy as superior to religion, which was stuck in representational modes of thought. Like the Faylasufs again, Hegel drew his conclusions about the Absolute from the working of the individual mind, which he described as caught up in a dialectical process which mirrored the whole.

His philosophy seemed ludicrously optimistic to Arthur Schopenhauer (1788–1860), who had defiantly scheduled his lectures at the same time as Hegel's in Berlin in 1819, the year of the publication of his book *The World as Will and Idea*. There was, Schopenhauer believed, no Absolute, no Reason, no God, no Spirit at work in the world: nothing but brute instinctive will to live. This bleak vision appealed to the darker spirits of the Romantic movement. It did not discount all the insights of religion, however. Schopenhauer believed that Hinduism and Buddhism (and those Christians who had asserted that everything was vanity) had arrived at a just conception of reality when they had claimed that every thing in the world was an illusion. Since there was no "God" to save us, only art, music and a discipline of renunciation and compassion could bring us a measure of serenity. Schopenhauer had no time for Judaism and Islam, which had in his view an absurdly simplistic and purposive view of history. In this he proved prescient: we shall see that in our own century, Jews and Muslims have found that their old view of history as a theophany is no longer tenable in the same way. Many can no longer subscribe to a God who is Lord of History. But Schopenhauer's view of salvation was close to Jewish and Muslim perceptions that individuals must create a sense of ultimate meaning for themselves. It had nothing in common with the Protestant conception of the absolute sovereignty of God, which meant that men and women could contribute nothing toward their own salvation but were entirely dependent upon a deity outside themselves.

These old doctrines about God were increasingly condemned as flawed and inadequate. The Danish philosopher Søren Kierkegaard (1813–55) insisted that the old creeds and doctrines had become idols, ends in themselves and substitutes for the ineffable reality of God. True Christian faith was a leap out of the world, away from these fossilized human beliefs and outmoded attitudes, into the unknown. Others, however, wanted to root humanity in this world and to cut off the notion of a Great Alternative. The German philosopher Ludwig Andreas Feuerbach (1804–72) argued that God was simply a human projection in his influential book *The Essence of Christianity* (1841). The idea of God had alienated us from our own nature by positing an impossible perfection over against our human frailty. Thus God was infinite, man finite; God almighty, man weak; God holy, man sinful. Feuerbach had put his finger on an essential weakness in the Western tradition which had always been perceived as a danger in monotheism. The kind of projection which pushes God outside the human condition can result in the creation of an idol. Other traditions had found various ways of countering this danger, but in the West it was unfortunately true that the idea of God had become increasingly externalized and had contributed to a very negative conception of human nature. There had been an emphasis on guilt and sin, struggle and strain in the religion of God in the West ever since Augustine, which was alien, for example, to Greek Orthodox theology. It is not surprising that philosophers such as Feuerbach or Auguste Comte (1798–1857), who had a more positive view of humanity, wanted to get rid of this deity which had caused widespread lack of confidence in the past.

Atheism had always been a rejection of a current conception of the divine. Jews and Christians had been called "atheists" because they denied pagan notions of divinity, even though they had faith in a God. The new atheists of the nineteenth century were inveighing against the particular conception of God current in the West rather than other notions of the divine. Thus Karl Marx (1818–1883) saw religion as "the sigh of the oppressed creature . . . the *opium* of the people, which made this suffering bearable."[16] Even though he adopted a Messianic view of history that was heavily dependent upon the Judeo-Christian tradition, he dismissed God as irrelevant. Since there was no meaning, value or purpose outside the historical process, the idea of God could not help humanity. Atheism, the negation of God, was also a waste of time. Yet "God" was vulnerable to the Marxist critique, since he had often been used by the establishment to approve a social order in which the rich man sat in his palace while the poor man sat at its gate. This was not true of the whole of monotheistic religion, however. A God who condoned social injustice would have appalled Amos, Isaiah or Muhammad, who had used the idea of God to quite different ends that were quite close to the Marxist ideal.

Similarly, the literal understanding of God and scripture made the faith of many Christians vulnerable to the scientific discoveries of the period. Charles Lyell's *Principles of Geology* (1830–33), which revealed the vast perspectives of geological time, and Charles Darwin's *The Origin of Species* (1859), which put forward the evolutionary hypothesis, seemed to contradict the biblical account of creation in Genesis. Since Newton, creation had been central to much Western understanding of God, and people had lost sight of the fact that the biblical story had never been intended as a literal account of the physical origins of the universe. Indeed, the doctrine of creation *ex nihilo* had long been problematic and had entered Judaism and Christianity relatively late; in Islam the creation of the world by al-Lah is taken for granted, but there is no detailed discussion of how this happened. Like all other Koranic speech about God, the doctrine of creation is only a "parable," a sign or a symbol. Monotheists in all three religions had regarded the creation as a myth, in the most positive sense of the word: it was a symbolic account which helped men and women to cultivate a particular religious attitude. Some Jews and Muslims had deliberately created imaginative interpretations of the creation story that departed radically from any literal sense. But in the West there had been a tendency to regard the Bible as factually true in every detail. Many people had come to see God as literally and physically responsible for everything that happens on earth, in rather the same way as we ourselves make things or set events in motion.

There were, however, a significant number of Christians who saw immediately that Darwin's discoveries were by no means fatal to the idea of God. In the main, Christianity has been able to adapt to the evolutionary theory, and Jews and Muslims have never been as seriously disturbed by the new scientific discoveries about the origins of life: their worries about God have, generally speaking, sprung from quite a different source, as we shall see. It is true, however, that as Western secularism has spread, it has inevitably affected members of other faiths. The literalistic view of God is still prevalent, and many people in the Western world—of all persuasions—take it for granted that modern cosmology has dealt a death-blow to the idea of God.

Throughout history people have discarded a conception of God when it no longer works for them. Sometimes this has taken the form of a violent iconoclasm, as when the ancient Israelites had torn down the shrines of the Canaanites or when the prophets railed against the gods of their pagan neighbors. In 1882 Friedrich Nietzsche resorted to similarly violent tactics when he proclaimed that God was dead. He announced this cataclysmic event in the parable of the madman who ran into the marketplace one morning, crying, "I seek God! I seek God!" When the supercilious bystanders asked where he imagined God had gone—had he run away, perhaps, or emigrated?—the madman glared at them. " 'Where has God gone?' he called out. 'I mean to tell you. We have killed him,—you and I! We are all his murderers!' " An unimaginable but irreversible event had torn mankind from its roots, thrown the earth off course and cast it adrift in a pathless universe. Everything that had previously given human beings a sense of direction had vanished. The death of God would lead to unparalleled despair and panic. "Is there still an above and below?" cried the madman in his anguish. "Do we not stray, as though through an infinite nothingness?"[17]

Nietzsche realized that there had been a radical shift in the consciousness of the West which would make it increasingly difficult to believe in the phenomenon most people described as "God." Not only had our science made such notions as the literal understanding of creation an impossibility, but our greater control and power made the idea of a divine overseer unacceptable. People felt that they were witnessing a new dawn. Nietzsche's madman insisted that the death of God would bring about a newer, higher phase of human history. To become worthy of their deicide, human beings would have to become gods themselves. In *Thus Spake Zarathustra* (1883), Nietzsche proclaimed the birth of the Superman who would replace God; the new enlightened man would declare war upon the old Christian values, trample upon the base mores of the rabble and herald a new, powerful humanity which would have none of the feeble Christian virtues of love and pity. He also turned to the ancient myth of perpetual recurrence and rebirth, found in such religions as Buddhism. Now that God was dead, this world could take his place as the supreme value. Whatever goes comes back; whatever dies blooms again; whatever breaks is joined anew. Our world could be revered as eternal and divine, attributes that had once applied only to the distant, transcendent God.

The Christian God, Nietzsche taught, was pitiable, absurd and "a crime against life."[18] He had encouraged people to fear their bodies, their passions and their sexuality and had promoted a puling morality of compassion which had made us weak. There was no ultimate meaning or value and human beings had no business offering an indulgent alternative in "God." Again, it must be said that the Western God was vulnerable to this critique. He had been used to alienate people from their humanity and from sexual passion by means of a life-denying asceticism. He had also been made into a facile panacea and an alternative to life here below.

Sigmund Freud (1856–1939) certainly regarded belief in God as an illusion that mature men and women should lay aside. The idea of God was not a lie but a device of the unconscious which needed to be decoded by psychology. A personal god was nothing more than an exalted father-figure: desire for such a deity sprang from infantile yearnings for a power-ful, protective father, for justice and fairness and for life to go on forever. God is simply a projection of these desires, feared and worshipped by human beings out of an abiding sense of helplessness. Religion belonged to the infancy of the human race; it had been a necessary stage in the transition from childhood to maturity. It had promoted ethical values which were essential to society. Now that humanity had come of age, however, it should be left behind. Science, the new *logos*, could take God's place. It could provide a new basis for morality and help us to face our fears. Freud was emphatic about his faith in science, which seemed almost religious in its intensity: "No, our science is not an illusion! An illusion it would be to suppose that what science cannot give we can get else-where."[19]

Not all psychoanalysts agreed with Freud's view of God. Alfred Adler (1870–1937) allowed that God was a projection but believed that it had been helpful to humanity; it had been a brilliant and effective symbol of excellence. C. G. Jung's (1875–1961) God was similar to the God of the mystics, a psychological truth, subjectively experienced by each individ-ual. When asked by John Freeman in the famous *Face to Face* interview whether he believed in God, Jung replied emphatically: "I do not have to believe. I *know!*" Jung's continued faith suggests that a subjective God, mysteriously identified with the ground of being in the depths of the self, can survive psychoanalytic science in a way that a more personal, anthropomorphic deity who can indeed encourage perpetual immaturity may not.

Like many other Western people, Freud seemed unaware of this inter-nalized, subjective God. Nevertheless he made a valid and perceptive point when he insisted that it would be dangerous to attempt to abolish religion. People must outgrow God in their own good time: to force them into atheism or secularism before they were ready could lead to an unhealthy denial and repression. We have seen that iconoclasm can spring from a buried anxiety and projection of our own fears onto the "other." Some of the atheists who wanted to abolish God certainly showed signs of strain. Thus, despite his advocacy of a compassionate ethic, Schopenhauer could not cope with human beings and became a recluse who communicated only with his poodle, Atman. Nietzsche was a tenderhearted, lonely man, plagued by ill health, who was very different from his Superman. Eventually he went mad. He did not abandon God joyously, as the ecstasy of his prose might lead us to imagine. In a poem delivered "after much trembling, quivering and self-contortion," he makes Zarathustra plead with God to return:

> No! come back,
> With all your torments!
> Oh come back
> To the last of all solitaries!
> All the streams of my tears
> Run their course for you!
> And the last flame of my heart—
> It burns up to *you*!
> Oh come back
> My unknown God! My pain! my last—happiness.[20]

Like Hegel's, Nietzsche's theories were used by a later generation of Germans to justify the policies of National Socialism, a reminder that an atheistic ideology can lead to just as cruel a crusading ethic as the idea of "God."

God had always been a struggle in the West. His demise was also attended by strain, desolation and dismay. Thus in *In Memoriam*, the great Victorian poem of doubt, Alfred Lord Tennyson recoiled in horror from the prospect of a purposeless, indifferent nature, red in tooth and claw. Published in 1850, nine years before the publication of *The Origin of Species*, the poem shows that Tennyson had already felt his faith crumbling and himself reduced to

> An infant crying in the night;
> An infant crying for the light
> And with no language but a cry.[21]

In "Dover Beach," Matthew Arnold had lamented the inexorable with-drawal of the sea of faith, which left mankind wandering on a darkling plain. The doubt and dismay had spread to the Orthodox world, though the denial of God did not take on the precise lineaments of Western doubt but was more in the nature of a denial of ultimate meaning. Fyodor Dostoyevsky, whose novel *The Brothers Karamazov* (1880) can be seen to describe the death of God, articulated his own conflict between faith and belief in a letter to a friend, written in March 1854:

> I look upon myself as a child of the age, a child of unbelief and doubt; it is probable, nay, I know for certain, that I shall remain so to my dying day. I have been tortured with longing to believe—am so, indeed, even now; and the yearning grows stronger the more cogent the intellectual difficulties that stand in the way.[22]

His novel is similarly ambivalent. Ivan, described as an atheist by the other characters (who attribute to him the now famous maxim: "If God does not exist, all is permitted"), says unequivocally that he does believe in God. Yet he does not find this God acceptable, since he fails to provide ultimate meaning for the tragedy of life. Ivan is not troubled by evolutionary theory but by the suffering of humanity in history: the death of a single child is too high a price to pay for the religious perspective that all will be well. We shall see later in this chapter that Jews would come to the same conclusion. On the other hand, it is the saintly Alyosha who admits that he does not believe in God—an admission that seems to burst from him unawares, escaping from some uncharted reach of his unconscious. Ambivalence and an obscure sense of dereliction have continued to haunt the literature of the twentieth century, with its imagery of wasteland and of humanity waiting for a Godot who never comes.

There was a similar malaise and disquiet in the Muslim world, though it sprang from quite a different source. By the end of the nineteenth century, the *mission civilisatrice* of Europe was well under way. The French had colonized Algiers in 1830, and in 1839 the British colonized Aden. Between them they took over Tunisia (1881), Egypt (1882), the Sudan (1898) and Libya and Morocco (1912). In 1920, Britain and France carved up the Middle East between them into protectorates and mandates. This colonial project only made a more silent process of Westernization official, since Europeans had been establishing a cultural and economic hegemony during the nineteenth century in the name of modernization. Technicalized Europe had become the leading power and was taking over the world. Trading posts and consular missions had been established in Turkey and the Middle East which had undermined the traditional structure of these societies long before there was actual Western rule. This was an entirely new kind of colonization. When the Moghuls had conquered India, the Hindu population had absorbed many Muslim elements into its own culture, but eventually the indigenous culture had made a comeback. The new colonial order transformed the lives of the subject people permanently, establishing a polity of dependence.

It was impossible for the colonized lands to catch up. Old institutions had been fatally undermined, and Muslim society was itself divided between those who had become "Westernized" and the "others." Some Muslims came to accept the European assessment of them as "Orientals," lumped indiscriminately with Hindus and Chinese. Some looked down on their more traditional countrymen. In Iran, Shah Nasiruddin (1848–96) insisted that he despised his subjects. What had been a living civilization with its own identity and integrity was gradually being transformed into a bloc of dependent states that were inadequate copies of an alien world. Innovation had been the essence of the modernizing process in Europe and the United States: it could not be achieved by imitation. Today anthropologists who study modernized countries or cities in the Arab world such as Cairo point out that the architecture and plan of the city reflects domination rather than progress.[23]

On their side Europeans had come to believe that their culture was not only superior at the present time but had always been in the van of progress. They often displayed a superb ignorance of world history. Indians, Egyptians and Syrians had to be Westernized for their own good. The colonial attitude was expressed by Evelyn Baring, Lord Cromer, consul general in Egypt from 1883 to 1907:

> Sir Alfred Lyall once said to me: "Accuracy is abhorrent to the Oriental mind. Every Anglo-Indian should always remember that maxim." Want of accuracy, which easily degenerates into untruthfulness, is in fact the main characteristic of the Oriental mind.
>
> The European is a close reasoner; his statements of fact are devoid of ambiguity; he is a natural logician, albeit he may not have studied logic; he is by nature sceptical and requires proof before he can accept the truth of any proposition; his trained intelligence works like a piece of mechanism. The mind of the Oriental, on the other hand, like his picturesque streets, is eminently wanting in symmetry.

His reasoning is of the most slipshod description. Although the ancient Arabs acquired in a somewhat higher degree the science of dialectics, their descendants are singularly deficient in the logical faculty. They are often incapable of drawing the most obvious conclusions from any simple premises of which they may admit the truth.[24]

One of the "problems" that had to be overcome was Islam. A negative image of the Prophet Muhammad and his religion had developed in Christendom at the time of the Crusades and had persisted alongside the anti-Semitism of Europe. During the colonial period, Islam was viewed as a fatalistic religion that was chronically opposed to progress. Lord Cromer, for example, decried the efforts of the Egyptian reformer Muhammad Abduh, arguing that it was impossible for "Islam" to reform itself.

Muslims had little time or energy to develop their understanding of God in the traditional way. They were engaged in a struggle to catch up with the West. Some saw Western secularism as the answer, but what was positive and invigorating in Europe could only seem alien and foreign in the Islamic world, since it had not developed naturally from their own tradition in its own time. In the West, "God" was seen as the voice of alienation; in the Muslim world it was the colonial process. Cut off from the roots of their culture, people felt disoriented and lost. Some Muslim reformers tried to hasten the cause of progress by forcibly relegating Islam to a minor role. The results were not at all as they had expected. In the new nation-state of Turkey, which had emerged after the defeat of the Ottoman empire in 1917, Mustafa Kemal (1881–1938), later known as Kemal Atatürk, tried to transform his country into a Western nation: he disestablished Islam, making religion a purely private affair. Sufi orders were abolished and went underground; the *madrasahs* were closed and the state training of the *ulema* ceased. This secularizing policy was symbolized by the banning of the fez, which reduced the visibility of the religious classes and was also a psychological attempt to force the people into a Western uniform: "to put on the hat" instead of the fez came to mean "to Europeanize." Reza Khan, Shah of Iran from 1925 to 1941, admired Atatürk and attempted a similar policy: the veil was banned; mullahs were forced to shave and wear the kepi instead of the traditional turban; the traditional celebrations in honor of the Shii Imam and martyr Husayn were forbidden.

Freud had wisely seen that any enforced repression of religion could only be destructive. Like sexuality, religion is a human need that affects life at every level. If suppressed, the results are likely to be as explosive and destructive as any severe sexual repression. Muslims regarded the new Turkey and Iran with suspicion and fascination. In Iran there was already an established tradition whereby the mullahs opposed the shahs in the name of the people. They sometimes achieved extraordinary success. In 1872, when the shah sold the monopoly for the production, sale and export of tobacco to the British, putting Iranian manufacturers out of business, the mullahs issued a *fatwa* forbidding Iranians to smoke. The shah was forced to rescind the concessions. The holy city of Qom became an alternative to the despotic and increasingly draconian regime in Teheran. Repression of religion can breed fundamentalism, just as inadequate forms of theism can result in a rejection of God. In Turkey, the closure of the *madrasahs* led inevitably to the decline of the authority of the *ulema*. This meant that the more educated, sober and responsible element in Islam declined, while the more extravagant forms of underground Sufism were the only forms of religion left.

Other reformers were convinced that forcible repression was not the answer. Islam had always thrived on contact with other civilizations, and they believed that religion was essential for any deep and long-lasting reform of their society. There was a great deal that needed to change; much had become backward-looking; there was superstition and ignorance. Yet Islam had also helped people to cultivate serious understanding: if it were allowed to become unhealthy, the spiritual well-being of Muslims all over the world would also suffer. The Muslim reformers were not hostile to the West. Most found Western ideals of equality, freedom and brotherhood congenial, since Islam shared the values of Judeo-Christianity which had been such an important influence in Europe and the United States. The modernization of Western society had—in some respects—created a new type of equality, and the reformers told their people that these Christians seemed to live better Islamic lives than the Muslims. There was enormous enthusiasm and excitement at this new encounter with Europe. The wealthier Muslims were educated in Europe, absorbed its philosophy, literature and ideals, and came back to their own countries eager to share what they had learned. At the beginning of the twentieth century, almost every single Muslim intellectual was also an ardent admirer of the West.

The reformers all had an intellectual bias, and yet they were also nearly all associated with some form of Islamic mysticism. The more imaginative and intelligent forms of Sufism and Ishraqi mysticism had helped Muslims in previous crises, and they turned toward them again. The experience of God was not regarded as a clog but as a force for transformation at a deep level that would hasten the transition to modernity. Thus the Iranian reformer Jamal ad-Din al-Afghani (1838–87) was an adept of the Ishraqi mysticism of Suhrawardi at the same time as he was a passionate advocate of modernization. As he toured Iran, Afghanistan, Egypt and India, al-Afghani attempted to be all things to all men. He was capable of presenting himself as a Sunni to Sunnis, a Shii martyr to Shiis, a revolutionary, a religious philosopher and a parliamentarian. The mystical disciplines of Ishraqi mysticism help Muslims to feel at one with the world around them and to experience a liberating loss of the boundaries that hedge in the self. It has been suggested that al-Afghani's recklessness and adoption of different roles had been influenced by the mystical discipline, with its enlarged concept of self.[25] Religion was essential, though reform was necessary. Al-Afghani was a convinced, even a passionate theist, but there is little talk of God in *The Refutation of the Materialists*, his only book. Because he knew that the West valued reason and regarded Islam and Orientals as irrational, al-Afghani tried to describe Islam as a faith distinguished by its ruthless cult of reason. In fact, even such rationalists as the Mutazilis would have found this description of their religion strange. Al-Afghani was an activist rather than a philosopher. It is, therefore, important not to judge his career and convictions by this one literary attempt. Nevertheless, the depiction of Islam in a way calculated to fit what is perceived as a Western ideal shows a new lack of confidence in the Muslim world that would shortly become extremely destructive.

Muhammad Abduh (1849–1905), al-Afghani's Egyptian disciple, had a different approach. He decided to concentrate his activities in Egypt alone and to focus on the intellectual education of its Muslims. He had had a traditional Islamic upbringing, which had brought him under the influence of the Sufi Sheikh Darwish, who had taught him that science and philosophy were the two most secure paths to the knowledge of God. Consequently when Abduh began to study at the prestigious al-Azhar mosque in Cairo, he was soon disillusioned by its antiquated syllabus. Instead he was attracted to al-Afghani, who coached him in logic, theology, astronomy, physics and mysticism. Some Christians in the West felt that science was the enemy of faith, but Muslim mystics had often used mathematics and science as an aid to contemplation. Today Muslims in some of the more radical mystical sects of the Shiah, such as the Druzes or the Alawis, are particularly interested in modern science. In the Islamic world there are grave reservations about Western politics but few find it a problem to reconcile their faith in God with Western science.

Abduh was excited by his contact with Western culture and was especially influenced by Comte, Tolstoy and Herbert Spencer, who was a personal friend. He never adopted a wholly Western lifestyle, but liked to visit Europe regularly to refresh himself intellectually. This did not mean that he abandoned Islam. Far from it; like any reformer, Abduh wanted to return to the roots of his faith. He therefore advocated a return to the spirit of the Prophet and the first four Rightly Guided Caliphs (*rashidun*). This did not entail a fundamentalist rejection of modernity, however. Abduh insisted that Muslims must study science, technology and secular philosophy in order to take their place in the modern world. The Shariah Law must be reformed to enable Muslims to get the intellectual freedom they required. Like al-Afghani, he also tried to present Islam as a rational faith, arguing that in the Koran reason and religion had marched hand in hand for the first time in human history. Before the career of the Prophet, revelation had been attended by miracles, legends and irrational rhetoric, but the Koran had not resorted to these more primitive methods. It had "advanced proof and demonstration, expounded the views of disbelievers and inveighed against them rationally."[26] The attack against the Faylasufs mounted by al-Ghazzali had been immoderate. It had caused division between piety and rationalism, which had affected the intellectual standing of the *ulema*. This was apparent in the outdated curriculum of al-Azhar. Muslims should, therefore, return to the more receptive and rational spirit of the Koran. Yet Abduh pulled back from a totally reductionist rationalism. He quoted the *hadith*: "Reflect upon God's creation but not upon his nature or else you will perish." Reason cannot grasp the essential being of God which remains shrouded in mystery. All that we can establish is the fact that God does not resemble any other being. All the other questions that exercise theologians are simply frivolous and are dismissed by the Koran as *zanna*.

In India the leading reformer was Sir Muhammad Iqbal (1877–1938), who became for the Muslims of India what Gandhi was for the Hindus. He was essentially a contemplative—a Sufi and an Urdu poet—but he also had a Western education and a doctorate in philosophy. He was filled with enthusiasm for Bergson, Nietzsche and A. N. Whitehead and tried to reinvigorate Falsafah in the light of their insights, seeing himself as a bridge between East and West. He was dismayed by what he saw as the decadence of Islam in India. Ever since the decline of the Moghul empire in the eighteenth century, the Muslims of India had felt in a false position. They lacked the confidence of their brethren in the Middle East, where Islam was on home ground. Consequently they were even more defensive and insecure before the British. Iqbal attempted to heal the disturbance of his people by a creative reconstruction of Islamic principles through poetry and philosophy.

From such Western philosophers as Nietzsche, Iqbal had imbibed the importance of individualism. The whole universe represented an Absolute which was the highest form of individuation and which men had called "God." In order to realize their own unique nature, all human beings must become more like God. That meant that each must become *more* individual, *more* creative and must express this creativity in action. The passivity and craven self-effacement (which Iqbal put down to Persian influence) of the Muslims of India must be laid aside. The Muslim principle of *ijtihad* (independent judgment) should encourage them to be receptive to new ideas: the Koran itself demanded constant revision and self-examination. Like al-Afghani and Abduh, Iqbal tried to show that the empirical attitude, which was the key to progress, had originated in Islam and passed to the West via Muslim science and mathematics during the Middle Ages. Before the arrival of the great confessional religions during the Axial Age, the progress of humanity had been haphazard, dependent as it was upon gifted and inspired individuals. Muhammad's prophecy was the culmination of these intuitive efforts and rendered any further revelation unnecessary. Henceforth people could rely on reason and science.

Unfortunately individualism had become a new form of idolatry in the West, since it was now an end in itself. People had forgotten that all true individuality derived from God. The genius of the individual could be used to dangerous effect if allowed absolutely free rein. A breed of Supermen who regarded themselves as Gods, as envisaged by Nietzsche, was a frightening prospect: people needed the challenge of a norm that transcended the whims and notions of the moment. It was the mission of Islam to uphold the nature of true individualism against the Western corruption of the ideal. They had their Sufi ideal of the Perfect Man, the end of creation and the purpose of its existence. Unlike the Superman who saw himself as supreme and despised the rabble, the Perfect Man was characterized by his total receptivity to the Absolute and would carry the masses along with him. The present state of the world meant that progress depended upon the gifts of an elite, who could see beyond the present and carry humanity forward into the future. Eventually everybody would achieve perfect individuality in God. Iqbal's view of the role of Islam was partial, but it was more sophisticated than many current Western attempts to vindicate Christianity at the expense of Islam. His misgivings about the Superman ideal were amply justified by events in Germany during the last years of his life.

By this time, the Arab Muslims of the Middle East were no longer so confident about their ability to contain the Western threat. The year 1920, when Britain and France marched into the Middle East, became known as the *am-al-nakhbah*, the Year of the Disaster, a word that has connotations of cosmic catastrophe. Arabs had hoped for independence after the collapse of the Ottoman empire, and this new domination made it seem that they would never control their own destiny: there was even a rumor that the British were going to hand over Palestine to the Zionists, as though its Arab inhabitants did not exist. The sense of shame and humiliation was acute. The Canadian scholar Wilfred Cantwell Smith points out that this was exacerbated by their memory of past greatness: "In the gulf between [the modern Arab] and, for instance, the modern American, a matter of prime significance has been precisely the deep difference between a society with a memory of past greatness and a sense of present greatness."[27] This had crucial religious implications. Christianity is supremely a religion of suffering and adversity and, in the West at least, has arguably been most authentic in times of trouble: it is not easy to square earthly glory with the image of Christ crucified. Islam, however, is a religion of success. The Koran taught that a society which lived according to God's will (implementing justice, equality, and a fair distribution of wealth) could not fail. Muslim history had seemed to confirm this. Unlike Christ, Muhammad had not been an apparent failure but a dazzling success. His achievements had been compounded by the phenomenal advance of the Muslim empire during the seventh and eighth centuries. This had naturally seemed to endorse the Muslim faith in God: al-Lah had proved to be extremely effective and had made good his word in the arena of history. Muslim success had continued. Even such catastrophes as the Mongol invasions had been overcome. Over the centuries, the *ummah* had acquired an almost sacramental importance and had disclosed the presence of God. Now, however, something seemed to have gone radically wrong with Muslim history, and this inevitably affected the perception of God. Henceforth many Muslims would concentrate on getting Islamic history back onto the rails and making the Koranic vision effective in the world.

The sense of shame was exacerbated when closer acquaintance with

Europe revealed the depth of Western contempt for the Prophet and his religion. Muslim scholarship was increasingly devoted to apologetics or to dreaming of past triumphs—a dangerous brew. God was no longer center stage. Cantwell Smith traces this process in a close examination of the Egyptian Journal *Al-Azhar* from 1930 to 1948. During that time, the journal had two editors. From 1930 to 1933 it was run by Al-Khidr Husain, a traditionist of the best sort, who saw his religion as a transcendent idea rather than a political and historical entity. Islam was an imperative, a summons to future action, rather than a reality which had been fully achieved. Because it is always difficult—even impossible—to incarnate the divine ideal in human life, Husain was not dismayed by past or present failures of the *ummah*. He was confident enough to criticize Muslim behavior, and the words "ought" and "should" run through all the issues of the journal during his time in office. Yet it is also clear that Husain could not imagine the predicament of a person who wanted to but found that he could not believe: the reality of al-Lah is taken for granted. In one early issue, an article by Yusuf al-Dijni had outlined the old teleological argument for the existence of God. Smith notes that the style was essentially reverential and expressed an intense and lively appreciation of the beauty and sublimity of nature which revealed the divine presence. Al-Dijni had no doubt that al-Lah existed. His article is a meditation rather than a logical demonstration of God's existence, and he was quite unconcerned that Western scientists had long since exploded this particular "proof." Yet this attitude was outdated. The circulation of the magazine slumped.

When Farid Wajdi took over in 1933, the readership doubled. Wajdi's prime consideration was to assure his readers that Islam was "all right." It would not have occurred to Husain that Islam, a transcendent idea in the mind of God, might require a helping hand from time to time, but Wajdi saw Islam as a human institution under threat. The prime need is to justify, admire and applaud. As Wilfred Cantwell Smith points out, a profound irreligiousness pervades Wajdi's work. Like his forebears, he constantly argued that the West was only teaching what Islam had discovered centuries earlier but, unlike them, he scarcely referred to God. The human reality of "Islam" was his central concern: and this earthly value had in some sense replaced the transcendent God. Smith concludes:

> A true Muslim is not a man who believes in Islam—especially Islam in history; but one who believes in God and is committed to the revelation through his Prophet. The latter is there sufficiently ad-

mired. But commitment is missing. And God appears remarkably
seldom throughout these pages.[28]

Instead, there is instability and lack of self-esteem: the opinion of the
West has come to matter too desperately. People like Husain had understood religion and the centrality of God but had lost touch with the
modern world. People who were in touch with modernity had lost the
sense of God. From this instability would spring the political activism
which characterizes modern fundamentalism, which is also in retreat from
God.

The Jews of Europe had also been affected by hostile criticism of their
faith. In Germany, Jewish philosophers developed what they called "the
Science of Judaism," which rewrote Jewish history in Hegelian terms to
counter the charge that Judaism was a servile, alienating faith. The first
to attempt this reinterpretation of the history of Israel was Solomon
Formstecher (1808–89). In *The Religion of the Spirit* (1841), he described
God as a world Soul, immanent in all things. This Spirit did not depend
upon the world, however, as Hegel had argued. Formstecher insisted that
it lay beyond the reach of reason, reverting to the old distinction between
God's essence and his activities. Where Hegel had decried the use of
representational language, Formstecher argued that symbolism was the
only appropriate vehicle for God-talk, since he lay beyond the reach of
philosophical concepts. Nevertheless, Judaism had been the first religion
to arrive at an advanced conception of the divine and would shortly show
the whole world what a truly spiritual religion was like.

Primitive, pagan religion had identified God with nature, Formstecher
argued. This spontaneous, unreflective period represented the infancy of
the human race. When human beings had attained a greater degree of
self-consciousness, they were ready to progress to a more sophisticated
idea of divinity. They began to realize that this "God" or "Spirit" was
not contained in nature but existed above and beyond it. The prophets
who had arrived at this new conception of the divine preached an ethical
religion. At first they had believed that their revelations had come from
a force outside themselves, but gradually they understood that they were
not dependent upon a wholly external God but were inspired by their
own Spirit-filled nature. The Jews had been the first people to attain this
ethical conception of God. Their long years in exile and the loss of their
Temple had weaned them from reliance upon external props and controls.
They had thus advanced to a superior type of religious consciousness,
which enabled them to approach God freely. They were not dependent

upon mediating priests nor cowed by an alien Law, as Hegel and Kant had argued. Instead they had learned to find God through their minds and individuality. Christianity and Islam had tried to imitate Judaism, but with less success. Christianity, for example, had retained many pagan elements in its depiction of God. Now that Jews had been emancipated, they would soon achieve complete liberation; they should prepare for this final stage in their development by casting aside the ceremonial laws that were a hangover from an earlier, less developed stage of their history.

Like the Muslim reformers, the exponents of the Science of Judaism were anxious to present their religion as a wholly rational faith. They were particularly eager to get rid of Kabbalah, which had become an embarrassment since the Shabbetai Zevi fiasco and the rise of Hasidism. Consequently Samuel Hirsch, who published *The Religious Philosophy of the Jews* in 1842, wrote a history of Israel which ignored the mystical dimension of Judaism and presented an ethical, rational history of God, which focused on the idea of liberty. A human being was distinguished by the ability to say "I." This self-consciousness represented an inalienable personal freedom. Pagan religion had not been able to cultivate this autonomy, since in the very early stages of human development, the gift of self-consciousness seemed to come from above. Pagans had located the source of their personal liberty in nature and believed that some of their vices were unavoidable. Abraham, however, had refused this pagan fatalism and dependence. He had stood alone in the presence of God in total command of himself. Such a man will find God in every aspect of life. God, the Master of the Universe, has arranged the world to help us to attain this inner freedom, and each individual is educated to this end by none other than God himself. Judaism was not the servile faith that Gentiles imagined. It had always been a more advanced religion than, for example, Christianity, which had turned its back on its Jewish roots and reverted to the irrationality and superstitions of paganism.

Nachman Krochmal (1785–1840), whose *Guide for the Perplexed of Our Time* was published posthumously in 1841, did not recoil from mysticism like his colleagues. He liked to call "God" or the "Spirit" "Nothing," like the Kabbalists, and to use the Kabbalistic metaphor of emanation to describe God's unfolding revelation of himself. He argued that the achievements of the Jews were not the result of an abject dependence upon God, but of the workings of the collective consciousness. Over the centuries, the Jews had gradually refined their conception of God. Thus at the time of the Exodus God had had to reveal his presence in miracles. By the time of the return from Babylon, however, the Jews had attained a more advanced perception of the divine and signs and wonders were no longer necessary. The Jewish conception of the worship of God was not the slavish dependence that the *goyim* imagined, but corresponded almost exactly to the philosophic ideal. The only difference between religion and philosophy was that the latter expressed itself in concepts, while religion used representational language, as Hegel had pointed out. Yet this type of symbolic language was appropriate, since God exceeds all our ideas about him. Indeed, we cannot even say that he exists, since our experience of existence is so partial and limited.

The new confidence brought by emancipation was dealt a harsh blow with the outbreak of a vicious anti-Semitism in Russia and Eastern Europe under Tsar Alexander III in 1881. This spread to Western Europe. In France, the first country to emancipate the Jews, there was an hysterical surge of anti-Semitism when the Jewish officer Alfred Dreyfus was wrongly convicted of treason in 1894. That same year, Karl Lueger, a notable anti-Semite, was elected Mayor of Vienna. Yet in Germany before Adolf Hitler came to power, Jews still imagined that they were safe. Thus Hermann Cohen (1842–1918) still seemed preoccupied with the metaphysical anti-Semitism of Kant and Hegel. Concerned above all with the accusation that Judaism was a servile faith, Cohen denied that God was an external reality that imposes obedience from on high. God was simply an idea formed by the human mind, a symbol of the ethical ideal. Discussing the biblical story of the Burning Bush, when God had defined himself to Moses as "I am what I am," Cohen argued that this was a primitive expression of the fact that what we call "God" is simply being itself. It is quite distinct from the mere being*s* that we experience, which can only participate in this essential existence. In *The Religion of Reason Drawn from the Sources of Judaism* (published posthumously in 1919), Cohen still insisted that God was simply a human idea. Yet he had also come to appreciate the emotional role of religion in human life. A mere ethical idea—such as "God"—cannot console us. Religion teaches us to love our neighbor, so it is possible to say that the God of religion—as opposed to the God of ethics and philosophy—*was* that affective love.

These ideas were developed out of all recognition by Franz Rosenzweig (1886–1929), who evolved an entirely different conception of Judaism which set him apart from his contemporaries. Not only was he one of the first existentialists, but he also formulated ideas that were close to the oriental religions. His independence can perhaps be explained by the fact that he had left Judaism as a young man, become an agnostic and then considered converting to Christianity before finally returning to Orthodox

Judaism. Rosenzweig passionately denied that the observance of the Torah encouraged a slavish, abject dependence upon a tyrannical God.
Religion was not simply about morality but was essentially a meeting
with the divine. How was it possible for mere human beings to encounter
the transcendent God? Rosenzweig never tells us what this meeting was
like—this is a weakness in his philosophy. He distrusted Hegel's attempt
to merge the Spirit with man and nature: if we simply see our human
consciousness as an aspect of the World Soul, we are no longer truly
individuals. A true existentialist, Rosenzweig emphasized the absolute
isolation of every single human being. Each one of us is alone, lost and
terrified in the vast crowd of humanity. It is only when God turns to
us that we are redeemed from this anonymity and fear. God does not
reduce our individuality, therefore, but enables us to attain full self-
consciousness.

It is impossible for us to meet God in any anthropomorphic way. God
is the Ground of being, so bound up with our own existence that we
cannot possibly talk *to* him, as though he were simply another person like
ourselves. There are no words or ideas that describe God. Instead the
gulf between him and human beings is bridged by the commandments of
the Torah. These are not just proscriptive laws, as the *goyim* imagine.
They are sacraments, symbolic actions that point beyond themselves and
introduce Jews to the divine dimension that underlies the being of each
one of us. Like the Rabbis, Rosenzweig argued that the commandments
are so obviously symbolic—since they often have no meaning in themselves—that they drive us beyond our limited words and concepts to the
ineffable Being itself. They help us to cultivate a listening, waiting attitude so that we are poised and attentive to the Ground of our existence.
The *mitzvot* do not work automatically, therefore. They have to be appropriated by the individual so that each *mitzvah* ceases to be an external
command but expresses *my* interior attitude, *my* inner "must." Yet although the Torah was a specifically Jewish religious practice, revelation
was not confined to the people of Israel. He, Rosenzweig, would meet
God in the symbolic gestures that were traditionally Jewish, but a Christian would use different symbols. The doctrines about God were not
primarily confessional statements, but they were symbols of interior attitudes. The doctrines of creation and revelation, for example, were not
literal accounts of actual events in the life of God and the world. The
myths of revelation expressed our personal experience of God. Creation
myths symbolized the absolute contingency of our human existence, the
shattering knowledge of our utter dependence upon the Ground of being

which made that existence possible. As Creator, God is not concerned with his creatures until he reveals himself to each one of them, but if he were not the Creator, that is, the Ground of all existence, the religious experience would have no meaning for humanity as a whole. It would remain a series of freak occurrences. Rosenzweig's universal vision of religion made him suspicious of the new political Judaism that was emerging as a response to the new anti-Semitism. Israel, he argued, had become a people in Egypt, not in the Promised Land, and would only fulfill its destiny as an eternal people if it severed its ties with the mundane world and did not get involved with politics.

But Jews who fell victim to the escalating anti-Semitism did not feel that they could afford this political disengagement. They could not sit back and wait for the Messiah or God to rescue them but must redeem their people themselves. In 1882, the year after the first pogroms in Russia, a band of Jews left Eastern Europe to settle in Palestine. They were convinced that Jews would remain incomplete, alienated human beings until they had a country of their own. The yearning for the return to Zion (one of the chief hills of Jerusalem) began as a defiantly secular movement, since the vicissitudes of history had convinced the Zionists that their religion and their God did not work. In Russia and Eastern Europe, Zionism was an offshoot of the revolutionary socialism that was putting the theories of Karl Marx into practice. The Jewish revolutionaries had become aware that their comrades were just as anti-Semitic as the Tsar and feared that their lot would not improve in a communist regime: events proved that they were correct. Accordingly ardent young socialists such as David Ben-Gurion (1886–1973) simply packed their bags and sailed to Palestine, determined to create a model society that would be a light to the Gentiles and herald the socialist millennium. Others had no time for these Marxist dreams. The charismatic Austrian Theodor Herzl (1860–1904) saw the new Jewish venture as a colonial enterprise: under the wing of one of the European imperial powers, the Jewish state would be a vanguard of progress in the Islamic wilderness.

Despite its avowed secularism, Zionism expressed itself instinctively in conventionally religious terminology and was essentially a religion without God. It was filled with ecstatic and mystical hopes for the future, drawing on the ancient themes of redemption, pilgrimage and rebirth. Zionists even adopted the practice of giving themselves new names as a sign of the redeemed self. Thus Asher Ginzberg, an early propagandist, called himself Ahad Ha'am (One of the People). He was now his own man because he had identified himself with the new national spirit, though he did not think that a Jewish state was feasible in Palestine. He simply wanted a "spiritual center" there to take the place of God as the single focus of the people of Israel. It would become "a guide to all the affairs of life," reach "to the depths of the heart" and "connect with all one's feelings." Zionists had reversed the old religious orientation. Instead of being directed toward a transcendent God, Jews sought fulfillment here below. The Hebrew term *hagshamah* (literally, "making concrete") had been a negative term in medieval Jewish philosophy, referring to the habit of attributing human or physical characteristics to God. In Zionism, *hagshamah* came to mean fulfillment, the embodiment of the hopes of Israel in the mundane world. Holiness no longer dwelt in heaven: Palestine was a "holy" land in the fullest sense of the word.

Just how holy can be seen in the writings of the early pioneer Aaron David Gordon (d. 1922), who had been an Orthodox Jew and Kabbalist until the age of forty-seven, when he was converted to Zionism. A weak and ailing man with white hair and beard, Gordon worked in the fields beside the younger settlers, leaping around with them at night in ecstasy, crying "Joy! . . . Joy!" In former times, he wrote, the experience of reunion with the land of Israel would have been called a revelation of the Shekinah. The Holy Land had become a sacred value; it had a spiritual power accessible to the Jews alone which had created the unique Jewish spirit. When he described this holiness, Gordon used Kabbalistic terms that had once been applied to the mysterious realm of God:

> The soul of the Jew is the offspring of the natural environment of the land of Israel. *Clarity*, the depth of an infinitely clear sky, a clear perspective, *mists of purity*. Even the divine unknown seems to disappear in this clarity, slipping from *limited manifest light* into *infinite hidden light*. The people of this world understand neither this clear perspective nor this luminous unknown in the Jewish soul.[29]

At first this Middle Eastern landscape had been so different from Russia, his natural fatherland, that Gordon had found it frightening and alien. But he realized that he could make it his own by means of labor (*avodah*, a word that also refers to religious ritual). By working the land, which Zionists claimed had been neglected by the Arabs, the Jews would conquer it for themselves and, at the same time, redeem themselves from the alienation of exile.

The socialist Zionists called their pioneering movement the Conquest of Labor: their *kibbutzim* became secular monasteries, where they lived in common and worked out their own salvation. Their cultivation of the land led to a mystical experience of rebirth and universal love. As Gordon explained:

> To the extent that my hands grew accustomed to labor, that my eyes and ears learned to see and hear and my heart to understand what is in it, my soul too learned to skip upon the hills, to rise, to soar—to spread out the expanses it had not known, to embrace all the land round about, the world and all that is in it, and to see itself embraced in the arms of the whole universe.[30]

Their work was a secular prayer. In about 1927, the younger pioneer and scholar Avraham Schlonsky (1900–73), who worked as a road builder, wrote this poem to the land of Israel:

> Dress me, good mother, in a glorious robe of many colors,
> and at dawn lead me to my toil.
> My land is wrapped in light as in a prayer shawl.
> The houses stand forth like frontlets;
> and the rocks paved by hand, stream down like phylactery straps.
> Here the lovely city says the morning prayer to its creator.
> And among the creators is your son Avraham,
> a road-building bard in Israel.[31]

The Zionist no longer needs God; he himself is the creator.

Other Zionists retained a more conventional faith. The Kabbalist Abraham Isaac Kook (1865–1935), who served as the Chief Rabbi for Palestinian Jewry, had had little contact with the Gentile world before his arrival in the Land of Israel. He insisted that as long as the concept of serving God was defined as the service of a particular Being, separate from the ideals and duties of religion, it would not be "free from the immature outlook which is always focused in particular beings."[32] God was not another Being: En Sof transcended all human concepts such as personality. To think of God as a particular being was idolatry and the sign of a primitive mentality. Kook was steeped in Jewish tradition, but he was not dismayed by the Zionist ideology. True, the Laborites believed that they had shaken off religion, but this atheistic Zionism was only a phase. God was at work in the pioneers: the divine "sparks" were trapped in these "husks" of darkness and were awaiting redemption. Whether they thought so or not, Jews were in their essence inseparable from God and were fulfilling God's plan without realizing it. During the exile, the Holy Spirit had departed from his people. They had hidden the Shekinah away in synagogues and study halls, but soon Israel would become the spiritual center of the world and reveal the true conception of God to the Gentiles.

This type of spirituality could be dangerous. The devotion to the Holy Land would give birth to the idolatry of Jewish fundamentalism in our own day. Devotion to historical "Islam" has contributed to a similar fundamentalism in the Muslim world. Both Jews and Muslims were struggling to find meaning in a dark world. The God of history seemed to have failed them. The Zionists had been right to fear the final elimination of their people. For many Jews, the traditional idea of God would become an impossibility after the Holocaust. The Nobel Prize winner Elie Wiesel had lived only for God during his childhood in Hungary; his life had been shaped by the disciplines of the Talmud, and he had hoped one day to be initiated into the mysteries of Kabbalah. As a boy, he was taken to Auschwitz and later to Buchenwald. During his first night in the death camp, watching the black smoke coiling to the sky from the crematorium where the bodies of his mother and sister were to be thrown, he knew that the flames had consumed his faith forever. He was in a world which was the objective correlative of the Godless world imagined by Nietzsche. "Never should I forget that nocturnal silence which deprived me, for all eternity, of the desire to live," he wrote years later. "Never shall I forget these moments which murdered my God and my soul and turned my dreams to dust."[33]

One day the Gestapo hanged a child. Even the SS were disturbed by the prospect of hanging a young boy in front of thousands of spectators. The child who, Wiesel recalled, had the face of a "sad-eyed angel," was silent, lividly pale and almost calm as he ascended the gallows. Behind Wiesel, one of the other prisoners asked: "Where is God? Where is He?" It took the child half an hour to die, while the prisoners were forced to look him in the face. The same man asked again: "Where is God now?" And Wiesel heard a voice within him make this answer: "Where is He? Here He is—He is hanging here on this gallows."[34]

Dostoevsky had said that the death of a single child could make God unacceptable, but even he, no stranger to inhumanity, had not imagined the death of a child in such circumstances. The horror of Auschwitz is a stark challenge to many of the more conventional ideas of God. The remote God of the philosophers, lost in a transcendent *apatheia*, becomes intolerable. Many Jews can no longer subscribe to the biblical idea of God who manifests himself in history, who, they say with Wiesel, died in Auschwitz. The idea of a personal God, like one of us writ large, is fraught with difficulty. If this God is omnipotent, he could have prevented the Holocaust. If he was unable to stop it, he is impotent and useless; if he could have stopped it and chose not to, he is a monster. Jews are not the only people who believe that the Holocaust put an end to conventional theology.

Yet it is also true that even in Auschwitz some Jews continued to study the Talmud and observe the traditional festivals, not because they hoped that God would rescue them but because it made sense. There is a story that one day in Auschwitz, a group of Jews put God on trial. They charged him with cruelty and betrayal. Like Job, they found no consolation in the usual answers to the problem of evil and suffering in the midst of this current obscenity. They could find no excuse for God, no extenuating circumstances, so they found him guilty and, presumably, worthy of death. The Rabbi pronounced the verdict. Then he looked up and said that the trial was over: it was time for the evening prayer.

11

Does God Have a Future?

A s we approach the end of the second millennium, it seems likely that the world we know is passing away. For decades we have lived with the knowledge that we have created weapons that could wipe out human life on the planet. The Cold War may have ended, but the new world order seems no less frightening than the old. We are facing the possibility of ecological disaster. The AIDS virus threatens to bring a plague of unmanageable proportions. Within two or three generations, the population will become too great for the planet to support. Thousands are dying of famine and drought. Generations before our own have felt that the end of the world is nigh, yet it does seem that we are facing a future that is unimaginable. How will the idea of God survive in the years to come? For 4000 years it has constantly adapted to meet the demands of the present, but in our own century, more and more people have found that it no longer works for them, and when religious ideas cease to be effective they fade away. Maybe God really is an idea of the past. The American scholar Peter Berger notes that we often have a double standard when we compare the past with our own time. Where the past is analyzed and made relative, the present is rendered immune to this process and our current position becomes an absolute: thus "the New Testament writers are seen as afflicted with a false consciousness rooted in *their* time, but the analyst takes the consciousness of *his* time as an unmixed intellectual blessing."[1] Secularists of the nineteenth and early twentieth centuries saw atheism as the irreversible condition of humanity in the scientific age.

There is much to support this view. In Europe, the churches are emptying; atheism is no longer the painfully acquired ideology of a few intellectual pioneers but a prevailing mood. In the past it was always produced by a particular idea of God, but now it seems to have lost its inbuilt relationship to theism and become an automatic response to the experience of living in a secularized society. Like the crowd of amused people surrounding Nietzsche's madman, many are unmoved by the prospect of life without God. Others find his absence a positive relief. Those of us who have had a difficult time with religion in the past find it liberating to be rid of the God who terrorized our childhood. It is wonderful not to have to cower before a vengeful deity, who threatens us with eternal damnation if we do not abide by his rules. We have a new intellectual freedom and can boldly follow up our own ideas without pussyfooting around difficult articles of faith, feeling all the while a sinking loss of integrity. We imagine that the hideous deity we have experienced is the authentic God of Jews, Christians and Muslims and do not always realize that it is merely an unfortunate aberration.

There is also desolation. Jean-Paul Sartre (1905–80) spoke of the God-shaped hole in the human consciousness, where God had always been. Nevertheless, he insisted that even if God existed, it was still necessary to reject him, since the idea of God negates our freedom. Traditional religion tells us that we must conform to God's idea of humanity to become fully human. Instead, we must see human beings as liberty incarnate. Sartre's atheism was not a consoling creed, but other existentialists saw the absence of God as a positive liberation. Maurice Merleau-Ponty (1908–61) argued that instead of increasing our sense of wonder, God actually negates it. Because God represents absolute perfection, there is nothing left for us to do or achieve. Albert Camus (1913–60) preached a heroic atheism. People should reject God defiantly in order to pour out all their loving solicitude upon mankind. As always, the atheists have a point. God had indeed been used in the past to stunt creativity; if he is made a blanket answer to every possible problem and contingency, he can indeed stifle our sense of wonder or achievement. A passionate and committed atheism can be more religious than a weary or inadequate theism.

During the 1950s, Logical Positivists such as A. J. Ayer (1910–91) asked whether it made sense to believe in God. The natural sciences provided the only reliable source of knowledge because it could be tested empirically. Ayer was not asking whether or not God existed but whether the idea of God had any meaning. He argued that a statement is meaningless if we cannot see how it can be verified or shown to be false. To say

"There is intelligent life on Mars" is not meaningless since we can see how we could verify this once we had the necessary technology. Similarly a simple believer in the traditional Old Man in the Sky is not making a meaningless statement when he says: "I believe in God," since after death we should be able to find out whether or not this is true. It is the more sophisticated believer who has problems, when he says: "God does not exist in any sense that we can understand" or "God is not good in the human sense of the word." These statements are too vague; it is impossible to see how they can be tested; therefore, they are meaningless. As Ayer said: "Theism is so confused and the sentences in which 'God' appears so incoherent and so incapable of verifiability or falsifiability that to speak of belief or unbelief, faith or unfaith, is logically impossible."[2] Atheism is as unintelligible and meaningless as theism. There is nothing in the concept of "God" to deny or be skeptical about.

Like Freud, the Positivists believed that religious belief represented an immaturity which science would overcome. Since the 1950s, linguistic philosophers have criticized Logical Positivism, pointing out that what Ayer called the Verification Principle could not itself be verified. Today we are less likely to be as optimistic about science, which can only explain the world of physical nature. Wilfred Cantwell Smith pointed out that the Logical Positivists set themselves up as scientists during a period when, for the first time in history, science saw the natural world in explicit disjunction from humanity.[3] The kind of statements to which Ayer referred work very well for the objective facts of science but are not suitable for less clear-cut human experiences. Like poetry or music, religion is not amenable to this kind of discourse and verification. More recently linguistic philosophers such as Antony Flew have argued that it is more rational to find a natural explanation than a religious one. The old "proofs" do not work: the argument from design falls down because we would need to get outside the system to see whether natural phenomena are motivated by their own laws or by Something outside. The argument that we are "contingent" or "defective" beings proves nothing, since there could always be an explanation that is ultimate but not supernatural. Flew is less of an optimist than Feuerbach, Marx or the Existentialists. There is no agonizing, no heroic defiance but simply a matter-of-fact commitment to reason and science as the only way forward.

We have seen, however, that not all religious people have looked to "God" to provide them with an explanation for the universe. Many have seen the proofs as a red herring. Science has been felt to be threatening only by those Western Christians who got into the habit of reading the scriptures literally and interpreting doctrines as though they were matters of objective fact. Scientists and philosophers who find no room for God in their systems are usually referring to the idea of God as First Cause, a notion eventually abandoned by Jews, Muslims and Greek Orthodox Christians during the Middle Ages. The more subjective "God" that they were looking for could not be proved as though it were an objective fact that was the same for everybody. It could not be located within a physical system of the universe, any more than the Buddhist nirvana.

More dramatic than the linguistic philosophers were the radical theologians of the 1960s who enthusiastically followed Nietzsche and proclaimed the death of God. In *The Gospel of Christian Atheism* (1966), Thomas J. Altizer claimed that the "good news" of God's death had freed us from slavery to a tyrannical transcendent deity: "Only by accepting and even willing the death of God in our experience can we be liberated from a transcendent beyond, an alien beyond which has been emptied and darkened by God's self-alienation in Christ."[4] Altizer spoke in mystical terms of the dark night of the soul and the pain of abandonment. The death of God represented the silence that was necessary before God could become meaningful again. All our old conceptions of divinity had to die before theology could be reborn. We were waiting for a language and a style in which God could once more become a possibility. Altizer's theology was a passionate dialectic which attacked the dark God-less world in the hope that it would give up its secret. Paul Van Buren was more precise and logical. In *The Secular Meaning of the Gospel* (1963), he claimed that it was no longer possible to speak of God acting in the world. Science and technology had made the old mythology invalid. Simple faith in the Old Man in the Sky was clearly impossible, but so was the more sophisticated belief of the theologians. We must do without God and hold on to Jesus of Nazareth. The Gospel was "the good news of a free man who has set other men free." Jesus of Nazareth was the liberator, "the man who defines what it means to be a man."[5]

In *Radical Theology and the Death of God* (1966), William Hamilton noted that this kind of theology had its roots in the United States, which had always had a utopian bent and had no great theological tradition of its own. The imagery of the death of God represented the anomie and barbarism of the technical age, which made it impossible to believe in the biblical God in the old way. Hamilton himself saw this theological mood as a way of being Protestant in the twentieth century. Luther had left his cloister and gone out into the world. In the same way, he and the other Christian radicals were avowedly secular men. They had walked away from the sacred place where God used to be to find the man Jesus in their neighbor out in the world of technology, power, sex, money and the city. Modern secular man did not need God. There was no God-shaped hole within Hamilton: he would find his own solution in the world.

There is something rather poignant about this buoyant sixties optimism. Certainly, the radicals were right that the old ways of speaking about God had become impossible for many people, but in the 1990s it is sadly difficult to feel that liberation and a new dawn are at hand. Even at the time, the Death of God theologians were criticized, since their perspective was that of the affluent, middle-class, white American. Black theologians such as James H. Cone asked how white people felt they had the right to affirm freedom through the death of God when they had actually enslaved people in God's name. The Jewish theologian Richard Rubenstein found it impossible to understand how they could feel so positive about Godless humanity so soon after the Nazi Holocaust. He himself was convinced that the deity conceived as a God of History had died forever in Auschwitz. Yet Rubenstein did not feel that Jews could jettison religion. After the near-extinction of European Jewry, they must not cut themselves off from their past. The nice, moral God of liberal Judaism was no good, however. It was too antiseptic; it ignored the tragedy of life and assumed that the world would improve. Rubenstein himself preferred the God of the Jewish mystics. He was moved by Isaac Luria's doctrine of *tsimtsum*, God's voluntary act of self-estrangement which brought the created world into being. All mystics had seen God as a Nothingness from which we came and to which we will return. Rubenstein agreed with Sartre that life is empty; he saw the God of the mystics as an imaginative way of entering this human experience of nothingness.[6]

Other Jewish theologians have also found comfort in Lurianic Kabbalah. Hans Jonas believes that after Auschwitz we can no longer believe in the omnipotence of God. When God created the world, he voluntarily limited himself and shared the weakness of human beings. He could do no more now, and human beings must restore wholeness to the Godhead and the world by prayer and Torah. The British theologian Louis Jacobs, however, dislikes this idea, finding the image of *tsimtsum* coarse and anthropomorphic: it encourages us to ask *how* God created the world in too literal a manner. God does not limit himself, holding his breath, as it were, before exhaling. An impotent God is useless and cannot be the meaning of human existence. It is better to return to the classic explanation that God is greater than human beings and his thought and ways are not ours. God may be incomprehensible, but people have the option of trusting this ineffable God and affirming *a* meaning, even in the midst of meaninglessness. The Roman Catholic theologian Hans Kung agrees with Jacobs, preferring a more reasonable explanation for tragedy than the fanciful myth of *tsimtsum*. He notes that human beings cannot have faith in a weak God but in the living God who made people strong enough to pray in Auschwitz.

Some people still find it possible to find meaning in the idea of God. The Swiss theologian Karl Barth (1886–1968) set his face against the Liberal Protestantism of Schleiermacher, with its emphasis on religious experience. But he was also a leading opponent of natural theology. It was, he thought, a radical error to seek to explain God in rational terms not simply because of the limitations of the human mind but also because humanity has been corrupted by the Fall. Any natural idea we form about God is bound to be flawed, therefore, and to worship such a God was idolatry. The only valid source of God-knowledge was the Bible. This seems to have the worst of all worlds: experience is out; natural reason is out; the human mind is corrupt and untrustworthy; and there is no possibility of learning from other faiths, since the Bible is the only valid revelation. It seems unhealthy to combine such radical skepticism in the powers of the intellect with such an uncritical acceptance of the truths of scripture.

Paul Tillich (1868–1965) was convinced that the personal God of traditional Western theism must go, but he also believed that religion was necessary for humankind. A deep-rooted anxiety is part of the human condition: this is not neurotic, because it is ineradicable and no therapy can take it away. We constantly fear loss and the terror of extinction, as we watch our bodies gradually but inexorably decay. Tillich agreed with Nietzsche that the personal God was a harmful idea and deserved to die:

> The concept of a "Personal God" interfering with natural events, or being "an independent cause of natural events," makes God a natural object beside others, an object among others, a being among beings, maybe the highest, but nevertheless *a* being. This indeed is not only the destruction of the physical system but even more the destruction of any meaningful idea of God.[7]

A God who kept tinkering with the universe was absurd; a God who interfered with human freedom and creativity was a tyrant. If God is seen as a self in a world of his own, an ego that relates to a thou, a cause separate from its effect, "he" becomes *a* being, not Being itself. An omnipotent, all-knowing tyrant is not so different from earthly dictators who made everything and everybody mere cogs in the machine which they controlled. An atheism that rejects such a God is amply justified.

Instead we should seek to find a "God" above this personal God. There is nothing new about this. Ever since biblical times, theists had been aware of the paradoxical nature of the God to which they prayed, aware that the personalized God was balanced by the essentially transpersonal divinity. Each prayer was a contradiction, since it attempted to speak to somebody to whom speech was impossible; it asked favors of somebody who had either bestowed them or not before he was asked; it said "thou" to a God who, as Being itself, was nearer to the "I" than our own ego. Tillich preferred the definition of God as the Ground of being. Participation in such a God above "God" does not alienate us from the world but immerses us in reality. It returns us to ourselves. Human beings have to use symbols when they talk about Being-itself: to speak literally or realistically about it is inaccurate and untrue. For centuries the symbols "God," "providence" and "immortality" have enabled people to bear the terror of life and the horror of death, but when these symbols lose their power there is fear and doubt. People who experience this dread and anxiety should seek the God above the discredited "God" of a theism which has lost its symbolic force.

When Tillich was speaking to laypeople, he preferred to replace the rather technical term "Ground of being" with "ultimate concern." He emphasized that the human experience of faith in this "God above God" was not a peculiar state distinguishable from others in our emotional or intellectual experience. You could not say: "I am now having a special 'religious' experience," since the God which is Being precedes and is fundamental to all our emotions of courage, hope and despair. It was not a distinct state with a name of its own but pervaded each one of our normal human experiences. A century earlier Feuerbach had made a similar claim when he had said that God was inseparable from normal human psychology. Now this atheism had been transformed into a new theism.

Liberal theologians were trying to discover whether it was possible to believe and to belong to the modern intellectual world. In forming their new conception of God, they turned to other disciplines: science, psychology, sociology and other religions. Again, there was nothing new in this attempt. Origen and Clement of Alexandria had been Liberal Christians in this sense in the third century when they had introduced Platonism into the Semitic religion of Yahweh. Now the Jesuit Pierre Teilhard de Chardin (1881–1955) combined his belief in God with modern science. He was a paleontologist with a special interest in prehistoric life and drew upon his understanding of evolution to write a new theology. He saw the whole evolutionary struggle as a divine force which propelled the universe from matter to spirit to personality and, finally, beyond personality to God. God was immanent and incarnate in the world, which had become a sacrament of his presence. De Chardin suggested that instead of concentrating on Jesus the man, Christians should cultivate the cosmic portrait of Christ in Paul's epistles to the Colossians and Ephesians: Christ in this view was the "omega point" of the universe, the climax of the evolutionary process when God becomes all in all. Scripture tells us that God is love, and science shows that the natural world progresses towards ever-greater complexity *and* to greater unity in this variety. This unity-in-differentiation was another way of regarding the love that animates the whole of creation. De Chardin has been criticized for identifying God so thoroughly with the world that all sense of his transcendence was lost, but his this-worldly theology was a welcome change from the *contemptus mundi* which had so often characterized Catholic spirituality.

In the United States during the 1960s, Daniel Day Williams (b. 1910) evolved what is known as Process theology, which also stressed God's unity with the world. He had been greatly influenced by the British philosopher A. N. Whitehead (1861–1947), who had seen God as inextricably bound up with the world process. Whitehead had been able to make no sense of God as an-other Being, self-contained and impassible, but had formulated a twentieth-century version of the prophetic idea of God's pathos:

> I affirm that God does suffer as he participates in the ongoing life of the society of being. His sharing in the world's suffering is the supreme instance of knowing, accepting, and transforming in love the suffering which arises in the world. I am affirming the divine sensitivity. Without it, I can make no sense of the being of God.[8]

He described God as "the great companion, the fellow-sufferer, who understands." Williams liked Whitehead's definition; he liked to speak of God as the "behavior" of the world or an "event."[9] It was wrong to set the supernatural order over against the natural world of our experience. There was only one order of being. This was not reductionist, however. In our concept of the natural we should include *all* the aspirations, capacities and potential that had once seemed miraculous. It would also include our "religious experiences," as Buddhists had always affirmed. When asked whether he thought God was separate from nature, Williams would reply that he was not sure. He hated the old Greek idea of *apatheia*, which he found almost blasphemous: it presented God as remote, uncaring and selfish. He denied that he was advocating pantheism. His theology was simply trying to correct an imbalance, which had resulted in an alienating God which was impossible to accept after Auschwitz and Hiroshima.

Others were less optimistic about the achievements of the modern world and wanted to retain the transcendence of God as a challenge to men and women. The Jesuit Karl Rahner has developed a more transcendental theology, which sees God as the supreme mystery and Jesus as the decisive manifestation of what humanity can become. Bernard Lonergan also emphasized the importance of transcendence and of thought as opposed to experience. The unaided intellect cannot reach the vision it seeks: it is continually coming up against barriers to understanding that demand that we change our attitudes. In all cultures, human beings have been driven by the same imperatives: to be intelligent, responsible, reasonable, loving and, if necessary, to change. The very nature of humanity, therefore, demands that we transcend ourselves and our current perceptions, and this principle indicates the presence of what has been called the divine in the very nature of serious human inquiry. Yet the Swiss theologian Hans Urs von Balthasar believes that instead of seeking God in logic and abstractions, we should look to art: Catholic revelation has been essentially Incarnational. In brilliant studies of Dante and Bonaventure, Balthasar shows that Catholics have "seen" God in human form. Their emphasis on beauty in the gestures of ritual, drama and in the great Catholic artists indicates that God is to be found by the senses and not simply by the more cerebral and abstracted parts of the human person.

Muslims and Jews have also attempted to look back to the past to find ideas of God that will suit the present. Abu al-Kalam Azad (d. 1959), a notable Pakistani theologian, turned to the Koran to find a way of seeing God that was not so transcendent that he became a nullity and not so personal that he became an idol. He pointed to the symbolic nature of the Koranic discourse, noting the balance between metaphorical, figurative and anthropomorphic descriptions, on the one hand, and the constant reminders that God is incomparable on the other. Others have looked back to the Sufis for insight into God's relationship with the world. The Swiss Sufi Frithjof Schuon revived the doctrine of the Oneness of Being (*Wahdat al-Wujud*) later attributed to Ibn al-Arabi, which asserted that since God is the *only* reality, nothing exists but him, and the world itself is properly divine. He qualifies this with the reminder that this is an esoteric truth and can only be understood in the context of the mystical disciplines of Sufism.

Others have made God more accessible to the people and relevant to the political challenge of the time. In the years leading up to the Iranian revolution, the young lay philosopher Dr. Ali Shariati drew enormous crowds from among the educated middle classes. He was largely responsible for recruiting them against the shah, even though the mullahs disapproved of a good deal of his religious message. During demonstrations, the crowds used to carry his portrait alongside those of the Ayatollah Khomeini, even though it is not clear how he would have fared in Khomeini's Iran. Shariati was convinced that Westernization had alienated Muslims from their cultural roots and that to heal this disorder they must reinterpret the old symbols of their faith. Muhammad had done the same when he had given the ancient pagan rites of the *hajj* a monotheistic relevance. In his own book *Hajj*, Shariati took his readers through the pilgrimage to Mecca, gradually articulating a dynamic conception of God which each pilgrim had to create imaginatively for him- or herself. Thus, on reaching the Kabah, pilgrims would realize how suitable it was that the shrine is empty: "This is not your final destination; the Kabah is a sign so that the way is not lost; it only shows you the direction."[10] The Kabah witnessed to the importance of transcending all human expressions of the divine, which must not become ends in themselves. Why is the Kabah a simple cube, without decoration or ornament? Because it represents "the secret of God in the universe: God is shapeless, colorless, without simularity, whatever form or condition mankind selects, sees or imagines, it is not God."[11] The *hajj* itself was the antithesis of the alienation experienced by so many Iranians in the postcolonial period. It represents the existential course of each human being who turns his or her life around and directs it toward the ineffable God. Shariati's activist faith was dangerous: the Shah's secret police tortured and deported him and may even have been responsible for his death in London in 1977.

Martin Buber (1878–1965) had an equally dynamic vision of Judaism as a spiritual process and a striving for elemental unity. Religion consisted entirely of an encounter with a personal God, which nearly always took place in our meetings with other human beings. There were two spheres: one the realm of space and time where we relate to other beings as subject and object, as I-It. In the second realm, we relate to others as they truly are, seeing them as ends in themselves. This is the I-Thou realm, which reveals the presence of God. Life was an endless dialogue with God, which does not endanger our freedom or creativity, since God never tells us *what* he is asking of us. We experience him simply as a presence and an imperative and have to work out the meaning for ourselves. This meant a break with much Jewish tradition, and Buber's exegesis of traditional texts is sometimes strained. As a Kantian, Buber had no time for Torah, which he found alienating: God was not a lawgiver! The I-Thou encounter meant freedom and spontaneity, not the weight of a past tradition. Yet the *mitzvot* are central to much Jewish spirituality, and this may explain why Buber has been more popular with Christians than with Jews.

Buber realized that the term "God" had been soiled and degraded, but he refused to relinquish it. "Where would I find a word to equal it, to describe the same reality?" It bears too great and complex a meaning, has too many sacred associations. Those who do reject the word "God" must be respected, since so many appalling things have been done in its name.

> It is easy to understand why there are some who propose a period of silence about "the last things" so that the misused words may be redeemed. But this is not the way to redeem them. We cannot clean up the term "God" and we cannot make it whole; but, stained and mauled as it is, we can raise it from the ground and set it above an hour of great sorrow.[12]

Unlike the other rationalists, Buber was not opposed to myth: he found Lurianic myth of the divine sparks trapped in the world to be of crucial symbolic significance. The separation of the sparks from the Godhead represent the human experience of alienation. When we relate to others, we will restore the primal unity and reduce the alienation in the world.

Where Buber looked back to the Bible and Hasidism, Abraham Joshua Heschel (1907–72) returned to the spirit of the Rabbis and the Talmud. Unlike Buber, he believed that the *mitzvot* would help Jews to counter the dehumanizing aspects of modernity. They were actions that fulfilled God's need rather than our own. Modern life was characterized by depersonalization and exploitation: even God was reduced to a thing to be manipulated and made to serve our purposes. Consequently religion became dull and insipid; we needed a "depth theology" to delve below the structures and recover the original awe, mystery and wonder. It was no use trying to prove God's existence logically. Faith in God sprang from an immediate apprehension that had nothing to do with concepts and rationality. The Bible must be read metaphorically like poetry if it is to yield that sense of the sacred. The *mitzvot* should also be seen as symbolic gestures that train us to live in God's presence. Each *mitzvah* is a place of encounter in the tiny details of mundane life and, like a work of art, the world of the *mitzvot* has its own logic and rhythm. Above all, we should be aware that God needs human beings. He is not the remote God of the philosophers but the God of pathos described by the prophets.

Atheistic philosophers have also been attracted by the idea of God during the second half of the twentieth century. In *Being and Time* (1927) Martin Heidegger (1899–1976) saw Being in rather the same way as Tillich, though he would have denied that it was "God" in the Christian sense: it was distinct from particular beings and quite separate from the normal categories of thought. Some Christians have been inspired by Heidegger's work, even though its moral value is called into question by his association with the Nazi regime. In *What Is Metaphysics?*, his inaugural lecture at Freiburg, Heidegger developed a number of ideas that had already surfaced in the work of Plotinus, Denys and Erigena. Since Being is "Wholly Other," it is in fact Nothing—no thing, neither an object nor a particular being. Yet it is what makes all other existence possible. The ancients had believed that nothing came from nothing, but Heidegger reversed this maxim: *ex nihilo omne qua ens fit*. He ended his lecture by posing a question asked by Leibniz: "Why are there beings at all, rather than just nothing?" It is a question that evokes the shock of surprise and wonder that has been a constant in the human response to the world: why should anything exist at all? In his *Introduction to Metaphysics* (1953), Heidegger began by asking the same question. Theology believed that it had the answer and traced everything back to Something Else, to God. But this God was just another being rather than something that was wholly other. Heidegger had a somewhat reductive idea of the God of religion—though one shared by many religious people—but he often spoke in mystical terms about Being. He speaks of it as a great paradox; describes the thinking process as a waiting or listening to Being and seems to experience a return and withdrawal of Being, rather as mystics feel the absence of God. There is nothing that human beings can do to think Being into existence. Since the Greeks, people in the Western world have tended to forget Being and have concentrated on beings instead, a process that has resulted in its modern technological success. In the article written toward the end of his life titled "Only a God Can Save Us," Heidegger suggested that the experience of God's absence in our time could liberate us from preoccupation with beings. But there was nothing we could do to bring Being back into the present. We could only hope for a new advent in the future.

The Marxist philosopher Ernst Bloch (1885–1977) saw the idea of God as natural to humanity. The whole of human life was directed toward the future: we experience our lives as incomplete and unfinished. Unlike animals, we are never satisfied but always want more. It is this which has forced us to think and develop, since at each point of our lives we must transcend ourselves and go on to the next stage: the baby must become a toddler, the toddler must overcome its disabilities and become a child, and so forth. All our dreams and aspirations look ahead to what is to come. Even philosophy begins with wonder, which is the experience of the not-knowing, the not-yet. Socialism also looks forward to a utopia, but, despite the Marxist rejection of faith, where there is hope there is also religion. Like Feuerbach, Bloch saw God as the human ideal that has not yet come to be, but instead of seeing this as alienating he found it essential to the human condition.

Max Horkheimer (1895–1973), the German social theorist of the Frankfurt school, also saw "God" as an important ideal in a way that was reminiscent of the prophets. Whether he existed or not or whether we "believe in him" is superfluous. Without the idea of God there is no absolute meaning, truth or morality: ethics becomes simply a question of taste, a mood or a whim. Unless politics and morality somehow include the idea of "God," they will remain pragmatic and shrewd rather than wise. If there is no absolute, there is no reason that we should not hate or that war is worse than peace. Religion is essentially an inner feeling that there *is* a God. One of our earliest dreams is a longing for justice (how frequently we hear children complain: "It's not fair!"). Religion records the aspirations and accusations of innumerable human beings in the face of suffering and wrong. It makes us aware of our finite nature; we all hope that the injustice of the world will not be the last word.

The fact that people who have no conventional religious beliefs should keep returning to central themes that we have discovered in the history of God indicates that the idea is not as alien as many of us assume. Yet during the second half of the twentieth century, there has been a move away from the idea of a personal God who behaves like a larger version of us. There is nothing new about this. As we have seen, the Jewish scriptures, which Christians call their "Old" Testament, show a similar process; the Koran saw al-Lah in less personal terms than the Judeo-Christian tradition from the very beginning. Doctrines such as the Trinity and the mythology and symbolism of the mystical systems all strove to suggest that God was beyond personality. Yet this does not seem to have been made clear to many of the faithful. When John Robinson, Bishop of Woolwich, published *Honest to God* in 1963, stating that he could no longer subscribe to the old personal God "out there," there was uproar in Britain. A similar furor has greeted various remarks by David Jenkins, Bishop of Durham, even though these ideas are commonplace in academic circles. Don Cupitt, Dean of Emmanuel College, Cambridge, has also been dubbed "the atheist priest": he finds the traditional realistic God of theism unacceptable and proposes a form of Christian Buddhism, which puts religious experience before theology. Like Robinson, Cupitt has arrived intellectually at an insight that mystics in all three faiths have reached by a more intuitive route. Yet the idea that God does not really exist and that there is Nothing out there is far from new.

There is a growing intolerance of inadequate images of the Absolute. This is a healthy iconoclasm, since the idea of God has been used in the past to disastrous effect. One of the most characteristic new developments since the 1970s has been the rise of a type of religiosity that we usually call "fundamentalism" in most of the major world religions, including the three religions of God. A highly political spirituality, it is literal and intolerant in its vision. In the United States, which has always been prone to extremist and apocalyptic enthusiasm, Christian fundamentalism has attached itself to the New Right. Fundamentalists campaign for the abolition of legal abortion and for a hard line on moral and social decency. Jerry Falwell's Moral Majority achieved astonishing political power during the Reagan years. Other evangelists such as Maurice Cerullo, taking Jesus' remarks literally, believe that miracles are an essential hallmark of true faith. God will give the believer anything that he asks for in prayer. In Britain, fundamentalists such as Colin Urquhart have made the same claim. Christian fundamentalists seem to have little regard for the loving compassion of Christ. They are swift to condemn the people they see as the "enemies of God." Most would consider Jews and Muslims destined for hellfire, and Urquhart has argued that all oriental religions are inspired by the devil.

There have been similar developments in the Muslim world, which have been much publicized in the West. Muslim fundamentalists have toppled governments and either assassinated or threatened the enemies of Islam with the death penalty. Similarly, Jewish fundamentalists have settled in the Occupied Territories of the West Bank and the Gaza Strip with the avowed intention of driving out the Arab inhabitants, using force if necessary. Thus they believe that they are paving a way for the advent

of the Messiah, which is at hand. In all its forms, fundamentalism is a
fiercely reductive faith. Thus Rabbi Meir Kahane, the most extreme
member of Israel's Far Right until his assassination in New York in 1990:

> There are not several messages in Judaism. There is only one. And
> this message is to do what God wants. Sometimes God wants us to
> go to war, sometimes he wants us to live in peace. . . . But there is
> only one message: God wanted us to come to this country to create
> a Jewish state.[13]

This wipes out centuries of Jewish development, returning to the Deuteronomist perspective of the Book of Joshua. It is not surprising that people
who hear this kind of profanity, which makes "God" deny other people's
human rights, think that the sooner we relinquish him the better.

Yet, as we saw in the last chapter, this type of religiosity is actually a
retreat from God. To make such human, historical phenomena as Christian "Family Values," "Islam" or "the Holy Land" the focus of religious
devotion is a new form of idolatry. This type of belligerent righteousness
has been a constant temptation to monotheists throughout the long history
of God. It must be rejected as inauthentic. The God of Jews, Christians
and Muslims got off to an unfortunate start, since the tribal deity Yahweh
was murderously partial to his own people. Latter-day crusaders who
return to this primitive ethos are elevating the values of the tribe to
an unacceptably high status and substituting man-made ideals for the
transcendent reality which should challenge our prejudices. They are also
denying a crucial monotheistic theme. Ever since the prophets of Israel
reformed the old pagan cult of Yahweh, the God of monotheists has
promoted the ideal of compassion.

We have seen that compassion was a characteristic of most of the
ideologies that were created during the Axial Age. The compassionate
ideal even impelled Buddhists to make a major change in their religious
orientation when they introduced devotion (*bhakti*) to the Buddha and
bodhisattvas. The prophets insisted that cult and worship were useless
unless society as a whole adopted a more just and compassionate ethos.
These insights were developed by Jesus, Paul and the Rabbis, who all
shared the same Jewish ideals and suggested major changes in Judaism in
order to implement them. The Koran made the creation of a compassionate and just society the essence of the reformed religion of al-Lah. Compassion is a particularly difficult virtue. It demands that we go beyond
the limitations of our egotism, insecurity and inherited prejudice. Not

surprisingly, there have been times when all three of the God-religions have failed to achieve these high standards. During the eighteenth century, deists rejected traditional Western Christianity largely because it had become so conspicuously cruel and intolerant. The same will hold good today. All too often, conventional believers, who are not fundamentalists, share their aggressive righteousness. They use "God" to prop up their own loves and hates, which they attribute to God himself. But Jews, Christians and Muslims who punctiliously attend divine services yet denigrate people who belong to different ethnic and ideological camps deny one of the basic truths of their religion. It is equally inappropriate for people who call themselves Jews, Christians and Muslims to condone an inequitable social system. The God of historical monotheism demands mercy not sacrifice, compassion rather than decorous liturgy.

There has often been a distinction between people who practice a cultic form of religion and those who have cultivated a sense of the God of compassion. The prophets fulminated against their contemporaries who thought that temple worship was sufficient. Jesus and St. Paul both made it clear that external observance was useless if it was not accompanied by charity: it was little better than sounding brass or a tinkling cymbal. Muhammad came into conflict with those Arabs who wanted to worship the pagan goddesses alongside al-Lah in the ancient rites, without implementing the compassionate ethos that God demanded as a condition of all true religion. There had been a similar divide in the pagan world of Rome: the old cultic religion celebrated the status quo, while the philosophers preached a message that they believed would change the world. It may be that the compassionate religion of the One God has only been observed by a minority; most have found it difficult to face the extremity of the God-experience with its uncompromising ethical demands. Ever since Moses brought the tablets of the Law from Mount Sinai, the majority have preferred the worship of a Golden Calf, a traditional, unthreatening image of a deity they have constructed for themselves, with its consoling, time-honored rituals. Aaron, the high priest, presided over the manufacture of the golden effigy. The religious establishment itself is often deaf to the inspiration of prophets and mystics who bring news of a much more demanding God.

God can also be used as an unworthy panacea, as an alternative to mundane life and as the object of indulgent fantasy. The idea of God has frequently been used as the opium of the people. This is a particular danger when he is conceived as an-other Being—just like us, only bigger and better—in his own heaven, which is itself conceived as a paradise of earthly delights. Yet originally, "God" was used to help people to concentrate on this world and to face up to unpleasant reality. Even the pagan cult of Yahweh, for all its manifest faults, stressed his involvement in current events in profane time, as opposed to the sacred time of rite and myth. The prophets of Israel forced their people to confront their own social culpability and impending political catastrophe in the name of the God who revealed himself in these historical occurrences. The Christian doctrine of Incarnation stressed the divine immanence in the world of flesh and blood. Concern for the here and now was especially marked in Islam: nobody could have been more of a realist than Muhammad, who was a political as well as a spiritual genius. As we have seen, later generations of Muslims have shared his concern to incarnate the divine will in human history by establishing a just and decent society. From the very beginning, God was experienced as an imperative to action. From the moment when—as either El or Yahweh—God called Abraham away from his family in Haran, the cult entailed concrete action in this world and often a painful abandonment of the old sanctities.

This dislocation also involved great strain. The Holy God, who was wholly other, was experienced as a profound shock by the prophets. He demanded a similar holiness and separation on the part of his people. When he spoke to Moses on Sinai, the Israelites were not allowed to approach the foot of the mountain. An entirely new gulf suddenly yawned between humanity and the divine, rupturing the holistic vision of paganism. There was, therefore, a potential for alienation from the world, which reflected a dawning consciousness of the inalienable autonomy of the individual. It is no accident that monotheism finally took root during the exile to Babylon, when the Israelites also developed the ideal of personal responsibility, which has been crucial in both Judaism and Islam.[14] We have seen that the Rabbis used the idea of an immanent God to help Jews to cultivate a sense of the sacred rights of the human personality. Yet alienation has continued to be a danger in all three faiths: in the West the experience of God was continually accompanied by guilt and by a pessimistic anthropology. In Judaism and Islam there is no doubt that the observance of Torah and Shariah has sometimes been seen as a heteronymous compliance with an external law, even though we have seen that nothing could have been further from the intention of the men who compiled these legal codes.

Those atheists who preached emancipation from a God who demands such servile obedience were protesting against an inadequate but unfortunately familiar image of God. Again, this was based on a conception of the divine that was too personalistic. It interpreted the scriptural image of God's judgment too literally and assumed that God was a sort of Big Brother in the sky. This image of the divine Tyrant imposing an alien law on his unwilling human servants has to go. Terrorizing the populace into civic obedience with threats is no longer acceptable or even practicable, as the downfall of communist regimes demonstrated so dramatically in the autumn of 1989. The anthropomorphic idea of God as Lawgiver and Ruler is not adequate to the temper of post-modernity. Yet the atheists who complained that the idea of God was unnatural were not entirely correct. We have seen that Jews, Christians and Muslims have developed remarkably similar ideas of God, which also resemble other conceptions of the Absolute. When people try to find an ultimate meaning and value in human life, their minds seem to go in a certain direction. They have not been coerced to do this; it is something that seems natural to humanity.

Yet if feelings are not to degenerate into indulgent, aggressive or unhealthy emotionalism, they need to be informed by the critical intelligence. The experience of God must keep abreast of other current enthusiasms, including those of the mind. The experiment of Falsafah was an attempt to relate faith in God with the new cult of rationalism among Muslims, Jews and, later, Western Christians. Eventually Muslims and Jews retreated from philosophy. Rationalism, they decided, had its uses, especially in such empirical studies as science, medicine and mathematics, but it was not entirely appropriate in the discussion of a God who lay beyond concepts. The Greeks had already sensed this and developed an early distrust of their native metaphysics. One of the drawbacks of the philosophic method of discussing God was that it could make it sound as though the Supreme Deity were simply an-other Being, the highest of all the things that exist, instead of a reality of an entirely different order. Yet the venture of Falsafah was important, since it showed an appreciation of the necessity of relating God to other experiences—if only to define the extent to which this was possible. To push God into intellectual isolation in a holy ghetto of his own is unhealthy and unnatural. It can encourage people to think that it is not necessary to apply normal standards of decency and rationality to behavior supposedly inspired by "God."

From the first, Falsafah had been associated with science. It was their initial enthusiasm for medicine, astronomy and mathematics which had led the first Muslim Faylasufs to discuss al-Lah in metaphysical terms. Science had effected a major change in their outlook, and they found that they could not think of God in the same way as their fellow Muslims. The philosophic conception of God was markedly different from the Koranic vision, but Faylasufs did recover some insights that were in danger of being lost in the *ummah* at that time. Thus the Koran had an extremely positive attitude to other religious traditions: Muhammad had not believed that he was founding a new, exclusive religion and considered that all rightly guided faith came from the One God. By the ninth century, however, the *ulema* were beginning to lose sight of this and were promoting the cult of Islam as the one true religion. The Faylasufs reverted to the older universalist approach, even though they reached it by a different route. We have a similar opportunity today. In our scientific age, we cannot think about God in the same way as our forebears, but the challenge of science could help us to appreciate some old truths.

We have seen that Albert Einstein had an appreciation of mystical religion. Despite his famous remarks about God not playing dice, he did not believe that his theory of relativity should affect the conception of God. During a visit to England in 1921, Einstein was asked by the Archbishop of Canterbury what were its implications for theology. He replied: "None. Relativity is a purely scientific matter and has nothing to do with religion."[15] When Christians are dismayed by such scientists as Stephen Hawking, who can find no room for God in his cosmology, they are perhaps still thinking of God in anthropomorphic terms as a Being who created the world in the same way as we would. Yet creation was not originally conceived in such a literal manner. Interest in Yahweh as Creator did not enter Judaism until the exile to Babylon. It was a conception that was alien to the Greek world: creation *ex nihilo* was not an official doctrine of Christianity until the Council of Nicaea in 341. Creation is a central teaching of the Koran, but, like all its utterances about God, this is said to be a "parable" or a "sign" (*aya*) of an ineffable truth. Jewish and Muslim rationalists found it a difficult and problematic doctrine, and many rejected it. Sufis and Kabbalists all preferred the Greek metaphor of emanation. In any case, cosmology was not a scientific description of the origins of the world but was originally a symbolic expression of a spiritual and psychological truth. There is consequently little agitation about the new science in the Muslim world: as we have seen, the events of recent history have been more of a threat than has science to the traditional conception of God. In the West, however, a more literal understanding of scripture has long prevailed. When some Western Christians feel their faith in God undermined by the new science, they are probably imagining God as Newton's great Mechanick, a personalistic notion of

God which should, perhaps, be rejected on religious as well as on scientific grounds. The challenge of science might shock the churches into a fresh appreciation of the symbolic nature of scriptural narrative.

The idea of a personal God seems increasingly unacceptable at the present time for all kinds of reasons: moral, intellectual, scientific and spiritual. Feminists are also repelled by a personal deity who, because of "his" gender, has been male since his tribal, pagan days. Yet to talk about "she"—other than in a dialectical way—can be just as limiting, since it confines the illimitable God to a purely human category. The old metaphysical notion of God as the Supreme Being, which has long been popular in the West, is also felt to be unsatisfactory. The God of the philosophers is the product of a now outdated rationalism, so the traditional "proofs" of his existence no longer work. The widespread acceptance of the God of the philosophers by the deists of the Enlightenment can be seen as the first step to the current atheism. Like the old Sky God, this deity is so remote from humanity and the mundane world that he easily becomes *Deus Otiosus* and fades from our consciousness.

The God of the mystics might seem to present a possible alternative. The mystics have long insisted that God is not an-Other Being; they have claimed that he does not really exist and that it is better to call him Nothing. This God is in tune with the atheistic mood of our secular society, with its distrust of inadequate images of the Absolute. Instead of seeing God as an objective Fact, which can be demonstrated by means of scientific proof, mystics have claimed that he is a subjective experience, mysteriously experienced in the ground of being. This God is to be approached through the imagination and can be seen as a kind of art form, akin to the other great artistic symbols that have expressed the ineffable mystery, beauty and value of life. Mystics have used music, dancing, poetry, fiction, stories, painting, sculpture and architecture to express this Reality that goes beyond concepts. Like all art, however, mysticism requires intelligence, discipline and self-criticism as a safeguard against indulgent emotionalism and projection. The God of the mystics could even satisfy the feminists, since both Sufis and Kabbalists have long tried to introduce a female element into the divine.

There are drawbacks, however. Mysticism has been regarded with some suspicion by many Jews and Muslims since the Shabbetai Zevi fiasco and the decline of latter-day Sufism. In the West, mysticism has never been a mainstream religious enthusiasm. The Protestant and Catholic Reformers either outlawed or marginalized it, and the scientific Age of Reason did not encourage this mode of perception. Since the 1960s, there has been a fresh interest in mysticism, expressed in the enthusiasm for Yoga, meditation and Buddhism, but it is not an approach that easily consorts with our objective, empirical mentality. The God of the mystics is not easy to apprehend. It requires long training with an expert and a considerable investment of time. The mystic has to work hard to acquire this sense of the reality known as God (which many have refused to name). Mystics often insist that human beings must deliberately create this sense of God for themselves, with the same degree of care and attention that others devote to artistic creation. It is not something that is likely to appeal to people in a society which has become used to speedy gratification, fast food and instant communication. The God of the mystics does not arrive readymade and prepackaged. He cannot be experienced as quickly as the instant ecstasy created by a revivalist preacher, who quickly has a whole congregation clapping its hands and speaking in tongues.

It is possible to acquire some of the mystical attitudes. Even if we are incapable of the higher states of consciousness achieved by a mystic, we can learn that God does not exist in any simplistic sense, for example, or that the very word "God" is only a symbol of a reality that ineffably transcends it. The mystical agnosticism could help us to acquire a restraint that stops us rushing into these complex matters with dogmatic assurance. But if these notions are not felt upon the pulse and personally appropriated, they are likely to seem meaningless abstractions. Secondhand mysticism could prove to be as unsatisfactory as reading the explanation of a poem by a literary critic instead of the original. We have seen that mysticism was often seen as an esoteric discipline, not because the mystics wanted to exclude the vulgar herd but because these truths could only be perceived by the intuitive part of the mind after special training. They mean something different when they are approached by this particular route, which is not accessible to the logical, rationalist faculty.

Ever since the prophets of Israel started to ascribe their own feelings and experiences to God, monotheists have in some sense created a God for themselves. God has rarely been seen as a self-evident fact that can be encountered like any other objective existent. Today many people seem to have lost the will to make this imaginative effort. This need not be a catastrophe. When religious ideas have lost their validity, they have usually faded away painlessly: if the human idea of God no longer works for us in the empirical age, it will be discarded. Yet in the past people have always created new symbols to act as a focus for spirituality. Human beings have always created a faith for themselves, to cultivate their sense of the wonder and ineffable significance of life. The aimlessness, alienation, anomie and violence that characterize so much of modern life seem to indicate that now that they are not deliberately creating a faith in "God" or anything else—it matters little what—many people are falling into despair.

In the United States, we have seen that ninety-nine percent of the population claim to believe in God, yet the prevalence of fundamentalism, apocalypticism and "instant" charismatic forms of religiosity in America is not reassuring. The escalating crime rate, drug addiction and the revival of the death penalty are not signs of a spiritually healthy society. In Europe there is a growing blankness where God once existed in the human consciousness. One of the first people to express this dry desolation— quite different from the heroic atheism of Nietzsche—was Thomas Hardy. In "The Darkling Thrush," written on December 30, 1900, at the turn of the twentieth century, he expressed the death of spirit that was no longer able to create a faith in life's meaning:

> I leant upon a coppice gate
>   When Frost was spectre-grey
> And Winter's dregs made desolate
>   The weakening eye of day.
> The tangled bine-stems scored the sky
>   Like strings of broken lyres,
> And all mankind that haunted nigh
>   Had sought their household fires.
>
> The land's sharp features seemed to be
>   The Century's corpse outleant,
> His crypt the cloudy canopy,
>   The wind his death-lament.
> The ancient pulse of germ and birth
>   Was shrunken hard and dry,
> And every spirit upon earth
>   Seemed fervourless as I.
>
> At once a voice arose among
>   The bleak twigs overhead
> In a full-hearted evensong
>   Of joy illimited;
> An aged thrush, frail, gaunt, and small,

In blast-beruffled plume,
Had chosen thus to fling his soul
  Upon the growing gloom.

So little cause for carolings
  Of such ecstatic sound
Was written on terrestrial things
  Afar or nigh around,
That I could think there trembled through
  His happy good-night air
Some blessed Hope, whereof he knew
  And I was unaware.

Human beings cannot endure emptiness and desolation; they will fill the vacuum by creating a new focus of meaning. The idols of fundamentalism are not good substitutes for God; if we are to create a vibrant new faith for the twenty-first century, we should, perhaps, ponder the history of God for some lessons and warnings.

Glossary

Alam al-mithal (Arabic) The world of pure images: the archetypal world of the imagination that leads the Muslim mystic and contemplative philosopher to God.

Alem (plural, *ulema*) (Arabic) Muslim cleric.

Apatheia (Greek) Impassibility, serenity and invulnerability. These characteristics of the God of the Greek philosophers became central to the Christian conception of God, who was considered impervious to suffering and change.

Apophatic (Greek). Silent. Greek Christians came to believe that all theology should have an element of silence, paradox and restraint in order to emphasize the ineffability and mystery of God.

Archetype The original pattern or prototype of our world, which was identified with the divine world of the ancient gods. In the pagan world, everything here below was seen as a replica or copy of a reality in the celestial world. See also *alam al-mithal*.

Ashkenazim (Hebrew corruption of "Allemagne"). The Jews of Germany and parts of Eastern and Western Europe.

Atman (Hindi) The sacred power of *Brahman* (q.v.), which each individual experiences within him or herself.

Avatar In Hindu myth, the descent of a god to earth in human form. More generally used of a person who is believed to embody or incarnate the divine.

Axial Age The term used by historians to denote the period 800–200 BCE, a time of transition during which the major world religions emerged in the civilized world.

Aya (plural, *Ayat*) (Arabic) Sign, parable. In the Koran, the manifestations of God in the world.

Banat al-Lah (Arabic) The Daughters of God: in the Koran, the phrase refers to the three pagan goddesses al-Lat, al-Uzza and Manat.

Baqa (Arabic) Survival. The return of the Sufi mystic to his enhanced and
   enlarged self after his climactic absorption (*'fana*) in God (q.v.).
Batin (Arabic) The inner meaning of the Koran. A *batini* is a Muslim who
   devotes himself to the esoteric, mystical understanding of the faith.
Bhakti (Hindi) Devotion to the person of the *Buddha* (q.v.) or to the Hindu
   gods who had appeared on earth in human form.
Bodhisattva (Hindi) The Buddhas-to-be. Those who have delayed their own
   private *nirvana* (q.v.) in order to guide and save suffering, unenlightened
   humanity.
Brahman The Hindu term for the sacred power that sustains all existing
   things; the inner meaning of existence.
Breaking of the Vessels A term in the Kabbalism of Isaac Luria that describes the
   primal catastrophe, when the sparks of divine light fell to the earth and
   were trapped in matter.
Buddha (Hindi) The enlightened one. The title applies to the numerous men
   and women who have attained *nirvana* (q.v.), but it is often used of
   Siddhartha Gautama, the founder of Buddhism.

Dhikr (Arabic) The "remembrance" of God prescribed in the Koran. In Sufism
   dhikr takes the form of a recitation of the name of God as a mantra.
Dogma Used by Greek Christians to describe the hidden, secret traditions of
   the Church, which could only be understood mystically and expressed
   symbolically. In the West, dogma has come to mean a body of opinion,
   categorically and authoritatively stated.
Dynameis (Greek) The "powers" of God. A term used by Greeks to denote
   God's activity in the world, which is to be regarded as quite distinct from
   his inaccessible essence.

Ecstasy (Greek) Literally, "a going out of the self." Applied to God, it indicates
   a *kenosis* (q.v.) of the hidden God who transcends his introspection to make
   himself known to humanity.
El The old *High God* (q.v.) of Canaan, who seems also to have been the God
   of Abraham, Isaac and Jacob, the fathers of the people of Israel.
Emanation A process whereby the various grades of reality were imagined to
   flow from a single, primal source, which the monotheists identified as God.
   Some Jews, Christians and Muslims, including philosophers and mystics,
   preferred to use this ancient metaphor to describe the origins of life than
   the more conventional biblical story of an instantaneous creation of all
   things by God in a moment of time.
En Sof (Hebrew: "without end"). The inscrutable, inaccessible and unknowable essence of God in the Jewish mystical theology of *Kabbalah* (q.v.).
Energeiai (Greek: "energies") God's "activities" in the world, which enable us
   to glimpse something of him. Like *dynameis* (q.v.), the term is used to
   distinguish the human conception of God from the ineffable and
   incomprehensible reality itself.
Enuma Elish The Babylonian epic recounting the creation of the world,
   chanted during the New Year Festival.
Epiphany The appearance of a god or goddess on earth in human form.

Falsafah (Arabic) Philosophy. The attempt to interpret Islam in terms of ancient Greek rationalism.

'Fana (Arabic) Annihilation. The ecstatic absorption in God of the Sufi mystic.

Faylasuf (Arabic) Philosopher. Used of Muslims and Jews in the Islamic empire who were dedicated to the rational and scientific ideals of *Falsafah* (q.v.).

Getik (Persian) The earthly world in which we live and which we can experience with our senses.

Godhead The inaccessible, hidden source of the reality that we know as "God."

Goy (plural, *goyim*) (Hebrew) Non-Jews or Gentiles.

Hadith (plural, *ahadith*) (Arabic) The traditions or collected maxims of the Prophet Muhammad.

Hajj (Arabic) The Muslim pilgrimage to Mecca.

Hesychasm, hesychast From the Greek *hesychia*: interior silence, tranquillity. The silent contemplation cultivated by Greek Orthodox mystics which eschewed words and concepts.

High God The supreme deity worshipped by many peoples as the sole God, creator of the world, who was eventually superseded by a pantheon of more immediate and attractive gods and goddesses. Also known as *Sky God*.

Hijra (Arabic) The migration of the first Muslims from Mecca to Medina in 622 CE, an event that marks the beginning of the Islamic era.

Holiness In Hebrew *kaddosh*: the absolute otherness of God; the radical separation of the divine from the profane world.

Holy Spirit Term used by Rabbis, often interchangeably with *Shekinah* (q.v.) to denote God's presence on earth. A way of distinguishing the God we experience and know from the utterly transcendent divinity which forever eludes us. In Christianity the Spirit would become the third "person" of the Trinity.

Homoousion (Greek) Literally, "made of the same stuff or substance." The controversial term used by Athanasius and his supporters to express their conviction that Jesus was of the same nature (*ousia*) as God the Father and was, therefore, divine in the same way as he.

Hypostasis (Greek) The exterior expression of a person's inner nature, as compared with *ousia* (essence) (q.v.), which represents a person or object seen from within. An object or person viewed from the outside. Term used by the Greeks to describe the three manifestations of the hidden essence of God: as Father, Son and Spirit.

Idolatry The worship or veneration of a human or man-made reality instead of the transcendent God.

Ijtihad (Arabic) Independent reasoning.

Ilm (Arabic) The secret "knowledge" of God, which Shiite Muslims believe to have been the sole possession of the *Imams* (q.v.).

Imam (Arabic) In the *Shiah* (q.v.) the Imam is a descendent of Ali, Muhammad's son-in-law. Imams were revered as *avatars* (q.v.) of the divine. Sunni Muslims, however, simply use the term to describe the person who leads the prayers in the mosque.

Incarnation The embodiment of God in human form.

Ishraq (Arabic) Illumination. The Ishraqi school of philosophy and spirituality was founded by Yahya Suhrawardi.

Islam (Arabic) Surrender [to God].

Jahiliyyah (Arabic) The time of ignorance: the term used by Muslims to describe the pre-Islamic period in Arabia.

Kabah (Arabic) The cube-shaped granite shrine dedicated to al-Lah in Mecca.

Kalam (Arabic) Literally, "debates." Muslim theology: the attempt to interpret the Koran in a rational way.

Kenosis (Greek) Self-emptying.

Kerygma (Greek) Term used by the Greek Christians to denote the public teaching of the Church, which can be expressed clearly and rationally, as opposed to its *dogma* (q.v.), which could not.

Logos (Greek) Reason; definition; word. God's "Logos" was identified by Greek theologians with the *Wisdom* (q.v.) of God in the Jewish scriptures or with the Word mentioned in the prologue of St. John's Gospel.

Madrasah (Arabic) College of Islamic studies.

Mana Term originally used in the South Sea Islands to describe the unseen forces that pervade the physical word and were experienced as sacred or divine.

Menok (Persian) The heavenly, archetypal realm of being.

Merkavah (Hebrew) Chariot. See *Throne Mysticism*.

Mishnah (Hebrew) The code of Jewish law, collated, edited and revised by the early Rabbis, known as the *tannaim* (q.v.). The code, divided into six major units and sixty-three minor ones, is the basis of the legal discussion and commentaries of the *Talmud* (q.v.).

Mitzvah (plural, *mitzvot*) (Hebrew) Commandment.

Muslim (Arabic) One who surrenders him or herself to God.

Mutazilah (Arabic) The Muslim sect which attempted to explain the Koran in rational terms.

Nirvana (Hindi) Literally "cooling off" or "going out" like a flame; extinction. Term used by Buddhists to denote the ultimate reality, the goal and fulfillment of human life and the end of pain. Like God, the end of the monotheistic quest, it is not capable of definition in rational terms but belongs to a different order of experience.

Numinous From the latin *numen*: spirit. The sense of the sacred, of transcendence and *holiness* (q.v.) which has always inspired awe, wonder and terror.

Oikumene (Greek) The civilized world.

Orthodox, Orthodoxy Literally, "right teaching." Term used by the Greek Christians to distinguish those who adhered to the correct doctrines of the

Church from heretics, such as the Arians or Nestorians, who did not. The term is also applied to the traditional Judaism which adheres to a strict observance of the Law.

Ousia (Greek) Essence, nature. That which makes a thing what it is. A person or object seen from within. Applied to God, the term denotes that divine essence which eludes human understanding and experience.

Parzuf (plural, *parzufim*) (Hebrew) Countenance. Like the *personae* (q.v.) of the Trinity; some types of *Kabbalah* (q.v.) have imagined the inscrutable God revealing himself to humanity in a number of different "countenances," each of which has distinctive features.

Patriarchs The term used of Abraham, Isaac and Jacob, the ancestors of the Israelites.

Persona (plural, *personae*) (Latin) The mask worn by an actor to define the character he is presenting to the audience and make his voice audible in the theater. The term preferred by the Western Christians to denote the three *hypostases* (q.v.) of the Trinity. The three "persons" are Father, Son and Spirit.

Pir (Arabic) The spiritual director of Muslim mystics.

Prophet One who speaks on God's behalf.

Rig-Veda The collection of odes, dating from 1500–900 BCE, which expressed the religious beliefs of the Aryans who invaded the Indus valley and imposed their faith on the indigenous people of the subcontinent.

Sefirah (plural, *sefiroth*) (Hebrew) "Numerations." The ten stages of God's unfolding revelation of himself in *Kabbalah* (q.v.). The ten *sefiroth* are:

1. Kether Elyon: The Supreme Crown.
2. Hokhmah: Wisdom.
3. Binah: Intelligence.
4. Hesed: Loving-kindness.
5. Din: Stern Judgment.
6. Tifereth: Beauty.
7. Netsakh: Endurance.
8. Hod: Majesty.
9. Yesod: Foundation.
10. Malkuth: Kingdom. Also called *Shekinah* (q.v.).

Sephardim The Jews of Spain.

Shahadah The Muslim proclamation of faith: "I bear witness that there is no god but al-Lah and that Muhammad is his Messenger."

Shariah The Islamic Holy Law, based on the Koran and the *hadith* (q.v.).

Shekinah From the Hebrew *shakan*: to pitch one's tent. The rabbinic term for God's presence on earth to distinguish a Jew's experience of God from the ineffable reality itself. In *Kabbalah* it is identified with the last of the *sefiroth* (q.v.).

Shema The Jewish proclamation of faith: "Listen (*shema*) Israel; Yahweh is our God, Yahweh is One!" (Deuteronomy 6:4)

Shiah The Party of Ali. Muslim *Shiis* believe that Ali ibn Abi Talib (son-in-law and cousin of the Prophet Muhammad) and the *Imams* (q.v.), his descendants, should lead the Islamic community.

Shiur Qomah (Hebrew) The Measurement of the Height. A controversial fifth-century mystical text describing the figure that Ezekiel saw enthroned on the heavenly chariot.

Sky God See *High God*.

Sufi, Sufism The mystics and mystical spirituality of Islam. The term may derive from the fact that the early Sufis and ascetics preferred to wear the coarse garments made of wool (Arabic, *SWF*) favored by Muhammad and his companions.

Sunnah (Arabic) Practice. Those customs sanctioned by tradition supposed to imitate the behavior and actions of the Prophet Muhammad.

Sunnah; Sunni The *ahl al-sunnah*: term used to denote the majority group of Muslims whose Islam is based upon the Koran, the *hadith* and the *sunnah* (q.v.) and upon the *Sharia* (q.v.) rather than upon the devotion to the *Imams* (q.v.) as expressed by the *Shiah* (q.v.).

Talmud (Hebrew) Literally, "study" or "learning." The classical rabbinic discussions of the ancient code of Jewish Law. See also *Mishnah*.

Tannaim (Hebrew) The first generations of rabbinic scholars and legists who collated and edited the ancient code of oral Jewish Law, known as the *Mishnah* (q.v.).

Taqwa (Arabic) God-consciousness.

Tariqa (Arabic) An order of *Sufi* mystics (q.v.).

Tawhid (Arabic) Unity. This refers to the divine unity of God and also to the integration required of each Muslim, who strives to surrender wholly to God.

Tawil The symbolic, mystical interpretation of the Koran advocated by such esoteric sects as the Ismailis.

Tfillin (Hebrew) The black boxes known as phylacteries, containing the text of the *Shema*, which Jewish men and boys who have attained majority wear fastened to their foreheads and left arms near the heart during the morning service, as commanded by Deuteronomy 6:4-7.

Theophany A manifestation of God to men and women.

Theoria (Greek) Contemplation.

Throne Mysticism An early form of Jewish mysticism, which focused upon the description of the heavenly chariot (*Merkavah*) seen by the Prophet Ezekiel and which took the form of an imaginary ascent through the halls (*hekhaloth*) of God's palace to his heavenly throne.

Tikkun (Hebrew) Restoration. The process of redemption described in the Kabbalism of Isaac Luria, whereby the divine sparks scattered during the *Breaking of the Vessels* (q.v.) are reintegrated with God.

Torah (Hebrew) The Law of Moses as outlined in the first five books of the Bible: Genesis, Exodus, Leviticus, Numbers and Deuteronomy, which are also collectively known as the Torah.

Traditionists The *ahl al-hadith*: the people of the *hadith*. Those Muslims who interpreted the Koran and the *hadith* (q.v.) literally in order to oppose the rationalistic tendencies of the *Mutazilah* (q.v.).

Tsimtsum (Hebrew) Shrinking, withdrawal. In the mysticism of Isaac Luria, God is imagined contracting into himself in order to make a space for creation. It is, therefore, an act of *kenosis* (q.v.) and self-limitation.

Ulema See *alem*.

Ummah (Arabic) The Muslim community.

Upanishads Hindu scriptures composed during the *Axial Age* (q.v.) from the eighth to the second centuries BCE.

Veda (plural, *Vedas*) See *Rig-Veda*.

Wisdom In Hebrew *Hokhmah* and in Greek *Sophia*. The personification of God's divine plan in the scriptures. A method of describing his activity in the world, which comes to stand for the human perception of God as opposed to the inaccessible reality itself.

Yahweh The name of God in Israel. Yahweh may originally have been the god of another people, adopted by Moses for the Israelites. By the third and second centuries BCE, Jews no longer pronounced the holy name, which is written YHWH.

Yoga A discipline early evolved by the people of India, which "yokes" the powers of the mind. By means of its techniques of concentration, the Yogi acquires an intense and heightened perception of reality, which seems to bring with it a sense of peace, bliss and tranquillity.

Zanna (Arabic) Guesswork. Term used in the Koran for pointless theological speculation.

Ziggurat Temple-tower built by the Sumerians in a form found in many other parts of the world. Ziggurats consist of huge stone ladders which men could climb to meet their gods.

Notes

Quotations from the Jewish and Christian scriptures are taken from *The Jerusalem Bible*.

Quotations from the Koran are from *The Message of the Qur'an*, translated and explained by Muhammad Asad, Gibraltar, 1980.

1 In the Beginning . . .

1. Mircea Eliade, *The Myth of the Eternal Return or Cosmos and History*, trans. Willard R. Trask, (Princeton, 1954).
2. From "The Babylonian Creation" in N. K. Sandars (trans.), *Poems of Heaven and Hell from Ancient Mesopotamia* (London, 1971), p. 73.
3. Ibid., p. 99.
4. Pindar, Nemean VI, 1–4, *The Odes of Pindar*, trans. C. M. Bowra, (Harmondsworth, 1969), p. 206.
5. Anat-Baal Texts 49:11:5, quoted in E. O. James, *The Ancient Gods* (London, 1960), p. 88.
6. Genesis 2:5–7.
7. Genesis 4:26; Exodus 6:3.
8. Genesis 31:42; 49:24.
9. Genesis 17:1.
10. *Iliad* XXIV, 393, trans. E. V. Rieu, (Harmondsworth, 1950), p. 446.
11. Acts of the Apostles 14:11–18.
12. Genesis 28:15.
13. Genesis 26:16–17. Elements of J have been added to this account by E, hence the use of the name Yahweh.
14. Genesis 32:30–31.
15. George E. Mendenhall, "The Hebrew Conquest of Palestine," *The Biblical Archeologist* 25, 1962; M. Weippert, *The Settlement of the Israelite Tribes in Palestine* (London, 1971).
16. Deuteronomy 26:5–8.
17. L. E. Bihu, "Midianite Elements in Hebrew Religion," *Jewish Theological*

Studies, 31; Salo Wittmeyer Baron, *A Social and Religious History of the Jews*, 10 vols., 2nd ed. (New York, 1952–1967), I. p. 46.

18. Exodus 3:5–6.
19. Exodus 3:14.
20. Exodus 19:16–18.
21. Exodus 20:2.
22. Joshua 24:14–15.
23. Joshua 24:24.
24. James, *The Ancient Gods*, p. 152; Psalms 29, 89, 93. These psalms date from after the Exile, however.
25. 1 Kings 18:20–40.
26. 1 Kings 19:11–13.
27. *Rig-Veda* 10:29, in R. H. Zaener, trans. and ed., *Hindu Scriptures* (London and New York, 1966), p. 12.
28. *Chandogya Upanishad* VI.13, in Juan Mascaró, trans. and ed., *The Upanishads* (Harmondsworth, 1965), p. 111.
29. Kena Upanishad I, in Mascaró, trans. and ed., *The Upanishads*, p. 51.
30. Ibid., 3, p. 52.
31. Samyutta-Nikaya, Part II: Nidana Vagga, trans. and ed. Leon Feer, (London, 1888) p. 106.
32. Edward Conze, *Buddhism: its Essence and Development* (Oxford, 1959), p. 40.
33. Udana 8.13, quoted and trans. in Paul Steintha, *Udanan* (London 1885), p. 81.
34. *The Symposium*, trans. W. Hamilton, (Harmondsworth, 1951), pp. 93–4.
35. *Philosophy*, Fragment 15.
36. *Poetics* 1461 b, 3.

2 *One God*

1. Isaiah 6:3.
2. Rudolf Otto, *The Idea of the Holy, An Inquiry into the Non-rational Factor in the Idea of the Divine and Its Relation to the Rational*, trans. John W. Harvey (Oxford, 1923), pp. 29–30.
3. Isaiah 6:5.
4. Exodus 4:11.
5. Psalms 29, 89, 93. Dagon was the god of the Philistines.
6. Isaiah 6:10.
7. Matthew 13:14–15.
8. Inscription on a cuneiform tablet quoted in Chaim Potok, *Wanderings, History of the Jews* (New York, 1978), p. 187.
9. Isaiah 6:13.
10. Isaiah 6:12.
11. Isaiah 10:5–6.
12. Isaiah 1:3.
13. Isaiah :11–15.
14. Isaiah 1:15–17.
15. Amos 7:15–17.
16. Amos 3:8.

17. Amos 8:7.
18. Amos 5:18.
19. Amos 3:1–2.
20. Hosea 8:5.
21. Hosea 6:6.
22. Genesis 4:1.
23. Hosea 2:23–24.
24. Hosea 2:18–19.
25. Hosea 1:2.
26. Hosea 1:9.
27. Hosea 13:2.
28. Jeremiah 10; Psalms 31:6; 115:4–8; 135:15.
29. The translation of this verse is by John Bowker, *The Religious Imagination and the Sense of God* (Oxford, 1978), p. 73.
30. See Genesis 14:20.
31. 2 Kings 32:3–10; 2 Chronicles 34:14.
32. Deuteronomy 6:4–6.
33. Deuteronomy 7:3.
34. Deuteronomy 7:5–6.
35. Deuteronomy 28:64–8.
36. 2 Chronicles 34:5–7.
37. Exodus 23:33.
38. Joshua 11:21–2.
39. Jeremiah 25:8, 9.
40. Jeremiah 13:15–17.
41. Jeremiah 1:6–10.
42. Jeremiah 23:9.
43. Jeremiah 20:7, 9.
44. In China, Tao and Confucianism are seen as two facets of a single spirituality, concerning the inner and outer man. Hinduism and Buddhism are related and can both be seen as a reformed paganism.
45. Jeremiah 2:31, 32; 12:7–11; 14:7–9; 6:11.
46. Jeremiah 32:15.
47. Jeremiah 44:15–19.
48. Jeremiah 31:33.
49. Ezekiel 1:4–25.
50. Ezekiel 3:14–15.
51. Ezekiel 8:12.
52. Psalm 137.
53. Isaiah 11:15, 16.
54. Isaiah 51:9, 10. This would be a constant theme. See Psalms 65:7; 74:13–14; 77:16; Job 3:8; 7:12.
55. Isaiah 46:1.
56. Isaiah 45:21.
57. Isaiah 43:11, 12.
58. Isaiah 55:8, 9.
59. Isaiah 19:24, 25.
60. Exodus 33:20.

61. Exodus 33:18.
62. Exodus 34:29–35.
63. Exodus 40:34, 35; Ezekiel 9:3.
64. Cf. Psalms 74 and 104.
65. Exodus 25:8, 9.
66. Exodus 25:3–5.
67. Exodus 39:32, 43; 40:33; 40:2, 17; 31:3, 13.
68. Deuteronomy 5:12–17.
69. Deuteronomy 14:1–21.
70. Proverbs 8:22, 23, 30, 31.
71. Ben Sirah 24:3–6.
72. The Wisdom of Solomon 7:25–26.
73. *De Specialibus Legibus*, 1:43.
74. *God Is Immutable*, 62; *The Life of Moses*, 1:75.
75. *Abraham*, 121–23.
76. *The Migration of Abraham*, 34–35.
77. Shabbat 31a.
78. Aroth de Rabba Nathan, 6.
79. Louis Jacobs, *Faith* (London, 1968), p. 7.
80. Leviticus Rabba 8:2; Sotah 9b.
81. Exodus Rabba 34:1; Hagigah 13b; Mekilta to Exodus 15:3.
82. Baba Metzia 59b.
83. Mishna Psalm 25:6; Psalm 139:1; Tanhuma 3:80.
84. Commenting on Job 11:7; Mishna Psalm 25:6.
85. Thus Rabbi Yohannan b. Nappacha: "He who speaks or relates too much of God's praise will be uprooted from this world."
86. Genesis Rabba 68:9.
87. B. Berakoth 10a; Leviticus Rabba 4:8; Yalkut on Psalm 90:1; Exodus Rabba.
88. B. Migillah 29a.
89. Song of Songs Rabba 2; Jerusalem Sukkah 4.
90. Numbers Rabba 11:2; Deuteronomy Rabba 7:2 based on Proverbs 8:34.
91. Mekhilta de Rabbi Simon on Exodus 19:6. Cf. Acts of the Apostles 4:32.
92. Song of Songs Rabba 8:12.
93. Yalkut on Song of Songs 1:2.
94. Sifre on Deuteronomy 36.
95. A. Marmorstein, *The Old Rabbinic Doctrine of God, The Names and Attributes of God* (Oxford, 1927), pp. 171–74.
96. Niddah 31b.
97. Yalkut on 2 Samuel 22; B. Yoma 22b; Yalkut on Esther 5:2.
98. Jacob E. Neusner, "Varieties of Judaism in the Formative Age," in Arthur Green, ed., *Jewish Spirituality*, 2 vols. (London 1986, 1988), I, pp. 172–73.
99. Sifre on Leviticus 19:8.
100. Mekhilta on Exodus 20:13.
101. Pirke Aboth 6:6; Horayot 13a.
102. Sanhedrin 4:5.
103. Baba Metziah 58b.
104. Arakin 15b.

3 A Light to the Gentiles

1. Mark 1:18, 11.
2. Mark 1:15. This is often translated: "The Kingdom of God is at hand," but the Greek is stronger.
3. See Geza Vermes, *Jesus the Jew* (London, 1973); Paul Johnson, *A History of the Jews* (London, 1987).
4. Matthew 5:17–19.
5. Matthew 7:12.
6. Matthew 23.
7. T. Sof. 13:2.
8. Matthew 17:2.
9. Matthew 17:5.
10. Matthew 17:20; Mark 11:22–23.
11. Astasahasrika 15:293 in Edward Conze, *Buddhism: its Essence and Development* (Oxford, 1959), p. 125.
12. *Bhagavad-Gita, Krishna's Counsel in War* (New York, 1986), XI, 14, p. 97.
13. Ibid., XI:21, p. 100.
14. Ibid., XI:18, p. 100.
15. Galatians 1:11;14.
16. See, for example, Romans 12:5; 1 Corinthians 4:15; 2 Corinthians 2:17, 5:17.
17. 1 Corinthians, 1:24.
18. Quoted by Paul in the sermon put on his lips by the author of the Acts of the Apostles 17:28. The quotation probably came from Epimanides.
19. 1 Corinthians 15:4.
20. Romans 6:4; Galatians 5:16–25; 2 Corinthians 5:17; Ephesians 2:15.
21. Colossians 1:24; Ephesians 3:1, 13; 9:3; 1 Corinthians 1:13.
22. Romans r:12–18.
23. Philippians 2:6–11.
24. John 1:3.
25. 1 John 1:1.
26. Acts of the Apostles 2:2.
27. Ibid., 2:9, 10.
28. Joel 3:1–5.
29. Acts of the Apostles 2:22–36.
30. Ibid., 7:48.
31. Quoted in A. D. Nock, *Conversion, The Old and the New in Religion from Alexander the Great to Augustine of Hippo* (Oxford, 1933), p. 207.
32. *Ad Baptizandos*, Homily 13:14, quoted in Wilfred Cantwell Smith, *Faith and Belief* (Princeton, 1979), p. 259.
33. Account given by Irenaeus, *Heresies*, I.1.1. Most of the writings of the early "heretics" were destroyed and survive only in the polemics of their orthodox opponents.
34. Hippolytus, *Heresies*, 7.21.4.
35. Irenaeus, *Heresies*, 1.5.3.
36. Hippolytus, *Heresies*, 8.15.1–2.
37. Luke 6:43.
38. Irenaeus, *Heresies*, 1.27.2.

39. Tertullian, *Against Marcion*, 1.6.1.
40. Origen, *Against Celsus*, 1.9.
41. *Exhortation to the Greeks*, 59.2.
42. Ibid., 10.106.4.
43. *The Teacher*, 2.3.381.
44. *Exhortation to the Greeks*, 1.8.4.
45. *Heresies*, 5.16.2.
46. Enneads, 5.6.
47. Ibid., 5.3.11.
48. Ibid., 7.3.2.
49. Ibid., 5.2.1.
50. Ibid., 4.3.9.
51. Ibid., 4.3.9.
52. Ibid., 6.7.37.
53. Ibid., 6.9.9.
54. Ibid., 6.9.4.
55. Jaroslav Pelikan, *The Christian Tradition, A History of the Development of Doctrine*, 5 vols., I. *The Emergence of the Catholic Tradition* (Chicago, 1971), p. 103.

4 Trinity: The Christian God

1. The source is Gregory of Nyssa.
2. In a letter to Eusebius, his ally, and in the Thalia, quoted in Robert C. Gregg and Dennis E. Groh, *Early Arianism, A View of Salvation* (London, 1981), p. 66.
3. Arius, *Epistle to Alexander*, 2.
4. Proverbs 8:22. Quoted on pp. 81–82.
5. John I.3.
6. John I.2.
7. Philippians 2:6–11, quoted on p. 105.
8. Arius, *Epistle to Alexander* 6.2.
9. Athanasius, *Against the Heathen*, 41.
10. Anthanasius, *On the Incarnation*, 54.
11. This differs from the doctrinal manifesto usually known as the Nicene Creed, which was actually composed at the Council of Constantinople in 381.
12. Athanasius, *On the Synods of Ariminium and Seleucia*, 41.1.
13. Athanasius, *Life of Antony*, 67.
14. Basil, *On the Holy Spirit*, 28.66.
15. Ibid.
16. Gregory of Nyssa, *Against Eunomius*, 3.
17. Gregory of Nyssa, *Answer to Eunomius's Second Book*.
18. Gregory of Nyssa, *Life of Moses*, 2.164.
19. Basil, Epistle 234.1.
20. Oration, 31.8.
21. Gregory of Nyssa, *Not Three Gods*.
22. G. L. Prestige, *God in Patristic Thought* (London, 1952), p. 300.
23. Gregory of Nyssa, *Not Three Gods*.

24. Gregory of Nazianzus, *Oration*, 40:41.
25. Gregory of Nazianzus, *Oration*, 29:6–10.
26. Basil, Epistle, 38:4.
27. *On the Trinity* vii.4.7.
28. *Confessions* 1.1., trans. Henry Chadwick (Oxford, 1991), p. 3.
29. Ibid., VIII vii (17), p. 145.
30. Ibid., VIII xii (28), p. 152.
31. Ibid., VIII xii (29), pp. 152–53. Passage from St. Paul, Romans 13:13–14.
32. Ibid., X xvii (26), p. 194.
33. Ibid., V xxvii (38), p. 201.
34. Ibid.
35. *On the Trinity* VIII.ii.3.
36. Ibid.
37. Ibid., X.x.14.
38. Ibid., X.xi.18.
39. Ibid.
40. Andrew Louth, *The Origins of the Christian Mystical Tradition* (Oxford, 1983), p. 79.
41. Augustine, *On the Trinity* xiii.
42. Ibid.
43. *Enchyridion* 26.27.
44. *On Female Dress*, I, i.
45. Letter 243, 10.
46. *The Literal Meaning of Genesis*, IX, V, 9.
47. Letter XI.
48. Ibid.
49. *The Celestial Hierarchy*, I.
50. *The Divine Names*, II, 7.
51. Ibid., VII, 3.
52. Ibid., XIII, 3.
53. Ibid., VII, 3.
54. Ibid., I.
55. *Mystical Theology*, 3.
56. *The Divine Names*, IV, 3.
57. *Ambigua*, Migne, PG 91. 1088c.

5 Unity: The God of Islam

1. Muhammad ibn Ishaq, *Sira*, 145, quoted in A. Guillaume, trans., *The Life of Muhammad* (London, 1955), p. 160.
2. Koran 96:1. In his translation, Muhammad Asad supplements the elliptical language of the Koran by adding words in brackets.
3. Ibn Ishaq, *Sira*, 153, in Guillaume, trans., *A Life of Muhammad*, p. 106.
4. Ibid.
5. Jalal ad-Din Suyuti, *al-itiqan fi'ulum al aq'ran* in Rodinson, *Mohammed*, trans. Anne Carter (London, 1971), p. 74.
6. Bukhari, Hadith 1.3, quoted in Martin Lings, *Muhammad, His Life Based On the Earliest Sources* (London, 1983), pp. 44–45.
7. "Expostulation and Reply."

8. Koran 75:17–19.

9. Koran 42:7.

10. Koran 88:21–22.

11. Koran 29:61–63.

12. Koran 96:6–8.

13. Koran 80:24–32.

14. Koran 92:18; 9:103; 63:9; 102:1.

15. Koran 24:1, 45.

16. Koran 2:158–59.

17. Koran 20:114–15.

18. Ibn Ishaq, *Sira* 227 in Guillaume, trans., *The Life of Muhammad*, p. 159.

19. Ibid., 228, p. 158.

20. George Steiner, *Real Presences, Is there anything* in *what we say?* (London, 1989), pp. 142–43.

21. Koran 53:19–26.

22. Karen Armstrong, *Muhammad: A Western Attempt to Understand Islam* (London, 1991), pp. 108–17.

23. Koran 109.

24. Koran 112.

25. Quoted in Seyyed Hossein Nasr, "God" in *Islamic Spirituality: Foundation*, which he also edited (London, 1987), p. 321.

26. Koran 2:11.

27. Koran 55:26.

28. Koran 24:35.

29. Armstrong, *Muhammad*, pp. 21–44; 86–88.

30. Koran 29:46.

31. Ibn Ishaq, *Sira* 362 in Guillaume, trans., *A Life of Muhammad*, p. 246.

32. This is Muhammad Asad's translation of *ahl al-kitab*, usually rendered "the people of the Book."

33. Koran 2:135–36.

34. Ali Shariati, *Hajj*, trans. Laleh Bakhtiar (Teheran, 1988), pp. 54–56.

35. Koran 33:35.

36. Quoted in Seyyed Hossein Nasr, "The Significance of the *Sunnah* and *Hadith*" in *Islamic Spirituality*, pp. 107–8.

37. I John 1.1.

38. W. Montgomery Watt, *Free Will and Predestination in Early Islam* (London, 1948) p. 139.

39. Abu al-Hasan ibn Ismail al Ashari, *Malakat* 1.197, quoted in A. J. Wensinck, *The Muslim Creed, Its Genesis and Historical Development* (Cambridge, 1932), pp. 67–68.

6 The God of the Philosophers

1. Translated by R. Walzer, "Islamic Philosophy," quoted in S. H. Nasr, "Theology, Philosophy and Spirituality" in *Islamic Spirituality: Manifestations* (London, 1991), which he also edited, p. 411.

2. Because they both came from Rayy in Iran.

3. Quoted in Azim Nanji, "Ismailism," in S. H. Nasr, *Islamic Spirituality: Foundation*, which he also edited (London, 1987), pp. 195–96.

4. See Henri Corbin, *Spiritual Body and Celestial Earth, From Mazdean Iran to Shiite Iran*, trans. Nancy Pearson, (London, 1990) pp. 51–72.

5. Ibid., p. 51.

6. Rasai'il I, 76, quoted in Majid Fakhry, *A History of Islamic Philosophy* (New York and London, 1970), p. 193.

7. Rasai'l IV, 42, in ibid., p. 187.

8. *Metaphysics XII*, 1074b, 32.

9. *Al-Mundiqh al-Dalal*, trans. in W. Montgomery Watt, *The Faith and Practice of Al Ghazzali* (London, 1953), p. 20.

10. Quoted in John Bowker, *The Religious Imagination and the Sense of God* (Oxford, 1978), p. 202.

11. When Western scholars read his work, they assumed that al-Ghazzali *was* a Faylasuf.

12. *Mundiqh*, in Watt, *The Faith and Practice of Al Ghazzali*, p. 59.

13. Bowker, *The Religious Imagination and the Sense of God*, pp. 222–26.

14. Koran 24:35, quoted on p. 176–77.

15. *Mishkat al-Anwar*, quoted in Fakhry, *A History of Islamic Philosophy*, p. 278.

16. *Kuzari*, Book II, quoted in J. Abelson, *The Immanence of God in Rabbinic Literature* (London, 1912), p. 257.

17. Koran 3:5.

18. Listed in Fakhry, *A History of Islamic Philosophy*, pp. 313–14.

19. Listed in Julius Guttman, *Philosophies of Judaism, the History of Jewish Philosophy from Biblical Times to Franz Rosenzweig*, trans. David W. Silverman (London and New York, 1964), p. 179.

20. Quoted in Abelson, *The Immanence of God in Rabbinic Literature*, p. 245.

21. For early crusading attitudes, Karen Armstrong, *Holy War, The Crusades and their Impact on Today's World* (New York, 1991, London, 1992) pp. 49–75.

22. *Exposition of the Celestial Hierarchy*, 2.1.

23. *Periphsean*, Migne, PL, 426C–D.

24. Ibid., 4287 B.

25. Ibid., 680 D–681–A.

26. Ibid.

27. Vladimir Lossky, *The Mystical Theology of the Eastern Church* (London, 1957), pp. 57–65.

28. *Monologion* I.

29. *Proslogion* I.

30. *Proslogion*, 2. Commenting on Isaiah 7:9.

31. John Macquarrie, *In Search of Deity; An Essay in Dialectical Theism* (London, 1984), pp. 201–2.

32. Epistle 191.1.

33. Quoted in Henry Adams, *Mont Saint-Michel and Chartres* (London, 1986), p. 296.

34. Armstrong, *Holy War*, pp. 199–234.

35. Thomas Aquinas, *De Potentia*, q.7, a.5. ad.14.

36. *Summa Theologiae* ia, 13, 11.

37. *The Journey of the Mind to God*, 6.2.

38. Ibid., 3.1.

39. Ibid., 1.7.

7 The God of the Mystics

1. John Macquarrie, *Thinking About God* (London, 1957), p. 34.
2. Hagigah 14b, quoting Psalms 101:7; 116:15; 25:16.
3. Quoted in Louis Jacobs, ed., *The Jewish Mystics* (Jerusalem, 1976, London, 1990), p. 23.
4. 2 Corinthians 2:2–4.
5. The Song of Songs, 5:10–15.
6. Translated in T. Carmi, ed. and trans., *The Penguin Book of Hebrew Verse* (London, 1981), p. 199.
7. Koran 53:13–17.
8. *Confessions* IX, 24, trans. Henry Chadwick (Oxford, 1991), p. 171.
9. Joseph Campbell (with Bill Moyers), *The Power of Myth* (New York, 1988), p. 85.
10. Annemarie Schimmel, *And Muhammad Is His Messenger: The Veneration of the Prophet in Islamic Piety* (Chapel Hill and London, 1985), pp. 161–75.
11. *Confessions* IX:24, trans. Chadwick, p. 171.
12. Confessions IX, 25, pp. 171–72.
13. Ibid.
14. *Morals on Job*, v. 66.
15. Ibid., xxiv. 11.
16. *Homilies on Ezekiel* II, ii, 1.
17. *Commentary on the Song of Songs*, 6.
18. Epistle 234.1.
19. *On Prayer*, 67.
20. *Ibid.*, 71.
21. *Ambigua*, PG.91.1088c.
22. Peter Brown with Sabine MacCormack, "Artifices of Eternity," in Brown, *Society and the Holy in Late Antiquity* (London, 1992), p. 212.
23. Nicephoras, *Greater Apology for the Holy Images*, 70.
24. *Theological Orations* I.
25. *Ethical Orations* 1.3.
26. *Orations* 26.
27. *Ethical Orations* 5.
28. *Hymns of Divine Love* 28.114–15, 160–2.
29. *Encyclopaedia of Islam* (1st ed. Leiden 1913), entry under "Tasawwuf."
30. Trans. R. A. Nicholson, quoted in A. J. Arberry, *Sufism, An Account of the Mystics of Islam* (London, 1950), p. 43.
31. Quoted in R. A. Nicholson, *The Mystics of Islam* (London, 1963 ed.), p. 115.
32. *Narrative*, quoted in Marshall G. S. Hodgson, *The Venture of Islam, Conscience and History in a World Civilization*, 3 vols. (Chicago, 1974), I., p. 404.
33. Quoted in Arberry, *Sufism*, p. 59.
34. Quoted in Nicholson, *The Mystics of Islam*, p. 151.
35. Quoted in Arberry, *Sufism*, p. 60.
36. Koran 2:32.
37. *Hiqmat al-Ishraq*, quoted in Henri Corbin, *Spiritual Body and Celestial Earth, From Mazdean Iran to Shiite Iran*, trans. Nancy Pearson, (London, 1990), pp. 168–69.
38. Mircea Eliade, *Shamanism*, p. 9, 508.

39. J.-P. Sartre, *The Psychology of the Imagination* (London, 1972), passim.
40. *Futuhat al Makkiyah* II, 326, quoted in Henri Corbin, *Creative Imagination in the Sufism of Ibn Arabi*, trans. Ralph Manheim (London, 1970), p. 330.
41. *The Diwan, Interpretation of Ardent Desires*, in ibid., p. 138.
42. *La Vita Nuova*, trans. Barbara Reynolds (Harmondsworth, 1969), pp. 29–30.
43. *Purgatory* xvii, 13–18, trans. Barbara Reynolds (Harmondsworth, 1969), p. 196.
44. William Chittick, "Ibn al-Arabi and His School" in Sayyed Hossein Nasr, ed. *Islamic Spirituality: Manifestations* (New York and London, 1991), p. 61.
45. Koran 18:69.
46. Quoted in Henri Corbin, *Creative Imagination in Ibn al-Arabi*, p. 111.
47. Chittick, "Ibn Arabi and His School," in Nasr, ed., *Islamic Spirituality*, p. 58.
48. Majid Fakhry, *A History of Islamic Philosophy* (New York and London, 1970), p. 282.
49. R. A. Nicholson, *The Mystics of Islam*, p. 105.
50. R. A. Nicholson, ed., *Eastern Poetry and Prose* (Cambridge, 1922), p. 148.
51. *Masnawi*, I, i, quoted in Hodgson, *The Venture of Islam*, II, p. 250.
52. Quoted in *This Longing, Teaching Stories and Selected letters of Rumi*, trans. and ed. Coleman Banks and John Moyne (Putney, 1988), p. 20.
53. "Song of Unity," quoted in Gershom Scholem, *Major Trends in Jewish Mysticism*, 2nd ed., (London, 1955), p. 108.
54. Ibid., p. 11.
55. In Gershom Scholem, ed. and trans. *The Zohar, The Book of Splendour* (New York, 1949), p. 27.
56. Ibid.
57. Scholem, *Major Trends in Jewish Mysticism*, p. 136.
58. Ibid., p. 142.
59. Quoted in J. C. Clark, *Meister Eckhart, An Introduction to the Study of his Works with an Anthology of his Sermons* (London, 1957), p. 28.
60. Simon Tugwell, "Dominican Spirituality," in Louis Dupre and Don. E. Saliers, eds. *Christian Spirituality III* (New York and London, 1989), p. 28.
61. Quoted in Clark, *Meister Eckhart*, p. 40.
62. Sermon, "Qui Audit Me Non Confundetur," in R. B. Blakeney, trans., *Meister Eckhart, A New Translation* (New York, 1957), p. 204.
63. Ibid., p. 288.
64. "On Detachment," in Edmund Coledge and Bernard McGinn, eds. and trans. *Meister Eckhart, the Essential Sermons, Commentaries, Treatises and Defence* (London, 1981), p. 87.
65. *Theophanes*, PG. 932D. (My italics.)
66. Homily, 16.
67. Triads 1.3.47.

8 A God for Reformers

1. *Majma'at al-Rasail*, quoted in Majid Fakhry, *A History of Islamic Philosophy* (New York and London, 1970), p. 351.
2. Marshall G. S. Hodgson, *The Venture of Islam, Conscience and History in a World Civilization*, 3 vols. (Chicago, 1974), II, pp. 334–60.

3. *Kitab al hikmat al-arshiya*, quoted in Henri Corbin, *Spiritual Body and Celestial Earth, From Mazdean Iran to Shiite Iran*, trans. Nancy Pearson, (London, 1990), p. 166.

4. Quoted in M. S. Raschid, *Iqbal's Concept of God* (London, 1981), pp. 103–4.

5. Quoted in Gershom Scholem, *Major Trends in Jewish Mysticism*, 2nd ed. (London, 1955), p. 253.

6. Ibid., p. 271; for Lurianic Kabbalah see also Scholem, *The Messianic Idea in Judaism and Other Essays in Jewish Spirituality* (New York, 1971), pp. 43–48; R. J. Zwi Weblosky, "The Safed Revival and its Aftermath," in Arthur Green, ed., *Jewish Spirituality*, 2 vols. (London, 1986, 1988), II; Jacob Katz, "Halakah and Kabbalah as Competing Disciplines of Study" in ibid.; Laurence Fine, "The Contemplative Practice of Yehudim in Lurianic Kabbalah," in ibid.; Louis Jacobs, "The Uplifting of the Sparks in later Jewish Mysticism," in ibid.

7. *The Mountain of Contemplation*, 4.

8. Thomas à Kempis, *The Imitation of Christ*, trans. Leo Sherley Poole, (Harmondsworth, 1953), I, i, p. 27.

9. Richard Kieckhafer, "Major Currents in Late Medieval Devotion," in Jill Raitt, ed., *Christian Spirituality: High Middle Ages and Reformation* (New York and London, 1989), p. 87.

10. Julian of Norwich, *Revelations of Divine Love*, trans. Clifton Wolters, (London, 1981), 15, pp. 87–88.

11. *Enconium Sancti Tomae Aquinatis*, quoted in William J. Bouwsme, "The Spirituality of Renaissance Humanism," in Raitt, *Christian Spirituality*, p. 244.

12. Letter to his brother Gherado, December 2, 1348, in David Thompson, ed., *Petrarch, a Humanist among Princes: An Anthology of Petrarch's Letters and Translations from His Works* (New York, 1971), p. 90.

13. Quoted in Charles Trinkaus, *The Poet as Philosopher: Petrarch and the Formation of Renaissance Consciousness* (New Haven, 1979), p. 87.

14. *Of Learned Ignorance*, I.22.

15. *On Possibility and Being in God*, 17.5.

16. Norman Cohn, *Europe's Inner Demons* (London, 1976).

17. Quoted in Alister E. McGrath, *Reformation Thought, An Introduction* (Oxford and New York, 1988), p. 73.

18. *Commentary on Psalm* 90.3.

19. *Commentary on Galatians* 3.19.

20. Quoted in McGrath, *Reformation Thought*, p. 74.

21. I Corinthians 1.25.

22. *Heidelberg Disputation*, 21.

23. Ibid., 19–20.

24. Ibid.

25. Quoted in Jaroslav Pelikan, *The Christian Tradition, A History of the Development of Dogma*, 5 vols., IV, *Reformation of Church and Dogma* (Chicago and London, 1984), p. 156.

26. *Commentary on Galatians* 2.16.

27. *Ethical Orations* 5.

28. *Small Catechism* 2.4. Quoted in Pelikan, *Reformation of Church*, p. 161. (My italics.)

29. Alastair E. McGrath, *A Life of John Calvin, A Study in the Shaping of Western Culture* (Oxford, 1990) p. 7.

30. Quoted in McGrath, ibid., p. 251.

31. *Institutes of the Christians Religion*, I, xiii, 2.

32. Quoted in Pelikan, *Reformation of Church*, p. 327.

33. Zinzendorf, quoted in ibid., p. 326.

34. Quoted in McGarth, *Reformation Thought*, p. 87.

35. McGrath, *A Life of Calvin*, p. 90.

36. William James, *The Varieties of Religious Experience*, ed. Martine E. Marty (New York and Harmondsworth, 1982), pp. 127–85.

37. John Bossy, *Christianity in the West, 1400–1700* (Oxford and New York, 1985), p. 96.

38. McGrath, *A Life of Calvin*, pp. 209–45.

39. R. C. Lovelace, "Puritan Spirituality: the Search for a Rightly Reformed Church," in Louis Dupre and Don E. Saliers, eds., *Christian Spirituality: Post Reformation and Modern* (New York and London, 1989), p. 313.

40. The Spiritual Exercises 230.

41. Quoted in Hugo Rahner SJ, *Ignatius the Theologian*, trans. Michael Barry (London, 1968), p. 23.

42. Quoted in Pelikan, *The Christian Doctrine and Modern Culture (Since 1700)* (Chicago and London, 1989), p. 39.

43. Lucien Febvre, *The Problem of Unbelief in the Sixteenth Century, the Religion of Rabelais*, trans. Beatrice Gottlieb (Cambridge, Mass., and London, 1982), p. 351.

44. Ibid., pp. 355–6.

45. Quoted in J. C. Davis, *Fear, Myth and History, the Ranters and the Historians* (Cambridge, 1986), p. 114.

46. McGrath, *A Life of John Calvin*, p. 131.

47. Quoted in Robert S. Westman, "The Copernicans and the Churches," in David C. Lindberg and Ronald E. Numbers, eds., *God and Nature; Historical Essays in the Encounter Between Christianity and Science* (Berkeley, Los Angeles and London, 1986), p. 87.

48. Psalm 93:1; Ecclesiasticus 1:5; Psalm 104:19.

49. William R. Shea, "Galileo and the Church," in Lindberg and Numbers, eds., *God and Nature*, p. 125.

9 Enlightenment

1. Text taken from Blaise Pascal, *Pensées*, trans. and ed. A. J. Krailsheimer (London, 1966), p. 309.

2. *Pensées*, 919.

3. Ibid., 198.

4. Ibid., 418.

5. Ibid., 919.

6. Ibid., 418.

7. Romans 1.19–20.

8. René Descartes, *A Discourse on Method etc*, trans. J. Veitch (London, 1912), 2.6.19.

9. René Descartes, *Discourse on Method, Optics, Geometry and Meteorology*, trans. Paul J. Olscamp (Indianapolis, 1965), p. 263.

10. Ibid., p. 361.

11. Quoted in A. R. Hall and L. Tilling, eds., *The Correspondence of Isaac Newton*, 3 vols. (Cambridge, 1959–77), December 10, 1692, III, pp. 234–35.

12. January 17, 1693, in ibid., p. 240.

13. Isaac Newton, *Philosophiae Naturalis Principia Mathematica*, trans. Andrew Motte, ed. Florian Cajavi (Berkeley, 1934), pp. 344–46.

14. "Corruptions of Scripture," quoted in Richard S. Westfall, "The Rise of Science and Decline of Orthodox Christianity. A Study of Kepler, Descartes and Newton," in David C. Lindberg and Ronald L. Numbers, eds., *God and Nature; Historical Essays on the Encounter between Christianity and Science* (Berkeley, Los Angeles and London, 1986), p. 231.

15. Ibid., pp. 231–32.

16. Quoted in Jaroslav Pelikan, *The Christian Tradition, A History of the Development of Doctrine*, 5 vols., V *Christian Doctrine and Modern Culture (Since 1700)* (Chicago and London, 1989), p. 66.

17. Ibid., p. 105.

18. Ibid., p. 101.

19. Ibid., p. 103.

20. *Paradise Lost*, Book III, Lines 113–19, 124–28.

21. François-Marie de Voltaire, *Philosophical Dictionary*, trans. Theodore Besterman (London, 1972), p. 357.

22. Ibid., p. 57.

23. Quoted in Paul Johnson, *A History of the Jews* (London, 1987), p. 290.

24. Baruch Spinoza, *A Theologico-Political Treatise*, trans. R. H. M. Elwes (New York, 1951), p. 6.

25. Quoted in Pelikan, *Christian Doctrine and Modern Culture*, p. 60.

26. Ibid., p. 110.

27. Quoted in Sherwood Eliot Wirt, ed., *Spiritual Awakening: Classic Writings of the eighteenth century devotions to inspire and help the twentieth century reader* (Tring, 1988), p. 9.

28. Albert C. Outler, ed., *John Wesley: Writings*, 2 vols. (Oxford and New York, 1964), pp. 194–96.

29. Pelikan, *Christian Doctrine and Modern Culture*, p. 125.

30. Ibid., p. 126.

31. Quoted in George Tickell SJ, *The Life of Blessed Margaret Mary* (London, 1890), p. 258.

32. Ibid., p. 221.

33. Samuel Shaw, *Communion with God*, quoted in Albert C. Outler, "Pietism and Enlightenment: Alternatives to Tradition," in Louis Dupre and Don E. Saliers, eds., *Christian Spirituality: Post Reformation and Modern* (New York and London, 1989), p. 245.

34. Ibid., p. 248.

35. Norman Cohn, *The Pursuit of the Millennium, Revolutionary Millennarians and Mystical Anarchists of the Middle Ages* (London, 1970 ed.), p. 172.

36. Ibid., p. 173.
37. Ibid., p. 174.
38. Ibid., p. 290.
39. Ibid., p. 303.
40. Ibid., p. 304.
41. Ibid., p. 305.
42. Quoted in Wirt, ed., *Spiritual Awakening*, p. 110.
43. Quoted in ibid., p. 113.
44. Alan Heimart, *Religion and the American Mind. From the Great Awakening to the Revolution* (Cambridge, Mass., 1968), p. 43.
45. "An Essay on the Trinity," quoted in ibid., pp. 62–63.
46. Quoted in ibid., p. 101.
47. Remarks of Alexander Gordon and Samuel Quincey, quoted in ibid., p. 167.
48. Gershom Scholem, *Sabbati Sevi* (Princeton, 1973).
49. Quoted in Gershom Scholem, "Redemption Through Sin," in *The Messianic Idea in Judaism and Other Essays on Jewish Spirituality* (New York, 1971), p. 124.
50. Ibid., p. 130.
51. Ibid.
52. Ibid.
53. Ibid., p. 136.
54. Quoted in Scholem, "Neutralisation of Messianism in Early Hasidism," in ibid., p. 190.
55. Scholem, "Devekut or Communion with God," in ibid., p. 207.
56. Louis Jacobs, "The Uplifting of the Sparks," in Arthur Green, ed., *Jewish Spirituality*, 2 vols. (London, 1986, 1988), II, pp. 118–21.
57. Ibid., p. 125.
58. Scholem, "Devekuth," in *The Messianic Idea in Judaism*, pp. 226–27.
59. Arthur Green, "Typologies of leadership and the Hasidic Zaddick," in *Jewish Spirituality* II, p. 132.
60. *Sifra De-Zeniuta*, trans. R. J. Za. Werblowsky, in Louis Jacobs, ed., *The Jewish Mystics* (Jerusalem, 1976 and London, 1990), p. 171.
61. Ibid., p. 174.
62. Arnold H. Toynbee, *A Study of History*, 12 vols. (Oxford 1934–61), X, p. 128.
63. Albert Einstein, "Strange is Our Situation Here on Earth," in Jaroslav Pelikan, ed., *Modern Religious Thought* (Boston, 1990), p. 204.
64. Quoted in Rachel Elin, "HaBaD: the Contemplative Ascent to God," in Green, ed., *Jewish Spirituality* II, p. 161.
65. Ibid., p. 196.
66. Quoted in Michael J. Buckley, *At the Origins of Modern Atheism* (New Haven and London, 1987), p. 225.
67. "A Letter to the Blind for Those Who See," in Margaret Jourdain, trans. and ed., *Diderot's Early Philosophical Works* (Chicago, 1966), pp. 113–14.
68. Paul Heinrich Dietrich, Baron d'Holbach, *The System of Nature: or Laws of the Moral and Physical World*, trans. H. D. Robinson, 2 vols. (New York, 1835), I, p. 22.
69. Ibid., II, p. 227.

70. Ibid., I, p. 174.
71. Ibid., II, p. 232.

10 The Death of God?

1. M. H. Abrams, *Natural Supernaturalism: Tradition and Revolution in Romantic Literature* (New York, 1971), p. 66.
2. November 22, 1817, in *The Letters of John Keats*, ed. H. E. Rollins, 2 vols. (Cambridge, Mass., 1958), pp. 184–85.
3. To George and Thomas Keats, December 21 (27?), 1817, in ibid., p. 191.
4. *The Prelude* II, 256–64.
5. "Lines Composed a Few Miles Above Tintern Abbey," 37–49.
6. "Expostulation and Reply"; "The Tables Turned."
7. "Tintern Abbey," 94–102.
8. "Ode To Duty"; *The Prelude* XII, 316.
9. "Introduction" to *The Songs of Experience*, 6–10.
10. *Jerusalem* 33:1–24.
11. Ibid., 96:23–28.
12. F. D. E. Schliermacher, *The Christian Faith*, trans. H. R. Mackintosh and J. S. Steward (Edinburgh, 1928).
13. Ibid., p. 12.
14. Albert Ritschl, *Theology and Metaphysics*, 2nd ed. (Bonn, 1929), p. 29.
15. Quoted in John Macquarrie, *Thinking About God* (London, 1978), p. 162.
16. "Contribution to the Critique of Hegel's 'Philosophy of the Right,' " in Jaroslav Pelikan, ed., *Modern Religious Thought* (Boston, 1990), p. 80.
17. Friedrich Nietzsche, *The Gay Science* (New York, 1974), No. 125.
18. Friedrich Nietzsche, *The Antichrist* in *The Twilight of the Gods and The Antichrist*, trans. R. J. Hollingdale (London, 1968), p. 163.
19. Sigmund Freud, *The Future of an Illusion* (standard ed.), p. 56.
20. Friedrich Nietzsche, *Thus Spake Zarathustra, A Book for Every One and No One*, trans. R. J. Hollingdale, London, 1961, p. 217.
21. Alfred, Lord Tennyson, *In Memoriam* liv, 18–20.
22. Quoted by William Hamilton in "The New Optimism—From Prufrock to Ringo" in Thomas J. J. Altizer and William Hamilton, eds., *Radical Theology and the Death of God* (New York and London, 1966).
23. Michael Gilsenan, *Recognizing Islam, Religion and Society in the Modern Middle East* (London and New York, 1985 ed.), p. 38.
24. Evelyn Baring, Lord Cromer, *Modern Egypt*, 2 vols. (New York, 1908), II, p. 146.
25. Roy Mottahedeh, *The Mantle of the Prophet, Religion and Politics in Iran* (London, 1985), pp. 183–84.
26. *Risalat al-Tawhid*, quoted in Majid Fakhry, *A History of Islamic Philosophy* (New York and London, 1971), p. 378.
27. Wilfred Cantwell Smith, *Islam in Modern History* (Princeton and London, 1957), p. 95.
28. Ibid., p. 146, also pp. 123–60 for the analysis of *Al-Azhar*.
29. Quoted in Eliezer Schweid, *The Land of Israel: National Home or Land of Destiny*, trans. Deborah Greniman (New York, 1985), p. 158. Kabbalistic terms in italics.

30. Ibid., p. 143.
31. "Avodah," 1–8, trans. by T. Carmi (ed. and trans.), *The Penguin Book of Hebrew Verse* (London, 1981), p. 534.
32. "The Service of God," quoted in Ben Zion Bokser ed. and trans., *The Essential Writings of Abraham Isaac Kook* (Warwick, N.Y., 1988), p. 50.
33. Elie Wiesel, *Night*, trans. Stella Rodway (Harmondsworth, 1981), p. 45.
34. Ibid., pp. 76–77.

11 Does God Have a Future?

1. Peter Berger, *A Rumour of Angels* (London, 1970), p. 58.
2. A. J. Ayer, *Language, Truth and Logic* (Harmondsworth, 1974), p. 152.
3. Wilfred Cantwell Smith, *Belief and History* (Charlottesville, 1985), p. 10.
4. Thomas J. J. Altizer, *The Gospel of Christian Atheism* (London, 1966), p. 136.
5. Paul Van Buren, *The Secular Meaning of the Gospel* (London, 1963), p. 138.
6. Richard L. Rubenstein, *After Auschwitz, Radical Theology and Contemporary Judaism* (Indianapolis, 1966), passim.
7. Paul Tillich, *Theology and Culture* (New York and Oxford, 1964), p. 129.
8. Alfred North Whitehead, "Suffering and Being," in *Adventures of Ideas* (Harmondsworth, 1942), pp. 191–92.
9. *Process and Reality* (Cambridge, 1929), p. 497.
10. Ali Shariati, *Hajj*, trans. Laleh Bakhtiar (Teheran, 1988), p. 46.
11. Ibid., p. 48.
12. Martin Buber, "Gottesfinsternis, Betrachtungen zur Beziehung zwischen Religion und Philosophie," quoted in Hans Kung, *Does God Exist? An Answer for Today*, trans. Edward Quinn, (London, 1978), p. 508.
13. Quoted in Raphael Mergui and Philippa Simmonot, *Israel's Ayatollahs; Meir Kahane and the Far Right in Israel* (London, 1987), p. 43.
14. Personal responsibility is also important in Christianity, of course, but Judaism and Islam have stressed it by their lack of a mediating priesthood, a perspective that was recovered by the Protestant Reformers.
15. Philipp Frank, *Einstein: His Life and Times* (New York, 1947), pp. 189–90.

Suggestions for Further Reading

General

Baillie, John, *The Sense of the Presence of God* (London, 1962).
Berger, Peter, *A Rumour of Angels* (London, 1970).
(ed.) *The Other Side of God, A Polarity in World Religions* (New York, 1981). An illuminating series of essays on the conflict between an interior and an external God of ultimate reality.
Bowker, John, *The Religious Imagination and the Sense of God* (Oxford, 1978). *Problems of Suffering in Religions of the World* (Cambridge, 1970). Two erudite yet highly readable books on world religions.
Campbell, Joseph, *The Hero with a Thousand Faces* (Princeton, 1949). (with Bill Moyers) *The Power of Myth* (New York, 1988). The text of the popular television series on mythology in traditional society and the major religions.
Cupitt, Don, *Taking Leave of God* (London, 1980). A challenging and passionate plea for a "Christian Buddhism"—a spirituality without an external, realistic God.
Eliade, Mircea. One of the major experts on comparative spirituality: essential reading.
The Myth of the Eternal Return or Cosmos and History (trans. Willard J. Trask, Princeton, 1954).
The Sacred and the Profane (trans. Willard J. Trask, New York, 1959).
The Quest; History and Meaning in Religion (trans. Willard J. Trask, Chicago, 1969).
James, William, *The Varieties of Religious Experience* (New York and Harmondsworth, 1982). A classic work which is still relevant and stimulating.
Katz, Steven T. (ed.), *Mysticism and Religious Traditions* (Oxford), 1983. Useful essays on the relationship between dogma and mysticism in the world religions.

Louth, Andrew, *Discerning the Mystery, An Essay on the Nature of Theology* (Oxford, 1983). Highly recommended; a slim volume that goes to the heart of the matter.

Macquarrie, John, *Thinking about God* (London, 1975).
In Search of Deity. An Essay in Dialectical Theism. Two excellent books on the meaning of the Christian God and the limits and uses of reason in the religious quest.

Otto, Rudolf, *The Idea of the Holy, An Inquiry into the Non-rational Factor in the Idea of the Divine and its Relation to the Rational* (trans. John W. Harvey, Oxford, 1923). A classic and essential book.

Smart, Ninian, *The Philosophy of Religion* (London, 1979). Academic and helpful essays.
The Religious Experience of Mankind (New York, 1969, Glasgow 1971). An extremely useful survey.

Smith, Wilfred Cantwell. Three superb and inspiring books from an outstanding Canadian scholar:
Belief and History (Charlottesville, 1977).
Faith and Belief (Princeton, 1979).
Towards a World Theology (London, 1981).

Ward, Keith, *The Concept of God* (Oxford, 1974). A useful summary of some Western Christian ideas.

Woods, Richard (ed.), *Understanding Mysticism* (London and New York, 1980).

Zaehner, R. H., *Mysticism—Sacred and Profane* (London, 1957).

The Bible

Albright, W. F., *Yahweh and the Gods of Canaan* (London, 1968).

Alter, Robert and Kermode, Frank (eds.), *The Literary Guide to the Bible* (London, 1987). Includes some exciting work by major scholars on both Jewish and Christian scriptures.

Bartlett, John R., *The Bible, Faith and Evidence* (London, 1990). An excellent, scholarly and readable introduction.

Childs, Brerand S., *Myth and Reality in the Old Testament* (London, 1959).

Driver, G. R., *Canaanite Myths and Legends* (Edinburgh, 1956).

Fishbane, Michael, *Text and Texture, Close Readings of Selected Biblical Texts* (New York, 1979). Highly recommended.

Fohrer, G., *A History of Israelite Religion* (New York, 1972).

Fox, Robin Lane, *The Unauthorised Version, Truth and Fiction in the Bible* (London, 1991). A readable, scholarly and extremely entertaining look at the Bible from the historian's point of view.

Frankfort, H., *The Intellectual Adventure of Ancient Man* (Chicago, 1946).

Gaster, T. H., *Thespis, Ritual, Myth and Drama in the Ancient Near East* (New York, 1950).

Heschel, Abraham, J., *The Prophets*, 2 vols., (New York, 1962). A classic: essential and inspiring reading.

Hooke, S. H., *Middle Eastern Mythology, From the Assyrians to the Hebrews* (London, 1963). A very useful, popular summary.

Josipovici, Gabriel, *The Book of God, A Response to the Bible* (New Haven and

London, 1988). A sensitive and original look at the Bible from the point of view of a literary specialist.

Kaufmann, Yehezkel, *The Religion of Israel, From its Beginnings to the Babylonian Exile* (trans. and abridged by Moshe Greenberg, Chicago and London, 1961). An accessible version of a classic work of scholarship.

Nicholson, E. W., *God and His People* (London, 1986). Excellent.

Pederson, J., *Israel: its Life and Culture* (trans. H. Milford, Copenhagen and London, 1926). Another seminal work.

Smith, Mark S., *The Early History of God; Yahweh and the Other Deities in Ancient Israel* (San Francisco, 1990). A scholarly, detailed study.

The New Testament

Bornkamm, Gunther. Two major and influential works:
Jesus of Nazareth (London, 1960).
Paul (London, 1971).

Bowker, John, *Jesus and the Pharisees* (Cambridge, 1983). Excellent study by an inspiring scholar.

Bultmann, Rudolf, *Jesus Christ and Mythology* (London, 1960).

Davies, W. D., *Paul and Rabbinic Judaism* (London, 1948).

Hick, John (ed.), *The Myth of God Incarnate* (London, 1977). A controversial but stimulating series of essays by major British scholars.

Kasemann, Ernst, *Perspectives on Paul* (London, 1971).

Moule, C. F. D., *The Origin of Christology* (Cambridge, 1977).

Sanders, E. P. Two scholarly and important books:
Paul and Palestinian Judaism (London, 1977).
Jesus and Judaism (London, 1989).

Theissen, Gerd, *The First Followers of Jesus, A Sociological Analysis of the Earliest Christianity* (trans. John Bowden, London, 1978).

Vermes, Geza, *Jesus the Jew* (London, 1973). A very valuable study.

Wilson, R. Mc L., *Gnosis and the New Testament* (Oxford, 1968).

The Rabbis

Abelson, J., *The Immanence of God in Rabbinical Literature* (London, 1912). A work that brings the Talmud to life.

Belkin, Samuel, *In His Image, the Jewish Philosophy of Man as Expressed in Rabbinic Tradition* (London, 1961). An excellent book that shows the relevance of the Rabbis to today's world.

Finkelstein, L., *Akiba, Scholar, Saint and Martyr* (Cleveland, 1962).

Kaddushin, Max, *The Rabbinic Mind* (2nd ed., New York, 1962).

Marmorstein, A., *The Old Rabbinic Doctrine of God; I: The Names and Attributes of God* (London, 1927).
Studies in Jewish Theology (eds. J. Rabinowits and M. S. Law, Oxford, 1950).

Montefiore, C. G., and Loewe, H. (eds.), *A Rabbinic Anthology* (New York, 1974).

Moore, George F., *Judaism in the First Centuries of the Christian Era*, 3 vols. (Oxford, 1927–30).

Neusner, Jacob, *Life of Yohannan ben Zakkai* (Leiden, 1962).
Schechter, Solomon, *Aspects of Rabbinic Theology* (New York, 1909).

Early Christianity

Chadwick, Henry, *The Early Church* (London, 1967).
   Early Christian Thought and the Classical Tradition (Oxford, 1966).
Geffcken, J., *The Last Days of Greco-Roman Paganism* (London, 1978). Excellent.
Grant, R. M., *Gnosticism and Early Christianity* (Oxford and New York, 1959).
Fox, Robin Lane, *Pagans and Christians in the Mediterranean World from the
   Second Century AD to the Conversion of Constantine* (London, 1986).
   Indispensable.
Frend, W. H. C., *Martyrdom and Persecution in the Early Church, A Study of the
   Conflict from the Maccabees to Donatus* (Oxford, 1965). A fascinating study of
   the Persecutions, which also contains much useful information about
   general matters.
Kelly, J. N. D., *Early Christian Creeds* (London, 1950).
   Early Christian Doctrines (London, 1958).
Liebeschuetz, J. H. W. G., *Continuity and Change in Roman Religion* (Oxford,
   1979). Probably the best account of the subject.
Lilla, Salvatore, R. C., *Clement of Alexandria: A Study in Christian Platonism and
   Gnosticism* (Oxford, 1971).
Nock, A. D., *Early Christianity and Its Hellenistic Background* (Oxford, 1904).
   *Conversion, The Old and the New in Religion from Alexander the Great to
   Augustine of Hippo* (Oxford, 1933). A classic and illuminating work.
Pagels, *The Gnostic Gospels* (London, 1970).
   Adam, Eve and the Serpent (London, 1988).
Payne, Robert, *The Holy Fire: The Story of the Fathers of the Eastern Church*
   (New York, 1957).

The Fathers of the Church and the Trinity

Brown, Peter. Erudite, eloquent books by one of the most inspiring scholars
   of the period: essential reading.
   Augustine of Hippo: A Biography (London, 1967).
   Religion and Society in the Age of St. Augustine (Chicago and London, 1972).
   The Making of Late Antiquity (Cambridge, Mass., and London, 1978).
   Society and the Holy in Late Antiquity (London, 1982).
Chesnut, R. C., *Three Monophysite Christologies* (Oxford, 1976). Highly
   recommended.
Danielou, Jean, *The Origins of Latin Christianity* (Philadelphia, 1977).
Gregg, Robert C. and Groh, Dennis E., *Early Arianism—A View of Salvation*
   (London, 1981).
Grillmeier, Aloys, *Christ in Christian Tradition: Apostolic Age to Chalcedon* (New
   York, 1965).
Lacugna, Catherine Mowry, *God For Us, The Trinity and Christian Life* (Chicago
   and San Francisco, 1973, 1991).
Louth, Andrew, *The Origins of the Christian Mystical Tradition. From Plato to*

Denys (Oxford, 1981). A superb account which shows how the doctrines were rooted in religious experience.
Denys the Areopagite (London, 1989).

McGinn, Bernard and Meyendorff, John (eds.), *Christian Spirituality: Origins to the Twelfth Century* (London, 1985). Excellent essays by leading scholars on the whole period, but especially illuminating contributions on the Trinity.

Meyendorff, John, *Byzantine Theology, Historical Trends and Doctrinal Themes* (New York and London, 1975). An excellent general account and particularly interesting on the Trinitarian and Christological issues.
Christ in Eastern Christian Thought (New York, 1975).

Murray, Robert, *Symbols of Church and Kingdom, A Study in Early Syriac Tradition* (Cambridge, 1975).

Pannikkar, Raimundo, *The Trinity and the Religious Experience of Man.* A brilliant book, which links Trinitarian theology with other religious traditions.

Pelikan, Jaroslav, *The Christian Tradition, A History of the Development of Doctrine*, 5 vols. An indispensable series. For this period:
I: *The Emergence of the Catholic Tradition (100–600)* (Chicago and London, 1971).
II: *The Spirit of the Eastern Tradition (600–1700)* (Chicago and London, 1974). For Maximus the Confessor.
III: *The Growth of Medieval Theology (600–1300)* (Chicago and London, 1978). For Anselm of Canterbury and the Latin understanding of Trinity and Christology.

Prestige, G. L., *God in Patristic Thought* (London, 1952). Particularly helpful on the technical Greek terms.

Williams, Rowan, *Arius, Heresy and Tradition* (London, 1987).

The Prophet Muhammad and Islam

Andrae, Tor, *Mohammed, the Man and his Faith* (trans. Theophil Menzel, London, 1936). Some of this is outdated, but there are useful insights.

Armstrong, Karen, *Muhammad, a Biography of the Prophet* (London, 1991, and San Francisco, 1992).

Gimaret, Daniel, *Les Noms Divins en Islam: Exégèse Lexicographique et Théologique* (Paris, 1988).

Hodgson, Marshall G. S., *The Venture of Islam, Conscience and History in a World Civilisation*, 3 vols. (Chicago and London, 1974). Far more than a history of Islam: Hodgson sets the development of the tradition in a universal context. Essential reading.

Jafri, H. M., *Origins and Early Development of Shia Islam* (London, 1981).

Lings, Martin, *Muhammad, His Life Based on the Earliest Sources* (London, 1983).

Khan, Muhammad Zafrulla, *Islam, Its Meaning for Modern Man* (London, 1962).

Nasr, Seyyed Hossein. An inspiring Iranian scholar. Highly recommended.
Ideals and Realities of Islam (London, 1971).
Islamic Spirituality, 2 vols. *I: Foundation* (London and New York, 1987).
II: Manifestations (London and New York, 1991).

Rahman, Fazlur, *Islam* (Chicago, 1979). Perhaps the best one-volume study.

Rodinson, Maxime, *Mohammad* (trans. Anne Carter, London, 1971). A
    secularist interpretation by a Marxist scholar.
Ruthven, Malise, *Islam and the World* (London, 1984).
Von Grunebaum, G. E., *Classical Islam, A History (600–1258)* (trans.
    Katherine Watson, London, 1970).
Watt, W. Montgomery. Useful books by a prolific author:
    Muhammad at Mecca (Oxford, 1953).
    Muhammad at Medina (Oxford, 1956).
    Islam and the Integration of Society (London, 1961).
    Muhammad's Mecca: History and the Qur'an (Edinburgh, 1988).
Wensinck, A. J., *The Muslim Creed, Its Genesis and Historical Development*
    (Cambridge, 1932). A fascinating work of scholarship.

Falsafah, Kalam and Theology in the Middle Ages

Al-Farabi, *Philosophy of Plato and Aristotle* (trans. and introduced by Muhsin
    Mahdi, Glencoe, Ill., 1962). An excellent presentation of the Faylasufs'
    position.
Corbin, Henri, *Histoire de la philosophie islamique* (Paris, 1964).
Fakhry, Majid, *A History of Islamic Philosophy* (New York and London, 1970).
    A scholarly and readable account to the present day which includes
    theological developments.
Gilson, Étienne, *The Spirit of Medieval Philosophy* (London, 1936).
Guttmann, Julius, *Philosophies of Judaism; The History of Jewish Philosophy from
    Biblical Times to Franz Rosenzweig* (London and New York, 1964). Essential
    reading.
Husik, I., *A History of Medieval Jewish Philosophy* (Philadelphia, 1940).
Leaman, Oliver, *An Introduction to Medieval Islamic Philosophy* (Cambridge,
    1985).
McCarthie, Richard, *The Theology of al-Ashari* (Beirut, 1953).
Meyendorff, John, *Gregory Palamas and Orthodox Spirituality* (New York, 1974).
Morewedge, P. (ed.), *Islamic Philosophical Theology* (New York, 1979).
    (ed.) *Islamic Philosophy and Mysticism* (New York, 1981).
    The Metaphysics of Avicenna (London, 1973).
Netton, I. R., *Muslim Neoplatonists, An Introduction to the Thought of the Brethren
    of Purity* (Edinburgh, 1991).
Pegis, Anton C., *At the Origins of the Thomistic Notion of Man* (New York,
    1963). A brilliant study of the Augustinian roots of Western scholasticism.
Pelikan, Jaroslav, *The Christian Tradition, A History of the Development of
    Doctrine*, 5 vols.
    II: *The Spirit of Eastern Christendom (600–1700)*, (Chicago and London, 1974).
    III: *The Growth of Medieval Theology (600–1300)*, (Chicago and London, 1978).
Rosenthal, F., *Knowledge Triumphant, The Concept of Knowledge in Medieval Islam*
    (Leiden, 1970).
Sharif, M. M., *A History of Muslim Philosophy* (Wiesbaden, 1963). Uneven but
    good on ar-Razi and al-Farabi.
Von Grunebaum, G. E., *Medieval Islam* (Chicago, 1946).
Watt, W. Montgomery, *The Formative Period of Islamic Thought* (Edinburgh, 1973).

Free Will and Predestination in Early Islam (London, 1948).
Muslim Intellectual: The Struggle and Achievement of Al-Ghazzali (Edinburgh, 1963).

Mysticism

Affifi, A. E., *The Mystical Philosophy of Ibnu 'l-Arabi* (Cambridge, 1938).

Arberry, A. J., *Sufism: An Account of the Mystics of Islam* (London, 1950).

Bakhtiar, L., *Sufi Expression of the Mystic Quest* (London, 1979).

Bension, Ariel, *The Zohar in Muslim and Christian Spain* (London, 1932).

Blumenthal, David, *Understanding Jewish Mysticism* (New York, 1978).

Butler, Dom Cuthbert, *Western Mysticism, The Teaching of Saints Augustine, Gregory and Bernard on Contemplation and the Contemplative Life, Neglected Chapters in the History of Religion* (2nd ed., London, 1927).

Chittick, William C., *The Sufi Path of Love: The Spiritual Teachings of Rumi* (Albany, 1983).

Corbin, Henri. Three highly recommended books:
Avicenna and the Visionary Recital (trans. W. Trask, Princeton, 1960).
Creative Imagination in the Sufism of Ibn Arabi (trans. W. Trask, London, 1970).
Spiritual Body and Celestial Earth, From Mazdean Iran to Shiite Iran (trans. Nancy Pearson, London, 1990). Excellent on the *alam al-mithal*.

Green, Arthur, *Jewish Spirituality, Volume I* (London, 1986).

Gruenwold, Ithamar, *Apocalyptic and Merkavah Mysticism* (Leiden, 1980).

Jacobs, Louis (ed.), *The Jewish Mystics* (Jerusalem, 1976, and London, 1990).

Leclercq, J. (ed.), *Spirituality of the Middle Ages* (London, 1968).

Lossky, Vladimir, *The Mystical Theology of the Eastern Church* (London, 1957). Essential reading.

Marcus, Ivan G., *Piety and Society: The Jewish Pietists of Medieval Germany* (Leiden, 1981).

Massignon, Louis, *The Passion of al-Hallaj*, 4 vols. (trans. H. Mason, Princeton, 1982). A classic work.

Nasr, Seyyed Hossein (ed.), *Islamic Spirituality: I: Foundations* (London, 1987). *II: Manifestations* (London, 1991).

Nicholson, Reynold A., *The Mystics of Islam* (London, 1914). A useful introduction.

Schaya, Leo, *The Universal Meaning of the Kabbalah* (London, 1971).

Schimmel, A. M., *Mystical Dimensions of Islam* (Chapel Hill, 1975).
The Triumphant Sun: A Study of Mawlana Rumi's Life and Work (London and the Hague, 1978).

Scholem, Gershom G. The major authority: essential reading. *Major Trends in Jewish Mysticism*, 2nd ed. (London, 1955).
(ed.) *The Zohar, The Book of Splendour* (New York, 1949).
On the Kabbalah and Its Symbolism (New York, 1965).
Jewish Gnosticism, Merkabah Mysticism and Talmudic Tradition (New York, 1960).

Smith, Margaret, *Rabia the Mystic and Her Fellow Saints in Islam* (London, 1928).

Temple, Richard, *Icons and the Mystical Origins of Christianity* (Shaftesbury, 1990).
Valiuddin, Mir, *Contemplative Disciplines in Sufism* (London, 1980).

The Reformation Period

Bossy, John, *Christianity in the West, 1400–1700* (Oxford and New York, 1985). An excellent short study.
Collinson, P., *The Religion of Protestants* (London, 1982).
Crew, P. Mack, *Calvinist Preaching and Iconoclasm in the Netherlands* (Cambridge, 1978). Good on the smashing of images.
Delumeau, Jean, *Catholicism Between Luther and Voltaire: a New View of the Counter-Reformation* (London and Philadelphia, 1977). Uneven, but some useful information.
Evennett, H. O., *The Spirit of the Counter-Reformation* (Cambridge, 1968).
Febvre, Lucien, *The Problem of Unbelief in the Sixteenth Century* (trans. Beatrice Gottlieb, Cambridge, Mass., 1982).
Green, Arthur (ed.), *Jewish Spirituality, Volume I* (London, 1988). Some excellent articles on Lurianic Kabbalah.
McGrath, Alister E., *The Intellectual Origins of the European Reformation* (Oxford and New York, 1987).
  Reformation Thought, An Introduction (Oxford and New York, 1988).
  A Life of John Calvin: A Study in the Shaping of Western Culture (Oxford, 1990).
Nuttall, G. F., *The Holy Spirit in Puritan Faith and Experience* (Oxford, 1946).
Pelikan, Jaroslav, *The Christian Tradition, A History of the Development of Doctrine*, 5 vols., IV: *Reformation of Church and Dogma* (Chicago and London, 1984).
Potter, G., *Zwingli* (Cambridge, 1976).
Raitt, Jill. (ed.), in collaboration with McGinn, Bernard and Meyendorff, John, *Christian Spirituality: High Middle Ages and Reformation* (New York, 1988, and London, 1989).
Trinkaus, Charles, *In Our Image and Likeness: Humanity and Divinity in Italian and Humanist Thought*, 2 vols. (London, 1970).
  with Oberman, H. (eds.), *The Pursuit of Holiness in Late Medieval and Renaissance Religion* (Leiden, 1974).
Williams, G. H., *The Radical Reformation* (Philadelphia, 1962).
Wright, A. D., *The Counter-Reformation, Catholic Europe and the Non-Christian World* (London, 1982).

The Enlightenment Period

Altmann, Alexander, *Essays in Jewish Intellectual History* (Hanover, N.Y., 1981).
  Moses Mendelssohn: A Biographical Study (Alabama, 1973).
Buber, Martin, *Hasidism and Modern Man* (New York, 1958).
  Jewish Mysticism and the Legend of Baal Shem (London, 1932).
Buckley, Michael J., *At the Origins of Modern Atheism* (New Haven and

London, 1987). A penetrating examination of atheism and orthodoxy in the eighteenth-century Christian West.

Cassirer, Ernst, *The Philosophy of Enlightenment* (Princeton, 1951).

Cohn, Norman, *The Pursuit of the Millennium, Revolutionary Millennarians and Mystical Anarchists of the Middle Ages* (London, 1957). Includes a section on the Ranters and incarnationalists of Puritan England.

Cragg, Gerald G., *The Church in the Age of Reason 1648–1789* (Harmondsworth and New York, 1960).

Reason and Authority in the Eighteenth Century (Cambridge, 1964).

Dupre, Louis and Saliers, Don E. (eds.), *Christian Spirituality: Post Reformation and Modern* (New York and London, 1989).

Gay, Peter, *The Enlightenment, An Interpretation*, 2 vols. (New York, 1966).

Guardini, Romano, *Pascal for Our Time* (trans. Brian Thompson, New York, 1966).

Haller, William, *The Rise of Puritanism* (New York, 1938).

Heimert, Alan, *Religion and the American Mind: From the Great Awakening to the Revolution* (Cambridge, Mass., 1968).

Lindberg, David C. and Numbers, Ronald L. (eds.), *God and Nature, Historical Essays on the Encounter between Christianity and Science* (Berkeley, Los Angeles and London, 1986).

Outler, Albert C., *John Wesley* (Oxford and New York, 1964).

Ozment, S. E., *Mysticism and Dissent* (New Haven and London, 1973).

Pelikan, Jaroslav, *The Christian Tradition, A History of the Development of Doctrine*, 5 vols.:

V: *Christian Doctrine and Modern Culture (Since 1700)* (Chicago and London, 1989).

Scholem, Gershom G., *The Messianic Idea in Judaism and Other Essays on Jewish Spirituality* (New York, 1971). Essays on Sabbatarianism and Hasidism.

Sabbati Sevi (Princeton, 1973).

God in the Modern Period

Ahmed, Akbar S., *Postmodernism and Islam, Predicament and Promise* (London and New York, 1992).

Altizer, Thomas J. J. and Hamilton, William, *Radical Theology and the Death of God* (New York and London, 1966).

Baeck, Leo, *The Essence of Judaism* (New York, 1948).

Barth, Karl, *The Knowledge of God and the Service of God* (trans. J. M. L. Haire and I. Henderson, London, 1938).

Balthasar, Hans Urs von, *The Glory of the Lord*, 3 vols. (Edinburgh, 1982–86).

Love Alone: The Way of Revelation (London, 1968).

Chadwick, Owen, *The Secularization of the European Mind in the 19th Century* (Cambridge, 1975).

Cone, James H., *Black Power and Black Theology* (New York, 1969).

D'Antonio, Michael, *Fall from Grace; The Failed Crusade of the Christian Right* (London, 1990).

De Chardin, Pierre Teilhard, *The Divine Milieu: An Essay on the Interior Life* (New York, 1987).

The Phenomenon of Man (New York, 1959).

Heschel, Abraham J., *The Insecurity of Freedom* (New York, 1966).
God in Search of Man (Philadelphia, 1959).
Hussain, Asaf, *Islamic Iran, Revolution and Counter-Revolution* (London, 1985).
Iqbal, Mohammed, *Six Lectures on the Reconstruction of Religious Thought in Islam* (Lahore, 1930).
Keddie, Nikki R. (ed.), *Religion and Politics in Iran, Shi'ism from Quietism to Revolution* (New Haven and London, 1983).
Kook, Abraham Isaac, *The Essential Writings of Abraham Isaac Kook* (ed. and trans. Ben Zion Bokser, Warwick, N.Y., 1988).
Kung, Hans, *Does God Exist? An Answer for Today* (trans. Edward Quinn, London, 1978).
Malik, Hafeez, *Iqbal, Poet-Philosopher of Pakistan* (New York, 1971).
Masterson, Patrick, *Atheism and Alienation, A Study of the Philosophic Sources of Contemporary Atheism* (Dublin, 1971).
Mergui, Raphael and Simonnot, Philippe, *Israel's Ayatollahs: Meir Kahane and the Far Right in Israel* (London, 1987).
Mottahedeh, Roy, *The Mantle of the Prophet, Religion and Politics in Iran* (London, 1985). Highly recommended.
O'Donovan, Leo (ed.), *A World of Grace, An Introduction to the Themes and Foundations of Karl Rahner's Theology* (New York, 1978).
Schleiermacher, Friedrich Daniel Ernst, *On Religion, Speeches to its Cultured Despisers* (New York, 1958).
The Christian Faith (trans. H. R. Mackintosh and J. S. Steward, Edinburgh, 1928).
Riches, John (ed.), *The Analogy of Beauty: The Theology of Hans Urs von Balthasar* (Edinburgh, 1986).
Robinson, J. A. T., *Honest to God* (London, 1963).
Exploration into God (London, 1967).
Rosenzweig, Franz, *The Star of Redemption*, 3 vols. (New York, 1970).
Rubenstein, Richard L., *After Auschwitz, Radical Theology and Contemporary Judaism* (Indianapolis, 1966).
Schweid, Eliezer, *The Land of Israel: National Home or Land of Destiny* (trans. Deborah Greniman, New York, 1985).
Smith, Wilfred Cantwell, *Islam in Modern History* (Princeton and London, 1957). A brilliant and prescient study.
Steiner, George, *Real Presences, Is there anything in what we say?* (London, 1989).
Tillich, Paul, *The Courage to Be* (London, 1962).
Tracy, David, *The Achievement of Bernard Lonergan* (New York, 1971).
Whitehead, A. N., *Process and Reality* (Cambridge, 1929).
Religion in the Making (Cambridge, 1926).

Index

Karen Armstrong, one of the foremost commentators on religious affairs, is the bestselling author of *A History of God* (1993), *The Battle for God* (2000), *Islam: A Short History* (2000), and *Buddha* (2001), among many other books. Having spent seven years as a Roman Catholic nun, she left her order in 1969 and took a B.Litt. at Oxford, taught modern literature at the University of London, and headed the English department of a public girls' school. She became a freelance writer and broadcaster in 1982, and in 1983 she worked in the Middle East on a six-part documentary television series on the life and works of St. Paul. Her other television work has included "Varieties of Religious Experience" (1984) and "Tongues of Fire" (1985); the latter resulted in an anthology by that name on religious and poetic expression. In 1996 she participated in Bill Moyers's television series "Genesis." She teaches at the Leo Baeck College for the Study of Judaism and the Training of Rabbis and Teachers and was awarded the 1999 Muslim Public Affairs Council Media Award. She regularly contributes reviews and articles to newspapers and journals.